A Companion to Diaspora and Transnationalism

Edited by

Ato Quayson and Girish Daswani

WILEY Blackwell

This edition first published 2013
© 2013 Blackwell Publishing Ltd

Blackwell Publishing was acquired by John Wiley & Sons in February 2007. Blackwell's publishing program
has been merged with Wiley's global Scientific, Technical, and Medical business to form Wiley Blackwell.

Registered Office
John Wiley & Sons Ltd, The Atrium, Southern Gate, Chichester, West Sussex, PO19 8SQ, UK

Editorial Offices
350 Main Street, Malden, MA 02148-5020, USA
9600 Garsington Road, Oxford, OX4 2DQ, UK
The Atrium, Southern Gate, Chichester, West Sussex, PO19 8SQ, UK

For details of our global editorial offices, for customer services, and for information about how to apply for
permission to reuse the copyright material in this book please see our website at www.wiley.com/
wiley-blackwell.

The right of Ato Quayson and Girish Daswani to be identified as the authors of the editorial material in
this work has been asserted in accordance with the UK Copyright, Designs and Patents Act 1988.

Library of Congress Cataloging-in-Publication Data is available on request

A catalogue record for this book is available from the British Library.

Cover image: Spencer Keeton Cunningham, *Me and My _____*, 7 × 5', acrylic, oil, goldleaf, latex, and spray
paint on canvas, 2013.
Cover design by Nicki Averill Design and Illustration

Set in 10.5/13 pt Minion by Toppan Best-set Premedia Limited
Printed in Malaysia by Ho Printing (M) Sdn Bhd

1 2013

Contents

A Companion to Diaspora
and Transnationalism

Wiley Blackwell Companions in Cultural Studies

Advisory editor: David Theo Goldberg, University of California, Irvine

This series provides theoretically ambitious but accessible volumes devoted to the major fields and subfields within cultural studies, whether as single disciplines (film studies) inspired and reconfigured by interventionist cultural studies approaches, or from broad interdisciplinary and multidisciplinary perspectives (gender studies, race and ethnic studies, postcolonial studies). Each volume sets out to ground and orientate the student through a broad range of specially commissioned articles and also to provide the more experienced scholar and teacher with a convenient and comprehensive overview of the latest trends and critical directions. An overarching Companion to Cultural Studies will map the territory as a whole.

1. A Companion to Film Theory
Edited by Toby Miller and Robert Stam

2. A Companion to Postcolonial Studies
Edited by Henry Schwarz and Sangeeta Ray

3. A Companion to Cultural Studies
Edited by Toby Miller

4. A Companion to Racial and Ethnic Studies
Edited by David Theo Goldberg and John Solomos

5. A Companion to Art Theory
Edited by Paul Smith and Carolyn Wilde

6. A Companion to Media Studies
Edited by Angharad Valdivia

7. A Companion to Literature and Film
Edited by Robert Stam and Alessandra Raengo

8. A Companion to Gender Studies
Edited by Philomena Essed, David Theo Goldberg, and Audrey Kobayashi

9. A Companion to Asian American Studies
Edited by Kent A. Ono

10. A Companion to Television
Edited by Janet Wasko

11. A Companion to African American Studies
Edited by Lewis R. Gordon and Jane Anna Gordon

12. A Companion to Museum Studies
Edited by Sharon Macdonald

13. A Companion to Lesbian, Gay, Bisexual, Transgender, and Queer Studies
Edited by George E. Haggerty and Molly McGarry

14. A Companion to Latina/o Studies
Edited by Juan Flores and Renato Rosaldo

15. A Companion to Sport
Edited by David L. Andrews and Ben Carrington

16. A Companion to Diaspora and Transnationalism
Edited by Ato Quayson and Girish Daswani

Notes on Contributors

Ali Albarghouthi is a PhD candidate at the University of Waterloo–Wilfrid Laurier University joint program in Religious Studies in Waterloo, Ontario. His work is based on interviews he conducted with American and Canadian academics and religious leaders. It focuses on *ijtihad* and its role in redefining religious norms and reinterpreting the *Shari'ah* in the West and how *ijtihad* is used to (de)construct religious authority. He is also interested in the influence of the North American culture(s) on Muslim (re)interpretation of primary religious sources and shifting notions of religiosity, Islamic modernism and liberalism, progressive Islam, the formative period of Islam, and Islamic heterodoxy.

Hakem Al-Rustom is the Manoogian Simone Foundation Postdoctoral Fellow and Lecturer in the Department of History at the University of Michigan, Ann Arbor. His doctoral thesis investigated the silenced past of postgenocide Armenians in Turkey since 1923. He specializes in the intersection between anthropology and history, ethnographic silences, political emotions, and settler colonialism. His research provides alternative approaches to the study of Middle Eastern and post-Ottoman societies, and interrogates the politics of "minorities"/"majorities" in governing population diversity with reference to Armenians, Arab Jews, Christians in the Middle East, and Muslims in Europe. He is the co-editor of *Edward Said: A Legacy of Emancipation and Representation* (with Adel Iskandar, 2010).

Emmanuel Akyeampong is Professor of History and African and African American Studies at Harvard University. Akyeampong's research interests include social and cultural history, comparative slavery, environment, and the history of disease and medicine. His publications include: *Between the Sea and the Lagoon: An Eco-Social History of the Anlo of Southeastern Ghana, c.1850 to Recent Times* (2001) and *A Dictionary of African Biography* (6 vols, with Henry Louis Gates Jr, 2012).

Garrett Wallace Brown is Reader in Political Theory and Global Ethics in the Department of Politics, University of Sheffield. His interests include Kantian political and legal theory, cosmopolitanism, global health governance, international legal theory, globalization theory and issues lying at the interface between political theory and international relations. He has published *Grounding Cosmopolitanism: From Kant to the Idea of a Cosmopolitan Constitution* (2009), co-edited (with David Held) *The Cosmopolitanism Reader* (2010), and is currently finishing a co-edited book (with Gavin Yamey and Sarah Wamala) *Global Health Policy* (forthcoming).

Maggie Cummings is Assistant Professor in the Department of Anthropology at the University of Toronto, Scarborough. For the past decade, she has conducted research on modernity, gender, and social transformation in Port Vila, Vanuatu. In addition to her current study of ni-Vanuatu migrant workers, she is conducting an ethnographic study of long-distance runners, embodied ethics, and corporate charities such as the Run for the Cure. She is co-author of *Cultural Anthropology: A Problem-Based Approach* (with Richard H. Robbins, Sherri N. Larkin and Karen McGarry, 2nd Canadian edn, 2013).

Girish Daswani is Assistant Professor in Anthropology at the University of Toronto. He is a social anthropologist with a special interest in Ghana, the anthropology of religion, the anthropology of Christianity, the anthropology of ethics, and diaspora and transnationalism. He conducted multi-sited research with members of a Ghanaian Pentecostal church in southern Ghana and London. His work looks at how Pentecostalism – its religious intermediaries, ideologies, and rituals – subjectively frames and facilitates church members' ideas of religious transformation and overseas travel. He is currently working on a book manuscript focusing on the ethical lives of Pentecostal church members in both Ghana and London.

Ayona Datta is Senior Lecturer in the School of Geography at the University of Leeds. She has an interdisciplinary background in architecture, environmental design and planning, with broad research interests in the social and cultural processes shaping notions of home, belonging, and citizenship in cities like London, Delhi, Mumbai, and Izmir. She has published in *Economy and Planning C*, *Antipode*, and *Urban Studies*. Her book *The Illegal City: Space, Law and Gender in a Delhi Squatter Settlement* was published in 2012.

Jigna Desai is Associate Professor in the Department of Gender, Women, and Sexuality Studies and Asian American Studies Program at the University of Minnesota. Her research interests include transnational feminist, Asian American, diasporic, queer, and disability cultural studies. She is the author of *Beyond Bollywood: The Cultural Politics of South Asian Diasporic Film* (2004), and co-edited *The Bollywood Reader* (2009) and *Asian Americans* (forthcoming). She has also published widely in journals such as *Social Text*, *Journal of Asian American Studies*, and *Meridians*.

Hilary Parsons Dick is an Assistant Professor of International Studies at Arcadia University, PA. Her forthcoming book *Words of Passage: Discourse and the Imagined Lives of Mexican Migrants* examines how everyday talk about migration from Mexico to the United States functions both as a critique of the failures of class mobility in Mexico and as a site for the production and potential transformation of gender inequality. Her new research examines the discourses of nation-state sovereignty in local immigration policies in Pennsylvania, with a focus on the ways these discourses function as code for forms of racial difference. She is particularly interested in how the display of "documents of identification" has become a key site for the defense of nation-state boundaries.

Edhem Eldem is a Professor at the Department of History of Boğaziçi University, Istanbul, and has taught as visiting professor at Berkeley and Harvard Universities and at the EHESS (Paris), and as a Fellow at the Wissenschaftskolleg zu Berlin. He has worked on the Levant trade, Ottoman funerary epigraphy, the socioeconomic development of Istanbul, the Ottoman Bank, archaeology in the Ottoman empire, and late Ottoman first-person narratives and biographies. Among his publications are *Pride and Privilege. A History of Ottoman Orders, Medals and Decorations* (2004); *Death in Istanbul. Death and its Rituals in Ottoman-Islamic Culture* (2005); *Consuming the Orient* (2007); *L'épitaphe ottomane musulmane XVIe-XXe siècles* (2007); and *Un Ottoman en Orient. Osman Hamdi Bey en Irak, 1869–1871* (2010).

Carmela Garritano is an Associate Professor of English at the University of Saint Thomas in Saint Paul, MN. She is author of *African Video Movies and Global Desires: A Ghanaian History* (2013).

Paul Christopher Johnson is a Professor in the Department of History and at the Center for Afroamerican and African Studies, University of Michigan, Ann Arbor, where he is also Director of the Doctoral Program in Anthropology and History. His books include *Secrets, Gossip, and Gods: The Transformation of Brazilian Candomblé* (2002), which received a Best Book Award from the American Academy of Religion, and *Diaspora Conversions: Black Carib Religion and the Recovery of Africa* (2007), which was awarded the Wesley Logan Prize of the American Historical Association for the best book on African diaspora history. Current work includes editing a book entitled "The Work of 'Possession' in Black Atlantic Religions" and a new project provisionally called "Vanishing: Religion and the Purification of Spirits," associated with a 2008 Guggenheim award.

Ananya Jahanara Kabir is Professor of English Literature at the Department of English, King's College, London. In 2010 she was curator of an exhibition on South Asian women artists working on conflict. She is the author of, most recently, *Territory of Desire: Representing the Valley of Kashmir* (2009) and *Partition's Post-Amnesias: 1947, 1971 and Modern South Asia* (forthcoming). Her research work concerns memorialization, modernity, trauma, and cultural belonging, and she is currently leading a European Research Council-funded project which will re-examine global modernity through the lens of African-derived kinaesthetics: "Modern Moves: Kinetic Transnationalism and Afro-Diasporic Rhythm Cultures."

Timm Lau is Assistant Professor of Cultural Anthropology at King Fahd University of Petroleum and Minerals. From 2010 to 2011, Dr Lau held a postdoctoral research fellowship at the University of Calgary, where he undertook research on Tibetan economic adaptation in Canada funded by the AXA Research Fund. He is co-editor of *How Do We Know? Evidence, Ethnography and the Making of Anthropological Knowledge* (with Liana Chua and Casey High, 2008) and has written several journal articles and book chapters on the Tibetan diaspora.

Anna Lindley is a lecturer in the Department of Development Studies at the School of Oriental and African Studies, University of London. Her research focuses on the relationships between processes of migration, conflict, and development, with particular interest in displacement and refugee issues, transnationalism and remittances, migration policy processes, and, increasingly, education, skills and mobility. She is the author of *The Early Morning Phonecall: Somali Refugees' Remittances* (2010).

Ken MacDonald teaches in the Department of Human Geography and City Studies, the Center for Diaspora and Transnational Studies, and the Center for Critical Development Studies at the University of Toronto. His research is grounded in ethnographic practice and he has ongoing research interests in a number of areas that seek to understand the role of transnational processes in the reproduction of cultural formations. Some of this work has appeared in *Antipode*, *India Review*, *Geoforum*, and *Comparative Studies in Society and History*.

Rachel Mairs is a Postdoctoral Fellow at the Joukowsky Institute for Archaeology and the Ancient World, and the Department of Egyptology and Ancient Western Asian Studies, at Brown University. Her research focuses on ethnic identity and multilingualism in Hellenistic period Egypt and Central Asia. She is the author of *The Hellenistic Far East: Archaeology, Language and Identity in Greek Central Asia* (forthcoming) and the literature review *The Archaeology of the Hellenistic Far East: A Survey* (2011).

Seán McLoughlin is Senior Lecturer in the School of Philosophy, Religion and the History of Science at the University of Leeds. His research focuses mainly on ethnographic approaches to the study of religion, ethnicity, diaspora, and identity among British South Asians and he is currently chair of the Muslims in Britain Research Network. His publications include the co-edited volumes *European Muslims and the Secular State* (with Jocelyne Cesari, 2005), *Diasporas: Concepts, Intersections, Identities* (with Kim Knott, 2010), and *Writing the City in British Asian Diasporas* (with William Gould, Ananya Jahanara Kabir, and Emma Tomalin, 2013).

Monir Moniruzzaman is an Assistant Professor in the Department of Anthropology and the Center for Ethics and Humanities in the Life Sciences at Michigan State University. Moniruzzaman's research examines illegal organ trafficking in Bangladesh, through the ethnography of kidney sellers. His research has been published in *Medical Anthropology Quarterly*, presented at the US Congress Human Rights Commission, and transformed into an art installation piece at a Toronto gallery.

Julian Murphet is Professor of Modern Film and Literature and Director of the Center for Modernism Studies at the University of New South Wales. He is the author of *Literature and Race in Los Angeles* (2001) and *Multimedia Modernism* (2009), and of various articles on modernism, postmodernism, race, and film.

Rani Neutill is a Mellon Postdoctoral Fellow in the English Department at Johns Hopkins University. Her research interests are at the intersections of postcolonial studies, literary theory, Asian American studies, studies in trauma and psychoanalysis, film studies, and transnational feminism. She is currently working on a manuscript entitled "Sitting in Sadness: Partition, Mourning, Diaspora," which looks at representations of the trauma of the Partition of India.

Michelle Obeid is a Lecturer in Social Anthropology at the University of Manchester. Her research interests include social change in the mundane experiences of mobility. Her current work focuses on Arab immigrants in London and the social and political projects they undertake in the process of building new lives and homes. Her published work includes "Searching for the Ideal Face of the State in a Lebanese Border Town" (2010) and "The Trials and Errors of Politics: Municipal Elections at the Lebanese Border" (2011).

Kevin Lewis O'Neill is Assistant Professor at the University of Toronto. He is author of *City of God: Christian Citizenship in Postwar Guatemala* (2010), and co-editor of *Genocide: Truth, Memory, and Representation* (with Alexander L. Hilton, 2009) and *Securing the City: Neoliberalism, Space, and Insecurity in Postwar Guatemala* (with Thomas Kedron, 2011).

Rajeev S. Patke is Director of the Division of Humanities at Yale-NUS College and Professor of English at the National University of Singapore. He is the author of *The Long Poems of Wallace Stevens* (1985), *Postcolonial Poetry in English* (2006), and *Modernist Literature and Postcolonial Studies* (forthcoming) and co-author of *The Concise Routledge History of Southeast Asian Writing in English* (with Philip Holden, 2010); editor of *Anthology of Southeast Asian Writing in English* (2011) and co-editor of *A Historical Companion to Postcolonial Literatures: Continental Europe and its Empires* (with Prem Poddar and Lars Jensen, 2006).

Ato Quayson is Professor of English and Founding Director of the Center for Diaspora and Transnational Studies at the University of Toronto. He has published widely in the areas of postcolonial studies and cultural theory, African studies, urban studies, disability studies, and in diaspora and transnationalism. His publications include: *Calibrations: Reading for the Social* (2003) and *Aesthetic Nervousness: Disability and the Crisis of Representation* (2007). He is general editor of the two-volume *Cambridge History of Postcolonial Literature* (2012) and has also co-edited (with Tejumola Olaniyan) *African Literature: An Anthology of Literary Theory and Criticism* (2007).

Carina Ray is Assistant Professor of African History at Fordham University and a social historian of race and sexuality in colonial and post-independence Africa. Her forthcoming book is entitled *Crossing the Color Line: Race, Sex, and the Contested Politics of Colonial Rule in Ghana*. She is co-editor (with Jeremy Rich) of *Navigating African Maritime History* and (with Salah M. Hassan) of *Darfur and the Crisis of Governance in Sudan: A Critical Reader* (both 2009).

Ann Reed is Assistant Professor in the Department of Anthropology at the University of North Dakota. Her research interests include globalization, tourism, identity, and economic development. Her ethnographical work examines Ghana's slavery heritage sites and Pan-African festivals used to attract diaspora Africans for pilgrimage tourism. She is the author of "The Commemoration of Slavery Heritage: Tourism and the Reification of Meaning" (2012), and is currently writing a book entitled "Pilgrimage Tourism of Diaspora Africans to Ghana." Although she continues to carry out long-term field research in Ghana, she recently embarked upon an interdisciplinary project investigating the sociocultural impacts of the oil boom in western North Dakota.

Meena Sharify-Funk is an Associate Professor of Religion and Culture at Wilfrid Laurier University in Waterloo, Canada. She specializes in Islamic studies with a focus on contemporary Muslim thought and identity and has written and presented a number of articles and papers on women and Islam, Islamic hermeneutics, and the role of cultural and religious factors in peacemaking. Her current research focuses on the construction of contemporary Canadian Muslim identity in a post 9/11 world, following on from her first book, *Encountering the Transnational: Women, Islam, and the Politics of Interpretation* (2008) which examined the impact of transnational networking on Muslim women's identity, thought, and activism. She has also co-edited *Cultural Diversity and Islam* (with Abdul Aziz Said, 2003) and *Contemporary Islam: Dynamic, Not Static* (with Abdul Aziz Said and Mohammed Abu-Nimer, 2006).

Anna Shternshis is Al and Malka Green Associate Professor of Yiddish and Diaspora Studies and the Associated Director of the Center for Jewish Studies at the University of Toronto. She is author of *Soviet and Kosher: Jewish Popular Culture in the Soviet Union, 1923–1939* (2006), and articles on Soviet and post-Soviet Jewish culture and identity, including "Between Red and Yellow Stars: Ethnic Identity of

Soviet Jewish Veterans of World War II in New York, Toronto and Berlin" (2011) and "White Concert Piano from the Real Shtetl: Material Culture and Ethnic Identity in the Post-Soviet Jewish Urban Community" (2010). She is currently working on two book projects, "Jewish Heart in the Soviet Body," examining the life of Soviet Jews born in the 1920s, and a study of the evacuation and escape of Soviet Jewish civilians during World War II.

T.T. Sreekumar is Associate Professor at the Mudra Institute of Communication, Ahmedabad (MICA), India. He is the author of *ICTS and Development in India: Perspectives on the Rural Network Society* (2011) and is currently working on two projects exploring technoculture in Asia focusing on youth and new media environments in South Asian and South East Asian countries and on the Islamic home film movement in globalized Southwest Asia. He has published articles in *Media, Culture & Society*, *Information Society*, *Third World Quarterly*, *Development & Change*, *Science, Technology & Society*, *International Journal of Technology Management*, *Journal of Contemporary Asia*, and *South Asian Journal*, among others.

Wisdom J. Tettey is Professor and Dean of the Faculty of Creative and Critical Studies at the University of British Columbia, Canada, and Coordinator of the Ghana Diaspora Educational and Professional Network. His research expertise and interests are in the areas of mass media and politics in Africa; ICTs, civic engagement, and transnational citizenship; the political economy of globalization and ICTs; brain drain, diaspora knowledge networks, and higher-education capacity building in Africa. He has published extensively in these areas, and is author/co-author and editor/co-editor of several books, including *African Media and the Digital Public Sphere* (2009), *The Public Sphere and the Politics of Survival: Voice, Sustainability, and Public Policy in Ghana* (2010), and *Challenges of Developing and Retaining the Next Generation of Academics: Deficits in Academic Staff Capacity in African Universities* (2010).

Takeyuki (Gaku) Tsuda is Associate Professor of Anthropology in the School of Human Evolution and Social Change at Arizona State University. His primary academic interests include international migration, diasporas, ethnic minorities, ethnic and national identity, transnationalism and globalization, ethnic return migrants, and the Japanese diaspora in the Americas. He is the author of *Strangers in the Ethnic Homeland: Japanese Brazilian Return Migration in Transnational Perspective* (2003) and editor of *Local Citizenship in Recent Countries of Immigration: Japan in Comparative Perspective* (2006) and *Diasporic Homecomings: Ethnic Return Migration in Comparative Perspective* (2009).

Pnina Werbner is Professor Emerita of Social Anthropology, Keele University. She is author of the Manchester Migration Trilogy (1990–2003). She edited *Anthropology and the New Cosmopolitanism: Rooted, Feminist and Vernacular Perspectives* (2008), and several theoretical collections on hybridity, multiculturalism, migration, and citizenship. She was Director of the project New African Migrants in the Gateway City (Economic and Social Research Council), and of Keele University, In the Footsteps of Jesus and the Prophet: Sociality, Caring and the Religion Imagination in the Filipino Diaspora (Arts and Humanities Research Council). She is currently recipient of a Wenner Gren award to complete the writing of a book on the Manual Workers Union and other public service unions in Botswana.

Chapter 1

Introduction – Diaspora and Transnationalism
Scapes, Scales, and Scopes
Ato Quayson and Girish Daswani

It is also a part of morality not to be at home in one's own home.

Theodor Adorno (2006)

The fierce disagreement that broke out in the late 1990s between the US Patent and Trademark Office and India over the patenting of the name "basmati" allows us a small window into the complexities of diaspora and transnationalism. RiceTec, a firm headquartered in Alvin, TX, that markets products such as Jasmati, Kasmati, and Texmati to over 20,000 supermarkets and other outlets in North America, sought a patent for a cross-breed of American long-grain rice. The patent would also have granted RiceTec the power to control basmati rice production in North America and the right to collect fees from farmers who sought to plant it. This was offensive to India, who argued that the name "basmati," which means "fragrant one" and is grown predominantly in the Punjab region of the country, must only be applied to rice from India. They suggested that basmati rice ought to have the same status as cognac or champagne, which are protected trademark names of certain alcoholic beverages deriving from the relevant regions of France. The Indians' scientific and commercial reasons were also supported by powerful cultural and nationalistic appeals. In response, the All India Rice Exporters Association stated in their deposition to the US Patent and Trademark Office: "You cannot build a monument anywhere and call it the Taj Mahal. There is only one Taj Mahal and that is in India" (Krieger 2005: 2–3). As Ken MacDonald shows in his discussion of the transnational circulation of cheese (CHAPTER 17), the link between cultural aura and commercial merchandizing for certain agricultural products establishes

A Companion to Diaspora and Transnationalism, First Edition.
Edited by Ato Quayson and Girish Daswani.
© 2013 Blackwell Publishing Ltd. Published 2013 by Blackwell Publishing Ltd.

a series of social and economic relationships across the entire spectrum of both production and consumption. It is the localization of such names that guarantees their cultural aura, and thus their niche status amongst the many other products that compete for consumer attention. In other words, there is a cultural economy to such agricultural products that relies entirely on the idea of cultural authenticity, which is folded into the product being consumed as a mark of cosmopolitan consumption.

The Taj Mahal is a labor of love and not simply a finished product of work. This example contrasts two forms of making, "work" and "labor" (Arendt 1998). For Indians, the label "basmati" represents not simply a finished market product, but a labor involving the daily life-producing activities that go into the making of home and locality. It is precisely through a labor of love, and not simply a labeling of a thing, that home and a longing for the past is created. The fact that there are also thousands of Indian grocery stores catering to the nostalgic needs of the large Indian communities across North America and elsewhere did not necessarily feature in the debate between the US Patent and Trademark Office and the All India Rice Export- ers Association. Yet the cultural economy of basmati invoked in the debate may be taken as extending well beyond the immediate confines of the patent disagreement itself. Such shops have become a veritable switchboard of nostalgic exchanges between diasporic communities and the homelands from which they hail. Whether among the Indian, Ghanaian, or Trinidadian community, a visit to the local ethnic supermarket is not solely for the purchase of goods and products from the home- land. Rather, it is also significantly about the exchange of news from home, gossip about the local community, lamentations about the recalcitrance of children, and the general renewal of the sense of participating in another culture that is richer and more complex than the one that they happen to be sojourners in (Hage 1997; Mankekar 2002). It is part of the complex affective economy of diaspora, which also incorporates monuments, heirlooms, and many material objects in both the public and private spheres. At the same time, the basmati story also tells us something about the intersecting *scapes* (the links between culture and economy), *scales* (the multiple levels of farmers, shops, and people that the patent decision would have impacted, in India and North America), and *scopes* (the spatio-temporal vectors that define nation and its variant social imaginaries).

Transnationalism and diaspora are two key concepts by which to organize our understanding of nation, identity, and globalization in today's world. They are also terms that are often used interchangeably. These two concepts tend to overlap with globalization theories in describing the conditions that give rise to new forms of migration, mobility, and mediatization. This volume shows that while there is no simple resolution to these intersections, there is a need to understand how these concepts and categories articulate with and against each other. Taken together, the concepts of diaspora and transnationalism promise a broad understanding of all the forms and implications that derive from the vast movements of populations, ideas, technologies, images, and financial networks that have come to shape the world we live in today. If the keywords that have organized the fields of diaspora and transnational studies thus far have involved historically charged terms (i.e., nation, nationalism, ethnicity, culture, politics, economics, society, space, place, homeland, home, narrative, representation, alienation, nostalgia, and all their cognates), it is because the conditions they pertain to are so variegated that their understanding requires a multifocal, and indeed interdisciplinary, approach. The chapters in this volume address these entanglements from a variety of perspectives and will cover a wide range of topics and methodological approaches.

Conceptual Categories

Though subject to varied emphases and disciplinary investments, the contemporary concept of diaspora involves an understanding of the shifting relations between homelands and host nations from the perspective both of those who have moved, whether voluntarily or not, and of the recipient societies in which they find themselves. While diasporas emerge out of dispersals, not all dispersals lead to diasporas. For example the violent dispersals that took place in Libya and the Ivory Coast in 2011 as a consequence of the political turmoil in those two countries may not necessarily lead to the formation of diasporas, whereas the Russian invasion and subsequent occupation of Afghanistan from 1979 to 1989, which led to massive dispersals of Pashtuns and other Afghani tribes into Pakistan and surrounding areas, did coalesce into a diaspora. Indeed, the central feature of the Afghani dispersal came to intensify an ethno-political and religious ideology to be articulated in the institutional form of the Taliban, incubated and hatched in the diaspora in the late 1990s, which in its turn came to cultivate a strong affiliation with the transnational network represented by Al-Qaeda. This would satisfy criteria for what Gabriel Sheffer describes in *Diaspora Politics* as an ethno-political diaspora (Sheffer 2003).

For a diaspora to emerge out of the dispersal of a given population a number of conditions have to be met. Among other things these often include the time-depth of dispersal and settlement in other locations; the development of a myth of the homeland; the attendant diversification of responses to homeland and host nation; the evolution of class segmentation and conflict within a given diaspora alongside the concomitant evolution of an elite group of cultural and political brokers; and the ways in which contradictions among the various class segments end up reinforcing different forms of material and emotional investment in an imaginary ideal of the homeland. Sometimes a utopian impulse serves to place the quest for the homeland in the vicinity of an active nationalism, as in the classic case of Jews at the turn of the nineteenth century and Palestinians in our contemporary period, and of the Irish diaspora nationalism following from the dispersals that took place from the middle of the nineteenth century. And yet the stake in a spatial homeland is neither always stable nor indeed consonant with the interests of a given diaspora, as Hakem al-Rustom shows for the Armenians of France (CHAPTER 28). It is the utopian idealization and the work of political and cultural brokers that gives the homeland ultimate salience within diasporic consciousness, whether this ensues in a return-to-homeland movement or not (Armstrong 1976; Brah 1996; Clifford 1997; Cohen 2008; Dufoix 2009; Sheffer 2003; Tölölyan 2000).

A diaspora, of whatever character, must not be perceived as a discrete entity but rather as being formed out of a series of contradictory convergences of peoples, ideas, and even cultural orientations. As Takeyuki Tsuda points out (CHAPTER 10), the circulations of diasporas between places of sojourn and their homelands may also come to generate different attachments to the idea of nation, either by deflating romantic notions of the national homeland and/or intensifying modes of identification with the erstwhile places of sojourn, or by conflating homeland and host nation into a new configuration of unanticipated doubled nostalgias. Following Hilary Parsons Dick on the contrapuntal lives of Mexican non-migrants (CHAPTER 24), diaspora is best understood, as Brah (1996) has noted, as the product of *diaspora space* involving a range of social and moral relationships that continually structure and restructure it. For diaspora space is inhabited not only by those who have migrated and their descendants but, equally, by those who are constructed and represented as indigenous. In other words, the concept of diaspora space (as opposed to that of diaspora) includes the entanglement of genealogies of dispersion with those of "staying put" (Brah 1996: 18).

As a paired term to diaspora, transnationalism on the other hand focuses on various flows and counterflows and the multi-striated connections they give rise to. Transnationalism encompasses not only the movement of people, but also of notions of citizenship, technology, forms of multinational governance, and the mechanisms of global markets. While diasporas are often understood to be a subset of transnational communities, the latter are taken to be an expansion of the overall conceptual scale of the former. As an analytical category transnational communities are understood to transcend diasporas because such communities may not be derived primarily or indeed exclusively from the forms of co-ethnic and cultural identification that are constitutive of diasporas, but rather from elective modes of identification involving class, sexuality, and even professional interest. Thus transnational communities may include the gay communities worldwide that wage daily battles across different frontiers for recognition of their rights to marriage; Buddhist communities outside of the religion's traditional homelands of India, China, and Japan that find common ground through involvement in certain rituals, practices, and non-violent ideologies across borders; or environmentalists who routinely traverse the circuits of international forums to assert common cause for a better-managed world. All such groups come to share strongly held objectives and communal values that are nonetheless quite different from the co-ethnic identifications that are taken to define diasporas.

While several displaced persons may be included within the umbrella of diaspora (such as exiles, refugees, guest-workers, asylum-seekers, etc.) it is the term *migrant community* that is most often used interchangeably with *diaspora* in scholarly accounts. "Migrant" is also the most prominent in everyday non-scholarly and bureaucratic usages. Even though we will also be using the two terms interchangeably, it is important to note some subtle shifts in the uses of the term between migration studies and diaspora studies over the past decade or so. These shifts become pertinent to the way that the links between diaspora and transnationalism may be conceived at the present time. As Pnina Werbner notes (CHAPTER 6), at the most formulaic level the difference between the two terms may be seen in the degree to which, within migration studies, particularly in the American scholarly literature, nation and society were taken to be coterminous, in the sense that migrants were assumed to ultimately integrate or assimilate into the country of settlement, with the nation then assumed to be the main horizon for understanding migrant relations across national borders. The social typologies of settlement and sojourn in the host nation and the problematics of citizenship were for example among the favored topics of migration studies. In an attempt to move away from what some have termed methodological nationalism (i.e., scholarly research which takes the nation-state as a "natural" container for understanding "the social and political form of the modern world" – e.g., Wimmer and Glick Schiller 2002: 302), recent studies in transnationalism have taken the nation-state as merely one agent in a more complex variety of global actors. As nation and society became progressively severed as concepts, the latter, now extended across different national boundaries, began to provide a different set of analytics for the study of social formations as well as for the ethnicities and political relationships that were thought to be their constituent parts. Against the stress on borders, transnationalism examines their permeability, transcendence, or irrelevance. Werbner argues, however, against simplistic notions of "simultaneity" that the transnational social field cannot be taken as continuous and homogeneous. Instead it is "ruptured" to "create new configurations and clusterings." Thus in Arjun Appadurai's much cited *Modernity at Large* (1996) the standard anthropological concept of ethnicity is only taken as a starting point for elaborating the fractal social relations that connect different scapes bearing an impact on identity formation. These include the financescapes, ideoscapes, and imagescapes in his well-known nomenclature. We might also add the significance of netscapes, or the possibilities opened up by social networking and the new technologies that help us imagine forms of community across borders and the consolidation of diasporic identities connected to different spaces (Ong 2008). While nations have still remained relevant in the study of diasporas and transnationalism, they are no longer the default mode of exemplification. The elasticity of societies, their self-imaginings as transcending national boundaries, the articulation of social identities, and the long *durée* of dispersal that in certain instances goes well beyond the formation of modern nation-states as we know them today, have all provided fresh ways for thinking about migrant lives in their interconnected global frameworks. If old usages of migration implied the rubric of the nation-state, diaspora emphasizes community plus the circuits and circulations that fundamentally undergird migrant social identities across borders.

When tied to demography the concept of transnationalism, on the other hand, has grown out of the understanding that migrants do not easily substitute old homes for new ones in a straightforward way (Basch, Glick Schiller, and Blanc 1994). Instead, scholarly research on transnationalism views the lives of migrants and those who remain behind as simultaneously connected between two or more nation-states, where homeland ties are a defining part of a transnational profile that incorporates recursive modes of nostalgia, sometimes lodged in both homelands and the nations of sojourn at once (Portes, Guarnizo, and Landolt 1999). The variety of such movements, which have been variously described as transnational "circuits" (Rouse 1991, 1992), "networks" (Hannerz 1996), "social fields" (Levitt and Glick Schiller 2004), "social spaces" (Faist 2000, 2011) and "chain migration" (Werbner 2002), allow for an investigation of both the broad social, economic, and cultural processes in which migrant diasporas are embedded, and the more inter-personal relationships of which they continue to be a part. The study of the trans-national also includes "trans-social" spaces, where "place" at the subnational level becomes a lens through which to study intersecting social relations at different spatial levels and moments in time (Pries 2009). It is widely recognized that, just as there are different ways of studying transnationalism (e.g., from above and below, at the borders), there are also multiple ways of being transnational, since trans-nationalism includes a multiplicity of historical trajectories or *pathways* that affect people in different ways (Werbner 1999; Grillo 2007). These multiple phenomena are then taken to exemplify the nature and intensities of the multi-striated flows that shape the modern world. More importantly, it is also understood that migrant and diasporic networks may make an impact at different levels of society in both the host nation and the homelands from which migrants and their parents came from originally. For the implications of translocality cannot be limited to the two locations that have most framed migrants' identities. The translocality of migrants means that their senses of themselves draw on the inflections and emphases pro-vided by other communities of co-ethnics in other parts of the world. As Khachig Tölölyan points out in another context, "diasporas are resolutely multilocal and polycentric, in that what happens to kin communities in other areas of dispersion as well as in the homeland consistently matter to them" (2007: 651). Furthermore, as liberal multicultural policies relating to minorities within host nations are dif-ferentiated in relation to subnational groups, autochthonous communities with prior rights to land, and newly arrived immigrant/diasporic communities, they come to impact on the nature of the alliances and interrelations that such minority groups establish amongst themselves, and between them and other such entities in other national domains. This also inflects their transnationalist orientations (see especially Kymlicka 2007: 61–87).

The Study of Diasporas and Diaspora Studies

Unlike the hitherto readily recognizable sociopolitical field of area studies, which has its own hemispheric demarcations and distinctive disciplinary emphases, diasporas transcend nations, areas and regions and have arguably existed since the dawn of human history. Yet in terms of specific institutions, conferences, journals, and professional scholarship diaspora studies can only be dated confidently from the middle of the twentieth century. There have always been differences between how diasporas represent themselves – emic uses – and how they are converted into an object of study under the rubric of diaspora studies – etic uses (Tölölyan 2007). It was only in 1965 that the historian George Shepperson made a scholarly case for viewing all peoples of African descent outside the continent as constituting a diaspora. As Brent Hayes Edwards points out (2003: 49), this crystallized the biblical resonances and figurations of Africans in the New World into a scholarly discourse explicitly in dialogue with the longstanding Jewish traditions behind the term *diaspora* itself. It also helped to expand and augment the purview of the classic diasporas, namely the Jewish, the Greek, and the Armenian. Since at least the early 1990s the term has been appropriated by and for the description of many other groups, both newer and older. Such groups have come to include the Chinese, the Indian, the Nigerian, the Caribbean, and the Somali diasporas, among many others, each of which has generated active transnational networks and internet communities as well as a steady stream of scholarly labor. With the establishment of the journal *Diasporas* by the Armenian American Khachig Tölölyan in 1991, the field progressively acquired scholarly coherence with a visible set of debates and practitioners. In 2004 the UK Arts and Humanities Research Board (now Council, hereafter AHRC) instituted for the first time the US$12 m Diaspora, Migration and Identities Program. The program's web site asserted that its main aim was "to research, discuss and present issues related to diasporas and migration, and their past and present impact on subjectivity and identity, culture and the imagination, place and space, emotion, politics and sociality."[1] Its funding was not limited to any ethnic or cultural group but encompassed all diasporas within the United Kingdom, with a studied attempt to explore areas of overlap between the social sciences and the humanities. The presence of institutional support in the form of organizations such as the AHRC coincided also with a large range of governmental programs and policies instigated by countries in many parts of the world that sought to target and stimulate active homeland interest from their diasporas. This includes countries as varied as India, China, Zimbabwe, Trinidad & Tobago, and Brazil. As Jignai Dessa and Rani Neutill show (CHAPTER 13), the new status that the diaspora acquired for Indian policymaking was mirrored in the emergence of a new character type in Bollywood cinema of the 1990s – the non-resident Indian or NRI – constructed out of a social imaginary of liberation, sexual adventurousness, and fresh female roles shaped within diasporic urban spaces that hitherto carried a different valence in the films. And in 2005 the African Union declared its African diaspora the "sixth region" of the continent, thus putting a continental spin on what had already been evolving within the domain of national policies.[2]

A broad contrast in diaspora studies may be seen when we compare Robin Cohen's *Global Diasporas* (2008), Stephane Dufoix's *Diasporas* (2008) and Avtar Brah's *Cartographies of Diaspora* (1996) on the one hand and Marianne Hirsch's *The Generation of Postmemory: Visual Cultures after the Holocaust* (2012) and the work of Paul Gilroy (1993) and James Clifford (1997) on the other. Cohen and Dufoix, elaborating on the suggestive essay by William Safran (1991), set out highly productive typologies of diasporas, while Brah's work explores the intersections of race, gender, class, sexuality, and ethnicity among South Asian diasporic communities in different parts of the world. For her part Hirsch builds upon her earlier "Post-Memories of Exile" essay from 1997, to focus on the ways in which the experiences of trauma after the Holocaust have impacted upon the field of visuality and memorialization for the children of Holocaust survivors and various others who bear witness to the violent events of the twentieth century. At the same time, Paul Gilroy's *The Black Atlantic* (1993) and James Clifford's *Routes: Travel and Translation in the Late Twentieth Century* (1997) are well known as offering models for rethinking the hybridities of diaspora. However, the distinction between Cohen, Dufoix, and Brah on the one hand and Hirsch, Gilroy, and Clifford on the other may be seen as between the outlining of social typologies and the attempt to describe the intangible elements of nostalgia, memory, and desire that elude the typologies of the social sciences. In a comprehensive view, both social science and humanities approaches are imperative for understanding the full spectrum of the significations of diaspora. The arts of memory, the dialectics of place, the affective economies of dispersal, the ethnographies of nostalgia, the intersubjectivities of social identity, and the citational practices that ground senses of cultural particularity outside the homeland (such as in names, family photographs, special community journals, movies, etc.), along with social categories and identities (village of provenance, race, class, gender, generational differences, the dynamics of (in)habitation facilitated by the host nation, etc.) are all crucial for understanding diasporas. All such features are part of the sometimes strategic/instrumental but always expressive configuration of diasporicity, the salience and intensity of whose elements is also shaped by the character of historical epochs in which they are articulated (Dufoix 2008).

Dispersals and Transnationalism

The history of the term *diaspora* reveals the polysemy of the historical context from which it first emerged and the further complications that came to be attached to it in subsequent usage. "Diaspora" first appears in the Septuagint, the Greek version of the Pentateuch or Torah. According to most scholars, the first Greek translation of the Torah probably took place in third-century BCE Alexandria for the benefit of the Jews living in that city, who then spoke more Greek than Hebrew, as well as for the practical purpose of allowing the Jewish laws to be recognized and accessed by Ptolemaic law courts (Modrzejewski 1997; Cohen 2008; Dufoix 2008; Rajak 2009). The largest Jewish community outside of Jerusalem at the time, the Jews of Hellenistic Alexandria belonged to the cultural intersection of two worlds: Jewish and Greek. It is precisely this intersecting context that led Hellenized Jews to craft a Greek neologism aimed at expressing a Biblical reality devoid of Greek equivalent. The Greek noun "diaspora" was coined after the verb *diaspeirô* (from *dia*, "through" and *speirô*, "to sow"), which literally means "to disperse" or "to scatter" (hence, by extension, "to take root elsewhere"). "Diaspora" did not originally translate into, or have the dramatic weight of, the Hebrew word *galuth* (exile, captivity), with which it later came to be associated after the destruction of the Second Temple by the Romans in 70 CE and "the disappearance of a Jewish political center – especially after the failure of the Bar Kochba revolt" (135 CE) (Dufoix 2008: 55; see also Boyarin and Boyarin 2002). Rather, it is first employed in reference to God's curse and threat of dispersal of the Jews if they do not respect his divine commandments. It is hence true to say that Jewish translators created a word that designated the potential, and not actual, dispersal of the Jewish people.

While the history of the Jewish diaspora illustrates the most extensive emic and etic reflections on diaspora, it is the dispersals dating from the early modern period that provide the horizon in which we might understand the broader transnational configurations of the world today that transcend the Jewish example. The process of imperial and colonial expansion from Europe proceeded in two main phases, which overlapped and were both tied to the formation of the global political economy. The first expansion of modernity (1492–1650 CE) was set in motion primarily by the Spanish and Portuguese monarchs in the long sixteenth century, while the second modernity (1650–1945) saw a decisive shift away from the multiple repercussions of Iberian ambition towards the interests of England, France, the Netherlands, and Germany. Each historical phase of modernity also generated its own internal and external imaginative borders. In the first modernity the expansion of Spain into the Americas coincided with their expulsion of Arabs and Jews from their lands in the name of blood purity, while a concomitant assumption of the heathen status of the natives they encountered in what later became Latin America was also maintained. The second modernity on the other hand saw the progressive construction of the uncivilized Other (Chinese, African, Caribbean, Southeast Asian) who needed to be reformed through the light of reason and colonial governmentality (Grosfoguel 2007: 94–104; also Mignolo 2000).

Scholars of colonialism and empire generally concede that the period from the sixteenth century represents the largest movement of human population in world history, with some estimates of as much as 60 million for the period. With the entire world population standing at 1.2 billion by 1850, the population dispersals from the sixteenth century onward then represent a dramatic movement of the world's population stock. The population movements that took place in the period are however normally reported in segments; it was not until the 1905 census of the British empire that we get a detailed picture for the first time of many of these population dispersals, particularly for the English-speaking world (see Maas 2003; Christopher 2008). And it is only when we take all these population dispersals together, as opposed to piecemeal or separately, that we get a proper picture of world history from the perspective of the mobility of populations and their implications for understanding the transnational character of social relations among different regions of the world.

The reasons for and character of population dispersals contrast in different historical phases. However, from a diaspora and transnational perspective, a handy overlap may be seen between the character of largely voluntary migrations from

Europe from the sixteenth to the mid-nineteenth century, and the more instrumentalized character of population dispersals that marked first the period of transatlantic slavery from the sixteenth to the nineteenth centuries and then, from the high
point of formal colonialism, from the mid-nineteenth century into the first half of
the twentieth. As Emmanuel Akyeampong adroitly shows (CHAPTER 9), transatlantic slavery had an impact not only on the constitution of hybrid societies in the New
World and Europe but also on the ways in which wage labor and regimes of factory
work came to later be defined (see also Williams 1944; Baucom 2005). As Simon
Gikandi argues in *Slavery and the Culture of Taste* (2011) the cultivation of modern
taste in Western societies and the violence of slavery did not inhabit separate
domains but were co-constitutive in the first and abiding instance. Even though
population dispersal became instrumentalized as a central component of colonial
governmentality, it is important to note that this process began first in Europe itself.
Thus while the seventeenth century in particular was to be characterized by vast
movements of populations from Europe to different parts of the world – instigated
by dire demographic transitions, famine and agricultural blight, acute living and
social conditions due to population explosion, and the rabid religious persecutions
and zeal for renewal that marked the Reformation and Counter-Reformation of the
period – these population dispersals were also managed with respect to race, class,
and also law-and-order prerogatives.

   In 1620 the English philosopher and politician Sir Francis Bacon called for a
study of monsters, "of everything . . . which is new, rare, and unusual in nature"
(Linebaugh and Rediker 2000: 39). Through this study landless peasants, orphans,
pirates, Anabaptists, the Irish, gypsies, Africans, and other types of "vagabonds"
were compared to a "hydra-headed monster" that needed to be controlled and later
exploited. The British empire at the time was expanding and these "monsters" served
as important sources of labor in the colonies. Thus for the British, whereas West
Africa had long been considered unsuitable for a penal colony in favor of Australia,
a settlement was still established in Sierra Leone for the settling of London's black
poor from 1786 to 1791. The resolution of issues of poverty in Britain through the
movement of segments of its own population was not limited exclusively to the
plight of the black poor but also included the dispersal of poor children to Australia,
South Africa, and the Americas. As early as 1618 a hundred "vagrant" children in
London were rounded up and transported to the colony of Virginia. They were set
to work as indentured laborers under slave-like conditions, the policies of enforced
child migration continuing piecemeal throughout the colonial period. Orphaned
children ended up being sent off to the Cape of Good Hope in South Africa and
the Swan River colony in Australia in 1832, and to New Brunswick and Toronto in
Canada in 1833. An estimated 150,000 poor children were transferred in this way
until the outbreak of World War II, with at least 80,000 of these being sent to Canada
alone. Many of the children ended up in dastardly conditions of servitude.[3]

   While some revisionist imperial historians with an eye to identifying the positive
effects of empire have argued that colonial policy was often confused and unsystematic (Ferguson 2002; Darwin 2009), it remains the case that, certainly in the case

of the British, conditions were created for the transfer of large populations during the colonial period, and that these groups were dispersed between different regions of the empire. A similar phenomenon of intra-colonial dispersals were also to mark French and Dutch colonialism, while Spain and Portugal played a key role first in the dispersion of Jews in the medieval period, and subsequently in the long phase of the Atlantic slave trade. In fact, it would not be hyperbolic to suggest that colonialism relied essentially on the instrumentalization of population dispersal as a key component of governmentality. Whether with the direct establishment of administrative and bureaucratic arrangements in the conversion of what were initially trade outposts (as in much of Africa, India, and Southeast Asia), or in the context of settler colonies (as in Australia, Canada, Latin America, and, arguably, Ireland), or in the case of post-plantation economies (as in Sri Lanka, Jamaica, and Malaysia), colonial governmentality invariably involved the creation of conditions for the dispersal of populations, some of which came to coalesce into diasporas (see CHAPTER 8). And in several instances, as in the indentured labor policies that took effect from the 1830s, population dispersal was systematic and designed to meet particular economic ends. In contrast, the enforced dispersal of Jews from Eastern Europe to North and South America and Israel that took place from the late nineteenth century was tied to the spasmodic nature of nation-state formation within Europe itself. Whether with regard to Russia, Germany, Poland, or other European countries of Eastern Europe, each phase of national splintering or imperial expansion involved the isolation of Jews as anomalous citizens who were submitted to violent attack and dispersal. The political and economic vagaries of the nation-state form are also responsible for the ongoing dispersal of people from the global south to the global north in our contemporary period. From at least the postwar period, when Europe actively encouraged labor migration from its former colonies, and then magnified several fold after the economic collapse of the early 1970s, people from Third World countries have had to flee famine, wars, religious persecution, and oppressive and incoherent political systems to become sojourners in foreign lands. It is a profound irony, then, that despite the moral panic often expressed in many parts of Europe and North America today at the prospect of immigrants and asylum-seekers on their borders, the period of extensive migrations from Europe during the seventeenth century and after was marked by the same forces that have underpinned the desperate movement of populations from the global south to the global north from the latter part of the twentieth century. These include spasmodic nation-states, famine and natural disasters, inter-ethnic conflicts, and religious persecutions. If the imaginative connection between the two modernities of European expansion already noted, and between Europe and the various lands that were "discovered," is displayed in the relentless dissemination of letters, reports, paintings, chronicles, and travel narratives penned by sailors, merchants, travelers, and colonial officials, it is also important to acknowledge that these media have not remained exclusively within the privileged purview of Europeans. As Julian Murphet shows (CHAPTER 3), once we expand our understanding of the word media to include different forms and modalities of representation that dispersed peoples have always carried along with them, we find that the diasporas that were created out of the various processes of dispersal not only deployed similar media for the self-representation of their conditions, but also came to completely alter the terms by which these media might be understood in the first place. As a starting point to understanding the relation between media and diaspora, Murphet asks that we revise our understanding of orality and its uses. For well before Facebook people told collective stories of where they came from and where they hoped to be going. In certain instances, as with the Torah, orality coalesced into ethical dicta and recommendations for surviving the traumas of dispersal that were progressively to be written down and later disseminated via other forms of representation. In yet other instances material objects also came to be invested with the aura of the homeland and become the bearers of the arts of memory. As Rachel Mairs points out (CHAPTER 6), the more than 70 garrison diasporas that were formed following Alexander the Great's military expeditions in the fourth century BCE, which spread from Alexandria in Egypt as far as Kandahar in Afghanistan and Khujand in Tajikistan, came to carry traces of Greece through the material culture and architecture that were transposed from their homeland into the new environments. Archaeological findings in some of the garrisons in Central Asia and India suggests that they knew Greek drama, philosophy, and literature, with a Greek transcription for a fragment found in Kandahar even bearing an oblique reference to Homer.

Transnationalism and the Question of the Nation-State

If diasporas are the exemplary communities of the transnational moment (Tölölyan 1991), then when did transnationalism become understood as a separate phenomenon in the first place? Scholars have pointed to the 1910s, when "transnationalism" was used to criticize classical frameworks within international migration and to challenge a calculating and rationalist model of the migrant as *homo economicus* (Isotalo 2009: 62). Bourne (1916) first used the word "transnationalism" to refer to a state in which migrants maintain cultural ties to their home countries. He was challenging the assumptions of an American "melting pot" scenario, which assumed that new migrants had to assimilate fully into their country of residence (Ernste, Van Houtum, and Zoomers 2009). The concept fell out of use until the 1970s, when transnationalism had some cache within the domain of international relations (Nye 1976). It was only in the early 1990s that transnationalism (like diaspora) became a popular concept, extending itself across different scholarly fields and serving as a useful critique of global development theories. Going beyond the "bipolar model" (Rouse 1991), this interdisciplinary field emphasizes the ways in which migrants build transnational social fields that cut across geographic, cultural, and political borders. Examining the spatialization of the "nation" through cultural "flows" between borders and the production of transnational "hybrid" subjects proved to become an influential and exciting field that cross-cut the social sciences and humanities. Studies in transnationalism challenged the boundaries of the nation-state and the stability of its borders and criticized policy-oriented research aiming at better managing and assimilating migrant populations.

In their attempts to move away from a simplistic model of linear migration and assimilation or integration paradigms, scholars have paid attention to the multiple ties and transnational connections that migrants maintain with their homeland (Basch, Glick Schiller, and Blanc 1994). The technologies of travel and long-distance communication have become cheaper and more easily accessible, allowing social networks and modern infrastructures to easily link nation-states over vast distances (Vertovec 2004; Wilding 2006). More recent examples of long-distance nationalism also show how migrants contribute to a national effort in their home countries, through the sending of remittances and the use of media technology (Glick Schiller and Fouron 2001). For example the financial remittances and political lobbying of overseas migrants, in Europe and North America, have contributed to the formalization of new nation-states, such as Eritrea (Bernal 2004) and Croatia (Winland 2007). Furthermore, as Anna Lindley shows (CHAPTER 18), remittances have become such a routine feature of diasporic and transnational lives that it has become an inescapable aspect of understanding such lives (see also Sirkeci, Cohen, and Ratha 2012). Another interest has been in the role of the nation-state, and the creation of new laws, to allow a more flexible or dual citizenship in order to bring political support and economic capital into these "homeland" countries from the overseas diaspora (Ong 1999; Goldring 2002; Østergaard-Nielsen 2003). India's Person of Indian Origin law, which has been in force since 2005, grants people of Indian origin (up to four generations removed), or those married to persons of Indian origin, who are not citizens of India, an overseas citizenship of India. This law has encouraged more Indians living abroad, as well as those who have never lived in India, to "return" and invest in India's economy – transforming what was described as a "brain drain" to a "brain circulation" (Saxenian 2006).

While much of the earlier writing on citizenship has been tied to the legal-political dimensions of the nation-state, scholarship in transnational studies has also allowed for a more complex understanding of citizenship and its cognates. Apart from its legal aspects, scholars also consider the everyday processes of subject-making and contradictory experiences involved in claims to citizenship (Ong 1996; Brown, CHAPTER 4). Citizenship is understood not simply as a legal entity but as a cultural category as well as a form of (self-)disciplinary power. Rather than being merely subjects of power, many migrants take on the responsibility of shaping the environments in which they sojourn as well as establishing the terms of the porous boundaries that govern the relationships between themselves and others. Approaching migrants as political actors helps to demonstrate how they are connected through fields of power and a web of social networks. Alongside a focus on social networks, attention is also given to how the "social world is perceived in a *placial way*," which means that where you are matters and that a specific place or neighborhood is always already linked to other social networks elsewhere (Gielis 2009: 273–275; Brown 2005; Olwig 2007) Family relationships, occupational networks, as well as ties to civic associations and religious institutions, matter. These networks make a difference to the migrant or transnational experience that is built around a specific location. The shift in analytical focus has also brought attention to the unequal power relationships, neoliberal restructuring, and interlinking of neighborhoods and cities on a global scale, simultaneously drawing on migration and urban studies (Sassen 1991, 2001; Smith 2001; Glick Schiller 2009; Glick Schiller and Çağlar 2011; Patke, CHAPTER 23). The importance of space and place also extends to the work that has been done on labor migrants, especially female domestic workers, the (self-)disciplinary effects of their workplace, and the spatial dynamics of power in the "home-space" (Constable 2007; Parreñas 2001; Huang and Yeoh 2007; Yeoh and Hang 2010). Another growing research interest is the study of the material culture and affective realities of migrant worlds, where the senses (tastes, sights, smells, touch) and feelings, and the material practices of travel and place collide, converge, and collapse in different ways, and through which place comes to be reappropriated by people (Napolitano 2007; Basu and Coleman 2008; Miller 2008).

Accustomed though we are to seeing many parts of today's urban world as multicultural and accommodating the interactions of variant migrant ethnicities, it must be remembered that certain periods in history have also provided important exemplars of cultural mixing. From the manuscript fragments lodged in the Cairo Geniza, S.D. Gotein's magisterial *A Mediterranean Society* (1967–1993) provides us with a complex picture of the multiple ways in which Jews and Arabs interacted in Mediterranean medieval society, and the truly global reach of these interactions. More recently, Natalie Rothman's *Brokering Empire: Trans-Imperial Subjects Between Venice and Istanbul* (2011) displays a similarly variegated picture. The book is set mainly in the Venice of the 1550s–1670s and focuses on the cultural mediation performed by various actors, including the famed dragomans (translators), Venetian commercial brokers, traders, converts, and a host of other personages. *Brokering Empire* is literally teeming with cultural ethnicities and social functions: Jews, Armenians, Ottoman ambassadors, and Arabs, along with a plethora of Venetian commercial and political elites. As she adroitly shows, the composite households of commercial brokers acted as switchboards of interchange between "locals" and "foreigners" and thus provided a theater for the ongoing recalibration of these categories. From a diaspora and transnational studies perspective, the central attraction of the book lies in Rothman's modeling of the idea of mediation, circulation, and the structuring and rupturing of ethno-cultural boundaries across trans-imperial locations. And, as Edhem Eldem shows (CHAPTER 12), the terms of cosmopolitanism in Istanbul of the mid-nineteenth century was to take account of a shift in linguistic registers among the elite, from the Italian that had been dominant throughout the Mediterranean basin to the French that was gradually coming to dominance in newspapers and other media of cultural dissemination alongside the equally strong Ottoman discourse that had been bequeathed to the city after several centuries of the empire. As he shows, religious and ethnic communities – Arabs, Greeks, Bulgarians, Serbs, Albanians, Russians, Syriacs, and Nestorians – were all part of the complex milieu that defined Istanbul's cosmopolitanism well into the twentieth century and which, if we take his earlier work (Eldem 2011) on the herit-age of Ottoman archaeology, alongside Rothman's and those of various others, shows that both Istanbul and Venice have historically been highly intercultural locations.

While we are urged to look beyond a purely "ethnic lens" (Glick Schiller, Çağlar, and Guldbrandsen 2006), and not to overlook the "non-national or even a-national cultural patterns" (Wilding 2007: 345), the nation-state remains an important player that continues to impact the field of transnational studies. The ongoing importance of nation-states in shaping the daily lives of its citizens and residents means that people are influenced by transnationalism whether they travel or not, as Avtar Brah (1996) has pointed out. By default of belonging to or residing in a nation-state that is itself constituted by the circulation of populations across borders, whether in Europe, Africa, South Asia, or Latin America, one is already connected transnationally in inclusive and exclusive, positive and negative ways. "Home" can be looked upon as an exotic place where various kinds of foreign Others arrive from the outside. These outsiders await designation (visa student, contract labor, guest-worker, foreign talent), and such acts of naming determine how they are received, their length of residence, social status, and access to economic and state resources. The category of "migrant" also commonly applies to second/third generations, even if they are citizens; consider Germany, where Turkish people cannot get German citizenship; and Israel, where despite the large number of Arab Israeli citizens, it has been very difficult for other non-Jews, say from Africa or South America, to gain citizenship in the country. In this way the transnational becomes personal and the personal is always political. While migrant groups are often invited to help build a country's economy, many are also described as a danger and a threat, especially in times of socioeconomic instability. If the nation is defined as a symbolic community that shares state borders, nationalism becomes "the political utilization of the symbol nation through discourse and political activity, as well as the sentiment that draws people into responding to this symbol's use" (Verdery 1996: 227).

Popular sentiments linked to a sense of nationalism created along the lines of "common blood," "dominant race," or "people of the soil" are often used to create fear and hostility against outsiders who are seen to be "swarming" into the country and changing its moral fabric. In many countries, from Singapore to the United Kingdom, from the Netherlands to Nigeria, and from the USA to Argentina, migra-tion has become a common topic of conversation. In many of these conversations, which include political speeches, newspapers and magazine articles, and online blogs, migrants are described as an invading force, unable to integrate fully into the resident society. Migrants become perfect scapegoats for national distress, which is perceived as resulting from exogenous forces; by projecting the blame onto the Other the national Self is preserved. While earlier policies of segregation (for example to "import labor and not people" in Germany or to "remain white and monocultural" in Australia) have generally been abandoned in favor of a policy of multiculturalism (Castles 2007: 31; Kymlicka 2007), this policy also serves in some countries as a form of moral compartmentalization built on the ideology of tolerance. However, as history teaches us, tolerance can easily turn into intolerance, and hospitality into hostility (Derrida 2000; Adorno 2006: 103).

Between October 2010 and February 2011 the leaders of three prosperous European countries lamented what they described as the failure of multiculturalism. German chancellor Angela Merkel, Nicolas Sarkozy, then president of France, and UK prime minister David Cameron publicly stated that they no longer believed different cultural communities could comfortably coexist in their countries side by side. They described this idea of multiculturalism as being in conflict with the dominant values of their respective countries (Angela Merkel called it Germany's Christian values). Instead, they argued, every migrant culture should work hard to integrate and assimilate within the dominant culture of their resident country. Their opinions, while potentially far-reaching, were mainly directed at the Muslim community and its potential links with a "homegrown Islamic terrorism." However, this political rhetoric is not exclusively used for a single group. The "Latino Other" in the USA, for example, is also described as people who are "unable or unwilling to integrate into the social and cultural life . . . they seal themselves off from the larger society, reproducing cultural beliefs and behaviors antithetical to a modern life" (Chavez 2008: 177). Ironically, a shared ideology of humanitarianism collectively expressed through attention to human rights does not always preclude a society or nation-state from hostility to immigrants (Fassin 2005; Isatalo 2009). Especially after 9/11, the migrant Other, along with the refugee and asylum-seeker, has often come to be seen as a threat to national security. Such forms of political scapegoating conveniently feed back into a call for increasing homeland securitization against the threats of immigration. However, much of the fear that nationals feel toward immigrants may itself be a by-product of the incoherent internal transformations of capitalism, which are ideologically masked in the discourse of the nation-state. As Glick Schiller (2009: 31) aptly puts it:

> It is not putative hordes of illegal aliens or migrants' transnational connections that are threatening the majority of people in the imperial core countries. Rather . . . anti-immigrant rage and subjective feelings of despair, the precariousness of life, and life's unmet aspirations reflect and speak to the global fragility and exploitative character of contemporary capitalism, its restructuring of economies, labor regimes, and states, and its dependence on war and plunder.

Nostalgia, Moral Imagination, and Ethics

The term nostalgia, which is derived from the Greek *nostos* ("to return home") and *algos* ("pain"), was originally intended to refer to a medical condition and physical ailment. Coined in the seventeenth century by a Swiss medical student, Johannes Hofer, nostalgia was used to describe the pathological homesickness of Swiss soldiers serving outside the fatherland who were pining for their mountain landscapes (1934: 45). It was in the late eighteenth and nineteenth centuries, with the advent of Freudian psychoanalysis, that nostalgia became seen as a process interior to the self and, by the end of the nineteenth century, nostalgia came to refer to a longing for a specific place and time that had since been lost (Wernick, cited in Wilson 2005: 23; Boym 2002).

Nostalgia is now commonly associated with rupture from, and the desire to one day return to, a place called home. It is also associated with the mourning for the impossibility of return, at least to a home as one remembers it. Avtar Brah (1996) has pointed out that the diasporic nostalgia for home is equally a site for diaspora identity politics. As she explains, this "homing" desire is not necessarily the same as wanting to return to a physical place, since, as we noted earlier, not all diasporas sustain an ideology of return (p. 180). Her distinction between "homing desire" and "desire for homeland" is a suggestive one as the desire of returning home does not reflect the more complex reality of the nostalgic desire for homeland. Elaborating on the work of Ghassan Hage (1997) and others, Michelle Obeid (CHAPTER 21) draws a fascinating picture of a displaced Palestinian family now resident in London and how they attempt to create a sense of home and homeliness away from the Occupied Territories. The family's café business produces a reconfiguration of the boundary between public and private, since the large upstairs room of their house is used as the café's parlor, which is also serviced by the same kitchen used by the household itself. The duality of this café's parlor space means that it comes to underwrite two seemingly distinctive affective fields, that of providing the household with a communal space for congregation and the breaking of bread, and a space in which stories of the vagaries of being a Palestinian and Arab in London are constantly rehearsed as clients meet regularly in the café to exchange tales from their various homelands. For the youngest generation of grandchildren who have known no other scene of familial congregation, the parlor performs the function of generating affective proliferation and of structuring the intimate secrecy of domestic spaces in a manner similar to that described by Gaston Bachelard in *The Poetics of Space* (1958). And yet the "Gazāwi" family's labored construction of a sense of home through their café business does not entirely obliterate the fact that they are a displaced family facing injunctions against return to their homeland because of Israel's policies of security containment in the Occupied Territories following political events there in 1997. As Daniel Barber points out in *On Diaspora: Christianity, Religion, and Secularity* (2011: 54–61), one of the defining features of diaspora is the dialectical relation between integrity and discontinuity, spatialized as a form of deteritorialization.[4] The particular theoretical model he deploys, which is both highly focused and yet also depends on insights from theology, philosophy, Christianity, structuralism, and ethics, does not allow him to talk about the affectivity involved in this pairing of integrity and discontinuity. But once we begin to look more closely at the grounds for bringing the two terms together we come to find that affectivity is central to both integrity and discontinuity and their mutual implication in diaspora. If integrity is not a pre-given condition of being (lodged perhaps in the authenticity of homeland culture, for example) but rather unfolds as a restless (re-)production of an account of one's self (Butler 2005), then it is in the necessity

for establishing the inter-particularities of everyday life, in, say, gaining competence
in the language and culture of the host society whilst also mastering the arts of
memory of one's own culture, that establishes for the diaspora an oscillatory relationship between integrity and discontinuity. This oscillatory movement is never
supposed to be fully resolved in favor of one or the other pole but only creatively
contained as defining a realm of open possibility. Nostalgia may then be seen as
both future-oriented and utopian (in a secular as well as in a religious register),
even as it is tied to an ineluctable sense of things past.

If the moral imagination is also an important component of both diaspora and
transnationalism it is because it helps produce a narrative of possibilities, hopes,
and social roles of appropriate conduct as well as models for action that are made
meaningful by allowing individuals to take on the active narrative positions of
migrant, victim, hero, survivor, community builder, transnational actor, and so on.
The moral imagination, however, is not without constraints or limits, and is always
refracted through various discourses and by the politics of place or the several places
that are knitted together for a given diaspora. Nation-states, regions, cities, and
neighborhoods continue to provide a spatial and legal framework for how different
diasporic groups self-identify and are allowed to organize themselves, and these
spatial constraints also act as dialectical determinants of a moral imagination. At
the same time the moral imagination also includes projects of self-fashioning that
take into account the ethical lives of people as they participate in remaking themselves as members of a virtue-community intersecting with other communities
within the same location and further afield. It is at the conjuncture of the crossing
of borders, along with the pressures of shaping a coherent understanding of the Self
within a diaspora far from the homeland, that ethical deliberation and action
become important considerations to the study of diasporas and their transnational
realities. While diasporas evoke a future time that foregrounds ritual practice and
performance which is in tension with, yet also participates in, the creation of a
distant homeland in the present, transnationalism points to an irony and tension
between the personal and group ambitions to transcend geographical, social, and
economic boundaries and the political and cultural barriers and boundary-making
processes that accompany such movement and mobility.

Working alongside a moral imagination, ethics is not simply a matter of following rules and conforming to, or transgressing, social norms. It is through radical
ethical positioning also that one becomes less concerned with *what* the boundaries
of home are, and more interested in seeking answers to the more unsettling *why*
questions concerning the reasons for the continuity of alienation, persecution, and
suffering for one's own group and those of others. Jewish tradition installs this
ethical concern as a central aspect of the rituals of the Pesach feast. It is a matter of
reflection, when the means (the journey) and not the ends (the results) of life's
decision-making processes become important considerations to an imagination of
home and its relation to discontinuity and Otherness. Within this framework ethics
draws attention to the moral judgments people must make regarding their dreams,
aspirations, desires, fears, and vague ideas in deciding how to live a good life, and

how to deal with incommensurable cultural values made visible between the homeland and the spaces of sojourn.

Salman Rushdie reflects on the nuance of migrant ethical imagination in his *Imaginary Homelands* thus (1991: 124–125):

> The effect of mass migrations has been the creation of radically new types of human being: people who root themselves in ideas rather than places, in memories as much as in material things; people who have been obliged to define themselves – because they are so defined by others – by their otherness; people in whose deepest selves strange fusions occur, unprecedented unions between what they were and where they find themselves. The migrant suspects reality: having experienced several ways of being, he understands their illusory nature. To see things plainly, you have to cross a frontier.

In these remarks Rushdie is clearly privileging the experience of displacement, suggesting that it creates an inherent epistemological payout that allows the diasporic to see the world in a fuller and more complex manner. But this diasporic privilege has to be countered by the more sober understanding proffered by Theodor Adorno (2006). Adorno connects home, alienation, and morality most poignantly in the telling aphorism from *Minima Moralia* (published in 1951) that forms the epigraph to our chapter: "It is also a part of morality not to be at home in one's own home." The point being made here is that alienation has a performative effect in generating an orientation toward homeliness that incorporates a necessary skepticism toward normalization. At a more profound level, this link between home, alienation, and morality also suggests the foundation for a new social contract. For if it is also a part of morality *not* to be at home *in one's own home*, then one does not need to be an immigrant to experience the creative restlessness produced by not being at home. We can readily see how a philosophical critic of the Enlightenment who himself suffered exile and witnessed persecution could produce such a fertile aphorism. Recall that the subtitle to *Minima Moralia* is "Reflections on a Damaged Life." In Adorno's usage the aphorism forces us to tarry with the particular, which at the same time is being idiosyncratically connected to a critique of the totality of social relations that are undergirded by capital and that thus produce the conditions for a damaged life in the first instance. To tarry with the particular yet couple this with the unpredictable and subtle links to a social totality may also be taken as a methodological necessity for the study of diaspora and transnationalism. For each detail in these two fertile and intersecting fields is a threshold of fresh interpretative possibilities that allows us to sense the complex layerings of what is past, passing, and still to come.

Organization of the Book

Each chapter in this volume was included on the basis of being able to combine general theories of diaspora and transnationalism with specific examples and case

studies. The book's sectional divisions must be seen as overlapping and mutually
reinforcing, rather than distinct and exclusive. For example, despite the fact that
they happen to appear in different Parts and that they focus on different case
studies, there is much in common between the chapters by Emmanuel Akyeampong (CHAPTER 9) and Ann Reed (CHAPTER 31); or Pnina Werbner (CHAPTER 6)
and Takeyuki Tsuda (CHAPTER 10); or Seán McLoughlin (CHAPTER 7), Meena
Sharify-Funk and Timm Lau (CHAPTER 29), and Paul Christopher Johnson
(CHAPTER 30); or Ayona Datta (CHAPTER 5) and Rajeev Patke (CHAPTER 23); or
Garret Brown (CHAPTER 4) and Hakem al-Rustom (CHAPTER 28) – to take just a
few examples of thematic clustering. It is thus important for teaching purposes to
read as many of the chapters as possible and to see the variety of ways in which
they might be fruitfully paired for students. Part I, Transnationalism and Diaspora
Through the Disciplines, provides models for discussing diaspora and transnationalism from a variety of disciplinary perspectives. The aim is to identify a small
cluster of themes from each discipline and to see how these are transformed in the
context of the two key terms. The list of disciplines in this section is meant to be
suggestive rather than exhaustive, and we hope that further work will be done to
identify the ways in which other disciplines and interdisciplinary models such as
international relations, public health, law, and public policy will provide further
insights about the salience of conceptual categories such as diaspora and transnationalism. Girish Daswani (CHAPTER 2) examines the ways in which anthropology has been historically invested in questions concerning transnationalism and diaspora,
as well as how these two terms converge and their respective limits within the discipline. Julian Muphet (CHAPTER 3) offers an outline of the relationship between
media studies and diaspora and how different forms of media interact with one
another in diaspora. Garrett W. Brown (CHAPTER 4) discusses some of the more
relevant debates about what constitutes a "political community," analyzing the
primary overlaps between the study of diaspora and transnationalism and contemporary themes in the discipline of political science. From the perspective of media
studies, Ayona Datta (CHAPTER 5) is interested in the role of cities in the making of
migrant identities and the importance of shifting our scale of inquiry from the
transnational to the urban. Drawing on migration studies and from an anthropological perspective, Pnina Werbner (CHAPTER 6) emphasizes the multivalence of
diasporic notions of home and belonging and the limits of "simultaneity," as expressed
by migrants in their transnational social relations. Seán McLoughlin (CHAPTER 7)
looks at why religion is sometimes a problematic and understudied category and
goes on to present an overview of how it has been studied in relation to diaspora
and transnationalism. In addition to the chapters already discussed above, Ato
Quayson (CHAPTER 8) points to the importance of diaspora for understanding
the main conditions of production and reception that fall under the rubric of
postcolonialism.

    The chapters in Part II, Backgrounds and Perspectives, provide broad overviews
of the processes of migratory flows and counterflows and the character of the historical interculturalism that has had an impact on different parts of today's world.

Akyeampong's discussion of slavery and indentured labor (CHAPTER 9) is complemented by Tsuda's lively discussion (CHAPTER 10) of the many patterns by which homeland return may be traced and the variety of configurations that the simultaneous attachments to lands of sojourn and to homelands produce for such migrants. The chapters by Ray on interracial sex in the making and dissolution of the British empire (CHAPTER 11) and by Eldem on Istanbul's cosmopolitanism (CHAPTER 12) both return to earlier historical periods to trace the character of intercultural formations and the implications that might be drawn from these for understanding cosmopolitanism. Part III, The Aesthetics of Transnationalism and Diaspora, attends to a number of creative cultural vectors that have become central to understandings of the two terms. As Desai and Neutill (CHAPTER 13), Garritano (CHAPTER 14), and Kabir (CHAPTER 15) show, from Bollywood to Nollywood and salsa, diasporic communities have established highly productive creative dialogues at the intersection of materiality, the new social media, and the dynamics of creative embodiment in a transnational world. Part IV, Overviews and Case Studies, is our longest section and offers a cornucopia of case studies and examples drawn from a variety of regions and diasporic/transnational groups. For example, technology (Sreekumar, CHAPTER 32; Tettey, CHAPTER 20), specific historical, ethno-cultural, political, and social discourses (Obeid, CHAPTER 21; Cummings, CHAPTER 22; Mairs, CHAPTER 26; al-Rustom, CHAPTER 28; and Reed, CHAPTER 31), the complex inter-relays of leisure, material culture, and the commercialization of body parts (MacDonald, CHAPTER 17; Moniruzzam, CHAPTER 27) and the new transnational economic nexus represented by the increase in remittances worldwide (Lindley, CHAPTER 18), make this section a rich and ready resource for teaching and further research. It is our hope that the chapters in this volume will individually and collectively be taken as a gift offering to the study of diaspora and transnationalism for students, researchers, and policymakers alike and that it will stimulate further insight, research, and discussion in the years to come.

Acknowledgments

We would like to express our gratitude to Evan Snyder, the very able and patient research assistant on this project, and to Janey Fisher, our magnificent copy editor.

Notes

1   See the website of the Diaspora, Migration, and Identities Program, at http://www.diasporas.ac.uk/, accessed January 30, 2013.
2   The process to make the diasporas the "sixth region" started in May 2003 when President Wade of Senegal moved for its adoption at the first Extraordinary Meeting of the Assembly of Heads of State in Addis Ababa, Ethiopia. The Council of Ministers then made a declaration at its ordinary meeting in May in 2005 in Addis Ababa and the first African

Union Diaspora Ministerial Conference was held in Johannesburg, South Africa, from November 16 to 18, 2007. The most significant development was the decision to amend the Constitutive Act of the African Union (AU) to include Article 3(q), which "invites and encourages the full participation of the African Diaspora as an important part of our Continent, in the building of the African Union." I am grateful to my colleague Thomas Tieku at the University of Toronto for pointing me to the relevant sections of the AU documents regarding the declaration.

3 For a further discussion of the founding of Sierra Leone and of the dispersal of children, see Ato Quayson (2012: 8–10); also "Child immigration," National Maritime Archives and Library information sheet 9, National Museums Liverpool, at www.diduknow.info/emigrants/media/child_emigration.rtf, accessed January 30, 2013; Bean and Melville (1989); Bagnell (2001).

4 Barber's argument is much more complex than can be conveyed here. But the argument with respect to terms such as immanence, Christian declaration, apocalyptic rupture, and the discontinuity of signification is so suggestive in its interdisciplinary effervescence as to provide a really stimulating model for thinking about diaspora as a philosophical concept as opposed to just a sociological one.

References

Adorno, T. 2006. *Minima Moralia: Reflections on a Damaged Life*, trans. E.F.N. Jephcott. London: Verso. (First published 1951.)

Appadurai, A. 1996. *Modernity at Large*. Minneapolis: Minnesota University Press.

Arendt, H. 1998. *The Human Condition*, 2nd edn. Chicago: University of Chicago Press. (First published 1958.)

Armstrong, J. 1976. "Mobilized and proletarian diasporas." *American Political Science Review*, 70: 393–408.

Bachelard, G. 1994. *The Poetics of Space*. New York: Beacon Books.

Bagnell, K. 2001. *The Little Immigrants: The Orphans Who Came to Canada*. Toronto: Dundurn Press.

Barber, D.C. 2011. *On Diaspora: Christianity, Religion, and Secularity*. Eugene, OR: Cascade Books.

Basch, L., Glick Schiller, N., and Blanc, C.S. 1994. *Nations Unbound: Transnational Projects, Postcolonial Predicaments, and De-Territorialized Nation-States*. London: Gordon Breach.

Basu, P. and Coleman, S. 2008. "Introduction: Migrant worlds, material cultures." *Mobilities*, 3(3): 313–330.

Baucom, I. 2005. *Specters of the Atlantic: Finance Capital, Slavery, and the Philosophy of History*. Durham, NC: Duke University Press.

Bean, P. and Melville, J. 1989. *Lost Children of the Empire*. London: Unwin Hyman.

Bernal, V. 2004. "Eritrea goes global: Reflections on nationalism in a transnational era." *Cultural Anthropology*, 19(1): 3–25.

Bourne, R. 1916. "Trans-national America." *Atlantic Monthly*, 118: 86–97.

Boyarin, J. and Boyarin, D. 2002. *Powers of Diaspora: Two Essays on the Relevance of Jewish Culture*. Minneapolis: University of Minnesota Press.

Boym, S. 2001. *The Future of Nostalgia*. New York: Basic Books.

Brah, A. 1996. *Cartographies of Diaspora: Contesting Identities*. London: Routledge.

Brown, J.N. 2005. *Dropping Anchor, Setting Sail: Geographies of Race in Black Liverpool*. Princeton: Princeton University Press.

Butler, J. 2005. *Giving an Account of One's Self*. New York: Fordham University Press.

Castles, S. 2007. "The factors that make and unmake migration policies." In A. Portes and J. DeWind (eds) *Rethinking Migration: New Theoretical and Empirical Perspectives*, pp. 29–61. New York: Berghan Books.

Chavez, L.R. 2008. *The Latino Threat: Constructing Immigrants, Citizens, and the Nation*. Stanford: Stanford University Press.

Christopher, A.J. 2008. "The quest for a census of the British Empire, 1840–1940." *Journal of Historical Geography*, 34(2): 268–285.

Clifford, J. 1997. *Routes: Travel and Translation in the Late Twentieth Century*. Cambridge, MA: Harvard University Press.

Cohen, R. 2008. *Global Diasporas: An Introduction*, 2nd edn. London: Routledge. (First published 1996.)

Constable, N. 2007. *Maid to Order in Hong Kong: Stories of Filipina Workers*. Ithaca, NY: Cornell University Press.

Darwin, J. 2009. *The Empire Project: The Rise and Fall of the British World System, 1830–1970*. Cambridge: Cambridge University Press.

Derrida, J. 2000. "Hospitality," trans. Barry Stocker and Forbes Morlock. *Angelaki: Journal of the Theoretical Humanities*, 5(3): 3–18. (First published Paris, 1997.)

Dufoix, S. 2008. *Diasporas*, trans. William Rodamor. Berkeley: University of California Press.

Edwards, B.H. 2003. *The Practice of Diaspora: Literature, Translation, and the Rise of Black Internationalism*. Boston, MA: Harvard University Press.

Eldem, E. 2011. "From blissful indifference to anguished concern: Ottoman perceptions of antiquities, 1799–1869." In Z. Bahrani, Z. Çelik, and E. Eldem (eds) *Scramble for the Past: A Story of Archaeology in the Ottoman Empire, 1753–1914*, pp. 281–330. Istanbul: SALTI/Garanti Kültür.

Ernste, H., Van Houtum, H., and Zoomers, A. 2009. "Trans-world: Debating the place and borders of places in the age of transnationalism." *Tijdschrift voor Economische en Social Geografie*, 100(5): 577–586.

Faist, T. 2000. "Transnationalization in international migration: Implications for the study of citizenship and culture." *Ethnic and Racial Studies*, 23: 189–222.

Faist, T. 2011. "Transnationalization and development: Toward an alternative agenda." *Social Analysis*, 53(3): 38–59.

Fassin, D. 2005. "Compassion and repression: the moral economy of immigration policies in France." *Cultural Anthropology* 20(3): 362–387.

Fassin, D. 2011. "Policing borders, producing boundaries: the governmentality of immigration in dark times." *Annual Review of Anthropology*, 40: 213–226.

Ferguson, N. 2002. *Empire: The Rise and Demise of the British World Order and the Lessons for Global Power*. New York: Basic Books.

Gielis, R. 2009. "A global sense of migrant places: Towards a place perspective in the study of migrant transnationalism." *Global Networks*, 9(2): 271–287.

Gikandi, S. 2011. *Slavery and the Culture of Taste*. Princeton: Princeton University Press.

Gilroy, P. 1993. *The Black Atlantic: Modernity and Double Consciousness*. Cambridge, MA: Harvard University Press.

Glick Schiller, N. 2009. "A global perspective on migration and development." *Social Analysis*, 53(3): 14–37.

Glick Schiller, N. and Çağlar, A. 2011. "Migrants and cities." In N. Glick Schiller and A. Çağlar (eds) *Locating Migration: Rescaling Cities and Migrants*. Ithaca, NY: Cornell University Press.

Glick Schiller, N. and Fouron, G.E. 2001. *Georges Woke Up Laughing: Long-Distance Nationalism and the Search for Home*. Durham, NC: Duke University Press.

Glick Schiller, N., Çaglar, A., and Guldbrandsen. T.C. 2006. "Beyond the ethnic lens: Locality, globality, and born-again incorporation." *American Ethnologist*, 33(4): 612–633.

Goldring, L. 2002. "The Mexican state and transmigrant organizations: Negotiating the boundaries of membership and participation." *Latin American Research Review*, 37: 55–99.

Gotein, S.D. 1967–1993. *A Mediterranean Society: The Jewish Communities of the Arab World as Portrayed in the Documents of the Cairo Geniza*. Berkeley: University of California Press.

Grillo, R. 2007. "Betwixt and between: Trajectories and projects of transmigration." *Journal of Ethnic and Migration Studies*, 33(2): 199–217.

Grosfoguel, R. 2007. "World-system analysis and postcolonial studies: a call for a dialogue from the "coloniality of power" approach." In R. Krishnaswamy and J.C. Hawley (eds) *The Post-Colonial and the Global*, pp. 94–104. Durham, NC: Duke University Press.

Hage, G. 1997. "At home in the entrails of the West: Multiculturalism, ethnic food and migrant home-building." In H. Grace, G. Hage, L. Johnson, *et al.* (eds) *Home/World: Space, Community and Marginality in Sydney's West*, pp. 99–153. Annandale: Pluto Press.

Hannerz, U. 1996. *Transnational Connections: Culture, People, Places*. London: Routledge.

Hirsch, M. 2012. *The Generation of Postmemory: Writing and Visual Culture after the Holocaust*. Durham, NC: Duke University Press.

Hofer, J. 1934. "Medical dissertation on nostalgia," trans. C.K. Anspach. *Bulletin of The Institute of the History of Medicine*, 2(6): 376–391. (First published 1688.)

Huang, S. and Yeoh, B.S.A. 2007. "Emotional labour and transnational domestic work: the moving geographies of 'maid abuse' in Singapore." *Mobilities*, 2(2): 195–217.

Isotalo, R. 2009. "Policing the transnational: On implications for migrants, refugees, and scholarship." *Social Analysis*, 53(3): 60–84.

Krieger, J. 2005. *Globalization and State Power: Who Wins When America Rules?* London: Pearson Longman.

Kymlicka, W. 2007. "The forms of liberal multiculturalism." In *Multicultural Odysseys: Navigating the New International Politics of Diversity*, pp. 61–85. Oxford: Oxford University Press.

Levitt, P. and Glick Schiller, N. 2004. "Conceptualizing simultaneity: a transnational social field perspective on society." *International Migration Review*, 38: 1002–1039.

Linebaugh, P. and Rediker, M. 2000. *The Many-Headed Hydra: Sailors, Slaves, Commoners and the Hidden History of the Revolutionary Atlantic*. London: Verso.

Maas, W. 2003. "Population and demographics." In M.E. Page (ed.) *Colonialism: An International Social, Cultural, and Political Encyclopedia*, Volume 2, p. 479–481. Santa Barbara, CA: ABC-CLIO.

Mankekar, P. 2002. "'India shopping': Indian grocery stores and transnational configurations of belonging." *Ethnos*, 67(1): 75–98.

Mignolo, W. 2000. *Local Histories/Global Designs: Essays on the Coloniality of Power, Subaltern Knowledges, and Border Thinking*. Princeton: Princeton University Press.

Miller, D. 2008. "Migration, material culture and tragedy: Four moments in Caribbean migration." *Mobilities* 3(3): 397–413.

Modrzejewski, J.M. 1997. *The Jews of Egypt: From Rameses II to Emperor Hadrian*. Princeton: Princeton University Press.

Napolitano, V. 2007. "Of migrant revelations and anthropological awakenings." *Social Anthropology*, 15(1): 71–87.

Nye, J.S. Jr. 1976. "Independence and interdependence." *Foreign Policy*, 22: 130–161.

Olwig, K.F. 2007. *Caribbean Journeys: An Ethnography of Migration and Home in Three Family Networks*. Durham, NC: Duke University Press.

Ong, A. 1996. "Cultural citizenship as subject-making: Immigrants negotiate racial and cultural boundaries in the United States." *Cultural Anthropology*, 37(5): 737–762.

Ong, A. 1999. *Flexible Citizenship: The Cultural Logics of Transnationality*. Durham, NC: Duke University Press.

Ong, A. 2008. "Cyberpublics and diaspora politics among transnational Chinese." In J.X. Inda and R. Rosaldo (eds) *The Anthropology of Globalization*, pp. 167–183. Oxford: Blackwell.

Østergaard-Nielsen, E.K. 2003. "The politics of migrant's transnational political practices." *International Migration Review*, 37: 760–786.

Parreñas, R.S. 2001. *Servants of Globalization: Women, Migration and Domestic Work*. Stanford, CA: Stanford University Press.

Portes, A, Guarnizo, L.E., and Landolt, P. 1999. "The study of transnationalism: Pitfalls and promise of an emergent research field." *Ethnic and Racial Studies*, 22: 217–298.

Pries, L. 2009. "Transnationalisation and the challenge of differentiated concepts of space." *Tijdschrift voor Economische en Social Geografie*, 100(5): 587–597.

Quayson, A. 2012. "Introduction: Postcolonial literature in a changing historical frame." In A. Quayson (ed.) *The Cambridge History of Postcolonial Literature*, Volume 1, pp. 1–29. Cambridge: Cambridge University Press.

Rajak, T. 2009. *Translation and Survival: The Greek Bible of the Ancient Jewish Diaspora*. Oxford: Oxford University Press.

Rothman, N. 2011. *Brokering Empire: Trans-Imperial Subjects Between Venice and Istanbul*. Ithaca, NY: Cornell University Press.

Rouse, R. 1991. "Mexican migration and the social space of postmodernism." *Diaspora*, 1: 8–23.

Rouse, R. 1992. "Making sense of settlement: Class transformation, cultural struggle and transnationalism among Mexican migrants in the United States." In N. Glick Schiller, L. Basch, and C.S. Blanc (eds) *Towards a Transnational Perspective on Migration*, pp. 25–52. New York: New York Academy of Sciences.

Rushdie, S. 1991. *Imaginary Homelands: Essays and Criticism, 1981–1991*. London: Granta.

Safran, W. 1991. "Diasporas in modern societies: Myths of homeland and return." *Diaspora: A Journal of Transnational Studies*, 1(1): 83–99.

Sassen, S. 1999. *Guests and Aliens*. New York: New Press.

Sassen, S. 2001. *The Global City: New York, London, Tokyo*. Princeton: Princeton University Press.

Saxenian, A. 2006. *The New Argonauts: Regional Advantage in a Global Economy*. Cambridge, MA: Harvard University Press.

Serkeci, I., Cohen, J.H., and Ratha, D. (eds) 2012. *Migration and Remittances During the Global Financial Crisis and Beyond*. Washington, DC: World Bank Publications.

Sheffer, G. 2003. *Diaspora Politics: At Home Abroad*. Cambridge: Cambridge University Press.

Smith, M.P. 2001. *Transnational Urbanism: Locating Globalization*. Oxford: Blackwell.

Tölölyan, K. 1991. "Rethinking diaspora(s): Stateless power in the transnational moment." *Diaspora: A Journal of Transnational Studies*, 5(1): 3–36.

Tölölyan, K. 2000. "Elites and institutions in the Armenian transnation." *Diaspora: A Journal of Transnational Studies*, 9(1): 107–136.

Tölölyan, K. 2007. "The contemporary discourse of diaspora studies." *Comparative Studies of South Asia, Africa and the Middle East*, 27(3): 647–655.

Verdery, K. 1996. "Transnationalism, nationalism, citizenship, and property: Eastern Europe since 1989." *American Ethnologist*, 25(2): 291–306.

Vertovec, S. 2004. "Migration and other modes of transnationalism: Towards conceptual cross-fertilization." *International Migration Review*, 38: 970–1001.

Werbner, P. 1999. "Global pathways: Working class cosmopolitans and the creation of transnational ethnic worlds." *Social Anthropology*, 7(1): 17–35.

Werbner, P. 2002. *The Migration Process: Capital, Gifts and Offerings Among Manchester Pakistanis*. Oxford: Berg.

Wilding, R. 2006. "'Virtual' intimacies? Families communicating across transnational contexts." *Global Networks: A Journal of Transnational Affairs*, 6(2): 125–142.

Wilding, R. 2007. "Transnational ethnographies and anthropological imaginings of migrancy." *Journal of Ethnic and Migration Studies*, 33(2): 331–348.

Williams, E. 1944. *Capitalism and Slavery*. Chapel Hill: University of North Carolina Press.

Wilson, J.L. 2005. *Nostalgia: Sanctuary of Meaning*. Lewisburg, PA: Bucknell University Press.

Wimmer, A. and Glick Schiller, N. 2002. "Methodological nationalism and beyond: Nation building, migration, and the social sciences." *Global Networks*, 2(4): 301–334.

Winland, D.N. 2007. *We Are Now a Nation: Croats Between "Home" and "Homeland."* Toronto: University of Toronto Press.

Yeoh, B. and Huang, S. 2010. "Transnational domestic workers and the negotiation of mobility and work practices in Singapore's home-spaces." *Mobilities*, 5(2): 219–236.

Part I

Transnationalism and Diaspora
Through the Disciplines

Chapter 2

The Anthropology of Transnationalism and Diaspora

Girish Daswani

Can we speak of the anthropology of transnationalism and diaspora? This chapter seeks to answer this question in three ways. In briefly addressing the history of anthropology, I argue that in many ways anthropology has always been about the "trans-" and the "nation" in its study of cultural differences elsewhere. It is in the broader anthropological spirit of understanding the conjunctions of cultural meaning and social change that ethnographic studies on diaspora and transnationalism are located. Secondly, I show that while anthropologists have been working on these questions for some time, there is an important need to understand how we use conceptual categories such as transnationalism and diaspora, and how they are distinct (or not) from each other and other categories that have become used synonymously with them, such as globalization. Finally, I identify some major themes that have emerged and look at anthropology's contributions to the dialogue around transnationalism and diaspora. This chapter is by no means an exhaustive review of the literature on transnationalism and diaspora within anthropology. Instead it explores the trajectory of the transnational and diasporic in anthropology, while paying attention to methods, differences between heuristic concepts, and to the main areas of research anthropology has contributed to. I see this intervention as the beginning of a conversation around how anthropology can contribute to a dialogue that is inherently interdisciplinary.

The "Trans-" and the "Nation" of Anthropology

Anthropologists have always been concerned about the "trans-" and the "nation" through their research on people's rootedness in specific sites and their historical

A Companion to Diaspora and Transnationalism, First Edition.
Edited by Ato Quayson and Girish Daswani.
© 2013 Blackwell Publishing Ltd. Published 2013 by Blackwell Publishing Ltd.

movements across space and time. In the late nineteenth and early twentieth centuries, anthropologists asked questions about how sociopolitical organizations and cultures "elsewhere" (described as "savage" or "primitive" societies) come together, develop, and spread. Evolutionism, for example, emphasized the growing complexity of culture over time. Diffusionism, on the other hand, was more concerned about the transmission of ideas or cultural "traits" between places. Although both shared a diachronic perspective, they offered different explanations for the question of how cultures change. While this earlier trend in anthropology focused on the diffusion or evolution of people and their cultural ideas over time, another group took a synchronic perspective in studying other cultures and their political organization in the non-Western world, asking comparative questions about their own (Western) societal development and the role of kinship, political society, and the nation in that development process. Taking different approaches to the study of human evolution and the human condition, anthropologists shared a focus on the comparative development of social and cultural traits within specific areas, and shared efforts to compare these findings across regional, colonial, and national contexts.

These works continue to contribute to contemporary anthropological discussions. However in sometimes choosing to focus on the internal dynamics of a given society, practically comprehending the field site as an imaginary sealed laboratory, many earlier ethnographies have been informed by colonialism and Enlightenment ideas, and driven by the assumption that "culture" could be easily mapped onto enclosed places and bounded units of analysis (Gupta and Ferguson 1997a; Appadurai 1996). Anthropology has since experienced different phases of self-examination, through an engagement with neo-Marxist, feminist, postmodern, and postcolonial auto-critiques between the late 1960s and the end of the twentieth century (e.g., Ortner 1984). The earlier (synchronic) sociocultural anthropology that focused on describing the social structures and cultures of "natives" led to the self-criticism and self-reflexivity of the 1980s. A more radical critique came with James Clifford and George Marcus' book *Writing Culture* (1986), in which many of the contributors sought to highlight the representational characteristics of ethnography, including its effect of naively presenting cultural wholes or integrated societies. Rather than taking emplaced difference as the field's starting point, in their wake, many anthropologists began highlighting the limitations of a bounded culture concept and turned to the study of transnational construction of differences.

There has been a re-evaluation of longstanding assumptions regarding spatially fixed ideas of cultures and a concomitant shift away from "tribe study" and "village studies" as the site of cultural production and social change (Gupta and Ferguson 1997b; Hannerz 1987, 1989). Ideas around the "bounded society" as a perfect microcosm of larger sociopolitical units have been challenged and the ways in which anthropological texts are produced called into question (Geertz 1973: 23–24; 1988). One criticism of this postmodern turn in anthropology is its overemphasis on the subjective narrative above "objective facts" and "independent social structures" (Gellner 1992: 29). However these different perspectives are not incommensurable or mutually exclusive. While anthropologists have become more reflective when

considering the connection between society, culture, and social change, it is important to remember that criticisms of the earlier body of work within anthropology
do not detract from their valuable ethnographic contributions and analytical insights.
Anthropologists have adapted, and continue to adapt, their research questions
according to the larger social and cultural changes affecting people's lives. They have
also responded to a call for new techniques for conducting fieldwork, through which
to reflect upon the ways in which the local and global are ever intertwined and
implicated in each other.

Anthropologists and other ethnographers have been sensitive to population
movements and the multifaceted nature of social relationships that span "home"
and "elsewhere." One need only think of the Chicago School and the Manchester
School, two centers of urban ethnographic research in the mid-twentieth century.
While studies in villages, and of village life, continue to be important, urban ethnography has drawn attention to issues of city life, rural–urban migration, residential neighborhoods, kinship connections, and trans-local grassroots organizations,
amongst others. The Manchester School of Social Anthropology, which was founded
by Max Gluckman in the 1950s, trained anthropologists who used situational analysis and extended case methods in understanding social change in colonial Africa
(Gluckman 1963; Mitchell 1956; Epstein 1958). Many Manchester School anthropologists paid particular attention to African migration to cities and urban environments, which included a greater number of interactions with strangers. They asked
questions around the dynamics of change and continuity, individual agency and
social structure, and how new collective identities were reconstructed around people's movement. One product of the Manchester School was Abner Cohen (1969),
who studied the Hausa Quarter in Ibadan, southern Nigeria, where an urban
migrant neighborhood became a new context for ethnic socialization that produced
subtle shifts in collective self-understanding, a process he described as detribaliza-
tion and retribalization. Cohen described how a newly arriving Hausa trader in
Ibadan, while sharing an ethnic *category* could not simply join the already existing
ethnic *group* until his Hausa identity "[became] the expression of his involvement
in a web of live social relationships which arise from current, mutual interests within
a new social setting" (1969: 29). Developed as an ethnographic tool in the late 1960s
and early 1970s the social network approach became a popular way to study the
connections and interaction within and between migrant groups, in cities like
London, and in different urban surroundings in southern Africa, as well as in Sicily
and Nova Scotia (Mitchell 1974). It was used to overcome the weaknesses of a
community-centered approach in anthropology, "which sometimes missed the fact
that significant social relations were not bounded by the idea of community" (Kapferer 2005: 112).

In other words while "cultures" and "communities" are social constructs that
spatially connect, and disconnect, people in real ways, its effects are never simply
constructed but are also determined through relationships. Anthropology is committed to understanding the extension, negotiation, and hierarchical nature of these
social relationships across space and time and within specific places. If cultural

differences are established through connections across space, as well as inscribed in space, it is establishing a connection to others through fieldwork that sociocultural anthropology is known for, and this is, as Sidney Mintz (2000: 177) eloquently put it, "the silver lining to any cloud that hangs over our discipline."

Rethinking Cultural Difference through Multiple Connections

While the classic notion of fieldwork is characterized by the anthropologist who travels to a specific field site to do participant observation, multi-sited research projects that span more than one location have also become more common. If Branislow Malinowski is credited with moving anthropological practice from the "verandah" into the "field," this new shift is toward studying several "fields" of interaction, in which actors are involved. While ethnography remains "the key research practice and emblem of cultural anthropology as a distinctive form of knowledge production" it is no longer based on the assumption that research in one location that produces culture (Marcus 1998: 231). In line with multi-sited fieldwork methods (Marcus 1995; Gardner 1999; Clifford 1992, 1994), and a "cosmopolitan ethnography" (Appadurai 1996: 52; Stoller 1997, 2002), anthropologists also take into account the wider context in which the "local" is positioned and the ways in which "locality" circulates and is reconstructed through multiple sites of social and linguistic interaction. From online communities to stock markets, global religious movements, and the world of activism, anthropologists cover a very diverse range of field sites, while continuing to spend extended periods of time in learning the language of these social worlds and the cultural ingredients from which they are built. In cases where our interlocutors are mobile, spatially dispersed, and a part of larger social networks, the advice to "follow the people" (Marcus 1995) makes good sense. But doubts about the depth and quality of global-oriented fieldwork surface from time to time (Mintz 2000; Hirsch *et al.* 2007; Marcus 2006: 115).

Anthropological research continues to be driven by our interlocutors' lives, their activities, the questions they ask about the world, and how they address them. For Mark-Anthony Falzon (2004) who studied the Sindhi diaspora, moving between different locations and sites of entrepreneurial and family networks, spread around the world, was the only way to understand what it meant to be culturally "Sindhi." For my own research on Ghanaian Pentecostals in London and southern Ghana, multi-sited fieldwork was an important way to understand what my interlocutors meant when they said to me that Pentecostalism and Christian life in Ghana and London were very different. However to assume that the anthropology of transnationalism has completely moved away from studies of locality and toward a new multi-sited or global fieldwork approach is not quite accurate. As I mentioned before, earlier anthropologists were already asking questions about the diffusion and evolution of culture, albeit with a different conceptual apparatus.

Anthropologists recognize that people do not have to travel to imagine and discuss the impact of new (dis-)connections or to be affected by the increased mobility and changes around the world. As Mintz (1998: 120) puts it, that a "community" can be thought to comprehend at the same time a place in California and a place in Mexico because some of the people in those two places are connected, really does not mean that the unilocal communities have stopped existing, nor that bilocal communities are unprecedented. Most people in almost any community do not migrate. Most stay put.

Working with non-migrants in Mexico, Hilary Dick (2010; CHAPTER 24, this volume) also describes how migrant discourse and images of a "beyond here" are equally mobile and connect people across the United States–Mexico border. Online communities are another example of how virtual places create social and affective interaction that simultaneously connects people from different parts of the world (Boelstroff 2009; Wilson and Peterson 2002).

To phrase the ethnographic problem in another way: instead of starting with an analysis of "global force" (Burawoy 2000) or the juxtaposition between the global and the local, many anthropologists have also started by reiterating the questions asked by ordinary people about the "global" (Moore 2004) and the "local" (Lambek 2011); and in the case of the latter, questions that include: "what are the centres and limits of our lived worlds"; and "what are the spaces for sustained ethical practice, meaningful work, effective political action?" (Lambek 2011: 198). A multi-sited approach does not decrease the importance of the local nor diminish the importance of the imaginative reach of those who remain in one place. Multiple sites of fieldwork should not be the result of a prior theoretical agenda, or reflective of the ethnographers' own transnational identity, but initiated from the specific cultural and historical conditions that concern our interlocutors' worlds.

Moreover, many of the earlier studies by anthropologists continue to be relevant to the study of mobility and shifting cultural identities. For example Malinowski's (1922) interest in the kula exchange demonstrated how the complexity of these circular movements of ceremonial exchange were central to the cultural lives of the Trobriand islanders. E. E. Evans-Pritchard (1940), in *The Nuer*, describes a segmentary organization in which personal identity is relative to the social context in which one finds oneself. One's identity and where one considers "home" are always situated in cultural understandings of place, as well as located within a structure of power relationships, but they are also context-dependent, experienced according to different forms of interpellation, and interpreted according to interpersonal considerations such as the social distance and closeness between speakers. Growing up in Singapore, I learnt to alternate between separate yet overlapping designations of identity. In everyday conversations and as well as bureaucratic-speak, I was "Singaporean" in the context of citizenship, "Indian" in the context of race (as printed on my national identity card), and "Sindhi" in the context of my family's linguistic and diasporic background; a scalar representation of self that intersected along different conjunctions of nationality, transnationality, race, and diaspora. How is one's identity construed as global, transnational, or diasporic and at what moments in time? One consideration in understanding what an anthropology of transnationalism and diaspora might look like is perceiving the ways in which these terms overlap. There is a need to review how concepts such as globalization, transnationalism, and diaspora, have been deployed, many times interchangeably, and to what purposes, and also to what extent they differ from each other.

Disentangling Transnationalism from Globalization

Globalization as a concept has been used to refer to the dramatic transformation of the modern world – an economic and societal transformation brought about by political shifts (the end of the Cold War for example), technological and communications advancements (internet, cell phones, social networking sites), and economic restructuring associated with neoliberal capitalism (opening up of former trade barriers, structural adjustment policies). In many ways globalization theories draw from but seek to move past Wallerstein's world-systems theory of the 1970s and 1980s. As post-Fordist production methods allow transnational corporations to move factories to any site that offers cheap labor and tax deductions, and as structural adjustment policies supported by the International Monetary Fund and World Bank steer less developed countries toward neoliberal policies that open them up to self-interested private investment, anthropologists invoke globalization to speak about the inequalities, the disjunctures, and the friction experienced when global capital arrives (see Inda and Rosaldo 2008). Globalization theories have come to describe what Steven Gregory (2007) calls "the Devil behind the mirror," the dissonance between what transnational capital promises and the reality on the ground.

The term *globalization* has also become a dumping ground for all sorts of different meanings, and theoretical battles over what it is and what it is not (Cooper 2005). In the literature on globalization scholars claim that our world is dissolving into a network society or a "space of flows" (Castells 1998; Urry 2001, 2004) and becoming increasingly deterritorialized (Appadurai 1996). They have also argued that the rise of global connections is causing the decline of the nation-state in its relative importance to other trans-statal connections (Hannerz 1996; Appadurai 1996). Arjun Appadurai's idea (1996: 31) of the "imagination as a social practice" has opened up a productive space for theorizing about the shifting interconnections between the "local" and "global." In particular, Appadurai suggested considering how various "-scapes" of the imaginary are constituted despite geospatial disjunctures and discontinuities, and enumerated the following possibilities: ethnoscapes, mediascapes, technoscapes, financescapes, and ideoscapes. As much as Appadurai's ideas have helped shape anthropological work on globalization, there is an unresolved tension between his claims of rupture and the particular cultural contexts and historical specificities of how these ruptures take place (Heyman and Campbell 2009). Alongside questions of what is changing globally, it is also important to consider how "the global" is imaginatively "conjured" (Tsing 2000; Moore 2004). The "global" is what Henrietta Moore (2004: 73) calls a "concept-metaphor," a term "whose exact meanings can never be specified in advance" but only "defined in practice and in context." Transnationalism, on the other hand, is generally used in less abstract ways to address the cultural specificities of these changing global conditions, as they are experienced by people in, and through, nation-states, and when addressing questions of the nation and nationalism, citizenship and diaspora.

In the Afterword to her book *Flexible Citizenship* Aihwa Ong (1999: 241–242) proposes "an anthropology of transnationality" that is critical of "totalizing discourses of globalization." She suggests that "a newer generation of anthropologists who are freeing themselves from the binarims of older models" will be able to take into account "the complex interplay between capitalism, the nation-state, and power dynamics in particular times and places." By exploring the nuances of transnational lives, anthropologists have pointed to the ways in which different groups, who have unequal access to global processes, move across geographical, social, and economic boundaries, where rupture and immobility matter, and where nation-states continue to play an important role in mediating border crossings of diasporic groups and policing citizenship.

Diaspora and Transnationalism

Historically, the social sciences have reproduced the nation as the "normal" – central and natural – container for organizing research and interpreting its findings. As a consequence, directly or indirectly, scholarship has reproduced cultural hierarchies where minorities and immigrant groups have remained the "Other" within pre-existing national societies. The study of diaspora and transnationalism has allowed us to challenge such a methodological nationalism and to better understand and interrogate both the imaginaries in which people see themselves connected to each other, and the different ways that transnational movements and affiliations are situated across borders simultaneously. Yet in using terms like *diaspora* and *transnationalism* to challenge the constraints of the nation-state, how much of the distinctions between these two categories are we taking for granted? Often these categories tend to bleed into each other. Just as there are different ways of being diasporic, there are multiple ways of being transnational, since both categories include a multiplicity of historical trajectories and lived experiences that effect people in different ways.

Scholars like James Clifford (1994, 1996) have argued that diaspora populations do not share the same theoretical point of origin as immigrants, in that they do not necessarily come from an "elsewhere." For Clifford, diasporas operate in a somewhat alternative public space that cannot be reduced to national boundaries. This is because, as he states (1994: 307), "Positive articulations of diaspora identity reach outside the normative territory and temporality (myth/history) of the nation-state." Others have since echoed this concern, recognizing that the limits of diaspora theory come from analysis that "privileges categories generated by the modern forms of the nation-state" (Axel 2002: 235). Transnational migration theories, on the other hand, have often defined transnational identities as those which cross "multiple national borders" (Ramji 2006: 646). So while transnational migration theories still give preference to nation-states and use them as key points of reference in migration and other circulations, diaspora communities are seen to move beyond this and, as Clifford discusses, do not easily fit into linear migration models of assimilation or transnational migration theories. A way forward, and perhaps a way out of this conundrum, is in thinking about how different modes of temporality are utilized when imagining and performing a diaspora consciousness (connections to a distant and imagined homeland) and transnational migration (the crossing of national borders and the simultaneity between discontinuous space-times).

While diasporas tend to evoke an idea of rupture and a sacred time that foregrounds rituals, performances, and embodied practices that allow people to reconnect with and re-create "homeland," transnationalism points to an irony and tension between the personal and group ambitions to transcend geographical, social, and economic boundaries, and the political and cultural barriers and boundary-making process that accompany such movement and mobility. Where "the transnational" might be inadequate in "exploring the complex relationships that are maintained between people and places" (Wilding 2007: 343), diaspora becomes useful in understanding the work of the imagination and social memory, in underlying notions of "home" and "nation" beyond these movements across space. I now proceed to look at how diaspora and transnationalism emerge as concepts of analysis and point to the ambiguities that surround them.

Diasporas, Homeland, and Place-Making

Diaspora commonly refers to different kinds of migrant groups who have left their homeland but who continue to share a religious, ethno-national, or national identity. Since the mid-1980s, and through the 1990s, diaspora has expanded in meaning, to include more groups of people and placing more importance to the non-center and hybridity as central to diasporic identities. Asylum-seekers, refugees, exiles, forced migrants, immigrants, expatriates, guest workers, trading communities, and ethnic communities of various kinds, have come to be described as in diaspora or as tokens of a single diaspora. Some scholars have tried to retain a sense of consistency to a word, described as stretched to the point of potential irrelevance. Rogers Brubaker (2005) for example, has argued that diaspora should consist of at least three core elements: dispersion, homeland orientation, and boundary maintenance. Robin Cohen (2009) has also suggested holding on to the notion of "homeland," distinguishing diaspora according to how people orientate to homeland differently. The challenge for scholars is to account for the political-historical complexities of different types of diaspora, while acknowledging that the idea of a homeland and practices of place-making are important ingredients to any definition of diaspora.

Given these different ways of imagining diaspora, and experiencing diasporic identity, how do we proceed to use the term? If diaspora is distinguished from other migratory experience because it invokes a multiplicity of meanings, which evades the linear model of assimilation and integrationist paradigms, then is diaspora simply about different ways of desiring a home that one no longer lives in? Diasporas are characteristic of a spatial longing, as well as a temporal desire, for an imagined past and future. Through his work on the Sikh longing for Khalistan, a homeland that is yet to exist, Brian Axel (2004: 27) looks at how this particular Khalistani Sikh subjectivity is produced through knowledge production. He argues that, "diaspora, rather than a community of individuals dispersed from a homeland, may be understood more productively as a globally mobile category of identification." Describing this Sikh diaspora as the outcome of histories of violence and internet mediation, he offers a view of diaspora "as a *process* productive of disparate temporalities (anteriorities, presents, futurities), displacements, and subjects." Similarly Patrick Eisenlohr (2006), in describing Mauritian "Indian" attempts to make India the ancestral homeland – through making modern Hindi the ancestral language and through re-creating religious performances – takes into account the divergent temporal orders that shape the relationship between diaspora and homeland. He points out that a linear conception of "empty, homogenous" time is not the only chronotope in imagining the nation. Rather, the invocation of the mythical "time of the ancestors" is another way of establishing a temporal equivalence and simultaneity between the "past" and "now," "there" and "here." These works reveal the ways in which the diasporic subject is crafted, and emerges, in different ways, and how performances and performative utterances evoke strong feelings of attachment to an imagined place of origin.

Diaspora, then, is not merely a transnational phenomenon. It is also about imagining and planting roots, in a place or multiple places, while sharing or contesting memories of having arrived from elsewhere. Looking at how diaspora communities are represented and imagine themselves as members of a community has become an important ethnographic contribution to how race, sexuality, nation, and gender become articulated in one place. Jacqueline N. Brown's (2005) ethnography on the black community in Liverpool is a good example of how this port city, a former center of the African slave trade, has become invested with local meanings and shifting identities of what it means to be black in Britain. These Liverpool-born blacks create and contest different categories of social relations and constructions of personhood, between themselves, between themselves and other black communities, and between themselves and white communities. Liverpool city becomes a signifier, a place through which to understand the power asymmetries and shifting relations within the black community, as well as how these different groups draw on diasporas's resources, based on gendered and generational differences and the politics of racial categories (Brown 2005). Being *here*, in this place, matters. These questions of relatedness and place-making have also been important for anthropologists whose work look at the context of home-making and family networks that are grounded in specific localities (Olwig 2007; CHAPTER 21, this volume). At the same time, community and home are created, not in one place, but across several sites of interaction. Roger Rouse's (1991) idea of "transnational migrant circuits" continues to be useful in understanding how the migration of family members and close kin between two or more localities is not a linear movement between distinct places, but a matter of spatially extended relationships that continue to circulate through people, money, goods, and information.

The literature on return migration has also helped shift attention to the different experiences of ethnic diasporas who, when returning to a place they call home, experience a simultaneous sense of rupture and alienation. The desire of returning to one's homeland, in ethnographic examples such as Japanese Brazilians returning to Japan for economic employment (Tsuda 2003), Gujarati Hindus in London returning to Gujarat for retirement (Ramji 2006), or Jamaicans from the United States and Britain resettling in Jamaica (Horst 2007), is in a lived tension with the reality of return. Returning home never quite plays out as expected, as "home" might have become unfamiliar in the time they were away. Different factors affect the experience of return, including their social status when they return, when and why they left their homeland and the frequency and types of communication they maintained while away. Ethnic migrants who return home often find themselves caught betwixt-and-between two or multiple worlds and social-economic realities. They begin to question where "home" truly is and whether they should have returned in the first place. Many continue to maintain connections to the places they lived in for so many years, reproducing the sociality, culinary tastes, and material intimacies of their previous host society. "Home" is not defined by the return but through the different ways in which intimate connections and disconnections are made.

Settler-colonial nations that have narratives of coming from elsewhere, like the United States, Canada, and Australia, or of return, like Israel, also pose important questions about the traumatic effects of settlement, on indigenous social life. Elizabeth Povinelli (2002) who works with indigenous Australians has written about these settler-colonial liberal states as a "liberal diaspora." According to Povinelli the ideology of liberalism – which includes "elaborations of the enlightenment idea that society should be organized on the basis of rational mutual understanding" (2002: 6) – travels well and transforms itself in different diasporic settings. In exploring liberal multiculturalism from the perspective of Australian indigenous social life Povinelli argues that the ethics of multiculturalism perpetuates unequal systems of power by demanding that indigenous subjects identify with an impossible standard of authentic traditional culture. The inequities of such a liberal multiculturalism arise not from its weak commitment to difference but from its even stronger vision of national cohesion. Multicultural ideologies thus serve to reinforce liberal regimes through which nostalgia for an authentic past becomes an important driving force behind the construction of citizenship and political subjectivity.

Citizenship and Political Subjectivity

While the rise of a post-national imagination has allowed people around the world to move back to the countries of their parents and ancestors and, in some cases, to mobilize and hold these nation-states (especially authoritarian ones) accountable, we also need to remember that the authoritative force and violence of the nation-state is not a thing of the past. The rhetoric of protecting national borders and the policing of internal group boundaries converge in bureaucratic regimentation and violent forms of policing and oppression. We should be wary of understanding the transnational movement of people and images across borders as merely a product of the increasing role of modern media and the decreasing role of the nation-state (Appadurai 1996). Examples of state power and oppression force us to pay more attention to the limits of transnationalism and to the ethical concerns of citizenship, to "the process by which, at the threshold of the modern era, natural life begins to be included in the mechanisms and calculations of state power, and politics turns into biopolitics" (Agamben 1998: 5).

While the concept "transnationalism" challenges a traditional state-centric paradigm, the nation-state continues to be an important analytical consideration. More than simply studying the integration processes of migrants in receiving countries, or tracing the movements of people around the world who are escaping exploitative conditions at home, anthropologists pay attention to migrants' political subjectivity. While much of the earlier writing on citizenship has been tied to the legal-political aspects of the nation-state, anthropological scholarship has allowed for a more complex understanding of citizenship, through which people become subjects of power relations. Citizenship is not simply a legal claim, or about public-civic participation, but also operates as a form of governmentality and as disciplinary power (Foucault 2008). The broader Gramscian question that frequently returns and begs to be asked is: How do forms of normative coercion become taken as "common sense"? In other words how do institutions of identity formation operate to naturalize difference, and what is being rendered invisible through its apparent transparency? The response of anthropology has generally been to reject the "given" or fixed nature of conceptual formations that present identity as a stable phenomenon in favor of an approach that sees it as a part of a conceptualized subject formation. Take for example Fredrik Barth's (1969) influential research amongst the Pathans of the Swat Valley in Pakistan, which led him to argue that a concept like "ethnicity" is historically constructed in specific moments, when social groups culturally distinguish themselves from each other. While Barth's study did not address citizenship *per se*, his focus on the social constructedness of identity continues to be helpful in moving beyond questions of *who* is a citizen, and toward questions that ask about *what processes* make a citizen at any moment in time and space.

Anthropologists studying immigration in North America and Europe have analyzed concepts such as race and ethnicity in immigrant discourse, as they emerge in everyday discourses of power and political representations. They ask questions such as: How does the racial categorization of immigrants in Europe take on the "new savage slot" (Silverstein 2005)? How does talk about "illegal aliens" in the United States become commonly conflated with the term "Mexican immigrants" (Dick 2011a; De Genova 2002)? How do national categories such as "multiculturalism," "diversity," and "ethnicity" become "polite ways of avoiding the charged politics of 'race'" (Dick and Wirtz 2011)? While migratory movement across borders, and within borderlands, especially in the Mexican–US context, have been the focus of ongoing anthropological research (Urciuoli 1995; Alvarez 1995; Dick 2011b), more recent work on ethnic migrant groups in Britain has also been sensitive to the idea of migrant identity as a process, informed by the cultural dynamics of these groups, and being rooted in Britain through moral ideas and values about belonging (A. Shaw 1988; P. Werbner 2002; Fumanti and Werbner 2010; Fumanti 2010).

For many immigrant communities in diaspora, the idea of "return" is no longer important, since they no longer see, or never saw, themselves "in" diaspora. Rather than a desire to return to their homeland, they see themselves belonging to their country of residence, which is in many cases also their country of birth. They continue to live in these countries even in the face of abuse and challenges made to their claims of citizenship. In some cases, undocumented migrants fulfill certain criteria or are able to prove their rootedness in order to be granted legal residency. Take for example the second-generation children of Latin American (non-Jewish) labor migrant parents, who have lived in Israel for most, if not all, of their life. They were prevented from being deported, like the children of many other labor migrant groups, because they could speak Hebrew like Israelis and thus appeared native (Paz 2011). The images and reports of these children in the Israeli media, confirming their cultural assimilation and patriotism, served to crystallize national public and nationalist sentiments in their favor. In such cases "return" may be an idea that has no personal significance for members of a diaspora. We therefore need to understand diaspora as a contested and historical relation, which is brought into being through different processes.

Refugees and Asylum-Seekers

Refugees – the classic case for defining diaspora – are a diaspora that share a theme of displacement and exile from a homeland. However, just as there are many kinds of diasporas, there are many different types of refugee – from the camp refugee who awaits return, to those who work and participate in economic and social life outside the camps, to the refugees who have settled elsewhere but continue to see themselves in exile from their homeland, to those who consider themselves in exile or are displaced but who are not granted refugee status. Refugees, even if they have fled from the same homeland, can share different realities of coexistence. The extension of refugee status is not a natural condition but involves a process of becoming and comes into existence through acts of interpellation. Take for example Greek Cypriots fleeing their homes during the invasion of the Turkish army in 1974. Peter Loizos (1981) describes how the Greek Cypriots learn that they have become refugees through the media and after hearing others use the word "refugee" to designate them. While initially resentful, they slowly come to terms with the fact that they can no longer return to their previous homes and lives. According to Loizos (1981) these refugees shared a preoccupation with a sense of loss and remembering the things of the past – the land, houses, and social relations that they embodied. Yael Navaro-Yashin (2009) takes up this point from the perspective of Turkish Cypriot refugees who are forced to live with the memory of previous social relations through these same houses, land, and objects they appropriated from the Greek Cypriots.

In Liisa Malkki's work (1995, 1996) on Hutu refugees from Burundi, living in Tanzania, the purity of the past is preserved through historical narratives produced in refugee camps, while they await their eventual return. These camp refugees see their refugee status as a moral condition that is productive and meaningful. For the refugee camp administrators, who represent them to the outside world, however, these "refugees" become judged according to their ability to perform victimhood and effectively become speechless subjects. While camp refugees reproduced the narrative of being victims, "merchant refugees," who lived outside the camps and engage in commerce, attracted the criticism of both "camp refugees and their administrators" who agreed "on the point that a rich refugee was a contradiction in terms" (Malkki 1996: 382). While refugees are the objects of humanitarian intervention and biased media representations, Timm Lau (CHAPTER 19) also shows how Tibetan refugees in India and Canada, who engage in business and trade, are able to create long-term relationships and maintain local affiliations, irrespective of the camp and the imagined homeland.

The "human rights" discourse, which applies to asylum-seekers and refugees, may be set up as a universal value but exists selectively and is contingent upon specific national contexts and processes of selective application and enforcement. In the late 1980s and the 1990s, nation-state discourses on asylum-seekers and refugees in Europe and North America shifted from one of humanitarianism to one of securitization. These state measures, which have increased since September 2001, have come to define our moral world where moments of compassion and expressions of sympathy serve to redeem a country from humanitarian obligation (Fassin 2005). Borders have become more securitized and there has been an increasing moral panic over Islam, asylum-seekers, refugees, and illegal immigrants and an increasingly intimate surveillance over diaspora populations that state institutions associate with their national enemies (Howell 2011). The idea that immigrants pose a cultural threat to the nation serves to normalize anti-immigration arguments, which claim "that immigrants steal jobs, exploit public services, and pose security risks" (Vertovec 2011: 242). However "far from being clandestine aliens sneaking in through deserts, on boats, or in trucks" most undocumented migrants in these parts of the world "are long-term residents in the receiving country where they live, work, and marry, and start a family, but where they always remain in a state of precariousness that facilitates their exploitation" (Fassin 2011: 218).

Traveling Suitcase Trade

The label "migrant" matters less when applied to traveling routes that are circular in nature, when the settled immigrant is replaced by the stranger, entrepreneur, the suitcase trader, and the smuggler. While trading communities, such as the Hausa of West Africa, are ethnic diasporas that capitalize on solidarity and make use of ties of kinship, religion, politics, and finance, to circulate goods and information between frontiers, the itinerant traders I focus on here are more influenced by informal networks, changing trade routes, and new business opportunities as they arise. What becomes more important to those who never settle are the circular movements and routes of travel, and the individual relationships of dependence and trust that form around them. The souks and bazaars of Istanbul, Damascus, Naples, Marseilles, and Paris are centers of convergence for these traders, who speak multiple languages and whose job it is to know their clients' worlds well enough to make a profit from their sales. From the sales of cloth to secondhand car markets, to the trade in illegal contraband items, they facilitate the transport of goods and luxury items, across borders, through airports, ports, and highways, moving back and forth in search of business. Writing about suitcase commerce Michel Peraldi (2005) describes the changes in different travel routes traversed by North African and Arab communities: "The pioneers of the Istanbul route were young Algerians, Tunisians or Moroccans hired by Armenian shop-keepers in the Egyptian Bazaar to serve the occidental tourist clientele. They all had university backgrounds, were perfectly fluent in French and often spoke English. They arrived in the wake of cohorts of European tourists heading for Aghia Sophia" (p. 50).

The Algerian suitcase-traders Peraldi writes about are not cosmopolitan, in the strict sense of the word, but mainly young men, affected by the social turmoil and chaos within Algeria, the closure of European borders, and the inability to claim a position of status in Algerian society. Many, having cut off ties with Algeria, move between multiple worlds without fully belonging to any. Similarly Congolese *sapeurs*, from Congo-Kinshasa and Congo-Brazzaville, travel to Paris to sell African foods, beauty products, wax-print cloth, and music, amongst other items. These well-dressed young men in suits form social relations between localities rather than territories and carry out clandestine commercial activity. Initially part of a 1970s movement called *La Sape*, made up of unemployed young men from Brazzaville who wore Parisian designer clothing and enjoyed an ostentatious lifestyle, these traders sought adventure but were also escaping the political and economic turmoil of their countries (MacGaffey and Bazenguissa-Ganga 2000). Like Algerian suitcase-traders in Istanbul, Congolese *sapeurs* in Paris work on the margins of society and the law. They include cultural brokers, entrepreneurs, and even tricksters, who confront the prejudices and chaos of their lives by relying on the trust of personal relationships and constructing their own systems of value. They are examples of how distinctions between the formal and informal economy are not useful when trying to understand how the informal economy is a central part of the global financial system (Nordstrom 2007; Hull and James 2012). While they engage in business networks across multiple borders, they are different from other trading communities, such as the Sindhi cosmopolitans described by Falzon (2004), a diasporic business community who reproduce home wherever they live, through kinship connections across the world.

The Home and Transnational Kinship

Home is a place for reconnecting and reconstructing networks of people, images, labor, culinary practices and memories of relatedness. The reconstruction of the household as a place for dwelling and relatedness requires both a labor of love and disciplinary forms of practice. Households are systems of redistribution that link people to kinship systems, rural and urban organizations, regional and economic structures, the state, and wider transnational contexts (Moore 1992). As Michelle Obeid (CHAPTER 21) demonstrates, economic production and labor do not take place outside the home but participate in the reconstitution of the homeland for a Palestinian family who start a café in London. Women are involved in productive and reproductive labor within the household but also link households to wider forms of socialization and transnational modes of belonging. The examples of migrant women from less developed countries who earn their living as sex workers, or domestic workers for families in first world countries, have brought a new focus on the emotional labor of transnational sex and care (Parreñas 2001; Ehrenreich and Hochschild 2003). While aspirations and ambitions for a better life in the West are important reasons for participating in sex tourism (Brennan 2004), transnational marriages (Thai 2003), and internet romances (E. Johnson 2007), these relationships are more often than not accompanied by the performance of cultural and gendered stereotypes that play into heteronormative male fantasies. The internet has played an increasingly important role in recruiting female labor and in the commodification of intimacy and romance. In the hopes of traveling to the West, many women present themselves as docile and deferential bodies of labor.

Domestic workers, who help raise children and care for the elderly in the households of comparatively richer countries, fall under the gaze of disciplinary agents and self-disciplinary mechanisms of power that work to control their movements (Constable 2007; Yeoh and Huang 2010). Such disciplinary power extends to the home countries of these female migrants. For example Rhacel Parreñas (2003, 2005), describing how domestic work creates a "crisis of care" in the Philippines, also reveals how the Filipino media articulate moral judgments about female workers who leave their children in the care of others while overseas, questioning their role as "good" mothers. Other ethnographic work on transnational adoption (Volkman 2005; Howell 2006; Howell and Marre 2006), intergenerational family networks (Smith 2006; Olwig 2007; Coe 2008), and the migration of children (Coe 2012; Gardner 2012; Olwig 2012), have allowed anthropologists to ask important questions around the normative assumptions of motherhood, biological parenthood, the importance of homeland and return, as well as the role of kinship and care in these different contexts.

Transnational Religions and Religious Diasporas

It has become increasingly important not only to understand how religions become global but also how religious movements and ideologies are closely intertwined with the transnational networks and movements of people across the globe (Vertovec 2000; Levitt 2001; Beyer 2006; Hüwelmeier and Krause 2010; Csordas 2010). Reconnecting with a traditional religious milieu is as much a part of transnational networks as belonging to global religions such as Hinduism, Buddhism, Judaism,

Christianity, and Islam. The recent flows of African American tourists who return
to Ghana to learn about their ancestral roots and for spiritual pilgrimages (Holsey
2008; McCaskie 2008; CHAPTER 31, this volume), and the spread of African diasporic
religions around the world (Clarke 2004; Matory 2005, 2010; P. Johnson 2007),
cannot be understood in isolation from the earlier transregional and transnational
flows of traffic – of people, ritual commodities, and deities (Allman and Parker
2006; R. Werbner 1989; Baum 1999; R. Shaw 2002).

While some religions travel well due to portable practices and transposable messages (Csordas 2010), movement and travel are also part of the very nature of spirits
and deities, who are involved in their own hierarchical networks of association and
who come into presence through their hosts at home and abroad (Sinha 2005;
Lambek 2010; Drotbohm 2010; Fjelstad 2010). Anthropologists have also explored
how religious ideologies and personalities mediate and ethically negotiate economic
migration and overseas travel (Pandolfo 2007; Daswani 2010), how spiritual movements like Yoga and Qigong become international (Van der Veer 2010; Frøystad
2010), as well as how pilgrims and spiritual tourists travel to centers of religious
faith, in order to fulfill spiritual obligations, seek divine blessings, and renew sacred
vows (Coleman 2000, 2002; Bajc, Coleman, and Eade 2007; Badone 2008; Young
2010). Transnational Islam and transnational Christianity have also become popular
topics of intellectual discussion, given their increasing public visibility around the
globe, around which questions about secularization and the role of religion in the
public sphere become commonly asked.

There are many ways to understand the relationship between transnationalism
and religions like Islam and Christianity. One possible way would be to think about
transnational Christianity/Islam as a dimension of migration, mediatization, and
missionization around the world. These religions spread through the migration of
their religious adherents, through the role of the media, religious texts, and the
internet in transmitting and sharing information, and through the role of religious
organizations in spreading and interpreting their message. Another way would be
to characterize the general attributes that each religion shares, as a discursive tradition, while paying attention to regional, national, and cultural differences within
each religious movement (Asad 1986; Cannell 2006; Robbins 2003). As anthropologists have argued, there is no one "Islam" or "Christianity." Clifford Geertz (1968),
in comparing Islamic reform movements in Indonesia and Morocco, has shown
how the religion is shaped by national, historical, and cultural boundaries. John
Bowen (2004a, 2004b), who writes about Islam in France, shows how matters of
scriptural interpretation (*ijtihâd*) are debated and linked to the work of transnational
Muslim scholars. Muslim public intellectuals in France encourage Muslims "to rethink
Islamic practices in terms of the broader objectives of the Qur'an, or in terms of
similarities between Islamic law and European legal systems" (Bowen 2004b: 890).

Transnational religion is not only political but has political relevance in other
spheres of life. Practices of ethical self-fashioning in Egypt, which are about the
micro-politics of how religious ideas inform bodily language and politics, have
become important ways to understand how religious subjects are involved in acts

of self-discipline and participate in redefining their cities of residence (see Mahmood 2005; Hirschkind 2006). Rather than an autonomous sphere, separate from "the secular", transnational Pentecostal communities are implicated in political spiritualities and participate in redefining their social climate through prayer and fasting (Marshall 2009; O'Neill 2010). Belonging to an imagined transnational religious community becomes an important way to momentarily step outside ethnic or national boundaries, whether through the idea of the Muslim *umma* or Christian citizenship. This transcendental logic of belonging is a powerful way of bringing religious migrants together, in presenting worldviews that are holistic within that virtue-community, even if they are in tension with the values of the host society.

Conclusion

For transnationalism and diaspora to exist there have to be criteria, internal to each, which help define their public definitions, their moral articulations, and their interpersonal usage and limits, as they converge in different contexts of practice and social action. While understanding the interconnections between an elsewhere and cultural identities has always been at the heart of the anthropological quest, there is a need for anthropologists to look continually at the concepts we use and to understand why we use them and whether they continue to reflect the concerns of our interlocutors. This chapter has provided different examples of how anthropologists have engaged with questions within the study of transnationalism and diaspora. Being aware of how we use concepts, as *emic* and *etic* categories of application, as well as how they are distinguished from each other or not, is an important part of our intellectual endeavor. While it is not always easy to make clear distinctions between diaspora and transnationalism, we should be aware of how our own interlocutors struggle with articulating their own desires, hopes, aspirations, and ambitions for transcending boundaries and barriers, alongside the continual re-creation of ideas of nostalgia for home and homeland. A historical analysis of when diasporas emerge and how they are articulated, or when and how transnationalism becomes a lived reality, has also to take into account the questions people ask themselves regarding the horizons of their own mobility, migration, and movement, and its concomitant limits. In summarizing the differences between diaspora and transnationalism, I return to my earlier question, regarding how we can understand these concepts given that they are commonly used interchangeably.

As concepts that are good to think with and as analytic terms in anthropology, diaspora and transnationalism designate different spatial temporalities and forms of social activity that need to be accounted for. Transnationalism can be described as a process that involves trans-border engagements and simultaneity between two or more nation-states, a social field that connects one or more migrant communities through the flows of communication technology, goods, finance, and people. It also includes historically shifting routes and pathways of travel as well as political processes of inclusion (incorporation/assimilation) and exclusion (illegality/marginality) that coexist within one or more nationalist frameworks. Diasporas, which are often involved in transnational circuits of exchange and circulation, include a different order of spatial temporality that makes it possible to become a diasporic subject. Diasporic subjects are created out of a nostalgic longing for the past and a desired future, which is constructed through affective and corporeal attachments to multiple sites as well as through narratives and objects of emotional investment in the present. Also, becoming diasporic requires an acknowledgment of sacrifice, whether a personal and collective sacrifice in the present or from previous generations – such as being forced to give something up or spending long stretches of time away from the place one truly desires to be. Such sacrifice, which in some ways requires an ending of life, is also about creating a new beginning and, for some, fulfilling the desire to eventually return home. Writing about sacrifice and beginnings, Michael Lambek (2007) distinguishes between two kinds of beginning that are interconnected: transitive and intransitive. While the transitive aspect of beginning focuses on continuity, intransitive beginnings require constant conceptual clarification and focus instead on radical starting points. Transitive and intransitive beginnings are both important for understanding diasporas, since they provide a narrative of continuity or cultural authenticity in the present and a mythical structure of rupture from the past.

In outlining possible ways of understanding transnationalism and diaspora I am not suggesting a sufficient approach to locating these terms across different contexts. Instead I see them as complementary to (1) a historical and cultural analysis of diaspora and transnationalism as *emic* and *etic* categories, (2) understanding diaspora and transnationalism as different space-time convergences, and (3) describing diaspora and transnationalism as processes of ethical self-fashioning. Also, we have to acknowledge that as much as we try to conceptually separate these domain terms, they are not internally consistent and can come together in unexpected ways through questions such as: How do migrants negotiate their desires for a better life elsewhere, alongside the limits of group belonging, social or gendered boundaries, and physical borders? How do ethnic migrants or members of diaspora make moral judgments about their own community and others that they live alongside? How do they balance their multiple and possibly conflicting commitments between different social and moral worlds they are attached to, either in one place or between home and away? These are only some possibilities of convergence, which highlight the instability of terms and which are a part of a longer conversation in an anthropology of transnationalism and diaspora – a conversation still in the making.

Acknowledgments

I want to thank Alejandro Paz, my colleague at the Department of Anthropology, University of Toronto, for reading a draft of this chapter and providing me with generous comments.

References

Agamben, G. 1998. *Homo Sacer: Sovereign Power and Bare Life*, trans. Daniel Heller-Roazen. Stanford: Stanford University Press.

Allman, J. and Parker, J. 2006. *Tongnaab: The History of a West African God*. Bloomington: Indiana University Press.

Alvarez, R.R. Jr 1995. "The Mexican–US border: the making of an anthropology of borderlands." *Annual Review of Anthropology*, 24: 447–470.

Appadurai, A. 1996. *Modernity at Large: Cultural Dimensions of Globalization*. Minneapolis: University of Minnesota Press.

Asad, T. 1986. "The idea of an anthropology of Islam." *Occasional Papers Series*, Washington, DC: Institute for Contemporary Arab Studies, Georgetown University.

Axel, B.K. 2002. "The diasporic imaginary." *Public Culture*, 14(2): 411–428.

Axel, B.K. 2004. "The context of diaspora." *Cultural Anthropology*, 19(1): 26–60.

Badone, E. 2008. "Pilgrimage, tourism and the Da Vinci Code at Les-Saintes-Maries-de-la-Mer, France." *Culture and Religion*, 9(1): 23–44.

Bajc, V., Coleman, S., and Eade, J. 2007. "Introduction: Mobility and centring in pilgrimage." *Mobilities*, 2(3): 321–329.

Barth, F. 1969. *Ethnic Groups and Boundaries: The Social Organization of Culture Difference*. Boston, MA: Little Brown.

Baum, R. 1999. *Shrines of the Slave Trade: Diola Religion and Society in Precolonial Senegambia*. New York: Oxford University Press.

Beyer, P. 2006. *Religions in Global Society*. London: Routledge.

Boelstroff, T. 2009. *Coming of Age in Second Life: An Anthropologist Explores the Virtually Human*. Princeton: Princeton University Press.

Bowen, J.R. 2004a. "Beyond migration: Islam as a transnational public space." *Journal of Ethnic and Migration Studies*, 30(5): 879–894.

Bowen, J.R. 2004b. "Does French Islam have borders? Dilemmas of domestication in a global religious field." *American Anthropologist*, 106(1): 43–55.

Brennan, D. 2004. *What's Love Got to Do with It? Transnational Desires and Sex Tourism in the Dominican Republic*. Durham, NC: Duke University Press.

Brown, J.N. 2005. *Dropping Anchor, Setting Sail: Geographies of Race in Black Liverpool*. Princeton: Princeton University Press.

Brubaker, R. 2005. "The 'diaspora' diaspora." *Ethnic and Racial Studies*, 28(1): 1–19.

Burawoy, M. 2000. "Introduction: Reaching for the global." In M. Burawoy (ed.) *Global Ethnography: Forces, Connections, and Imaginations in a Postmodern World*, pp. 1–40. Berkeley: University of California Press.

Cannell, F. 2006. "Introduction: The anthropology of Christianity." In F. Cannell (ed.) *The Anthropology of Christianity*, pp. 1–50. Durham, NC: Duke University Press.

Castells, M. 1998. *The Information Age: Economy, Society and Culture*, Volume III: *End of Millennium*. Oxford: Blackwell.

Clarke, K.M. 2004. *Mapping Yoruba Networks: Power and Agency in the Making of Transnational Communities*. Durham NC: Duke University Press.

Clifford, J. 1992. "Traveling cultures." In J. Flinn (ed.) *Fieldwork and Families: Constructing New Models for Ethnographic Research*, pp. 1–21. Honolulu: Honolulu University Press.

Clifford, J. 1994. "Diasporas." *Cultural Anthropology*, 9: 302–338.

Clifford, J. 1997. *Routes: Travel and Translation in the Late Twentieth Century*. Cambridge, MA: Harvard University Press.

Clifford, J. and Marcus, G.E. (eds) 1986. *Writing Culture: The Poetics and Politics of Ethnography*. Berkeley: University of California Press.

Coe, C. 2008. "The structuring of feeling in Ghanaian transnational families." *City and Society*, 20(2): 222–250.

Coe, C. 2012. "Growing up and going abroad: How Ghanaian children imagine transnational migration." *Journal and Ethnic and Migration Studies*, 38(6): 913–931.

Cohen, A. 1969. *Custom and Politics in Urban Africa: A Study of Hausa Migrants in Yoruba Towns*. Berkeley and Los Angeles: University of California Press.

Cohen, R. 2009. "Solid, ductile and liquid: Changing notions of homeland and home in diaspora studies." In E. Ben-Rafael and Y. Sternberg (eds) *Transnationalism: Diasporas and the Advent of a New (Dis)order*, pp. 117–134. Leyden: Brill.

Coleman, S. 2000. "Meaning of movement, place and home in Walsingham." *Culture and Religion*, 1(2): 153–169.

Coleman, S. 2002. "Do you believe in pilgrimage?: *Communitas*, contestation and beyond." *Anthropological Theory*, 2(3): 355–368.

Constable, N. 2007. *Maid to Order in Hong Kong: Stories of Filipina Workers*. Ithaca, NY: Cornell University Press.

Cooper, F. 2005. *Colonialism in Question: Theory, Knowledge, History*. Berkeley: University of California Press.

Csordas, T.J. 2010. "Introduction: Modalities of transnational transcendence." In T.J. Csordas (ed.) *Transnational Transcendence: Essays on Religion and Globalization*, pp. 1–30. Berkeley: University of California Press.

Daswani, G. 2010. "Ghanaian Pentecostal prophets: Travel and (im)-mobility." In G. Hüwelmeier and K. Krause (eds) *Traveling Spirits. Migrants, Markets, And Moralities*, pp. 67–82. New York: Routledge.

De Genova, N.P. 2002. "Migrant 'illegality' and deportability in everyday life." *Annual Review of Anthropology*, 31: 419–447.

Dick, H.P. 2010. "Imagined lives and modernist chronotopes in Mexican nonmigrant discourse." *American Ethnologist*, 37(2): 275–290.

Dick, H.P. 2011a. "Making immigrants illegal in small-town USA." *Journal of Linguistic Anthropology*, 21(S1): 35–55.

Dick, H.P. 2011b. "Language and migration to the United States." *Annual Review of Anthropology*, 40: 227–240.

Dick, H.P. and Wirtz, K. 2011. "Racializing discourses." Special issue, *Journal of Linguistic Anthropology*, 21(S1): 2–10.

Drotbohm, H. 2010. "Haunted by spirits: Balancing religious commitment and moral obligations in Haitian transnational fields." In G. Hüwelmeier and K. Krause (eds) *Traveling Spirits: Migrants, Markets and Mobilities*, pp. 36–51. New York: Routledge.

Ehrenreich, B. and Hochschild, A.R. (eds) 2003. *Global Women: Nannies, Maids and Sex Workers in the New Economy*. New York: Holt/Metropolitan Books.

Eisenlohr, P. 2006. *Little India: Diaspora, Time and Ethnolinguistic Belonging in Hindu Mauritius*. Berkeley: University of California Press.

Epstein, A.L. 1958. *Politics in an Urban African Community*. Manchester: Manchester University Press.

Evans-Pritchard, E.E. 1940. *The Nuer: A Description of the Modes of Livelihood and Political Institutions of a Nilotic People*. Oxford: Clarendon Press.

Falzon, M. 2004. *Cosmopolitan Connections: The Sindhi Diaspora, 1860–2000.* Leiden: Brill.

Fassin, D. 2005. "Compassion and repression: the moral economy of immigration policies in France." *Cultural Anthropology,* 20(3): 362–387.

Fassin, D. 2011. "Policing borders, producing boundaries. The governmentality of immigration in dark times." *Annual Review of Anthropology,* 40: 213–226.

Fjelstad, K. 2010. "Spirited migrations: the travels of *Len Dong* spirits and their mediums." In G. Hüwelmeier and K. Krause (eds) *Traveling Spirits: Migrants, Markets and Mobilities,* pp. 52–66. New York: Routledge.

Foucault, M. 2008. *The Birth of Biopolitics: Lectures at the College de France, 1978–1979,* trans. G. Burchell. Basingstoke: Palgrave Macmillan.

Frøystad, K. 2010. "The return path: Anthropology of a Western yogi." In T.J. Csordas (ed.) *Transnational Transcendence: Essays on Religion and Globalization,* pp. 279–304. Berkeley: University of California Press.

Fumanti, M. 2010. "'Virtuous citizenship': Ethnicity and encapsulation among Akan-speaking Ghanaian Methodists in London." *African Diaspora,* 3: 13–42.

Fumanti, M. and Werbner, P. 2010. "The moral economy of the African diaspora: Citizenship, networking and permeable ethnicity." *African Diaspora,* 3: 3–12.

Gardner, K. 1999. "Location and relocation: Home, 'the field' and anthropological ethics (Sylhet Bangladesh)." In C.W. Watson (ed.) *Being There: Fieldwork in Anthropology,* pp. 49–73. London: Pluto Press.

Gardner, K. 2012. "Transnational migration and the study of children: an introduction." *Journal of Ethnic and Migration Studies,* 38(6): 889–912.

Geertz, C. 1968. *Islam Observed: Religious Development in Morocco and Indonesia.* Chicago: University of Chicago Press.

Geertz, C. 1973. *Interpretation of Cultures.* New York: Basic Books.

Geertz, C. 1988. *Works and Lives: The Anthropologist as Author.* Stanford: Stanford University Press.

Gellner, E. 1992. *Postmodernism, Reason and Religion.* London: Routledge.

Gluckman, M. 1963. *Order and Rebellion in Tribal Africa.* New York: Free Press of Glencoe (Macmillan).

Gregory, S. 2007. *The Devil Behind the Mirror: Globalization and Politics in the Dominican Republic.* Berkeley: University of California Press.

Gupta, A. and Ferguson, J. 1997a. *Culture, Power, Place: Explorations in Critical Anthropology.* New York: Columbia University Press.

Gupta, A. and J. Ferguson. 1997b. *Anthropological Locations: Boundaries and Grounds of a Field Science.* Berkeley: University of California Press.

Hannerz, U. 1987. "The world in creolisation." *Africa,* 57(4): 546–559.

Hannerz, U. 1989. "Notes on the global ecumene." *Public Culture,* 1(2): 66–75.

Hannerz, U. 1996. *Transnational Connections: Culture, People, Places.* London: Routledge.

Heyman, J.M. and Campbell, H. 2009. "The anthropology of global flows: a critical reading of Appadurai's 'Disjuncture and difference in the global cultural economy.'" *Anthropological Theory,* 9(2): 131–148.

Hirsch, E., Kapferer, B., Marton, E., and Tsing, A. 2007. "Anthropologists are talking about anthropology after globalization." *Ethnos,* 72(1): 102–126.

Hirschkind, C. 2006. *The Ethical Soundscape: Cassette Sermons and Islamic Counterpublics.* New York: Columbia University Press.

Holsey, B. 2008. *Routes of Remembrance: Refashioning the Slave Trade in Ghana.* Chicago: University of Chicago Press.

Horst, H. 2007. "'You can't be in two places at once': Rethinking transnationalism through Jamaican return migration." *Identities: Global Studies in Culture and Power*, 14: 63–83.

Howell, S. 2006. *The Kinning of Foreigners: Transnational Adoption in a Global Perspective*. Oxford: Bergahn Books.

Howell, S. 2011. "Muslims as moving targets: External scrutiny and internal critique in Detroit's mosques." In N. Abraham, A. Shryock, and S. Howell (eds) *Arab Detroit 9/11: Life in the Terror Decade*, pp. 151–185. Detroit: Wayne State University Press.

Howell, S., and Marre, D. 2006. "To kin a foreign child in Norway and Spain: Notions of resemblances and the achievement of belonging." *Ethnos*, 4: 293–316.

Hull, E., and James, D. 2012. "Introduction: Popular economies in South Africa." *Africa: Journal of the International Africa Institute*, 82(1): 1–19.

Hüwelmeier, G. and Krause, K. 2010. "Introduction." In G. Hüwelmeier and K. Krause (eds) *Traveling Spirits: Migrants, Markets, and Moralities*, pp. 1–16. New York: Routledge.

Inda, J.X. and Rosaldo, R. 2008. "Tracking global flows." In J.X. Inda and R. Rosaldo (eds) *The Anthropology of Globalization: A Reader*, 2nd edn, pp. 3–46. Oxford: Wiley Blackwell.

Johnson, E. 2007. *Dreaming of a Mail-Order Husband: Russian-American Internet Romance*. Durham, NC: Duke University Press.

Johnson, P.C. 2007. *Diaspora Conversions: Black Carib and the Recovery of Africa*. Berkeley: University of California Press.

Kapferer, B. 2005. "Situations, crisis, and the anthropology of the concrete: the contribution of Max Gluckman." *Social Analysis*, 49(3): 85–122.

Lambek, M. 2007. "Sacrifice and the problem of beginning: Mediations from Sakalava mythopraxis." *Journal of the Royal Anthropological Institute*, 13: 19–38.

Lambek, M. 2010. "Traveling spirits: Unconcealment and undisplacement." In G. Hüwelmeier and K. Krause (eds) *Traveling Spirits: Migrants, Markets and Mobilities*, pp. 17–35. New York: Routledge.

Lambek, M. 2011. "Catching the local." *Anthropological Theory*, 11(2): 197–221.

Levitt, P. 2001. *Between God, Ethnicity, and Country: An Approach to the Study of Transnational Religion*. Transnational Communities Working Paper WPTC-01-13, University of Oxford.

Loizos, P. 1981. *The Heart Grown Bitter: A Chronicle of Cypriot War Refugees*. Cambridge: Cambridge University Press.

Mahmood, S. 2005. *Politics of Piety: The Islamic Revival and the Feminist Subject*. Princeton: Princeton University Press.

Malinowski, B. 1922. *Argonauts of the Western Pacific: An Account of Native Enterprise and Adventure in the Archipelagos of Melanesian New Guinea*. London: Routledge.

Malkki, L. 1995. *Purity and Exile: Violence, Memory and National Cosmology Among Hutu Refugees in Tanzania*. Chicago: University of Chicago Press.

Malkki, L. 1996. "Speechless emissaries: Refugees, humanitarianism, and dehistoricization." *Cultural Anthropology*, 7(3): 377–404.

Marcus, G.E. 1995. "Ethnography in/of the world system: the emergence of multi-sited ethnography." *Annual Review of Anthropology*, 24(1): 95–117.

Marcus, G.E. 1998. *Ethnography Through Thick and Thin*. Princeton: Princeton University Press.

Marcus, G.E. 2006. "Where have all the tales of fieldwork gone?" *Ethnos* 71(1): 113–122.

Marshall, R. 2009. *Political Spiritualities: The Pentecostal Revolution in Nigeria*. Chicago: University of Chicago Press.

Matory, J.L. 2005. *Black Atlantic Religion: Tradition, Transnationalism and Matriarchy in the Afro-Brazilian Candomblé*. Princeton: Princeton University Press.

Matory, J.L. 2010. "The many who dance in me: Afro-Atlantic ontology and the problem with 'transnationalism.'" In T.J. Csordas (ed.) *Transnational Transcendence: Essays on Religion and Globalization*, pp. 231–262. Berkeley: University of California Press.

McCaskie, T.C. 2008. "*Akwantemfi* – 'In mid-journey': an Asante shrine today and its clients." *Journal of Religion in Africa*, 38: 57–80.

MacGaffey, J. and Bazenguissa-Ganga, R. 2000. *Congo-Paris: Transnational Traders on the margins of the Law*. Oxford: James Currey.

Mintz, S. 1998. "The localization of anthropological practice." *Critique of Anthropology*, 18(2): 117–133.

Mintz, S. 2000. "Sow's ears and silver linings: a backward look at ethnography." *Current Anthropology*, 41(2): 169–189.

Mitchell, J.C. 1956. *The Kalela Dance*. Rhodes-Livingstone paper 27, Manchester: Manchester University Press.

Mitchell, J.C. 1974. "Social networks." *Annual Review Anthropology*, 3: 279–299.

Moore, H.L. 1992. "Households and gender relations: the modelling of the economy." In S. Ortiz and S. Lees (eds) *Understanding Economic Processes*, pp. 131–148. Monographs in Economic Anthropology, 10, Lanham, MD: University Press of America.

Moore, H.L. 2004. "Global anxieties: Concept-metaphors and pre-theoretical commitments in anthropology." *Anthropological Theory*, 4(1): 71–88.

Navaro-Yashin, Y. 2009. "Affective spaces, melancholic objects: Ruination and the production of anthropological knowledge." *Journal of the Royal Anthropological Institute*, 15: 1–18.

Nordstrom, C. 2007. *Global Outlaws: Crime, Money, and Power in the Contemporary World*. Berkeley: University of California Press.

Olwig, K.F. 2007. *Caribbean Journeys: An Ethnography of Migration and Home in Three Family Networks*. Durham, NC: Duke University Press.

Olwig, K.F. 2012. "The care chain, children's mobility and the Caribbean migration tradition." *Journal of Ethnic and Migration Studies*, 38(6): 933–952.

Ong, A. 1999. *Flexible Citizenship: The Cultural Logics of Transnationality*. Durham, NC: Duke University Press.

O'Neill, K.L. 2010. *City of God: Christian Citizenship in Postwar Guatemala*. Berkeley: University of California Press.

Ortner, S. 1984. "Theory in anthropology since the sixties." *Comparative Studies in Society and History*, 26(1): 126–166.

Pandolfo, S. 2007. "'The burning': Finitude and the politico-theological imagination of illegal immigration." *Anthropological Theory*, 7(3): 329–363.

Parreñas, R.S. 2001. *Servants of Globalization: Women, Migration and Domestic Work*. Stanford, CA: Stanford University Press.

Parreñas, R.S. 2003. "The care crisis in the Philippines: Children and transnational families in the new global economy." In B. Ehrenreich and A. Hochschild (eds) *Global Women: Nannies, Maids and Sex Workers in the New Economy*, pp. 39–54. New York: Metropolitan Books.

Parreñas, R.S. 2005. *Children of Global Migration: Transnational Families and Gendered Woes*. Stanford: Stanford University Press.

Paz, A. 2011. "Memories of diaspora: Publics, ethnicity and the process of recognizing children of undocumented labor migrants in Israel." Paper presented at the

Workshop on Language, Interaction, and Social Relations, University of Toronto Mississauga, April.

Peraldi, M. 2005. "Algerian routes: Emancipation, deterritorialisation and transnationalism through suitcase trade." *History and Anthropology*, 16(1): 47–61.

Povinelli, E.A. 2002. *The Cunning of Recognition: Indigenous Alterities and the Making of Australian Multiculturalism*. Durham, NC: Duke University Press.

Ramji, H. 2006. "British Indians returning 'home': an exploration of transnational belonging." *Sociology*, 40(4): 645–662.

Robbins, J. 2003. "On the paradoxes of global Pentecostalism and the perils of continuity thinking." *Religion*, 33: 191–199.

Rouse, R. 1991. "Mexican migration and the social space of postmodernism." *Diaspora: A Journal of Transnational Studies*, 1(1): 8–23.

Shaw, A. 1988. *A Pakistani Community in Britain*. Oxford: Blackwell.

Shaw, R. 2002. *Memories of the Slave Trade: Ritual and the Historical Imagination in Sierra Leone*. Chicago: Chicago University Press.

Silverstein, P. 2005. "Immigration racialization and the new savage slot: Race, migration, and immigration in the new Europe." *Annual Review of Anthropology*, 34: 363–384.

Sinha, V. 2005. *A New God in the Diaspora? Muneeswaran Worship in Contemporary Singapore*. Singapore: Singapore University Press.

Smith, R.C. 2006. *Mexican New York: Transnational Lives of New Immigrants*. Berkeley: University of California Press.

Stoller, P. 1997. "Globalizing method: the problems of doing ethnography in transnational spaces." *Anthropology and Humanism*, 22(1): 81–94.

Stoller, P. 2002. "Crossroads: Tracing African paths on New York City streets." *Ethnography*, 3(1): 35–62.

Thai, H. 2003. "Clashing dreams: Highly educated brides and low-wage US husbands." In B. Ehrenreich, and A. Hochschild (eds) *Global Women: Nannies, Maids and Sex Workers in the New Economy*, pp. 230–253. New York: Metropolitan Books.

Tsing, A. 2000. "The global situation." *Cultural Anthropology*, 15(3): 327–360.

Tsuda, T. 2003. *Strangers in the Ethnic Homeland: Japanese Brazilian Return Migration in Transnational Perspective*. New York: Columbia University Press.

Urciuoli, B. 1995. "Language and borders." *Annual Review of Anthropology*, 24: 525–546.

Urry, J. 2001. *Sociology Beyond Societies: Mobilities for the Twenty-First Century*. London: Routledge.

Urry, J. 2004. "Small worlds and the new 'social physics.'" *Global Networks*, 4: 109–130.

Van der Veer, P. 2010. "Global breathing: Religious utopias in India and China." In T.J. Csordas (ed.) *Transnational Transcendence: Essays on Religion and Globalization*, pp. 263–278. Berkeley: University of California Press.

Vertovec, S. 2000. *The Hindu Diaspora: Comparative Patterns*. London: Routledge.

Vertovec, S. 2011. "The cultural politics of nation and migration." *Annual Review of Anthropology*, 40: 241–256.

Volkman, T.A. (ed.) 2005. *Cultures of Transnational Adoption*. Durham, NC: Duke University Press. Werbner, R. 1989. *Ritual Passage, Sacred Journey: The Process and Organization of Religious Movement*. Washington, DC: Smithsonian Institution.

Werbner, P. 2002. *Imagined Diasporas Among Manchester Muslims*. Oxford: James Currey.

Wilding, R. 2007. "Transnational ethnographies and anthropological imaginings of migrancy." *Journal of Ethnic and Migration Studies*, 33(2): 333–348.

Wilson, S.M. and Peterson, L.C. 2002. "The anthropology of online communities." *Annual Review Anthropology*, 31: 449–467.

Yeoh, B. and Huang, S. 2010. "Transnational domestic workers and the negotiation of mobility and work practices in Singapore's home-spaces." *Mobilities*, 5(2): 219–236.

Young, D. 2010. "Engaging others: Religious conviction and irony in the Holy Lands." In M. Lambek (ed.) *Ordinary Ethics: Anthropology, Language, and Action*, pp. 351–367. New York: Fordham University Press.

Chapter 3

Communication and Media Studies

Julian Murphet

In another version of the radical truism according to which, while the center is most often indifferent to the doings of the periphery, the periphery cannot afford *not* to be fully conversant with the operations of the center, mainstream media studies and theory remain aloof from the interventions that historians, sociologists, and anthropologists of the world's various diasporas have been making in recent years (see Naficy 1999; King and Wood 2001; Cottle 2000; Karim 2003a). Nothing could be more damaging to the truth claims of media studies and communications theory themselves, since what appears to be keeping media institutions and forms vibrantly alive today are their complex appropriations by networked communities not bound by national territories or monolithic state ideologies. It is partly insofar as the diasporas of the contemporary world – the vast migrations, exilic transplantations, violent deportations, and refugee trails that characterize our unique planetary situation – have made use of the diverse array of residual, dominant, and emergent media, that those media are extended in their use and value beyond the routine circulation of centrist ideologies and the sterile recapitulation of information. And in what must be the pivotal node in the turbulent confluence of "diaspora" and "communications" as concepts, it is precisely as "diasporas" (virtual or otherwise) that the most interesting and exciting new media collectives are being enjoined to identify themselves – since what the internet has enabled (for all with access to it) is more or less what the peoples of the various diasporas have been experiencing for much longer periods: transmigratoriness, deterritorialization, and the opportunity to invent new mediatized "identities" in *unheimlich* situations. Yet scan the established literature as you may for signs of a reasoned engagement with these potent homologies and connections, your search will be in vain (see the otherwise

A Companion to Diaspora and Transnationalism, First Edition.
Edited by Ato Quayson and Girish Daswani.
© 2013 Blackwell Publishing Ltd. Published 2013 by Blackwell Publishing Ltd.

excellent anthologies and readers Chun and Keenan 2006; Thorburn and Jenkins 2003; and Wardrip-Fruin and Montfort 2003). The term *diaspora* appears in not one of the indices of the major textbooks in the field, and this despite the fact that diaspora studies has been generating research that is both cutting-edge and innovative with regard to media studies for some 15 years. It is a situation begging for theoretical critique, and if we cannot offer that here we can at least sketch out the outlines of a conceptual fieldmap to explore the *méconnaissance* between diaspora and media studies.

Historical Tectonics

Taking diaspora back to its geopolitical roots in the *Galuth* or *Tefutzot*, the violent scattering of Israel's seeds in the deserts of Khorasan and the urban spaces of Babylon, Antioch, and Alexandria, we can sense immediately the degree to which the reactive recuperation of a national identity and ethno-religious continuity across the diasporic checkerboard depended upon a single, privileged media form: the book. Indeed, the degree to which the Sefer Torah, as a portable scroll, managed to bind the scattered tribes of Israel into a single "imagined community" despite the loss of nationhood, is a remarkable proof of what henceforth will be taken to be an axiom of diaspora formations: *no diaspora without media*. That is to say, in no case can the concept "diaspora" be applied to a minority collective without the existence of media to make that affirmation tangible. Otherwise, a displaced collective is simply absorbed into the host culture, or eradicated altogether. Whether it is the retellings of oral folklore, the circulation of songs, the scribal tradition of textual transcription and preservation, or the priestly avocation of textually sanctioned religious instruction, what renders an uprooted community properly diasporic (rather than simply defeated or lost) is the persistence, within determinate media, of practices that stem, ideally, from originary practices predating the "scattering" itself. But this ideal of continuity is very often precisely that; and what may turn out to be closer to the truth is that this insistence on mediatized performances of "belonging" marks them as more the product of an interruption in continuity than as genuine consistencies. Indeed, it would be arguable that the Torah as the focal point of Hebraic "identity" dated precisely from the moment that the first Babylonian exiles returned to Judea and reconstituted their *ethnie* in a determinate negation of the diaspora, a move that a later Zionism would only exaggerate in other, more modern, media (see Comay 1981; Barclay 1996). Dialectically enough, it would thus be the supercharged value of the book in exile that ultimately conferred a redoubled nationalist power upon it once the "return of the natives" could consecrate it in the Temple of Jerusalem. Nationalist consciousness as such would be the product of a mediatic construction of identity in exile; it is the medium that brings the message of this identity home.

What recent scholarship in the field of media history has been teaching us is that media are to be understood not in isolation from one another, or individually, but as bound together in complex ecologies (see Tabbi 1997; Fuller 2005; Murphet 2009). Mediatic ecosystems not only interact within historically situated technological environments, themselves tethered to the economic development of a given social formation, but they effectively "determine" (a loaded term if ever there was one) the range of expressive, communicational, and affective resources available to a given community. Tending, like their circumambient social systems, towards homeostasis, media ecologies distribute the socially sensible according to the demands of the wider economy (divisions of labor, the functioning of ideology, caste and class structures, etc.), in a hierarchical arrangement that traditionally apportions literacy to the priestly caste, numeracy to the merchant class, and "popular cultural" physical media to the laboring masses. And yet such ecologies perforce differ from place to place on the world map, in a topology of uneven developments whose contours become particularly evident to those communities that for whatever reason have been obliged to traverse a number of social domains. It is thus that, in a unique relationship that has yet to be adequately formulated, diasporas are (so to speak) the privileged "media" through which extant media systems come into contact with one another and lose some of their homeostatic conservatism. In an uncanny reversal of conceptual orthodoxies, human diasporic phenomena are *the media of media systems*, allowing for the deformation of established communicational functions and techniques in host societies according to a logic of interference and hybridity that engenders cultural rebirth and transformation.

Without the Jewish diaspora and the widespread diffusion of Ashkenazi Jews across northern and eastern Europe, there would never have been the specific Hebraic recalibration of "German" media institutions (such as literature and music) that would ultimately give rise to the evental originality of a Heine, a Mahler, or a Kafka. As Deleuze and Guattari (1986) famously describe Kafka's genius:

> A minor literature doesn't come from a minor language; it is rather that which a minority constructs within a major language. . . . Kafka marks the impasse that bars access to writing for the Jews of Prague and turns their literature into something impossible – the impossibility of not writing, the impossibility of writing in German, the impossibility of writing otherwise. (p. 16)

Kafka, hailed by the Kabbala, the rabbinical tradition and the dream of Zion, instead deterritorializes that inherited media system by forcing a passage through the dominant, Middle European one. The opportunity is precisely one of linguistic systems out of all alignment with one another: "the situation of the German language in Czechoslovakia, as a fluid language intermixed with Czech and Yiddish, will allow Kafka the possibility of invention" (Deleuze and Guattari 1986: 20).

So, there are media ecologies, and there are diasporic trajectories that both link and derange these ecologies. In order to grasp this remarkably craggy and dialectical terrain, I propose the notion of "historical tectonics" – a way of thinking dynamic flows of peoples and media as if they were geological plates in movement, here pressing up against each other and forming alpine peaks of expressive intensity, there uncoupling from one another and opening up troughs of cultural desert. Paul Gilroy's notion of the "black Atlantic" (1993) is one such experiment in historical tectonics. Although the concept of "media" scarcely informs Gilroy's account of the exhilarating cultural hybridizations consequent upon the Atlantic slave trade, his attention to the forms of black musical expression is a guide to understanding how diaspora and the media systems of a number of discrete territories mutually inform each other's impure evolution.

In the unrepeatable historical tectonics of the black Atlantic, three media systems interpenetrate along the line of flight described by West Africans sold and stolen into American slavery: the highly developed Enlightenment ecologies of Great Britain, Portugal, Spain, and other trading nations, the more rudimentary media system of the postcolonial USA and other Western hemispheric colonies, and the traditional congeries of media sustaining the various African kingdoms (of Benin, Koya, Khasso, and many others) whence the slaves were taken in the first place. If most of these kingdoms were illiterate, that only placed greater weight on media such as instrumental and vocal music, and oral narrative, which were to determine the peculiar manner in which the interweaving of European and American media ecologies would be inflected by subsequent slave practices. Gilroy (1993), by way of Edward Glissant, particularly notes the preponderance of West African physical cultural forms (gesture, dance, priest-magicianship, *vodun* ritual, *griot* musician-ship, drum and kora, and so on), rather than written ones, since it is that passage through the performing body that characterizes the historical tectonic in question.

> The oral character of the cultural settings in which diaspora musics have developed presupposes a distinctive relationship to the body – an idea expressed with exactly the right amount of impatience by Glissant: "It is nothing new to declare that for us music, gesture, dance are forms of communication, just as important as the gift of speech. This is how we first managed to emerge from the plantation: aesthetic form in our cultures must be shaped from these oral structures." (Gilroy 1993: 75)

But shaped only by way of their passage through European musical structures and American instrumental culture.

"How did the West African influence survive in New Orleans and blend with European music?" asks Marshall Stearns in his classic (1970) history of jazz (p. 44).

> Two steps in the process seem to be clear: private *vodun* ceremonies and public performances in Congo Square. The first preserved African music – and especially rhythm – in the midst of its rituals; and the second forced the same music – without as much of the ritual – out into the open where it could easily influence and be influenced by European music.

Diasporic derangements of European sound systems were variable, as Lafcadio Hearn remarked in New Orleans in 1880: "the melancholy, quavering beauty and weirdness of the Negro chant are lightened by the French influence, or subdued and deepened by the Spanish" (quoted in Bisland 1906: 189). As one media system interacts with another under the specific impetus of a deterritorialized collective, such inflections and mutations not only allow a diasporic community to assert its traditions (as the West African funeral was "continued" in the unique New Orleans tradition of the black funeral parade), but dislocate the cultural coordinates of the host society in the process and help to create the conditions for cultural renaissance (as the black funeral parade altered the very meaning of public musical performance in the USA).

Historical tectonics, in which migrations of people and clashes between unevenly developed media systems crystallize into unprecedented conditions for cultural invention, are the under-theorized spaces in which media history and diaspora studies ought properly to be converging. That they are not, yet, is testament to the blindness of established media studies to the ways in which large-scale movements of human bodies have, at least since the *Galuth*, been modifying and deterritorializing the media ecologies they traverse; above all in the modern period and beyond.

Costs of Representation

One of the defining features of modernity was the manner in which, thanks to technological change and mass mediatization, the world suddenly shrank in size. Railroads, steamships, telegraphs, telephones, motor-cars and motion pictures, all notably "desevered" the large distances between planetary regions, creating new technical folds and juxtapositions between them. This outer constriction was felt as an inner expansion, and the black box for that double perspectival shift was generally specified as a mechanical medium. Gerald Stanley Lee wrote in 1913: "The telephone changes the structure of the brain. Men live in wider distances, and think in larger figures, and become eligible for nobler and wider motives" (p. 65). One of these "nobler motives" made peculiarly possible by these new forms of transportation and mechanical mediation was of course imperialism itself. The mediatized ability to "live in wider distances" is not simply a metaphorical figure; it describes the technological umbilicus feeding existential sustenance to the imperial enterprise. But imperialism, in its "civilizing" aspect, putting new media systems in direct contact with colonized subjects, also configured new torsional zones of local cultural and political ferment. The printing press, in particular, was a critical resource for establishing counter-imperial cultural formations in the Indian subcontinent and numerous African colonies. Indeed, the material wellsprings of insurgent nationalism in the colonized world are to be located in the mediatic deposits of empire's glittering hegemony – mail routes, education, newspapers, telegraph offices, steamers, railroads, and photography. In Benedict Anderson's well-known argument, if the printing press enabled the emergence of imperialist nationalism as such in Europe, so too did it enable the rise of indigenous nationalism in Europe's scattered colonies. Thanks to the imposed media system of British rule in India, for instance, a McCauleyite ideology could propose forcing a wedge between the local elites and the working masses, precisely by "Anglicizing" them through the literary machine:

textbooks, poetry, novels, histories, and so on. "A sort of mental miscegenation is intended," notes Anderson (2006: 91), thereby giving rise to the further speculation that imperialism succeeds in its hegemony by technically "alienating" the elites from their own national culture – that is, by inducting them via its imported media into a virtual, *internal diaspora*, which triggers the material sequel of sons being sent to Oxbridge to complete their education. Virtual diaspora becomes actual, and the ends of empire are satisfied; but only ironically. For these same diasporic elites are almost always the cadres amongst whom indigenous nationalism takes mature root and develops a fighting consciousness – a consciousness made effective by its medial integuments, its literate expressions and publicized, broadcast forms.

There is perhaps no greater proof of this tactical reappropriation of the very means of cultural subjugation than the path to victory of that quintessential diasporic nationalist, Mohandas K. Gandhi. Leaving India at age 18, and not returning permanently until he was 46, Gandhi traced a rootless path through the British Natal colony in South Africa and England's education system, and learned about his own "Indianness" on the hoof. As Antoinette Burton has speculated (1998: 73), "there was something about being in temporary or permanent exile that nurtured resistance." That "something," Robert Young (2001) has argued, was the modern media system itself. In a brilliant series of reflections, Young details Gandhi's use of the printing press in exile, in a number of self-edited journals; his deployment of a cyclostyle machine "secretly carried about the countryside"; the syndication of his articles throughout the world; and his frequent use of international news agencies. "Few politicians of his time used the power of journalism to the same degree as Gandhi. He utilized the extensive print culture of India to maximum effect" (Young 2001: 330). After a number of years, "his life became a publicity event. As a result, it is comprehensively documented in photographs, films, and sound recordings: Gandhi must have been one of the most photographed politicians of the twentieth century." The result is an extraordinary and paradoxical legacy, for a man so vociferously committed to an "anti-modern" independent India. "In Gandhi's hands, the Indian liberation struggle took the form of the first media war, the first media revolution. . . . Gandhi was the first anticolonial activist to use the contemporary media as a forum to stage his non-violent tactics of resistance, using high technology to facilitate the communicative power of the soul-force of *satyagraha*" (Young 2001: 330–331).

The same could be said for many of the critical figures in the heroic period of decolonization: Senghor's "16 years of wandering," coining the concept of *négritude* whilst mastering linguistics at the École pratique des hautes études (EPHE); Kwame Nkrumah being inducted via telephone into Trotskyist cells in New York City; Patrice Lumumba distributing party leaflets in Belgium; Ho Chi Minh walking the Harlem streets with Marcus Garvey and writing magazine articles on sport in Paris; Franz Fanon demobbed to Toulon via Casablanca, then studying psychiatry and writing plays in Paris; and so forth. There is scarcely a Third World national liberation figure who wasn't both an educationally alienated diasporic intellectual, and a hands-on pragmatist within the modern media ecology. Just as the exiled Jews in

Babylon fashioned a militant nationalist subjectivity around the material potency of the Pentateuch, and then brought it home, so too the pioneers of tricontinental nationalist revolt stoked the flames of resistant consciousness on the hearth of imperial mechanical media, and returned with messages about indigenous sovereignty propagated by cosmopolitan means of production. The paradoxes are such that, while fully endorsing the passage through the foreign, dominant media system as the only possible path to modern liberated political self-consciousness, one must also be prepared to face the inevitable costs of such dialectical vacillation.

Richard Wright (1954), recounting his first visit to the West Coast of Africa, describes a group of "young African students," around 1952. What he perceives is an unprecedented globalization of the capacity to think beyond empire; although the students dream of extirpating the British nomination of their homeland and "renaming many of their towns, rivers, villages," their saturation by media emanating from Europe and the East determines how they envisage social change itself.

> The methods of imperialists have made it easy for these boys to embrace the idea of "masses", and the masses they have in mind are black masses. . . . Of Communism *per se* they wanted none, but they keenly appreciated the moral panic into which Russia had thrown the Western world. And they were aware of the huge mass of empiric material available about the techniques of making uprisings, general strikes, all kinds and degrees of actions that could paralyse the economic activities of imperialist powers. (Wright 1954: 28)

Wright captures a unique historical tectonic, in which returning African diasporic nationalists have yet to feel the gravitational pull of America's intercalated media empire, and incline instead to the leaflets and speeches of Soviet propaganda as roadmaps to national liberation. Ghana was then a land of some 4 million, and as Wright observes (1954: 55), "though still mainly tribal, though 90 per cent illiterate, they wanted to be free of an alien flag, wanted the sovereignty of their own will in their own land." When Nkrumah tells a crowd of his people that his American guest is a novelist, they respond with incomprehension. "'The ideological development here is not very high,'" Nkrumah confides to Wright. "'There are but two or three of us who know what we are doing'" (1954: 63). Suddenly the stakes are exposed in stark relief. For the gap here between literate elites versed in cosmopolitan media systems (which include novels and reportage), and illiterate masses living in unalleviated village orality, is so vast that for a moment the entire postcolonial experiment threatens to topple into its own contradictions. However available the imperial media system is to tactical reappropriations and insurgent applications, the deep structure of its increasingly global ecology preserves inequalities that are ontologically embedded.

For the media of modernity are in essence broadcast media, "one-way" streets that neither invite dialogical reply nor proffer themselves for widespread popular ownership. Typewriters and cameras may be relatively affordable (though not if you are a Yoruba peasant in 1950), but the means of mechanical reproduction (printing labs, photomechanical presses, recording studios, publishing houses, radio trans-mitters, etc.) most certainly are not. "For the longest time in cultural history," writes Wolfgang Ernst, "storage of data and the means of operating them have been kept separately" (2006: 111). This separation between storage and operation, between the capacity to construct media messages and the means to disseminate them, has clear sociological effects and causes. The analog nature of these mechanical and then increasingly electrical media – their isomorphisms of wavelength, imprint, mark, and index – ties them to situations and to embodiment, and thus to determinate social forms: to local divisions of labor, to specializations of storage and processing, and disparities of ownership over original and copy. But the disposition of these linked media within global patterns of inequality and exploitation means that such divisions inevitably get played out in colonial situations as power imbalances that not even the most fervent of egalitarian "contents" can burst from within their technical "forms." Colonial diaspora, of the elites, can certainly refashion that iniq-uitous disposition: hijacking modern media technologies to foment resistance and militant subjectivities; contributing to a counter-current of "Third Worldist" infor-mation growth; and compiling a new world archive of anti-imperial documents. But the retroactive pressure of the media system itself on all such political seizures is more often than not deleterious, since in every postcolonial situation where it is reproduced, it carries within it the selfish gene of a monopoly of information and a radical imbalance of access to the means of cultural production.

Demographies of the New Media

What follows the "modernist" phase of nationalist liberation and consolidation by way of diasporic media professionalization, is our own bewildering planetary moment, whose most prototypical features are – precisely – the mass migratory movements of unprecedented numbers of human bodies, and the instauration of a "World Wide Web" of digital-mediatic convergence wherein immediate, light-speed transfers of textual, visual, audible, and other species of data make redundant the hitherto melancholy cast of long-distance physical separation (Jenkins 2006). If diaspora, as a structure of feeling and badge of identity, had previously been limited to the experience of exceptionally punished communities (and of the exceptionally privileged members of others), today it must be said that diaspora is the veritable dominant of global experience; but it is so exactly inasmuch as it is sustained by the given conditions of global media. When every major world city is literally that – traversed by the layered migratory histories of innumerable "post-national" collec-tives and communities – and when high-tech war pushes ever greater numbers out on the endless paths of asylum-seeking to add still more "multiculture" to every national space, it is urgent to point out that all of this is as much a matter of rep-resentation as it is of sheer demography and human geography. For those earlier national "self-consciousnesses" of modern political liberations are now fractalized and subdivided into hyphenated *groupuscules* by a quantum leap in the means of communication. Mass migration and the new era of mass communication heralded by the internet are two sides of an infinitely looping Möbius strip; and we can take Michael Hardt's and Antonio Negri's words for it:

> Along with the flight from the so-called Third World there are flows of political refugees and transfers of intellectual labor power, in addition to the massive movements of the agricultural, manufacturing and service proletariat. The legal and documented movements are dwarfed by clandestine migrations: the borders of national sovereignty are sieves. . . . In effect, what pushes from behind is, negatively, desertion from the miserable cultural and material conditions of imperial reproduction; but positively, what pulls forward is the wealth of desire and the accumulation of expressive and productive capacities that the processes of globalization have determined in the consciousness of every individual and social group – and thus a certain hope. (Hardt and Negri 2000: 213)

The passage is as interesting for what it does not say as for what it does. For what are "the wealth of desire and the accumulation of expressive and productive capacities" but paraphrases for the new media ecology itself, its infinite capacity to industrialize desire and metastatize "expressive capacities" along a continuum of intensively capitalized profit motives? The attractive moment behind the enormous population transfers of our time is the delirious capability of the new media to advertise themselves, everywhere at once, as opportunities, not now for national liberation, but for the attainment of happiness itself. Every description of the new media situation tends of its own accord to transform into an apologia:

> The computer and communication revolution of production has transformed labouring practices in such a way that they all tend toward the model of information and communication technologies. Interactive and cybernetic machines become a new prosthesis integrated into our bodies and minds and a lens through which to redefine our bodies and minds themselves. The anthropology of cyberspace is really a recognition of the new human condition. (Hardt and Negri 2000: 291)

The "new human condition," I want to suggest, is simultaneously the "anthropology of cyberspace" and the "massive movements" of diasporas – neither of which is actually comprehensible without the other. It is important, amidst all the celebration of this transformation of social existence, to offer minatory warning sounds about premature celebrations of deterritorialization as such. The critical factor is always to hold in mind the second axiom hazarded in this chapter: the digital revolution is insufficiently understood until its contemporaneity with the explosion of human movement is grasped as immanent to its historical meaning.

It is not simply that the omnipresent nodes and terminals of the information revolution solicit patterns of migration and settlement today; it is also that all current migratory patterns are themselves immediately media phenomena, made meaningful by their light-speed representation in state, corporate multinational, and "NGO" media platforms. Exhaustively catalogued and categorized into hyphenated "group" identities, whose specific social value will vary from space to space, transnational diasporic formations are socially constructed media phenomena often before they are geopolitical facts. To suggest that we are inundated by diasporic "information" is to belittle the sober truth that media industries today thrive on nothing so much as the circulation of legal and illegal "migrancy" as a global ideologeme: facile reactionary panic buttons, liberal heart-bleeding, angry defensive self-representation, "neutral" UN statistics, NGO activism and aid, and the daily horror of drowned children and suffocated mothers. Indeed, take away the daily diet of sensational diasporic "stories" and the world's media empires would implode on their own bloated mass, like beached whales. The *dramatis personae* of these stories is today virtually innumerable: Roma, Kurds, Palestinians, other Arabs, Sudanese, Somalis, Afghanis, Iraqis, Iranians, Tamils, Mexicans – the list stretches indefinitely to take in virtually the entire Third World; and within each of these large national descriptors, regional and faith-based subdivisions further specify the ethno-religious complexion of every migrant under the sun. Such, it would seem, is largely the function of the media today: to fill in every blank spot in an ever-changing color-by-number snapshot of global "diversity" – precisely to keep the liberal white bourgeoisie of the developed world anxiously informed about the rising tide of Otherness at their feet.

Of course, there is the other side of the equation, where most contemporary studies of "media and diaspora" pitch their tents: the uses made by immigrant communities of the new network media. David Palumbo-Liu (1999: 355) makes a pertinent case that "'diaspora' does not consist in the fact of leaving Home, but in having that factuality available to representation as such – we come to 'know' diaspora only as it is psychically identified in a narrative form that discloses the various ideological investments. . . . It is that narrative form that locates the representation of diaspora in its particular chronotope." Decoding this into media-theoretical language, what this means is that diaspora are sustained only through media use; and the fast-changing nature of media ecologies in recent history tells us that the "narrative forms" available to migrant communities have been intrinsically altered by the technological infrastructure itself. If there are no diasporas without narratives, there are no narratives without media: media systems transmute the quality and quantity of "story" through which a diaspora can be embodied and felt as an existential structure. So, studies of a Kurdish TV station broadcast from London; internet communities among diasporic Burundians; or Tamil nationalist web sites (see Hassanpour 2003; Kadende-Kaiser 2000; Whitaker 2004) suggest the infinite diversity of close-reading situations in a cultural studies vein that are available to a diasporic analysis of media use. Time and again, however, such studies are haunted by their opposite; since although, as Karim H. Karim writes (2003b: 5), "diasporas are often viewed as forming alternatives to the structures of worldwide capitalism, . . . in many instances they are participants in transnational economic activity." The perils of representation, already stark in the modern epoch, today seem unresolvable.

The purely corporate nature of multinational media conglomerates (such as Google, Microsoft, Apple, Facebook, and many others) could not have escaped the conduct of researchers into this burgeoning field. Analysts of diasporic appropriations of convergence culture often remark upon the implicit tension between the "particularism" of the community in question, and the "universal" means of representation through which these particularisms make manifest their identities today. Insofar as young people are the drivers of this "Web 2.0" usage, indeed, Marie Gillespie (2000) is justified in making the preliminary remark in a study of South Asian diasporic media use that "transnational youth programming, dominated by Americanized teen consumer culture (MTV's 'McCulture'), encourages a self-perception as a world-teenager, and mobilizes transnational identifications around consumption practices" (p. 165). To enter such a media terrain, which brings to light the implicit equation between globalization and Americanization, is at one level to liquidate cultural specificity – to become a "world teenager," which is pre-emptively a transnational and deterritorialized category, prior to its admixture with any ethno-religious scattering, since the multinational corporate system, as it were, "got there first," before the world's diasporas could place any existential claims upon it. Today the "world teenager" recognizes herself as such in Tehran and Abuja, even prior to her subsequent displacement to Sydney or Oakland, thanks to the aggressive and ubiquitous "hailings" of her in any number of articulated media outlets: magazines, shop-front windows, television programming, radio broadcasts, and so on. When in her new home she begins to implement the resources of the Web to facilitate her, and her community's, sense of "belonging" to a transnational imaginary, then, she does so in an immanently schizophrenic fashion. She is at once her national, ethnic, and religious past, and her mediatized present, and both in a deterritorialized sense. Gillespie notes (2000: 168):

> By articulating new kinds of spatial and temporal relationships, communications technologies can transform the politics of representation and the modes of identification available to migrant and diaspora groups. New developments in media are arguably now reducing the importance of geopolitical borders and spatial and temporal boundaries, and so threatening the vitality and significance, even the viability of national cultures, at the same time as they increase the significance of diaspora cultures.

The fact is that all such "representation" is grist to the mill of the digital hegemon, indifferent as it is in essence to the provenance of any specific data-stream entered into its matrix. What matters is that the information spreads, that it creates networks of users who sustain the ever-increasing systemic domination of culture by computational methods. To be sure, these "processes dissolve distances and suspend time, and in doing so create new and unpredictable forms of connection, identification and cultural affinity, but also of dislocation and disjuncture between people, places and cultures" (Gillespie 2000: 169). But none of this seems peculiar to diasporic media use.

Consider two other transnational communities: academics, as members of what Slavoj Žižek calls the "symbolic class"; and bankers. The fact that today a great part of their work takes "place" outside of any geographical space, but on the sprawling international circuits of digitally coded information, means that such groups are less "national" formations than they are dislocated transnational communities sustained by media systems – a fact only amplified by the growing numbers of immigrants in their physically located ranks. If, as Hardt and Negri (2000: 291) write, "the computer and communication revolution of production has transformed labouring practices in such a way that they all tend toward the model of information and communication technologies," what that means is that they also tend towards the model of diasporic communities. To the extent that the global economy is dominated by networked technology, so too is it dominated by diasporic relations. The relationship is genetic, not accidental. Angie Chabram Dernersesian writes (1994: 286): "Just having a transnational identity is not something to be romanticized or something only we have: everyone in the world has one, thanks to the global culture of communications and the far reaching grip of capitalist formations."

Finally, however, it is worth wondering about this categorical "everyone." If issues of access and divisions between storage and operation characterized the modern media ecology, the postmodern one is not unaffected by lingering inequalities of distribution. For every relatively affluent community of, say, migrant Muslims in London, with newly abundant media forms targeting their purses and constructing enticing identities for them, there are other diasporic formations without any significant media presence, and who effectively continue to fall off the world map of constituted identities. Of the former it has been written: "If market conditions allow, the ongoing development and diversification of Muslim style media and the advent of a new generation of style mediators look likely to provide a forum for the creation, expression, and contestation of Muslim identities" (Lewis 2010: 31). For an instance of the latter, however, it is sobering indeed to read the work of Epifanio San Juan Jr (2001), on the plight of the world's most invisible diaspora: the 10 million and more Filipino women and women currently engaged in domestic labor in Saudi Arabia, Singapore, the USA, Mexico, and elsewhere. These expatriates "communicate" with the homeland, to be sure, but principally by way of the weekly monetary transfers to their familial homes that constitute 14 percent of domestic GDP; and by way of the six coffins a day that bear their exhausted bodies home for burial. It is a diaspora like many others, but one whose stakes are exacerbated by two peculiarities: the absence of any evident transnational media links sustaining an expatriate Filipino "imagined community," and the invisibility of the diaspora as such to the media ecology itself. San Juan, without conceptualizing the function of media institutions in this situation, asks a round of rhetorical questions:

Can Filipino migrant labor mount a collective resistance against globalized exploitation? Can the Filipino diaspora expose also the limits of genetic and/or procedural notions of citizenship? In what ways can the Filipino diaspora serve as a paradigm for analysing and critically unsettling the corporate globalization of labor and the reification of identities in the new millennium?" (San Juan 2001: 9)

With this last question, the rub is really touched. For you cannot "mount a collective resistance" today without sophisticated mediatic means, and it is those means precisely which work rapidly to congeal a "reification of identities" in our corporate media environment. The double-bind of diasporic media "representation" is hereby crystallized: to force a way through the dominant media system is immediately to submit to the endemic capitalist structures that govern its every application – it is to submit to a regulative "identity" that will adapt a community-in-formation to the dictates of the market; and yet, to abstain or stand aloof from these networked deterritorializations of self and home is to consign oneself to the outer limits of visibility, where only the most two-dimensional of social images hold sway (such as, for instance, the "hard-working Filipina domestic"). There is yet to be a thoroughgoing evaluation of this dilemma.

References

Anderson, B. 2006. *Imagined Communities*, rev. edn. New York: Verso.

Barclay, J.M.G. 1996. *Jews in the Mediterranean Diaspora: From Alexander to Trajan (323 BCE–117 CE)*. Berkeley: University of California Press.

Bisland, E. (ed.) 1906. *The Life and Letters of Lafcadio Hearn*, Volume 1. Boston, MA: Houghton Mifflin.

Burton, A. 1998. *At the Heart of the Empire: Indians and the Colonial Encounter in Late-Victorian Britain*. Berkeley: University of California Press.

Chun, W.K. and Keenan, T. (eds) 2006. *New Media, Old Media: A History and Theory Reader*. New York: Routledge.

Comay, J. 1981. *The Diaspora Story: The Epic of the Jewish People Among the Nations*. London: Weidenfeld & Nicholson.

Cottle, S. (ed.) 2000. *Ethnic Minorities and the Media*. Buckingham: Open University Press.

Deleuze, G. and Guattari, F. 1986. *Kafka: Toward a Minor Literature*, trans. D. Polan. Minneapolis: University of Minnesota Press.

Dernersesian, A.C. 1994. "'Chicana! Rican? no, Chicana-Riqueña!': Refashioning the transnational connection." In D. Goldberg (ed.) *Multiculturalism: A Critical Reader*, pp. 269–295. Oxford: Basil Blackwell.

Ernst, W. 2006. "Dis/Continuities: Does the archive become metaphorical in multi-media space?" In W.K. Chun and T. Keenan (eds) *New Media, Old Media*, pp. 105–125. New York: Routledge.

Fuller, M. 2005. *Media Ecologies: Materialist Energies in Art and Technoculture*. Cambridge, MA: MIT Press.

Gillespie, M. 2000. "Transnational communications and diaspora communities." In S. Cottle (ed.) *Ethnic Minorities and the Media*, pp. 164–179. Buckingham: Open University Press.

Gilroy, P. 1993. *The Black Atlantic: Modernity and Double Consciousness*. London: Verso.

Hardt, M. and Negri, A. 2000. *Empire*. Cambridge, MA: Harvard University Press.

Hassanpour, A. 2003. "Diaspora, homeland, and communication technologies." In K.H. Karim (2003a), pp. 76–88.

Jenkins, H. 2006. *Convergence Culture: Where Old and New Media Collide*. New York: New York University Press.

Kadende-Kaiser, R.M. 2000. "Interpreting language and cultural discourse: Internet communication among Burundians in the diaspora." *Africa Today*, 47(2): 120–148.

Karim, K.H. (ed.) 2003a. *The Media of Diaspora*. London: Routledge.

Karim, K.H. 2003b. "Mapping diasporic mediascapes." In K.H. Karim (2003a), pp. 1–17.

King, R. and Wood, N. (eds) 2001. *Media and Migration: Constructions of Mobility and Difference*. London: Routledge.

Lee, G.S. 1913. *Crowds: A Moving-Picture of Democracy*. New York: Doubleday, Page & Co.

Lewis, R. 2010. "Marketing Muslim lifestyle: a new media genre." *Journal of Middle East Women's Studies*, 6(3): 58–90.

Murphet, J. 2009. *Multimedia Modernism: Literature and the Anglo-American Avant-Garde*. Cambridge: Cambridge University Press.

Naficy, H. (ed.) 1999. *Home, Exile, Homeland: Film, Media, and the Politics of Place*. New York: Routledge.

Palumbo-Liu, D. 1999. *Asian/American*. Stanford: Stanford University Press.

San Juan, E. Jr. 2001. "Interrogating transmigrancy, remapping diaspora: the globalization of laboring Filipinos/as." *Discourse*, 23(3): 52–74.

Stearns, M.W. 1970. *The Story of Jazz*. Oxford: Oxford University Press.

Tabbi, J. 1997. *Reading Matters: Narrative in the New Media Ecology*. Ithaca, NY: Cornell University Press.

Thorburn, D. and Jenkins, H. (eds) 2003. *Rethinking Media Change: The Aesthetics of Transition*. Cambridge, MA: MIT Press.

Wardrip-Fruin, N. and Montfort, N. (eds) 2003. *The New Media Reader*. Cambridge, MA: MIT Press.

Whitaker, M.P. 2004. "Tamilnet.com: Some reflections on popular anthropology, nationalism, and the internet." *Anthropological Quarterly*, 77(3): 469–498.

Wright, R. 1954. *Black Power: A Record of Reactions in a Land of Pathos*. New York: Harper & Brothers.

Young, R.J.C. 2001. *Postcolonialism: An Historical Introduction*. Oxford: Blackwell.

Chapter 4

Diaspora, Transnationalism, and Issues in Contemporary Politics

Garrett Wallace Brown

Diaspora, transnational identities, and the study of politics have had a long, complex, and often under-explored relationship. Some basic aspects of this relationship can be seen in the overlap between politics and identity formation in the tale of what is often considered as the first prototypical diaspora: the Jewish Exodus. As this history suggests, through various claims to empire, religion, political and territorial ownership, and political obligation, the Babylonian king Nebuchadnezzar wielded the full force of the Mesopotamian empire to end the revolt of the Jewish king Zedekiah. This political struggle ended with the Mesopotamian king brutally smashing both the religious (by destroying Solomon's temple) and political (by cruelly executing key military, political, and religious figures) foundations of King Zedekiah, which lead to the exodus and eventual dispersal of the Jews from what they often regard as their ancestral homeland (Clifford 1994). Even a cursory examination of these events helps to highlight that theoretical debates about the political economics of empire, political obligation, political identity, and the politics of border creation have a bearing on how we might understand the multifarious complexities involved in the spread of the Jewish diaspora as well as the deeply political and ideational relationships involved with corresponding images of homeland. In addition, the discipline of politics has immediate relevance for how we might analyze existing political relationships between other diaspora, migrants, transnational networks, and their societies of settlement. For a key question and theme throughout the history of political thought, as well as in diaspora studies, is how to define a political community and what combination of moral, cultural, and institutional structures need to exist in order to sustain a common political identity,

A Companion to Diaspora and Transnationalism, First Edition.
Edited by Ato Quayson and Girish Daswani.
© 2013 Blackwell Publishing Ltd. Published 2013 by Blackwell Publishing Ltd.

legitimate political authority, and long-term political solidarity. These questions continue to have general relevance to both classical and broadened conceptions of diaspora, as well as to understanding emerging transnational identities that inevitably arise from migration and global movements, whether they result from expulsion or choice.

The implications for the way we address the questions about what constitutes a political community are significant, for there is also a form of politics (and political rhetoric) that is deeply connected with the more unfortunate histories involved with transnational identities and diaspora. To highlight just one historical example, the language and negative connotation of diaspora was effectively incorporated into Nazi propaganda and policy (despite the fact that the Nazis were appealing to their own image of a reconnected German diaspora), where Jews and Gypsies were cast as "rootless cosmopolitans," who were "inherent traitors to their countries" without political allegiance to the state or to peoples outside of their immediate religious or cultural communities (Jaspers 1961: 62). As a result, these members of diaspora were portrayed as a politically and culturally destructive element to society that must be removed in order to foster a state of elevated political and cultural solidarity. In this case, strong communitarian claims for the maintenance of strict racial, cultural, and political identification relationships, and for the establishment of political borders of inclusion and exclusion required to foster them, were deemed antithetical to diasporic identities or to individuals who saw themselves as networked into more than one community. This negative portrayal of diasporic and transnational identity has had several expressions and forms throughout modern political thought, from destructive communist ideologies to "weed out" transnational "bourgeoisie imperialists" (Carew Hunt 1957: 36) to more contemporary arguments suggesting a "clash of civilizations" and the erosion of American values resulting from large-scale Mexican migration into the United States (Huntington 2004). In either a pejorative sense, or in terms of positive contribution, the language of diaspora and transnationalism has been, and continues to be, involved in debates about "political community" and it has long been embedded in our political thinking, whether explicitly or implicitly, destructively or in defense.

As a way to capture some of these complex relationships more systematically, the purpose of this chapter is to examine four primary areas of overlap between contemporary themes in politics and their links to the study of diaspora and transnationalism. To do so, the chapter will be divided into five primary sections. The first section will attempt to outline some common characteristics and conceptualizations of diaspora and transnationalism and to locate four key intersections with contemporary politics. From this, the following sections will map out those political intersections as they relate to the relationship between host states and transnational groups; intra-group political mobilization; the role of transnational groups as non-state/kin-state actors; and the role of emerging transnational and cosmopolitan identities in global politics.

Nevertheless, before beginning it is important to set the parameters. First, this chapter will not attempt to resolve current conceptual debates about the definitions of diaspora or explore the many methodological issues surrounding its application in social science. Although these debates are heuristically valuable, they have been explored in greater depth elsewhere (Braziel and Mannur 2003), as well as within the dedicated chapters of this *Companion*. Second, this chapter will not seek to resolve current conceptual and theoretical problems regarding the definitional distinctions between diaspora and transnationalism. Again, this is an extremely nuanced debate, the results of which are ongoing, and these debates have been explored in more sophisticated detail elsewhere (Baubóck and Faist 2010). Third, this chapter does not purport to cover the entire spectrum of debate and argument involving diaspora and transnationalism as found in the broad discipline of political science. To do so would require its own dedicated volume and significant attention to detailed studies and empirical research. As a result, the aim of this chapter is to map out four key debates in contemporary politics as they pertain to issues of diaspora and transnationalism. Although this will leave many subjects unexplored and will only loosely touch upon the field, it will nevertheless expose some key research overlaps. Since the interdisciplinary relevance of diaspora and transnationalism has only recently started to be seriously explored within the study of politics, the targeted overview provided here will highlight areas for continued interdisciplinary development.

Relating Diaspora and Transnationalism to the Study of Politics

There is an active debate between scholars who specialize in the study of diaspora and transnationalism about how to conceptualize, theorize, and apply these concepts. In addition, there is ongoing debate regarding whether or not the concept of diaspora actually captures something distinct in our social and political experiences, or whether newer theories of transnationalism offer a more analytically robust concept for understanding contemporary global and national transformations (Anthias 1998; Soyal 2000). Putting aside these important debates, and relying on a more detailed analysis elsewhere (Baubóck and Faist 2010), most scholars attempt to distinguish diaspora from transnationalism by suggesting that diaspora specifically denotes the movement of religious or national groups, forced or voluntary, from one or more territorial nation-state to another, where these groups maintain strong ideational bonds to other members of that group beyond immediate borders and/or to a common imagined homeland. Within this broad definition there are at least four key characteristics that are common to most definitions of diaspora. First, the use of the term diaspora has traditionally related to a specific focus on the causes of migration or dispersal either through a traumatic experience of removal, as with the Jewish exodus mentioned above, or more recently, through the socioeconomic movement of people via labor and trade (Cohen 2010). Second, the term diaspora has been used to denote a sense of strong group identity that maintains a corresponding notion of an imagined homeland, which often includes a desire to return to, or to maintain strong political, social, and cultural ties with, this ancestral home-land (Safran 1991). Third, diaspora studies have often been concerned with how diasporic groups integrate (or do not) into their host countries and about how these groups often suffer negative reactions from the host population (Alba 2003). In general, these studies have focused on common perceptions that migrant groups are reluctant to fully integrate into the country of settlement and on the resulting discrimination that is often perpetrated by the host country's majority (Cortiade, Djuric, and Williams 1993: 7–12; Bauer, Lofstrom, and Zimmerman 2001). Fourth, the term diaspora has also been related to questions of trans-border ethnic identity and a sense of co-responsibility and/or a sense of sustained special obligations to other members of the diaspora regardless of proximity (Werbner 2002). In an attempt to condense these common characteristics together for use in the study of politics, Adamson and Demetriou (2007: 497) have suggested that:

> A diaspora can be identified as a social collectivity that exists across state borders and that has succeeded over time to 1) sustain a collective national, cultural or religious identity through a sense of internal cohesion and sustained ties with a real or imagined homeland and 2) display an ability to address the collective interests of members of the social collectivity through a developed internal organizational framework and transnational links.

The common features associated with diaspora have often been considered to offer analytical distinction from the study of transnationalism, which maintains an approach that focuses on other social networks and identification relationships that cross state borders, organizational boundaries and cultures. These can include many diasporic forms of transnational identity (Baubök 2010), but in general terms the use of transnationalism has tended to reflect a broader description of global social formations resulting from international business relations, internet social network-ing, global travel, global consumerism, and other processes of globalization that operate outside and across international borders. According to Thomas Faist (2010), the key distinction between the study of diaspora and transnationalism is that "diaspora approaches focus on aspects of collective identity, while transnational approaches take their cue from cross-border mobility." As Faist suggests, "trans-national communities encompass diasporas, but not all transnational communities are diasporas" (p. 21). However, it should be noted that many shared transnational spaces do in fact create a sense of common identity and shared experience, but that in contrast to traditional definitions of diaspora, these identities tend to be less dynamic and not always tightly connected to a shared homeland, ethnic identity, and/or other cultural signifiers. This is because a transnational identity may be connected strictly to a political cause or identity, such as environmental activism or anti-globalization, and this identity formation can be purposely set in opposition to more nationalist or cultural appeals. In order to further a distinction, many scholars also suggest that a diaspora will tend to have a multigenerational compo-nent regarding collective identity or a recognized identity over time (Marienstras

1989), whereas transnationalism refers to broader experiences of trans-border migration, the associated experiences of movement or networking, and the resulting formation of transnational spaces and communities (Vertovec 1999; Kastoryano 2000).

As was previously mentioned, there is considerable debate between scholars regarding the exact peculiarities that separate transnationalism and the study of diaspora and whether it is conceptually, theoretically, and methodologically appropriate to classify them as representing distinct analytical categories. In many ways the lines between diaspora and transnationalism have been blurred to a point of synthesis and differentiation is often difficult. Nevertheless, there are compelling arguments to suggest that both terms are still able to capture unique empirical experiences, while at the same time realizing that they also fail to capture other empirical experiences that seemingly sit outside the generalizations of either approach. Although these debates cannot be explored here, and in order to pinpoint key links to politics, it is possible to locate at least four primary areas where contemporary political thought can be seen to immediately intersect with transnationalism and the study of diaspora. In these cases, a common feature relates to the quality and strength of transnational identities and their relationship to political obligation and solitary political community. First, if we agree that the aforementioned definitions of diaspora and transnationalism capture something about human experiences and the movement of groups from one location to another, then questions about existing political boundaries, their political inclusiveness, and how these political communities relate with transnational groups has relevance in explaining how these experiences are lived and understood. In other words, one question, and one key area of research in politics, pertains to investigating the politics of citizenship and inclusion between the host population and the members of various migrant groups of settlement. Second, and primarily in relation to the study of diaspora, another clear set of political questions relates to how these transnational groups politically mobilize themselves, what political and cultural iconography is assembled in order to maintain a sense of common membership, and what sorts of group behavior can be recognized as having a distinct political dimension. In this regard, a second key question in understanding the links between transnational identities, diasporas, and politics involves examining whether or not these groups can be seen to act as an effective political organization. If so, how and who mobilizes this group, and what amalgamation of rhetoric, iconography, and national identity is utilized to foster this sense of political solidarity and membership? Third, if many transnational and diasporic groups maintain cultural, spiritual, political, and economic links to a real or imagined homeland, then another set of questions pertains to the quality of existing political solidarities across borders and what mixture of internal (settlement group) and external (homeland) motivations are involved with efforts to politically mobilize transnational groups and for what end. Fourth, if the phenomenon of globalization and the creation of transnational identities continues to expand, as many globalization scholars suggest, then what effects will these expanding forces have in transforming structures of global governance, in altering the makeup of cultures, nations, and states, and in relation to the creation of new cosmopolitan identities.

Therefore, where a relationship between politics, diaspora, and transnationalism is most clearly interlinked is in relation to issues of identity formation and how these particular identities help to shape, and/or are shaped by, various political organizations and institutional structures. In other words, identity formation and its connection to ongoing debates about political solidarity, either within states or between groups across borders, is a relevant factor in understanding the quality of transnational relationships and their normative significance. Although this has been presented in rather simple terms and it is certainly far more nuanced than suggested above, it is useful to focus on these key areas of overlap. To reiterate, it has been suggested that these areas relate specifically to: (1) the political relationship between hosts and migrants, either diasporic or transnational; (2) issues of political mobilization within diasporic or transnational groups; (3) the international implications of political solidarities that exist between diasporic and transnational groups and their imagined homeland(s) or imagined co-nationals; and (4) the degree to which emerging transnational identities are fostering, or could foster, new cosmopolitan political identities and institutions. It is in relation to exploring each of these intersections in more detail that this chapter now turns.

Identity and the Boundaries of Political Citizenship

This chapter began by discussing two experiences associated with the history of the Jewish diaspora. The first was the story of the sacking of the Jewish kingdom by Nebuchadnezzar and the armies of the Mesopotamian empire. This event unfortunately represents a very common theme in human history; namely, a political and physical act of violence by one identifiable group on another and the resulting mass movement of people beyond their borders. The second experience related the politicalized violence of Nazi Germany against the Jews, which through a mixture of racial, ethnic, and cultural references resulted in systematic policies to target, expel, and then eliminate those viewed as a threat to the solidaristic aspirations of the greater German Reich. In both cases a relationship between identity and political obligation acted as a key driver. Furthermore, in both cases, a common "need" for political solidarity and strict lines of inclusion and exclusion were appealed to. What these highlight, like many similar events in human history, is that in the history of political thought a link is often made between the need for a solidaristic form of communal identity and a corresponding form of political obligation, and that the political pursuit to strengthen this link can have dire consequences for those who are viewed to lie outside of the community.

As with the examples above, a dedication to this assumption has often resulted in the expulsion or refusal of migrants (Sniderman, Hagerdoorn, and Prior 2004) and has led to high levels of suspicion concerning immigrants within host countries (Mayda 2006). We can see the manifestation of such thinking in the behavior of many modern states, particularly from more authoritarian political organizations, which often appeal to aspects of ethno-nationalism as an easy means to mobilize political support for their regimes. Acts like Idi Amin's removal of the Indian diaspora from Uganda in the 1970s illustrate the immediate effectiveness of appealing to ethno-nationalism, while at the same time highlighting the brutal human and economic consequences that can result long term (Howard 1995). Yet, these sorts of solidaristic appeals are not solely reserved for more totalitarian regimes. Similar claims for an essentialist form of common identity, as a necessary requirement of political citizenship, are also generated in Western countries where a strong tradition of human rights and universal suffrage is present. For there is intense debate within contemporary Western political thought concerning issues of group recognition (Taylor 1994), multicultural inclusion (Kymlicka 1995, 2001), and about the limits to which liberal institutions can/should tolerate religious, cultural, and political diversity (Barry 2001). Within these debates, reference to the cultural identities of migrants and diasporic groups are often implicitly and explicitly made. Furthermore, it is often argued that certain forms of migration could potentially weaken democratic nation-states, since "multination states cannot survive unless the various national groups have allegiance to the larger political community they cohabit . . . and [maintain] a form of national identity" (Kymlicka 1995: 13).

As a result, one particularly robust debate within the study of politics has centered on migration into Western liberal democratic states and how it is possible to foster a common national identity from people of widely diverse cultural and national backgrounds. Underpinning this debate is the question whether increased transnationalism and migrant identities weaken the common national fabric and as a result threaten the common political values that are necessary for state stability, governance, and mutually consistent systems of social justice. For some liberal political theorists, Western democratic states must remain impartial to new cultural, transnational, and migrant demands for special recognition by enforcing human rights impartially and by requiring a level of assimilation and formal acceptance of existing democratic practices and values (Kukathas 2003; Barry 2001). This is because, by doing so, these values present a common source for political identification and if properly constituted, can generate a cross-cultural sense of *constitutional patriotism* from which a solidary sense of citizenship can be fostered regardless of one's specific cultural or national backgrounds (Habermas 1996: 499). In contrast, some multiculturalists have maintained that it is important to recognize that "different communities have different needs . . . and both justice and the need to foster a common sense of belonging require such measures as group-differentiated rights, culturally differentiated applications of laws and policies, state support for minority institutions, and a judicious program of affirmative action" (Parekh 2000). As a culturally sensitive supplement to assimilationist models, and as a way to counter the dominating "enculturative" effects of Western majorities, a multicultural approach seeks to emphasize "the importance of culture of the individual member of society and for groups" and "stresses the right of different cultures not merely to exist but to be recognized and acknowledged within a state or territory" (Peele

2006: 198). Nevertheless, these discussions within political thought are ongoing and without broad normative consensus. As everyday political discourse suggests, multicultural inclusion continues to be a highly charged and polarizing issue and there are growing announcements that the "multicultural experiment has failed" (Bekheet 2010). In addition, the impetus behind resolving these debates has become increasingly more relevant as the forces of globalization create new transnational spaces and the movement of people across borders.

On a quantitative level, there has been considerable research conducted in countries concerning host attitudes to immigration as well as in determining what factors elicit negative or less negative sentiments towards immigration and migrant settlers. By means of cross-country survey data political scientists have been able to locate several explanatory variables with regard to what factors correlate with negative perceptions of immigration and migrant residency. These studies generally focus on host perceptions of a "threat" from immigration and seek to rank these perceived threats against existing beliefs about national identity and solidarity. The "usual suspects" include threat perceptions regarding the negative economic impact of immigration (Facchini and Mayda 2009), the threat of ethnic and racial imbalance posed by mass immigration (Lewin-Epstein and Levanon 2004), the threat to national culture, ways of living, and shared values (Sides and Citrin 2007), and in regards to a threat to national education systems (Hainmueller and Hiscox 2007). In many cases these studies have sought to examine how these perceived threats are actually based on misperception and by doing so, have attempted to empirically expose these threats as socially constructed fallacies. However, as the effects of globalization and the movement of peoples and transnational identities grow, issues regarding citizenship, the boundaries of political inclusion, and the maintenance of national solidarity will certainly become more acute, strained, and in need of conceptual and empirical re-evaluation.

Although existing research is able to expose many host perceptions, when surveying the literature within the study of politics it is common to see that the scope of research is largely restricted to general issues of immigration and migration as they relate specifically to a rooted and consistent national identity of the host population. The problem is that this can often lead to what Wimmer and Glick Schiller have described as "methodological nationalism" and the acceptance "of national borders as the borders of society and as the necessary institutional nexus for citizenship" (Wimmer and Glick Schiller 2002; Glick Schiller 2010). As a result, although they have certainly touched upon issues of transnational identities and how host perceptions of these "foreign" identities can form individual attitudes about immigration policy, these studies can also suffer from methodological and theoretical shortcomings that stymie a more nuanced and holistic explanation within the study of politics.

On a methodological level, there has traditionally been a failure to separate the study of diasporic communities from other transnational groups, and there is a tendency to lump all migrant groups inappropriately together as representing a single independent variable that threatens a consistent dependent variable (i.e., the assumed national solidarity of the state). Nevertheless, by doing so these studies often fail to examine how a diasporic group or other strong transnational identities are different or how they might elicit different reactionary and/or more negative attitudes about certain kinds of migrants. In addition, many studies have tended to ignore subgroup distinctions within various transnational groups and have as a result rendered these groups as thoroughly consistent entities. By doing so, this methodological stance can help to foster the suggestion that all immigrants face similar challenges from the country of settlement or that they experience largely uniform experiences. In the case of diaspora, if we agree that a diaspora delineates a robust condition of identity and special obligation between co-nationals that exists beyond borders, then it is important to understand in what ways these stronger cultural, economic, or political ties might affect threat perceptions within host societies and what political and social reactions they elicit. *Prima facie*, one would expect that diasporic identities might be seen by host populations to be a far greater "threat" (rightly or wrongly) than other immigrants who are perceived as assimilating more easily into the host population (Morawska 2002). Moreover, certain diasporic groups (such as American Jews) might be seen as more compatible with existing national values as opposed to other groups (as is often claimed of Muslim groups in Europe and the USA). Although there has been an effort to recognize greater differentiation between groups since the 9/11 attacks, particularly in regards to the experiences of Muslim migrants (Bunzl 2005), on the whole over-generalizations about migrants and existing national identities remain a mainstay lacuna in contemporary political thought.

Consequently, this raises several theoretical concerns regarding the lack of conceptual clarity about the interplay between culture, nationality, and ethnicity and how these concepts are meant to ground a common sense of group identity and political solidarity. This is because there is often an unexplained conflation between these concepts that is not always fully explored or delineated within the study of politics. In terms of culture, contemporary political thought is rife with claims for or against "the culturalization of identity" and with corresponding normative prescriptions premised on the assumption of clearly delineated cultural identities (Barry 2001: 305). As Seyla Benhabib (2002: 2) has suggested, "culture has become a ubiquitous synonym for identity, an identity marker and differentiator." In exposing this problem, Benhabib has argued that many contemporary political debates about multiculturalism and political inclusion are based on a *reductionist sociology of culture* that posits three faulty assumptions about group entities: (1) that cultures are clearly delineable wholes; (2) that each person belongs to one culture and that a description of that culture is possible; and (3) that subgroup variants pose no important analytical problems (2002: 2). The epistemological problem is that within many political debates about culture and political community the definition of one term is usually uncritically presented as being self-evident or is substantiated through an immediate appeal to the internal aspects of another contestable term (i.e., nationality based on ethnicity; or ethnicity based on culture; or nationality based on culture). By doing so without critical assessment, this often creates conceptual, theoretical, and methodological problems of essential contestability and infinite regress, where claims to culture become fetishized beyond the reach of critical analysis (Brown 2009: 128–130). In other words, it would seem that one immediate problem facing the study of diaspora and transnationalism in politics, where interdisciplinary research would be useful (Bauböck 2010), relates to a better exploration of the dynamics that underwrite cultural appeals as they relate to citizenship, so that we can understand what normative weight should be assigned to them in our thinking about constructing political communities and new forms of political solidarity.

To be clear, this is not to argue that a substantive political community can exist without a common sense of solidarity, for all political theorists agree that some form of solidarity is required for a mutually consistent political order. However, what is not clear, and where disagreement persists, is in regards to what foundational elements are required to constitute this mutual sense of political obligation. As mentioned above, in terms of nationality and national identity there is a tendency to render the nation, the state, and their current borders as being unitary, stable, fixed, and representative of a united national culture and citizenry. The grounding for what constitutes a national culture has often included claims to an imagined community (Anderson 1983), constructed nationalism (Miller 2007), common language and territory (Taylor 1995), ethnic, racial, and religious similarities (A. Smith 1986), collective memories (Miller 2000), cultural similarities (Kymlicka 2001), contractarian commitments (Rawls 1971), or shared history and/or mission (Miller 2000). Many theorists see solidary national identities as the result of self-referential group practice that can be positively identified through the examination of group rites, myths, and rituals of *belonging* (Gellner 1983). Some multiculturalists have attempted to conceptualize the existence of solidary national communities historically, in that national groups can be seen to exhibit politically *shared lives* (Parekh 2000). Other classifications of national identity suggest that it is based on a notion of group *recognition* (or misrecognition), where a delineated group derives its sense of collective self from their identification relationships with external groups who acknowledge them (Young 1990).

The current problem is that it is becoming more and more apparent that these traditional conceptualizations of culture, ethnicity, and nationality as representing the essential foundations for political community and obligation are becoming gradually unable to capture analytically many transformative and stretching effects of globalization upon existing and newly forming political communities. Although there have been promising innovations within political theory to respond to these concerns (Held 1995; Carens 2000; Tinnevelt and Verschraegen 2006; Cabrera 2010; Bauböck 2010), there seemingly remains a sizable need for cross-disciplinary discussion in terms of the changing nature of ethnic identities (Radhakrishnan 2003), the metamorphic quality of cultural identity (Hall 1990), sociological transformations (Delanty 2000; Kendall, Woodward, and Skrbis 2010), and emerging cosmopolitan identities based on common global risks (Beck 2006). It is perhaps here where the study of diaspora and transnationalism has its most important intersections with contemporary political thought and with the expanding discussions about global politics.

The Political Mobilization of Diaspora and Transnational Groups

Another area of investigation that requires further development within the study of mainstream politics relates to how transnational groups, diasporic or not, internally mobilize themselves in order to construct communal relationships between members over time, and to what degree various forms of mobilization can be understood as having a distinct political dimension. As Martin Sokefeld (2006) has suggested in relation to the study of diaspora, these groups represent "imagined transnational communities which unite segments of people that live in territorially separate locations" and these relationships will need certain "opportunity structures," "mobilizing processes," and social "framings" in order for an imagined sense of community to be socially reproduced into more collective sentiments of actual community. In this regard, transnational identities are undoubtedly formed; however, the strength and longevity of these identification relationship depend on social and political mobilizations to reproduce collective self-definition and to motivate participation and support for a regenerated sense of community. As Sokefeld (2006) suggests, the strength and longevity of these mobilizations have a unique quality in diasporas, but there is also a significant level of measurable mobilization that can be seen in many politically motivated forms of transnational movement.

In relation to the previous section, one key feature of diaspora regeneration and the strengthening of transnational identities relates to *opportunities structures* that exist within host countries as well as between the group members themselves. For example, in terms of the country of settlement, the legal and political environment will have to be sufficiently tolerant and open to allow for the political and social activities of various transnational groups to flourish. If the "threats" felt by the host population are significantly intolerant to a politics of difference, then the opportunity structures for communal interfacing will be limited. However, this very restriction of difference may itself create a politically charged atmosphere of "us and them," from which a sense of self-identity is generated and regenerated. Furthermore, there has to be sufficient opportunity for communication between group members as well as with other international groups and institutions. In this regard, when studying the politics of transnationalism, one particular area of interest relates to the opportunity structures available for identity reproduction and what set of political and legal conditions exist that will either repress or enhance diasporic and transnational organization.

An additional area of interest resides in how diasporic and transnational groups politically *mobilize* themselves and how these activities can help to generate and socially reproduce notions of common identity and solidary. As Sokefeld (2006) suggests, these practices can include simple forms of association such as having a designated community hall for neighborhood events, or include more politically explicit practices such as group demonstrations, lobbying, and other forms of direct political activism. In these cases, political questions arise in regard to which elites are actively attempting to mobilize the group and for what purpose; what mechanisms are utilized to retain old members and to recruit new members into the social fabric of the transnational group? By responding to these questions, a distinct framework for making empirical links between the study of diaspora, transnationalism, and politics becomes possible and of great heuristic worth.

Lastly, as Sokefeld and others suggest, any form of group mobilization requires a certain set of *frames* in which collective imagination and self-definition can be generated. In this sense, one key question for the study of politics, as it relates to transnationalism and diaspora, involves what combination of iconography, shared history, and common "roots" to an imagined homeland are propagated in order to regenerate a sense of common identity and political organization. Moreover, a further question pertains to how certain appeals to these images generate distinct group responses and how these responses can have a greater ability to mobilize political action. One recent example of this type of research relates to studies on "homegrown terrorism" and with its attempt to decipher the mixture of iconography, religious teachings, and normative signifiers (*jihad* or *umma*) employed to recruit new members and to elicit politically motivated obligation (Mandaville 2001). Although there have been increased efforts within the study of politics to examine many of these aspects, particularly after 9/11, this area of research has remained by and large unattended by many scholars of politics and it therefore represents a largely untapped area for future interdisciplinary research.

Transnational Groups as Non-State and Kin-State Political Actors

Since the 1990s the study of transnationalism and diasporas has gained significant momentum in international relations (IR), specifically as these concepts relate to emerging transnational networks and their role as non-state actors (Risse-Kappen 1995; Tarrow 2005). In particular, there has been growing interest in how diaspora and transnational groups act as politically motivated agents to pursue international agendas in their countries of settlement, in their countries of origin, and/or within the international community. Within this research there have been broadly two areas of focus. The first looks at diasporic and transnational civil society groups as a positive force for democratization in global governance (Kaldor 2001), as a revenue stream for development (Newland and Patrick 2004), and for their role in promoting democratic change or conflict resolution within their country of origin (Shain 2002; Koinova 2009). Examples of how diasporic and transnational groups can promote peace and conflict resolution can be witnessed in the Ethiopian diaspora's attempt to bring warring factions together for peace negotiations (Koser 2007) and with the role of prominent Irish Americans to bring about the Good Friday Agreement by suppressing IRA fundraising efforts within the Irish American community (Cochrane 2007).

The second area of focus relates to transnational actors as potential sources for inflaming conflict between global actors (Al-Qaeda) or in perpetuating civil conflicts within their country of origin (diasporic support for the Tamil Tigers). One interesting aspect of this research suggests that diasporic and transnational groups relate to their country of origin differently depending on how they were "dispersed" from their homeland. For example, in cases of political expulsion, there is seemingly direct correlation between forced exodus due to civil conflict and a willingness to help armed resistance in the home country through fundraising, the political lobbying of host governments, the purchasing of arms, or increasingly, by returning to engage directly in civil conflict (Adamson 2005; Lyons 2006). As Gabriel Sheffer has suggested (2003: 244), "whereas stateless diasporas often choose separatist strategies in regard to their homelands, most state-linked entities tend to opt for communalism." This suggests that transnational and diasporic networks have distinctive and complex political characteristics in regards to their lived histories and in relation to how these groups identify with existing political regimes in their countries of origin.

Furthermore, it would seem that categorizing the role of diaspora and transnational groups as non-state actors is immensely difficult and that the political agendas involved are not as clear-cut or autonomously generated as they are commonly understood to be. As Hazel Smith and Paul Stares suggest (2007: 7), diasporas and transnational groups can often be both "peace-makers" and "peace-wreckers" when pursuing their international agendas. Moreover, some groups, as was the case with the Eritrean diaspora, can pursue contradictory and seemingly counterproductive agendas that instigate both peace-making and peace-wrecking simultaneously. In addition, diasporic and transnational groups can often adopt the political values associated with their host countries and amalgamate them with their own homeland nationalist aspirations. By doing so, many transnational groups appeal to these values instrumentally in order to influence political change within their countries of origin as well as from the international community. As Maria Koinova suggests (2010: 53):

> Diasporas use the universalist creed of liberalism instrumentally in order to increase their political clout with Western governments while simultaneously pursuing nationalist projects related to their country of origin. They do so by 1) using *discourses* about democratization, peace and reconciliation and 2) occasionally endorsing minimal democratic *procedures*. They do not, however, promote a full-fledged version of liberalism and they fall short of supporting liberal democratic values.

Although the role of diaspora and transnational groups as non-state actors has elicited increased interest within IR, this research has often tended to view these political relationships as unidirectional. Namely, a considerable amount of the research in IR has focused on how diasporic or transnational groups effect change in their country of origin. What is less studied in politics, but is of increased importance for understanding transnational networks, is how these groups politically mobilize themselves across borders or how homeland states seek to engage with their transnational populations. For example, there is strong evidence to suggest that states actively seek to form economic, social, and political relationships with their diasporic or transnational groups in order to propagate a larger notion of "kin-state." As Myra Waterbury suggests (2010: 135), states will often appeal to notions of "global nation" and target specific populations abroad in order to gain geopolitical advantage, to elicit internal political pressure on settlement countries and to gain access to various external resources. The motivations and tools used to create such links are diverse, multifaceted and context specific (Fitzgerald 2006; Itzigsohn 2000; Shain 2007). Nevertheless, there is general consensus that transnational networks are growing as the spatial-temporal *distanciation* of globalization "stretches" social systems across territories, identities, economies, and cultural lifeworlds. It is because of this that the role of transnational groups as non-state or kin-state actors will be of increasing importance within the study of global politics and this represents an area where stronger links to the study of diaspora and transnationalism will be necessary.

Globalization, Political Community, and Emerging Cosmopolitan Identities

As alluded to above, there are strong indicators that suggest that the world is becoming increasingly interdependent, interrelated, mobile, and subject to pressing issues of global cohabitation. In the study of politics, this has generated significant debate regarding how to reconceptualize traditional notions of citizenship and political inclusion, and there are at least two important areas where questions of transnationalism and the study of global politics immediately intersect. These intersections concern questions about the scope of justice under conditions of increased globalization and the extent to which these processes of globalization are creating cosmopolitan solidarities and the political foundations for "world citizenship."

As was discussed in the second section, a common debate within Western political thought pertains to the scope of justice and to the necessary conditions of national solidarity required to create a flourishing social and political community. For more cosmopolitan-minded scholars, duties of justice should not be confined to existing political borders, for cosmopolitans argue that there are ethical obligations of justice that transcend political, cultural, and geographic borders on both moral and institutional grounds (Caney 2005; Beitz 2010). However, for more communitarian-minded scholars, justice cannot apply at the global level because the international environment lacks key institutional and communal structures. Since justice requires authoritarian structures to enforce mutual obligations (Nagel 2005) as well as the existence of robust identification relationships of mutual reciprocity between co-nationals (Miller 2007), the idea of justice beyond borders remains an unintelligible chimera. Because of these disagreements, there has been a continued debate about what sorts of duties we could/should have to those beyond our borders and whether those duties would be compatible with the demands of a globalizing world as well as with the "special obligations" that continue to exist between co-nationals.

To better understand this debate, it is important to highlight that these positions are underpinned by two opposing ontological claims. On one hand, cosmopolitans assert that globalization and its transnational spaces have effectively created inter-dependency to the point where it resembles something like the conditions of social cooperation and economic institutionalism that motivate both communitarian and contractarian concerns for the establishment of domestic justice. In this regard, for many cosmopolitans, the current global order and its transnational structure represent the basic institutional conditions analogous to the conditions under which many traditional political theorists argue justice should apply. As Charles Beitz suggests (2010: 93), "if evidence of global economic and political interdependence shows the existence of a global scheme of social cooperation, we should not view national boundaries as having fundamental moral significance." Brian Barry (1998) adds to this claim by suggesting that all theories of liberal justice demand a level of impartiality and that this requirement, when applied globally, "shows itself to be distinctive in its denial that membership of a society is of deep moral significance when the claims that people can legitimately make on one another are addressed" (p. 145).

On the other hand, critics of the cosmopolitan approach contend that globalization and the transformational aspects of transnationalism have been "exaggerated" and that there is still "considerable scope for national policy making" and direct cultural appeals when determining the boundaries of justice and political membership (Kymlicka 1999: 114; Miller 2007; Nagel 2005). For scholars like David Miller (2007), national and communal sentiments are important and necessary conditions for establishing the motivations for, and the reciprocal conditions of, social justice. As Miller emphasizes, by being indifferent to these communal forms of justice, cosmopolitanism dismantles key elements of communal belonging and pursues this theory against the intrinsic values embroiled within existing special duties between community members.

In this case, the argument about the scope of justice also rests on an empirical assessment about whether or not there is enough of an identification relationship between peoples at the global level to motivate duties of justice and whether transnational spaces are actually creating a sense of cosmopolitan citizenship (Cabrera 2010) or promoting cultural distinctiveness and anti-cosmopolitan sentiments (Saul 2005; Urry 2007). In other words, the debate about global justice also involves evaluations about current sentiments regarding universal humanity, our identification with this common humanity, and whether these new transnational identities are strong enough to provide a "global horizon" for cosmopolitan citizenship (Vertovec and Cohen 2002).

There are many ways in which to interpret the transformative properties of globalization in relation to the formation of cosmopolitan solidarities and imagined global citizenship. For some, emerging global interconnections denote a limiting degree of separation between peoples of the world and the construction of meaningful social and political allegiances that reach beyond borders (Cohen and Rai 2000). For others, the complex affiliations related to global civil society has generated new transnational spaces from which local identities are being fused with a global collective consciousness and that this condition forms a "virtually networked" political society (Castells 2000). In determining the foundations of these cosmopolitan solidarities, scholars generally employ two techniques. The first technique is to locate common universal principles that encompass all human activities and cultural structures. By locating common human traits like human reason, a universal requirement for basic needs, or the capacity to be harmed, cosmopolitan scholars seek to encourage a common humanity that transcends immediate political and cultural boundaries. Through these investigations, cosmopolitans seek to foster "globally aware" educational processes (Nussbaum 2008), the codification of global norms (Habermas 2006), and a universal understanding of global society in the face of escalating risks (Beck 2006). The second technique, and one of growing interest within the study of transnationalism, is to suggest that individuals already have multifarious cultural identities and influences and that human beings already identify with a multiplicity of obligations beyond current political borders. If individuals already have multilayered obligations, then it is possible for human beings, as well as various cultures, to accommodate a cosmopolitan identity as part of an existing set of layered obligations (Appiah 2006). What is missing in terms of political solidarity, argue many cosmopolitans, are systems of global governance that correspond to existing and growing transnational identities that can capture an emerging global condition of "overlapping communities of fate" (Held 2010). As Held and others have suggested, there "is a paradox of our time" where "the issues we must grapple with are growing extensively and intensely and, yet, the means for addressing these are weak and incomplete" (2010: 293). It is here, between the global and the local, between traditional obligations of solidarity and new global horizons, where the study of diaspora, transnationalism, and politics collide. It is also here where new and innovative research is required not only to create stronger links between these fields of study, but also to capture more succinctly the ways in which our everyday lives are interlocked with expanding transnational spaces, global experiences and the political implications that result from an increasingly globalized world.

References

Adamson, F. 2005. "Globalization, transnational political mobilization, and networks of violence." *Cambridge Review of International Affairs*, 18(1): 31–49.

Adamson, F. and Demetriou, M. 2007. "Remapping the boundaries of 'state' and 'national identity': Incorporating diasporas into IR theorizing." *European Journal of International Relations*, 13(4): 489–526.

Alba, R. 2003. *Remaking the American Mainstream: Assimilation and Contemporary Immigration.* Cambridge, MA: Harvard University Press.

Anderson, B. 1983. *Imagined Communities: Reflections on the Origins and Spread of Nationalism.* London: Verso.

Anthias, F. 1998. "Evaluating 'diaspora': Beyond ethnicity." *Sociology,* 32(3): 557–580.

Appiah, K.A. 2006. *Cosmopolitanism: Ethics in a World of Strangers.* New York: Norton.

Barber, B. 1984. *Strong Democracy: Participatory Politics for a New Age.* Los Angeles: University of California Press.

Barry, B. 1998. "International society from a cosmopolitan perspective." In D. Maple and T. Nardin (ed.) *International Society: Diverse Ethical Perspectives,* pp. 144–164. New Jersey: Princeton University Press.

Barry, B. 2001. *Culture and Equality.* Cambridge, MA: Harvard University Press.

Bauböck, R. 2010. "Cold constellations and hot identities: Political theory questions about transnationalism and diaspora." In Bauböck and Faist (2010), pp. 295–323.

Bauböck, R. and Faist, T. (eds) (2010) *Diaspora and Transnationalism: Concepts, Theories and Methods.* Amsterdam: Amsterdam University Press.

Bauer, T., Lofstrom, M., and Zimmermann, K. 2001. "Immigration policy, assimilation of immigrants, and natives' sentiments toward immigrants: Evidence from 12 OECD countries." Working Paper, Center for Comparative Immigration Studies, University of California, San Diego.

Beck, U. 1999. *World Risk Society.* Cambridge: Polity Press.

Beck, U. 2006. *Cosmopolitan Vision.* Cambridge: Polity Press.

Beckheet, D. 2010. "German chancellor calls multicultural experiment a failure," *Voice of America,* October 28. at http://www.voanews.com/content/german-chancellor-calls-multiculturalism-experiment-a-failure-106133534/129241.html, accessed March 4, 2013.

Beitz, C. 2010. "Justice and international relations." In G.W. Brown and D. Held (eds) *The Cosmopolitanism Reader,* pp. 85–99. Cambridge: Polity Press.

Benhabib, S. 2002. *The Claims of Culture: Equality and Diversity in the Global Era.* Princeton: Princeton University Press.

Braziel, J. and Mannur, A. (eds) 2003. *Theorizing Diaspora.* Oxford: Blackwell.

Brown, G.W. 2009. *Grounding Cosmopolitanism: From Kant to the Idea of a Cosmopolitan Constitution.* Edinburgh: Edinburgh University Press.

Bunzl, M. 2005. "Between anti-Semitism and Islamophobia: Some thoughts on the New Europe." *American Ethnologist,* 32: 499–508.

Cabrera, L. 2010. *The Practice of Global Citizenship.* Cambridge: Cambridge University Press.

Caney, S. 2005. *Justice Beyond Borders.* Oxford: Oxford University Press.

Carens, J. 2000. *Culture, Citizenship and Community.* Oxford: Oxford University Press.

Carew Hunt, R.N. 1957. *A Guide to Communist Jargon.* London: Geoffrey Bles.

Castells, M. 2000. *The Rise of the Network Society.* Oxford: Blackwell.

Clifford, J. 1994. "Diasporas." *Current Anthropology,* 9(3): 302–338.

Cochrane, F. 2007. "Civil society beyond the state: the impact of diaspora communities on peace building." *Global Media Journal,* 2(2): 19–29.

Cohen, R. 2010. *Global Diasporas: An Introduction,* 2nd edn. Abingdon: Routledge.

Cohen, R. and Rai, S. (eds) 2000. *Global Social Movements.* London: Athlone Press.

Cortiade, M., Djuric R., and Williams, P. 1993. "Terres d'asile, terre d'exile: l'Europe tsigane." Special issue, *Ethnies,* 8(15): 7–137.

Delanty, G. 2000. *Citizenship in a Global Age: Society, Culture and Politics*. Buckingham: Open University Press.

Facchini, G. and Mayda, M. 2009. "Does the Welfare State affect individual attitudes toward immigrants? Evidence across the countries." *Review of Economics and Statistics*, 91(2): 295–315.

Faist, T. 2010. "Diaspora and transnationalism: What kind of dance partners?" In Bauböck and Faist (2010), pp. 9–35.

Fitzgerald, D. 2006. "Rethinking emigrant citizenship." *New York University Law Review*, 81(1): 90–116.

Gellner, E. 1983. *Nations and Nationalism*. Oxford: Blackwell.

Glick Schiller, N. 2010. "A global perspective on transnational migration: Theorizing migration without methodological nationalism." In Bauböck and Faist (2010), pp. 109–131.

Habermas, J. 1996. *Between Facts and Norms*. Cambridge: Polity Press.

Habermas, J. 2006. *The Divided West*. Cambridge: Polity Press.

Hainmueller, J. and Hiscox, M. 2007. "Educated preferences: Explaining attitudes toward immigrants in Europe." *International Organization*, 61: 399–442.

Hall, S. 1990. "Cultural identity and diaspora." In J. Rutherford (ed.) *Identity: Community, Culture and Difference*, pp. 222–237. London: Lawrence & Wishart.

Held, D. 1995. *Democracy and the Global Order*. Cambridge: Polity Press.

Held, D. 2010. "Reframing global governance: Apocalypse soon or reform!" In G.W. Brown, and D. Held (eds) *The Cosmopolitanism Reader*, pp. 293–312. Cambridge: Polity Press.

Howard, R. 1995. "Civil conflict in Sub-Sahara Africa: Internally generated causes." *International Journal*, 51 (winter): 27–53.

Huntington, S. 2004. *Who Are We? Challenges to America's National Identity*. New York: Simon & Schuster.

Itzigsohn, J. 2000. "Immigration and the boundaries of citizenship: The institutions of immigrants' political transnationalism." *International Migration Review*, 34(4): 1126–1154.

Jaspers, K. 1961. *The Question of German Guilt*. New York: Capricorn Books.

Kaldor, M. 2001. *New and Old Wars: Organized Violence in a Global Era*. Cambridge: Polity Press.

Kastoryano, R. 2000. "Immigration, communautés transnationales et citoyenneté." *Revue International des Sciences Sociales*, 165: 353–359.

Kendall, G., Woodward, I., and Skrbis, Z. 2010. *The Sociology of Cosmopolitanism: Globalization, Identity, Culture and Government*. Basingstoke: Palgrave Macmillan.

Koinova, M. 2009. "Diasporas and democratization in the post-Communist world." *Communist and Post-Communist Studies*, 42(1): 41–64.

Koinova, M. 2010. "Diasporas and international politics: Utilizing the universalistic creed of liberalism for particularistic and nationalist purposes." In Bauböck and Faist (2010), pp. 149–167.

Koser, K. 2007. "African diaspora and post-conflict reconstruction: an Eritrean case study." In Smith and Stares (2007), pp. 239–252.

Kukathas, C. 2003. *The Liberal Archipelago: A Theory of Diversity and Freedom*. Oxford: Oxford University Press.

Kymlicka, W. 1995. *Multicultural Citizenship*. Oxford: Oxford University Press.

Kymlicka, W. 1999. "Citizenship in the era of globalization." In I. Shapiro and C. Hacker-Coredon (eds) *Democracy's Edges*, pp. 112–126. Cambridge: Cambridge University Press.

Kymlicka, W. 2001. *Politics in the Vernacular: Nationalism, Multiculturalism and Citizenship.* Oxford: Oxford University Press.

Lewin-Epstein, N. and Levanon, A. 2004. "National identity and xenophobia in an ethnically divided society." *International Journal of Multicultural Societies*, 7(2): 90–119.

Lyons, T. 2006. "Diasporas in homeland conflict." In M. Kahler and B. Walter (eds) *Territoriality and Conflict in an Era of Globalization*, pp. 111–132. Cambridge: Cambridge University Press.

Mandaville, P. 2001. *Transnational Muslim Politics: Reimagining the Umma.* New York: Routledge.

Marienstras, R. 1989. "On the notion of diaspora." In G. Chaliand (ed.) *Minority Peoples in the Age of Nation-States*, pp. 119–125. London: Pluto Press.

Mayda, A. 2006. "Who is against immigration? A cross-country investigation of individual attitudes to immigrants." *Review of Economics and Statistics*, 88(3): 510–530.

Miller, D. 2000. *Citizenship and National Identity.* Cambridge: Polity Press.

Miller, D. 2007. *National Responsibility and Global Justice.* Oxford: Oxford University Press.

Morawska, E. 2002. "Immigrant transnationalism and assimilation: a variety of combinations and the analytic strategy it suggests." In E. Morawska, and C. Joopke (eds) *Toward Assimilation and Citizenship in Liberal States*, pp. 133–176. Basingstoke: Palgrave Macmillan.

Nagel, T. 2005. "The problem of global justice." *Philosophy and Public Affairs*, 33(2): 113–147.

Newland, K. and Patrick, E. 2004. "Beyond remittances: the role of diaspora in poverty reduction in their countries of origin." Washington DC: Migration Policy Institute.

Nussbaum, M. 2008. "Toward a globally sensitive patriotism." *Daedalus*, 137(3): 78–93.

Parekh, B. 2000. *Rethinking Multiculturalism.* Basingstoke: Palgrave.

Peele, G. 2006. "The politics of multiculturalism." In P. Dunleavy, R. Heffernan, P. Cowley, and C. Hay (eds) *Developments in British Politics*, Volume 8. Basingstoke: Palgrave Macmillan.

Radhakrishnan, R. 2003. *Theory in an Uneven World.* Oxford: Blackwell.

Rawls, J. 1971. *A Theory of Justice.* Cambridge, MA: Harvard University Press.

Risse-Kappen, T. (ed.) 1995. *Bringing Transnational Relations Back In: Non-State Actors, Domestic Structures, and International Institutions.* Cambridge: Cambridge University Press.

Safran, W. 1991. "Diasporas in modern societies: Myths of homeland and return." *Diaspora*, 1(1): 83–99.

Saul, J. 2005. *The Collapse of Globalism.* New York: Atlantic Books.

Shain, Y. 2002. "The role of diasporas in conflict perpetuation and resolution." *SAIS Review*, 22(summer): 115–144.

Shain, Y. 2007. *Kinship and Diasporas in International Affairs.* Ann Arbor: University of Michigan Press.

Sheffer, G. 2003. *Diaspora Politics: At Home Abroad.* Cambridge: Cambridge University Press.

Sides, J. and Citrin, J. 2007. "European opinion about immigration: the role of identities, interests and information." *British Journal of Political Science*, 37: 477–504.

Smith, A. 1986. *The Ethnic Origins of Nations.* Oxford: Blackwell.

Smith, H. and Stares, P. (eds) 2007. *Diasporas in Conflict: Peace-Makers and Peace-Wreckers.* Tokyo: United Nations University Press.

Sniderman, P., Hagerdoorn, L., and Prior, M. 2004. "Predisposing factors and situational triggers: Exclusionary reactions to immigrant minorities." *American Political Science Review*, 98(1): 35–49.

Sokefeld, M. 2006. "Mobilizing in transnational space: a social movement approach to the formation of diaspora." *Global Networks*, 6(3): 265–284.

Soyal, Y. 2000. "Citizenship and identity: Living in diasporas in post-war Europe." *Ethnic and Racial Studies*, 23(1): 1–15.

Tarrow, S. 2005. *The New Transnational Activism*. Cambridge: Cambridge University Press.

Taylor, C. 1994. *Multiculturalism: Examining the Politics of Recognition*. Princeton: Princeton University Press.

Taylor, C. 1995. *Philosophical Arguments*. Cambridge MA: Harvard University Press.

Tinnevelt, R. and Verschraegen, G. 2006. *Between Cosmopolitan Ideals and State Sovereignty*. Basingstoke: Palgrave Macmillan.

Urry, J. 2007. *Mobilities*. Cambridge: Polity Press.

Vertovec, S. 1999. "Conceiving and researching transnationalism." *Ethnic and Racial Studies*, 22(2): 447–462.

Vertovec, S. and Cohen, R. 2002. *Conceiving Cosmopolitanism: Theory, Context and Practice*. Oxford: Oxford University Press.

Waterbury, M. 2010. "Bridging the divide: Toward a comparative framework for understanding kin state and migrant-sending state diaspora politics." In Bauböck and Faist (2010), pp. 131–149.

Werbner, P. 2002. "The place which is diaspora: Citizenship, religion, and gender in the making of Chaordic transnationalism." *Journal of Ethnic and Migration Studies*, 28(1): 119–133.

Wimmer, A. and Glick Schiller, N. 2002. "Methodological nationalism and beyond: Nation building, migration, and the social sciences." *Global Networks*, 2(4): 301–334.

Yack, B. 2002. "Multiculturalism and the political theorists." *European Journal of Political Theory*, 1(2): 107–119.

Young, I. 1990. *Justice and the Politics of Difference*. Princeton: Princeton University Press.

Chapter 5

Diaspora and Transnationalism in Urban Studies

Ayona Datta

Diaspora, Transnationalism, and Urban Studies

Diaspora and transnationalism have been the two driving concepts through which migration and movement have been defined in the past decade. On the one hand, Avtar Brah's classic definition of diaspora (2006: 196) as "a matrix of economic, political and cultural inter-relationships which construct the commonality between various components of a dispersed group" provides us with the conceptual and analytical grounds to examine forms of identity and belonging in a transnational world. Following on her important work, the increasing breadth and range of research on diaspora and transnationalism in recent years has alerted us to the need to look for diasporic formations not just in terms of power relations, but also across spaces and scales of the global, national, regional, and local. Transnationalism, on the other hand, forms one of the key theoretical and analytical lens through which nation-states have responded to the migration and movement of people globally. Transnationalism, which began as a deterritorialized concept, has in more recent years grounded itself into examining more material, embodied, and cultural processes of transnational identity formations in and across different spaces. Taken together, diaspora and transnationalism are both important concepts in order to understand when, how, and under what circumstances people leave, settle, return, and resettle and how their decisions are shaped by structural, political, social, cultural, and subjective processes at different scales.

In this chapter, I focus on the relevance of diaspora and transnationalism to the broad and interdisciplinary field of urban studies, in order to argue that embodied,

A Companion to Diaspora and Transnationalism, First Edition.
Edited by Ato Quayson and Girish Daswani.
© 2013 Blackwell Publishing Ltd. Published 2013 by Blackwell Publishing Ltd.

material, and corporeal encounters within cities and urban spaces are critical to the making of contemporary diasporic and transnational spaces and identities. I argue that while the multifaceted notions of transnationalism and diaspora in their relations to people and power have significantly shaped the debates on identity, multiculturalism, and cosmopolitanism, it is only very recently that their implications for thinking about spaces physically, materially, and geographically is coming to the forefront. The geographical "turn" in diaspora and transnationalism, as the movement of goods, ideas, people, and capital across (and beyond) nation-states, allows us to explore more situated politics of power that shape migrants' relations to other spaces and scales.

Diaspora and transnationalism are the two concepts which I suggest have much to contribute to the study of urban spaces, city cultures, and everyday life in cities, and in turn a focus on cities and urban spaces is also critical to understanding the forces that shape diasporic and transnational identities across space and over time. As Brah (2006) notes, diaspora offers a critique of fixity, while simultaneously recognizing home-making practices, and therefore counters the ideology of "return" so implicit in the discourses of migration. Diaspora therefore poses the question of location in structural, material, social, and subjective terms. This is important in a context where historically diaspora-making has been strongly associated with dislocation and displacement – particularly in the work on refugees, asylum-seekers, and holocaust survivors (Koser 2007). Breaking this understanding means that diasporic space can be associated both with those who have moved and those who are considered relatively fixed.

Recent empirically driven work in diaspora and transnationalism studies has implicitly or explicitly used an urban lens to highlight what I see as an increased significance of cities as the sites where diasporic and transnational lives are lived, contested, and imagined (Amin 2002; Beaverstock 2002; Blunt 2003; Bretell 2003; Cairns 2004; Chacko 2008; Datta 2012; Kothari 2008; Sandercock 2003; Smith 2001). In this chapter, I am particularly interested in framing cities as laboratories in the making of identities, difference, otherness, and the production of home and belonging during the movement/immobility of people. This comes at a time when cities are becoming increasingly important players in shaping the structural processes and politics of migration, diasporic identity formation and transnationalism – a notion common among those supporting the "global city" hypothesis (Sassen 1991). At the same time, there is another corrective lens developing around the notion of individual agencies of migrants where migrant experiences and encounters in everyday urban life are seen as important in understanding how cities are made and transformed by migrants over time. It is now increasingly accepted that migrants' experiences across urban spaces, neighborhoods, rental homes, shops, hotels, public transport, and so on are also part of the structuring effects of globalization. While researchers have sought to position this latter approach as the more grounded or "bottom-up" approaches to the global-city hypothesis, to globalization (Smith and Guarnizo 1998), and broadly speaking to migration itself, I will explore how we can take this now widely acknowledged understanding of diasporic and transnational cities beyond its mere analytical bottom-up approach. I ask how we can understand the social, cultural, and political connections between urban, diasporic, and transnational lives. How are we to observe these connections, research them in real places, and what might our shift in the scale towards the urban tell us about the geopolitical dimensions of migrant diasporic and transnational identities?

Transnationalism from Above and Below

For some time now, transnationalism from above and transnationalism from below have been the two opposing but related concepts whence urban studies have begun exploring both trends and experiences of migration. *Transnationalism from above* has primarily examined the flows and movements of people across the globe, demographics, and population change. This is not to say that migrants' lives have not been important in transnational research; rather that their lives have been examined largely through economic, political, and social networks between sending and receiving national contexts, thus signifying the primacy of nation-states. It has also largely focused on socioeconomic and cultural assimilation, using evidence from census and survey data (Lie 1995). Its relevance to cities has tended to concentrate on high-end professional or low-skilled migration in global cities – a mode of enquiry made popular by Sassen's (1998) global-city hypothesis. Sassen notes transnationalism as having facilitated a "portability of national identity," or a notion of multiple citizenships in different global cities, which has led to a considerable academic exploration of the notion of rights and responsibilities around immigration, national belonging, and multiculturalism (Hannerz 1996; Vertovec and Cohen 2002). This recent interest in transnational and global cities however is largely based on an economistic turn in migration research, which has focused on business and entrepreneurial activities of migrants in global cities on the one hand, and on disempowered migrant working lives on the other (May *et al.* 2008; McDowell 2003). However, the notion that national identity is "portable" and that migrants are often able to carry with them assemblages of citizenships with unhindered access to national territories and uninhibited routes through national borders has been criticized widely as a notion that is based on the experiences of the white male Western professional elite. On the other hand, the fact that the global city tends to exclude low-income or unskilled migrants has also been critiqued for its top-down lens that tends to sideline migrant agencies in favor of passive victimhood to structural conditions of citizenship and belonging.

Transnationalism from below as an opposition to the globalizing tendencies of migration research in the 1980s and 1990s attempts to address much of the critique around the loss of migrant agencies through a shift in focus towards subjective processes of citizenship, identity formation, and home-making practices. Transnationalism from below is a largely corrective analytical lens which focuses on the agency of the local (Smith and Guarnizo 1998) that works simultaneously with the structuring tendencies of nation-states and sovereign territories. Smith and Guarnizo argue for an awareness of the individual experiences and subjectivities of those who move while also providing a way to study how these are shaped by wider structural and global forces. As Lie (1995) notes, both in sociology and anthropology there has been a scholarly turn towards exploring connectedness and the simultaneous experiences of being here and there through the use of concepts such as diaspora and transnationalism. Much of this turn however tends to focus on links across nation-states. This has been identified by Wimmer and Glick Schiller (2002: 302) in their coining of the term "methodological nationalism" whereby analytical tools and concepts have been colored by the self-evidence of a world ordered into nation-states. This has resulted in a situation according to Levitt and Khagram (2004: 5) in which, "the terms 'transnational' or 'transnationalism' or 'transnationality' are partly misnomers, in that they imply that the only things we are interested in are the dynamics across or beyond nation states, or within the (nation-) state system."

A new and emerging body of research has more modestly called for the nation to be seen in a less deterministic fashion. This does not mean the nation has become irrelevant. As Aiwha Ong (1999: 15) so effectively illustrates, migrants' lives are still touched by its "juridical-legislative systems, bureaucratic apparatuses, economic entities, modes of governmentality, and war-making capabilities." But the framing of migrant experiences singularly through the scale of the nation and national belonging perpetuates the silencing of other scales and spaces during migration research. As Ley (2004: 155) notes, "there is a need to re-incorporate other scales, including the regional, the national and the supranational but not yet global, such as the European Union and other continental-scale trading networks." The driving question then is how do we reference these other scales without losing sight of the nation?

Transnational Urbanism

The often opposing forces of the transnationalism debate which positioned scholars along the above-and-below divide, fall roughly parallel with the structure–agency divide. In discussing transnationalism from above, scholars often gave too much preponderance to sovereign power vested in the state while stripping the migrant of any agency and rendering them as passive victims. The transnationalism from below debate on the other hand, often valorized the agency of the migrant, leading to an aestheticization and exotification of migrant lives. This opposition has been critiqued in recent years as the problem of defining diaspora and transnationalism through the lens of the nation. Michael Peter Smith (2001) suggests that the challenge does not proceed from the nature of local–global connections so prevalent in transnationalism research; rather it is a problem of scope and scale of analysis. Given that diasporic and transnational processes are multidimensional and multi-scalar, Smith asks how we can better capture the dynamic and temporal processes that shape migrants as both socially and spatially situated subjects. His proposal is to examine this through a lens of "transnational urbanism," which directs attention to the making and remaking of cities through migrant agencies, even as cities have increasingly begun to play an important role in globalization and migration. As he explained (2001: 5):

> transnational social actors are materially connected to socio-economic opportunities, political structures, or cultural practices found in cities at some point in their transnational communication circuit, e.g. transnational cities as sources of migrant employment, the means to deploy remittances, the acquisition of cultural and physical capital, consumption practices, political organising networks, or life style images; or [because] . . . they maintain transnational connections by using advanced means of communication and travel, which because of their simultaneity, indirectly implicate transnational actors in an orbit of cosmopolitan ideas, images, technologies, and socio-cultural practices that have historically been associated with the culture of cities.

For Smith, transnational urbanism captured "a sense of distanciated yet situated possibilities for constituting and reconstituting social relations" that enabled them to "forge the translocal connections and create the translocalities that increasingly sustain new modes of being-in-the-world" (2005: 237). This meant contextualizing migrant experiences in the city, by articulating how their everyday lives simultaneously incorporated aspects of being "there" and "here." Smith was particularly interested in how migrants are transforming both their cities of origin and of settlement, deploying a conscious use of the term "urbanism" which denotes a process, not a product. For Smith transnational urbanism is therefore a power relation "from in-between" – a continuous process that is shaped somewhere between the state and the citizen. For Smith, this process takes shape in the city.

The key message in Smith's work and my argument further on in this chapter is that cities continue to be significant as "mediators of local and global power, as well as the human foundation of contemporary transnationalism." Smith's contribution to urban studies is both conceptual and methodological. He proposes that we use an "agency-oriented" urban theory in which we see migrants as active agents in the making of cities and transnational spaces. Smith (2003) illustrated this through a political notion of transnationalism, where migrants on the Mexican–American border were not just making connections across political boundaries of nation-states; they were also situating these connections within urban spaces through local encounters and networks. Smith argued that the cooptation of transnational migrants by party elites into state development projects is actively resisted by the migrant leaders themselves, who see this as a way of obstructing the development of transnational civil society across national borders. Smith's discussions of this form of active political transnationalism captures the emplacement of migrants' lives within local contexts in order to understand how localized interactions make way for distanciated, yet situated possibilities for constituting and reconstituting social relations from near and far.

Smith therefore reinforces that we need to focus more on cities as sites of diaspora, transnationalism, and globalization. This is both a conceptual and methodological provocation, since it involves a rescaling of theories of transnationalism and diaspora

onto more territorial and spatial realms, as well as finding different ways to investigate the multiple sites and processes of transnational urbanism within the city.
Following on this cue, I will now discuss four aspects of cities that make the "urban"
relevant to the study of diaspora and transnationalism. Indeed cities are part of the
past, present, and future of migrant lives – an understanding that relates to what
has often been proposed as the roots/routes of migrant itineraries. Cities are places
of origin/departure for migrants, as well as places of destination. In more recent
years, cities have also been mapped along migrants' return journeys as well as
lifecycle/circulatory journeys across the world. What can we learn then from refo-
cusing our attention onto the social and spatial processes of the "urban"? How is
the urban shaped by diasporic and transnational migrant groups? How do cities
themselves shape the diasporic and transnational experiences and imaginations of
migrants?

Cities as Places of Origin/Departure

Cities as places of origin of migrants are often related to the experiences and imaginations of migrants who are forced or coerced to move across national and territorial boundaries. The "left-behind" city has occupied vivid and powerful nostalgic
spaces within the memories of political émigrés after World War II (Shallcross
2002), and in more contemporary times among refugees and asylum-seekers. They
are often related to the "roots" of migrants (Wessendorf 2007) – the sending context,
which has shaped debates around local development (Faist 2008), home-town associations (Çağlar 2006) and brain-drain (Raghuram 2009) in origin countries, as
well as notions of home and belonging in a global world in recent years.

Roots is a powerful linguistic, cultural, and social framing of the complex process
of leaving, moving, settling, and possibilities of return. It has shaped countless
debates in academia and popular culture, notwithstanding the highly successful
dramatization of Alex Haley's book *Roots* where a ninth-generation African American brought to the USA via the slave trade goes in search of his roots in a village in
The Gambia. If anything, the roots concept highlights the potent politicization of
questions of "origin" even amongst those understood to be ordinary Americans in
contemporary US society. It also evokes a continuous longing and nostalgia for that
which has been left behind both spatially and temporally, imagined often as the
original, the authentic, the unchanged – the place from where a migrant started his/
her journey. Understandably then, the notion of roots has become an important
conceptual tool through which to evoke questions of home and belonging to sending
contexts, particularly among diasporic communities who desire the left-behind
home/land and often have no means of return whether for structural or social
reasons.

The importance of the city within this discourse of roots has been explored by
a number of scholars (Blunt 2007; Foner 1997; Mountz and Wright 1996). Blunt (2007)
in particular examined the notion of the "diasporic city" through the material and

imaginative practices and networks of the London-based Brahmo and Jewish communities from Calcutta and Jerusalem. In this notion of diaspora, the city rather than the nation was imagined as home. Blunt argued that migrants' highly embodied and situated memories and experiences of living in these cities of origin connected them across a transnational diasporic space of nostalgia, longing, and belonging. It emerged that memories and experiences of everyday lives in the spaces and places of these cities formed part of the wider construction of identity, belonging, and self for transnational Jewish and Brahmo migrants in ways that were intensely connected to actually existing urban spaces and places in the past and present. Thus diasporic belonging was not just imagined, it was also embodied in urban spaces – evoked through the senses of sight, touch, smell, and sound that differentiated but also connected cities like London, Jerusalem, and Calcutta. Blunt argued that these cities were therefore part of a diasporic transnational space – forging connections between migrants' multiple individual subjectivities and collective experiences of home, belonging, and Otherness.

Diasporic belonging to cities of origin has remained a continuous framework for investigation around notions of home and belonging to new contexts. From a social and cultural perspective, the left-behind home has been re-narrated through migrants' stories, photographs, food, diaries, household objects, music, artwork, and films. Material culture has remained important in these narrations. Tolia-Kelly (2004) investigated this through objects in the South Asian home which evoke notions of diasporic belonging. She argued that visual cultures (which include photographs, pictures, and paintings) in the everyday lives of South Asian migrant families in the United Kingdom depict symbolic and material relationships with past landscapes which are made meaningful in their placement in the new home in the United Kingdom. For Tolia-Kelly this placement allowed for the exploration of home-making in new contexts but most crucially also embodied connections to landscapes experienced pre-migration, including sensory connections with past homes, natures, and family life.

The debate in the study of diasporic cities has therefore been about their relationships to home-making in the present. The making and imagining of homes/cities left behind due to current home-making practices relates to the notion of what home means in a context of migration, movement, and transnationalism. This is succinctly summarized by Ahmed and colleagues (2003) who ask, insightfully, what is the relationship between leaving home and the imagining of home? From the perspective of urban studies, we might then also ask what is the relationship between cities left behind to the process of making home and belonging to cities of destination and resettlement?

Cities as Places of Destination/Settlement

Destination cities shape a critical politics of location within diaspora and transnationalism in contemporary times, since most global and local migrations, be they rural or urban, regional or international, often have cities as their destination. In urban studies there is now a powerful debate around the coming of an urban age, which refers to the prediction that globally more people will be living in cities than any other location by 2030. Destination cities as sites of employment, livelihoods, and desirable lifestyles have come to occupy the frontiers of migratory routes and imaginations. The impact of these debates is apparent not just in urban studies, but also in popular culture through films, art, installations, exhibitions, novels, and so on.

The most prolific debate around transnationalism and diaspora in cities of destination has perhaps taken shape around the existence of migrant and ethnic neighborhoods in Western cities (Chacko 2008; Lin 1998; Pacyga 1991). While migrant neighborhoods, particularly Polish and Italian ones, have been common in US cities since World War II, the new migrant neighborhoods that comprise African, Asian, or Chinese populations have come under recent scrutiny by the state. Labeling them somewhat negatively as "ethnoscapes," Appadurai (1991) noted that migrant neighborhoods are the sites of violent battles of power between state and citizen. These ethnoscapes are where parochialism and anti-cosmopolitanism are seen to reside – in more recent times, these have also been conceptualized as breeding grounds for terrorism. Ethnoscapes therefore are often places where sovereign authority is established through the force of law in order to create compliant and controllable migrants.

In popular culture too, representations of migrants to cities in the West are usually voyeuristic at best and assert victimhood at worst. We see this even in highly acclaimed movies like *Dogville* which though sympathetic to migrants' lives and satirical about society's normative ideologies and dogmas, produce nevertheless a migrant subjecthood that is doomed from their moment of arrival. *Dogville* was particularly interesting in that it has no props, no buildings, and virtually no built environment – only architectural plans of the street and houses along it through which the figure of the immigrant (a single female and already symbolically assigned to victimhood through its gendering) entered, left, and was finally confined. The absence of a built environment is telling since it evokes the question of where is this place, who is this community, who is the migrant? This was intentional – in that the director Lars von Trier wanted to suggest that this can happen in any community, in any place, to any migrant in any American city or town.

A more material investigation of the home-making practices of migrants in destination cities has emerged in recent years, which emphasizes the built environment in contrast to the absence of it in films like *Dogville*. Home-making in destination cities engages with architectural styles and layouts to examine the wider cultural politics of citizenship, nationhood, identity, and belonging. Examining architecture for/by migrants in the form of migrant neighborhoods, expat towns, and retirement/second homes, Cairns (2004) noted how these architectural forms are made through the mobility of ideas, people, and building styles across national territories. From the perspective of a transnational migrant, the new home in a foreign land can be the site where a number of insecurities and anxieties of separation, longing, and memory can be played out through its walls and built elements, as discussed by Jacobs (2004) in the houses occupied by Chinese immigrants in Australia. Examining the "monster homes" of the Chinese in Vancouver suburbs, Mitchell (2004) further highlights how local protests against the architectural styles of these homes are also part of the wider contestations around citizenship, identity, and belonging of transnational migrants.

That Western cities in the Anglo-American world have seen a rise in migration of people from the global south since the twentieth century is widely acknowledged. The influx of new social groups from different racial, ethnic, and religious backgrounds into spaces that were earlier considered largely white and Christian have transformed cities into contested sites of negotiations of identities between migrants and host communities. These negotiations are often based on normative understandings of race, religion, nationality, and so on, evident in recent confrontations around what it means to be American, British, French, Muslim, Christian, European, or even first/second-generation migrants within cities such as New York, Los Angeles, London, Paris, and many others. New and more recent research on migrant social groups suggest more complex processes of home-making in destination cities, which draw attention away from the binary portrayals of ethnoscapes or *Dogville*. They suggest that cities are central in conceptualizing Otherness and fostering notions of inclusiveness, belonging, and citizenship among migrants through processes of cosmopolitanism (Appiah 2006; Vertovec and Cohen 2002), cosmopolitics (Cheah and Robbins 1998), mongrelization (Sandercock 2003), and the creation of micro-publics (Amin 2002). In other words, scholars have called for a view of cities in the West as socially, culturally, and materially transformed through a politics of difference negotiated in urban spaces.

What does it mean then to live with difference in transnational cities? This is a key question asked in the European Research Council-sponsored project LIVDIFF that aims to examine everyday accounts of living with Others (Valentine 2008). Aiming to understand how encounters with Others across European cities are mediated through migrants' transnational histories, cosmopolitan attitudes, diasporic belonging, national identity, and particular positionalities of gender, race, ethnicity, and citizenship, the LIVDIFF project recognizes cities as key sites of migrants' experiences of home(s) and belonging in a mobile world. In examining how living with difference is both personal and political, it establishes again the centrality of cities in anchoring memory, nostalgia, remembering, belonging, inclusion, and openness to others during the making of homes in Western transnational cities.

Cities as Places of "Return"

More recently cities have been drawn into debates of return migration. As much of the second- and even third-generation migrants and diasporic groups reach more advanced stages in their life cycle, cities of (diasporic) origin have increasingly begun to see a form of migration of these groups returning to their (diasporic) homeland. This has been particularly salient in the return of migrant groups from Anglo-American cities to their diasporic homeland in Greece, Turkey, India, and more specifically in migrant investments in (future) houses in their left-behind cities (Klaufus 2006; Lothar and Mazzucato 2009). Often labeled as "counter-diasporic" migration (Christou and King 2006) this has become common among middle-class migrants associated with an imputed readjustment and assimilation within its spaces.

While return migration to one's diasporic homeland might be a personal choice related to the desire to live with those with whom one shares cultural, social, and historical narratives, Christou and King (2006) note, however, that counter-diasporic migration is often disappointing to those who return. Particularly amongst second- and third-generation return migrants who may not even have had any embodied experience of the city left behind, return migration might evoke similar feelings of exclusion and alienation that first-generation migrants felt in Western cities of destination. The city of their home/land that they desired to return to had always been imagined and desired through nostalgia and memory, mythologized through stories narrated to them by older family members who had migrated. Christou (2011) notes that counter-diasporic migration is made possible only through the "myths of homeland" that reimagines a left-behind city as the site of "original" identity and site of homeliness. In reality, return/counter-diasporic migration never achieves the closure or completion that migrants desire; rather it produces in them a disillusionment of return and often fresh negotiations to make a home for themselves within a city that seems familiar yet is experienced through the eyes of a migrant. Cities of return therefore are significant sites of the negotiation of diasporic origins, reinforcing and producing new differences along class, capital, and generation within transnational connections.

Return migration is embedded within the dynamics and geopolitics of migration through the power vested within individual migrants' relationships to class, social networks, and cultural/economic capital. We can ask the question, who has the power or choice of return and who possess the social, cultural, and economic capital to make a home in their city of diasporic origin?

Cities as Places of Transit/Life-Cycle Cities

Even as cities are mapped along counter-diasporic routes, a new role of the city as a place of transit has emerged. This is mostly associated with what is known as "circular migration" identified by Ley and Kobayashi (2005) as part of continuous movement on the part of migrants. In this form of migration to and from cities, particular social groups are said to be participating in migration during various life-cycle changes – marriage, parenting, children moving out, and retirement (Gustafson 2001). This conceptualization is based on a critique of return migration to cities which Ley and Kobayashi argue does not capture the dynamic, temporal, and intergenerational nature of decisions around when to move and to where. They critique return migration in its similarity to other forms of migration which convey a sense of closure or finality. Instead they argue for a more temporal and incomplete nature of movement across cities in a transnational world that corrects the conventional immigration-assimilation narrative of migration. They note that migration is better described as continuous throughout life rather than completed at a definitive moment. Ley and Kobayashi report from their research in Hong Kong with middle-class "returnees" from Canada (2005: 111):

> Focus groups held in Hong Kong with middle-class returnees from Canada disclose that migration is undertaken strategically at different stages of the life cycle. The return trip to Hong Kong typically occurs for economic reasons at the stage of early or mid-career. A second move to Canada may occur with teenage children for education purposes, and even more likely is migration at retirement when the quality of life in Canada becomes a renewed priority. Strategic switching between an economic pole in Hong Kong and a quality of life pole in Canada identifies each of them to be separate stations within an extended but unified social field.

This form of migration is arguably most common among the hypermobile – global business elites, or journalists, or diplomats. But it is also common among those enacting "routinized sojourning" (Gustafson 2001) as part of their retirement lifestyles. This form of migration is relevant to a stage in their life cycle which coincides with a desire for "multilocal adaptation" and "translocal normality" rather than settlement and assimilation. Gustafson suggests that this is also a result of the hypermobility of individuals and families as professionals or as tourists during earlier periods of their life, which brings about a desire for retaining the "normalcy" of "routinized sojourning." Similar to counter-diasporic migration, circular migration across cities is a choice made from social, economic, and politically privileged positions of middle-class white Western professional families.

Translocal Cities

There is another perspective on diaspora and transnationalism which has perhaps received less attention in urban studies. This is a notion of translocality, or connections that are made between and across locales. Translocality as a concept is not new – it has been proposed by various scholars across disciplines of anthropology, geography, and international relations as a way to highlight the importance of connections across borders which are not necessarily confined to nation-states (Oakes and Schein 2006) as well as the increased deterritorialization of linkages across national boundaries. Appadurai (1991, 1995) proposed that translocality could no longer be associated with territoriality, a critique that was essentially directed towards the insularity of anthropological imagination within bounded communities. Instead Appadurai suggested that we examine different ways that translocality has exploded the attachment to place, by increasing cross-border virtual linkages facilitated by media and communications. In geography and urban studies recently, translocality has been proposed as a subset of transnationalism (Velayutham and Wise 2005) in the guise of a grounded transnationalism. This notion was deployed particularly by Smith (2001) who suggested that translocality be seen as a way that deterritorialized transnational connections were emplaced through local politics, encounters, experiences, and economies.

In our work on translocal geographies (Brickell and Datta 2011), we proposed that translocality be seen as "a fractured collection of mundane spaces and places that produces connections (both social and material) with other spaces, places and locales within and beyond the city" (p. 17). Using a framework of translocal geographies we were able to underscore the contribution of geography and urban studies to transnationalism and vice versa. We suggested that the role and position of the migrant within a number of spaces and scales, as well as the connections that might exist or be made possible between these spaces and scales, constituted the translocal geographies of those who moved as well as those who decided to remain immobile. Drawing upon the multiple (and often divergent) ways that translocality was described in current literature, we sought to give it conceptual coherence by reflecting upon this through the notion of *habitus* (Bourdieu 2002), arguing that emplacement within local contexts was shaped through migrants' accumulation of social, cultural, and economic capital across various spaces and scales. We then asked the following questions: At which scale was the local situated? What were the temporal dynamics of this local in making connections with other scales? How was the local emplaced through migrants' personal stories and experiences of leaving, settlement return, and re-return? How was this emplacement simultaneously material, affective, and corporeal?

In my work, I have found it conceptually and empirically important to situate the "local" within cities, neighborhoods, homes, and urban spaces (Hall and Datta 2010). In my research on East European builders in London, migrating after the European Union expansion in 2004 (Datta 2008, 2009a, 2009b, 2012; Datta and Brickell 2009), I wanted to explore how new migrants in the global city made sense of their location and experiences within its spaces, and how their work as builders of the global city shaped their relationship to home(s). I was less interested in the statistics of migration (although that formed the context), but more in the individual and collective agencies of new migrant workers who made the city through their bodily labors. I argued that cities are places of sight, sound, smell, touch – a variety of sensual experiences. These experiences evoke memories of attachment to other similar places, which are affective, emotional, and sensual. They cannot be captured through a singular lens of nationhood, diaspora, or transnationalism. In other words, I have argued that transnationalism cannot exist without a continuous process of translocal home-making among migrants in cities of origin, destination, and return.

Central to this line of enquiry has been the interrelationship between urban (social and spatial) transformations and home-building – the very corporeal and embodied act of putting together a home in the city for oneself or for others.

Examining the notion of home-making through its building elements, its socio-technical processes, and through cultural and relational understandings of home in different contexts, highlighted an intersectional politics of gender, race, ethnicity, and nationality enacted through the making of diasporic and transnational working lives in a global city such as London (Datta 2008, 2009a, 2009b, 2011). It brought forth a different notion of home that is lived in its absence, which one sustains in order to sustain one's role within a patriarchal family in a left-behind city that one might return to in the future, or which one builds for others in order to make a living in a city of destination (Datta 2008). Taken from this perspective, different home(s) (that one is absent from, inhabits, and builds for others) can then be mapped onto the cities where they are located. These homes through their relative meanings and building elements produce local–local connections across cities and national territories. These translocal links made through very material, corporeal, and affective meanings of homes, have not only made cities (as the location of these homes) central to my investigations of transnational lives and migrant experiences, but, as Conradson and Latham argue (2005), have highlighted that urban life and everyday mobilities are integral aspects of transnationalism. It has brought into view the corporeal, material, relational, and temporal dynamics of transnational urbanism, but it has not necessarily remained focused primarily on the nation-state.

I have suggested that social, cultural, and material specificity is of crucial importance in understanding the context in/through which the histories of departure and possibilities of return are produced. Cities are important sites of these motivations since, as Smith (2001) notes, they provide an intense concentration of opportunities – of better job prospects, better social mobility, and ultimately better lifestyles. For me this has meant an ontological shift from researching "extraordinary" migrant lives in the city to examining ordinary lives as lived by those who might identify themselves as migrants at any time in their lives. It has meant looking not specifically at migrants *per se* but at the interchanges between migrants and hosts during acts of building; it has meant looking at how ordinary lives in the city were shaped by these interchanges; and it has meant looking at how migrants find affective spaces within wider structures of urban exclusion, where they can enact embodied and subjective performances that are other than those of migrants. I have called this notion the *translocal city* (Datta 2011: 77, emphasis added).

> The notion of the translocal city then takes on the linkages between locality and mobility in a number of ways. First, I argue that while transnational mobility brings participants to London, local experiences of mobility within the spaces of public transport, streets, and parks transforms [sic] the city into a range of urban sites which are constructed in relation to other localities and neighbourhoods within and beyond the city. I take this as the condition of translocality – although they show heightened mobility across national and local spaces, *their experiences within these urban sites are simultaneously highly emplaced.*

Seeing the city as a place of translocal experiences plays into the discourses of transnationalism from below, or a grounded transnationalism, without reinforcing the assumption that every experience references the nation. My point here is that the nation continues to persist as a structural constraint or facilitator (depending on which social class and group of migrants we are referring to) of movement, yet in day-to-day experiences of home, belonging, and Otherness, it is those memories of particular material spaces, encounters, and objects that continue to produce migrant identities. I proposed a *translocal imagination* which visualized these linkages through participant photography.

Material, Visual, and Embodied Spaces of Translocal Cities

The translocal imagination emphasizes migrant experiences and agencies in making and transforming urban spaces and experiences, making ordinary lives in the city through work, housing, and leisure in ways that make the global-city hypothesis irrelevant to their everyday lives (Datta 2012). This inclination towards the affective, embodied, and material aspects of transnational space is usually discounted in urban studies research or left to the realm of cultural studies. What I have found critical however is that it is within the spaces of the affective city that migrants otherwise excluded from the successes of the global city find ways to make a home in the city.

Employing methods that reflected these concerns – semi-structured interviews and participant photography – in order to produce a different visual and narrative account of the city, I have called these "visual narratives" (Datta 2012). Participant photographs were used as interview triggers to bring the absent everyday spaces and places of migrants into an interview setting. Visual narratives have been useful in engaging with migrants who had difficulty expressing themselves in English and therefore used photographs as a form of visual language to convey specific feelings, attitudes, and experiences of their urban lives. Using visual narratives of transnational urban life has provided evidence of the making of transnational homes through personal and subjective accounts, and in doing so has retrieved a sense of agency for migrants themselves to construct and experience the city on their own terms. Visual narratives also diverge greatly from conventional urban pictorial and documentary approaches to the city that have often situated the observer as static and distanced from the migrant subject, and have produced aestheticized and objectified migrant representations. In relocating the observer as the mobile migrant in photographs, my deployment of visual narratives has indicated the assembling of a migrant self through the spatio-temporal dynamics of different scales and the multiplicities of everyday urban life.

Visualizing migrant lives through the eyes of the migrants themselves allows us to further situate and emplace transnational and diasporic lives within the "urban." It brings about an important shift from understanding transnationalism as border crossing to understanding it as an assemblage of everyday life in cities and urban spaces. It presents very vividly the differences between migrants' "real" and imagined spaces that are evident in photographs of their "routes" through the city during daily journeys between home, work, leisure, and shopping. It presents how migrants are able to find within a city's rapidly changing neighborhoods a sense of "homeliness" and possible routes of return to home/land. And it constructs a different version of ordinary urban lives that are produced from migrants' personal histories, and their material, corporeal, and affective landscapes of transnationalism and diaspora.

Conclusions: An Urban Diaspora?

What will an urban scale of analysis tell us about the making of diasporas and transnational lives? I began with this question in order to examine the contribution that diaspora and transnationalism can make to urban studies and vice versa. This is not a novel question – the city has explicitly or implicitly remained central to questions of migration, transnational border crossings, and diasporic home-making practices. However, shifting the scale of research from the transnational to the urban has some distinct consequences. First, it resituates diaspora and transnational away from one life-changing event of movement to a series of smaller ordinary events of everyday mobility, and in doing so it highlights that we need to reconceptualize the relationship between transnational border crossings and urban dwelling more seriously. This would entail a destabilizing of the divides between near and far, home and abroad, migration and mobility, national and urban. Second, by utilizing participatory and visual narratives, the notion of the translocal city brings about a mixing of the political and personal – an essential step towards understanding how and why people build home(s), feel a sense of belonging, and are involved in urban life in ways that are not just to do with survival in a new context. This perspective takes the translocal on an equal footing with the transnational in order to reflect migrant agencies in diasporic home-making practices.

Finally, the notion of a translocal city maps the city along migrants' transnational and diasporic home-making practices. This means that the city continuously remains as a referent during migrant mobilities – not just in terms of decisions around leaving, settlement, return, and sojourning, but also in terms of everyday decisions around work, accommodation, leisure, food, socializing, and so on. Repositioning the city in this manner means acknowledging an "urban turn" in transnationalism and diaspora. It means acknowledging that the translocal city encompasses the varied nature of interactions (including mobility) that has led to an onset of the "urban age," while also emphasizing that this urban age owes much to the individual and collective agencies of the variety of migrants across the world.

References

Ahmed, S.C., Casteneda, C., Fortier, A., and Sheller, M. (eds) 2003. *Uprootings/Regroundings, Questions of Home and Migration.* New York: Berg Publishers.

Amin, A. 2002. "Ethnicity and the multicultural city: Living with diversity." *Environment and Planning A*, 34: 959–980.

Appadurai, A. 1991. "Global ethnoscapes: Notes and queries for a transnational anthropology." In R.G. Fox (ed.) *Recapturing Anthropology: Working in the Present*, pp. 191–210. Santa Fe: School of American Research Press.

Appadurai, A. 1995. "The production of locality." In R. Fardon (ed.) *Counterworks: Managing the Diversity of Knowledge*, pp. 208–229. London: Routledge.

Appiah, K.A. 2006. *Cosmopolitanism: Ethics in a World of Strangers*. London: Penguin Books.

Beaverstock, J. 2002. "Transnational elites in global cities: British expatriates in Singapore's financial district." *Geoforum*, 33(4): 525–538.

Blunt, A. 2003. "Collective memory and productive nostalgia: Anglo-Indian homemaking at McCluskieganj." *Environment and Planning D*, 21(6): 717–738.

Blunt, A. 2007. "Cultural geographies of migration: Mobility, transnationality and diaspora." *Progress in Human Geography*, 31(5): 684–694.

Bourdieu, P. 2002. "Habitus." In J. Hillier and E. Rooksby (eds) *Habitus: A Sense of Place*, pp. 27–36. Aldershot: Ashgate.

Brah, A. 2006. *Cartographies of Diaspora: Contesting Identities*. London: Routledge.

Bretell, C. 2003. "Bringing the city back: Cities as contexts for immigrant incorporation." In N. Foner (ed.) *American Arrivals: Anthropology Engages the New Immigration*, pp. 163–195. Santa Fe: School of American Research Press.

Brickell, K. and Datta, A. (eds) 2011. *Translocal Geographies: Spaces, Places, Connections*. Farnham: Ashgate.

Çağlar, A. 2006. "Hometown associations, the rescaling of state spatiality and migrant grassroots transnationalism." *Global Networks*, 6: 1–22.

Cairns, S. (ed.) 2004. *Drifting: Architecture and Migrancy*. London: Routledge.

Chacko, E. 2008. "Washington: From bi-racial city to multi-ethnic gateway." In M. Price and L. Benton-Short (ed.) *Migrants to the Metropolis: The Rise of Immigrant Gateway Cities*, pp. 203–226. Syracuse, NY: University of Syracuse Press.

Cheah, P. and Robbins, B. (eds) 1998. *Cosmopolitics: Thinking and Feeling beyond the Nation*. Minneapolis: University of Minnesota Press.

Christou, A. 2011. "Narrating lives in (e)motion: Embodiment and belongingness in diasporic spaces of home and return." *Emotion, Space and Society*, 4: 249–257.

Christou, A. and King, R. 2006. "Migrants encounter migrants in the city: the changing context of "home" for second-generation Greek-American return migrants." *International Journal of Urban and Regional Research*, 30(4): 816–835.

Conradson, D. and Latham, A. 2005. "Transnational urbanism: Attending to everyday practices and mobilities." *Journal of Ethnic and Migration Studies*, 31(2): 227–233.

Datta, A. 2008. "Building differences: Material geographies of home(s) among Polish builders in London." *Transactions of the Institute of British Geographers*, 33(4): 518–531.

Datta, A. 2009a. "Places of everyday cosmopolitanisms: East European construction workers in London." *Environment and Planning A*, 41(2): 353–370.

Datta, A. 2009b. "'This is special humour': Visual narratives of Polish masculinities in London's building sites." In K. Burrell (ed.) *After 2004: Polish Migration to the UK in the "New" European Union*, pp. 189–210. Aldershot: Ashgate.

Datta, A. 2011. "Translocal geographies of London: Belonging and otherness among Polish migrants after 2004." In K. Brickell and A. Datta (2011), pp. 73–91.

Datta, A. 2012. "'Where is the global city?' Visual narratives of London among East European migrants." *Urban Studies*, 49(8): 1725–1740.

Datta, A. and Brickell, K. 2009. "'We have a little bit more finesse as a nation': Constructing the Polish worker in London's building sites." *Antipode: A Radical Journal of Geography*, 41(4): 439–464.

Faist, T. 2008. "Migrants as transnational development agents: an inquiry into the newest round of the migration-development nexus." *Population, Space, and Place*, 14: 21–42.

Foner, N. 1997. "What's new about transnationalism? New York immigrants today and at the turn of the century." *Diaspora*, 6: 355–375.

Guarnizo, L. and Smith, M.P. 1998. "The locations of transnationalism." In Smith and Guarnizo (1998), pp. 3–34.

Gustafson, P. 2001. "Retirement migration and transnational lifestyles." *Ageing and Society*, 21: 371–394.

Hall, S. and Datta, A. 2010. "The translocal street: Shop signs and local multi-culture along Walworth Road, London." *City, Culture and Society*, 1(2): 69–77.

Hannerz, U. 1996. *Transnational Connections: Culture, People, Places*. London: Routledge.

Jacobs, J.M. 2004. "Too many houses for a home: Narrating the house in the Chinese diaspora." In Cairns (2004), pp. 164–183.

Klaufus, C. 2006. "Globalization in residential architecture in Cuenca, Ecuador: Social and cultural diversification of architects and their clients." *Environment and Planning D*, 24: 69–89.

Koser, K. 2007. "Refugees, transnationalism and the state." *Journal of Ethnic and Migration Studies*, 33(2): 233–254.

Kothari, U, 2008. "Global peddlers and local networks: Migrant cosmopolitanisms." *Environment and Planning D*, 26: 500–516.

Levitt, P. and Khagram, S. 2004. *The Transnational Studies Reader: Intersections and Innovations*. London: Routledge.

Ley, D. 2004. "Transnational spaces and everyday lives." *Transactions of the Institute of British Geographers*, 29: 151–164.

Ley, D. and Kobayashi, A. 2005. "Back to Hong Kong: Return migration or transnational sojourn." *Global Networks*, 5(2): 1470–2266.

Lie, J. 1995. "From international migration to transnational diaspora." *Contemporary Sociology*, 24(4), July: 303–306.

Lin, J. 1998. *Reconstructing Chinatown: Ethnic Enclave, Global Change*. Minneapolis: University of Minnesota Press.

Lothar, S. and Mazzucato, V. 2009. "Constructing homes, building relationships: Migrant investments in houses." *Tijdschrift voor Economische en Sociale Geografie*, 100(5): 662–673.

May, J., Wills, J., Datta, K. *et al.* 2008. "Keeping London working: Global cities, the British state and London's new migrant division of labour." *Transactions of the Institute of British Geographers*, 32: 151–167.

McDowell, L. 2003. "Masculine identities and low paid work: Young men in urban labour markets." *International Journal of Urban and Regional Research*, 27(4): 828–848.

Mitchell, K. 2004. "Conflicting landscapes of democracy and dwelling in Canada." In Cairns (2004), pp. 142–163.

Mountz, A. and Wright, R.A. 1996. "Daily life in the transnational migrant community of San Augustin, Oaxaca and Poughkeepsie, New York." *Diaspora*, 5(3): 403–428.

Oakes, T. and Schein, L. (eds) 2006. *Translocal China, Linkages, Identities, and the Reimagining of Space*. London: Routledge.

Ong, A. 1999. *Flexible Citizenship: The Cultural Logics of Transnationality*. Durham, NC: Duke University Press.

Pacyga, D.A. 1991. *Polish Immigrants and Industrial Chicago*. Chicago: University of Chicago Press.

Raghuram, P. 2009. "Caring about brain drain in a post-colonial world." *Geoforum*, 40: 25–33.

Sandercock, L. 2003. *Cosmopolis II: Mongrel Cities in the Twenty-First Century*. London: Continuum.

Sassen, S. 1991. *The Global City: New York, London, Tokyo*. Princeton: Princeton University Press.

Sassen, S. 1998. *Globalization and Its Discontents*. New York: New York Press.

Shallcross, B. 2002. *Framing the Polish Home: The Postwar Literary and Cultural Constructions of Hearth, Nation, and Self*. Athens: Ohio University Press.

Smith, M.P. 2001. *Transnational Urbanism: Locating Globalization*. Oxford: Blackwell.

Smith, M.P. 2003. "Transnationalism, the state, and the extraterritorial citizen." *Politics and Society*, 31(4): 467–502.

Smith, M.P. and Guarnizo, L.E. (eds) 1998. *Transnationalism from Below*. New Brunswick: Transaction Publishers.

Tolia-Kelly, D. 2004. "Locating processes of identification: Studying the precipitates of re-memory through artefacts in the British Asian home." *Transactions of the Institute of British Geographers*, 29(3): 314–329.

Valentine, G. 2008. "Living with difference: Reflections on geographies of encounter." *Progress in Human Geography*, 32(June): 323–337.

Velayutham, S. and Wise, A. 2005. "Moral economies of a translocal village: Obligation and shame among South Indian transnational migrants." *Global Networks*, 5(1): 27–47.

Vertovec, S. and Cohen, R. 2002. *Conceiving Cosmopolitanism: Theory, Context and Practice*. Oxford: Oxford University Press.

Wessendorf, S. 2007. "'Roots migrants': Transnationalism and 'return' among second-generation Italians in Switzerland." *Journal of Ethnic and Migration Studies*, 33(7): 1083–1102.

Wimmer, A. and Glick Schiller, N. 2002. "Methodological nationalism and beyond: Nation–state building, migration and the social sciences." *Global Networks*, 2: 301–334.

Chapter 6

Migration and Transnational Studies

Between Simultaneity and Rupture

Pnina Werbner

Introduction: "You Can Never Return Home"

Stuart Hall famously summed up the painful predicament of international migration as the dawning realization that one can never return home.[1] Overseas migration sets in motion a process of dislocation along with the encounter with new social environments and landscapes. Over time, these change migrants' consciousness, their intimate knowledge, and taken-for-granted expectations, while in their absence the countries and friends they left behind change too, often to the extent that on their return they find they are no longer in the same country. Describing himself as a "cosmopolitan by default," Hall (2008) reflects on the sense of loss, noting that "every diaspora has its regrets":

> Although you can never go back to the past, you do have a sense of loss. There is something you have lost. A kind of intimate connection with landscape, and family, and tradition, which you lose. I think this is the fate of modern people – we have to lose them, but [we believe] we are going to go back to them. (pp. 349–350)

The sense of lost intimacy – the knowing of a place and all its taken-for-granted ways of thinking, interacting and "systems of relevancies" – was first theorized by Alfred Schütz in "The Homecomer" (1945), a foundational article on the sociology of everyday life:

> Home means one thing to the man who never has left it, another thing to the man who dwells far from it, and still another to him who returns. "To feel at home" is an

---

A Companion to Diaspora and Transnationalism, First Edition.
Edited by Ato Quayson and Girish Daswani.
© 2013 Blackwell Publishing Ltd. Published 2013 by Blackwell Publishing Ltd.

expression of the highest degree of familiarity and intimacy. . . . There is no need to define or redefine situations which have occurred so many times or to look for new solutions of old problems hitherto handled satisfactorily. (p. 370)

Migration initiates a process in which such intimacies are shattered. The "community of space," of vivid, ongoing face-to-face relationships, is lost and cannot be regained since, as Schütz recognizes, time is "irreversible." "The homecomer is not the same man who left. He is neither the same for himself nor for those who await his return" (1945: 374, 375). Hall also recognizes this predicament (2008: 350):

So in my history, as it happens, my generation stayed at home and got deeply involved in writing the history of the nation. And I wasn't there. I was watching it from afar. So I wasn't enclosed in that. So I see now the limits of that [the national project]. . . . And when I came to England, I couldn't be a member of this one either [i.e., of England], because I was already deracinated from it, you know, although I've chosen to live here and marry into it, and so on. I'm not a part of the conception of the nation. So I'm a cosmopolitan by default. I have to find my way, like many of us, amongst many attachments, many identifications, none of them old. I have to recognise how limited that is. And I have to, I've tried to, maintain what I would call the openness of the horizon to that which I am not, the experiences I have not had.

Migration creates a sense of "double consciousness," an awareness, as W.E.B. Du Bois (1994) argues in relation to American blacks, of seeing oneself through the eyes of others; a doubling up of a subject's sense of belonging and alienation. Migrants and return migrants share a sense of being split: "One ever feels his two-ness, – an American, a Negro: two souls, two thoughts, two unreconciled strivings" (Du Bois 1994: 5). So too, migration and diaspora engender a split subject, a fractured reality (Gilroy 1993: 126). A homecomer must manage the insider and outsider perspectives simultaneously, seeing herself through the often disapproving eyes of those who stayed at home. Paradoxically, however, the experience of strangerhood has its own attraction. In Schütz's words (1945: 375): "To a certain extent, each homecomer has tasted the magic fruit of strangeness, be it sweet or bitter. Even amid the overwhelming longing for home there remains the wish to transplant into the old pattern something of the novel goals, of the newly discovered means to realize them, of the skills and experiences acquired abroad."

The reversal of time, the disruption of intimate knowledge, the experience of double consciousness and the growing sense of regret and loss challenge simplistic theorizations of transnationalism as an uninterrupted social field, or of "transmigrants" as mobile subjects unproblematically participating in more than one nation-state. However frequent the communication and travel between a migrant's home country and country of migration, over time the gap between the two gradually widens and cannot be easily sutured: seen in the *longue durée,* history and memory are made elsewhere, whether at home or in the diaspora. The unproblematic assumption in transnational theory of uninterrupted, continuing, intimate, taken-for-granted sociality across homeland and diaspora misrecognizes the critical phenomenological question of how intimate knowledge is sustained over discontinuous space and time.[2]

This implies that the sense of "simultaneity" experienced by migrants in their transnational social relations, of sharing space in a continuous social field (Levitt and Glick Schiller 2004) reflects only a partial truth, hiding from participants themselves ruptures that become apparent when and if migrants return home, on holiday and especially to live. Nevertheless, the *illusion of simultaneity* remains a powerful experiential force, especially within transnational families, defining migrants' sense of self and subjectivity, and more so in the age of easy Skype and mobile phone connectivity, an issue I return to below.[3]

As summarized by Glick Schiller (e.g., Glick Schiller and Fouron 2002), transnationalism emerged as something of a parochial American argument: it denied an alleged prevailing American melting-pot ideology which assumed that immigrants arriving in the New World would cut their ties with their homeland and "assimilate" to become true Americans. This rupturing of relationships was itself an illusion, however, as Foner, for example (1997, 2002), argued for early European migrations to the USA, although World War II cut many immigrants off from their European families and home towns. In any case, ethnicity in America has remained a potent force, as Glazer and Moyniham argued (1963) in another kind of critique of assimilationist theory. Equally open to debate was the alleged "methodological nationalism" of migration studies – the conflation of "society" and the state, an accusation taken up in another context by sociologists of globalization (see, e.g., Beck 2006: 32–34; Wimmer and Glick Schiller 2002). This was the view that privileged state borders and minimized significant cross-border migrant relationships, both personal and political. Rather than separate nation-states, what needed to be recognized was a continuous "social field." Here the transnationalists drew on both Bourdieu's and the Manchester School of Anthropology's theorizing of the social field as encompassing migrants' sites of departure and destination (Levitt and Glick Schiller 2004: 1009; Bourdieu 1985; R. Werbner 1984). Immigrants were really "transmigrants," living in between; all the more so as new contemporary modes of communication across borders enabled them to straddle different countries, keeping in touch with those left behind as never before. A final term added to the conceptual armory of the transnationalists has been "long-distance nationalism," grasped in a benign, emancipatory sense that subverts the original notion of "long-distance nationalism *without responsibility*," specifically used by Anderson (1994) to refer to diaspora groups' considerable financial support for religious or nationalist extremists in their countries of origin.

This chapter considers some of these issues as they have been tackled in contemporary innovative research on international migration and return migration. I leave aside here the obvious truth that well before the "invention" of transnational theory to describe international migration, diaspora theory was built around the continuing sentimental, practical, and political loyalties of ethnic groups to countries and places beyond the nation-state. So too, the opening up of nation-states to trade and imperialism was an early feature of capitalist expansion recognized by Marx and Weber.

In the developing world, well before Basch, Glick Schiller, and Blanc wrote their (1993) manifesto, scholars in Africa and elsewhere were debating the implication of "circulatory" labor migration, which has indeed remained a typical pattern in many parts of the world.

Without going into the widely debated question, then, of what is "new" in transnational approaches, I argue here for the need to probe the complex emotional and moral dimensions of transnational migration that lead to ruptures and created new configurations and clustering in the transnational migration field. A distinctive recent challenge to simplistic, optimistic notions of transnational migration has come from Ghassan Hage (2002, 2012), whose study of a Lebanese extended family living across four continents led him to formulate the notion of migration "guilt," loss, and rupture. Others, like Mirca Madiano and Daniel Miller (2011), have probed the limits of new communication media in creating intimacy and co-presence among Filipino mothers and children. A third central strand in contemporary transnational migration theory has looked at the plight of undocumented migrants who are blocked from traveling back and forth to their homelands. Thus Ali Nobil Ahmad (2009, 2011) argues perceptively that in contrast to the early depiction of immigrants to Britain as fostering a "myth of return," for the contemporary wave of undocumented Pakistani migrants to Europe there is, instead, a "myth of arrival." Another innovative strand in transnational migration scholarship is that of second-generation "return" migrations, which probes the painful dilemmas and paradoxes encountered by "returnees" that signal ruptures rather than continuities in the transnational field. Beyond these, and somewhat in answer both to Hage's pessimism and to over-optimistic theories of transnationalism, are theories of international migration and diaspora that recognize the mediation of multiple, intersecting, newly formed moral "communities" or circles of trust in the migration context (P. Werbner 2002a), and migrants' situational management of multiple valorized identities, even in destinations where their stay is restricted by legal work contracts (Sabar 2010; Fumanti 2010; Liebelt 2011).

In this latter respect too, the dismissal of the nation-state by transnational theorists as an instance of methodological nationalism is ironically denied by migrants themselves. A good deal of recent scholarly research on international migration shows how migrants map the world in terms of the rights, entitlements, and visa regulations allowed to newcomers and workers by various countries. Thus research on Pakistanis, black Africans, or Filipino female migrants shows how the rules regulating work permits and residency in different nation-states are highly significant for them (Liebelt 2008; Ahmad 2009). Intercontinental marriages and mail-order brides are a familiar strategy linked to such understandings of legal differentials between states. The moral economy of migration and citizenship is built around such mappings, identities, and socialities formed away from home, and rests on moral assumptions about the entitlements conferred by hard work, however menial.[4]

Despite invocations of simultaneity within the transnational social field, the ethnographies of Glick Schiller and Fouron (2002) and Levitt (2001) are both remarkable for repeatedly highlighting not continuities but painful ruptures separating migrants both within their new places of settlement *and* from their home communities, often despite their valiant efforts to support the folk back home or, alternatively, to sink roots in the place of migration. Hence, the message of Levitt's (2001) study of Dominican migrants living in Boston is highly pessimistic. Life in Boston is extremely hard for migrants. They live scattered throughout the city and meet only intermittently, since they often hold more than one full-time, menial job. Their community institutions are rudimentary, although they do fundraise for the home country. They often leave children behind in the homeland to be cared for by relatives. In the absence of parental discipline, however, children growing up on the island often lack discipline, are showered by parents with spending money as compensation for their absence, and end up with little education, relying on the expectation of future migration, and latterly on the growing drug trade, to make up for their lack of qualifications. Children growing up in Boston fare little better, coming back to empty homes since parents work long hours, and failing educationally.

The emotional bitterness and trauma suffered by families as a result of transnational migration are thus a key finding of the study. A further finding is that the sending town in the Dominican Republic gradually loses its best people to migration, leaving it underdeveloped and economically backward. Retiring migrants who return to the island rarely manage to convert their hard-earned savings into productive investments, and often end up as impoverished as when they set out on their travels. Levitt (2001: 11) introduces the notion of "social" remittances, which she defines as "the ideas, behaviors, and social capital that flow from receiving to sending communities. . . . tools with which ordinary individuals create global culture at the local level." On the whole, however, her examples are less than persuasive that international migration "from below" – that is, the migration of uneducated manual workers – really creates meaningful, radical lifestyle shifts in the home country. Given the global flow of ideas via the media, especially television and the internet, the growth of tourism, foreign investments, and in particular the influence of Dominican *élite* mobility (including transnational movement for higher education) and the impact of international NGOs, it seems that lasting processes of Westernization and modernization in the Dominican Republic are, in fact, the result primarily of globalization and cosmopolitization "from *above.*" Indeed, Levitt found that the town she studied remained stagnant, with returning migrants soon going back to their old ways. The book leaves us with an impression of a dependency economy being sucked into the international drug trade, with most transmigrants leading hard and joyless lives, and yet being envied by those left behind on the island.

Glick Schiller and Fouron's (2002) study is equally remarkable for the ruptures it describes as disrupting transnational relationships. They remark that when transmigrants return to Haiti they expect to step into their old roles, "just as one might anticipate going home and finally putting on old and comfortable clothes. But when they return, they and those who had stayed behind discover that a process of change has been occurring. . . . Home is not what they remember it to be. . . . It is as if the old clothes no longer fit." Instead of gratitude for remittances and gifts sent, they find "a crop of bitterness" "sown and reaped" (Glick Schiller and Fouron 2002: 84).

This points to a familiar theoretical question in diaspora and migration studies of the meaning and place of "home." If the yearning for home is seen as a defining feature of some diasporas – the Jews, the Greeks, the Armenians (Safran 1999: 83) – theorists of diaspora have challenged the centrality of a lost homeland for the definition of diaspora (e.g., Hall 1990: 235; Boyarin and Boyarin 1993). So too, whereas modern transnational migrants visit home frequently, indentured Indian migrants in the Caribbean, Amitav Ghosh has suggested, saw India as remote – a mythologized place of the "imagination" (1989). The question is, as Avtar Brah puts it (1996: 190):

> When does a location *become* home? What is the difference between "feeling at home" and staking a claim to a place as one's own? It is quite possible to feel at home in a place and, yet, the experience of social exclusions may inhibit public proclamations of the place as home. . . . Clearly, the relationship of the first generation to the place of migration is different from that of subsequent generations, mediated as it is by memories of what was recently left behind, and by the experiences of disruptions and displacement, as one tries to reorientate, to form new social networks, and learns to negotiate new economic, cultural and political realities.

While agreeing that one can move between "multiple homes," the question is whether, as Rapport and Dawson suggest (1998: 27), "as home becomes more mobile, so it comes to be seen as individuated and privatized." Second, once uprooted, can modern persons ever find a place that is "truly" home? (Peter Berger, cited in Rapport and Dawson 1998: 31). For overseas migrants, it seems, home is neither entirely individualized nor forever absent. Instead, it is always embedded in significant social relations and responds to migrants' moral engagements over the life course.

The difference between generations when it comes to "home," "ancestral home," and "homeland" is particularly salient in discussions of counter-diasporic movements of second- and third-generation migrants returning to a homeland they know only through parental memories and occasional visits (King and Christou 2009).[5] Returnees' double consciousness impacts upon them with the shocking revelation that rather than returning "home," they are regarded in their homeland as foreigners and aliens, a feature repeatedly documented in the literature on counter-diasporic second-generation return migrations (see, e.g., Christou 2002; Reynolds 2008). Some migrant groups have evolved a special term for returnees, such as the Filipino *balikbayan*, a term expanded to refer to different kinds of returnees as migration from the Philippines has grown (Szanton-Blanc 1996). In his masterly study of Japanese Brazilian return migrants to Japan, for example, Takeyuki Tsuda (2003) describes how, from being a relatively high-status ethnic group in Brazil, Japanese Brazilian workers in Japan found themselves denigrated and shunned by local Japanese, a rejection that engendered a growing realization of themselves as "Brazilian" – in their modes of interaction, sociality, and conviviality, in their egalitarian vision and in their human capacity to have fun and celebrate.

Pakistani Myths of Return and Arrival

From the start of their migration to Britain, Pakistani migrants fostered a "myth of return" to their homeland (Dahya 1974; Anwar 1979; Bolognani 2007). Bolognani argues that whereas for the first generation of migrants return has gradually been recognized as impossible in practical terms, second-generation Pakistanis born and bred in Bradford see return to Pakistan as a way of escaping stigmatization and limited career prospects in post-9/11 Britain. Where migrants have been legally compelled to return home to Pakistan, as is the case for migrants working in the Gulf, they typically suffer from what has been dubbed the "Dubai syndrome" (Bolognani 2007: 64). In Ballard's original formulation (1987), this refers to the jealousy generated by their newly acquired wealth not only among kin but among Pakistan's urban elite as well, who see the newly rich migrants' behavior as "misguided and disturbed" (p. 40; cf. also Donnan and Werbner 1991: 15–16). In Bolognani's usage, the term refers to the "mental distress" experienced by returnees (2007: 64).

Given their discourse of return, as the early generation of British Pakistani postwar migrants reached retirement age, one might expect an exodus of pensioners back to Pakistan. But early Pakistani returnees came back to Britain reporting that, accustomed as they were to the British ways of doing things it was impossible for them to deal with Pakistani red tape and corruption. Often, they lost all their savings.[6] Hence, although there is little data beyond anecdotal evidence (see Bolognani 2007; Bolognani *et al.* 2009) it would seem that most retired Pakistanis have chosen a pragmatic middle path. The majority had already built houses in their natal villages or, quite often, in the cities neighboring their village, and their state pensions enable them to spend part of the year, several months at a time, at home, in Pakistan, before returning home, to Britain, where children and grandchildren live. Pakistani children were in the past expected to go on prolonged visits to Pakistan in order to get to know the folks back home and experience the ambience of rural life nostalgically remembered by their parents (Bolognani 2007). Often young second-generation British Pakistanis feel misperceived and misunderstood by their compatriots in Pakistan (Cressey 2006: esp. 58–67). The transnational family among Pakistanis is sustained by frequent visiting back and forth and massive numbers of intercontinental marriages between Britain and Pakistan, with brides and grooms joining second-generation spouses, usually first cousins, living in the United Kingdom (see, e.g., Shaw and Charsley 2006). Charsley (2005), however, has documented some of the hardships experienced by *mangeteers,* incoming bridegrooms from Pakistan, living in their "English" wives' homes. Indeed, there is a growing literature on the problems associated with such intercontinental marriages (for a review see P. Werbner 2007).

In a twist on the aspirational "myth of return" of postwar Pakistani immigrants, Ali Nobil Ahmad's study of irregular migrants in Britain and Italy (2009, 2011) highlights the impossibility of *arrival.* Irregular Pakistani migrants live precarious lives, paying large sums of money in Italy in an attempt to regularize their stay, working long hours for little pay, mostly unable to buy a house or bring over their families. Rather than dreaming of going home to Pakistan, they aspire to find a country that will provide them with secure jobs, education, and housing. In a trenchant critique of transnational theory, Ahmad argues that its underlying optimistic narrative is misplaced. The social and financial capital accumulated by networking "from below" depends on the capitalist context of migration: Fordist Britain opened up well-paid job opportunities for South Asian migrants in the 1960s and 1970s, who also benefited from cheap housing and a growing demand for ethnic foods. In contemporary Britain draconian immigration restrictions, and in Italy high unemployment and housing costs, create endemic precarity. Ethnic networks fail to afford support while irregular migrants move between European countries and within Italy in their search for employment.

Ahmad's (2011) monograph draws on Bataille's psychoanalytic notion of eroticism as extreme risk-taking to critique the prevailing assumption that transnational migration is a rational process determined by "the family." Young Pakistani migrants to the United Kingdom and Europe, both in the earlier and in the present generations, embarked on international migration to escape patriarchal control and to see the wonders of another world glimpsed on the media or in encounters with young tourists; to experience *aiashi,* hedonistic pleasure, and fulfil *ghumna,* the desire to roam. Migrants often decide to migrate against the explicit wishes of parents or (if they are married) their wives. They wheedle money out of reluctant fathers in order to embark on a high-risk journey across the Middle East and Eastern Europe, managed by unscrupulous agents, often living without food or adequate water for weeks, transported in suffocatingly crowded vehicles and crossing dangerous rivers or the Mediterranean. Some never arrive. Others are sent back home, to Pakistan. Ahmad (2011), following Bataille, interprets this experience of extreme danger, as a form of eroticism, but the end result is a "poisoned chalice" (p. 175). Migrants' youthful, masculine dreams of mastery end for many in deep melancholia, as they eke out a meager living on long hours of work without leisure, unable to marry or bring wives over, in many cases equally unable to go back home even for visits.

This bleak vision of transnationalism and migration makes the point that whereas migrants cross many international borders and strike up a wide range of acquaintances across many ethnic and national groups, they remain deeply isolated and alienated in the place of migration. The transnational social field for them is ruptured at both ends, unable to repay the debts incurred for their journey, scattered in Italy but set apart by their lack of resources from fully joining the life enjoyed by the thriving British Pakistani community in the United Kingdom.

Virtuous Citizens and Mediated Ruptures: Virtual *Illusios* of the Social Field

Not all irregular migrants experience this type of isolation, however. Indeed, more remarkable has been the struggle by undocumented migrants in the United Kingdom, the USA, and Europe to demand the right to stay. The moral economy of migration rests on a sense of entitlement and national or civic membership that migrants develop for their societies of settlement, *even in the absence of formal papers.* Hence, in his analysis of Ghanaian Akan-speaking Methodists in London, Mattia Fumanti (2010) proposes reviving the Aristotelian notion of "virtuous" citizenship, defining the transnational social field more specifically in terms of distinctive flows rooted in the historical relationship of Britain to its former colonies. With or without legal status in Britain, Ghanaian Akan-speaking Methodists regard being law-abiding, hardworking taxpayers who contribute to their communities and church congregations both in Britain and in Africa as the hallmarks of a good citizen. As British Ghanaian Methodists see it, they are virtuous citizens because they ensure the welfare of fellow diasporans in Britain and family and community back home. Church and community thus mediate notions of belonging and citizenship and this is especially so for African Methodists, for whom the transnational church itself epitomizes British values and mores. Elsewhere, in Israel, Galia Sabar (2010) and Claudia Liebelt (2008) find that black African and Filipino migrant workers and carers make religious and moral claims to remain in the Holy Land, the center of Christianity, as virtuous Christians, while more recent African refugees to Israel from East Africa, the majority of them Muslims, claim citizenship by invoking a broader human rights discourse (Sabar 2010).

Nevertheless, the absence of legal travel documents and the precarity of their work and earnings severely restrict transnational migrants' ability to travel home frequently. We need to remind ourselves that transnational theory emerged among American migration scholars in response to new migrations to the USA from the Caribbean, Cuba, Mexico, and Latin America, all virtually on America's doorstep. Kasinitz (1992) reports, for example, that Brooklyn's proximity to Trinidad has meant that Trinidadian carnival artists regularly travel back and forth to New York to contribute and participate in the New York Carnival. For migrants elsewhere in the world, however, travel costs can be prohibitive, especially because going home involves an additional huge expenditure on gifts for a wide range of relatives. In such cases, old and new media become the main forms of transnational communication. The question is, can these substitute for the intimacy of face-to-face interactions?

A study by Miller and Madianou (2011) of UK Filipino women migrants' communication with their children answers definitively in the negative. Historically, when telephone costs were high and cell phone ownership rare, migrants to the United Kingdom from the Philippines communicated through letter-writing and cassette tapes. These often took several weeks to arrive by post. They thus lacked the "simultaneity" posited by the transnationalists, while having other intrinsic advantages: the letters, the authors tell us, were carefully crafted and could be carried around, read and re-read, while cassettes reproduced the voices of absent loved ones and in this sense were emotionally moving. Nowadays, however, almost everyone owns a cell phone and calls are much cheaper, especially from the United Kingdom *to* the Philippines, while text-messaging is virtually free. In addition, there are the options of email and Skype or Yahoo Messenger, though this requires both senders and receivers to own computers, have domestic access to broadband, and possess computer literacy. This is the case only for some more middle-class migrants. Hence Megha Amrith (2011) reports that in Singapore whereas Filipino domestic workers create intense sociality with one other on their Sundays off, Filipino nurses, most of whom hope to move on to other countries, spend virtually all their spare time on Yahoo Messenger talking to loved ones in the Philippines. But when these same migrants go home on visits, for example for annual fiestas, they discover that their children don't recognize them immediately. Return visits gather family from all over the world for an exhilarating time of "fun, reunions, eating, drinking and parties with family and friends" (Amrith 2011: 172). Amrith comments, however, that this "utopian Philippine experience is condensed into a period of two or three weeks. Home is longed for but never realistically considered as a place to live, even if migrants are not happy or successful overseas. Rather, it is a temporary space for the denial of the hardships of life overseas" (2011: 181).

It seems, then, that even when mothers and children possess the requisite technology and are able to hold lengthy conversations free on Skype, the sense of rupture – from the children's point-of-view – persists, as they informed Madianou and Miller (2011). True, mothers are better able to supervise carers by using Skype, or to help children with their homework. This allows them to cling to the *illusion of simultaneity*, of being intimately close to their children; they often Skype them daily and even leave Skype on continuously so events in the Philippine household can be viewed all day long. These migrant mothers can talk to and see their children in real time. But still the gap, the rupture, persists from the children's viewpoint.

This implies a sociological insight not fully theorized by the authors, related to human experience of sociality as *ontologically felt*: "authentic," "real," "genuine" social intimacy is *embodied and holistic*. In this case, for children in particular their daily emotional lives, the small events and interactions that make up their waking hours, the physical closeness, the touch, the hug, the daily nurture, are what count in their expectations from their mothers. When this embodied support is provided by carers, whether aunts, grandmothers, or fathers, it diminishes the ideal maternal role for them. This is so for young children while teenagers, often secretive, find it even harder at times to communicate from a distance. Life, however trivial, goes on elsewhere. By the time mothers arrive home, their children have grown up being cared for by others.

It is this ontological rupture, the unreality of even the most sophisticated media, that explains why Filipino migrant women, like most single migrants, call for their families to join them once their status is regularized. In the United Kingdom the newly emerging Filipino "community" in the twenty-first century is strikingly hetero-sexual, with both parents, husbands and wives, children and even grandchildren, organizing gatherings together with other families – in festivals, churches, and other celebrations. Even if these families still miss the Philippines and their loved ones left behind, as migrants often do, they appear to have reached a much greater sense of wholeness or completion in being reunited.

Migration "Guilt" and "Shame," "Pity" and "Sacrifice"

Even the most successful and legal transnational family migration, it has been suggested, nevertheless triggers complex emotional upheaval and personal crisis. For
Ghassan Hage (2002: 203) being born into and part of a community, nation, or
family is a "gift" that one repays through lifelong participation (just as, in Catholicism, life is a gift from God, to be repaid religiously). Transnational migration from
the Lebanon entails leaving the community that gave one a social life, and this
induces a state of guilt, especially evident when your community/nation/family is
going through hard times and you are not there to help, allowing others to pay the
debt for which you are collectively responsible. Forging a new community in the
place of settlement introduces new debts, of course. But this social participation in
the new place of settlement, including even hanging a picture on one's bare wall
(Hage 2012), can induce a further sense of debt to the community left behind. New
commitments are felt to be a "form of social treason: a sign that one has forgotten
about their [migrants'] original debt" (Hage 2002: 205). This sense of "distancing,"
of alienation and estrangement, can only be overcome momentarily through ges-
tures of "intensification" (p.201) that convey "a desire for proximity," a sense of
being "affectively implicated," a sign of (still) "caring" for the homeland (p. 201).

In a later paper Hage (2012) elaborates further on this Lacanian sense of rupture
that permeates migrants' subjectivity. In Boston and Venezuela two successful Lebanese migrants told him at different times that "there are no friends here." This was
not merely a statement of nostalgia or fact. It reflected the sense that before leaving
the Lebanon the migrant was a sensitive intellectual, interested in "ideas, poetry and
philosophy" (2012: 16). "But slowly it became all about money. I left poetry and
Gibran in the village. I left it just like I left the village itself that I loved, just as I left
my parents and just as I left my friends" (p. 17). The idealized, "whole" self cannot
be recaptured but it haunts the migrants just as the space of diaspora is "haunted"
by another place left behind. It is a kind of doubling up, just as return migration
creates a double consciousness. At the same time migrants are unwilling to admit
their "shame" in their country, a country that failed to sustain them and compelled
them to leave.

Shame can also be experienced collectively. Filipino migrants have been dubbed
"a nation of servants" because of their domestic service and caring role in many
societies worldwide. In the face of such definitions, nurses in Singapore feel "shame,
humiliation and disdain" (see Amrith 2010: 424). They counter this shameful
stereotype by stressing Filipinos' innate humanity, compassion, "pity," and family
loyalty, as well as professionalism – all of which are lacking in the Singaporeans
they treat. They moralize their migration as a sacrifice for the sake of their families
and their caring as a service to humanity and God. This transforming of transnational migration into a moral project, the *moralizing* of migration as an ethical
journey, also has the capacity to transform painful rupture into subjective and communal healing.

Transnational Migration as a Cultural Movement: Aesthetics, Ritual, and Moral Inscriptions

So far my discussion has broadly followed transnational theorists and their critics in focusing on "the individual" as she is embedded in transactional modes of sociality. Transnational social networks, in this prevailing approach, are conceived of as "linking" ethnic entrepreneurs to their homelands on a regular basis (Portes, Guarnizo, and Landolt 1999), connecting members of internationally dispersed families to one another, and creating shared activities across borders between "home" and "home town" associations or religious organizations, all of which generate regular "flows" of goods and money transnationally. But such a restricted methodological individualism, as advocated explicitly by Portes and colleagues, for example (1999: 220), fails to recognize that *transnationalism is above all a social and cultural movement that inscribes itself spatially, morally, and imaginatively in the dispersed places where migrants settle.* It is not simply individuals who travel; it is their rituals, popular culture, modes of celebration, protest, sport, leisure, and consumption; and with these their notions of hierarchy, honor and shame, customary ceremonial gift exchange, and cosmological ideas about God and human existence. As they move transnationally and come to be rooted locally in shared practice and performance, such symbolic complexes are elaborated, hybridized, creolized, revitalized, and redeployed by transnational migrants in their efforts to form circles of trust and in their agonistic vyings for power and distinction (P. Werbner 2002a, 2002b).

Elsewhere I have written at length about what I term this "translocation" of culture, the dislocation and transnational relocation of customary symbolic ways of living, worshipping, and celebrating from one country to another (e.g., P. Werbner 2005, 2012). Central for us here, however, is the question of what *effects* this transnational movement has. How do transposed symbolic complexes impact on transnational networking and migratory ruptures – the sense of incompleteness, loss, and alienation – or the illusion of simultaneity discussed so far in this chapter? One key consequence of transnational cultural movements is the *widening* of transnational networks and the incorporation of previous strangers into ethnic networks, while at the same time *prior* close relationships at "home" are shed. This relates to the way that migrants inscribe their presence symbolically on their new environment in order to build home and homeliness abroad (see, e.g., P. Werbner 2003, on this inscription). But this is not simply a matter of creating local community at the expense of cutting off transnational connections. Migrants form *new* transnational links in a myriad of ways – as by joining Sufi orders that extend between Pakistan, the United Kingdom, and the Middle East (P. Werbner 2003). Such religious networks are elective and voluntary, not simply determined by prior ascriptive links. Similarly, Ghanaian Pentecostals extend transnational links and moral relations where none existed before (Daswani 2010).

Ritual, celebration, and popular culture open up ways for migrants to forge new, morally grounded relationships with each other, to create Ghanaian, Pakistani, Filipino,

Sri Lankan, Indonesian, and Pan-South Asian spaces in an alien environment. In performing or celebrating bodily together, transnational migrants reshape their subjectivities spiritually and ethically. More broadly, new places of settlement enable transnational migrant workers as manual laborers or in caring jobs to reposition themselves, not merely as subjugated servants but as agents of their own destiny, pilgrims and cosmopolitan adventurers on a spiritual journey (Liebelt 2010).

Sometimes, no doubt, the transnational field is ruptured by migrant forging of significant new local socialities. Thus, previously Christian Filipinas who convert to Islam in Saudi Arabia grapple with the ethics and morality of second marriages and intimate relations with local Muslims while juggling commitments to their prior transnational families (Pingol 2010). Sri Lankan women migrants in Lebanon pursue erotic adventures as gender outlaws beyond the normalizing constraints of state, religious, and other international institutions (Smith 2010). Siblings in the "virtual village" that stretches from Mountain Province in the Philippines to Hong Kong and beyond contest the morality of traditional ritual sacrifice, with religious differences threatening to rupture transnational family relations (McKay 2010).

A remarkable feature of transnational migration is that similar cultural spaces and institutions are produced in different countries across the diaspora, often following predictable patterns – Filipinos create weekend places of assembly, shopping, and conviviality wherever they settle, from Central in Hong Kong to Lucky Plaza in Singapore to the old central bus station in Tel Aviv (Constable 2007; Liebelt 2013). Caribbean migrants celebrate huge carnivals in Notting Hill, Brooklyn, and a multitude of other cities (Cohen 1993; Kasinitz 1992). Italians, Peruvians, and Filipinos follow their sacred icons, imported transnationally, through the streets in fiesta celebrations (e.g., Orsi 1985; Paerregaard 2008; Tondo 2010). Similarly, transnational migrants establish a multitude of places of worship and welfare, national and rights associations often linked to the home country, reproducing the religious and civic diversity of their countries of origin. These are all examples of what I have called "chaordic transnationalism" (P. Werbner 2002c). They are predictable yet uncoordinated and unsupervised grassroots transnational creations "from below." Through such places, performances, and rituals migrants' presence is symbolically, bodily, and materially inscribed in rather similar ways wherever they settle, without any apparent central command structure. Despite being unorchestrated and situated in discontinuous social locales, such cultural movements are nonetheless organized in predictable ways, mobilizing migrants periodically around shared diasporic predicaments, desires, and imaginaries.

All this implies that migration opens up new horizons and possibilities for migrants wherever they journey, and that these come to be embodied materially, performatively, and spiritually in the place of settlement. But if religion, family, and politics are actively extended by migrants across the transnational social field, this does not imply that the field extends homogeneously and unproblematically. Instead, new relationships forged in the place of settlement mediate prior relations within and across space with those left behind. In their diasporic encounters, migrants creatively engage with the places and landscapes where they live and labor, sharing conviviality with others like themselves through ritual performance, pil-grimage journeys, mobilization for rights, religious worship, and new intimate relationships.

Transnational aesthetic and ritual translocation is not simply, it needs to be stressed, about ethnic boundary-making processes. Rather, it produces inversions of gender and generational authority, reconciles past with present and reconstitutes a sense of home and personal integrity in the face of rupture and disintegration. Tondo (2010), for example, argues that the Santo Niño fiesta imported from lowland Philippines to New Zealand transforms new spaces into diasporic "home." In dancing through the streets of Auckland and other cities in front of the imported icons of the Santo Niño and the Blessed Virgin Mary, migrants inscribe a tangible connection across space to home and family, at the same time transcending religion as private practice to assert a collective identity and public presence in New Zea-land's multicultural nation. Writing on Israel, Liebelt (2010) shows the creative fusion of pilgrimage, tourism, and migration achieved by migrants in their tran-snational journeys. Filipina pilgrimages to sacred and devotional sites in the Holy Land, she argues, sacralize the humdrum and sometimes degrading realities of their work and everyday circumstances, and enable them to transcend through perform-ance the "migrant" label assigned to them by contemporary migration regimes. Instead, they become pilgrims on a sacred life journey. In Jordan, Buddhist Sri Lankan women migrants go on pilgrimage to Christian sites and attend Christian churches, but this, Frantz (2010) argues, is not a case of "Buddhism transformed." Rather, it is a further instance of Buddhism's personalized and pluralist approach to the divine that enables ways of connecting with a local social geography of migra-tion while privately renewing migrant women's existential sense of connection to people and places back home.

Like ritual and morality, the transnational aesthetics of diaspora are "the sensual and performative medium through which diasporans enact their felt autonomy while laying claims to 'ownership' of the places and nations in which they settle" (Werbner and Fumanti 2013: 1). As Shenar (2013) stresses, migrants work hard to create an *ambiance,* a spatial sensorium imbued with multiple sensorial experiences that enrich their sense of self and connect them experientially to fellow migrants elsewhere in the world and in their homeland.

Conclusion: Towards a Critical Transnationalism

This chapter has argued for the need to go beyond methodological individualism as well as so-called methodological nationalism in order to identify the ruptures and interruptions in the transnational social field of migration. Such ruptures surface when transnational migrants return "home," when they remain in limbo as undocumented migrants, or, in the case of transnational families, at moments of illness or death (see Baldassar, Baldock, and Wilding 2007; Olwig 2002: esp. 212–215). Not even the new information and communication technologies (ICTs), imported films, music and satellite TV beamed directly from the homeland, or the alleged speeding up of international travel can overcome the gaping absence of the embodied, everyday, nurturing co-presence of a migrant's loved ones. As a cultural movement, I proposed, however, that the social universe of transnationalism is neither binary nor fixed at the moment of migration; on the contrary, it is expansive and incorporative, enabling new moral relationships in and across space as transnational migrants root themselves ontologically and experientially in their places of settlement – but without abandoning home. Indeed, through ritual and cultural performance the *illusion* of simultaneity sustains them on their transnational journeys.

Notes

1   The actual quotation from Stuart Hall is: "Migration is a one way trip, there is no 'home' to go back to" (1989: 44).
2   The challenge to simplistic assumptions of a continuous, uninterrupted "transnational field" has increasingly been voiced by scholars; for practical reasons, as among undocumented migrants (Nolin 2002), but more fundamentally as well (see Amit 2002's brilliant analysis). In a recent doctoral thesis, Laura Morosanu surveys this literature and shows that the young Romanian migrants in London she studied felt they could not sustain friendship networks at home in the absence of day-to-day interaction; that their friends in Romania had moved on in their familial and professional careers and no longer shared the same experiences. They nevertheless claimed that "soul friends" were still at home (Morosanu 2010).
3   One might refer here to Pierre Bourdieu's notion of the *illusio* permeating the social field (1992: 66–67).
4   In a conservative critique that points to the continuing centrality of nation-states in regulating and policing migration and perceptions of migrant populations (e.g., as potentially disloyal), Waldinger and Fitzgerald (2004: 1178) propose that whereas transnationalism seems to refer to loyalties *beyond* any nation-state, immigration scholars usually describe the very opposite: high particularistic attachments to two or more countries, the very antithesis of transnational civil society or, one might add, cosmopolitanism (on the latter see Werbner 2008). This may, perhaps, suggest an ambiguity in the term itself but transnationalism nevertheless remains useful for describing non-state relations across borders.
5   Another term often used is "repatriation," while the experiences of repatriats are sometimes described as "reverse culture shock."
6   Osella and Osella (2008) describe the experience of Muslim middle-class returnees from Britain to Kerala, who escape racism and perceived teenage decadence but find they cannot get used to the physical hardships and lack of amenities back home. In one case they opt to go to the Gulf which they regard as almost an extension of Kerala, less foreign than many towns in India itself. The authors' conclusion (2008: 170) is that migrants come to be ambivalent about all places, including Kerala itself; there is no longer an absolute sense of home, and their mobile lives become a balancing act to improve the fortunes and education of the immediate family.

References

Ahmad, A.N. 2009. "The myth of arrival: Pakistanis in Italy." In V.S. Kalra (ed.) *Pakistani Diasporas: Culture, Conflict, and Change*, pp. 63–82. Karachi: Oxford University Press.

Ahmad, A.N. 2011. *Masculinity, Sexuality and Illegal: Human Smuggling from Pakistan and Europe*. Farnham: Ashgate.

Amit, V. 2002. "Part I: an anthropology without community." In N. Rapport, and V. Amit (eds) *The Trouble with Community. Anthropological Reflections on Movement, Identity and Collectivity*, pp. 13–66. London: Pluto Press.

Amrith, M. 2010. "'They think we are just caregivers': the ambivalence of care in the lives of Filipino Medical workers in Singapore." *Asia Pacific Journal of Anthropology*, 11(3): 410–427.

Amrith, M. 2011. "Life in transit: the aspirations of Filipino medical workers in Singapore." PhD dissertation, University of Cambridge.

Anderson, B. 1994. "Exodus." *Critical Inquiry*, 20: 314–327.

Anwar, M. 1979. *The Myth of Return: Pakistanis in Britain*. London: Heinemann.

Baldassar, L., Baldock, C., and Wilding, R. 2007. *Families Caring Across Borders: Migration, Ageing and Transnational Caregiving*. Basingstoke: Palgrave Macmillan.

Ballard, R. 1987. "The political economy of migration: Pakistan, Britain and the Middle East." In J. Eades (ed.) *Migrants, Workers and the Social Order*, pp. 19–41. London: Tavistock.

Basch, L., Glick Schiller, N., and Blanc, C.S. 1993. *Nations Unbound: Transnational Projects, Postcolonial Predicaments and Deterritorialized Nation-States*. London: Routledge.

Beck, U. 2006. *The Cosmopolitan Vision*, trans. C. Cronin. Cambridge: Polity Press. (First published 2004.)

Blanc, C.S. 1996. "*Balikbayan*: a Filipino extension of the national imaginary and of state boundaries." *Philippine Sociological Review*, 44(1–4): 178–193.

Bolognani, M. 2007. "The myth of return: Dismissal, survival or revival? A Bradford example of transnationalism as a political instrument." *Journal of Ethnic and Migration Studies*, 33(1): 59–76.

Bolognani, M., Khawaja, R.Z., Khan, N.H., and Waheed, A. 2009. *Return Migrants in Pakistan*. London: Institute for Public Policy Research.

Bourdieu, P. 1985. "The social space and the genesis of groups." *Theory and Society*, 14(6): 723–744.

Bourdieu, P. 1992. *The Logic of Practice*. Cambridge: Polity Press. (Originally published 1980.)

Boyarin, D. and Boyarin, J. 1993. "Diaspora: Generation and the ground of Jewish identity." *Critical Inquiry*, 19: 693–725.

Brah, A. 1996. *Cartographies of Diaspora: Contesting Identities*. London: Routledge.

Charsley, K. 2005. "Unhappy husbands: Masculinity and migration in transnational Pakistani marriages." *Journal of the Royal Anthropological Institute*, 11(1): 85–105.

Christou, A. 2002. "Geographies of place, culture and identity in the narratives of second-generation Greek-Americans Returning 'Home.'" Working Paper 6, Sussex Centre for Migration Research.

Cohen, A. 1993. *Masquerade Politics: Explorations in the Structure of Urban Cultural Movements*. Berkeley: University of California Press.

Constable, N. 2007. *Maid to Order in Hong Kong. Stories of Migrant Workers*, 2nd edn. Ithaca, NY: Cornell University Press.

Cressey, G. 2006. *Diaspora Youth and Ancestral Homeland: British Pakistani/Kashmiri Youth Visiting Kin in Pakistan and Kashmir*. Leiden: Brill.

Dahya, B.1974. "The nature of Pakistani ethnicity in industrial cities in Britain." In A. Cohen (ed.) *Urban Ethnicity*, pp. 77–118. London: Tavistock.

Daswani, G. 2010. "Transformation and migration among members of a Pentecostal church in Ghana and London." *Journal of Religion in Africa*, 40: 442–474.

Donnan, H. and Werbner, P. 1991. "Introduction." In H. Donnan and P. Werbner (eds) *Economy and Culture in Pakistan: Migrants and Cities in a Muslim Society*. London: Macmillan.

Du Bois, W.E.B. 1994. *The Souls of Black Folk*. New York: Gramercy Books.

Foner, N. 1997. "What's new about transnationalism? New York immigrants today and at the turn of the century." *Diaspora*, 6: 355–375.

Foner, N. 2002. *From Ellis Island to JFK: New York's Two Great Waves of Immigration*. New Haven: Yale University Press/New York: Russell Sage Foundation.

Frantz, E. 2010. "Buddhism by other means: Sacred sites and ritual practice among Sri Lankan domestic workers in Jordan." *Asia Pacific Journal of Anthropology*, 11(3): 268–292.

Fumanti, M. 2010. "Virtuous citizenship, ethnicity and encapsulation among Akan speaking Ghanaian Methodists in London." *African Diaspora*, 3(1): 1–30.

Ghosh, A. 1989. "The diaspora in Indian culture." *Public Culture*, 2(1): 73–78.

Gilroy, P. 1993. *The Black Atlantic: Modernity and Double Consciousness*. London: Verso.

Glazer, N. and Moyniham, D.P. 1963. *Beyond the Melting Pot*. Cambridge, MA: MIT Press.

Glick Schiller, N. and Fouron, G.E. 2002. *Georges Woke Up Laughing: Long-Distance Nationalism and the Search for Home*. Durham, NC: Duke University Press.

Hage, G. 2002. "The differential intensities of social reality: Migration, participation and guilt." In G. Hage (ed.) *Arab Australians Today: Citizenship and Belonging*, pp. 192–205. Melbourne: Melbourne University Press.

Hage, G. 2012. "The everyday aesthetics of the Lebanese transnational family." ASA Firth Lecture, April 2–5, Delhi.

Hall, S. 1987. "Minimal selves." In L. Appignanesi (ed.) *Identity, the Real Me: Post-Modernism and the Question of Identity*, pp. 44–46. London: Institute of Contemporary Arts.

Hall, S. 1990. "Cultural identity and diaspora." In J. Rutherford (ed.) *Identity: Community, Culture, Difference*, pp. 222–237. London: Lawrence & Wishart.

Hall, S. 2008. "Cosmopolitanism, globalisation and diaspora: Stuart Hall in conversation with Pnina Werbner." In P. Werbner (ed.) *Anthropology and the New Cosmopolitanism: Rooted, Feminist and Vernacular Perspectives*, pp. 345–360. Oxford: Berg.

Kasinitz, P. 1992. *Caribbean New York: Black Immigrants and the Politics of Race*. Ithaca, NY: Cornell University Press.

King, R. and Christou, A. 2009. "Cultural geographies of counter-diasporic migration: Perspectives from the study of second-generation 'returnees' to Greece," *Population, Space, and Place*, 15: 103–119.

Levitt, P. 2001. *The Transnational Villagers*. Berkeley: University of California Press.

Levitt, P. and Glick Schiller, N. 2004. "Conceptualizing simultaneity: a transnational social field perspective on society." *International Migration Review*, 38(3): 1002–1039.

Liebelt, C. 2008. "On sentimental Orientalists, Christian Zionists, and 'working class cosmopolitans': Filipina domestic workers' journeys to Israel and beyond." *Critical Asian Studies*, 40(4): 567–586.

Liebelt, C. 2010. "Becoming pilgrims in the 'Holy Land': On Filipina domestic workers' struggles and pilgrimages for a cause." *Asia Pacific Journal of Anthropology*, 11(3): 245–267.

Liebelt, C. 2011. *Caring for the "Holy Land": Filipina Domestic Workers in Israel*. Oxford: Berghahn Books.

Liebelt, C. 2013. "Consuming pork, parading the virgin and crafting origami in Tel Aviv: Filipina care workers' aesthetic formations in Israel." Special issue, The Aesthetics of Diaspora, ed. M. Fumanti and P. Werbner, *Ethnos* 78(2). DOI:10.1080/00141844.2011.6 51483.

McKay, D. 2010. "A transnational pig: Reconstituting kinship among Filipinos in Hong Kong." *Asia Pacific Journal of Anthropology*, 11(3): 330–334.

Miller, D. and Madianou, M. 2011. *Migration and New Media: Transnational Families and Polymedia*. London: Routledge.

Morosanu, L. 2010. "From the uprooted to the rootless: Transnational social ties of Romanian migrants in London." Paper presented at the Oxford Graduate Migration Research Seminar, COMPAS, February 23, Oxford.

Nolin, C. 2002. "Transnational ruptures and sutures: Questions of identity and social relations among Guatemalans in Canada." *GeoJournal*, 56(1): 59–67.

Olwig, K.F. 2002. "A wedding in the family: Home-making in a global kin group." *Global Networks*, 2(3): 205–218.

Orsi, R.A. 1985. *The Madonna of 115th Street: Faith and Community in Italian Harlem, 1880–1950*. New Haven: Yale University Press.

Osella, C. and Osella, F. 2008. "Nuancing the migrant experience: Perspectives from Kerala, South India." In S. Koshy and R. Radhakrishnan (eds) *Transnational South Asians: The Making of a Neo-Diaspora*, pp. 146–178. Delhi: Oxford University Press.

Paerregaard, K. 2008. "In the footsteps of the Lord of the Miracles: the expatriation of religious icons in the Peruvian diaspora." *Journal of Ethnic and Migration Studies*, 34(7): 1073–1089.

Pingol, A. 2010. "Filipino women workers in Saudi: Making offerings for the here and now and hereafter." *Asia Pacific Journal of Anthropology*, 11(3): 394–409.

Portes, A., Guarnizo, L.E., and Landolt, P. 1999. "The study of transnationalism: Pitfalls and promise of an emergent research field." *Ethnic and Racial Studies*, 22(2): 218–237.

Rapport, N. and Dawson, A. 1998. "Home and movement: a polemic." In N. Rapport and A. Dawson (eds) *Migrants of Identity: Perceptions of Home in a World of Movement*, pp. 19–38. Oxford: Berg.

Reynolds, T. 2008. *Families, Social Capital and Caribbean Second-Generation Return Migration*. Working Paper 46, University of Sussex.

Sabar, G. 2010. "Israel and the 'Holy Land': the religio-political discourse of rights among African migrant labourers and African asylum seekers, 1990–2008." *African Diaspora*, 3(1): 43–76.

Safran, W. 1999. "Comparing diasporas: a review essay." *Diaspora*, 8(3): 255–291.

Schütz, A. 1945. "The homecomer." *American Journal of Sociology*, 50(5): 369–376.

Shaw, A. and Charsley, K. (2006) "Rishtas: Adding emotion to strategy in understanding British Pakistani transnational marriages." *Global Networks*, 6(4): 405–421.

Shenar, G. 2013. "Bollywood in Israel: Multi-sensual milieus, cultural appropriation and the aesthetics of diaspora transnational audiences." Special issue, The Aesthetics of Diaspora, ed. P. Werbner and M. Johnson, *Ethnos*, 78(2). DOI:10.1080/00141844.2011.651483.

Smith, M. 2010. "Erasure of sexuality and desire: State morality and Sri Lankan migrants in Beirut, Lebanon." *Asia Pacific Journal of Anthropology*, 11(3): 378–393.

Tondo, J.S.F. 2010. "Popular religiosity and the transnational journey: Inscribing Filipino identity in the Santo Niño Fiesta in New Zealand." *Asia Pacific Journal of Anthropology*, 11(3): 219–244.

Tsuda, T. 2003. *Strangers in the Ethnic Homeland: Japanese Brazilian Return Migration in Transnational Perspective*. New York: Columbia University Press.

Waldinger, R. and Fitzgerald, D. 2004. "Transnationalism in question." *American Journal of Sociology*, 109(5): 1177–1195.

Werbner, P. 2002a. *The Migration Process: Capital, Gifts and Offerings among British Pakistanis*, 2nd edn. Oxford: Berg. (Originally published 1990.)

Werbner, P. 2002b. *Imagined Diasporas among Manchester Muslims*. Oxford: James Currey/ Sante Fe, CA: School of American Research.

Werbner, P. 2002c. "The place which is diaspora: Citizenship, religion and gender in the making of chaordic transnationalism." *Journal of Ethnic and Migration Studies*, 28(1): 119–134.

Werbner, P. 2003. *Pilgrims of Love: The Anthropology of a Global Sufi Cult*. London: Hurst/ Bloomington: Indiana University Press.

Werbner, P. 2005. "The translocation of culture: Migration, community, and the force of multiculturalism in history." *Sociological Review*, 53(4): 745–768.

Werbner, P. 2007. "Veiled interventions in pure space: Shame and embodied struggles among Muslims in Britain and France." Special issue, "Authority and Islam," *Theory, Culture and Society*, 24(2): 161–186.

Werbner, P. 2008. *Anthropology and the New Cosmopolitanism: Rooted, Feminist and Vernacular Perspectives*. Oxford: Berg.

Werbner, P. 2012. "Migration and culture." In M. Rosenblum and D.Tichenor (eds) *The Oxford Handbook of the Politics of International Migration*, pp. 215–243. New York: Oxford University Press.

Werbner, P. and Fumanti, M. 2013. "The aesthetics of diaspora: Ownership and appropriation." Special issue, The Aesthetics of Diaspora, ed. P. Werbner, and M. Johnson. *Ethnos*, 78(2). DOI:10.1080/00141844.2011.651483.

Werbner, R. 1984. "The Manchester School in South Central Africa," *Annual Review of Anthropology* 13: 157–185.

Wimmer, A. and Glick Schiller, N. 2002. "Methodological nationalism and beyond: Nation-state building, migration and the social sciences." *Global Networks*, 2(4): 301–334.

Chapter 7

Religion, Religions, and Diaspora

Seán McLoughlin

Religions have a very significant place in the history of diaspora and transnationalism, whether in terms of the prototypical Babylonian exile of the Jews and their desire to return to Zion, or the universal horizons of Christian missionaries, Sufi orders, and Buddhist monks whose networks extended empires of faith across land and sea. However, across the contemporary Western academy "religion" is a problematic category. From the seventeenth century, early modern Europe gradually rationalized, compartmentalized, and domesticated religion, segregating it from secular power in line with the interests of emergent nation-states (Asad 1993). A substantive definition of "natural religion" also opened the way for comparison of a presumed universal in all societies, an autonomous and bounded essence "in some timeless realm (perhaps a realm of pure doctrine) outside of wider cultural patterns and history" (Flood 1999: 3). Indeed, as part of colonial projects, modern European models of religion were also globalized, with new religious elites in Asia, Africa, and beyond espousing reformed Hindu, Sikh, Muslim, and Buddhist neo-orthodoxies which mimicked Protestant Christianity.

Perhaps for this reason, then, religion has often been a concept "set apart" in the arts, humanities and social sciences, and has certainly received much less theoretical attention in diaspora and transnational studies than the closely related notions of ethnicity, race, nation, and hybridity. While some anthropologists have made key interventions, important cultural theorists like Paul Gilroy have not generally been moved to explore religion further, though his examination of black popular culture as a source of redemption draws upon the quasi-theological language of transcendence, for example, when he invokes "the transvaluation of all values" (1993: 36) and

A Companion to Diaspora and Transnationalism, First Edition.
Edited by Ato Quayson and Girish Daswani.

"the politics of transfiguration" (1993: 37–38). For its part, the study of religions, which is a multidisciplinary field encompassing quite diverse approaches to a shared object of study, has been slow to acknowledge the contemporary significance of diaspora and transnationalism (Baumann 2000). Some in the subfield of the history of religions, for instance, have been reluctant to embrace a wider use of the term, given its specific roots in Jewish theology. In the late 1990s one pioneering hand-book on "living religions" (Hinnells 1997) did include dedicated entries on diaspora, probably because the editor's own research included the contemporary life of Indian Zoroastrians (the Parsis) long since dispersed from Persia. Nevertheless, religion textbooks today, even in the field of sociology of religion, do not always feature diaspora and transnationalism, perhaps viewing them as specialized topics within the wider study of religions and globalization or religion and social change.

In the last decade, however, the situation across all disciplines has been changing rapidly. The growing recognition that globalization (or rather glocalization) entails "multiple modernities," and that the particularity of European models of seculariza-tion do not fit the rest of the world including the United States of America (USA), together with the securitization of a gated globe as a response to the terrorist attacks of 9/11 and its aftermath, have all created the circumstances in which religion can no longer be ignored or regarded as epiphenomenal by disciplines with a central interest in culture, society, and politics. Moreover, the same debates about culture and power in postmodernism and postcolonialism, which played a key role in reshaping diaspora studies in the 1990s, were also responsible for provoking the new wave of decolonized, anti-essentialist theory which (at about the same time) began to deconstruct the modern Western idea of "religion" in earnest. However, even if scholars can no longer reasonably treat it as an *a priori* cross-cultural and trans-historical phenomenon, "religion" is of course very much "out there" in public discourse. I support Flood's (1999) position that scholars can continue to employ the category in a taxonomic sense but that their analysis should be grounded in "utterance in the social world" (p. 233). Indeed, as we shall see, scholars of religion working out of the empirical study of diasporas and transnational migrants have been at the forefront of taking such an agenda forward, illuminating particularly the importance of spatial location for the study of religions in context and on the move (Tweed 1997, 2006; Vásquez and Marquardt 2003; Knott 2005; Vásquez 2011).

In what follows I present an overview of how religion has been studied in relation to diaspora and transnationalism, loosely adapting Cohen's (1997) mapping of the evolution of scholarship in diaspora studies to organize my discussion. As Vertovec reminds us (2004), some conceptual distinctions are also important: "Diasporas arise from some form of migration, but not all migration involves diasporic con-sciousness; all transnational communities comprise diasporas, but not all diasporas develop transnationalism" (p. 282). Drawing upon the examples of Judaism and the black Atlantic, then, I begin with reflections on religion in the paradigm of diaspora as a large-scale, traumatic scattering, exploring the role of religion in maintaining consciousness of a homeland connection, real or imagined, as well as a sense of peoplehood. Next, I consider the challenges of remaking home abroad as a religious minority, focusing on the literature concerning international migration to the United States and Western Europe from the 1960s, and highlighting similarities and differences in the relationships between religious organizations, ethnic identity, and hostland incorporation. After that, I illuminate the impact of a more transnational frame for studying religion and migration from the 1990s, underlining the embeddedness of actors simultaneously in at least two places, and what this means in terms of understanding everyday religious circulations of people, goods, capital, and ideas. In my penultimate section, I return attention to the more theoretical matters hinted at in this introduction, testing the utility of accepted distinctions between so-called "ethnic" and "universal" religions and their connections to people and place, thereafter considering an alternative schema which recasts the study of diasporic and transnational religion in terms of three distinctive spatialities. Finally, I sum up, pointing briefly to some possible future developments in the field.

Religion, Diaspora Consciousness, and the Reinvention of Tradition

> Diaspora refers to operations that are also trans-temporal, and which join multiple spaces through a work of imagination that links past, present and future. . . . [It] retrieves or invents a common origin and tradition and commemorates idealized geographic spaces as a way to dwell in an inhospitable present and perhaps bring about a return. . . . [It] often involves intense ritualized and momentary fusions of past and future. (Vásquez 2008: 163)

While the term *diaspora* is of Greek origin (*dia speiro*, "sowing over") and while the ancient Greeks thought of this mainly positively in terms of migration and colonization from 800 BCE, for more or less two thousand years the term was used predominantly in relation to an ancient Jewish "prototype" based on the trauma of dispersal and a troubled captivity and exile (Hebrew *galuth*) in Babylon (Cohen 1997). As the Psalm (137: 1, 4) puts it: "By the rivers of Babylon we sat down and wept at the memory of Zion. . . . How could we sing a song of Yahweh on alien soil?"[1] Today, it is no longer necessary to take Jewish theology as the only paradigm of dispersal. Indeed, Jews "are not a single people with a single origin and a single migration history" (Cohen 1997: 21); as well as a so-called "victim" diaspora in Cohen's typology, they have also been successful "labor" and "trade" diasporas. Nevertheless, the ancient Jewish example still usefully illustrates what Vásquez suggests above about diasporas being "trans-temporal" and religion's enabling role in this regard (cf. Tweed 1997). It was the Babylonians' capture of Jerusalem and destruction of its Temple in the sixth century BCE that saw the elite of the Kingdom of Judah exiled from the land promised to God's "chosen people." As Boyarin and Boyarin (1993: 719–722) argue, even while underlining a people's consciousness and memory of a homeland, diaspora calls this attachment into question, for Rabbis eventually responded to the realities of displacement and powerlessness by selectively reinventing Judaism as a religion of portable texts rather than temple sacrifice. They also developed a theology which deferred the question of final return and redemption to God, an ideology later challenged by Zionism. Thus, Baumann speaks (2000: 317) of a soteriological "pattern constituted by the fourfold course of sin or disobedience, scattering and exile as punishment, and finally return and gathering."

Eventually it was possible to return to Palestine but in many ways Jewish life had actually become more secure and cosmopolitan amongst the "communities in Alexandria, Antioch, Damascus, Asia Minor and Babylon [which] became centres of civilisation, culture and learning" (Cohen 1997: 5). Having remade new hostlands as Jewish spaces with institutions like synagogues, Jewry began to feel at home in the diaspora. Indeed, around the third century BCE the term "diaspora" itself became widely used in the Septuagint, the Greek translation of the Hebrew Bible for Jews in Alexandria. Notably, the term *galuth* was "*not* rendered into Greek by 'diaspora'" (Baumann 2000: 316) though the thrust of this neologism remained unfavorable in Jewish theology: "It was understood as a preparation for, an intermediate situation until, the final gathering of the scattered in Jerusalem by God's decree at the end of time" (Baumann 2010: 21). However, Cohen argues (1997: 6) that diaspora's "doleful" associations were also conveniently perpetuated by Christian theologians who read the (numerically relatively insignificant) scattering following the Roman destruction of the Second Temple in CE 70 as further punishment (for rejecting Christ and having him put to death). Interestingly, while itself a multi-ethnic people and lacking a homeland as such, the often persecuted early Christian Church gave Jewish notions of diaspora its own twist, seeing itself as a traveling and wandering people, commissioned to go out to the whole world and proclaim "the good news" of the Gospel, while awaiting the imminent coming of the kingdom of God (Baumann 2000: 20).

The study of diaspora was largely confined to Jewish studies until about the mid-1950s and 1960s, when the term began to emerge vis-à-vis other groups with experiences of large-scale scattering due to homeland traumas (Cohen 1997). At a time of decolonization in Africa and civil rights in the United States, raised black consciousness saw interest in African diaspora studies mushroom by the mid-1970s (Baumann 2000: 321). Decades earlier, in the 1920s and 1930s, social movements imagining a return to Africa as a homeland, including Garveyism and especially Ethiopianism/Rastafarianism in Jamaica and beyond, drew upon ancient biblical symbolism to spiritually and imaginatively overturn the ongoing legacy of African peoples' exodus and captivity in the "Babylon" of white oppression. While such movements themselves pointed to complex processes of religious hybridization in diaspora, perhaps one of the most significant texts of the 1970s explored such processes in relation to what Albert Raboteau (1978) calls the "invisible institution" of slave religion. From the early sixteenth until the mid-nineteenth centuries more than 12.5 million Africans were forcibly transported to the Caribbean and the Americas via Europe. Given the violence of this rupturing from the homeland, and subsequent efforts to control and eradicate African cultures' potential for group solidarity and resistance, it was impossible for religious traditions to be reconstructed "intact" under slavery (1978: 8). Aspects of mainly sub-Saharan African-based religiosities, including divination, ritual sacrifice, and spirit possession do all survive in the religiosity of slaves' descendants today and so represent a tangible link to generalized homeland origins. However, as Raboteau (1978: 16) explains, specific memories of liturgical seasons and rituals, myths, and languages, were "attenuated, replaced, and altered or lost." Thus, new syncretic religiosities emerged across the Americas and the Caribbean, with the importance of good relations with multiple gods in African-based traditions blending with other imported beliefs and practices including intercession by the Virgin Mary and the saints among Spanish and Portuguese Catholics. This is evident in both the Candomblé tradition of Brazil and Santería in Cuba, Puerto Rico, and the Dominican Republic. Of course, such mixed traditions have continued to travel, as Karen McCarthy Brown's (2001) portrait of *Mama Lola: A Vodou Priestess in Brooklyn* documents in the context of contemporary migration from Haiti to New York. Elsewhere, Joseph Murphy (1994) argues that transformed African-based religious traditions of "working the spirit" are evident, too, in the worship of black-led African American Protestant churches in the United States. As Boyarin and Boyarian have written, "Diasporic cultural identity teaches us that cultures are not preserved by being protected from "mixing" but probably can only continue to exist as a product of such mixing" (1993: 721).

Religious Organizations, Ethnic Distinctiveness, and Hostland Incorporation

In both Western Europe and North America the 1960s were a key moment in terms of new, non-European-origin, mainly labor-based, migration. By the 1980s the term *diaspora* eventually came to be used in some circles as an alternative to "immigrant," "ethnic minority," "guest-worker," "refugee," and so on (Tölölyan 1991), not least because it was seen as having more dignity by the groups in question. Nevertheless, migration, along with class, race, and ethnicity, remained the dominant scholarly frames for studying such matters. In terms of religious backgrounds, immigration to Western European cities has been predominantly into the working class and from the Muslim Middle East, South Asia, and Africa, though with significant other groups in the United Kingdom and elsewhere. A different picture emerges in the United States where a greater number of immigrant workers have been professionals; a 1996 pilot of the New Immigrant Survey also identified that at least two-thirds of post-1965 immigrants were Christian and some 42 percent Catholic, though four times as many as native-born Americans had a non-Jewish or Christian affiliation (Cadge and Ecklund 2007: 361). Research on religion and migration was somewhat limited until the 1980s, whether because of limited data, skepticism about the significance of religion vis-à-vis other categories, or perhaps even a lack of migrant-heritage researchers interested to take the topic forward (Ebaugh and Chafetz 2000). In any case, what work there has been has tended to be sociological and anthropological, typically focusing on one or more religious community organizations associated with a given tradition and from a particular homeland context, now relocated to a specific hostland city (Cadge and Ecklund 2007).

In the study of religions this pattern is evident, too, as an example of pioneering work in the United Kingdom will illustrate.[2] Since 1976, the Community Religions Project (CRP; http://www.leeds.ac.uk/crp), based at the University of Leeds, has published various case studies of religion locally in West Yorkshire and beyond. Reflecting on the reductionism of earlier social scientific studies, the CRP's lead researcher at the time, Kim Knott (1992), observed that few did more than examine religion as a marker "in the service of ethnicity" (p. 12). With a greater concern for the internal dynamics of religions, Knott (1986: 10) also developed one of the first attempts to map the factors interacting to produce diverse "new patterns and forms of religious behaviour, organisation, experience and self-understanding." This can be summarized briefly as follows: (1) *home traditions* (e.g., whether the religion is tied or not to a particular people/place); (2) *host traditions* (e.g., the general relationship of religion to the state); (3) *nature of the migration process* (e.g., whether it involves sojourning, settlement, or seeking refuge); (4) *nature of migrant group* (e.g., its size, ethnic and denominational diversity, geographical dispersion, and level of education); (5) *nature of host response* (e.g., social attitudes to integration, racism, and ecumenism; cf. Hinnells 1997; Vertovec 2000; McLoughlin 2009). With a particular focus on Hinduism, Islam, and Sikhism among Gujaratis, Punjabis, East African Asian "twice migrants," and Bengalis, CRP case studies illuminated the huge moral and economic investments made in establishing autonomous, often multi-functional, religious institutions, especially when it became necessary to transmit homeland traditions to the next generation. Rituals, which as Vásquez suggested (2008), create continuity with the past, were sometimes found to be "standardized" to accommodate ethnic differences in mixed congregations equally pressed for time and space, although if such congregations grew in size they became increasingly organized by cleavages of ethnicity and caste, denomination and sect, with religion often sanctifying social hierarchies (cf. McLoughlin and Zavos, forthcoming). Nevertheless, self-conscious of their minority status, and that this required the presentation of a comprehensible common front especially to the state and wider society, leaders' representations and rhetoric across religio-ethnic boundaries temporarily reasserted broader unities of religious "fusion" over "fission."

In the United States as in the United Kingdom, religion has rarely been seen by social scientists as a variable more or less independent of other factors; indeed, even today, "most of the current religion and immigration literature focuses on the ways immigrant religious organizations help to reinforce and maintain ethnicity" (Cadge and Ecklund 2007: 364). The ethnicity paradigm has a particularly significant history in the United States, with Herberg (1955), for instance, arguing that even while Southern and Eastern European immigrants had lost their ethno-national languages and customs, by the 1950s, paradoxically, it was maintaining their religious identity which was the key to third-generation Catholics and Jews finding their place in a society with not just one, but three, "melting pots." While we shall say more eventually about the disaggregation of religion from other cultural stuff (language, custom, and attachment to place), the more recent literature on non-European migration to the United States has underlined that identity is "ascribed" as well as "achieved" (Herberg took no account of African Americans or race), and that second generations may be more (not less) religious than their parents (as Herberg suggested) (Cadge and Ecklund 2007). However, Herberg's (1955) emphasis on religion and incorporation is alive and well especially in the United States, where religious congregations are readily identified as sites for migrants to access information about rights, services, and recognition; they also build social capital, providing opportunities for training and the chance to exercise leadership.

Regarding such debates about immigration and citizenship, Foner and Alba (2008) draw an interesting contrast between the location and function of religion in the United States and Western Europe. In the United States, religion is largely regarded as a pathway to incorporation, inclusion, respectability, and mobility for immigrants, whereas in Western Europe religion is generally regarded as a barrier to such things. Echoing aspects of Knott's framework, and allowing more or less for significant ideological differences, say between communitarianism in the United Kingdom and laicism in France (Cesari and McLoughlin 2005), Foner and Alba (2008) argue that this is the case mainly because of different configurations of religion in terms of both (1) the background of migrants and (2) the context of their reception. First, as we have seen, most US immigrants are Christians and so share the faith of the majority, whereas the 15 million Muslims in Western Europe represent the majority of its immigrants; Islam is thus a marker of difference, not similarity or Europeanization. Second, the USA is a more or less religious society, whereas, despite its Christian heritage, Western Europe is predominantly secularizing, further sharpening majority–minority distinctions. Third, the USA makes a mostly clear separation between religion and state, yet recognizes a place for religion in the mainstream of public life; thus, recognition is largely unproblematic with most sources of religious conflict concerning non-migrant conservative Christians. By contrast, in Western Europe religion–state relations still bear traces of a Christian past and this can make legalizing equal treatment more problematic; indeed, most religious conflicts concern Islam and are highly politicized, for example, in terms of veiling. This is exacerbated by Muslims' position as the immigrant group with the lowest social capital and highest disadvantage and by the fact that transnational Islam has become both a moral and political resource for the oppositional identities of some European Muslim youth.

Transnational Migrants and the Global Circulation of Religions

In the 1990s the social sciences were significantly impacted by globalization theory, which in migration studies meant a much stronger emphasis on transnationalism. Peggy Levitt makes a useful distinction between the two (2001a: 202): "Global processes tend to be de-linked from specific national territories while transnational processes are anchored in and transcend one or more nation-states." Elsewhere, she notes that, rather than more far-flung circuits, work on transnationalism has some-times been too focused on the relatively close geographical and historical linkages between the United States, Latin America, and the Caribbean (Levitt and Jaworsky 2007: 131). However, in her own work she has moved beyond a case study of Dominican Catholics in Boston and Miraflores (Levitt 2001b) to a comparative transnational study of Irish Catholics, Brazilian Protestants, Indian Hindus, and Pakistani Muslims in the United States (Levitt 2007). Of course, as the opening remarks of my introduction illustrated, religious transnationalism is nothing new. Furthermore, not all work on transnationalism and religion today is concerned with migration; religions create transnational spaces and civil societies which motivate and enable action across national borders in many different ways, including human-itarian donations, pilgrimage, volunteering, mission, and media consumption (Wuthnow and Offutt 2008). Nevertheless, migration remains our focus here and in general terms Levitt and Jaworsky argue (2007) that a "transnational optic" has allowed migration scholars to look beyond the dichotomy of homeland and hostland in much earlier work, and perhaps especially a "container" model of the nation-state concerned with hostland assimilation and integration. However, once again, migra-tion scholars "have largely overlooked the ways in which religious identities and practices also enable migrants to sustain memberships in multiple locations" (Levitt 2003: 847).

Even while making new homes abroad, then, migrants at different stages of life and the migration process are "simultaneously embedded" in more or less enduring and intense religious (as well as social, cultural, economic, and political) connec-tions across borders (Levitt and Jaworsky 2007: 130; Vásquez and Marquardt 2003). So, while, for example, the Iwa (saints, spirits) who possess Catholic Haitians have now come to divide their time transnationally between Ri Rivyé and Palm Beach county, Miami, some migrants from this community convert to Protestantism to free themselves from the obligation to homeland kin to support the rituals that keep their supernatural guardians contented. At the same time, a transnational frame also illuminates that homeland religion is frequently impacted by reverse flows of migrants' social remittances though Vásquez is right to speak of a "mobility regime" (2011: 294) constraining circulations. Other important asymmetries also remain, for example,

> Brazil has more than twice as many Catholics as the United States, but the United States has more than twice as many Catholic parishes as Brazil and the ratio of priests to parishioners is six times higher in the United States than in Brazil. Overall, Catholic and Protestant churches take in approximately nine times more money annually than churches in Brazil. (Wuthnow and Offutt 2008: 227)

Nevertheless, in Miraflores, Levitt reports (2001b) that Dominicans came to emulate their migrant compatriots who (often for social and pragmatic reasons) engaged much more formally with the Catholic Church in Boston than at home (a common pattern), whether in terms of the requirements of church-based baptism, lay contributions to the ritual and finances of the congregations or the time-constrained, organized sociality of after-mass coffee. While some in receipt of such social remittances in Miraflores put this down to becoming "more educated," they were also in receipt of financial remittances, and with higher incomes at their disposal could, for example, afford to engage in certain forms of organized religiosity such as pilgrimage to national shrines for the first time (Levitt 2001b: 159–179). Similarly, in her study of Sylhet in Bangladesh, Gardner (1995) argues that, amongst successful economic migrants and their families back home, completing the *Hajj* (pilgrimage to Mecca) is part of a modern, more rationalized and textualized, "Protestant" Islamic consciousness that is the product of ideas about religion encountered while working in Britain and especially Saudi Arabia (pp. 243–245).

Transnationalism (or translocalism) clearly operates, then, at multiple distinct yet interconnected spatial scales, including (1) the private, informal and hybrid interiority of the individual, as well as interpersonal and household relations and (2) the more collective, public and formally organized levels of associations and congregations. While factors such as immigration status, proximity to the homeland, the extent of dispersal and English-language fluency all nuance the extent to which engagement with transnational networks is informal, formal, or both (Ebaugh and Chafetz 2002: 854), these dimensions of everyday life are also routinely shaped to a greater or lesser extent at the scale of nation-states (homeland and hostland) and by transnational religious organizations. For instance, while the Turkish Ministry of Religious Affairs (Diyanet) takes a great interest in organizing Islamic institutions in Western Europe, Morocco has usually had less interest in this regard, meaning that the religious life of its migrants is more fragmented. In terms of transnational religious organizations, Levitt (2003) compares the distinctive authority structures among Catholics and Protestants in the United States, illustrating their divergent impacts. The Catholic Church represents "a vast, interconnected network" (2003: 855) of religious orders, schools, and so on which "facilitate transnational practices' (p. 854) such as sharing staff in the United States and Brazil; however, in its efforts to incorporate immigrants into multi-ethnic congregations with generic worship styles it can also ultimately de-ethnicize them (p. 856; cf. Herberg 1955). In contrast, Protestant churches, both mainline and start-up Pentecostal groups, have authority structures that are "less hierarchical" (p. 857) and so more flexible, which for groups like the Salvadorians has meant that, having established their churches, as diasporas they can remain focused on a homeland orientation without having "to create new, more inclusive identities to encourage newcomers to feel like they belonged to the US church" (p. 859).

Other transnational religious organizations operate as "franchises" or "chapters" of specific homeland religious movements (Levitt 2003) and with the more or less instant magnification of distant events since the 1980s especially the global media has seen such networks mobilize transnationally both in support of, and sometimes, leading causes in the homeland and beyond. Such events have included the storming of the Sikhs' Golden Temple at Amritsar by Indian government forces during 1984 (Tatla 1999), Hindu nationalists' destruction of the contested site of the Babri

Masjid (mosque) in Ayodhya, India, in 1992 (Vertovec 2000), and the trans-ethnic mobilizations opposing Western interventions in the Muslim world, from "Desert Storm" in Iraq in the early 1990s to the ongoing "War on Terror" in Afghanistan. Therefore, "long distance" religious transnationalism, whether amongst the followers of Babbar Khalsa in Vancouver, the Vishwa Hindu Parishad in London, or Jama'at-i-Islami in New York, might take a number of forms, including fundraising and charitable giving, lobbying governments and international human rights organizations, as well as supporting more militant activities.

Re-Mapping Diasporic and Transnational Religion: A Locative Approach

Theorizations of religion and diaspora have often focused on the question of whether a particular religious tradition, type of religion, or religions in general, can properly or usefully be described in terms of the concept of diaspora. "Religions can provide additional cement to bind a diasporic consciousness, but they do not constitute diasporas in and of themselves. . . . The myth and idealization of a homeland and a return movement are also conspicuously absent in the case of world religions . . . their programmes are extraterritorial rather than territorial" (Cohen 1997: 189). Following Cohen, Vertovec (2004) draws a distinction between "ethnic" religions such as Judaism, Sikhism, and Hinduism, which seem to "qualify" as diasporic because of their historic attachment to a particular people and/or place, and missionary or "world" religions with more "universal" horizons such as Christianity, Islam, and Buddhism (Prebish and Baumann 2002), about which he is more skeptical: "It broadens the term far too much to talk – as many scholars do – about the 'Muslim diaspora,' 'Catholic diaspora' . . . and so forth . . . are Muslims in Pakistan part of a diaspora religion because Islam is derived from and broadly centred on Mecca?" (2004: 281). However, this modernist, classificatory distinction between "universal" and "ethnic" religions is problematic because so-called "universal" religions have always been re-territorialized even as they have adapted to new environments, while especially under the conditions of globalized multiple modernities, so-called "ethnic" religions like "Hinduism" have been self-consciously re-articulated by at least some Hindus as "universal" "world religions" (Smart 1987; McLoughlin 2009). A more complex schema is therefore required to recast the different sorts of work that the same religious traditions can resource, both in terms of reinforcing territorial identities and transcending them.

One scholar who has developed "a theory of religion that made sense of the religious life of transnational migrants" (2006: 5), is Thomas Tweed. His earlier influential study (1997) examined the significance of the shrine of Our Lady of Charity, built to their national patron saint by Cuban Catholics in Miami, and the site of national flags as well as soil from the homeland. Elsewhere, he reminds us, too, that such examples illustrate that diasporic religion operates trans-temporally: "orienting them [migrants] in space and time . . . bridging then and now, here and there (Tweed 2002: 263). While he notes that the study of religions has generally "privileged time over space," he is equally concerned with spatiality, in particular, "displaced people's attempts to map, construct, and inhabit worlds of meaning" (1997: 93). Moving beyond the unhelpful dichotomization of religions tied to, or seemingly transcending, people/place, he adapts the ideas of study of religions scholar Jonathan Z. Smith, suggesting three different ways in which religions "can map and inhabit worlds of meaning": *locatively* (religion reinforces territorial locations and contributes to remaking new homes locally abroad); *translocatively* (religion enables linkages, especially symbolic linkages, across homeland locations old and new); *supralocatively* (religion transcends both homeland and hostland locations) (Tweed 1997: 94–95). Tweed also adds that religions map worlds of meaning both "horizontally" (in terms of social relations) and "vertically" (in terms of supernatural relations) but, as for his own work, he remains focused on the former because "members of the diaspora are propelled horizontally and not vertically" (1997: 139–40). More recently he has offered a further elaboration of such ideas including a definition of what "doing religion" – or "religioning" to use Malory Nye's (2000) term – entails: "religions are confluences of organic-cultural flows that intensify joy and confront suffering by drawing on human and superhuman forces to make homes and cross boundaries" (Tweed 2006: 54). So, deeply influenced by the spatial and aquatic metaphors which have come to define the study of diaspora and transnationalism, Tweed suggests that religions – theological narratives, social institutions, material artefacts, embodied rituals – are intimately concerned with "crossing and dwelling," moving across corporeal, territorial, and cosmic boundaries, as well as a felt need to be in place.

Tweed's schema is extremely illuminating. However, certainly in his study of Cuban Catholics in Miami, he says least about the supralocative dimension of his cartography. This is understandable given how clearly ethno-national the orientation of his respondents was. Nevertheless, as imagined spaces of individual and collective religious identification and belonging that have the potential to trump (however temporarily) the competing claims of homelands and hostlands, the supralocative is crucial, perhaps especially amongst later generations of migrants for whom homeland memories have become fractured and yet hostland affinity is compromised by exclusion. In a globalizing world where de- and extra-territorial imaginings are especially well enabled, supralocative religious spaces would seem to provide an interesting example of a "homing desire which is not the same thing as a desire for a 'homeland'" (Brah 1996: 179–180). Moreover, as Vásquez notes, religions may be considered unique because "they invoke supra-historical or trans-historical transcendence" (2011: 284) and can draw upon rich mythic, symbolic, and ritual resources in this regard. Before introducing the idea of the supralocative himself, however, Tweed (1997: 93) notes Smith's identification of a "utopian" religious map amongst ancient diasporas which "values transcending space or being no place." Indeed, while "being no place" suggests a number of possible spiritual, moral, and political projects, Vásquez underlines the fact that (2011: 284) "very often, religion adds a powerful utopian, millenarian, and even apocalyptic dimension to lived spaces, imagining a radical, perhaps even violent, inversion of the present, a rectification of all the traumas and unfulfilled longings, and a return to a timeless state of grace." Whatever their orientation, supralocative religious spaces should still be seen, of course, as emerging from particular time-space locations. Religious spaces are therefore simultaneously produced by supralocative, just as much as locative or translocative forces (cf. Knott 2005), with religious actors "religioning" performatively "across," "up," and "down" all of these scales in the course of everyday life.

Some Future Developments

The theoretical work of scholars like Tweed, Knott, and Vásquez in the last two decades has the potential to reposition the study of religions at the heart of diaspora and transnationalism studies; it invites wide-ranging, reciprocal engagement across the arts, humanities, and social sciences. While long since flagged as significant, there is still room for more work connecting theories of religion, diaspora, and transnationalism to the study of religions, travel, and mobility *per se*. In terms of more empirical work, Cadge and Ecklund (2007) suggest more analytically precise and problem-oriented research design to test individual variables, also arguing that future work must make systematic comparison more of a priority. Scholarship to date has often focused on diasporic and transnational religious organizations. Therefore greater attention to religion in everyday life and in public institutions is an area for development too, as is religion beyond organizations, whether as part of everyday life or in public institutions. Levitt (2003: 860) has called for longitudinal studies of multi-sited transnational migration reflecting on continuity and change across significant periods of time.

Notes

1 Biblical quotations are from the *New Jerusalem Bible*, 1985.
2 Similarly, since the 1990s, the Pluralism Project at Harvard University (www.pluralism.org, accessed February 5, 2013) has sought to chart the changing religious landscape of "Main Street USA," mainly through local case studies of congregations in major cities. For a related project in Canada, see www.religionanddiversity.ca, accessed February 5, 2013.

References

Asad, T. 1993. *Genealogies of Religion: Discipline and Reasons of Power in Christianity and Islam*. Baltimore: Johns Hopkins University Press.
Baumann, M. 2000. "Diaspora: Genealogies of semantics and transcultural comparison." *Numen*, 47(3): 313–337.

Baumann, M. 2010. "Exile." In K. Knott and S. McLoughlin (eds) *Diasporas: Concepts, Identities, Intersections*, pp. 9–23. London: Zed Books.

Boyarin, D. and Boyarin, J. (1993). "Diaspora: Generation and the Ground of Jewish Identity." *Critical Inquiry*, 19(4): 693–725.

Brah, A. 1996. *Cartographies of Diaspora*. London: Routledge.

Cadge, W. and Ecklund, E.H. 2007. "Immigration and religion." *Annual Review of Sociology*, 33: 359–379.

Cesari, J. and McLoughlin, S. 2005. *European Muslims and the Secular State*. Aldershot: Ashgate.

Cohen, R. 1997. *Global Diasporas: An Introduction*. London: Routledge (2nd edn 2008.)

Ebaugh, H.R. and Chafetz, J.S. 2002. *Religion Across Borders*. Walnut Creek, CA: Alta Mira.

Flood, G. 1999. *Beyond Phenomenology: Rethinking the Study of Religion*. London: Cassell.

Foner, N. and Alba, R. 2008. "Immigrant religion in the US and Western Europe: Bridge or barrier to inclusion?" *International Migration Review*, 42(2): 360–392.

Gardner, K. 1995. *Global Migrants, Local Lives: Travel and Transformation in Rural Bangladesh*. Oxford: Clarendon.

Gilroy, P. 1993. *The Black Atlantic: Modernity and Double Consciousness*. London: Verso.

Herberg, W. 1955. *Protestant, Catholic, Jew: An Essay on American Religious Sociology*. Garden City, NY: Doubleday.

Hinnells, J.R. (ed.) 1997. *The New Penguin Handbook of Living Religions*. London: Penguin Books.

Knott, K. 1986. *Religion and Identity, and the Study of Ethnic Minority Religions in Britain*. Leeds: Community Religions Project, Department of Theology and Religious Studies, University of Leeds.

Knott, K. 1992. *The Role of Religious Studies in Understanding the Ethnic Experience*. Leeds: Community Religions Project, Department of Theology and Religious Studies, University of Leeds.

Knott, K. 2005. *The Location of Religion: A Spatial Analysis*. London: Equinox Books.

Lefebvre, H. 1991. *The Production of Space*. Oxford: Blackwell.

Levitt, P. 2001a. "Transnational migration: Taking stock and future directions." *Global Networks*, 1(3): 195–216.

Levitt, P. 2001b. *The Transnational Villagers*. Berkeley: University of California Press.

Levitt, P. 2003. "'You know, Abraham was really the first immigrant': Religion and transnational migration." *International Migration Review*, 3: 847–873.

Levitt, P. (2007). *God Needs No Passport: Immigrants and the Changing American Religious Landscape*. New York: New Press.

Levitt, P. and Jaworsky, B.N. (2007). "Transnational migration studies: Past developments and future trends. *Annual Review of Sociology*, 33: 129–156.

McCarthy Brown, K. 2001. *Mama Lola: A Vodou Priestess in Brooklyn*. Berkeley: University of California Press.

McLoughlin, S. 2009. "Religion and diaspora." In J.R. Hinnells (ed.) *The Routledge Companion to the Study of Religion*, pp. 558–580. London: Routledge.

McLoughlin, S. and Zavos, J. forthcoming. "Writing religion in British Asian cities." In S. McLoughlin, W. Gould, A.J. Kabir, and E. Tomalin (eds) *Writing the City in British Asian Diasporas*. London: Routledge.

Murphy, J.M. 1994. *Working the Spirit: Ceremonies of the African Diaspora*. Boston, MA: Beacon Press.

Nye, M. 2000. "Religion, post-religionism, and religioning: Religious studies and contemporary cultural debates." *Method and Theory in the Study of Religion*, 12(3): 447–476.

Prebish, C.S. and Baumann, M. (eds) 2002. *Westward Dharma: Buddhism Beyond Asia*. Berkeley: University of California Press.

Raboteau, A. 1978. *Slave Religion: The Invisible Institution in the Antebellum South*. New York: Oxford University Press.

Smart, N. 1987. "The importance of diasporas." In S. Shaked, R.Y. Werblovsky, D.D. Shulman, and G.A.G. Strounka (eds) *Gilgul: Essays on Transformation, Revolution and Permanence in the History of Religions*, pp. 288–295. Leiden: Brill.

Tatla, D.S. 1999. *The Sikh Diaspora: The Search for Statehood*. London: UCL Press.

Tölölyan, K. 1991. "The nation state and its Other: in lieu of a Preface." *Diaspora: A Journal of Transnational Studies*, 1(1): 3–7.

Tweed, T.A. 1997. *Our Lady of the Exile: Diaspora Religion at a Cuban Catholic Shrine in Miami*. New York: Oxford University Press.

Tweed, T.A. 2002. "On moving across: Translocative religion and the interpreter's position." *Journal of the American Academy of Religion*, 70(2): 253–277.

Tweed, T.A. 2006. *Crossing and Dwelling: A Theory of Religion*. Cambridge, MA: Harvard University Press.

Vásquez, M.A. 2008. "Studying religion in motion: a networks approach." *Method and Theory in the Study of Religion*, 20: 151–184.

Vásquez, M.A. 2011. *More Than Belief: A Materialist Theory of Religion*. New York: Oxford University Press.

Vásquez, M.A. and Marquardt, M.F. 2003. *Globalizing the Sacred: Religion Across the Americas*, New Brunswick: Rutgers University Press.

Vertovec, S. 2000. *The Hindu Diaspora: Comparative Patterns*. London: Routledge.

Vertovec, S. 2004. "Religion and diaspora." In P. Antes, A.W. Geertz, and R. Warne (eds) *New Approaches to the Study of Religion: Textual, Comparative, Sociological, and Cognitive Approaches*. Berlin: de Gruyter.

Wuthnow, R. and Offutt, S. 2008. "Transnational religious connections." *Sociology of Religion*, 69: 209–232.

Chapter 8

Postcolonialism and the Diasporic Imaginary

Ato Quayson

Erich Auerbach writes from Princeton in 1952: "New outlooks on history and on reality have been revealed, and the view of the structure of inter-human processes has been enriched and renewed. We have participated – indeed, we are still participating – in a practical seminar on world history. . . . In any event, our philological home is the earth: it can no longer be the nation" (1969: 11, 17). While it is with respect to *Weltliteratur* that Auerbach makes his remarks, the conditions under which they were made must also be recalled in reflecting upon the remarks. Born in Berlin to Jewish parents in 1892, he was trained in the German philological tradition, earned his doctorate in 1921 and became a member of the faculty at the University of Marburg in 1929. The rise of Nazism in Germany forced Auerbach out of his position and in 1935 he took up exile in Istanbul, Turkey, where *Mimesis: The Representation of Reality in Western Literature* (2003) was completed in 1953. Auerbach produced *Mimesis* without access to his library, much of which had been left behind in fleeing Germany. The book then was written from the few books and fragmentary notes he had with him while in Istanbul. If, as one proverb puts it, a book is as the gateway to an entire city then Auerbach may be seen to have suffered two forms of exile, one from the land of his birth and the other from the comfort of his library. Auerbach's remarks may thus be fruitfully taken as also deriving from the sense of exile, mobility and circulation that he was subject to, and that in their turn are central to the condition of diaspora. Despite the sound intuition that undergirds his remarks, the ways by which we might establish the parameters of the "practical seminar on world history" remain strangely elusive. Even if postcolonial literary scholars have gone some way in elaborating the terms for such a practical seminar, its dimensions have been largely obscured by a number of problems,

A Companion to Diaspora and Transnationalism, First Edition.
Edited by Ato Quayson and Girish Daswani.
© 2013 Blackwell Publishing Ltd. Published 2013 by Blackwell Publishing Ltd.

among which are the still dominant models of methodological nationalism and the lamentable fact that postcolonial studies, while showing much interest in questions of transnationalism, has not as yet come to terms with the salience of diaspora for understanding the primary conditions of production and reception of much that falls under the rubric of postcolonialism.[1]

There are three main tasks that must be considered central to a practical seminar on world history today: first is to interrogate the assumption of the nation-state as the privileged horizon for literary history; second is to evaluate the implications of the vast range of voluntary and enforced movements of populations that have taken place in world history for their impact on the imagination; and third is to generate a supple model for interpreting literary texts in full view of their grounding in the recursive mobilities of the past and present time. This chapter will pursue these tasks from a combined postcolonial and diaspora studies perspective, starting with an elaboration of some of their overlaps and differences and then turning to the question of the diasporic imaginary. While referencing the processes of diasporization that took place during the colonial period, for heuristic purposes the literary texts to which we shall be turning in illustrating the diasporic imaginary will be drawn mainly from the period after 1945 to account for the ways in which such texts have reflected changes to social formations since World War II and the independence of many nations from the yoke of colonialism. A fuller account of how the long *durée* of diasporas from earlier periods may be connected to a postcolonial-type analysis will have to wait for another occasion.[2]

Methodological Nationalism and the Challenge of Mobility

Methodological nationalism implies the assumption that the nation is the natural container for understanding politics and society. This has been seriously questioned by scholars of migration and diasporas (Wimmer and Glick Schiller 2002; Werbner, CHAPTER 6). As Stephen Greenblatt notes in *Cultural Mobility: A Manifesto* (2010: 2):

> There is no going back to the fantasy that once upon a time there were settled, coherent, and perfectly integrated national or ethnic communities. To write convincing and accurate cultural analyses – not only of the troubled present but of centuries past – requires, to paraphrase Hamlet, more a chronicle of carnal, bloody, and unnatural acts than a story of inevitable progress from traceable origins. We need to understand colonization, exile, emigration, wandering, contamination, and unintended consequences, along with the fierce compulsions of greed, longing, and restlessness, for it is these disruptive forces that principally shape the history and diffusion of identity and language, and not a rooted sense of cultural legitimacy. At the same time, we need to account for the persistence, over very long time periods and the face of radical disruption of cultural identities which substantial numbers of people are willing to make extreme sacrifices, including life itself.

The problem, he goes on to point out, is that the established analytical tools we use operate on the assumption of the stability of cultures, "or that in their original or natural state, before they are disrupted or contaminated [they] are properly rooted in the rich soil of blood and land and that they are virtually motionless" (2010: 3). The assumption is so engrained that it has affected the ways in which entire disciplines are organized. This is not completely surprising, since most universities all over the world are funded from national budgets and it is in the interest of governments to replicate a sense of authenticity for their nation-states. The problem, of course, is that the nation-state as we know it today is a fairly recent product of human history. The Treaty of Westphalia of 1648 that set up the earliest model of nation-state sovereignty was based on the two central principles of territorial integrity and the absence of a role for external agents in domestic affairs. However, the treaty also signally ignored the widespread and intensified movements of population that were taking place in the same period, from the mass outward European migrations to the New World, to the Atlantic slave trade, both of which were in full flow at the time. The challenge of methodological nationalism is also strongly to be felt in postcolonial studies, where the often violent birth of nations following colonialism (think of India and Pakistan, Algeria and Angola) served to install an idea of the epochality of the nation-state, guaranteeing that it provided the preferred horizon for elaborating social, political, and cultural history. This is because decolonization had already succeeded in elevating the struggles and sacrifices of political elites against colonialism to the level of an ontological necessity and had thereby obliterated other modes of analysis that were not seen as central to that model.[3] In West Africa for example, it is only in the past decade or so that the history of slavery has begun to be taken seriously in schools and among the general public. This has been as much due to attempts to court tourism from the African American diaspora as to the emergence of fresh archives and methods of analysis.

Any critique of the methodological nationalism undergirding forms of postcolonial literary history must begin by re-examining the ways in which canonical writers in the field have so far been read. For it is true that many well-known canonical writers of the postcolonial tradition, such as Wole Soyinka, Raja Rao, Chinua Achebe, Ngugi wa Thiongo, Garcia Marquez, Assia Djebar, Anita Desai, Arundhati Roy, Bapsi Sidwha, and Salman Rushdie have written within a thematic of the nation-state and/or community (on the epochality of the nation-state and its implications for literary history, see Quayson 2012b). But even here the figure of the stranger or that of the one who arrives from a point outside of demarcated social or communal boundaries serves to unsettle the easy parameters of the nation-state form implicit in such writing. Thus a process of making strange afflicts both Okonkwo and Ezeulu, the central protagonists of Achebe's *Things Fall Apart* and *Arrow of God*, respectively. In each instance the final mark of their estrangement (both in the sense of alienation and becoming *unheimlich*, or "unhomely") is suggested in the journeys that they undertake away from their communities. Both journeys are involuntary and enforced, the return from which registers their ultimate alienation. With other well-known postcolonial writers the principle of strangerhood is tied to a lack of conformity to the horizon of established social norms, as in J.M. Coetzee's *The Life and Times of Michael K*, or Isabel Allende's *House of Spirits*, or, as is often

also the case, explicitly to that of the circularities of migration trauma, and dislocation, in Rushdie's *Satanic Verses*, Anne Michaels' *Fugitive Pieces*, Amitav Ghosh's *In
an Antique Land*, or Kiran Desai's *Inheritance of Loss*, to cite but a handful of well-
known examples. Zadie Smith's *White Teeth*, Ben Okri's *The Famished Road*, Keri
Hulme's *The Bone People* and much of Derek Walcott's poetry ("The Schooner
Flight," *Omeros*, and "The Prodigal" being the prime examples), provide a synthesis
of the two previous positions just mentioned, because in such writers the deep
desire for rootedness and home is strongly coupled to a romantic idealization of
strangerhood that then ends up unsettling any facile foundations for identity and
identification in the first instance, whether this be with the ideal of a homeland/
nation, or family, or even a singular and coherent community. For the diasporic
imaginary, on the other hand, the condition of strangerhood or estrangement is a necessary and inescapable dimension. We see this across a wide spectrum of diasporic
literature and film, from the writings of Sholem Aleichem that straddled the end of
the nineteenth century and the beginning of the twentieth, to Steven Spielberg's
Fievel Goes West, Atom Egoyan's *Calendar*, Zadie Smith's *White Teeth*, Dionne
Brand's *What We All Long For*, and almost all the writings of Toni Morrison. As
Georg Simmel (1971) notes, the sociological category of the stranger is the synthesis
of two seemingly contradictory properties, that of complete detachment from every
given point in space and its opposite, the attachment to a location: "The stranger is
an element of the group itself, not unlike the poor and sundry 'inner enemies' – an
element whose membership within the group involves both being outside it and
confronting it" (p. 144). And yet, as a thematic, strangerhood must properly be
thought of as occupying a continuum between affiliation/attachment and disaffiliation/
estrangement, with different points on that continuum helping to configure a text
as either postcolonial or diasporic. As we shall see later, the condition of strangerhood is by no means the only defining characteristic of the diasporic imaginary.
Suffice it to say for now, however, that the dynamic relationship between the implicit
or explicit assertion of the epochality of a particular space (nation, community,
society) as providing the dominant horizon for identity and identification is a
primary mark of postcolonial literature, while the oscillatory structure of strangerhood and its problematic relation to spatial epochality is one area that allows
diasporic writing both to overlap and to be sharply distinguished from postcolonialism. We shall have more to say on this in the final part of this chapter, when we
contrast the work of J.M. Coetzee and Toni Morrison as exemplars of postcolonial
and diasporic writing respectively.

The task of identifying the terms of our practical seminar must also include
revisiting the conditions under which postcolonial literatures were first studied and
indeed introduced into the curriculum. Ever since the early stages of postcolonial
literary studies, traceable to the now much-criticized model of Commonwealth
Literature that took off in the 1960s, and to the work of colonial discourse analysis
signaled especially by Edward Said's *Orientalism* of 1978, the field has been marked
by a number of key issues and interests. While journals such as the *Journal of Commonwealth Literature* (established 1964), *ARIEL* (1970), and later *Kunapipi* (1979)

and *Wasafiri* (1984) focused on what were considered shared features of literatures of the newly independent postcolonial nations, this first push at literary history was soon overtaken by the tendency toward the exemplification of a national or hemispheric consciousness.[4] Comparativism was much sought after but rarely achieved in the early works that inaugurated the field. But perhaps the most important feature of this early phase of Commonwealth literary study was that the historical contextualization of literature turned on grasping a largely inert background of cultural and other particulars, thus allowing the literatures from places such as, say, Nigeria, India, or Jamaica to be explained exclusively in terms of anthropological, social, political and other contextual historical details all framed within a largely unquestioned model of nation. In fact, this was installed as the key organizational principle of Commonwealth literature anthologies, with entries first placed under regional or hemispheric rubrics such as "Africa," "Asia," and "the Caribbean" and then subdivided further under nation-states, such as Kenya, Pakistan, and Trinidad (see, e.g., Thieme 1996; Walder 1998). With the publication of Said's *Orientalism* context was no longer a question of discrete historical details, but rather of the discursive ensemble of institutions, symbols, and ideas that infused presumed literary backgrounds. However, if the model of Commonwealth literature seemed to have had no place in it for contemplating the diasporic and transnational character of the social relations that were being formed in the very heyday of its original formation in the late 1960s and early 1970s, postcolonial literary study was not to fare much better. For both incarnations of the study of world literature from former colonies did not take into account the implications of mobility and movement for understanding the literary imagination. It is a telling irony that even as the nation-state was being installed as the privileged horizon for understanding the literatures of the postcolonial world, the populations that postcolonialism is exercised about have established a steady and increasingly widespread process of migration, starting from the threshold of independence onwards. Thus, from 1948 the *Empire Windrush* was to inaugurate the British practice of looking to the Caribbean and its former colonies for labor to help in postwar rebuilding. This new influx came to layer the already existing multicultural communities of places such as Liverpool, which had had a steady community of black and Asian sailors since the end of the nineteenth century (see Nassy Brown 2005; Carina Ray 2009). Instructively, there have been more African-born Africans migrating to the United States annually since 1970 than the annual average for the entire 400-year period of slavery. This amazing fact was posted on Barack Obama's campaign web site during the Democratic Party presidential nomination contest in 2008, but had previously been given wide circulation from an article by Sam Roberts (2005) published in the *New York Times*.[5] Similar figures can be cited for population movements out of South Asia, Latin America, and the Caribbean for the same period, all of which are areas prominent in postcolonial studies. While by the 1990s postcolonial studies had fully embraced terms such as hybridity, transnationalism, and in-betweenness and disavowed the main weaknesses inherent to Commonwealth literature, it did not attempt a systematic incorporation of the idea of diaspora into its model of theorizing literatures from the formerly colonized world. To put it starkly, postcolonial literary study is still in thrall to extant forms of methodological nationalism.

Colonial Space-Making and Its Impact on Diasporas

To be sure, the most recent phase of global population circulation from the formerly colonized world is not the most remarkable in human history. As discussed in the Introduction to this volume (CHAPTER 1), scholars of colonialism and empire generally concede that the period from the sixteenth century represents the largest movement of human population in history, with some estimates as high as 60 million for the period. With the entire world population standing at 1.2 bn by 1850, the population dispersals from the sixteenth century onward then represent a dramatic movement of the world's population stock. The population movements that took place in the period are however normally reported in segments, and focus either on the emigration of Europeans to other parts of the world, or on the forced movement of African labor into the New World during the phase of slavery, or on the transverse migrations around the edges of empire, such as between Australia and New Zealand or India and Canada. It was not until the 1905 census of the British empire that we get a collective picture for the first time of many of these population dispersals. And it is only when we take all these dispersals together, as opposed to piecemeal or separately, that we get a labile picture of world history from the perspective of mobility and circulation. In fact, as we shall see shortly, population dispersal appears to have been a central plank of colonial governmentality and space-making. Space-making itself involved not just the constitution of a geographically demarcated political reality but was first and foremost the projection of a series of sociopolitical dimensions onto geographic space. These sociopolitical dimensions involved society and politics as well as economy, culture, and a wide range of symbolic and discursive practices. Colonial space-making is thus to be understood in terms of the relations that were structurally generated and contested across interrelated vectors throughout the colonial encounter, with population dispersal being central to the entire process (for earlier and fuller accounts of the history of the term postcolonialism and its relation to space and space-making, see Quayson 2012a, 2012b). Bearing in mind the caveat that while diasporization was central to colonial space-making there were also many configurations of colonial space that were not mutually exclusive but rather mixed and overlapped in specific local contexts, we are then able to set out a typology of colonial space-making from which to identify the historical sources of different kinds of postcolonial/diasporic representations:[6]

(1) *Formal colonialism in ex-trading outposts.* This involved the direct establishment of colonial administrative and bureaucratic arrangements and the conversion of what were initially trade outposts into colonialism proper, as in much of Africa, India, and Southeast Asia.

(2)   *Colonialism in ex-plantation societies.* The transformation of ex-plantation societies into colonialism proper differed from place to place such as in Sri Lanka (coffee), Brazil, Jamaica, the Dominican Republic and much of the Caribbean (sugar), and Malaysia (rubber). All such contexts also involved the mixing of variant populations transferred from different parts of the world, in some instances producing tensions that may still be felt today. The literature of former plantation economies refracts these interracial and political realities, and we read about these in the novels of V.S. Naipaul, George Lamming, K.K. Seet, Jean Rhys, Jamaica Kincaid, K.S. Maniam, and Lloyd Fernando, among various others. In the case of Malaysia, to take one of the most fascinating examples, all Anglophone writing is produced by the migrant Chinese and Indian minorities that were brought into the country as laborers in the nineteenth century and that subsequently coalesced into distinctive communities by the middle of the twentieth. As Rajeev Patke (2013) notes, the colonial policy of educating Malays only in their native language but reserving English for the Chinese and the Indians meant that at independence in 1965 the declaration of Malay as national language immediately peripheralized the migrant communities. For French Mauritius, on the other hand, the roughly 25,000 Indian indentured laborers that arrived on the island came to encounter autochthonous groups as well as African slaves. Along with the evolution of a distinct language called Kreol, the hybrid cultural mixture that has developed on the island since the nineteenth century has not obliterated acute ethno-cultural dichotomies (Allen 2006; Prabhu 2007).

(3)   *Settler colonialism.* From the fifteenth century Europeans set out steadily on journeys to different parts of the world, originally to escape the economic and social vagaries of Europe, but subsequently transforming into settler colonies. This process was to impact especially on southern Africa, Canada, Australia, and Latin America, with Ireland arguably providing a test case of settler colonialism within Europe itself. In all such settler colonies the descendants of settlers developed an ambiguous love/hate relationship with the mother country on the one hand, and to the indigenous populations they encountered on the other. The literatures of settler colonies bear traces of these ambiguities and tensions and suggest a different disposition of postcolonial literary history from the previous colonial examples we have suggested. As Robert Young points out in a trenchant review of postcolonial studies (2012), the dynamics of settler colonial relations have not been properly attended to in the present configuration of the field. Without a doubt a diaspora perspective must also be coupled to one from postcolonial studies to provide comprehensive tools for the incorporation of settler colonialism into the field.

(4)   *Migration and diaspora in metropolitan Europe.* Setting aside the European population dispersals that took place from the fifteenth century onward, in the period of the consolidation of formal colonialism,[7] the population dispersals that took place were, if not deliberately intended policies of colonial governance (as with the settling of London's black poor in Sierra Leone (1786–1791), or the transportation of indentured South Asian and Chinese labor into East Africa and the Caribbean (1850s–1920s)), then definitely an unforeseen consequence of colonial policy and

of decolonization (as with the 1947 Partition of India and Pakistan and the traumatic dispersals that took place following that). All these processes, along with the transatlantic slave trade (1550s–1850s), have served to expand the original application of the term *diaspora* from the classic cases of Jews, Armenians, and Greeks to include other cultures (Cohen 2008; Dufoix 2008). As was noted in the Introduction to this volume, the term diaspora has also come to be applied to various other constituencies in both scholarly discourse and popular parlance. The politically spasmodic form of the nation-state has also been responsible for processes of dispersal and diasporization. First in nineteenth-century Europe and then in the postcolonial period, large population movements have been triggered by the sometimes peculiarly exclusionary and incoherent form of the nation-state. If the dispersal of Jews from Eastern Europe in the modern period was a direct result of their being considered as anomalous subjects/citizens of Russia, Poland, and then Germany as these countries were fissured and reconstituted in the nineteenth century,[8] then the nation-states of the Third World were also to generate mass migrations due to the economic hardships that afflicted them from the 1970s onwards. The root causes of the two migrations – Jewish and Third World – are by no means equivalent, yet it is useful to study both from a conjoined postcolonial and diaspora studies perspective to ensure that such movements do not come to serve the interests of hegemonic compartmentalization. Frantz Fanon was to note in *Black Skin, White Masks* that three quarters of Algerian Jewry acted as the "eyes and ears of the Revolution," thus firmly bringing together "diasporic Jewry and the history of anti-Semitism with the colonial struggle and anti-Black Racism" (Cheyette 2005: 75) and suggesting that all oppression must generate common cause rather than atomization. With specific respect to today's Europe we find that Britain, Germany, France, and The Netherlands may productively be understood as themselves being postcolonialized by internal diasporas from their erstwhile margins. From Samuel Selvon to Zadie Smith, Calixthe Beyala to Alain Mabanckou, Duallo Misipo to Zé do Rock (Claudio Marshulat) there is no shortage of examples of diasporic writing in Britain, France, and Germany respectively that allow us to see them and Europe in general as postcolonial (Lennox 2012; McLeod 2012).

The Diasporic Imaginary

Now to the diasporic imaginary[9] as an aspect of our practical seminar. As Daniel Barber suggests (2011: 54–64), a central dialectic of the diasporic condition is that between integrity and discontinuity encapsulated in the form of deterritorialization. From the early Greek etymological roots of the term *diaspora* – scattering over – through to the various categories of diasporization provided by Cohen (2008), Dufoix (2008), Sheffer (2003), and various others, diasporas have always implied a shifting set of relationships between different spaces and distances. Subjectivity is no longer tied exclusively to the immediacy of present location but rather extends to encompass all the other places of co-ethnic identification. Diasporic forms of social relations are especially intensified in the era of the internet and of social networking. Something happens to a co-ethnic in one part of the world and this is immediately put on Facebook, or Tweeted, or placed on an email list to ensure that other co-ethnics may know and relate to what has happened in a distant place (Hiller and Franz 2004). The increased interrelationality of social spaces in today's world is accounted for in the social sciences by the now widespread terminology of transnationalism such as transnational circuits, networks, social fields, and social spaces (see CHAPTER 1). And yet these terms do not divulge to us the affective economy of diaspora.

The affective economy of diaspora may be gleaned through a variety of instruments. Material objects such as private heirlooms and public monuments of various kinds encapsulate such an affective economy while songs, rituals, and stories provide narrative shape and justification. Depending on how the sense of the affective economy is expressed, it may become an instrument of mobilization and serve to define terms for the diasporic population. In W.E.B Du Bois' *Souls of Black Folk* (1903), for instance, the function of nostalgia is by no means limited to the imagining of a lost Africa. Rather, by drawing on the historical and sociological condition of black people in America Du Bois redefines their aspirations and expectations of an American modernity. Another means of gauging the affective economy is from ascertaining the degree to which the diaspora incorporates and responds to the interdiction against return (see Cohen 2008; Clifford 1997). Strictly speaking it is only where people have been dispersed due to violent political events such as invasion, occupation, or the coming-to-dominance of forms of exclusionary politics that the label of *victim diasporas* is justified. History is replete with examples of these, the classic cases being the Jews after the destruction of the Second Temple by the Romans in 70 CE, the Armenians following the Turkish genocide of 1915, and the Palestinians of our more modern times. But the interdiction against return may also operate under other guises, such as in the direct effect of long spatial distance from the homeland, or in extreme cases, when the homeland ceases to exist entirely, as was the case with certain parts of Lebanon when the geography of the region was divided and reorganized by Britain and France on the final collapse of the Ottoman empire in 1915. The Kurds, scattered across Turkey, Iraq, and Iran, represent another population whose claim to a unified homeland has to be negotiated across different nation-state spaces. Sometimes, as in the case of second- and third-generation survivors of the Jewish Holocaust described by Marianne Hirsch (1997), the homeland can never be returned to because it has either been obliterated or so exhaustively saturated with the negative memories of the traumatic events that took place there as to disavow any easy and untrammeled access to that space in the present. She terms this phenomenon the "post-memory of exile." Significantly, however, the interdiction against return may act as a means to memorial plenitude rather than aridity: "The deep sense of displacement suffered by the children of exile, the elegiac aura of the memory of a place to which one cannot return, creates, in my experience, a strange sense of plenitude rather than a feeling of absence" (Hirsch 1997: 422). We must assume, then, that the stronger the interdiction against return to the homeland, the more profound will be the affective economy for the relevant diaspora. Finally, the affective economy of diaspora may be used to refer to the problematic processes by which the homeland is inserted into the domain of consumption in the form of tourism, archeological sites, the sale of memorabilia, and the circulation of various tokens that signify attachment to the homeland.

While the fields of visual and material culture may be studied for clues to the diasporic imaginary (and these indeed are the subjects of Hirsch's *The Generation of Postmemory*, 2012), it seems to me that the domain of literature must be given privilege for the manner by which it binds affect to questions of ontology in both the content and form of narration. Whether in the genres of children's stories, folk tales, biblical accounts of the enigmas of rupture and arrival (*The Book of Exodus*), the *yizker bikher* or memorial books of the shtetls, or in the literary writings of Toni Morrison, S.G. Sebald, Amos Oz, Hanif Kureishi, Jhumpa Lahiri, Junot Diaz, and various others, the diasporic imaginary is encapsulated in a set of complex relationships between form, content, and affective economies. For the heuristic purposes of this chapter, however, I would like to isolate for discussion three elements that I consider to be central to the diasporic imaginary in literature, namely place, nostalgia, and what I want to term *genealogical accounting*.[10] We should acknowledge immediately that the categories of place and nostalgia are not exclusive to the diasporic imaginary, while genealogical accounting, on the other hand, must be taken as constitutive. It is important to note, also, that it is the overall configuration of all three elements that allows us to establish the character of the diasporic imaginary. In that respect, depending on the precise nature of the configuration of elements, some texts may be asserted to be strongly diasporic, while others may only be noted as expressing the diasporic imaginary in an attenuated form.

Within the diasporic imaginary the question of identity – Who am I? – is necessarily entangled with that of place – What is this place, and how does it affect who I am? (Massey 1994; for a more phenomenological view, see also Malpas 1999). This calls to mind Barber's (2011) point about the dialectical relationship in diaspora between integrity and discontinuity. Apart from the fact that for the diasporic, *this* place is always in some form of dialectical relation to *that place* and to an *elsewhere*, the dialectical relation may in certain instances produce breaches in the commonplace, an *unheimlich* of place, as it were. The *unheimlich* or "unhomeliness" of place is undergirded by the fraught dynamic of the links between ideas of homeland and host nation that take as their theater the *mind of the beholder* (i.e., the diasporic individual or community) in negotiating the present. For Sidra DeKoven Ezrahi (2000), writing about the themes of exile and homecoming in the modern Jewish imagination, this dynamic has historically produced affective attachments to simulacra of the original Jerusalem destroyed in 70 CE. The simulacra sometimes have entailed the amalgamation of elements from different diasporic locations ("little Jerusalems") that then interact with the idea of the homeland to produce different affective investments in the places of sojourn as well as supporting imagined utopias

(Ezrahi 2000: 36, 90–92, 153–155). For the African American community, Pharaonic Egypt and Ethiopia have provided sites for the production of simulacra. Given that the Africans who were sent to the New World came from diverse cultural and religious backgrounds, the race pride preached by versions of Afrocentrism had to be entirely dependent upon asserting the discursive value of such simulacra (for a useful evaluation and critique of Afrocentrism, see Howe 1998). It would thus be impossible to grasp the relationship between homeland and host nation solely through the exhaustive itemization of policies, rules, and regulations; that is the domain of a brute sociology. Rather, it is the way these rules impact upon the consciousness of the individual in their process of self-fashioning and the interruptions or otherwise that he or she experiences that help to shape a diasporic imaginary.

Overlapping markedly with the concept of space, nostalgia nonetheless turns out to be a highly elusive concept. Svetlana Boym (2001) has suggested that nostalgia is a primary condition of modernity itself. The idea that the present is always thought to be somehow a diversion from a past that was better than it emerges most strongly in the early modern period, especially in the lives of soldiers stationed away from home. As Boym puts it (2001: 5), from at least the seventeenth century, "nostalgia was not merely an individual anxiety but a public threat that revealed the contradictions of modernity and acquired greater political importance." What makes nostalgia relevant for our definitional purposes, however, is the fact that it is intimately tied to a sense of displacement, and that this displacement is foundational to the constitution of diasporic identity. Furthermore, as we have just noted with reference to Marianne Hirsch, it is possible to experience nostalgia for a place one has never encountered, in the form of a "post-memory" of exile.[11] The desire for a lost or even unknown landscape generates both constraints and possibilities for the imaginary. For many diasporics, nostalgia may be expressed not solely in relation to a particular landscape, but rather with respect to the form of social relationships centred by that landscape. Eva Hoffman captures the point adroitly in the first part of *Lost in Translation* (1989: 74–75):

No, I'm no patriot, nor was I ever allowed to be. And yet, the country of my childhood lives within me with a primacy that is a form of love. . . . All it has given me is the world, but that is enough. It has fed me language, perceptions, sounds, the human kind. It has given me the colors and the furrows of reality, my first loves. The absoluteness of those loves can never be recaptured: no geometry of the landscape, no haze in the air, will live in us as intensely as the landscapes that we saw as the first, and to which we gave ourselves wholly, without reservations. Later, of course, we learn how to be more parsimonious: how to parse ourselves into constituent elements, how to be less indiscriminate and foolish in our enthusiasms. But if we're not to risk falling into that other absurd, in which we come unpeeled from all the objects of the world, and they all seem equally two-dimensional and stale, we must somehow preserve the memory and the possibility of our childish, absurd affections. Insofar as we retain the capacity for attachment, the energy of desire that draws us toward the world and makes us want to live within it, we're always returning. All we have to draw on is that

first potent furnace, the uncomparing, ignorant love, the original heat and hunger for
the forms of the world, for the here and now.

Note certain keywords: language, perceptions, sounds, colors, reality, and love. The
passage itself speaks to a sense of completeness that is provided by these childhood
memories, something which, as she points out, is often compromised by the growing
necessity to stem one's enthusiasm for unmediated experience. The similarity of the
sentiments raised here to Wordsworth's famous "spots of time" in *The Prelude* is
quite telling and not entirely accidental. Hoffman points out that she picks up from
her Polish education "notions about flair, and panache, and sparks of inspiration –
tonalities of character that are the true Polish values, and that are encouraged by
my peers and my schoolteachers, not to speak of the Romantic Poetry we read"
(p. 71). We must note, however, that the passage is also a signifier of estrangement,
for even as she is expressing the intensification of her perspectival sensorium in
relation to Cracow, the aestheticization is also a means of severing the landscape of
her childhood from the framework of a traumatic Jewish history. This is actually
conscious and strategic, for later on in the narrative she makes an explicit identification with the style of Vladimir Nabokov, whom she assumes to have been able to
parenthesize his native Russia in order to be able to write freely about his own
experience. As Hoffman puts it (p. 197):

> I wish I could breathe a Nabokovian air. I wish I could have the Olympian freedom
> of sensibility that disdains, in his autobiography, to give the Russian Revolution more
> than a passing mention, as if such common events did not have the power to wreak
> fundamental changes in his own life, or as if it were vulgar, tactless, to dwell on
> something so brutishly, so crudely collective.

Similar devices of aestheticization are also deployed to great effect in the first part
of Anton Shammas' *Arabesques*; this may in its turn be distinguished from Mourid
Barghouti's *I saw Ramallah*, where although he is also writing about Palestine
Barghouti aims for a stark realism to show how little the Occupied Territories have
changed since his departure thirty years previously. In Amy Tan's *Joy Luck Club*, on
the other hand, the nostalgia for the homeland inheres in the form of nuggets of
Chinese wisdom that the mothers try to bequeath to their daughters through storytelling in America but which the children resolutely refuse, while for the people
in Hanuman House in V.S. Naipaul's *A House for Mr Biswas*, it is the enforced daily
puja rituals and what the Trinidadian Indian characters mistakenly consider to be
authentic borrowings from the Indian homeland that defines the terrain of nostalgia
for the them. Biswas finds this a source of extreme constriction rather than freedom,
and rebels accordingly. Yet even if he disavows the nostalgia represented in the daily
rituals he still struggles against the homelessness that his essentially nomadic condition defines so that his quest for a house for himself becomes a forward projection
of the nostalgia for an elusive domestic stability. As a final example, in Saidiya Hart-

man's *Lose Your Mother* (2004), her memoirs based on research on slavery in Ghana as a Fulbright scholar, the nostalgia comes from her choice of the dungeon, as opposed to the ancestral village, as inaugurating black diasporic identity. The choice, however, requires her to position all her interlocutors – her brother, various African Americans that have relocated to the homeland, and the several Ghanaians she meets in the course of her research – into a strict grid of ethical positions since they are all required by her to assert their relation to the originary moment of slave trauma. Clearly nostalgia in this instance is contaminated by the perception of the real inequalities that afflict black America today, thus unfolding into a single affective domain the dissatisfactions of the present time into the recognition of the trauma of the past. *Lose Your Mother* is remarkable for containing very little camaraderie and no laughter in a land that is abundant with both.

The third and to my mind most important element for defining the diasporic imaginary is genealogical accounting. A Hassidic story is told of a 4-year-old who keeps badgering his parents to allow him to have a quiet word alone with his 6-month-old baby sister. After much persistence, the parents let him into his sister's room one evening but eavesdrop anxiously behind the closed door to see what he might be up to. The little boy bends toward his sister and whispers to her earnestly: "I need you to tell me where we came from, because I am beginning to forget."[12] Genealogical accounting involves questions of ancestry, ethnicity, tradition, and culture and provides a distinguishing past to the person or community. Almost without fail, genealogical accounting also involves stories of the "how-we-got-here" variety, sometimes with detailed descriptions of the journey itself on foot, by ship, plane, train, and other means of transport. The "we" in the formulation just provided is not limited exclusively to the nuclear family unit but encompasses the stories of other figures such as aunts, uncles, cousins, and an extensive panoply of relations and acquaintances. Thus the genealogical accounting also produces a nexus of affiliations such that the fate of one person is seen to be inextricably tied to the fate of all others of the same group. Since family establishes the primary set of affective relationships for the individual, it is the genealogical accounting that provides the link between the individual and the entire community of co-ethnics, whether in the same location or further afield. The genealogical accounting may sometimes be expressed in the form of quest motif, where discovery is meant to restore the diasporic to a form of epistemological certainty about their identity. The form of the quest is rarely, if at all, pre-given, but has to be unearthed through acts of attentiveness and labor. The quest thematic of genealogical accounting is what we see in "Paul Bereyter," a short story in W.G. Sebald's *The Emigrants*, while in *Interpreter of Maladies* Jhumpa Lahiri mediates the theme through the eyes of a bewildered Indian child watching the drama of the violent birth of Bangladesh unfold on TV with her family and their Pakistani guest in "Mr Prizada Came to Dine." The detailing of the journey and the stories of how-we-got-here also perform the formal mnemonic function of defining the conceptual distance between the diasporic and the non-diasporics with whom they are required to interact. Finally, the genealogical accounting introduces a form of ethical imperative that is incorporated into the recognition of the past. Sometimes, as in the Jewish tradition of the Pesach or Passover prayer, the ethical imperative is incorporated as a central aspect of the ritual recalling the passage from the homeland into exile.

A question now presses itself to our attention, which we will have to attend to in a somewhat provisional manner before going on to discuss the distinctions to be drawn between postcolonial and diasporic literatures. The question turns on the differences that may be perceived between diasporic writing on the one hand, and exilic literature on the other. For even though it might be argued that these are cognates of each other, a conceptual distinction is important so as not to confuse the different emphases deployed in the two kinds of writing. To start with, all foundational narratives of exile involve destruction of the place called home, "or its being rendered illegitimate and contaminated, or taken over by conquerors and rival claimants" (Seidel 1986: 8). This is so close to the definition of victim diasporas as to make the two conditions practically indistinguishable, except of course that not all diasporas are generated out of violent conditions of dispersal. In other instances, however, exile is a chosen condition, particularly for intellectuals, writers, and artists who may feel that their homelands have erected too many constraints against their artistic self-realization. Even though it is the Bible that provides the most exhaustive typology of exilic conditions, from a strictly secular perspective by far the most sustained exploration of the condition is provided in Greek tragedy, where the condition of exile was termed *eremia*, variously glossed as solitude, wilderness, or uninhabited region. In texts as varied as Aeschylus' *Prometheus Bound* and *The Libation Bearers*, Sophocles' *Oedipus at Colonus*, *Ajax*, and *Philoctetes*, and Euripides' *Medea*, the condition of *eremia* or exile is given center stage. The twentieth century gives us many examples of writers who have adopted exile as a choice of being in the world, including James Joyce, Samuel Beckett, Eugene Ionesco, and Edward Said, among many others (see especially Papastergiadis 1993). We may then suggest that, since diasporas normally represent a more complex set of conditions of dispersal and sojourn that transcend those of exile, exilic literature be seen as a subset of diasporic writing and not necessarily coterminous with it.

The Same Difference? Postcolonial and Diasporic Literatures

Whereas many postcolonial texts may easily be read under the rubric of the diasporic imaginary, there is still a sharp distinction to be drawn between postcolonial and diasporic literature. But why is this so? Why does the work of say Wole Soyinka, J.M. Coetzee, and Gabriel Garcia Marquez fall exclusively under the rubric of postcolonialism, while that of Sam Selvon, Zadie Smith, Junot Diaz, or Toni Morrison fall securely under the rubric of diasporic literature? Since their work comfortably occupies the two domains Salman Rushdie and to some extent V.S. Naipaul appear to unsettle these dichotomies. But even with Rushdie, there is a sense that the nation-state performs the function of a performative epochality and that it is the oscillation between its repeated affirmations and its dissolution by way of heightened narrative experimentations that allows us to read him as an exemplary *griot* of the Indian condition as well as a diasporic writer. In elaborating a complex diasporic and transnational aesthetic in the course of his career, Rushdie has maintained a long-standing interest in moments of epochality as a creative inspiration for his best writing, whether the birth of India in *Midnight's Children*, of Pakistan in *Shame*, or of Islam in the *Satanic Verses*. However, after the infamous fatwa of 1989 Rushdie turned decisively away from the trope of the epochal, nation-state-inflected or not. He deploys a somewhat attenuated form of it in *The Moor's Last Sigh*, and by *The Ground beneath Her Feet* has abandoned the trope altogether. *Fury, Shalimar the Clown*, and *The Enchantress of Florence* have nothing epochal in them, but his latest, *Luka and the Fire of Life*, reprises the terrific storytelling for young adults of which he showed himself a master twenty years earlier in *Haroun and the Sea of Stories*.

A comparison of the oeuvre of J.M. Coetzee with that of Toni Morrison helps us come to a better understanding of the differences between postcolonial and diasporic literature. We should note, however, that the two authors have a number of features in common. First is that they both engage with the dialectics of place, such that to Coetzee's *In the Heart of the Country* or *Disgrace* we may readily pose Toni Morrison's *Jazz* or *Tar Baby*, all of which are place-centered in the extreme. Both writers also regularly touch on questions of embodiment and disability, such that to Coetzee's *The Life and Times of Michael K* and *Slow Man* we can readily pose Toni Morrison's *Sula* or *The Bluest Eye*. Some of Coetzee's novels even have a strong nostalgia for the past, as in say *Waiting for the Barbarians* and *In the Heart of the Country* and yet this nostalgia is never connected to an "elsewhere" conceived of as a homeland different from that of the present. In Coetzee the past may be better than the present, but it is not another country. In other words, nostalgia in Coetzee is a product of temporality rather than of spatiality. Furthermore, in Coetzee the crises that afflict his central protagonists are usually crises of a highly individualized kind. His characters rarely, if ever, bear a communal consciousness. Even though the works of other canonical postcolonial writers generally have heroes of a communal inflection, the central aspect of nostalgia connecting to time as opposed to place still applies. Thus in Soyinka's *Death and the King's Horseman* or Achebe's *Arrow of God*, or Marquez's *One Hundred Years of Solitude*, the central protagonists bear a heightened communal consciousness, and indeed a nostalgia for a pristine order of things. But this nostalgia is connected to an ideal of nation (with a small "n") as opposed to a sense of epic displacement from a clearly conceived homeland. And with other postcolonial writers such as Ngugi wa Thiongo, Ivan Vladislavic, Yvonne Vera, Dambudzo Marechera, Raja Rao, and Naguib Mahfouz, we get a strong nation-and-narration orientation that precludes their work from being considered under the rubric of diaspora at all. This contrasts dramatically with Morrison's novels, where in almost every instance nostalgia is spatialized as a place that has been lost and whose retrieval is the subject of utopian yearnings and constructions.

However, the real difference that marks one writer as postcolonial and the other as a writer of diaspora lies in the nature of the genealogical accounting that they illustrate in their novels.[13] In Coetzee, genealogical accounting is practically non-existent. There are no stories of the where-we-came-from variety. Contrastively, for Toni Morrison, even though she displays the thematic of genealogical accounting in an attenuated form in the early novels, such as *The Bluest Eye, Sula, Tar Baby*, and *Jazz*, the terms of how that thematic would later be elaborated are set in a quite strong way as early as *Song of Solomon* (1978). *Song of Solomon* is explicitly about the young African American Milkman Dead's quest for his African roots. He is put up to this by his aunt Pilate, a veritable spiritual *griot* in the African tradition if ever there was one. *Beloved*, the best known of Morrison's novels, is notable for staging the recovery of genealogical accounting as a way of coming to terms with the trauma of infanticide and slavery, while *Paradise* elaborates such narratives as part of the unsettling ideological matrix that supports the exclusive African American breaka-way community of Ruby. Her novel *Love* represents a hiatus from this thematic, with the genealogical accounting going back to the attenuated form evident in her earliest novels; but with *A Mercy* she returns to that mode with full force and this time even incorporates the accounts of a Native American character recalling the collective past of his people. The genealogical accounting that we find in various forms everywhere in her novels is one of the distinctive signatures of Toni Morrison's writings and allows us to see her clearly as a diasporic rather than a postcolonial or even exclusively an American writer. Forms of genealogical accounting can be seen seen in all the diasporic texts that we have named for illustration in this chapter. There is practically no text that presents itself as diasporic that does not have a form of genealogical accounting in it.

What then are the elements of the practical seminar that Auerbach wrote about several decades ago? An expansion of the historical sense and properly taking account of the contributions of diasporas to world history is fundamental. The accounts of diasporas that have been given to us by an army of social scientists, though useful, must be explored for ways to translate sociological categories into an understanding of the themes of loss, recovery, and identity that define the many different spaces and spheres of identification for the diasporic. The ultimate task, however, is to tarry with the terms of the literary text itself, to understand the nar-rative whorls and whirls and from these to see the ways in which ordinary people's struggle between integrity and discontinuity, attachment and disaffiliation may provide us handy windows for understanding the variegated world in which we live and how to live in it.

Acknowledgment

I want to say a special thanks to Anna Shternshis, my colleague at the Centre for Diaspora and Transnational Studies at the University of Toronto for reading through a draft version of this chapter and for providing generous comments.

Notes

1 On thoughtful contributions to the question of the worldliness of literature, see Gayatri Spivak (2003); Pascale Casanova (2004); David Damrosch (2003); Franco Moretti (2000); Emily Apter (2006). None of these, however, deploy a diasporic lens to their subject matter. And at the same time, the most trenchant critiques of postcolonialism that have emerged since its inception, such as those by E. San Juan Jr (2000), Benita Parry (2004), Aijaz Ahmad (2008), and Neil Lazarus (2010), have been mainly about the ethical implications of obscurantism, especially in the earliest forms of postcolonial theory, and also for its apparent disavowal of Marxism. None of these touched on what was the fundamental disjuncture between postcolonialism and diaspora.

2 Independence is itself an extremely problematic category for dating postcolonialism and its subject matters. The reason is that, strictly speaking, there are actually many dates that might be taken to inaugurate a postcolonial analysis (in the sense of coming "after" independence). For more on this, see Quayson (2012b).

3 Subaltern studies historiography was to provide a useful critique of nationalist historiography, but really from the perspective of non-elite actors, who they argued were responsible for reinterpreting nationalism in fundamentally new and significant ways. See Guha and Spivak (1988).

4 The reading of the main phases of postcolonial literary history to be seen in journals in the field is indebted to the superb piece by Ira Raja and Deepika Bahri (2012).

5 See also "The US foreign-born population: Trends and selected characteristics," at http://www.fas.org/sgp/crs/misc/R41592.pdf, accessed February 6, 2013; and "Profile of selected demographic and social characteristics: 2000, people born in Africa," at http://www.census.gov/population/cen2000/stp-159/STP-159-africa.pdf, accessed February 6, 2013.

6 The list here is only a shorthand for much more complicated distinctions between colonies, dominions, and protectorates, predominantly of the British empire. For a more complex picture, see the very helpful guide and explanation to the holdings of the Colonial Records Office in London, compiled by Mandy Banton (2008), and A.N. Porter (1991).

7 The period of formal colonialism may be taken to stretch from the date of the establishment of the reconstituted Colonial Office in 1854 to the end of World War II in 1945. See Banton (2008).

8 Jews were granted citizenship in Germany, France, and other West European countries in the nineteenth century. However in the Russian empire, they were subjects (not citizens), and were not granted full rights until after the Russian Revolution. So in the Russian empire up to the early twentieth century they were not anomalous citizens, but rather not citizens at all. Special thanks to Anna Shternshis for pointing out this historical nuance to me.

9 Brian Axel (2002) has a fascinating use of the term *diasporic imaginary* which is nevertheless quite different from what we seek to elaborate here. Focusing primarily on the case of the Sikh diaspora, he argues that the elaboration of Sikh subjectivity is not tied to a homeland at all, since the "homeland" of Khalistani was only an idea that was never allowed to materialize, but is rather constituted through the violence that is visited upon the bodies of Sikhs in India. An elaborate discourse of martyrdom and trauma is generated around the pictures of Sikhs who have been violently tortured and killed by the Indian government. These maimed rites then serve to constitute a distinct Sikh subjectivity. As

Axel puts it (2002: 426): "In my analysis of the Sikh diaspora, the homeland, as a utopian destination for Khalistani activism, is only one element of the diasporic imaginary – and, as such, must be understood as an affective and temporal process rather than a place." While I generally endorse the view that the homeland is not only a place but is also constituted through an affective economy, I would like to part ways with Axel on the fundamental ground that not all diasporas are created or even maintained through the violence of another entity (in this case the state of India). Vijay Mishra (2005) deploys the same term, drawing also on Lacanian theory, but in his case to illustrate the distinct formation of the Indian diaspora "old" and "new." The old Indian diaspora designates what we have described under the rubric of planter colonialism, while the new diaspora is part of the post-1960s era of globalization. Being an Indian from Fiji but residing and teaching in Australia, old and new coincide in unsettling ways in his own biography, thus allowing him to argue that the "homeland exists as an absence that acquires surplus meaning by the fact of diaspora" (2005: 2; see also Mishra 1996 for an earlier version of these reflections). This insightful proposition is elaborated more fully in Lorand Matory's *Black Atlantic Religion* (2005), where he argues, quite persuasively, that it was the returning African slaves from Bahia and those freed by the British from Sierra Leone coming back to western Nigeria in the nineteenth century that helped to constitute the Yoruba nation, and thus the homeland of their return. In Matory's argument the constitution of "Yorubanness" is a question of particular social dynamics as it is of the recursive religious practices of Candomblé/orisha worship.

10 I am using the singular formulation – genealogical accounting – only for rhetorical consistency because strictly speaking the longer a community has existed in the diaspora the more likely it will be that there are multiple, if not contradictory, forms of genealogical accounting. Genealogical accounting may also be differentiated in relation to class and gender, since these perspectives may dramatically alter the sense of what it is exactly that has been left behind.

11 Curiously enough, the field of consumer market research has also come up with the term *virtual nostalgia*, which is nostalgia for something one has never experienced before. This is used to great effect in generating desire for products. Ironically, many of these definitions come from market research (e.g., how to advertise products), but they do a great job classifying (some might say exploiting) nostalgia and its significance for one's identity. See for example Wallendorf and Arnould (1991), Holak and Havlena (1992), and Havlena and Holak (1996).

12 Eli Rubinstein recounted this beautiful story in a lecture at the University of Toronto titled "Stories to Heal a Broken World," March 30, 2011.

13 This also seems to be especially true for Yiddish literature, which is obsessed with genealogical accounting, both in terms of authors (Abramowitch is "literary grand-father" of Sholem Aleichem, and Peretz is the father of the literary family, etc.) as well as in novels themselves – fictional geography, connection between novels, and so on. Thanks again to Anna Shternshis for pointing this out to me.

References

Ahmad, A. 2008. *In Theory: Nations, Classes, Literatures*. London: Verso.

Allen, R. 2006. *Slaves, Freedmen and Indentured Laborers in Colonial Mauritius*. Cambridge: Cambridge University Press.

Apter, E. 2006. *The Translation Zone: A New Comparative Literature.* Princeton: Princeton University Press.

Auerbach, E. 1969. "Philology and *Weltliteratur*," trans. E. Said and M. Said. *The Centennial Review,* 13(1): 1–17. (Originally published 1952.)

Auerbach, E. 2003. *Mimesis: The Representation of Reality in Western Literature.* Princeton: Princeton University Press. (Originally published 1953.)

Axel, B.K. 2002. "The diasporic imaginary." *Public Culture* 14(2): 411–428.

Banton, M. 2008. *Administering Empire, 1801–1968,* 2nd edn. London: Institute of Historical Research. (Originally published 1994.)

Barber, D.C. 2011. *On Diaspora: Christianity, Religion, and Secularity.* Eugene, OR: Cascade Books.

Boym, S. 2001. *The Future of Nostalgia.* New York: Basic Books.

Casanova, P. 2004. *The Republic of Letters.* Boston, MA: Harvard University Press.

Cheyette, B. 2005. "Frantz Fanon and the black/Jewish imaginary." In M. Silverman (ed.) *Frantz Fanon's Black Skin, White Masks: New Interdisciplinary Essays,* pp. 74–99. Manchester: Manchester University Press.

Clifford, J. 1997. *Routes: Travel and Translation in the Late Twentieth Century.* Cambridge, MA: Harvard University Press.

Cohen, R. 2008. *Global Diasporas: An Introduction,* 2nd edn. London: Routledge. (First published 1996.)

Damrosch, D. 2003. *What is World Literature?* Princeton: Princeton University Press.

Du Bois, W.E.B. 1903. *The Souls of Black Folk.* Cambridge: Cambridge University Press.

Dufoix, S. 2008. *Diasporas,* trans. W. Rodamor. Berkeley: University of California Press.

Ezrahi, S.D. 2000. *Booking Passage: Exile and Homecoming in the Modern Jewish Imagination.* Berkeley: University of California Press.

Greenblatt, Stephen (ed.) 2010. *Cultural Mobility: A Manifesto.* Cambridge: Cambridge University Press.

Guha, R. and Spivak, G.C. (eds) 1988. *Selected Subaltern Studies.* Oxford: Oxford University Press.

Hartman, S. 2004. *Lose Your Mother: A Journey Along the Atlantic Slave Route.* New York: Farrar, Strauss & Giroux.

Havlena, W. and Holak, S. 1996. "Exploring nostalgia imagery using consumer collages." In K.P. Corfman and J. Lynch (eds) *Advances in Consumer Research,* pp. 35–42. Provo, UT: Association for Consumer Research, 1996.

Hiller, H. and Franz, T. 2004. "New ties, old ties and lost ties: the use of the internet in diaspora." *New Media and Society,* 6(6): 731–752.

Hirsch, M. 1997. "Past lives: Post-memories in exile." *Poetics Today,* 17(4): 659–686.

Hirsch, M. 2012. *The Generation of Postmemory: Writing and Visual Culture after the Holocaust.* Durham, NC: Duke University Press.

Hoffman, E. 1989. *Lost in Translation: Life in a New Language.* New York: Penguin.

Holak, S. and Havlena, W. 1992. "Nostalgia: an exploratory study of themes and emotions in the nostalgic experience." In J.F. Sherry Jr and B. Sternthal (eds) *Advances in Consumer Research.* Provo, UT: Association for Consumer Research.

Howe, S. 1998. *Afrocentrism: Mythical Pasts and Imagined Homes.* London: Verso.

Lazarus, N 2010. *The Postcolonial Unconscious.* Cambridge: Cambridge University Press.

Lennox, S. 2012. "Postcolonial writing in Germany." In A. Quayson (ed.) *The Cambridge History of Postcolonial Literature,* pp. 620–648. Cambridge: Cambridge University Press.

Malpas, J. 1999. *Place and Experience: A Philosophical Topography.* Cambridge: Cambridge University Press.

Massey, D. 1994. *Space, Place and Gender*. Minneapolis: Minnesota University Press.

Matory, L.J. 2005. *Black Atlantic Religion: Tradition, Transnationalism, and Matriarchy in the Afro-Brazilian Candomblé*. Princeton: Princeton University Press.

McLeod, J. 2012. "Postcolonial writing in Britain." In A. Quayson (ed.) *The Cambridge History of Postcolonial Literature*, Volume I. Cambridge: Cambridge University Press. 559–570.

Mishra, V. 1996. "The diasporic imaginary: Theorizing the Indian diaspora." *Textual Practice*, 10(3): 421–447.

Mishra, V. 2005. "The diasporic imaginary and the Indian diaspora." *Asian Studies Institute Occasional Lecture*, 2: 1–27. Wellington: Asian Studies Institute.

Moretti, F. 2000. "Conjectures on world literature." *New Left Review*, 1: 54–68.

Nassy Brown, J. 2005. *Dropping Anchor, Setting Sail: Geographies of Race in Black Liverpool*. Princeton: Princeton University Press.

Papastergiadis, N. 1993. *Modernity as Exile: The Figure of the Stranger in John Berger's Writing*. Cambridge: Cambridge University Press.

Parry, B. 2004. *Postcolonial Theory: A Materialist Critique*. London: Routledge.

Patke, R. 2013. "Postcolonial literature in Southeast Asia." In A. Quayson (ed.) *The Cambridge History of Postcolonial Literature*, Volume 1, pp. 352–384. Cambridge: Cambridge University Press.

Porter, A.N. (ed.) 1991. *Atlas of British Overseas Expansion*. London: Routledge.

Prabhu, A. 2007. *Hybridity: Limits, Transformations, Prospects*. New York: State University of New York Press.

Quayson, A. 2012a. "Introduction: Postcolonial literature in a changing historical frame." In A. Quayson (ed.) *The Cambridge History of Postcolonial Literature*, Volume 1, pp. 1–29. Cambridge; Cambridge University Press.

Quayson, A. 2012b. "Periods vrs concepts: Space making and the question of postcolonial literary history." *PMLA*, 127(2): 349–356.

Raja, I. and Bahri, D. 2012. "Key journals and institutions." In A. Quayson (ed.) *The Cambridge History of Postcolonial Literature*, Volume II, pp. 1151–1188. Cambridge: Cambridge University Press.

Ray, C. 2009. "'The white wife problem': Sex, race and the contested politics of repatriation to interwar British West Africa." *Gender and History*, 22(3): 628–646.

Roberts, S. 2005. "More Africans enter US than in the days of slavery." *New York Times*, February 21.

San Juan, E. Jr 2000. *Beyond Postcolonial Theory*. Basingstoke: Palgrave.

Seidel, M. 1986. *Exile and the Narrative Imagination*. New Haven: Yale University Press.

Sheffer, G. 2003. *Diaspora Politics*. Cambridge: Cambridge University Press.

Simmel, G. 1971. "The stranger." In D.N. Levine (ed.) *Georg Simmel: On Individuality and Social Forms*, pp. 143–149. Chicago: University of Chicago Press.

Spivak, G. 2003. *Death of a Discipline*. New York: Columbia University Press.

Thieme, J. 1996. *The Arnold Anthology of Post-Colonial Literatures in English*. London: Arnold.

Thomas, D. 2012. "Postcolonial writing in France." In A. Quayson (ed.) *The Cambridge History of Postcolonial Literature*, Volume I, pp. 604–619. Cambridge: Cambridge University Press.

Walder, D. 1998. *Post-Colonial Literatures in English: History, Language, Theory*. Oxford: Blackwell.

Wimmer, A. and Glick Schiller, N. 2002. "Methodological nationalism and beyond: Nation building, migration, and the social sciences." *Global Networks*, 2: 301–334.

Wallendorf, M. and Arnould, E.J. 1991. "'We gather today': Consumption rituals of Thanksgiving Day." *Journal of Consumer Research* 18(1): 13–31.

Young, R. 2012. "Postcolonial remains." *New Literary History* 43(1): 19–42.

Part II

Backgrounds and Perspectives

Chapter 9

Slavery, Indentured Labor, and the Making of a Transnational World

Emmanuel Akyeampong

Introduction

The multiculturalism and multiracialism that we have come to associate with the cosmopolitan modern society emerged from the flows of migrant labor between the sixteenth century and the end of the nineteenth century. Some of the flows were involuntary, such as African slavery to the New World from the sixteenth century. But slavery, the Asian and African indentured labor that replaced it from the 1830s, and the almost 50 million Europeans who migrated around the world over the long nineteenth century (c.1800–1914) were all propelled by the political economy of an emergent capitalism (Akyeampong 2000: 183–215; Northrup 1995). Labor moved towards sites of production involuntarily through capture and sale or voluntarily, sometimes by indenture, in search of greener pastures and fleeing economic misery. Slavery, diaspora, indentured labor, immigration have all intersected in the making of a transnational world. Our understanding of these historical processes has been deepened by more contemporary works that underscore the circularity of people, goods, and ideas even during the era of the export slave trade (Mann and Bay 2001). Matory (2005) has emphasized how Africa and its diaspora were not completely disconnected before the nineteenth century, and the need to view Atlantic communities as coeval contemporaries in historical time, building on Gilroy's (1993) concept of the "black Atlantic" connected by the ship. The result has been to link diaspora and transnationalism in the emphasis on circularity, and to push back historically the phenomenon of transnationalism or the ability of individuals to maintain simultaneously social networks in two different societies or worlds. This

A Companion to Diaspora and Transnationalism, First Edition.
Edited by Ato Quayson and Girish Daswani.
© 2013 Blackwell Publishing Ltd. Published 2013 by Blackwell Publishing Ltd.

chapter reviews the place of slavery and indentured labor in the making of a transnational world.

African Slavery in an Age of Modernity

Associating slavery and modernity sounds contradictory, considering how modernity has come to privilege free labor. But free labor as we understand it today, "voluntary labor not subject to legal compulsion" (Steinfield 1991: 13), is primarily a nineteenth-century invention, and before the nineteenth century free labor was not the dominant or natural form of labor. It is striking that African slavery to the New World would develop in the early modern period when slavery was in decline in Europe, displaced by serfdom, with some exceptions in urban contexts where urban slavery persisted. African slavery thus emerged in the early modern era within the context of nascent capitalism. Plantation slavery, the regimented labor that marked the cultivation of sugar cane, the skill of work in the sugar mill, where the whip was seldom used and incentives encouraged labor, brought together features of agrarian and industrial economies. The sugar mill presaged the modern factory. Eric Williams' thesis (1944) about the connection between plantation slavery in the British Caribbean and the rise of British capitalism has been attacked and revised, but has persisted as an important insight in interrogating the history of capitalism.[1]

Plantation slavery and sugar, which so transformed the New World, setting a model for the use of slave labor in the commercial production of tropical crops, had little connection with Africa and Africans in its inception. With a long history in South Asia and the Muslim world, Europeans first encountered sugar during the Crusades of the late medieval era (Mintz 1985; Curtin 1998). In this late medieval period, another ethnic group so characterized the institution of slavery internationally that they lent their name to the institution. These were the Slavs from the region around the Black Sea and the Caucasus Mountains. Seen as the quintessential slaves in the medieval period, Slavic slaves could be found all over the Old World, including in North and West Africa. But long before this medieval period in which Slavs came to characterize the face of slavery, slaves were held in the classical world. Ancient Athens in the sixth and fifth centuries BCE and Rome under the Republic and the Empire (from the early sixth century BCE to the collapse of Rome) have been described as "slave societies," that is societies where the social elite or the dominant propertied classes derived their wealth and power from their ownership of slaves. Moses Finley (1960: 53), reflecting on Greek civilization, commented on how the Greek "cities in which individual freedom reached its largest expression – most obviously Athens – were the cities where chattel slavery flourished." Slavery and freedom existed in a dialectical relationship, each defining itself as the mirror opposite of the other.

So how did the Slavs come to typify slavery in medieval Europe when serfdom was on the rise? Demand and supply reinforce each other in particular historic moments to generate "myths." In the middle and late medieval period, the European aristocracy in towns believed that Slavs were excellent domestic slaves; while in Muslim societies the Slav was seen as the talented soldier. Venetian merchants were instrumental in nurturing these myths and in supplying Slavic slaves to European cities and to Muslim powers from the mid-eighth century. Serf labor, and the invention of labor-saving devices over the medieval period – better plows, harnesses that enabled oxen and horses to pull heavier loads, horseshoes for better traction, water mills – depressed the demand for slave labor in agrarian settings. Urban, domestic slavery became the vogue. Italian merchants scoured the Slavic lands, convincing Slavic nobles who had trained their domestic slaves to sell them, and relocating them to other cities in Central and Western Europe (see, e.g., Stuard 1983). In the Muslim lands where the gap between Islamic ideology and political reality in the creation of the ideal Muslim government and society led to disillusioned citizens withdrawing from Muslim armies, slave soldiers, increasingly of Slavic origin, were brought in to replace jihadists (Pipes 1981). By the tenth century CE, Slavs had become the most numerous slave group in Europe and the Muslim lands, and by an interesting semantic shift they would bequeath their name to slavery. Latin was the language of bureaucracy in the medieval period. Administrators, seeking a word to describe the emerging class of serfs, chose the Latin word for slave, *servus*. But the medieval serf was very different from the Roman slave. In the search for a new word for true slaves, European administrators coined a new word derived from the ethnic group most numerous in the medieval slave trade, the Slavs. The word has cognates in all Western European languages: *slave* in English, *esclave* in French, *esclavo* in Spanish, *escravo* in Portuguese, *schiavo* in Italian, and *Sklave* in German (Philips 1988: 199).

The rise of the Ottoman empire in the late medieval period and its expansion to incorporate the Slavic lands in the 1450s cut off the traditional source of slaves in the Old World. This was at a time when the Crusades and the establishment of Crusader states in Syria and Palestine had brought European Crusaders and Italian merchants into contact with sugar cane and sugar production. The Black Death in the mid-fourteenth century reduced Europe's population by an estimated quarter to a third, making urban domestic servants scarce. In the late medieval period, African servants would be a mark of prestige among the British aristocracy. It has been noted that two African ladies occupied responsible positions in 1507 at the court of King James IV of Scotland, and Elizabeth I employed Africans at her court as entertainers (Shyllon 1982: 171). The use of African servile labor in the Atlantic economy was but a step away.

The maritime revolution spearheaded by Portugal and Spain from the early fifteenth century would bring these southern European powers into contact with the islands and coastlands of western Africa. The Americas were discovered between 1492 and 1504. An insignificant commodity at the outset, African slaves gradually increased in numbers and were exported to cities in Portugal and Spain as servants. They were also exported to Atlantic islands off the coast of western Africa, where the southern European powers continued their experimentation with sugar plantations with Italian financial and technical assistance. With the plantation complex perfected on these Atlantic islands, the discovery of the Americas provided the opportunity for the entire economic complex to be transplanted to the New World, and plantation societies emerged on a scale hitherto unknown. An internal African slave trade, the Muslim slave trade to the north and northeast, and the Atlantic slave trade would interact to create distinct patterns of enslavement. Africans preferred female slaves, valuing women for both production and reproduction (Robertson and Klein 1983). Young boys were also kept within Africa because of their ease of assimilation. The Muslim or oriental slave trade also preferred women and boys, the women becoming servants in Muslim societies where Muslim women were secluded, and the boys being trained as soldiers or becoming eunuchs. Muslim slaveholders had decided early, after major slave revolts, against the agricultural use of slaves. Adult males captured in warfare, not easily assimilated, were disposed off through the Atlantic trade. This explains why sex ratios in the Atlantic slave trade were about two-thirds male and one-third female (Manning 1990). By the cessation of the African export slave trade in the late nineteenth century, about 12 million Africans had been landed in the New World (Eltis *et al.* 1999; Eltis and Richardson 2008). An estimated 9 million Africans were exported to the Muslim world of North Africa and the Middle East between 600 and 1900 CE (Austen 1987: ch. 2). The export of slaves from Eastern Africa remained at low levels for much of the era of the slave trade until the nineteenth century, when Ralph Austen (1989: 21–44) calculates that some 800,000 Africans were removed from the African continent through the Indian Ocean trade, about 500,000 from the Red Sea Coast and a little over 300,000 from the Swahili coast. With French connivance, the Indian Ocean slave trade continued into the late nineteenth century with Mauritius and Reunion being the major importers of East African slaves.

Revolution, Nationalism, and Emancipation

By an interesting coincidence the bicentenary of the British abolition of the export slave trade (1807–2007) coincided with the fiftieth anniversary of Ghana's independence, and the celebration of a spate of other fiftieth independence anniversaries in Africa. Instructively, the histories of slavery, emancipation, and nationalism are connected in integral ways, as demonstrated in the eighteenth-century revolutions in America, France, and Haiti. The American Revolution (1776) witnessed the overthrow of British rule by its North American colony. Paradoxically, the founding fathers of the American nation affirmed the inalienable right of man to liberty as the basis to self-determination, while denying their slaves the same right. They declared their slaves of African descent or Afro-Americans to be of another race, and as a separate race excluded from the privileges of American nationhood (Fields 1990). The French Revolution from 1789 trumpeted the virtues of universal liberty, equality, and fraternity. The French revolutionaries logically abolished slavery and declared French citizenship open irrespective of color. The dictates of political economy and colonial politics later compelled the French revolutionaries to reimpose slavery in their Caribbean colonies and to narrow the eligibility for French citizenship. In the end, people of color and eventually slaves in Saint Domingue lost patience with the Parisian government and took their destiny into their own hands. They fought a brutal war from 1791 to 1803 to forge the new nation they called Haiti, making it the only successful slave revolution in history.[2] In all three revolutions that forged new nation-states, the question of slavery was central. Thomas Jefferson (1743–1826), a founding father of the American nation and author of the 1776 Declaration of Independence, understood these connections well, and he cautioned his fellow Americans to be on the alert once news of the Haitian revolution reached North America, as freedom could be infectious (Dubois and Garrigus 2006: 159–62).

In the wars of independence in Hispanic America, slave trade and slavery became entangled with the formation of nations. As colonists sought to expand alliances against their mother country, they emancipated slaves outright to encourage them to join the war of independence or they declared "free womb laws" that phased the elimination of slavery. Ada Ferrer (1994) has provided a brilliant examination of the role of blacks in the Cuban war of independence. The civil war in the United States over the nature of the nation resulted in the emancipation of slaves in 1865. Brazil, the last nation in the Americas to abolish slavery, started its slow progress in this direction by abolishing the slave trade in 1851, introduced free-womb legislation in 1871, and eventually emancipated slaves in 1888. Intriguingly, indentured labor that replaced slavery also stirred nationalism among migrants, leading to new nations in parts of Asia. Thus, slavery and indentured labor were at the heart of processes that produced the modern nation-state.

British Abolition of the Slave Trade and the Transition to Indentured Labor

It is worth noting that the first European power to abolish the export of African slaves was Denmark in 1803. Britain followed in 1807, and the United States in 1808. But it was Britain that assigned itself the duty of ensuring that slave ships did not leave the coasts of western African for the Americas. Through treaties with other European powers and Brazil, a leading slave dealer, the trade was brought to an effective halt in the mid-nineteenth century, the last slave ship leaving the Slave Coast for Cuba in 1867. Britain then extended its activities to the Indian Ocean. A complex mix of religious, political, and economic factors came together to transform Britain from a slave power in the eighteenth century into the world's leading opponent of slave trade and then slavery. David Eltis has demonstrated (1987: 15) that the Atlantic slave trade "was killed when its [economic] significance to the Americas and to a lesser extent to Europe was greater than at any point in its history." The Atlantic slave trade did not die a natural death; it was terminated by the most powerful nations of the Atlantic world when it was still a vibrant economic affair. Chris Brown (2006) and Maya Jasanoff (2011) have provided recent revisionary studies of British abolitionism. Northrup (1995:17) notes that for 27 years after the British abolition of the export slave trade in 1807, slave populations in the West Indies and Mauritius declined. British emancipation in 1834 only heightened labor concerns. Plantation slavery had ended, but the plantations still defined Caribbean economies. Britain had introduced an apprenticeship system when it passed emancipation within its dominion in 1834, hoping that apprenticeship would prepare ex-slaves for free wage labor.

But the last thing ex-slaves wanted was to continue to labor on plantations that had dictated a harsh work life and subverted their attempts to forge family and community. In the Americas and in the Cape Colony in South Africa, former slaves opted out of plantation labor (on emancipation and the fraught apprenticeship process in the Cape Colony, see Scully 1997; Mason 2003). Indeed, slaves had accelerated the timetable for emancipation, particularly with the Christmas Rebellion in Jamaica in 1831–1832, when over 60,000 slaves rose in open rebellion against plantation owners demanding more freedom and better working conditions. Slave resistance shortened the planned apprenticeship program. Within two months after the ending of apprenticeship, Jamaica was down to a quarter of its former labor force. The 1838 sugar crop rotted in the fields (Northrup 1995: 19–20). The British, the French, and other European nations turned to indentured labor, initially from Africa, and then from Asia. Between 1834 when the British abolished slavery and 1914 when World War I commenced, about 2 million Africans, Asians, and Pacific islanders signed up as indentured labor and were taken all over the world. The "recaptives" taken off slave ships in the first half of the nineteenth century and landed in Sierra Leone were among the first recruits in the British turn to indentured labor. Needing more workers, the British turned to British India, and by 1850 nearly 120,000 Indians had arrived in Mauritius, some 12,000 in British Guiana, and an additional 10,000 in Jamaica and Trinidad. From 1850 British West Indian planters would extend their search for indentured labor to the Chinese (Northrup 1995). The French would take African indentured laborers to Reunion, French Guiana, Martinique, and Guadeloupe in the mid-nineteenth century (Northrup 1995: 27). Rising demand for sugar throughout the nineteenth century made up for falling prices, expanding cultivation areas for sugar. Indian indentured laborers would be brought to Natal to grow sugar cane in the nineteenth century, the nucleus of the vibrant Indian community in present-day South Africa (Freund 1995). Indentured labor from the Pacific islands went to Australia and Fiji to grow sugar cane. Japanese and Filipino indentured laborers went to Hawaii and mainland United States, especially the west coast. Indentured labor was not limited to plantation agriculture, and over 60,000 Chinese laborers, for example, were brought to the Transvaal mines in South Africa at the beginning of the twentieth century (Northrup 1995: 59).

It is instructive that the end of indentured labor in India and China was associated with the rise of strong nationalist sentiment in these two countries (Northrup 1995: 143). A recent thesis (Ballasteros 2012) draws attention to the links between Filipino contract labor to Hawaii and mainland United States and the achievement of independence for Philippines. Annexed as American territory, Filipinos could immigrate to Hawaii and mainland United States to work. Northrup asserts (1995: x, 5) that indentured laborers in the nineteenth century had work experiences more in common with "free" migrants of the same era than with those of the slave trade. Indentured laborers were paid wages and received benefits such as free housing, medical care, and clothing. This did not necessarily translate into attractive work conditions. In 1924 Filipino contract workers in Hawaii struck against conditions of work. They clashed with police and in the ensuing violence 16 Filipino and four policemen were killed. This has gone down in Filipino history as the Hanapepe War. The result was a Filipino disillusionment with residence in Hawaii. Many returned home to the Philippines. There was a subsequent shift in Filipino patterns of immigration away from Hawaii to mainland United States and to California in particular. The rise in nativist attacks in California in the 1920s, and the conflation of Filipinos with other Asian immigrants in California was galling. This encouraged Filipino nationalists in a rather ironic twist to ally with American nativist politicians, who sought to exclude Asians from immigrating to the United States, and to press for political independence for the Philippines in the early 1930s on the understanding that Filipino immigrants would then be subject to the 1924 Immigration Act, which barred other Asians such as the Japanese and the Chinese from immigrating to the United States (Ballesteros 2012). Again, we are presented with the complex links between migrant labor, voluntary and involuntary, and nationalism. We are reminded that some of Gandhi's most formative experiences as a nationalist politician were in South Africa, mobilizing Indian workers.

Conclusion

This chapter has examined the place of slavery and slave trade in the making of a transnational world; a world marked by a multiracialism and multiculturalism forged through migration. From the 1880s, as indentured laborers finished their contracts, many opted to stay on. The consequence in the West Indies, for example, is that Indians from Asia would displace Africans in British and Dutch Guiana. Indians would constitute about a third of the population in Trinidad by 1921. In the Indian Ocean they were more numerous than Africans in Reunion and Mauritius, and outnumbered Europeans in Natal (Northrup 1995:148). There is a sense in which the diasporas created by indentured labor offered a reflexive space that facilitated or encouraged a revaluation of ties with the homeland. The regimen of work abroad, nativist attacks, and other experiences of sojourning abroad shaped nationalist sentiment and agitation among migrants. More mobile than the African slaves forced into involuntary servitude before them, indenture offered a foundation for transnationalism. But Lindsay's (1994) and Matory's (1999) work have underscored how transnationalism was also a phenomenon among ex-slaves in the nineteenth century, as slaves of Yoruba origins, recent entrants into the Atlantic slave trade, forged new ties to Lagos. These were at the center of the making of a Yoruba "nation." There is a sense in which the history of the modern world cannot be divorced from the historical processes of slavery and indentured labor.

Notes

1 For a restatement of the thesis, see Manning (1990). A 2011 conference on Slavery's Capitalism, organized by Brown University and Harvard University, revisited this important theme. For an important discussion which situates slaving in Africa in the context of Arab, European and African trade and accumulation, see Miller (2010).
2 For a good short history of the Haitian revolution, see Geggus (1989). The classic study on the Haitian revolution remains James (2001; first published in 1938). For a recent excellent study, see Dubois (2004).

References

Akyeampong, E. 2000. "Africans in the diaspora; the diaspora and Africa." *African Affairs*, 99(395): 183–215.

Austen, R. 1987. *African Economic History*. London: James Currey.

Austen, R. 1989. "The nineteenth century Islamic slave trade from East Africa (Swahili and Red Sea Coasts): a tentative census." In W.G. Clarence-Smith (ed.) *The Economics of the Indian Ocean Slave Trade in the Nineteenth Century*, pp. 21–44. London: Frank Cass.

Ballesteros, C. 2012. "Hanapepe! Massacre, migration, and the transnational origins of Philippine independence, 1924–1934." BA thesis, Harvard University.

Brown, C.L. 2006. *Moral Capital: Foundations of British Abolitionism*. Chapel Hill: University of North Carolina Press.

Curtin, P.D. 1998. *The Rise and Fall of the Plantation Complex*. Cambridge: Cambridge University Press.

Dubois, L. 2004. *A Colony of Citizens: Revolution and Slave Emancipation in the French Caribbean, 1787–1804*. Chapel Hill: University of North Carolina Press.

Dubois, L. and Garrigus, J.D. 2006. *Slave Revolutions in the Caribbean 1789–1804: A Brief History with Documents*. Boston, MA: Bedford/St Martin's.

Eltis, D. 1987. *Economic Growth and the Ending of the Trans-Atlantic Slave Trade*. New York: Oxford University Press.

Eltis, D. and Richardson, D. (eds) 2008. *Extending the Frontiers: Essays on the New Transatlantic Slave Trade Database*. New Haven: Yale University Press.

Eltis, D., Behrendt, S.D., Richardson, D. and Klein, H.S. 1999. *The Trans-Atlantic Slave Trade: A Database on CD-Rom*. Cambridge: Cambridge University Press.

Ferrer, A. 1994. *Insurgent Cuba: Race, Nation and Revolution, 1868–1898*. Chapel Hill: University of North Carolina Press.

Fields, B.J. 1990. "Slavery, race and ideology in the United States of America." *New Left Review*, I/181: 95–118.

Finley, M.I. 1960. "Was Greek civilization based on slave labor?" In M.I. Finley (eds) *Slavery in Classical Antiquity*, pp. 141–154. Cambridge: W. Heffer & Sons.

Freund, B. 1995. *Insiders and Outsiders: The Indian Working Class of Durban, 1910–1990*. Portsmouth, NH: Heinemann.

Geggus, D.P. 1989. "The Haitian Revolution." In F. Knight and C. Palmer (eds) *The Modern Caribbean*, pp. 21–51. Chapel Hill: University of North Carolina Press.

Gilroy, P. 1993. *The Black Atlantic: Modernity and Double Consciousness*. Cambridge, MA: Harvard University Press.

James, C.L.R. 2001. *The Black Jacobins: Toussaint L'Ouverture and the San Domingo Revolution*. London: Penguin Books. (First published 1938.)

Jasanoff, M. 2011. *Liberty's Exiles: American Loyalists in the Revolutionary World*. New York: Random House.

Lindsay, L. 1994. "'To return to the bosom of their fatherland': Brazilian immigrants in nineteenth-century Lagos." *Slavery and Abolition*, 15(1): 22–50.

Mann, K. and Bay, E.G. (eds) 2001. *Rethinking the African Diaspora: The Making of a Black Atlantic in the Bight of Benin and Brazil*. London: Frank Cass.

Manning, P. 1990. *Slavery and African Life: Occidental, Oriental, and African Slave Trades*. Cambridge: Cambridge University Press.

Mason, J.E. 2003. *Social Death and Resurrection: Slavery and Emancipation in South Africa*. Charlottesville: University of Virginia Press.

Matory, L. 1999. "The English professors of Brazil: on the diaspora roots of the Yoruba nation." *Comparative Studies in Society and History*, 41(1): 72–103.

Matory, L. 2005. *Black Atlantic Religion: Tradition, Transnationalism and Matriarchy in the Afro-Brazilian Candomblé*. New Jersey: Princeton University Press.

Miller, J.C. 2010. "Investing in poverty in Africa – financial aspects of global historical dynamics of commercialization." Paper presented at the Conference on Understanding African Poverty over the Longue Durée, Accra.

Mintz, S. 1985. *Sweetness and Power: The Place of Sugar in Modern History*. New York: Viking Penguin.

Northrup, D. 1995. *Indentured Labor in the Age of Imperialism, 1834–1922*. New York: Cambridge University Press.

Philips, W.D. Jr 1988. "Europe: the Middle Ages." In S. Drescher and S. Engerman (eds) *Historical Guide to World Slavery*, pp. 197–200. Oxford: Oxford University Press.

Pipes, D. 1981. *Slave Soldiers and Islam: The Genesis of Military System*. New Haven: Yale University Press.

Robertson, C. and Klein, M. (eds) 1983. *Women and Slavery in Africa*. Madison: University of Wisconsin Press.

Shyllon, F. 1982. "Blacks in Britain: a historical and analytical overview." In J.E. Harris (ed.) *Global Dimensions of the African Diaspora*, pp. 170–195. Washington, DC: Howard University Press.

Stuard, S.M. 1983. "To town to serve: Urban domestic slavery in medieval Ragusa." *Journal of Medieval History*, 9(3): 155–171.

Williams, E. 1944. *Capitalism and Slavery*. Chapel Hill: University of North Carolina Press.

Chapter 10

When the Diaspora Returns Home
Ambivalent Encounters with the Ethnic Homeland

Takeyuki Tsuda

Introduction: The Return of the Diaspora

In recent decades, the total volume of ethnic return migration has increased significantly. In contrast to the return migration of first-generation diasporic peoples who move back to their homeland (country of birth), *ethnic* return migration refers to later-generation descendants of diasporic peoples who "return" to their countries of ancestral origin after living outside their ethnic homelands for generations.[1] Although a number of scholars have examined how diasporas have continued to evolve through further migratory scattering, relatively few have studied how certain diasporic peoples have also been returning to their ethnic homelands, a form of diasporic "in-gathering" or the "unmaking of diasporas" (Münz and Ohliger 2003; Van Hear 1998: 6, 47–48; see also Clifford 1994: 304). In fact, certain diasporas are now characterized by a tension between centrifugal and centripetal migratory forces.

The most prominent example of diasporic return is that of the millions of Jews in the diaspora who have migrated to Israel since World War II. The largest group of Jewish ethnic return migrants has come from the former Soviet Union, more than 770,000 of whom entered Israel between 1990 and 1999 (see Levy and Weingrod 2005; Münz and Ohliger 2003; Remennick 2003). In Western Europe, 4 million ethnic German descendants from Eastern Europe return-migrated to their ethnic homeland between 1950 and 1999 (see Münz and Ohliger 2003). Other European countries, such as Spain, Italy, Greece, Poland, and Hungary have received much smaller populations of ethnic return migrants from Latin American and Eastern Europe (see Capo Zmegac, Vob, and Roth 2010; Cook-Martín and Viladrich 2009; Fox 2009; King and Christou 2010; Skrentny *et al.* 2009). After the collapse of the

A Companion to Diaspora and Transnationalism, First Edition.
Edited by Ato Quayson and Girish Daswani.
© 2013 Blackwell Publishing Ltd. Published 2013 by Blackwell Publishing Ltd.

Soviet Union, 2.8 million ethnic Russians living outside Russia in Eastern Europe, Central Asia, and the Caucasus returned to their ethnic homeland between 1990 to 1998 (see Pilkington 1998). In East Asia, close to a million second- and third-generation Japanese and Korean descendants scattered across Latin America, Eastern Europe, and China have return-migrated to Japan and Korea since the late 1980s (see Song 2009; Tsuda 2003a). China and Taiwan have also been receiving ethnic Chinese descendants from various Southeast Asian countries. There has even been limited ethnic return migration to various Southeast Asian countries as well. Although most diasporic "returnees" are labor migrants from poorer countries, there is also a smaller but growing population of professionals and students from developed countries in North America and Europe who migrate to their countries of ancestral origin.

Not only is the total volume of ethnic return migration quite substantial, it is generally long term or permanent in nature. Diasporic returnees in the Middle East and Europe often migrate in order to settle permanently in their countries of ethnic origin. Although some ethnic return migrants (especially in East Asia) are sojourners who intend to remain only a few years in their ancestral homelands (as labor migrants and target earners), a number of them are prolonging their stays and settling, often with family members (see Tsuda 1999). The exceptions here are professional and student migrants from the developed world, who generally remain in their ethnic homelands temporarily (see, e.g., Jain 2012).

The Causes of Diasporic Return

Economic motives and ethnic return migration

Most diasporic descendants are not returning to their ethnic homelands simply to reconnect with their ancestral roots or explore their ethnic heritage. Instead, they are generally migrating from less developed countries to more economically prosperous ancestral homelands (often in the developed world) in search of jobs, higher incomes, and a better standard of living. In this sense, diasporic return from the developing world initially appears to be another form of international labor migration caused by widening economic disparities between rich and poor countries.

Although ethnicity is generally not a "pull" factor that draws diasporic descendants to the ancestral homeland in search of ancestral heritage, it can be a "push" factor that forces them out of their country of birth. In the past, large ethnic return migration flows were instigated by ethno-political persecution caused by major geopolitical disruptions, such as the dissolution of empires, colonial regimes, and multi-ethnic states, and not by direct economic pressure *per se* (see Brubaker 1998; Capo Zmegac 2005, 2010). Nonetheless, ethnic discrimination can play a role even in cases of economically motivated return migration. For instance, continuing ethnic insecurity and discrimination in Eastern Europe sometimes worsened the socioeconomic situation of ethnic minorities in these countries, causing them to leave for their ancestral homelands (Brubaker 1998: 1059–1061; Fox 2003: 452; Pilkington 1998: 123–138; Remennick 1998: 247; 2007: 36–37, 42–43). In these cases, diasporic return migration is still motivated by underlying economic causes, but ethnic discrimination and persecution serve as an additional impetus that helps "push" diasporic descendants out of their countries of birth.

Ethnicity seems to play a greater role for ethnic return migrants from the developed world. Coming from rich countries, such individuals have much less economic incentive to migrate to their ethnic homelands (which are sometimes poorer countries) and therefore their numbers are quite limited. Although many are seeking professional, educational, or business investment opportunities in their countries of ancestral origin, the desire to reconnect with their ethnic roots and explore their cultural heritage seems to be a stronger motive compared to ethnic return migrants from poorer, developing countries. Asian Americans in East Asia cite the desire to explore their ethnic ancestry as a reason for return migration (see Kim 2009) as do Greek Americans in Greece (Christou 2006: 1050–1051) and Indian Americans in India (Jain 2012). A limited number of individuals from developed countries travel to their ancestral homelands as cultural heritage tourists in order to explore their ethnic roots, sometimes on organized tours sponsored by ethnic organizations and homeland governments (see, e.g., Kibria 2002; Louie 2004). The most notable examples of such organized ethnic tourism are to Israel, China, and South Korea.[2]

Transnational ethnic ties and diasporic return

Although diasporic returns have been caused more by economic pressures than by ancestral ties persisting across borders, such transnational ethnic affinities determine the direction of these migrant flows. In response to economic pressures, diasporic descendants have chosen to migrate to their ethnic homelands instead of to other advanced industrialized countries because of their nostalgic affiliation to their country of ethnic origin.

Most ordinary labor migration flows are structured by pre-existing social networks and institutional connections between sending and receiving countries, which provide transnational linkages enabling migrants to move across borders and relocate to foreign countries. In the case of ethnic return migration, however, most diasporic descendants have lost any substantial transnational social connections or cultural contacts with their countries of ethnic origin, except in a few cases where the ethnic homeland is located in a neighboring country. Therefore, the transnational ethnic ties that channel diasporic return migrants to their ethnic homelands are based on an imagined, nostalgic, ethnic affinity to an ancestral country which most have never visited.

Although most diasporic descendants have developed a nostalgic identification with their ethnic homelands, the strength of such sentimental ethnic attachments varies. For instance, Russian Jews do not have a strong transnational ethnic affiliation to Israel because of their cultural assimilation and suppression of nationalist sentiment among ethnic minorities in the former Soviet Union (see Remennick 2003). Others, like the Argentines of Spanish and Italian descent, do not have a strong awareness of their ethnic heritage, but develop an appreciation for it while recovering their homeland nationality (Cook-Martín, 2005).

Immigrant ethnic minorities sometimes develop strong transnational identifications with their countries of ethnic origin in response to the discriminatory exclusion and marginalization they experience in dominant society (e.g., see Espiritu 2003: 86–88; Levitt 2001: 19–20; Parreñas 2001: 55–59), which makes them feel that they do not fully belong to their countries of birth. For instance, ethnic Hungarian descendants in Romania feel solidarity with the greater Hungarian nation partly in response to their adversarial relations with majority Romanians. Ethnic Germans in Eastern Europe seem to have had analogous experiences in the past when faced with discrimination. Some ethnic minorities (such as Asian Americans and Japanese-descent *nikkeijin* in Latin America) are forever racialized as foreigners with essentialized cultural attachments to their native countries of origin because of their phenotypic differences from the mainstream populace; this can cause them to construct a romanticized view of their ethnic homeland as the country where they racially belong (Kim 2009; Louie 2004; Tsuda 2003a: ch. 2).

However, ethnic minorities can also develop relatively strong homeland attachments because their ethnic ancestry and countries of origin are constructed and portrayed in a favorable manner. Indeed, most diasporic descendants imagine their ancestral homelands from afar in rather idealized, romantic, if not mythical ways (see Cohen 1997: 184–185). Many of these positive images come from their parents and grandparents, whose nostalgic romanticization of their homeland is a product of their prolonged separation from their countries of origin (see Grossutti 2006; Kim 2009; von Koppenfels 2009; Tsuda 2003a: ch. 2; Viladrich 2005). Other images come from the globalized mass media and popular culture, which has become the primary means of imagining homelands from afar. Attachments to homelands are especially strong for diasporic peoples located in neighboring countries where ethno-cultural links exist across national borders, as with the Hungarian Romanians and Finland Swedes.

Therefore, when diasporic descendants are faced with economic pressures to emigrate, many naturally have turned to their ethnic homelands instead of migrating to other advanced industrialized nations because of their sentimental ethnic attachments to their countries of ancestral origin. Not only did these countries seem more ethnically accessible, it was presumed that their co-ethnic status would facilitate their immigrant social integration.

In addition, such transnational ethnic affiliations have been substantiated by homeland governments, which have adopted immigration and nationality policies that reach out to their diasporic descendants abroad and allow them to return to their ethnic homelands. Such policies of homeland governments are based on the essentialized assumption that these descendants of former emigrants, despite being born and raised abroad, would be culturally similar to the host populace because of their shared bloodline. Diasporic descendants have been imagined as an integral part of a broader, deterritorialized cultural nation of "co-ethnics" living in other countries but united by common descent (cf. Joppke 2005: 159), thus invoking a natural ethnic affinity between the nation-state and its diaspora. However, the specific reasons that made homeland governments decide to welcome back their ethnic descendants from abroad vary according to geographical region.

Ethnic return migration policies in Europe (and Israel) are generally based on an ethnic protection or ethnic affinity rationale based on the historical connection of these countries to their diasporic peoples abroad (cf. Skrentny *et al.* 2009; see also Joppke 2005: 23–24). In Israel and Germany, these policies were initially implemented to protect their diasporic peoples from ethnic persecution. When the state of Israel was established after the Holocaust, all Jews were granted the right to return to their ancestral homeland partly to provide them a safe haven from future persecution as well as to build up and strengthen the Jewish state (Joppke and Rosenhek 2009). Likewise, in Germany, ethnic German descendants expelled from Eastern Europe after World War II and those living in Communist countries during the Cold War were allowed to return as Aussiedler under the presumption of ethnic persecution.

In contrast, ethnic preferences in immigration policy and nationality law in other European countries (Spain, Italy, Greece, Hungary, Poland, and Russia) are based almost exclusively on an ethnic affinity rationale with diasporic descendants born abroad as part of a greater ethnic nation beyond state borders (Joppke 2005: 116–117, 245–246). Because of historical and racial ties to the diaspora, ethnic descendants are seen by their respective homeland governments as "our peoples" who therefore have a right to return to their ancestral homeland. Although some type of ethnic protection rationale can be invoked, the underlying justification is based on a sense of state responsibility/obligation toward their diasporic descendants abroad (Cook-Martín 2005; Joppke 2005: 246; Skrentny *et al.* 2009; de Tinguy 2003: 116–119).

Unlike their European counterparts, East Asian countries have invited back their diasporic descendants mainly for economic purposes (Skrentny *et al.* 2009; see also Joppke 2005: 158–159). Japan and South Korea have imported large numbers of ethnic return migrants in response to acute unskilled labor shortages caused by decades of economic prosperity coupled with low fertility rates. South Korea and China have encouraged wealthy and highly skilled ethnic descendants in the diaspora to return-migrate in order to promote economic investment from abroad and to tap their professional skills (see Cheng 2002: 91–92 and Skrentny *et al.* 2009). However, these countries generally decided to allow diasporic return because they assumed ethnic return migrants of shared descent and presumed cultural affinity would be easier to assimilate and integrate socially than other immigrants and would therefore not disrupt the country's ethno-racial balance.

Such ethnic immigration policies have been an important factor in facilitating diasporic return by enabling co-ethnic descendants abroad to secure access to their ancestral homelands by virtue of their ethnic heritage and descent (Van Hear 1998: 48). Many diasporic descendants have chosen to return-migrate to their ethnic homelands for economic reasons because of the much greater ease of entry compared to other countries of immigration (see, e.g., Tsuda 1999). If homeland governments had not openly admitted their diasporic descendants, most ethnic return migration flows would have remained quite small and many of the migrants would have headed to other advanced industrialized nations.

Ambivalent Homecomings: Ethnic and Socioeconomic Marginalization in the Ancestral Homeland

Although many ethnic return migrants feel a nostalgic ethnic affiliation to their countries of ancestral origin, because they have been living outside their ethnic homeland for generations, they are essentially "returning" to a foreign country from which their ancestors came. As a result, their diasporic homecomings are often quite ambivalent, if not negative, experiences. Despite initial expectations that their presumed ethnic affinity with the host society (as co-ethnics) would facilitate their social integration, they are often ethnically excluded as foreigners in their ancestral homelands because of their alien cultural differences (see also Capo Zmegac 2005: 199; 2010: 21–24). They are also socioeconomically marginalized as unskilled immigrant workers performing low-status jobs that are shunned by the host populace. Such negative ethnic receptions are disappointing, if not dismaying for many of ethnic return migrants and shatter their previously favorable, romantic images of their ethnic homeland (King and Christou 2010: 111–112; Stefansson 2004: 9; Tsuda 2003a: ch. 3).

Ethnic exclusion: Diasporic returnees as cultural foreigners

Many diasporic return migrants simply lack the linguistic and cultural competence necessary for acceptance as co-ethnics in their ancestral homelands. Since they have been born and raised in foreign countries, they have generally lost their ancestral language and customs, especially if they have lived outside their ancestral countries for many generations. A number of them have also been subject to past nationalist assimilation projects or ethnic discrimination in their countries of birth that suppressed minority cultures and diasporic allegiances to their ancestral homelands, especially in former communist regimes. This includes the Russification, secularization, and stigmatization of Soviet Jews (Remennick 1998), the ethno-cultural discrimination against ethnic German descendants in Eastern Europe, and the prohibition of Korean Chinese minority culture during the Chinese Cultural Revolution (Song 2009). Japanese-descent ethnic minorities in South America (especially in Brazil) and Spanish- and Italian-descent Argentines have also been historically influenced by nationalization projects, often under dictatorship regimes (Cook-Martín, 2005; Tsuda 2001).

Therefore, when these diasporic descendants "return" to their ethnic homelands, they are ethnically excluded as culturally different foreigners and strangers (see also Capo Zmegac 2005: 206–207). Despite their shared bloodline, their ethnic heritage is seemingly denied on cultural grounds by their ancestral compatriots when they are identified as foreign nationals. For instance: Jews from Russia in Israel are called "Russians"; ethnic Germans from Russia or Poland are labeled "Russians" or "Poles" in Germany; ethnic Hungarian descendants from Romania become "Romanians" in Hungary; Korean-descent Chosŏnjok from China become "Chinese" in South Korea; and Japanese descent *nikkeijin* from South America are seen as Brazilians, Peruvians, or simply *gaijin* (foreigners) in Japan. In this manner, co-ethnic descendants from abroad who were once seen as integral members of a deterritorialized and racialized ethnic nation based on a shared bloodline are now excluded from the ethno-national community on the basis of cultural difference.

Often, the alien cultural characteristics of ethnic return migrants are seen in a pejorative manner by the host society, especially if they come from countries that are less developed and lower in the global hierarchy of nations. In such cases, the national labels used by the host populace to refer to them (Russians, Romanians, Chinese, Brazilians, etc.) are based on negative stereotypes and prejudices toward these countries as economically backward and culturally inferior and can even be used as ethnic slurs. For instance, Israeli attitudes toward Russian Jews are influenced by negative mass-media stereotyping of Russians as "mafia men, prostitutes, and welfare mothers" and there is considerable suspicion about their secular lifestyle, lack of Jewishness, and foreignness (Remennick 2003; 2007: 154; Feldman 2003). Hungarians view their co-ethnics from Romania scornfully, with suspicion and disdain, as poor people from an inferior country who may even take jobs away from Hungarians (Fox 2003: 456–457). In South Korea, negative reports have proliferated about ethnic Korean Chosŏnjok, emphasizing their insufficient work ethic, untrustworthiness, over-Sinicized behavior and attitudes, and lack of Korean national loyalty (Song 2009). Japanese Brazilians are often viewed by mainstream Japanese as poor, lazy, easy-going, culturally inferior, overly individualistic, and noisy (Tsuda 2003a: ch. 2). Even Argentines of Spanish descent are seen as unreliable workers with a questionable work ethic (Cook-Martín and Viladrich 2009). In some countries with newer diasporic populations, like Russia, Japan, and South Korea, ethnic return migrants can be seen as descendants of traitors who left and betrayed the ethnic homeland or as descendants of poor, uneducated emigrants who could not survive economically and had to abandon their home country (Park 2006; Pilkington 1998: 168–171; Tsuda 2003a, ch. 2).

Because diasporic return migrants have prior expectations of ethnic belonging in their country of ancestral origin, most of them are quite surprised, if not shocked, by their ethnic rejection and social exclusion. As their previous idealized and nostalgic images of their ancestral country are seriously challenged, they become culturally alienated immigrant minorities whose members are strangers in their ethnic homeland. Although they were often minorities in their countries of birth because of their foreign racial descent, they again become ethnic minorities when they return to their country of ancestral origin, this time because of their cultural foreignness. Ethnic return migration is therefore not a type of diasporic consolidation or regrouping. It is instead producing new ethnic minorities through an increased consciousness of cultural heterogeneity among peoples of shared descent.

The level of ethnic marginalization experienced by diasporic return migrants varies, depending on the cultural and linguistic distance between them and the homeland populace. This is partly a function of the length of time that they have lived outside their homelands as well as their level of assimilation and loss of ethnic heritage in their countries of birth. It also depends on whether the homeland and its diasporic peoples are located in different cultural regions of the world. For instance, ethnic Korean Chosŏnjok from China returning to South Korea remain within the East Asian cultural region whereas Latin American *nikkeijin* returning to Japan are crossing a greater cultural divide. Ethnic return migrants moving from former communist to advanced capitalist countries also encounter significant cultural barriers associated with two very different socioeconomic systems.

In contrast, although Argentines of Spanish descent migrate across a vast geographical distance to Spain, they are in an ethnic homeland that shares a broader Hispanic culture and language because of its historical colonial ties to Argentina. Therefore, Spanish Argentines seem to enjoy greater ethnic acceptance in their homeland (see also Viladrich 2005) and the problems they encounter seem mainly to be related to their low-level immigrant jobs and socioeconomic marginalization (Cook-Martín and Viladrich 2009). In contrast, Argentines of Italian descent who return-migrate to Italy feel greater cultural and linguistic differences with the local populace and their social integration is more difficult (Grossutti 2006).

In general, diasporic descendants whose ethnic homelands are in neighboring countries tend to encounter fewer cultural difficulties upon return-migrating, since they tend to have much greater contact with the homeland, allowing them to maintain their cultural heritage. This is especially the case with the Finland Swedes, whose linguistic and cultural affinity with neighboring Sweden enable them to ethnically integrate quite successfully in their ancestral homeland. Another example is ethnic Russians who relocated during Soviet expansion to nearby communist countries, which were under Russian political and cultural influence for decades. As a result, ethnic Russian repatriates encounter fewer problems than other ethnic return migrants because they share a common Russian language and culture with the host populace (Ohliger and Münz 2003: 6–7; Pilkington 1998: 173–175; de Tinguy 2003: 125).

Socioeconomic marginalization: Dealing with degrading immigrant jobs

Diasporic returnees are also socioeconomically marginalized since they are frequently offered only low-status, unskilled immigrant jobs that are shunned by the majority populace. Because a number of them are from relatively well-educated, middle class backgrounds, ethnic return migration can involve considerable declassing and downward mobility. Although they are granted favorable immigrant legal status because of their racial ties to the host society as diasporic descendants, this does not give them privileged access to the labor market because of the linguistic and cultural barriers they face. In addition, their educational credentials and skills from developing countries are often not recognized or transferable in advanced capitalist countries (see, e.g., Remennick 2003: 277; 2009). Others are recruited specifically to fill unskilled labor shortages in their ethnic homelands and do not have the social network contacts needed to access higher-level jobs.

Many of the negative experiences that ethnic return migrants have in their homelands are therefore the result of their socioeconomic marginalization, which is often just as severe as other immigrant workers. Not only must they toil as unskilled, manual laborers in difficult, stigmatized jobs, they must cope with a serious decline in social status from former, respected middle-class occupations to degrading working-class jobs, which can have negative effects on self-worth and self-esteem and become a source of social class prejudice from the majority society. Even ethnic return migrants who have maintained their ancestral heritage and are less culturally alienated in their ethnic homelands often still have negative diasporic homecomings because of the degrading and low-status jobs they must endure (see Cook-Martín and Viladrich 2009; Fox 2003: 452–453; 2009).

Because of their marginalization as immigrant minorities, many ethnic return migrants remain socially unintegrated in their homelands. In some cases, they are segregated in immigrant ethnic communities and interact primarily amongst themselves in their own languages. Some of these communities, such as those of the ethnic German Aussiedler, Russian Jews in Israel, and Japanese-descent *nikkeijin* in Japan, have become quite cohesive and extensive with an array of ethnic businesses and services, as well as an active ethnic mass media, enabling many of them to conduct their daily lives without much contact with the local populace (see also Remennick 2003: 378–379; de Tinguy 2003: 124). In response to their social exclusion in their homelands, ethnic return migrants have withdrawn into their enclaved communities and subcultures, often resisting attempts by mainstream society to culturally assimilate and socially incorporate them (Remennick 2003: 382, 378–379; Tsuda 2003a: ch. 5).

Therefore, despite their racialized ethnic affinity with their ancestral homeland, the "homecomings" of ethnic return migrants are quite ambivalent and they often experience levels of ethnic and socioeconomic marginalization equivalent to ordinary labor migrants (see Ohliger and Münz 2003: 15). However, diasporic returnees often feel much more socially alienated than other immigrants because their stronger prior ethnic affiliation and identification with the homeland causes them to expect an ethnic homecoming befitting diasporic descendants returning to their land of ancestral origin. When it does not materialize and they are confronted by social exclusion instead, they feel more estranged and disillusioned than other immigrants who do not arrive with such ethnic expectations. Ironically therefore, the immigrant group that is most ethnically related to the host society can often experience the most social alienation.

Ethnic Return Migration from the First World: A More Positive Homecoming?

The ethnic reception of diasporic returnees from developed countries seems to be somewhat better for a number of reasons. Although they are just as culturally alien as their counterparts from developing countries and can be subject to some ethnic prejudice, they are generally more respected because of their First World origins. Most importantly, they are not socioeconomically marginalized in stigmatized working-class jobs because most of them return-migrate with relatively high status as professionals, business investors, or students, leading to a more positive reception and social experiences.

Ethnic return migrants from developed countries definitely benefit from the higher stature of their countries of birth and are not subject to the negative stereotypes attached to developing countries. For instance, Korean Americans in South Korea can be perceived as role models and valuable assets because they represent the English-speaking, internationally successful, global Korean. Such images are derived from past respect for the United States, as a source of prosperity, cultural capital, and popular culture in a globalized world (Park 2006). Nonetheless, they are still subject to negative attitudes about the United States and are also singled out for their lack of cultural competence as people who have become too Americanized (Kibria 2002; Kim 2009; Park 2006). As a result, they do not feel ethnically accepted as culturally different foreigners, although their social alienation and disappointment in their ethnic homeland are considerably less than among their Korean Chinese counterparts. Similar trends are observable among Japanese Americans in Japan, although their ethnic experiences seem more positive, partly because the Japanese generally have a more favorable attitude toward the United States than Koreans (Tsuda 2009).[3] The Finland Swedes seem to have the best of both worlds. As ethnic return migrants from First World Finland, they are socioeconomically well integrated in Sweden as middle-class professionals and students, and as diasporic descendants from a neighboring country, they are culturally similar to majority Swedes (Hedberg 2009).

Diasporic Return and Ethnic Identity

The negative ethnic reception and ambivalent homecomings experienced by many diasporic return migrants from the developing world in their countries of ethnic origin have a significant impact on their ethno-national identities. When confronted by social alienation as immigrant minorities, most ethnic return migrant groups seem to experience a decline in their transnational diasporic attachments to their ethnic homelands and a strengthening of nationalist identifications in response to their sociocultural differences with the homeland populace (see also Capo Zmegac 2005: 208–210). Others seek out alternative forms of ethno-national belonging as they reconsider their position in the diaspora. For most ethnic return migrants, therefore, a previously stronger diasporic consciousness based on their ancestral origins is replaced by more parochial ethnic identifications based on their different cultural backgrounds.

From transnational affinity to deterritorialized nationalism

In most cases, ethnic return migrants strengthen their nationalist attachments to their countries of birth in response to their ethnic and socioeconomic marginalization in their ancestral homelands. Not only do they realize that they are cultural foreigners who do not belong in their country of ethnic origin, they often develop negative perceptions of it because of the discrimination they face as ethnic minorities and their degrading work experiences. This causes them to distance themselves from their ancestral homeland by affirming their status as foreign nationals, which can become a defensive counter-identity asserted in opposition to the host society. Some of them also develop a renewed nationalist appreciation of their country of birth in response to their negative experiences in their country of ethnic origin. In this manner, the dislocations of migration can produce a form of "deterritorialized" migrant nationalism where national loyalties are articulated outside the territorial boundaries of the nation-state.

This deterritorialized nationalism among ethnic return migrants is quite ironic since most of them were ethnic minorities in their countries of birth who had never adopted strong nationalist identities. For instance, Japanese Brazilians were seen (and saw themselves) as a "Japanese" minority in Brazil and did not strongly identify with majority Brazilians. However, they suddenly embrace their "Brazilianness" in Japan to an extent they never had in Brazil (Tsuda 2003a: ch. 4). Likewise, Aussiedler were regarded as Germans in Russia, but are seen as Russians after return migration to Germany (von Koppenfels 2009). Korean Chinese were an ethnic Korean minority in China but see themselves as Chinese in South Korea (Song 2009). This resurgence of nationalist identification with the country of birth among ethnic return migrants is often accompanied by active engagement in its national cultural activities. Thus, we find Japanese Brazilians dancing samba (often for the first time) in their ethnic homeland of Japan and German Aussiedler singing Russian songs in Germany.

The strength of deterritorialized nationalism among diasporic return migrants depends on the level of ethnic alienation they experience in their ancestral homelands. For instance, although Argentines of Spanish descent in Spain become more aware of their Argentine backgrounds and culture when faced with an ambivalent ethnic homecoming, since they are more culturally similar to their Spanish hosts their assertion of nationalist difference seems to be less strong than other diasporic returnees (see also Viladrich 2005). In contrast, Italo-Argentine return migrants, who do not feel as much linguistic and cultural commonality with their Italian homeland, seem to develop a stronger nationalist attachment to Argentina (Grossutti 2006).

For other groups of ethnic return migrants, the assertion of nationalist difference in response to their negative diasporic homecoming is not based on an increased cultural attachment to their countries of birth but on a reaffirmation of their ancestral nationalities by claiming that they have maintained ethnic cultural traditions abroad better than their co-ethnics living in the homeland. This is the case with ethnic Hungarian descendants from Romania who return-migrate to Hungary. When they are socially excluded and labeled as Romanians by mainstream Hungarians, the Hungarian Romanians refuse to accept this ethnic categorization, and instead, claim a purer Hungarian identity (as the "real Hungarians"), which becomes a form of nationalist differentiation from their Hungarian hosts, who have supposedly been contaminated by modernity and are no longer truly Hungarian (Fox 2003: 458–459; 2009). Ethnic Russians who repatriate to Russia, Mongolian Kazakhs in Kazakhstan, as well as ethnic Greeks in Asia Minor and ethnic Croats in the former Yugoslavia, who return-migrate to their homelands seem to have analogous experiences (Capo Zmegac 2005: 212; Pilkington 1998: 168–171; de Tinguy 2003: 125).

In this manner, the ethnic encounter between diasporic descendants and their co-ethnics in the ancestral homeland often leads to exclusionary nationalist identities based on cultural difference rather than transnational identifications based on shared ethnic commonalities among peoples from different countries. Since most ethnic return migrants feel their ancestral heritage is denied by their negative reception in their homelands, few develop multiple transnational attachments to both their countries of birth and those of ethnic origin but come to identify more exclusively as nationals from a foreign country or claim a more authentic ethno-national identity that excludes their co-ethnics in the homeland. The sense of shared descent and bloodline that initially created transnational ethnic attachments across borders between diasporic descendants and their homeland populaces is overridden by the stark national cultural differences that emerge when these co-ethnics actually meet in the ancestral homeland. This is an example of how transnational mobility ironically creates a renewal of nationalist attachments instead of producing transnational, hybrid identifications across national borders.

Non-nationalist, diasporic identities

Although most ethnic return migrants redefine their identities in nationalist ways, some groups seem to adopt a non-nationalist ethnic identity as diasporic people whose sense of belonging cannot be defined in nationalist terms (see also King and Christou 2010: 114). This occurs among diasporic returnees who distance themselves from the host society in response to their negative ethnic homecoming but remain reluctant to embrace a nationalist identification with their country of birth for various reasons. For instance, when Japanese Peruvian returnees in Japan are denied their previous Japanese ethnic identities, they do not strengthen their nationalist identities as Peruvians because Peruvianness is not well regarded in Japan and the immigrant community contains illegal, non-Japanese-descent Peruvian nationals.

Instead, the Japanese Peruvians adopt a diasporic ethnic identity as *nikkei* (peoples of Japanese descent born and raised abroad), which serves as a means of cultural differentiation from the Japanese while also distancing themselves from illegal, non-*nikkei* Peruvians (Takenaka 2009).

It is also possible that ethnic return migrants who suffer considerable exclusion and discrimination in *both* their countries of birth and their ethnic homelands may adopt non-nationalist, diasporic ethnic identities that are not based on loyalty to either nation-state. This process of double marginalization seems to be the case with Korean Americans in South Korea, who do not feel completely at home either in the United States, where they are racialized minorities, or in South Korea, where they are cultural minorities. Thus diasporic return produces for them a heightened sense of hybridity and "inbetweenness," as people who are both American and Korean but not fully either (Kim 2009), causing some of them to use the diasporic term "Chaemi kyopo" (ethnic Korean descendants from America) to refer to themselves (Park 2006). Like the *nikkei* consciousness of the Japanese Peruvians, these Korean Americans are also adopting an identity as diasporic descendants abroad who do not belong to either their country of birth or of ethnic origin.[4]

Transnational identifications

Only a few ethnic return migrants from developed countries who enjoy a certain degree of social acceptance in their homelands seem to develop a transnational identification in which their allegiance to their countries of birth is accompanied by a strengthened attachment to their ethnic homelands. For instance, although Korean and Japanese Americans do experience some ethnic marginalization in their homelands (which can lead to a heightened sense of Americanness), their more positive reception and socioeconomic position leaves them with a greater appreciation and pride in their ethnic heritage (Kibria 2002). Therefore, some Korean Americans in Korea seem to appropriate a more cosmopolitan, transnational identity as "globalized Koreans" (Park 2006). A number of Japanese Americans in Japan also emerge from their sojourn with a transnational appreciation of their ethnic heritage as well as a greater cosmopolitan consciousness (Tsuda 2009).[5] This may also be so for the Finland Swedes, whose sociocultural integration and assimilation into Swedish society over time has been quite successful (see also Hedberg 2009). Since they eventually adopt a majority Swedish identity, while retaining their Finland Swede identities in private, they may be developing multiple, transnational affiliations to both Sweden and Finland.

Ethnic Return Migration, Immigrant Settlement, and the Changing Meanings of Home and Homeland

Diasporic return does not simply transform migrants' ethnic identities, it also causes them to reconsider the meaning of homeland. Ethnic return migrants technically have two homelands: the ethnic homeland, where their ethnic group originated, and the natal homeland, where they were born and raised. Unlike other types of immigrants, who are often part of the majority society in their natal homeland, most ethnic return migrants were ethnic minorities in their country of birth because of their foreign descent. However, when they return-migrate to their ethnic homeland, they become minorities all over again because of their foreign cultural upbringing, causing some of them to feel that they are a people without a homeland.

Quite often, the negative diasporic homecomings and sociocultural alienation experienced by most ethnic return migrants challenge their previously idealized and nostalgic affinity for their ethnic homeland. As a result, their country of ethnic origin comes to no longer feel like a homeland (cf. Christou 2006: 1048; Fox 2003: 457; Capo Zmegac 2005: 205) because it has lost the positive emotional affect as a place of desire and longing which make homelands meaningful. However, as is the case with Korean Chinese and Japanese Brazilians, when diasporic returnees are alienated from their ethnic homeland, they may redefine their natal homeland as the true homeland (Song 2009; Tsuda 2009; see also Pilkington 1998, 194; Capo Zmegac 2005: 206 for ethnic Russians and other groups). Although they did not initially regard their country of birth as a "homeland" *per se*, when they are separated from it through migration and are confronted by a negative ethnic reception abroad, they become "homesick" and develop positive nostalgic sentiments for their natal country as the place where they truly belonged. In this manner, homelands are often discovered through migration and physical absence, causing ethnic return migrants to prioritize their natal over their ethnic homeland.

At the same time, we must be careful to distinguish the concept of homeland from the concept of home. Although they are often conflated and used interchangeably in the literature (based on the assumption that "home" is located in the homeland; see, e.g., Espiritu 2003: 2, 11; Glick Schiller and Fouron 2001: 6; Parreñas 2001: 55–56), the two places do not always correspond for migrants. *Homeland* is a place of origin to which one feels emotionally attached whereas *home* is a stable place of residence that feels secure, comfortable, and familiar (see Constable 1999: 206–207; Markowitz 2004: 24; Stefansson 2004: 174). Whereas it is often the case that homeland is a place where individuals feel at home, home and homeland are not always the same place.

In fact, diasporic return can create a disconnection between home and homeland. This seems to be especially true for Korean Americans in South Korea. Although they do not feel as alienated from their country of ancestral origin as do their counterparts from the developing world, they certainly do not feel at home in their ethnic homeland. As a result, they eventually differentiate between South Korea as their homeland of racial origin and the United States as their home, where they feel more culturally familiar and comfortable (Kim 2009; see also Park 2006). In this case, it is the concept of home (not homeland) which shifts, from the place of racial belonging (South Korea) to the place of cultural belonging (United States).

Even if ethnic return migrants do not initially feel at home in their ethnic homeland, this has not prevented them from settling in the host society and eventually making it into a new home. Despite their ethnic and social alienation in their ancestral country, most of them are not returning to their countries of birth because of the greater economic opportunities and security they enjoy in the host society. Just as instrumental economic pressures (not ethnic affinity *per se*) initiated their return migration, it seems that such practical economic considerations and incentives again influence their decision to settle long term, if not permanently, in the ancestral country, even if it remains an ethnically inhospitable place where they are not socially well integrated.

The settlement of ethnic return migrants is causing another disjuncture between home and homeland. Although the ethnic "homeland" does not feel like a homeland to many of them, it has definitely become a home over time, as many have decided to settle long term with their families and have grown accustomed to life in these countries. As mentioned earlier, large return migrant groups such as Russian Jews, ethnic German Aussiedler, ethnic Russian repatriates, and Japanese-descent *nikkeijin* have created very cohesive immigrant ethnic communities with a wide range of ethnic businesses, various services, organizations, and churches, and an active ethnic media, all supported by extensive transnational economic, political, and social connections with their sending countries (see, e.g., Remennick 2003; de Tinguy 2003:124; Tsuda 2003a). Although they remain socially alienated in the host society, they feel well situated and comfortable living in these self-contained immigrant communities, where they can conduct their daily lives amongst family and compatriots in culturally familiar settings without much contact with mainstream society, while remaining actively in touch with their countries of birth. As a result, they have created a home away from the natal homeland. Undoubtedly, the immigrant host society does not have to be experienced as a homeland for it to be considered as a home. In fact, immigrants around the world have shown a remarkable ability to create homes in alienating, foreign places (see, e.g., Constable 1999: 208; Markowitz 2004: 25), and ethnic return migrants are no exception, enabling them to resist the negative effects of their social alienation and homesickness abroad (Tsuda 2003b). In this sense, the diaspora *has* truly come home.

Notes

1   Although ethnic return migration is often referred to as "co-ethnic migration," "ethnic affinity migration," or "ethnic migration" in the literature, these terms will generally not be used in this chapter because of their greater ambiguity.
2   Some white Americans of European descent have also returned to their ethnic homelands (as tourists or otherwise) in search of their ancestral roots (see, e.g., Basu 2005).
3   For American ethnic return migrants, the level of anti-American sentiment in their ethnic homelands has a significant impact on their host society reception (cf. Christou 2006a: 836–837).
4   An analogous process occurs among Korean Japanese ethnic return migrants in Japan (Kweon 2006). Some ethnic Germans also seem to adopt a non-nationalist, diasporic identity as Aussiedler who are neither Russian nor German (see von Koppenfels 2009).
5   This also seems to be the case with Chinese Americans on ethnic heritage tours in China (Louie 2004).

References

Basu, P. 2005. "Roots-tourism as return movement: Semantics and the Scottish diaspora." In M. Harper (ed.) *Emigrant Homecomings: The Return Movement of Emigrants, 1600–2000*, pp. 131–150. Manchester: Manchester University Press.

Brubaker, R. 1998. "Migrations of ethnic unmixing in the 'New Europe.'" *International Migration Review*, 32(4):1047–1065.

Capo Zmegac, J. 2005. "Ethnically privileged migrants in their new homeland." *Journal of Refugee Studies*, 18(2):199–215.

Capo Zmegac, J. 2010. "Introduction: Co-ethnic migrations compared." In Capo Zmegac *et al.* (2010), pp. 9–36.

Capo Zmegac, J., Vob, C., and Roth, K. (eds) *Co-Ethnic Migrations Compared: Central and Eastern European Contexts*. Berlin: Otto Sagner.

Cheng, L. 2002. "Transnational labor, citizenship and the Taiwan state." In A. Rosett, L. Cheng, and M.Y.K. Woo (eds) *East Asian Law: Universal Norms and Local Cultures*, pp. 85–105. New York: RoutledgeCurzon.

Christou, A. 2006. "Deciphering diaspora – Translating transnationalism: Family dynamics, identity constructions and the legacy of 'home' in second-generation Greek-American return migration." *Ethnic and Racial Studies*, 29(6):1040–1056.

Clifford, J. 1994. "Diasporas." *Cultural Anthropology*, 9(3): 302–338.

Cohen, R. 1997. *Global Diasporas: An Introduction*. Seattle: University of Washington Press.

Constable, N. 1999. "At home but not at home: Filipina narratives of ambivalent returns." *Cultural Anthropology*, 14(2): 203–228.

Cook-Martín, D. and Viadrich, A. 2009. "Imagined homecomings: the problem with similarity among ethnic return migrants in Spain." In T. Tsuda (ed.) *Diasporic Homecomings: Ethnic Return Migration in Comparative Perspective*, pp. 133–158. Stanford: Stanford University Press.

Cook-Martín, D. 2005 "The long way home or back door to the EU? Argentines' claims of ancestral nationalities." Paper presented to Diasporic Homecomings Conference, Center for Comparative Immigration Studies, University of California, San Diego, May.

de Tinguy, A. 2003. "Ethnic migrations of the 1990s from and to the successor states of the former Soviet Union: 'Repatriation' or privileged migration?" In Münz and Ohliger (2003), pp. 112–127.

Espiritu, Y.L. 2003. *Home Bound: Filipino American Lives Across Cultures, Communities, and Countries*. Berkeley: University of California Press.

Fox, J. 2003. "National identities on the move: Transylvanian Hungarian labour migrants in Hungary." *Journal of Ethnic and Migration Studies*, 29(3): 449–466.

Fox, J. 2009. "From national inclusion to economic exclusion: Transylvanian Hungarian ethnic return migration to Hungary." In T. Tsuda (ed.) *Diasporic Homecomings: Ethnic Return Migration in Comparative Perspective*, pp. 186–207. Stanford: Stanford University Press.

Glick Schiller, N. and Fouron, G.E. 2001. *Georges Woke Up Laughing: Long-Distance Nationalism and the Search for Home*. Durham, NC: Duke University Press.

Grossutti, J. 2006. "From Argentina to Friuli (1989–1994): a case of return migration?" Unpublished MS.

Hedberg, C. 2009. "Ethnic 'return' migration to Sweden: the dividing line of language." In T. Tsuda (ed.) *Diasporic Homecomings: Ethnic Return Migration in Comparative Perspective*, pp. 159–185. Stanford: Stanford University Press.

188 *Takeyuki Tsuda*

Jain, S. 2012. "For love and money: Second-generation Indian-Americans 'return' to India." *Ethnic and Racial Studies,* at http://www.tandfonline.com/doi/abs/10.1080/01419870.2011.641576?prevSearch=sonali%2Bjain&searchHistoryKey=, accessed March 8, 2013.

Joppke, C. 2005. *Selecting by Origin: Ethnic Migration in the Liberal State.* Cambridge, MA: Harvard University Press.

Joppke, C. and Rosenhek, Z. 2009. "Contesting ethnic immigration: Germany and Israel compared." In T. Tsuda (ed.) *Diasporic Homecomings: Ethnic Return Migration in Comparative Perspective,* pp. 73–99. Stanford: Stanford University Press.

Kibria, N. 2002. "Of blood, belonging, and homeland trips: Transnationalism and identity among second-generation Chinese and Korean Americans." In P. Levitt and M.C. Waters (eds) *The Changing Face of Home: The Transnational Lives of the Second Generation,* pp. 295–311. New York: Russell Sage.

Kim, N. 2009. "Finding our way home: Korean Americans, 'homeland' trips, and cultural foreignness." In T. Tsuda (ed.) *Diasporic Homecomings: Ethnic Return Migration in Comparative Perspective,* pp. 305–324. Stanford: Stanford University Press.

King, R. and Christou, A. 2010. "Cultural geographies of counter-diasporic migration: Perspectives from the study of second-generation 'returnees' to Greece." *Population, Space and Place,* 16(2): 103–119.

Kweon, S.-I. 2006. "Returning ethnic Koreans from Japan in Korea: Experiences and identities." Paper presented at the Conference on Korean Ethnic Return Migrants in South Korea, University of Auckland, New Zealand, November 27–28.

Levitt, P. 2001. *The Transnational Villagers.* Berkeley: University of California Press.

Levy, A. and Weingrod, A. 2005. *Homelands and Diasporas: Holy Lands and Other Places.* Stanford: Stanford University Press.

Louie, A. 2004. *Renegotiating Chinese Identities in China and the United States.* Durham, NC: Duke University Press.

Markowitz, F. 2004. "The home(s) of homecomings." In F. Markowitz and A. Stefansson (eds) *Homecomings: Unsettling Paths of Return,* pp. 21–33. Lanham, MD: Lexington Books.

Münz, R. and Ohliger, R. (eds) 2003. *Diasporas and Ethnic Migrants: Germany, Israel, and Post-Soviet Successor States in Comparative Perspective.* London: Frank Cass.

Ohliger, R. and Münz, R. 2003. "Diasporas and ethnic migrants in twentieth-century Europe: a comparative perspective." In Münz and Ohliger (2003), pp. 3–17.

Park, C.J. 2006. "Korean Americans in South Korea." Paper presented at the Conference on Korean Ethnic Return Migration, University of Auckland, New Zealand, November 27–28.

Parreñas, R.S. 2001. *Servants of Globalization: Women, Migration and Domestic Work.* Stanford: Stanford University Press.

Pilkington, H. 1998. *Migration, Displacement, and Identity in Post-Soviet Russia.* London: Routledge.

Remennick, L.I. 1998. "Identity quest among Russian Jews of the 1990s: Before and after emigration." In E. Krausz and G. Tulea (eds) *Jewish Survival: The Identity Problem at the Close of the Twentieth Century,* pp. 241–258. New Brunswick: Transaction Publishers.

Remennick, L.I. 2003. "A case study in transnationalism: Russian Jewish immigrants in Israel of the 1990s." In Münz and Ohliger (2003), pp. 370–384.

Skrentny, J., Chan, S., Fox, J.E., and Kim, D. 2009. "Defining nations in Asia and Europe: a comparative analysis of ethnic return migration policy." In T. Tsuda (eds) *Diasporic*

Homecomings: Ethnic Return Migration in Comparative Perspective, pp. 44–72. Stanford: Stanford University Press.

Song, C. 2009. "Brothers only in name: the alienation and identity transformation of Korean Chinese return migrants in South Korea." In T. Tsuda (ed.) *Diasporic Homecomings: Ethnic Return Migration in Comparative Perspective*, pp. 281–304. Stanford: Stanford University Press.

Stefansson, A.H. 2004. "Refugee returns to Sarajevo and their challenge to contemporary narratives of mobility." In L.D. Long and E. Oxfeld (eds) *Coming Home? Refugees, Migrants, and Those Who Stayed Behind*, pp.170–186. Philadelphia: University of Pennsylvania Press.

Takenaka, A. 2009. "Ethnic hierarchy and its impact on ethnic identities: a comparative analysis of Peruvian and Brazilian return migrants in Japan." In T. Tsuda (eds) *Diasporic Homecomings: Ethnic Return Migration in Comparative Perspective*, pp. 260–280. Stanford: Stanford University Press.

Tsuda, T. 1999. "The permanence of 'temporary' migration: the 'structural embeddedness' of Japanese Brazilian migrant workers in Japan." *Journal of Asian Studies*, 58(3): 687–722.

Tsuda, T. 2001. "When identities become modern: Japanese immigrants in Brazil and the global contextualization of identity." *Ethnic and Racial Studies*, 24(3): 412–432.

Tsuda, T. 2003a. *Strangers in the Ethnic Homeland: Japanese Brazilian Return Migration in Transnational Perspective*. New York: Columbia University Press.

Tsuda, T. 2003b. "Homeland-less abroad: Transnational liminality, social alienation, and personal malaise." In J. Lesser (ed.) *Searching for Home Abroad: Japanese Brazilians and Transnationalism*, pp. 121–161. Durham, NC: Duke University Press.

Tsuda, T. 2009. "Global inequities and diasporic return: Japanese American and Brazilian encounters with the ethnic homeland." In Takeyuki Tsuda (ed.) *Diasporic Homecomings: Ethnic Return Migration in Comparative Perspective*, pp. 227–259. Stanford: Stanford University Press.

Van Hear, N. 1998. *New Diasporas: The Mass Exodus, Dispersal and Regrouping of Migrant Communities*. Seattle: University of Washington Press.

Viladrich, A. 2005 "Going back home? Argentine return migrants in transnational perspective." Paper presented to Diasporic Homecomings Conference, Center for Comparative Immigration Studies, University of California, San Diego, May.

von Koppenfels, A. K. 2009. "From Germans to migrants: Aussiedler migration to Germany." In T. Tsuda (ed.) *Diasporic Homecomings: Ethnic Return Migration in Comparative Perspective*, pp. 103–132. Stanford: Stanford University Press.

Chapter 11

Interracial Sex and the Making of Empire

Carina Ray

In an oft-cited and widely critiqued essay, the historian of British empire, Ronald Hyam (1986b), claimed that "the expansion of Europe was not only a matter of 'Christianity and commerce,' it was also a matter of copulation and concubinage." To this he added, "Sexual opportunities were seized with imperious confidence" (p.35). In *Empire and Sexuality: The British Experience* (1990), Hyam further developed his contention that the sexual opportunities available abroad to Europe's empire builders were more than just a perk of imperial expansion; they were, he boldly claimed, what sustained the large numbers of European men who fanned out across the globe in the service of empire. Freed from repressive Victorian morality codes at home, European men could fulfill their libidinous desires with the colonies' sexually decadent "natives." Hyam's explorations of the complex role played by sex in the making of empire are characterized by a marked interest in what interracial sexual relations meant for British men and for imperialism. As one of his critics points out, his "imperialist centered approach" causes him to take "the position of the white male colonialists, imperial administrators and soldiers who staffed the British Empire, and he fails to link his discussion of sex and empire with any analysis of the power relations in the various situations which he describes"; nor does he offer any analysis of the "providers" of sexual opportunity – colonized women and girls, as well as colonized men and boys (Berger 1988: 84; for Hyam's response to Berger, see Hyam 1988; for other critiques, see Strobel 1992; Voeltz 1996). Hyam's approach, which perpetuates the erasure of the colonized found in outdated colonial histories, where Europeans, as agents of the "civilizing mission," were the center of attention, is particularly problematic precisely because interracial sexual relation-

A Companion to Diaspora and Transnationalism, First Edition.
Edited by Ato Quayson and Girish Daswani.
© 2013 Blackwell Publishing Ltd. Published 2013 by Blackwell Publishing Ltd.

ships are constituted through multiple histories; to take up only one of those histories is to tell only part of the story. It might not be possible to tell both sides of the story with parity in evidence, but we cannot let that prevent us from raising questions, even if we do not always answer them fully, about how colonized populations negotiated their sexual encounters with Europeans.

For all of its well-documented shortcomings, however, Hyam's work made a claim for the British empire that subsequent, more sophisticated scholarship substantiated, rather than contradicted, not only for Britain, but for Europe's other imperial powers more broadly: sex, and in particular interracial sex, was critical to the formation of empire.[1] Drawing on this extensive body of literature, this chapter brings together examples from the Americas, the Caribbean, Africa, and Asia in order to assess the multiple modalities of interracial sexual relationships as they unfolded over the *longue durée* of Europe's imperial expansion, beginning in the late fifteenth century and winding down in the mid-twentieth century with the wave of independence movements that swept across Africa, Asia, and parts of the Caribbean. This chapter illuminates the common threads running through this chronologically and geographically broad field of enquiry, as well as the diverse and divergent patterns in the historical development of these relationships.

A singular focus on temporality, geography, or even colonizing power does little in the way of explaining these commonalities and variations. Rather, the life histories of individual colonial projects provide the necessary context for understanding the different forms taken by interracial sexual relationships (marriage, concubinage, prostitution, rape) at particular historical moments and in particular locales and how this changed over time; the ideologies and anxieties that shaped their existence; the diverse systems of regulation devised to encourage, manage, control, penalize, criminalize, or prohibit interracial sex; and the kinds of relationships and categories of people that were marked out for different forms of regulation. In short, context is key. It matters greatly whether the unit of analysis is a settler colony, an administered colony, a colony under company rule, a slaveholding colony, or a colony with a large standing military. Equally, demographics matter: gender ratios across and within racial groups significantly influenced patterns of race mixture. Cultural beliefs and practices, not least among them attitudes about sex on the part of indigenous, enslaved, and European communities, also shaped practices and policies where interracial relationships were concerned.

Divided into three different overlapping sections, this chapter traces the common threads and divergent patterns that are discernible in the global history of interracial sex and the making of empire. It begins by attending to the dominant raced and gendered configuration of interracial sexual relationships – the colonizing male/colonized female dyad – while also addressing the question of relationships between colonized men and colonizing women. The second and third parts assess how the nature of different colonial encounters and their imperatives influenced patterns of interracial sexual relationships by drawing on examples from the Americas and Caribbean, where conquest and colonization were immediate, and Africa and Asia, where the era of formal colonization in the nineteenth century was generally preceded by centuries of trade-based relationships and company rule. Considerable effort has been made to provide the broadest possible coverage, both spatial and temporal; however not all areas and time periods are covered equally. The extensive references that accompany this chapter are intended to provide readers with sources for further consultation.

Common Threads/Divergent Patterns

The raced and gendered configuration of interracial sexual relationships

Colonial interracial sexual relations varied greatly across time and space, but were also remarkably consistent in their raced and gendered configuration: they almost always occurred between European men and indigenous women, or in the case of empires' slaveholding societies, enslaved or formerly enslaved non-native women. Imbalanced sex ratios among Europeans in the colonies offer a partial explanation for this pattern. From the earliest days of Europe's overseas exploration in the late fifteenth and sixteenth centuries, European women were largely absent from contact zones in Africa, Asia, the Americas, and Caribbean. Even in Latin America where the age of encounter quickly gave way to Spanish colonization and widespread set- tlement during the sixteenth century, the emigrant female Spanish population peaked at just below 30 percent. While their numbers increased in the following century – 42 percent of Spanish emigrants to New Spain were female as were 32 percent of emigrants to Peru between 1598 and 1621 – Spanish men still outnum- bered their female counterparts by a substantial margin in many places throughout Spain's New World empire (Horton 2001: 22–23; Sanchez-Abornoz 1984: 16–17, 21). Even as late as the nineteenth century in Cuba, white men still outnumbered white women (Stolcke 1989: 57). This partly accounts for the frequency with which white men cohabitated and/or married indigenous women and formed a range of different sexual and domestic arrangements with enslaved and free/d women of African descent throughout Spain's Caribbean and Latin American possessions.

Throughout Africa and Asia, contrary to popular perception, imbalanced sex ratios continued to be the status quo long after the age of exploration and conquest was over and, as Ann Stoler notes (1989: 638), "rough living and a scarcity of ameni- ties had become conditions of the past." It was not until the turn of the twentieth century that European women took up residency in the African and Asian colonies in sizable numbers and, even then, they were still outnumbered by their male coun- terparts. This was largely the case because colonial governments and private businesses variously restricted the emigration of European women to the colonies, refused employment to rank-and-file married male recruits, and only extended the privilege of bringing a wife to the colonies to men of rank or those who had successfully completed several tours of service and could demonstrate their ability to maintain their wives in a standard suitable to European womanhood (Stoler 1989: 637). Such practices influenced the colonies' demography in stark ways. In Britain's Gold Coast colony, at the late date of 1931, only 17 percent of the European male population were accompanied by their wives (Gold Coast Census: PRAAD, ACC, ADM 5/2/6). In the French colonies of Ivory Coast, Dahomey (Benin), and Congo, the 1904–1905 census recorded a total of 2,469 French-born men and only 236 French-born women (Tiryakian 1993). Improvement did not follow in the following decade and a half: by 1921 the European sex ratio in Ivory Coast was 1:25 (Stoler 1991: 53). Even in the settler colony of Madagascar, French-born women made up only 37 percent of the total French-born population. This statistic is striking given that by definition settler colonialism depended on the ability of the settler population to reproduce itself in large enough numbers to sustain a permanent occupation.

In colonial Asia during the twentieth century European demographics were less skewed, but they were never balanced and they varied greatly from place to place:

> While in the Netherlands Indies, the overall ratio of European women to men rose from 47:100 to 88:100 between 1900 and 1930, on Sumatra's plantation belt in 1920 there were still only 61 European women per 100 European men. . . . In Tonkin, European men (totaling more than 14,000) sharply outnumbered European women (just over 3000) as late as 1931 (Stoler 1989: 638).

These gender imbalances, as Stoler points out (2002: 2), resulted from how sexuality was managed, not the other way around: in other words interracial sexual relationships were not tolerated and/or encouraged because there were so few European women in the colonies; rather, there were so few European women in the colonies because colonial regimes found it more expedient to meet the sexual and domestic needs of European men through relationships with colonized women. When and where this was no longer the case, colonial administrators sought to increase the number of European women in the colonies as part of a wider set of efforts to bring interracial sexual relationships to an end. Rather than heralding their demise, such efforts pushed these relationships to the margins of colonial society, where they were carried out more clandestinely (Edwards 1998: 118).

While more balanced sex ratios might have decreased the frequency of interracial sexual relationships in some colonial settings, or at the very least diminished their visibility, this was not the case across the board and especially so in slaveholding societies. In colonial America's slaveholding south, sex – often coerced – between white slave masters and enslaved and/or free/d women, persisted long after the gender ratios in the white population evened out (D'Emilio and Freedman 1997: 35). During the eighteenth century in colonial Barbados, white women often marginally outnumbered white men; elsewhere in the West Indies, with the exception of Jamaica, by the second half of the eighteenth century sex ratios in the European population became relatively balanced as well, but this did not curb the frequency with which white men engaged in sexual relationships with black women (Beckles 1993: 70–71; Burnard 1991: 98). Clearly then, lack of sexual access to white women was not the primary factor driving white men into sexual relationships with black women. Indeed, the very nature of their sexual relationships with white women, structured by notions of respectability and expectations of paternal responsibility for any resultant offspring, may have heightened their libidinous desire for black women, with whom sexual contact was not subjected to the same kinds of morality codes. Given that these relationships reinforced rather than undermined racial domination, and reinscribed white male privilege (unlike white men, white women did not have immunity from the law and social custom to freely engage in sexual relations with black men), they formed an integral part of the system of white supremacy and patriarchy that was at the heart of chattel slavery.

Just as white men's unfettered sexual access to colonized/enslaved women embodied the raced and gendered power dynamics of empire, so too did the restricted sexual access of colonized/enslaved men and white women to one another. Across Europe's empires, sexual relationships between European women and indigenous or enslaved men in the colonies were comparatively rare. Cast as sexually depraved in general and fixated on white women in particular, colonized/enslaved men were seen as sexual threats to white women and by extension to race-based colonial power. Because in the colonial imagination it was unthinkable that all but the most degenerate white women would willingly engage in sexual relationships with colonized/enslaved men, rape became the primary paradigm through which such relationships were understood. Popularly known as the Black Peril, hysteria over the rape of white women gave way to draconian legislation. In early twentieth-century colonial contexts as diverse as Papua New Guinea and Southern Rhodesia, native men were put to death for the rape, attempted rape, or even suspected rape of white women (for Papua New Guinea, see Inglis 1974, 1975; for Southern Rhodesia, see McCulloch 2000). In a number of American colonies black men could be castrated for the attempted rape of white women and put to death if convicted of rape (D'Emilio and Freedman 2006: 163–209). And while lynching is typically a phenomenon associated with post-independence US history, there can be no doubt that in colonial America extrajudicial modes of punishment were also meted out to black men suspected of raping white women (on the history of lynching in colonial America, see Berg 2011). Neither the outbreak of Black Peril scares, nor the severity of punishments they provoked, correlated to actual incidences of rape. Instead these scares reveal how colonial communities' investments in protecting white women's sexual-cum-racial purity were often a means through which Europeans in the colonies shored up their interests and created racial unity during crises of control, whether real or perceived (Stoler 2002: 58).[2]

Although relationships between colonized/enslaved men and white women were typically a hidden facet of colonial life, this was not always the case, especially when both parties shared similar class status. In twentieth-century British West Africa, wealthy African men who had married white women in Europe were given permission to return home with their wives provided they were able to demonstrate to colonial authorities that they could provide their wives with a lifestyle befitting European womanhood. The stringent standards West Africans were required to meet are reflected in the very small number (six) of documented cases fitting this description (Ray 2009: 641). If, however, we expand our analysis to include the British metropole, relationships between black men and white women during the nineteenth and early twentieth centuries become significantly less exceptional. At the opposite end of the class spectrum, in the context of the early American colonies, it was not uncommon for white indentured female servants and black male servants and slaves to cohabit openly and some even married (Hodes 1997: 19–38; Finkelman 1997: 125). In South Africa's Witwatersrand during the late nineteenth and early twentieth centuries sexual relationships between black men and white women "developed most readily along class lines – those between [black] 'houseboys' and white female servants being relatively prominent" (Van Onselen 1982: 47, 49). In the latter two cases, the window of opportunity for these relationships closed as systems of racial domination intensified (a similar trend holds true for colonial Barbados; see Beckles 1989: 134). In the case of colonial America it was the entrenchment of racialized chattel slavery that ultimately led to laws criminalizing relationships between white women and black men, while upholding the right of white men to engage in sexual relationships with enslaved women (Millward 2010: 24). In South Africa the increasingly institutionalized system of racial segregation and domination that undergirded settler colonialism and ultimately culminated in the formation of the apartheid state in 1948, ruptured the common bonds that had previously brought white and black domestic workers together in ways that facilitated their romantic relationships.

Both the ubiquity of the colonizing male/colonized female dyad and the comparative rarity of relationships between indigenous and/or enslaved men and white women speak volumes about the raced and gendered nature of colonial power. Because this pattern was an enduring feature of empire, it places indigenous and/or enslaved women at the center of the making of empire in ways that require much greater attention to their lives within and beyond their relationships with European men. As Pamela Scully (2005a, 2005b) has aptly pointed out, the "victim/traitor dynamic that has shaped so much of the literature on indigenous women" involved with European men leaves little room for understanding the full complexities of their lives, including how the gendered cultural and sexual economies of local societies "created the conditions for particular kinds of interactions with powerful strangers" (para 28). The following sections make clear that indigenous communities often shored up their own interests by extending sexual and marriage rights to European men, but we know much less about how local women perceived and negotiated their relationships with European men.

Conquest/early settler colonization

When Portuguese explorers left the Iberian peninsula in the early fifteenth century in search of a sea route to the Indies, they ushered in the era of Europe's imperial expansion. Portuguese mariners spent much of that century exploring the western African coast before Bartolomeu Dias rounded the southernmost tip of the continent in 1488. A decade later Vasco da Gama finally reached Calicut in southern India. For Africa and Asia, Portuguese exploration paved the way for a protracted process of European empire building that began with trade and ended in formal colonization in the nineteenth century. Encounter in much of the Americas and the Caribbean proceeded along very different lines. Spain's maritime exploits in the New World at the end of the fifteenth century ushered in an era of almost immediate conquest and colonization for the regions' inhabitants.

Upon arrival or shortly thereafter Europe's invading settlers used a combination of military and germ warfare to achieve wide-scale theft of land in the New World, especially in the Caribbean, Latin America, and parts of North America. Evidence suggests that for native communities faced with the threat of extinction by Spain's invading armies, handing over native women to conquistadors, already a common practice among Amerindians, may very well have been a strategy of survival. During the invasion of Mexico, for instance, "chiefs sought to placate the invaders, or to cement alliances with them, by gifts of women" (Lunenfeld 1991: 327). The most famous instance of this, the relationship between Malintzin and Spanish conquistador Hernán Cortés, began when her Tabascan masters gave the enslaved Malintzin to Cortés "along with nineteen other women . . . in order to stave off war, avoid being conquered themselves, and to encourage Cortés to move on" (John Taylor 2000). Malintzin's linguistic prowess quickly distinguished her from the other women and Cortés soon took her as his interpreter and mistress. She later bore him a son. Although, as a woman, her role as a prominent interpreter and advisor to Cortés was unusual, her sexual relationship was not, nor was her subsequent marriage to another Spanish conquistador. In the years that followed conquest, both marriage and concubinage between indigenous women and European men became an integral component of Spanish America's settlement, as sex ratios in the European population remained imbalanced. In the highland areas of Mexico and the Andean region, where indigenous populations survived the Spanish American conquest in the largest numbers, these relationships produced a large *mestizo* population. By the mid-sixteenth century, however, Spanish colonists began to fear that their own prerogatives were being undermined by the growth of the *mestizo* population and in turn the Crown stopped encouraging marital unions between Spanish men and Christianized Indian women (Stoler 2002: 76). In addition to the native population, a sizable number of imported African slaves also supplied labor to the region's lucrative mining economy, and later plantation and livestock-raising economies (Florescano 1984: 164–165). Sexual relationships between European settlers and enslaved and free/d women gave rise to a population of mixed African and European descent, albeit much smaller than the *mestizo* population.

Where conquest was achieved through genocide, as in much of the Caribbean and North American colonies, or where indigenous labor was difficult to obtain, as in Brazil, Europe's settler colonial regimes relied almost exclusively on imported slave labor from Africa to achieve their economic objectives. Given the unequal power relationships that accompanied conquest and colonization, in large swathes of the New World interracial sexual relations were often characterized by coercion, especially in slaveholding societies, where the imbalance of power between colonizer and colonized was made more obscene by the relations of dominance between owner and owned. While rape was common elsewhere in the colonial world, in the slaveholding societies of the Americas and Caribbean it occurred with far greater frequency and impunity, and the line between coercion and consent was never clear.

In her analysis of creolization in the early French Caribbean, Doris Garraway (2005) deploys an alternative reading of the concept of libertinage, as "a sexual economy that undergirded exploitative power relations among whites, free people of color, and slaves," to show how interracial sex was implicated in the making of "the extreme segregationist regime that reached its apogee in the exceptionally brutal slave society of late-eighteenth-century Saint-Domingue" (p. xiii). There, as in other slaveholding societies, white men's sexual access to enslaved women was held as a right grounded not only in their privileged racial position, but also, as Carolyn West (2004) points out, in their portrayal of "enslaved women as promiscuous, immoral Jezebels who seduced their masters." "Consequently," West continues, "there were no legal or social sanctions against raping Black women" because they were always, in the minds of their masters, willing participants – they were in effect unrapeable (2004: 1491; also see D. White 1999; for the Caribbean see Beckles 1989: 142–143 and Garraway 2005: xiv). Such relations were not just about domination and desire, they were also about wealth and its reproduction. Both rape and consensual sex held out the possibility of literally reproducing slave masters' wealth, and hence the empire's wealth, when it resulted in pregnancy because the doctrine of *partus sequitur ventrem*, common in many parts of the New World, mandated that the offspring's legal status followed that of the mother (Garraway 2005; Davis 2002: 16).

From the perspective of enslaved women, given that their consent was not a prerequisite and resistance could have dire consequences, it is difficult to speculate about how they negotiated and experienced their sexual encounters with white men, except to say that their choices were made "in a context warped and circumscribed by slavery" (Brown 1996: 237; Millward 2010: 26). While sexual relationships with white men could result in manumission for enslaved women and/or their offspring, there were no guarantees. As Jessica Millward notes, "manumission laws were slaveholders' laws, and any space left for a slave to gain freedom through them was a loophole, not an open door" (p. 26). Still, according to Millward, "some shrewd and deliberate enslaved women maximized their relationships with those who owned them in order to provide a better future for themselves or their children" (p. 26). Over time, as the freed and free-born population increased, so too did the number of women whose relationships with white men were no longer defined primarily by their status as property; however, as historian Marisa Fuentes asks (2010: 565–566), "if 'freedom' meant free from bondage but not from social, economic and political degradation what does it mean to survive under such conditions?" Focusing on free/d women in Barbados, Fuentes argues that under these conditions the agency often ascribed to black women in their sexual relationships with white men elides the wholly unequal terrain upon which such relations were negotiated and the disparate outcomes they produced for individual women.

The emphasis here on the predominance of rape in slaveholding societies is not meant to suggest that more stable, if not equitable, arrangements, whether marriage or concubinage, were unheard of in some slaveholding societies. Verena Martinez-Alier's work on colonial Cuba has demonstrated that despite strong social sanctions against intermarriage, whites and blacks did marry, while many others openly cohabitated outside of marriage (Stolcke 1989). Nor do I want to suggest that rape was uncommon in non-slaveholding colonial societies. To be sure, rape and other forms of sexual exploitation of colonized women by European men were facets of colonial life that rarely received public censure precisely because, like enslaved women, non-enslaved colonized women were regarded as sexually available. The rape of native women, who were often cast as sexually licentious, was widespread not only in the North American colonies, but also in the westward conquest and colonization of the American frontier. In the case of colonial India, Ghosh (2006) notes that European men were frequently acquitted of rape charges "based largely on the understanding that native women who lived among Europeans and their acquaintances were assumed to be potential conjugal companions to European men and sexually available, thereby mitigating any accusation of rape" (p.197). In short, the very idea that a native woman could be raped could be called into question. Yet, in some colonial contexts indigenous women had recourse to a legal system that, in theory at least, regarded their rape as a criminal offense; enslaved women did not have that benefit. Underscoring this reminds us that the label "colonized" glosses over pronounced differences in status within colonized populations. Perhaps the most dramatic of these axes of difference was between enslaved and free, especially in areas where slavery outlived colonialism.

The other point to be made here is that neither concubinage nor marriage were guarantors of freedom from sexual violence or exploitation. In the colonial context, concubinage, a befittingly ambiguous term for an even more ambiguous phenomenon, generally referred to cohabitation outside marriage between European men and colonized women. As Stoler notes (2002: 59), this narrow definition:

> glossed a wide range of arrangements that included sexual access to a non-European woman as well as demands on her labor and legal rights to the children she bore. Thus, to define concubinage as cohabitation perhaps suggests more social privileges than most women who were involved in such relations enjoyed. Many colonized women combined sexual and domestic service within the abjectly subordinate contexts of slave or "coolie" and lived in separate quarters.

And although marriage came with a certain set of legal rights and protections, it did not necessarily protect colonized women from abuse, racial domination, or gendered oppression. These observations are particularly important to keep in mind as we move to the next section, which deals in large part with marriage and concubinage in the contexts of early colonial trading settlements, company rule, and late formal colonialism.

Trade, company rule, and late formal colonialism

Where trade, rather than outright conquest and colonization, dominated imperial agendas during the early centuries of Europe's overseas expansion, as was the case in much of littoral Africa and Asia, and even parts of northern North America, the power relations between Europeans and those with whom they came into contact were not as imbalanced as they would later become. In this context interracial sexual relations were often, but not always, a middle ground upon which Europeans and indigenous communities solidified economic, political, and social alliances. Indeed, European economic imperatives and the precarious position in which European men often found themselves, as outnumbered strangers in unfamiliar lands, meant that the vanguard of early traders and colonists depended on indigenous communities for their very survival. This continued to be the case into the nineteenth century in many parts of Africa and Asia. In this context indigenous women provided European men with more than just sex and language instruction, they also dispensed medical care and domestic services, and often served as cultural interpreters and partners in commercial exchanges (Stoler 2002: 49). Without overstating the case, where the balance of power between Europeans and indigenous communities was more equitable, interracial sexual relationships tended to be more consensual, at least as far as the men who brokered such relations on behalf of their female relatives and dependents were concerned. Europeans were in no position to seize "with imperious confidence" sexual opportunities with local women, without first securing the approval of their fathers, uncles, lineage heads, or other male power-holders, who typically controlled sexual access to female dependents. This point is important because it draws our attention to the fact that while some women brokered relationships with white men on their own, and others willingly cohabitated or married them at their families' behest, others were forced to accept arrangements that were not of their own choosing.[3]

A variety of sexual and domestic arrangements between indigenous women and European men played an integral role in rooting the European presence in areas where a long era of trade and company rule preceded formal colonization. In North America's Great Lakes region, where France lacked the manpower to colonize Native American lands through brute force and its interests were primarily economic, seventeenth- and eighteenth-century marriages between indigenous women and French traders and the kin networks they produced formed the bedrock of the region's lucrative fur trade. Intermarriage was not only an integral part of stranger integration and alliance-making between Europeans and Native Americans, it also placed Native American women and their *métis* offspring at the heart of the process of cultural transmission and adaptation (Sleeper-Smith 2001, esp. 38–46). While interracial marriage was common in the Great Lakes and elsewhere in Native American regions of North America, so too was the practice of providing temporary sexual access to Native women. Like intermarriage, this was part of a wider ideology of reciprocity and set of practices designed to display hospitality and to engender friendships and loyal trading relationships (Hurtado 1996: 60; the classic work on the idea of reciprocity in the making of Native American–European relationships in the Great Lakes Region is R. White 1991).

Spiritual beliefs also appear to have played a role in Native motivations for granting Europeans sexual access to native women, at least in the case of the Mandan and Hidatsa peoples of the Upper Missouri and other Great Plains Indians, who "believed that the coitus transferred power from one man to another, using the woman as a kind of transmission line" (Hurtado 1996: 60). Thus, both indigenous and European systems of patriarchy shaped the limits of indigenous women's control over their own bodies and sexuality. Although the grand narrative about interracial sex in the context of the fur trade remains focused on consensual relationships, however imperfectly defined, a lesser-known aspect of this history is the purchase of enslaved Native American women by fur traders for use as "wives" and the rape of Native American women (Hurtado 1996: 61; Carter and McCormack 2011: 342). This last point draws our attention, once again, to the need to pay attention to both the common threads and divergent patterns that characterize histories of interracial sex.

In littoral Africa and Asia, intermarriage and interracial cohabitation functioned similarly during the long period of trade and company rule that only gave way to formal colonialism in the nineteenth century. Some of our earliest information about these relationships comes from the Portuguese sphere of influence on the coast of West Africa. On the Upper Guinea coast during the sixteenth and seventeenth centuries, Portuguese traders were few in number, relatively autonomous, and although they were ostensibly there to trade on behalf of the Portuguese Crown, the Crown provided them with little in the way of protection, supervision, food supplies, or shelter. Instead, individual Portuguese traders had to develop reciprocal relationships with local African communities in order to meet their economic objectives and everyday needs. Through marital alliances with local women, Portuguese traders, like African strangers, were absorbed into host societies and through these attachments Africans attempted to derive the maximum benefit from the Portuguese traders in their midst (Brooks 1993: 38; also see Newitt 2010: 81). Pursuing interracial unions was as a strategy used not only by European men to advance their agendas, but also by African societies to shore up their interests. While these relationships were brokered with the benefit of the family and wider community in mind, some African women who married or cohabited with European traders were able to accumulate considerable wealth and power for themselves. The African and mixed-race women who became known as *nharas* in Guinea-Bissau and *signares* in Gorée and Saint-Louis, Senegal, as well as their counterparts on the Gold Coast, derived their wealth largely from the entrepreneurial niches they were able to carve out for themselves in the transatlantic slave trade. Thus, their fortunes were not only linked to European men and the wider Atlantic economy, but also to their exceptional skills and personal networks. If, as Amanda Vickery has noted for the eighteenth century (2011: 24), "women everywhere were more likely to garner prestige and power via men than by their own abilities or female contacts," the *nharas* and *signares* demonstrate that this was not a one-way street. In this early period of the colonial encounter in littoral Africa, European men's entrepreneurial successes were often realized through their relationships with African women. On the Upper Guinea coast, these unions gradually produced an identifiable Luso-African population and culture, through which both Africans and Europeans increasingly mediated their relationships (for the development of the Luso-African population and culture on the Upper Guinea coast, see Mark 2002; Brooks 2003).

Even at this early period, however, a divergent pattern in official policy had already emerged further south along the coast in the port of Elmina, where the Portuguese Crown disapproved of marital unions between local women and traders and officers who came to the Gold Coast under the auspices of the Crown (Feinberg 1989: 88; de Marees, van Dantzig, and Jones 1987: 217). Unlike the Portuguese on the Upper Guinea coast, who lived among local communities, most of their counterparts in Elmina resided within the confines of their coastal fort, São Jorge da Mina, built in 1481 to protect King João II's royal monopoly on trade (Boxer 1963: 11; Feinberg 1989: 88). As with the construction of the fort, all regulations were geared towards the promotion and protection of trade (Vogt 1979: 7–8). Thus, the administration's disapproval of intermarriage likely stemmed from concerns that access to local women's networks would increase opportunities for illicit trade. In short, the tightly controlled institutionalized trade in Elmina rendered these unions a threat rather than an asset to the Crown's economic interests.

In lieu of sanctioning stable unions with local women, the administration supplied officers with female slaves who tended to their domestic needs (Vogt 1979: 57). Their sexual needs were met through a system of prostitution, in which women, who were likely enslaved, were housed in the fort expressly for this purpose (Vogt 1979: 234, n. 63; on the likelihood that these women were slaves, see Akyeampong 1997: 146–49). Despite these provisions, some fortsmen also maintained liaisons with townswomen. The local contacts made through these relations may even partially account for the rampant illicit trade that was occurring between the fort's residents and local townspeople. Even if unsuccessful, the administration's disapproval of marital unions in favor of a system of prostitution must be understood as an explicit attempt to manage interracial sexual relations in a manner intended to advance the Crown's agenda on the Gold Coast.

When the Dutch wrested control of Elmina from the Portuguese in 1637, it signaled the end of Portuguese hegemony on the coast and ushered in an era of intense competition among Europeans for control over the coast's lucrative trading settlements. Whether it was the trading companies of the Dutch in Elmina, the Danes in Accra and Keta, or the Swedes and later the British in Cape Coast, all regulated interracial sexual relations in an attempt to stabilize the European male population, create and sustain local political and economic alliances, and groom the offspring of these unions for company service (Ray 2007: 36–53). As was the case on the Upper

202   *Carina Ray*

inea coast, coastal ethnic groups, such as the Fante and Ga, were drawing on their own precolonial traditions of using marriage alliances to foster stranger integration and strengthen their political and economic positions when they extended the privilege of marriage and/or cohabitation with local women to Europeans. These cases demonstrate that from the earliest moments of Europe's imperial expansion, the domain of interracial sexual relations was a space in which Europeans and Africans were actively working out the mechanics of encounter. Accordingly, it was in and around trading settlements, where interracial unions and the prominent Afro-European trading families they produced were prevalent, that hybrid cultural formations took root characterized by cultural transfer on both sides (see, e.g., Yarak 2003; Feinberg 1989; Everts 2002; Gocking 1999).

Asia's early colonial encounters were also shaped in large part by the relationships that European men forged with indigenous and Eurasian women. These relationships and the enduring matrilineal kin networks they produced became the bedrock of what Jean Taylor (1983) calls *mestizo* culture. While specifically referring to Indonesia, Taylor's (1983: xix) definition is useful because it considers the diversity in both local and European populations that constituted many early colonial enclaves:

> Mestizo characterizes a culture made up of many influences, extending beyond the Dutch and Indonesian. It underlines the fact that migrants on Dutch ships represented many states in Europe and that the local peoples amongst whom they lived included Indians, Japanese, Indonesians of all sorts, and people descended from an earlier meeting of East and West, from unions between Asians and Portuguese.

The gendered nature of immigration to Indonesia played a significant role in ensuring the longevity of *mestizo* culture's Asian influences. Because with few exceptions Dutch authorities prevented Dutch women from immigrating to Indonesia until the nineteenth century, Indies families were the product of relationships between European male immigrants and the locally born Asian or part-Asian women who were their wives, concubines, and slaves (Jean Taylor 1983: 15). Rarely sent to Europe, the female offspring of these unions, in turn, served as the bride pool for incoming European immigrants. Steeped in the cultural milieu of their mothers and Asian servants, they ensured the continuity not only of the Asian influences in *mestizo* culture, but also of the powerful kin networks that dominated the Dutch Indies until the nineteenth century. As Taylor notes (1983: 71), "crucial family links were not those between father and son but between a man and his in-laws. At the heart of the Indies clan were women, locally born and raised, who brought men into relationships of patron and protégé as father-in-law, son-in-law, and brothers-in-law." To be sure, not all interracial sexual relationships were marital in nature, many were fleeting, others were coerced. What is important to point out, however, is that they were an indispensable part of the way in which the early European presence established itself in parts of Asia, and, as we have already seen, West Africa, during the era in which Europe's interests in these regions were trade-based, rather than about large-scale territorial acquisition and direct political control. This ethos was characterized by the fact that throughout Asia and Africa it was trading companies, like the Dutch East Indies Company (VOC) and West India Company (GWC); Britain's Royal African Company and later the British African Company of Merchants; and the Swedish African Company, that presided over Europe's imperial presence in these regions.

The period of company rule in Asia and Africa was not, however, uniform in terms of the context that it provided for interracial sexual relationships. For instance, within a few decades of founding the VOC's settlement at the Cape of Good Hope, the Dutch made interracial marriages illegal in 1685. This is not surprising given that VOC rule at the Cape was less about trade and more about widespread territorial acquisition and conquest of native peoples. While much has been written about the ubiquity of interracial marriage and cohabitation in the Gold Coast during company rule, there was a darker side to this story. As the slave trade came to dominate the commercial life of the coast's trading settlements, women held captive in the bowels of Elmina and Cape Coast castles prior to embarking on the dreaded Middle Passage were raped by the European inhabitants of the castles. Scholarship has not yet established the extent of this practice, but it has been memorialized in the narratives that the castles' tour guides regularly tell visitors. This provides a stark reminder, yet again, of the significant role that a woman's status played in shaping her sexual encounters with European men and underscores a point made earlier about the link between slavery and rape. Needless to say European men could not rape with impunity the free townswomen of Elmina and Cape Coast; they reserved that treatment for enslaved women who could do little in the way of resisting their captors and were without kin who could protect them from the depravations of the slave trade.

As Europe's limited governance in service of trade transformed over the course of the nineteenth century into formal colonialism characterized by large-scale land acquisition and the institutionalization of territory-wide governance structures in Africa and Asia, often achieved through military conquest, colonial regimes were far less dependent on the good will and cooperation of indigenous communities. Although European men still had many of their sexual and domestic needs met through relationships with colonized women, colonial governments would come to view such relationships as a hindrance rather than a help to the new colonial dispensation. As a result, administrators and policymakers focused their attention on eradicating concubinage. It is instructive that marriage and prostitution were not the foci of these efforts. By the late nineteenth century interracial marriages recognized by the colonial state were largely a thing of the past, although mixed marriages contracted in accordance with native law and recognized by indigenous communities were not.[4] Prostitution was elevated above concubinage as the preferred method of meeting the sexual needs of European men who were not permitted or could not afford to marry full-blooded European women.

Ann Stoler's observation (2002: 51) that concubinage increasingly fell out of favor with colonial administrators, "when European identity and supremacy were

thought to be vulnerable, in jeopardy, or less than convincing" helps to make sense
of the timing of some of the better-known French and British efforts to bring the practice to an end. Typically, such efforts were undertaken as part and parcel of the
process of legitimizing, institutionalizing, and professionalizing the colonial service
in Asia and Africa. In French Cambodia, as part of Governor-General Doumer's
efforts to professionalize its ragtag colonial service at the turn of the twentieth
century he "took immediate steps to police the private lives of French administrators," which included instructing them "to avoid relationships with native concubines"
(Edwards 1998: 117–118). Similar injunctions against concubinage were soon made
elsewhere in Indochina. While interracial concubinage was never officially prohibited in French West Africa, by the second decade of the twentieth century colonial
administrators were no longer openly encouraging the practice and it was generally
frowned upon by colonial society, although it remained a common, if clandestine,
practice (Conklin 1998: 70; O. White 1999: 12). The French colony of Guinea
appears to have been exceptional in its efforts to ban concubinage (see Klein 2001:
153–154). Not surprisingly this change in attitude came on the heels of increased
colonial anxieties about the legal status and citizenship rights of the *métis* offspring
of these often-temporary unions.

   The early twentieth century also witnessed significant changes in official attitudes
and policies towards interracial sexual relationships throughout much of British
Africa and in many of Britain's Asian and Pacific colonies. In 1909, then secretary
of state for the colonies Lord Crewe issued a circular prohibiting concubinage between
native women and British officers in an effort to bring the latter's sex lives in line
with the new racial politics of British colonial rule in these areas, which emphasized
more than ever before the need to maintain social and (quite often) spatial distance
from subject populations. In this new dispensation, the notion of European (white)
prestige, which rested on claims of racial purity, cultural superiority, and moral
integrity of which sexual chasteness was a defining feature, was widely regarded as
the backbone of a successful colonial administration. Accordingly, interracial concubinage was condemned because colonial policymakers, like Lord Crewe, believed
that "it is not possible for any member of the administration to countenance such
practices without lowering himself in the eyes of the natives, and diminishing his
authority to an extent which will seriously impair his capacity for useful work in
the Service."[5] Although concubinage took many different forms and involved
varying degrees of intimacy and physical proximity, it was more likely to draw
colonial officers into intricate webs of social relations and obligation with local
families precisely because it was an ongoing relationship, unlike prostitution or
"occasional illicit acts" as one colonial office advisor put it (T.C. Macnaghten, 1908,
File minute for December 16: TNA, CO 533/52, no. 45005). Thus an officer's ability
to discharge his duties impartially was at risk. While the stated purpose of British
efforts to end concubinage was to ensure administrative efficiency, in practice they
revealed the inherent instability of colonial rule.

   If a broadly discernible pattern suggests that interracial sexual relationships move
from being a commonplace feature of Europe's early imperial expansion towards

condemnation and prohibition as of the late nineteenth century, numerous examples that do not fit this chronology caution against making sweeping temporal claims. Instead we need to focus on the developmental stages and exigencies of individual colonial projects, in order to better discern how "similar shifts in the rhythms of rule and sexual management" are linked to "similar patterns within specific colonial histories themselves" (Stoler 2002: 77). When such projects are occasioned by immediate conquest and colonization or become formalized, as trade gives way to conquest and the implementation and expansion of alien political rule, regardless of the century in which it occurs, anxieties around interracial sex appear to surface and/or intensify. Durba Ghosh (2006: 9–10) has convincingly shown that colonial anxieties around interracial sex, sexual morality, and racial prestige and purity, predate the late nineteenth century in India. The presence of these anxieties during the eighteenth century in India is largely explained by the fact that the British imperial project there was already firmly rooted, fairly formal, and rapidly growing, even in this earlier time period. As Ghosh puts it (2006: 2), "The expansion of the [East India] Company's territorial frontiers corresponded closely with growing anxieties about social frontiers and the ways in which they ought to be managed." Elsewhere in the British empire, these concerns came even earlier, while in others they came later: as we have already seen, laws penalizing or banning intermarriage and sex between whites and blacks in several North American colonies were introduced as early as the seventeenth century, yet throughout most of British Africa it was not until the early twentieth century, precisely when formal colonial rule had been established, that active efforts were made to curtail such relationships, and even then they were limited to colonial employees (Woodson 1918: 339–343; Hyam 1986a).

In the Dutch empire, anxieties about waning Dutch cultural purity and its relationship to the ubiquity of interracial sexual relationships initially surfaced during the period of VOC rule in Batavia, but became the subject of policy and prohibition after the VOC was dissolved at the end of the eighteenth century and the Dutch embarked on the complete colonization of the Indonesian archipelago. In the VOC's Cape settlement in South Africa, within the first few decades of its existence a combination of germ and military warfare against the Khoisan had strengthened company rule enough to lessen its dependence on Khoisan intermediaries. The life of Krotoa, a prominent young Khoisan woman, who became a translator and intermediary, is illustrative of this shift. In the decade following the settlement's founding in 1652, Krotoa was incorporated into Dutch settler society as the wife of a Danish surgeon and the mother of his three children. She also brokered diplomatic relationships between the Dutch settlers and the Khoisan, but as the Dutch replaced diplomacy with force in their quest to settle the Cape, they "no longer needed Krotoa's skills as a translator." After her husband's death and with the arrival of a new Governor who disparaged the Khoisan, Krotoa's children were taken from her and she was expelled from colonial society, dying alone on Robben Island in 1674 (Scully 2005b). While interracial sex between indigenous and enslaved women and European settlers remained a common feature of settler colonialism in the Cape, as noted earlier the Dutch outlawed interracial marriage as early as 1685.

In all of these instances, as Ghosh argues (2006: 10), seventeenth- and eighteenth-century anxieties over interracial sex cannot be explained by the rise of "scientific racism and biological claims about the genetic differences between Caucasians and others" in the nineteenth century. Rather, they are better understood as manifestations of internal developments within their respective colonial contexts. What is important, however, about nineteenth-century European racial theory is that it harnessed the power of science to legitimate the hierarchical organization of perceived racial groups in new ways and played a significant role in shaping policy and popular attitudes towards interracial sexual relations in ways that make the nineteenth century a watershed moment in the history of colonial interracial sexual relations (Fredrickson 2005: 107). This was accomplished largely through scientific racism's theorization of miscegenation as unnatural and the source of racial contagion and degeneracy through the production of mixed-race offspring who were regarded as a biologically inferior and subversive class of people. (Young 1995: 18). A preference for "pure types" emerged on the part of colonial powers that not only pathologized mixed-race people who were viewed as the very embodiment of impurity, but also indigenous people who were Europeanized and Europeans who were indigenized.

The specter of Haiti loomed large in shaping European anxieties about the colonies' mixed populations. The unprecedented magnitude and violence of the slave uprisings, and the leading role that many contemporary observers believed mixed-race Haitians played in organizing them, alarmed colonial powers everywhere.[6] Anxieties were particularly acute in colonies with large enslaved and/or mixed populations, like India, where a British observer (Viscount Vilencia, who visited the possessions of the East India Company at the turn of the nineteenth century) noted:

> The most rapidly accumulating evil of Bengal is the increase of half-caste children. . . . In every country where this intermediate caste has been permitted to rise, it has ultimately tended to its ruin. Spanish-America and San Domingo are examples of this fact. . . . Their increase in India is beyond calculation . . . it may be justly apprehended that this tribe may hereafter become too powerful for control. . . . With numbers in their favor, with a close relationship to the natives, and without equal proportion of the pusillanimity and indolence which is natural to them, what may not in the future time be dreaded from them? (Gist and Wright 1973: 13)

In France events in Haiti were invoked "as a dire warning" of what could happen to its other colonies if policies continued to alienate the *métis* population. One colonial administrator warned, "rejected by all sides, they will becomes *declasses*, and I would add, the most dangerous *declasses* from the point of view of maintaining European domination" (O. White 1999: 78). The Haitian case became a powerful trope in the European colonial imagination not only of the dangers of rule by force, but also of the prophylactic necessity of maintaining firm boundaries between colonized and colonizer. The lessons of Haiti and a half-century later the Indian Rebellion of 1857 (the Sepoy Mutiny), were not lost on the colonial policymakers who were charged with running Europe's second empire. The sexual boundary, above all others, became the subject of such intense scrutiny precisely because of the frequency with which it was transgressed even in the face of well-rehearsed arguments about the importance of racial endogamy to the maintenance of colonial rule.

Although little has been written about the link between interracial sexual relationships and the rise of anticolonialism, evidence suggests that we need to push beyond thinking about the roles these relationships played in the formation of empire to considering how they are implicated in its dissolution. In the introduction to *Empire and Sexuality* Ronald Hyam (1990) devotes a single, albeit lengthy, paragraph to listing numerous instances in areas as diverse as Canton, Kabul, South Africa, Kenya, and Bechuanaland, in which the sexual abuse of native women by European men provoked deep resentment, outbreaks of violence, and anticolonial resistance. He dismisses their significance, however, by concluding that "despite such occasional protests, the Afro-Asian world was remarkably accommodating to the sexual demands placed upon it" (1990: 2–3). His callous assertion is called into question by his own evidentiary list, but there are other examples too. The early South African nationalist, Sol Plaatje, as well as Frantz Fanon and Albert Memmi, two of the twentieth century's most important anticolonial intellectuals and activists, all made the domain of interracial sex a focus of their anticolonial politics. My own research on British West Africa reveals how the early vanguard of Gold Coast nationalists used their grievances over illicit sexual relationships between African women and European men to challenge the legitimacy of British colonial rule well before the onset of formal decolonization. Among these early nationalists was the prolific female columnist and playwright, Mabel Dove, who posited interracial sexual relationships, whether between African women and European men or between African men and European women, as an impediment to national development and pride (2004: 92). In offering us a glimpse of her critique of interracial sexual relations, Dove's writings remind us, once again, of how marginalized colonized women's experiences and perspectives remain to our understanding of the role interracial sexual relations played in the making and unmaking of empire.

Notes

1   Readers interested in what is arguably the most canonical study of interracial sex and empire should see Stoler (2002).

2   For an overview of the scholarship on Black Peril and the way in which different scholars have linked these scares to internal crises, economic or otherwise, within white communities, see the introduction to McCulloch (2000).

3   Arranged marriages were, of course, not unique to interracial relationships. Intra-racial and intra-ethnic marriages and cohabitation were also subject to similar kinds of familial control throughout most of the world at this time period.

4   More research on interracial customary marriages needs to be undertaken, but my own research for the Gold Coast confirms that European men continued to contract so-called native marriages with local women throughout the colonial period.

5   R.O.A. Crewe-Milnes, 1st Marquess of Crewe, "Crewe to the officer administering the government of the Gold Coast, 11 January 1909." PRAAD, ACC, ADM 12/1/31.
6   Scholars have increasingly turned their attention towards documenting the leadership roles of enslaved Africans in the Haitian revolution, thereby revising previously held assumptions about the centrality of mixed-race Haitians to the success of the revolution. See, for example, Fick (1990).

References

Akyeampong, E. 1997. "Sexuality and prostitution among the Akan of the Gold Coast c. 1650–1950." *Past and Present*, 156: 144–173.

Beckles, H.McD. 1989. *Natural Rebels: A Social History of Enslaved Black Women in Barbados*. New Brunswick: Rutgers University Press.

Beckles, H.McD. 1993. "White women and slavery in the Caribbean." *History Workshop Journal*, 36(1): 66–82.

Berg, M. 2011. *Popular Justice: A History of Lynching in America*. The American Ways series, Chicago: Ivan R. Dee.

Berger, M.T. 1988. "Imperialism and sexual exploitation: a response to Ronald Hyam's 'Empire and sexual opportunity.'" *Journal of Imperial and Commonwealth History*, 17(1): 83–89.

Boxer, C.R. 1963. *Race Relations in the Portuguese Colonial Empire, 1415–1825*. Oxford: Clarendon Press.

Brooks, G.E. 2003. *Eurafricans in Western Africa: Commerce, Social Status, Gender, and Religious Observance from the Sixteenth to the Eighteenth Century*. Western African Studies, Athens, GA: Ohio University Press.

Brown, K.M. 1996. *Good Wives, Nasty Wenches, and Anxious Patriarchs: Gender, Race, and Power in Colonial Virginia*. Chapel Hill, NC: University of North Carolina Press.

Burnard, T. 1991. "Inheritance and independence: Women's status in early colonial Jamaica." *William and Mary Quarterly*, 48(1): 93–114.

Carter, S. and McCormack, P.A. 2011. *Recollecting: Lives of Aboriginal Women of the Canadian Northwest and Borderlands*. The West Unbound, Social and Cultural Studies, Edmonton: AU Press.

Conklin, A. "Redefining 'Frenchness': France and West Africa." In J.A. Clancy-Smith and F. Gouda (eds) *Domesticating the Empire: Race, Gender, and Family Life in French and Dutch Colonialism*, pp. 65–83. Charlottesville: University Press of Virginia.

Davis, A. 2002. "Don't let nobody bother yo' principle/the sexual economy of American slavery." In S. Harley (ed.) *Sister Circle: Black Women and Work*, pp. 103–127. New Brunswick: Rutgers University Press.

de Marees, P., van Dantzig, A., and Jones, A. 1987. *Description and Historical Account of the Gold Kingdom of Guinea (1602)*. Oxford: Oxford University Press.

D'Emilio, J. and Freedman, E.B. 1997. *Intimate Matters: A History of Sexuality in America*, 2nd edn. Chicago: University of Chicago Press.

Dove, M. 2004. *Selected Writings of a Pioneer West African Feminist*, ed. S. Newell and A. Gadzekpo. Nottingham: Trent Books.

Edwards, P. 1998. "Womanizing Indochina: Fiction, nation, and cohabitation in colonial Cambodia, 1890–1930." In J.A. Clancy-Smith and F. Gouda, *Domesticating the Empire:*

Race, Gender, and Family Life in French and Dutch Colonialism, pp. 108–130. Charlottesville: University Press of Virginia.

Everts, N. 2002. "'Brought up well according to European Standards.' Helena Van Der Burgh and Wilhelmina Van Naarssen: Two Christian women from Elmina." In I. van Kessel (ed.) *Merchants, Missionaries and Migrants: 300 Years of Dutch-Ghanaian Relations*, pp. 101–109. Amsterdam: KIT Press.

Feinberg, H.M. 1989. *Africans and Europeans in West Africa: Elminans and Dutchmen on the Gold Coast During the Eighteenth Century*. Philadelphia: American Philosophical Society.

Fick, C.E. 1990. *The Making of Haiti: The Saint Domingue Revolution from Below*. Knoxville: University of Tennessee Press.

Finkelman, P. 1997. "Crimes of love, misdemeanors of passion: the regulation of race and sex in the colonial South." In C. Clinton and M. Gillespie (eds) *The Devil's Lane: Sex and Race in the Early South*, pp. 124–138. Oxford: Oxford University Press.

Florescano, E. 1984. "The formation and economic structure of the hacienda in New Spain." In L. Bethell (ed.) *Colonial Latin America*, pp. 153–188. Cambridge: Cambridge University Press.

Fredrickson, G.M. 2005. "Mulattoes and metis: Attitudes toward miscegenation in the United States and France since the seventeenth century." *International Social Science Journal*, 57(183): 103–112.

Fuentes, M.J. 2010. "Power and historical figuring: Rachael Pringle Polgreen's troubled archive." *Gender & History*, 22(3): 564–584.

Garraway, D.L. 2005. *The Libertine Colony: Creolization in the Early French Caribbean*. Durham, NC: Duke University Press.

Ghosh, D. 2006. *Sex and the Family in Colonial India: The Making of Empire*. Cambridge Studies in Indian History and Society, Cambridge: Cambridge University Press.

Gist, N.P. and Wright, R.D. 1973. *Marginality and Identity: Anglo-Indians as a Racially-Mixed Minority in India*. Monographs and Theoretical Studies in Sociology and Anthropology in Honour of Nels Anderson, 3. Leiden: Brill.

Gocking, R. 1999. *Facing Two Ways: Ghana's Coastal Communities under Colonial Rule*. Lanham, MD: University Press of America.

Hodes, M.E. 1997. *White Women, Black Men: Illicit Sex in the Nineteenth-Century South*. New Haven: Yale University Press.

Horton, M. Anore. 2001. *New Perspectives on Women and Migration in Colonial Latin America*, Plas Cuadernos, 4. Princeton: Program in Latin American Studies, Princeton University.

Hurtado, A.L. 1996. "When strangers met: Sex and gender on three frontiers." *Frontiers: A Journal of Women Studies*, 17(3): 52–75.

Hyam, R. 1986a. "Concubinage and the colonial service." *Journal of Imperial and Commonwealth History*, 14(3): 170–186.

Hyam, R. 1986b. "Empire and sexual opportunity." *Journal of Imperial and Commonwealth History*, 14(2): 34–89.

Hyam, R. 1988. "'Imperialism and sexual exploitation': a reply." *Journal of Imperial and Commonwealth History*, 17(1): 90–98.

Hyam, R. 1990. *Empire and Sexuality: The British Experience*. Manchester: Manchester University Press.

Inglis, A. 1974. *Not a White Woman Safe: Sexual Anxiety and Politics in Port Moresby, 1920–1934*. Canberra: Australian National University Press.

Inglis, A. 1975. *The White Women's Protection Ordinance: Sexual Anxiety and Politics in Papua.* London: Chatto & Windus/Sussex University Press.

Klein, M.A. 2001. "Review: Children of the French empire." *Journal of Interdisciplinary History*, 32(1): 153–154.

Lunenfeld, M. 1991. *1492 – Discovery, Invasion, Encounter: Sources and Interpretation.* Lexington, MA: D.C. Heath.

Mark, P. 2002. *"Portuguese" Style and Luso-African Identity: Precolonial Senegambia, Sixteenth-Nineteenth Centuries.* Bloomington: Indiana University Press.

McCulloch, J. 2000. *Black Peril, White Virtue: Sexual Crime in Southern Rhodesia, 1902–1935.* Bloomington: Indiana University Press.

Millward, J. 2010. "'The relics of slavery': Interracial sex and manumission in the American South." *Frontiers: A Journal of Women Studies*, 31(3): 22–30.

Newitt, M.D.D. 2010. *The Portuguese in West Africa, 1415–1670: A Documentary History.* Cambridge: Cambridge University Press.

Ray, C. 2007. "Policing sexual boundaries: the politics of race in colonial Ghana." PhD dissertation, Cornell University.

Ray, C. 2009. "'The white wife problem': Sex, race and the contested politics of repatriation to interwar British West Africa." *Gender & History*, 21(3): 628–646.

Sanchez-Albornoz, N. 1984. "The population of colonial Spanish America." In L. Bethell (ed.) *Colonial Latin America*, pp. 1–36. Cambridge: Cambridge University Press.

Scully, P. 2005a. "Indigenous women and colonial cultures: an introduction." Special issue, *Journal of Colonialism and Colonial History*, 6(3), ed. P. Scully: ch.1.

Scully, Pamela. 2005b. "Malintzin, Pocahontas, and Krotoa: Indigenous women and myth models of the Atlantic world." Special issue, *Journal of Colonialism and Colonial History*, 6(3), ed. P. Scully: ch. 2.

Sleeper-Smith, S. 2001. *Indian Women and French Men: Rethinking Cultural Encounter in the Western Great Lakes.* Native Americans of the Northeast series, Amherst: University of Massachusetts Press.

Stolcke, V. 1989. *Marriage, Class, and Colour in Nineteenth-Century Cuba: A Study of Racial Attitudes and Sexual Values in a Slave Society*, 2nd edn. Ann Arbor: University of Michigan Press.

Stoler, A.L. 1989. "Making empire respectable: the politics of race and sexual morality in 20th-century colonial cultures." *American Ethnologist*, 16(4): 634–660.

Stoler, A.L. 1991. "Carnal knowledge and imperial power: the politics of race and sexual morality in colonial Asia." In M. di Leonardo (ed.) *Gender at the Crossroads: Feminist Anthropology in the Post-Modern Era*, pp. 51–101. Berkeley: University of California Press.

Stoler, A.L. 2002. *Carnal Knowledge and Imperial Power: Race and the Intimate in Colonial Rule.* Berkeley: University of California Press.

Strobel, M. 1992. "Sex and work in the British empire." *Radical History Review*, 54: 177–186.

Taylor, Jean G. 1983. *The Social World of Batavia: European and Eurasian in Dutch Asia.* Madison: University of Wisconsin Press.

Taylor, John 2000. "Reinterpreting Malinche." *Ex Post Facto*, at http://malinche.info/blog/?p=139, accessed March 8, 2013.

Tiryakian, E.A. 1993. "White women in darkest Africa: Marginals as observers in no-woman's land." *Civilisations*, 41, at http://civilisations.revues.org/1706?lang=en, accessed March 9, 2013.

Van Onselen, C. 1982. *Studies in the Social and Economic History of the Witwatersrand, 1886–1914*. Johannesburg: Ravan Press.

Voeltz, R.A. 1996. "The British empire, sexuality, feminism and Ronald Hyam." *European Review of History*, 3(1): 41–45.

Vogt, J. 1979. *Portuguese Rule on the Gold Coast, 1469–1682*. Athens: University of Georgia Press.

West, C.M. 2004. "Black women and intimate partner violence." *Journal of Interpersonal Violence*, 19(12): 1487–1493.

White, D.G. 1999. *Ar'n't I a Woman?: Female Slaves in the Plantation South*, rev. edn. New York: W.W. Norton.

White, O. 1999. *Children of the French Empire: Miscegenation and Colonial Society in French West Africa, 1895–1960*. Oxford Historical Monographs, Oxford: Oxford University Press.

White, R. 1991. *The Middle Ground: Indians, Empires, and Republics in the Great Lakes Region, 1650–1815*, Cambridge Studies in North American Indian History. Cambridge: Cambridge University Press.

Woodson, C.G. 1918. "The beginnings of the miscegenation of the whites and blacks." *Journal of Negro History*, 3(4): 335–353.

Yarak, L. 2003. "A West African cosmopolis: Elmina (Ghana) in the nineteenth century." Paper presented at the Seascapes, Littoral Cultures, and Trans-Oceanic Exchanges, Library of Congress, Washington DC.

Young, R. 1995. *Colonial Desire: Hybridity in Theory, Culture, and Race*. London: Routledge.

Chapter 12

Istanbul as a Cosmopolitan City
Myths and Realities
Edhem Eldem

Prologue: The Birth Pangs of Levantine Cosmopolitanism

Issue 73 of the *Journal de Constantinople* (January 6, 1848), published in Istanbul, capital of the Ottoman Empire, boasted on its fourth page a rather dense and wordy advertisement for a department store located on the main (and only) artery of Pera (in Turkish, Beyoğlu), the "European" district of the city. A closer look at this advertisement reveals several layers of cultural porosity embedded in its text and format. The most striking, without doubt, is the strong, almost overwhelming, French context that permeates practically every detail. First, of course, the language itself, not only of the advertisement, but of the entire newspaper: The *Journal de Constantinople. Écho de l'Orient* was born in 1846 from the merger of two former French language newspapers, *L'Écho de l'Orient* (1838–1846) and the *Journal de Constantinople et des interêts orientaux* (1843–1846) (Groc and Çağlar 1985). French had started to become the dominant language among certain sectors of the urban population of the empire, gradually replacing Italian and the strongly Italianate lingua franca in use throughout most of the eastern Mediterranean basin. The use of French was still quantitatively limited, as it hardly went beyond the predictable circles of foreign communities, diplomatic circles, higher state officials, and the *crème* of the business community; yet in qualitative terms, there is no doubt that it had a relatively much greater weight and influence, and that this process of Gallicization would very rapidly spread throughout the empire.

The French reference in the advertisement was not limited to language. The name of the store itself, Grand Bazar Parisien, echoed the numerous references to France,

---

A Companion to Diaspora and Transnationalism, First Edition.
Edited by Ato Quayson and Girish Daswani.
© 2013 Blackwell Publishing Ltd. Published 2013 by Blackwell Publishing Ltd.

and more particularly to Paris, throughout the text: "cravates de Paris . . . étoffes, rubans et fleurs les plus à la mode de Paris, . . . nouveaux modèles de Paris, . . . prix fixes de Paris, . . . paquebot français de la Compagnie Rostand," and so on. In short, this was an advertisement in French, in a French-language newspaper, promoting merchandise dominated by French products and style. If it were not for the explicit references to Constantinople, the advertisement would have had its place in any daily in a French colonial city, say, Algiers.

Nevertheless, there were a few details that set the context of the advertisement apart from a purely French colonial one. These had to do with an effort at adapting the advertisement to rather particular local conditions, by using two separate calendars to promote sales, namely the Julian and the Gregorian, referred to respectively as *ancien style* and *nouveau style*. Thus customers were invited to buy gifts for the New Year based on the Julian, and for the Epiphany according to the Gregorian calendar. The latter date targeted the Latin and other foreign communities while the former was designed for the "Oriental" Christians, for whom the date was still December 25. This was why the first addressees of the whole advertisement, those who were urged to buy New Year gifts a week after Western New Year, were "MM. les Grecs, Arméniens, etc."

This way of identifying potential customers was, to say the least, rather surprising. The use of a religious taxonomy in itself was a strikingly particular way of dealing with the diversity of Ottoman society; but what was probably even more shocking was the strange way in which the two major religious groups were followed by a rather demeaning "etc." How should one interpret this clearly casual way of treating what may have been a multitude of other religious communities, evidently less important in the eyes of the owners of the Grand Bazar Parisien?

A closer look at this particular element of the advertisement reveals that things were probably a bit more complicated than our political correctness would have it. Indeed, a better understanding of the dismissive "etc." is possible by reflecting on who it did *not* include, rather than on who it might have done. Considering the context of New Year presents to be bought according to the Julian calendar, it was clear that the "western Christians" were not concerned; nor were the Muslims, obviously, to whom the Christian New Year, regardless of the calendar, did not make sense. Finally, the other major religious community, the Jews, had nothing to do with this tradition either, and were clearly not targeted by the advertisement. Under this light, it is clear that the number of religious or ethnic groups that were implicitly excluded from the count was limited: some Orthodox individuals who were not Greek – Bulgarians, Serbs, Albanians, or Russians – and some members of local Oriental Christian communities – Nestorians, Syriacs, or Chaldeans and the like. All in all, then, a very marginal section of the Christian population of the Ottoman capital, not to mention the fact that as early as 1848 many Orthodox subjects would have still accepted being lumped under the category of "Greek" as a predominantly confessional denomination.

What are we to make of this strange mix of ethno-religious identities and linguistic concerns? There is little doubt that this was the embodiment of a phenomenon that was new in more than one respect. First, the press itself, which had less than two decades of activity behind it, and had almost from the start adopted French as its medium for the propagation of ideas and information, was a novelty that targeted a very specific portion of Ottoman society consisting of the new bureaucratic elite – the *Tanzimat* reformers – of the top echelons of the foreign community, and possibly of a few local non-Muslims who were powerful or rich enough to frequent these circles. What the phrasing and contents of this advertisement suggested was that by the mid-nineteenth century, the elite targeted by the French press had expanded to include a sizeable number of local Christians of somewhat more modest profile, a kind of urban bourgeoisie, as it were. Culturally and, to a certain extent ideologically, this was the birth of what I shall call, for lack of a better term, *Levantine cosmopolitanism.*

The Slippery Grounds of Cosmopolitanism and Transnationalism

Cosmopolitanism and transnationalism are tempting words to describe the plurality and diversity characterizing Ottoman society – especially in the major urban centers of the empire – towards the turn of the twentieth century. Yet both terms rest on very slippery ground with regard to their true applicability to a wide variety of situations and to the rigor with which they can really be used as analytical concepts to describe Ottoman society or sections of it. To be sure, transnationalism seems somewhat more limiting, if only because of the implicit notion it carries of transcending the borders and limits of the nation-state at a time when in actual fact the latter hardly constituted the dominant model of political organization in the region under study. Moreover, if one were to use this term, even in a premodern or early modern context, the focus would inevitably have to be on those individuals and groups characterized by a high degree of mobility that allowed them to habitually cross those borders while engaging in their trade and establishing their networks.[1] While it is clear that the Ottoman capital did host a sizable population of transnational or trans-imperial nature – from foreign diplomats and traders to captains and seafarers, from traveling artists and missionaries to political refugees and dragomans – the real challenge concerns the possibility of defining the nature of the mixed social, cultural, ethnic, and religious fabric of the settled population of the imperial capital, as well as that of other major urban centers, generally lumped under the generic term of port cities.[2] Among a number of possible terms – plurality, pluralism, diversity, hybridity – cosmopolitanism seems to come closest to a social and cultural diversity resulting from the combined effect of the mixing of ethnic and/or religious groups of local or foreign origin, as suggested by the rather frequent use of the term in the context of nineteenth-century Ottoman society.

Yet the term is difficult to use, if only because it has been used too loosely and indiscriminately in a number of relatively recent works. In a concise essay published in 2005, Henk Driessen (2005) was among the first to critically review the weaknesses inherent to this literature. Following an overview of the nature of port cities and a closer look at the specific case of Izmir, Driessen engaged in a discussion of the concept of cosmopolitanism and the uses it was put to in Mediterranean urban studies. Based on a critique ranging from the tendency of scholars to take the concept for granted to their willingness to mistake for a reality what might have been only "nostalgic celebrations by elites of a lost world that never really existed," he insisted on the need for "a working definition" (Driessen 2005: 135–136) of a concept rendered all the more complicated by the fact that "'cosmopolitanism' is a Protean commonsense term referring to a rather elusive set of historical, social and cultural phenomena" (2005: 136–137). A few years later, Will Hanley (2008) took up the same issue in a somewhat more focused, but for that reason harsher, essay directed against the prevailing (mis)uses of "cosmopolitanism" in Middle East studies. Hanley's critique echoed Driessen's in many respects, especially with regard to the tendency to take Ottoman or Middle Eastern cosmopolitanism for granted, the propensity of observers to concentrate on an elitist formulation of the concept, and the feeling of nostalgia for a lost golden age or paradise that pervades most of these descriptions. Hanley additionally (2008: 1346–1347) gives particular attention to the fact that the discussion on cosmopolitanism in the Middle East has developed with little, if any, concern for the existing Western literature on the concept, from Kantian universalist ethic feeding into perpetual international peace to the renewed interest in the concept in political philosophy and cultural studies with respect to globalization and multiculturalism.

With much insight, Hanley insists on the fact that nineteenth-century cosmopolitanism often masks a colonial or quasi-colonial situation of domination and that, contrary to the image of inclusiveness and fluidity it generally conjures, in actual fact it depends largely on the exclusion of the majority from the mixed environment reserved to a wealthy, powerful, and mobile elite (2008: 1347–1348, 1352). This observation had already been made by Driessen, albeit less explicitly, by linking the development of port cities to the combined effect of Ottoman disintegration and Western imperialism, and by stressing that the label of cosmopolitanism applied only to certain categories of the population, and that such a lifestyle owed its existence to "the encounter between the non-Muslim Ottomans and the different communities of Western Europeans" (Driessen 2005: 138).

The problem, however, is that these incisive and most welcome critiques have much less to offer in terms of possible alternatives, correctives, or revisions to this evidently problematic concept. Driessen's predominantly anthropological approach leads him to conclude on the question of possible connections between the partly colonial context of late nineteenth-century cultural pluralism and present-day multiculturalism as it seems to be re-emerging in parts of the Mediterranean, without really proposing the kind of "working definition" he advocated at the start of his discussion (2005: 138–139). Hanley (2008) realistically proposes to "limit the purview of the concept," thereby avoiding the frequent mismatch caused by a perception that by far exceeds the very limited scope of a social and cultural reality confined to elites. Yet behind this pragmatic proposition lurk, on the one hand, the specter of universalism and the desire to comply with a proper understanding of the concept's own philosophical and historiographical background and, on the other, the fear that cosmopolitanism might become a smokescreen masking much more concrete social and political categories (pp. 1358–1361). One thus gets the impression that the advantages that can be derived from the avoidance altogether of this term are much greater than the somewhat romantic comfort that it offers for the description of the exotic hybridity of a mythical Ottoman *belle époque*. Should we then simply do away with this cumbersome and slippery concept and banish it from our historiographical vocabulary for fear of lapsing into facile Ottoman particularism?[3]

The Search for Ottoman Cosmopolitanism

Such radical measures could perhaps be avoided by adopting a more practical approach towards the possible uses of the term "cosmopolitanism." For one, I do not think that the quest for a universalist understanding of the concept and the expectation that the Ottoman case should somehow fall in line with Western philosophical and political ideals is likely to help. If anything, such a maximalist attitude would lead to the need to simply drop the term and replace it with more neutral ways of describing and defining the coexistence of different national, ethnic, and religious groups in Ottoman urban centers. Likewise, resorting to the etymology of the term to justify its use or not in a certain period of time seems to me a rather sterile exercise unless the comparison between its past and present uses is properly contextualized.[4] We know, for example, that one of the first documented uses of the word *cosmopolite* in French is by Guillaume Postel in his *République des Turcs* (1560) and that this use as an epithet for a "fluid" individual would persist until well into the nineteenth century. The use of the same adjective to describe a place or an environment appeared only in the 1820s, together with the derived term of *cosmopolitisme*, which had until then described the state of mind of a *cosmopolite*. Yet, while this information shows that the concept acquired the meaning most widely attached to it with regard to mixed societies more or less simultaneously with the rise of such an environment in the Ottoman empire, I am not convinced that this is reason enough to seek proof of its existence in the appearance or not in local languages of a proper translation of the term.[5]

Indeed, I would argue that the question is not to know whether certain inhabitants of the Ottoman capital – or of the major port cities – believed that they were cosmopolitan and lived in a cosmopolitan environment, and if so, whether their understanding of cosmopolitanism fits our present perceptions of the concept. Rather, what really counts is to ascertain whether we, as historians, can use this terminology to describe the social and cultural milieu of this bygone world. In fact, I would go one step further, and suggest that the real challenge is not to know whether we *can* use this term, but rather whether we *need* to do so. For if what we are studying can still be described and defined by resorting to less "loaded" terms than cosmopolitanism, such as pluralism, diversity, or even multiculturalism, then there probably is no justification to bring into the discussion a concept harking back to a number of philosophical and political issues exceeding by far the scope of an Ottoman *convivenza* of sorts.

Did the Ottoman *millet* system, which allowed for the coexistence of different religious and ethnic communities, constitute an early example of cosmopolitanism, distinct from the general tendency of religious homogenization observed in Europe? Generally speaking, it is true that until at least the end of the eighteenth century, Ottoman society seems to have thrived on diversity, while at the same time ensuring that the most basic boundaries between coexisting communities were maintained and respected. In an early modern society, it should probably not come as a surprise to note the existence of a general avoidance of inter-communal contacts, proximity, and other forms of association across the limits set by religion, and by other cultural forms of distinction. True, this rigidity should not be seen as cause for social and cultural immobilism. On the contrary, we know well that Ottoman society was characterized by a great degree of fluidity, both forced and voluntary, which made the crossing of such borders possible, and even rather frequent. Yet, it should be remembered that these crossings often, if not always, required an explicit change of identity, generally through conversion, which, while permitting movement, ended up confirming the importance of the boundaries between communities.

Not every form of diversity is cosmopolitan, and in the case of the Ottoman empire, the evidence suggests that the mixing of ethnic and religious groups was quite far from providing the kind of intercultural or multicultural environment and practices one would associate with cosmopolitanism. True, Istanbul looked under-standably cosmopolitan to the average European visitor who knew no such diversity at home; but that did not mean that this mixed environment was truly characterized by inter-communal fluidity and integration. Quite the contrary; one could claim that what made the existence and functioning of such a heterogeneous society pos-sible in the major urban centers of the empire was precisely the fact that these very diverse groups were able – and to a large extent encouraged – to erect barriers that kept them from mixing with others. Moreover, it should never be forgotten that at the root of the Ottoman *millet* system lay a very strict hierarchy that separated Muslims from non-Muslims, the latter being subjected to a form of segregation which, while granting them a great degree of autonomy, also made sure that their inferior status as *dhimmi*s was constantly maintained and reminded. In short, one should not mistake a system that tolerated the coexistence of cultural and ethnic diversity for a conscious policy geared towards promoting exchange and interaction among imperial subjects.

Obviously, what made the Ottoman system rather remarkable in contrast to contemporary European societies, was its seemingly endless capacity to absorb Otherness into its own body. The ways in which this absorption could be realized varied greatly in time and according to context. Enslavement in a wide variety of forms – constituted one of the major avenues of assimilation, from the young Christian boy "taken" into the formative track of the palace school to the Circassian and other women acquired by the imperial harem and grandee households, or from the manumitted domestic slave taking up his master's business to the war captive somehow finding his way to freedom through conversion. Apart from the fact that these and similar situations represented a rather marginal proportion of a dominantly stable social reality, one should not forget that such examples of mobility, striking as they may have been, depended on a radical change of identity, almost exclusively through conversion to Islam. Rather than a cosmopolitan environment, one would therefore have to talk of an Ottoman "melting pot" aiming at assimilating "foreign" elements by incorporating them into specific parts of the elite. While these outsiders were generally able to maintain clear and explicit traces of their original identities – language, culture, family, relations, nicknames – they were nevertheless subjected to a substantial level of "standardization" through conversion, education, formation, and the sheer participation in the customs, manners, and procedure of the body or group they joined. The diverse aspect of these elites was thus pushed to the background, well behind the new identity they had acquired. This may have been a premodern version of a multicultural environment, but it was certainly not cosmopolitanism.

True, there were some levels at which simple plurality and latent multiculturalism could be conducive to a form of cosmopolitanism, in the sense of a cultural and social praxis resulting from – as opposed to being tolerant of – diversity. Indeed, if one prerequisite of cosmopolitanism is the existence of a political intent or, at least, of a certain consciousness with respect to this particular sort of social porosity, a second and crucial one would be the capacity of that environment to produce a culture that would be different from the simple juxtaposition of several distinct cultures. In other words, a social environment can be qualified as truly cosmopolitan only as long as it is shaped by the diversity of its constituents, while they, in turn, are also transformed by the cosmopolitan cultural milieu they had contributed to form. There is little doubt that Ottoman society as a whole was subjected to some degree of transformation as a result of its mixed nature. Linguistic fluidity, eventually developing into multilingualism, and frequent examples of cultural or religious syncretism attest to the existence of such multicultural exchanges among sections of the population. Nevertheless, such examples lacked the sort of consciousness and intentionality that one would associate with a truly dynamic multiculturalism. On the contrary, they constituted cultural traits that were embedded in the social fabric and praxis of the masses, but without any explicit understanding or recognition of their hybrid nature.

Not surprisingly, the development of true multiculturalism – and potentially of cosmopolitanism – tends to be unequally distributed across the social spectrum. Typically, such forms of fluidity and porosity have never been the apanage of the middle classes, but have rather found much richer feeding grounds on the margins of society, at both extremes of the social ladder. In that respect, the Ottoman court, the palace and its immediate entourage, constituted one of the most likely recipients and producers of a mixed and hybrid culture, due to the attraction exerted on a wide spectrum of individuals of very diverse origins and cultures – men and women –

who were incorporated, sometimes forcibly, into the production and dynamics of court culture. An imperial system that could find architectural inspiration in Iran and in Egypt, as well as in France or Italy, or that could muster up the creative forces of Armenian, Greek, Muslim, and Jewish composers for its musical consumption, was in fact displaying the almost innate capacity of any premodern empire to feed on some form of cosmopolitan synergy. At the other end of the scale – admittedly, the bottom – there is little doubt that the lowlife of harbors and arsenals, brothels and taverns, represented another – yet very different – environment likely to produce its own culture stemming from, and feeding on, diversity; one that may not have been documented as thoroughly as that of the court and its entourage, but still a culture of which the traces clearly survive in such cultural products as the Levantine lingua franca – that colorful mix of Italian, Catalan, Greek, Arabic, and Turkish – which was spoken in most of the Mediterranean ports. There again, heterogeneity was the rule, with no forceful assimilation through religion or any other overriding identity: these were men and women whose extreme mobility had transformed them into a caste of wandering marginals. If any group fully deserved to be categorized as transnational or trans-imperial, it was probably these scores of sailors and other proletarians roaming the Mediterranean basin.

The Nineteenth Century

In the light of these observations, then, it would probably not be wrong to speak of the existence of a considerable degree of Ottoman cosmopolitanism in the early modern period, unequally distributed in space and time and along certain social strata, but more or less inherent to the nature of an empire and to the fluidity that was so characteristic of premodern societies and communities. The term may not apply equally well to all the major subcategories concerned: the elite may have practiced a form of controlled and assimiliationist multiculturalism, while the men peopling the sea and harbors constituted a perfect example of an early version of transnational mobility. For the great majority, however, there was hardly more than a basic level of coexistence and *convivenza*, a far cry from anything approaching cosmopolitanism.

And yet, by the second half of the nineteenth century most of the urban centers of the empire had developed a form of heterogeneity which most observers, past and present, did not hesitate to describe as a perfect example of cosmopolitanism. The temptation is understandably great to link this process to the traces of diversity and multiculturalism observed during the early modern period. Nineteenth-century cosmopolitanism was often seen as a modernized and transformed version of a pre-existing form of social and cultural fluidity. Interestingly, despite his very critical approach to the concept, Driessen (2005: 138) seems to have fully accepted this historical construct: "The cosmopolitics of the eastern Mediterranean port cities, involving multilingualism, religious plurality, openness, enterprising ethos, intercultural exchange and at least a weak form of tolerance were rooted in the Ottoman millet system of non-Muslim communities that were granted protection and relative autonomy." Yet, in my opinion, this is a very misleading vision of a process which was characterized by rupture rather than continuity.

One way of understanding the nature of nineteenth-century cosmopolitanism – which I have tentatively labeled "Levantine" – is to try to identify the main characteristics that set it apart from earlier forms of multiculturalism or near-cosmopolitanism. Among these, I would like to point especially at its globalizing ambition, if not character. Looking back at the advertisement I used to illustrate this phenomenon at the outset of this discussion, one cannot fail to notice that a major change with respect to the previous centuries is that the cultural reference uniting several groups was no longer Ottoman, but French. It had thus moved from an internal/local dimension centered on the elite of the empire to an external one, centered on Paris, but in fact aiming at connecting Istanbul to what was then considered to be the center of the civilized world. This was a form of global reference, as yet at an early stage of its formation, but already powerful enough to displace what had until then constituted the main center of attraction for local cultural diversity.

The new identities that were forged throughout the second half of the century were exceptional in their capacity and eagerness to emulate the new Western civilizational model offered by Western references. The phenomenon rested on a very sudden and extremely dense transformation of the empire under the combined effect of rising Western influence and of Westernization. Politically speaking, the influence of Western powers – now very explicitly named the Great Powers – was matched only by the willingness of the Ottoman bureaucratic elite itself to engage in the path of a systematic emulation of the Western model. From an economic perspective, the integration of the Ottoman Empire into the Western-dominated world economy had reached unprecedented levels, slowed down only by the sheer size and complexity of the empire. The infrastructure and institutions instrumental to this process of integration had started to mushroom throughout the Ottoman lands, most particularly in its major urban centers, starting with Istanbul. Banks, railways, insurance companies, municipalities, urban utilities, schools, theaters, and department stores exerted their powerful attraction on ever-increasing numbers of consumers, investors, traders, and wage-earners. The impact of these transformations was felt directly on the very outlook of the Ottoman capital: from a marginal and rather residential suburb of the city, the district of Pera developed into a full-fledged "European" district boasting all these innovations and gradually becoming a model for the urban development of the rest of the city.

By the end of the Crimean War, in 1856, the main characteristics of this new order had formed to a large extent. From an outpost of European presence in the Levant, business-dominated Galata and residential Pera had become the spearhead of an Ottoman project of integration with the West. This led to a two-fold transformation of part of the population of the Ottoman capital: on the one hand, the creation of a local middle class increasingly integrated with Western economic interests and cultural values; on the other, the steady influx of a growing number of immigrants and expatriates from a wide range of European countries. Some fifty years later, at the height of this process, the Ottoman capital would count no less than 130,000 foreign residents: this figure represented about 15 percent of the city's total population, more than its Armenian and Jewish communities put together (Karpat 1985: 168–169; Behar 1996: 55–58, 74). The phenomenon becomes even more striking if one considers that the overwhelming majority of this foreign population lived and worked in the combined area of Galata and Pera: in this extended district accounting for about a quarter of the capital city's population, the proportion of foreigners rose to unprecedented levels, justifying the "European" label observers generally attached to it.

This situation clearly draws a line between premodern imperial multiculturalism as it developed among certain circles under Ottoman rule and the new kind of Western-dominated fluidity that characterized the last decades of the empire. The main difference between the two had to do with the sudden shift in the center of gravity, as it were, of these two different worlds, from Istanbul and Ottoman power to Paris and Western civilization. Henk Driessen was wrong to assume that there should have been some form of continuity between the two; but he was right to describe the new order as "the product of a disintegrating Ottoman Empire and an expanding imperialism of the Great Powers of Europe" (2005:138).

Levantine Cosmopolitanism: A Flexible Praxis

Considering the major characteristics of this phenomenon, it would probably be wrong to label this new diversity as Ottoman, except in the very limited sense that it developed and blossomed in urban areas under Ottoman control. Even then, one could legitimately wonder if this political denomination might not bring a crippling limitation to the scope of the phenomenon by excluding certain regions that were not (or were no longer) under Ottoman control but still displayed a very similar form of multiculturalism. This is particularly true of Egypt – especially Alexandria – and of a number of North African cities under French colonial rule, such as Algiers and Tunis. Given this wider geographical distribution, one should perhaps concentrate on what cities like Istanbul, Izmir, Beirut, Alexandria, and Algiers may have had in common that might explain the existence of similar forms of cosmopolitanism throughout much of the eastern and southern Mediterranean basin. Two major, and to a large extent concomitant, factors come to mind: the colonial or quasi-colonial nature of the *rapport de forces* between the local society and the western powers of the time and the absence or extreme weakness of a political structure identifiable with the nation-state. At this point, and in order to bring some degree of differentiation from an openly colonial situation, "Levantine" comes in handy by providing a relevant geographical and cultural context. Indeed, the term "Levant" had traditionally been used to describe a geographical area extending from the coast of Dalmatia to Egypt, a rather close match with the broad definition of the eastern Mediterranean basin. "Levantine," however, had been to a large extent redefined culturally and politically during the nineteenth century. Until then, the term had been used – especially by the French – to describe rather indiscriminately all the inhabitants of the area, Muslims and non-Muslims alike, much like a synonym for "Ottoman subject," while Muslims were lumped under the collective appellation of "Turks." By the mid-nineteenth century, however, the meaning attached to this term had greatly changed: from an initially neutral and inclusive term, it had gradually moved in the direction of a derogatory label used to describe the hybrid identities of half-Westernized local non-Muslims and of Westerners who had "gone native" as a result of several generations of residence in the Ottoman lands. Considering that one of the dominant features of Levantine identity – as described by "real" Westerners – was an eagerness to integrate and assimilate into European culture, it becomes obvious that there was a serious overlap between this phenomenon and the kind of cosmopolitanism which developed in the Ottoman lands during the second half of the nineteenth century.[6]

Levantine cosmopolitanism, then, seems to have developed almost as a by-product of Westernization, with little more to offer than a superficial interface between a Western and Westernizing environment in the Eastern Mediterranean and its European sources of reference and inspiration. Indeed, a closer look at this wide array of communities reveals that their social, cultural, and ideological outlook lacked many of the criteria to be expected from a truly cosmopolitan situation. Most striking among these was the absence of a common culture resulting from inter-communal mixing and interaction. Rather than creating any common culture, this form of cosmopolitanism by and large adopted and imported, in pragmatic fashion, a number of already dominant Western cultural models, from the French language to Italian opera, from German architecture to British interior design, and from Parisian fashion to London-inspired business praxis. True, one could claim that the very eclectic way in which these external references were received and adopted, with results sometimes bordering on kitsch, constituted a culture by itself, not entirely devoid of a certain form of originality. Yet, there is very little, if anything, to suggest that any of the major actors of this plural world were conscious of doing, or willing to do, anything more than to emulate a composite model that had its sources and references in Europe.

And yet, the transformative power of this hybrid culture was truly remarkable in many respects. One needs only to look at the way in which some names were reshuffled and translated to get a sense of the leveling impact of Western influence on local non-Muslims. Ottoman imperial culture had traditionally exerted a limited degree of onomastic assimilation by promoting the use of Turkish names among Turkish-speaking Armenians, by disregarding family names among all non-Muslims, or by systematically adding the diminutive -*aki* at the end of Greek names.[7] Yet there was no comparison with in the extraordinary degree to which scores of Hovannes, Ohannes, Onnig, or Ioannis became Jean (and much more rarely John), or tens of Stephanos and Stepans, or Yorghis and Kevorks became Étienne or Georges (and occasionally Stephen or George). Obviously, this worked particularly well for "MM. les Grecs, Arméniens etc.," as the advertisement put it, whose Christian names could easily be translated into French and, if necessary, into any other European language;

but the practice also spread among a considerable portion of the Jewish community who easily Gallicized biblical names – Avram into Abraham, Elias into Élie, Jacob into Jacques, Moshe into Moïse – or simply adopted "modern" European names such as Albert, Charles, Henri, Léon, Maurice, or Robert.[8]

Once again, one cannot insist enough on the fact that only a section of the population participated in this new form of multiculturalism. One of the most telling indicators of this relative marginality was the phenomenon's very high dependence on the existence of a favorable environment. This environment, in its broadest sense, consisted of the very urban topography in which this new culture thrived and developed: Galata and Pera, where street signs and advertisements systematically made use of French before any other local language; where a widespread *alla franca* lifestyle formed a glaring contrast with the "traditional" makeup of the rest of the city; where architecture and urbanism recreated the looks of a European, albeit somewhat provincial, town; and where the major economic, political, and cultural institutions of integration with the West were concentrated. More specifically, however, one needs to understand that although it bore a superficial resemblance with respect to culture and ideology, Levantine cosmopolitanism was first and foremost a social praxis, which surfaced in those environments where it was of use or even of necessity. A typical example of such a context, probably the best ever, was that of the Imperial Ottoman Bank, itself a product and a catalyst of this very particular kind of hybrid modernity. A private bank formed by a mix of British- and French-dominated European capital, but functioning as a state bank and a bank of issue to the Ottoman government, the Ottoman Bank was the perfect embodiment of the new social, economic, and cultural environment that had formed in Istanbul and in the major urban centers of the empire during the second half of the nineteenth century. It employed a staff consisting of approximately one-third foreigners and two-thirds Ottoman nationals, the latter almost equally distributed among the major ethnic and religious categories of the empire (Eldem 1999a, 2002). The majority of this staff clearly reflected the profile described above: with the exception of underlings, they spoke an average of three languages, one of which was inevitably French; almost all had at some point or another received a Western-style education or formation; their costume reflected a strong commitment to external appearances consistent with the European model (Eldem 2005). A very considerable portion of the bank's almost exclusively urban customers mirrored a very similar profile: almost two-thirds of the upper-tier customers lived in Pera and worked in Galata; almost a quarter consisted of foreigners and more than half of non-Muslims (Eldem 1997); two-thirds of these individuals could – and more importantly, chose to – sign their name in French instead of their "ethnic" alphabet (Eldem 1995, 2007).

In the face of such diversity and of a conscious desire to belong to the greater world of Western civilization, one can hardly avoid using the term "cosmopolitanism," albeit within the very restrictive context of a "Levantine" society evolving in a quasi-colonial environment. More importantly, however, one needs to acknowledge the inevitable tensions and contradictions created by the coexistence of cosmopolitanism and its ideological opposite, nationalism. One common error has been to assume that the two were incompatible and to seek in cosmopolitanism a systematic rebuttal of nationalist and sectarian parochialism. This incompatibility disappears, however, the moment one is willing to view cosmopolitanism as a social praxis, rather than an ideology, thus allowing for a great deal of pragmatic flexibility in the face of the fluctuating equilibrium between a weak but familiar Ottoman state, a strong but distant Western influence, and the still diffuse but powerful surge of nationalist currents. Cosmopolitan as they may have been, the "moderns" of the Ottoman capital knew how to navigate from one identity to another, their allegiances shifting back and forth according to the political circumstances of the time. If Krikor or Dimitri could become Grégoire or Démètre in a cosmopolitan environment, they also knew exactly how to use their original names whenever necessary.

Even at its peak, this form of cosmopolitanism was bound to remain extremely marginal with respect to the bulk of the population of the empire and of the overall region. Indeed, the quaint and endearing image of Greeks, Armenians, Muslims, and Jews sharing space, business, and entertainment tends to mask the very real fact that the overwhelming majority of the population, across the board, was in fact held at bay from this protected and restrictive environment. In Istanbul, the difference between a Greek grocer working and living in the "traditional" district of Samatya and a Greek stockbroker working in Galata and living in Pera was probably as significant as the divide that separated a Muslim inhabitant of the conservative neighborhood of Eyüb, and a similarly Muslim bureaucrat working at a government ministry and residing on the shores of the Bosporus. In fact, the bureaucrat and the stockbroker may have shared a greater degree of common culture that set them equally apart from their respective brethren in faith. The consequence of this observation is that despite its inherent weaknesses, cosmopolitanism could have borne within itself a certain potential for class formation, beyond traditional solidarities of a religious or ethnic nature.

Yet whatever potential it may have had, Levantine cosmopolitanism soon fell victim to its own superficiality and fragility. After a brief and illusory moment of hope during the first three or four years that followed the Young Turk revolution of 1908, it became evident that any multicultural or pluralist scheme was bound to succumb to the force of nationalist currents. The latest and most destructive among these was Turkish/Islamic nationalism and its (eventually successful) attempts at redefining the empire along ethnic, linguistic, and cultural lines. It was this powerful thrust that eventually managed to transform former non-Muslim communities into de facto minorities, and to demonize any form of diversity that might have challenged new visions of ethnic, religious, and cultural homogeneity,

Epilogue: The Destruction and Reinvention of Cosmopolitanism

The destruction and eradication of ethnic, religious, and cultural diversity in the Ottoman Empire and Turkey is a tragic, but well-known story. The rise of Turkish and Islamic nationalism, combined with a series of regional and international con-flicts, set the destructive machine in motion, targeting almost simultaneously the Armenian and Greek communities, now viewed as a threat to the survival of the empire. Deportation, massacres, ethnic cleansing, and genocide were followed, in the early years of the Republic, by a population exchange aimed at finalizing through diplo-macy what a decade of war had left unfinished (Akçam 2006; Hirschon 2003). By 1936, at the peak of Kemalist power, the régime's international propaganda organ, *La Turquie kamâliste* could proudly claim to have reached modernity through homogeneity: "It was Kemalism which endeavored to establish, in the midst of such a divided continent, a modern State, provided with all the racial and cultural homo-geneity required by such a State. . . . [The Kemalist government's] stubborn struggle against the Greek invaders brought a final solution to the question of minorities, which had always caused the greatest troubles" (Atay 1936).[9]

Interestingly, Istanbul had been to a certain extent spared from all this destruc-tion. Most of its Armenian population had escaped deportation and annihilation, and its established Greek population had been exempted from the application of the population exchange agreement between Greece and Turkey (Anastassiadou and Dumont 2003: 6). Yet the city did lose the very foundations of its legitimacy, both as the capital of a now defunct empire and as the thriving center of a plural and diverse society. In a world where "cosmopolitan" had become the label most easily attached to the enemies of the nation and to those who betrayed the tenets of its sacrosanct unity and homogeneity, diversity, multilingualism, mobility, and differ-ence had become legitimate grounds for suspicion and exclusion. With its non-Muslim communities reduced to the status of minorities, Istanbul lost the very essence of its past glory.

However, the real backlash of nationalism would hit Istanbul only a few decades later. By targeting non-Muslims and most particularly Jews, the 1942 wealth tax confirmed the antisemite policies of the government, and contributed to the exodus of a considerable part of the city's Jewish population after 1948 to the newly estab-lished state of Israel (Aktar 2000). In 1955, a violent and state-sponsored pogrom unleashed against the Greek population left parts of the city in shambles and trig-gered the first massive departures towards Greece, repeated in 1964 and, for the remaining few, in 1974 (Güven 2006; Anastassiadou and Dumont 2003). If the Arme-nian population was not directly targeted by any similar aggression, it probably owes it partly to its much earlier exposure to violence and to its consequent capacity to lie low, as well as to its greater cultural and linguistic proximity to the Turkish majority.

In the wake of the 1980 military coup, the Turkish public started rediscovering, and to a large extent reinventing, Istanbul's "cosmopolitan" past. By the 1990s, nostalgic references to an assumed *belle époque* located in late-nineteenth and early-twentieth-century Pera had become a standard feature of scholarly, literary, and popular interest.[10] This movement was followed by a very conscious exploitation of this nostalgia in the development and gentrification of Beyoğlu/Pera. Shops, museums, and cultural centers started to be renamed with explicit references to the district's former social and topographic nomenclature (Örs 2002). Today, almost thirty years after the first signs of this revivalist movement, the claim to a multicultural and cosmopolitan past is still the dominant sales pitch of most stakeholders in the area, from the municipality to real-estate owners, and from a multitude of businesses to the throngs of visitors who flow daily to what is considered the city's main center for entertainment. The fact that it coincided with the liberalization of the Turkish economy and its rapid integration into the new global order, combined with a boom in tourism, greatly contributed to this process.

And yet, one can express very serious doubts as to the authenticity of this revivalist trend. It is rather ironic to observe that the sudden rediscovery of the lost multiculturalism of the former Ottoman capital came in at a time when the communities that were celebrated in this nostalgic recreation of an alleged cosmopolitanism had dwindled to less than 1 percent of the city's population. It is no coincidence either that this rediscovery coincided with the period during which the city experienced the speediest growth of its overall population, from some 2.7 million in 1980 to 5.4 million in 1985 and almost 9 million in 2000. Nor should one forget that the political and ideological context of the same period ran counter to a genuine and sincere recognition of multiculturalism and diversity as a social virtue. Rather, the political ambience under the Motherland Party (ANAP), which was then in power, was qualified as a "Turco-Islamic synthesis," according to which ethnic and cultural diversity was deemed positive only as long as it strengthened the perception of the Ottoman empire and of the Turkish republic as tolerant and magnanimous towards non-Muslim minorities. In short, then, the reinvention of cosmopolitanism in the 1980s and 1990s rested to a large extent on the combined effect of the lure of a booming urban economy and tourism, the comfort of celebrating the history of communities that had long been eliminated or forced into submission, and the thrill of upgrading Ottoman and Turkish history along the lines of a more "civilized" narrative.

Today, the shallowness of the process has become even more blatant as the Justice and Development Party (AKP) approaches its tenth year in power. For at least half this period, the present government has played the card of political and economic liberalism with great success, managing to increase its electoral base steadily. The comfort of a positive economic record has enabled it to move gradually in the direction of a more conservative stance, which, not unlike ANAP, feeds on the combination of Turkish nationalism and Sunni Islam. As a result, the city has now, more than ever, been enshrined in narratives that reject anything that may have occurred before 1453 or outside of the context of its Muslim/Turkish history. Perhaps one of the most telling indicators of this trend is the frequentation of its major museums. While the two major touristic destinations, namely Topkapı, the palace of the sultans, and Hagia Sophia, Justinian's basilica, received some 4 million and 3 million visitors, respectively, in 2011, the Archaeological Museum, located right between these two monuments, attracted a mere 400,000, almost half of which were non-paying visitors, in other words chain-gangs of school children.[11] Topkapı and Hagia Sophia are not really museums: the former is a palace that tries to be a museum and manages to be neither; the latter is a church that was converted to a mosque, and then to a museum as part of the secularist policies of the 1930s. Yet, they attract crowds of tourists, local and foreign, in quest of an "essential" value attached to these monuments. For Turks, Topkapı is a symbol of Ottoman – and therefore Turkish – glory, and an exhibit of Islamic holy relics; Hagia Sophia is a former mosque, perhaps even a place to be reconquered as it had been by Mehmed II in 1453. For Western tourists, Topkapı is the harem and the embodiment of a popular Orientalist vision of an exotic culture, while Hagia Sophia is a glorious remnant of a civilization that was wiped out by the Turks. The Archaeological Museum, however, although a *real* museum in the purest European tradition, fails to attract Turks who do not feel that it relates to "their" history; but it is also bypassed by most foreigners, who simply do not see it as a relevant destination in a city that should symbolize the Orient.

Istanbul's "Levantine" cosmopolitanism of a century ago may have been limited, superficial, socially skewed, and fraught with colonial undertones; it nevertheless had the merit of handling a very complex social and cultural structure with a relative degree of success. Its destruction at the hands of nationalism has left a void which the liberalization and globalization of the past decades has tried to fill by re-creating part of that environment and claiming to emulate its teachings. Interestingly, nationalism has proven to be much more resilient, and certainly not incompatible with globalization: it has thus managed to hijack the discourse of diversity and to turn it into a cosmetic extension of a dominantly ethnocentric narrative. Istanbul, whose history cannot be understood without listening to the mixed voices of its multicultural past, has become a global city, covered with a varnish of multiculturalism that barely hides an increasingly powerful nationalist historical construct.

Notes

1   A case in point is Natalie Rothman's (2012: 11–15) adaptation of the term transnational to an early modern Venetian context by using the expression "trans-imperial" to describe subjects engaged in an active process of brokerage between the Serenissima and the Ottoman capital.
2   For a discussion on whether the term port city applies to Istanbul, see, Eldem (1999b).
3   For a recent re-evaluation of the concept of cosmopolitanism in the eastern Mediterranean and its possible relation to class, see Gekas (2009).
4   On the complex relation between terms and concepts as they were used by the society and culture under study, on the one hand, and by the present-day historian, see Ginzburg (2012).
5   Hanley (2008: 1348) thus emphasizes that the local languages have only loan words to describe the concept and that these are of recent adoption and rarely comes close to the meaning implied in Middle East studies. In actual fact, efforts to translate the term go back at least to the 1830s, but they do tend to paraphrase the idea of an individual choice of being a citizen of the world and a habitual traveler. See, for example, Bianchi (1831: 94); Handjéri (1840: 545); Redhouse (1861: 183–184).
6   The term was "objectively" used to define and describe individuals issued from families of Western origin long established in the Ottoman lands, most typically Roman Catholic

Ottoman subjects. However, as the word had no real legal definition, it should rather be understood as a very elastic and subjective label attached to individuals who were considered to be somewhat attached to Europe without being *really* Western. This explains why it should have applied to "local" Catholics even if they acquired some European nationality, as well as to other non-Muslims who showed a great eagerness to be considered as Europeans. It also explains that the term was never used by members of the allegedly defined group themselves, but rather by Europeans who looked down upon these "wannabe" Westerners. The term used in Turkish to describe this group is rather telling of the same scornful vision, this time from an Ottoman-Muslim perspective: *tatlı su Frengi* or, literally, "sweet-water Franks." On the evolution of the term, see Eldem (2006). There are two major studies that focus particularly on Levantine society: Smyrnelis (2005) and Schmitt (2005).

7   The Ottoman bureaucracy is known for its propensity to treat non-Muslim names with a certain degree of carelessness and to disregard their existing family names or surnames, perhaps less so with Armenians due to the fact that they often bore Turkish names and surnames. Even by the nineteenth century, at a time when a growing number of non-Muslims served in the bureaucracy, these practices never entirely disappeared, as apparent in the systematic use of Kostaki for Konstantinos, Pavlaki for Pavlos, Yorgaki for Georghios, and so on.

8   This information is based on my research on the Imperial Ottoman Bank archives, more particularly on documents relating to the bank's customers and employees.

9   Falih Rıfkı Atay's editorial added a rather telling projection: "Following the present rhythm of increase, in a few years Turkey will have twenty millions of inhabitants expressing themselves in the same language, united under the same social and cultural consciousness."

10   Said Naum Duhani (1892–1970), the scion of a Christian Arab family, was the first author who harked back to a lost Pera in his melancholic *Vieilles gens vieilles demeures. Topographie sociale de Beyoğlu au XIXe siècle* (1947) and his nostalgic *Quand Beyoğlu s'appelait Péra. Les temps qui ne reviendront plus* (1956). Duhani's books, however, were still for "internal consumption," as it were: they were written in French and published in close sequence to the traumatic events of the 1940s and 1950s. In that sense, from the perspective of my argument, it is much more significant to note that Duhani's works were published in Turkish, the former twice in 1982 and 1984, and the latter in 1990. It should be no coincidence that Orhan Pamuk's first novel, *Cevdet Bey ve Oğulları* (*Cevdet Bey and His Sons*), published in 1982, started with a long description of Pera that was directly taken from Duhani's *Vieilles gens*. Finally, it is rather telling that it was in 1990 that Giovanni Scognamillo published his *Bir Levantenin Beyoğlu Anıları* (*The Recollections of a Levantine on Pera*), fascinating for the author's eagerness to define himself through an adjective that was always used with a pejorative and scornful twist.

11   The statistics are available at the Ministry of Culture and Tourism web site: http://dosim.kulturturizm.gov.tr, accessed February 11, 2013.

References

Akçam, T. 2006. *A Shameful Act: the Armenian Genocide and the Question of Turkish Responsibility*. New York: Metropolitan Books.

Aktar, A. 2000. *Varlık Vergisi ve Türkleştirme Politikaları* (The Wealth Tax and Turkification Policies). Istanbul: İletişim.

Anastassiadou, M. and Dumont, P. 2003. *Une mémoire pour la Ville: la communauté grecque d'Istanbul en 2003*. Istanbul: Institut français d'études anatoliennes.

Atay, F.R. 1936. "À ceux qui veulent savoir," *La Turquie kamâliste*, 12(April): 1.

Behar, C. 1996. *Osmanlı İmparatorluğu'nun ve Türkiye'nin Nüfusu 1500–1927*. (The population of the Ottoman empire and Turkey 1500–1927.) Ankara: Başbakanlık Devlet İstatistik Enstitüsü.

Bianchi, T.-X. 1831. *Vocabulaire français-turc*. Paris: Éverat.

Driessen, H. 2005. "Mediterranean port cities: Cosmopolitanism reconsidered." *History and Anthropology*, 16(1): 129–141.

Duhani, S.N. 1947. *Vieilles gens vieilles demeures. Topographie sociale de Beyoğlu au XIXe siècle*. Istanbul: Touring et automobile club de Turquie.

Duhani, S.N. 1956. *Quand Beyoğlu s'appelait Péra. Les temps qui ne reviendront plus*. Istanbul: La Turquie moderne.

Eldem, E. 1995. "Culture et signature: Quelques remarques sur les signatures de clients de la Banque Impériale Ottomane au début du XXe siècle." *Revue du Monde Musulman et de la Méditerranée. Oral et écrit dans le monde turco-ottoman*, 75–76(1–2): 181–195.

Eldem, E. 1997. "Istanbul 1903–1918: a quantitative analysis of a bourgeoisie." *Boğaziçi Journal*. Special issue, *Review of Social, Economic and Administrative Studies, Istanbul Past and Present*, 11(1–2): 53–98.

Eldem, E. 1999a. *A History of the Ottoman Bank*. Istanbul: Ottoman Bank Historical Research Centre.

Eldem, E. 1999b. "Istanbul: From imperial to peripheralized capital." In E. Eldem, D. Goffman, and B. Masters (eds), *The Ottoman City between East and West: Aleppo, Izmir and Istanbul*, pp. 135–206. Cambridge: Cambridge University Press.

Eldem, E. 2002. "Reshuffling nationality and ethnicity: The Ottoman Bank staff from empire to republic." In T. de Graaf, J. Jonker, and J.-J. Mobron (eds) *European Banking Overseas, 19th– 20th Century*, pp. 179–211. Amsterdam: ABN AMRO Historical Archives.

Eldem, E. 2005. "Les dossiers des employés de la Banque impériale ottomane." In K. Bendana, K. Boissevain, and D. Cavallo (eds) *Alfa. Maghreb et sciences sociales. Biographies et récits de vie*, pp. 45–62. Tunis: Institut de recherche sur le Maghreb contemporain.

Eldem, E. 2006. "'Levanten' Kelimesi Üzerine" (On the term "Levantine"). In A. Yumul and F. Dikkaya (eds) *Avrupalı mı Levanten mi?* (Europeans or Levantines?), pp. 11–22. Istanbul: Bağlam.

Eldem, E. 2007. "Signatures of Greek clients of the Imperial Ottoman Bank: a clue to cultural choices and behaviour?" In A. Frangoudaki and Ç. Keyder (eds) *Ways to Modernity in Greece and Turkey: Encounters with Europe, 1850–1950*, pp. 60–90. London: I.B. Tauris.

Gekas, S. 2009. "Class and cosmopolitanism: the historiographical fortunes of merchants in eastern Mediterranean ports." *Mediterranean Historical Review*, 24(2), December: 95–114.

Ginzburg, C. "Our words, and theirs: a reflection on the historian's craft, today." In S. Fellman and M. Rahikainen (eds) *Historical Knowledge: In Quest of Theory, Method and Evidence*, pp. 97–119. Cambridge: Cambridge Scholars Publishing.

Groc, G. and Çağlar, İ. 1985. *La presse française de Turquie de 1795 à nos jours: Histoire et catalogue*. Istanbul: Isis.

Güven, D. 2006. *6–7 Eylül Olayları*. (The events of September 6–7 [1955]). Istanbul: İletişim.

Handjéri, A. 1840. *Dictionnaire français-arabe-persan et turc*. Moscow: Université impériale, volume I.

Hanley, W. 2008. "Grieving cosmopolitanism in Middle East studies." *History Compass*, 6(5): 1346–1367.

Hirschon, R. (ed.) 2003. *Crossing the Aegean: The Consequences of the 1923 Greek-Turkish Population Exchange*. Oxford: Berghahn.

Karpat, K.H. 1985. *Ottoman Population 1830–1914: Demographic and Social Characteristics*. Madison: University of Wisconsin Press.

Örs, İlay. 2002. "Coffeehouses, Cosmopolitanism and Pluralizing Modernities in Istanbul." *Journal of Mediterranean Studies*, 12(1): 119–145.

Redhouse, J.W. 1861. *A Lexicon, English and Turkish*. London: Bernard Quaritch.

Rothman, N. 2012. *Brokering Empire. Trans-Imperial Subjects between Venice and Istanbul*. Ithaca, NY: Cornell University Press.

Schmitt, O.J. 2005. *Levantiner: Lebenswelten und Identitäten einer ethnokonfessionellen Gruppe im osmanischen Reich im "langen 19. Jahrhundert."* Munich: R. Oldenbourg.

Scognamillo, G. 1900. *Bir Levantenin Beyoğlu Anıları* (The recollections of a Levantine on Pera). Istanbul: Metis.

Smyrnelis, M.C. 2005. *Une société hors de soi: Identités et relations sociales à Smyrne aux XVIIIe et XIXe siècles*. Paris-Leuwen: Peeters.

Part III

The Aesthetics of Transnationalism and Diaspora

Chapter 13

The Anxieties of "New" Indian Modernity
Globalization, Diaspora, and Bollywood
Jigna Desai and Rani Neutill

While migration has led to the formation of South Asian communities around the world for centuries, the rubric of diaspora has only gained a foothold in the social imaginary and academic scholarship in the last few decades. Transnational communities and South Asian nation-states have recently begun to use "diaspora" as nomenclature to describe communities as well as the complex global social, affective, cultural, and political economies linking migrant communities and South Asian nation-states. The South Asian diaspora can be described by both the classical definition of diaspora, as formed through traumatic dispersal or exile (e.g., the 1947 Partition of India and Pakistan, and indentured servitude), and by the contemporary theorizations that understand diaspora broadly as a transnational formation in relation to postcoloniality, racial formations, and late capitalist globalization. Encompassing both of these definitions, the widespread and heterogeneous South Asian diasporas in the global north and south have their "origins in the modern period" and are embedded in the "three major world-historical forces that have shaped global modernity: capitalism, colonialism, and nationalism" (Koshy 2008: 3). In this chapter, we look to the global culture industry of Bollywood to understand the role and function of diaspora and globalization in producing "new" Indian modernities.

Like diaspora, it is only recently that Bollywood has become the subject of transnational academic scholarship. In this literature, scholars have noted the centrality of cinema and visual culture, and especially Hindi cinema, to India's sociocultural and political history, national imaginary, and modernity (see, e.g., Dwyer and Pinney 2002). Here, we turn to the relationship between diaspora and homeland as

A Companion to Diaspora and Transnationalism, First Edition.
Edited by Ato Quayson and Girish Daswani.
© 2013 Blackwell Publishing Ltd. Published 2013 by Blackwell Publishing Ltd.

articulated in the national media and public culture, specifically in the global media ecology of Bollywood. "Bollywood" is itself a contested term that, as many critics have pointed out, implies a belated and mimetic relationship to the West and its dominant media ecology, Hollywood.[1] Scholars have, nevertheless, marked Bollywood as an index of the transformation within Indian media. As Madhava Prasad posits (2003), "'Bollywood' may well provide insights into the changing modalities of Indian national identity in a globalizing world." We pursue this mode of inquiry to interrogate specifically what the Bollywood genre of NRI (non-resident Indian) films tells us about the changing modalities of India's globalization and nationalism in light of class, gender, and sexual politics. We do so by examining the desires and anxieties of the nation-state about diaspora, imagined and narrated as the NRI in this transnational media. The emergence and rise of Bollywood amidst India's liberalization and globalization has been well established elsewhere.[2] Scholars point to Bollywood as an exemplary site for understanding the changing modes of capitalism, nationalism, and globalization in India (see Chakravarty 1993; Virdi 2003; Prasad 1998; Desai 2004; Punathambekar and Kavoori 2008; and Ganti 2012). This chapter interrogates what the genre of the NRI film, as well the gendered figure of the NRI, tell us about the anxieties about globalization and diaspora within new Indian modernities.

The NRI in this case may be understood as the manifestation of a specific and narrow diaspora that is imagined, interpellated, romanticized, and reviled by the nation-state within the context of globalization. It should be noted that the figure of the NRI is located and narrated cinematically in only particular geographies (namely, migrant communities located in the global north such as the United States, Canada, Britain, and Australia) and is specifically of the Hindu middle class.[3] Bollywood's evocation of the NRI reflects the interconnected hopes, fears, and anxieties about diaspora's key role as a catalyst and conduit for the transnational flows of capital, technology, and culture between India and the global north.[4]

The NRI, a pivotal national and transnational figure, tells us much about the history of the political and affective economies between the diaspora and nation-state. The Indian state recently invested in configuring the NRI subject as a long-distance member of the nation. These shifts have been reflected in both citizenship and economic policies and national cultural formations such as Bollywood. The NRI is imagined as a political, cultural, and economic citizen-subject who is offered membership, access, and privileges of heightened citizenship in exchange for *his* – the economic NRI is more often than not, gendered male – economic and political investment. Simultaneously the NRI, a diasporic citizen of the Indian nation-state, should, as a good citizen, yearn nostalgically for the homeland, its values and culture, duplicating authentic tradition as much as possible in the diaspora. Bollywood is a critical node of production and consumption in this transnational political and affective economy, a site where nostalgia, desire, and attachment are produced and maintained. Many of the films of the 1990s and early 2000s – such as *Hum Aapke Hain Kaun . . . !* (1994), *Dilwale Dulhania Le Jayenge* (1995, dir. Aditya Chopra, and popularly referred to as *DDLJ*), *Dil To Pagal Hai* (1997), *Pardes* (1997, dir. Subhash Ghai), *Kuch Kuch Hota Hai* (1998), *Kabhi Khushi Kabhie Gham* (2001, dir. Karan Johar), *Dil Chahta Hai* (2001), and *Kal Ho Naa Ho* (2003, dir. Nikhil Advani) – give form to the shift in aesthetics, ethics, and politics of urban post-liberal India and, more specifically, the growing investment in the migrant communities, and the figure of the NRI. Tracing the political, aesthetic, and affective economies of NRI films gives us a sense of the history of India's globalization and the rise of Bollywood.

Diasporic Doubling and Death in Hindi Cinema

While Hindi cinema has deployed foreign locations as settings for several decades, these locales have functioned in multiple ways, sometimes attesting to the global mobility of Indian citizens, providing audiences a global view from an Indian vantage point, and/or marking a presence on the global stage of Indian (performative and political) actors. For example, Swiss mountain scenes within song-and-dance sequences have provided an opportunity to construct and perform a touristic gaze of the North. However, some films go beyond the picturization of the foreign locales, actually incorporating them into the film's diegesis. Migration features as an emerging motif in films of the late 1960s and early 1970s. These early films about diaspora, including *An Evening in Paris* (1967),[5] *Purab aur Paschim* (1970), and *Hare Rama Hare Krishna* (1971), function as warnings about the danger of leaving the homeland, assimilating into Western (colonial) cultures, and losing one's "Indianness" and homeland.[6] As such, the films caution against migration only as much as they caution against greater forces associated with globalization and Westernization as threats to cultural nationalism – for example, greed, gluttony, sexual promiscuity and depravity, dissolution of family, and hyperconsumption.

The distinction between the corrupt Westernized and the pure traditional woman has usually appeared in the oppositional characters of the vamp and the heroine, figures who are sometimes played by the same actress within Hindi cinema. The vamp has often represented the corrupt Westernization and modernization of the Indian woman whose sexual impropriety, greedy consumption, public dance performances, and immodest clothing mark her as the counterpoint to the chaste, selfless, sari-clad woman of tradition. In *Purab aur Paschim*, both mother and daughter have transgressed the acceptable gender and sexual norms and are depicted as depraved, immodest, and lustful; the daughter Preeti, however, is redeemable through a return to India and to proper gender norms. Both *An Evening in Paris* and *Hare Rama Hare Krishna* use the trope of the double to indicate the conflict presented by the sexualized woman. In the former film, Sharmila Tagore plays the double role of twins who are separated as youths and raised separately in India and Paris. In the latter film, the female protagonist psychically splits herself into an Indian self, Jasbir, and a Western self, Janice, to accommodate the binary. Significantly, in these latter films, the death of the wayward diasporic female proves to be the denouement of these cautionary melodramas allowing the transcendence and salvation of the pure Indian woman.

In *Hare Rama Hare Krishna*'s interrogation of transnational mobility, it is clear how a critique of hippie tourism and culture in the 1970s becomes intertwined with a narrative about the disintegration of the migrating family, gender normativity, and cultural identity in the diaspora. Directed by and starring Dev Anand, the film focuses on a wealthy family in Montreal. Bickering and taunting each other, the husband and wife display a clear disdain for each other and "traditional" marriage. The film pinpoints the Westernization of the couple as leading to the dissolution of the marriage and the family, devastating their two children – Prashant and Jasbir. When the parents divorce, the mother heads back to India with Prashant, while the father stays in Canada with Jasbir. Told that her mother and brother are dead, the adult Jasbir (Zeenat Aman), clearly lost and disoriented, joins Western hippie culture and becomes the Westernized Janice. A biting indictment of hippie culture – personified by throngs of hippie tourists traveling to the subcontinent – the film frames them as young people who are driven to South Asia by the failings of Western society. The failings of Western society – which is steeped in material wealth, but bereft of spirituality – have driven these youths to India and Nepal where tradition and modernity, spirituality and material wealth can abound. The adult Prashant (Dev Anand) embodies this new modernity that is distinct from "lost" Western modernity by synthesizing the traditional and the modern as a loving brother and a successful pilot.

The film deploys the narrative of diasporic Westernization and lack of morality, loss of culture and the indictment and danger of divorce as a site of engagement with anxieties about the increasing global mobility of South Asians, as well as tourism to South Asia by Western hippies. Marrying an ambivalent attitude to diasporic migration and the globalization of tourism, the film voices a discomfort and fascination with the increase in transnational flows and marks the extreme dangers that can result from such movements. At the end of the film, Jasbir (now Janice), kills herself. The camera zooms in on a shot of her parents while Janice, in a voice-over asks, "What have you given me besides birth?" The judgment here is clear: her death is not only her fault, but the fault of her parents, their migration and exposure to the failing morals and conceptions of family that constitutes the general lack of the West. Their separation and break from the "motherland" is what has caused the metaphorical death of Jasbir and the literal death of Janice. Since Jasbir has been tainted by Janice's Western-polluted ways, she cannot be recuperated as she speaks to her brother from the dead: "lifelong I kept pining for a brother. And when I found him, it was too late. Prashant, there is darkness all around. I won't be able to see you within this darkness. That's why I am going into the light."[7] The relationship between diaspora and homeland is configured here through the trope of familial kinship, with the homeland as both mother and brother to the diasporic migrant woman who only through death can return home to the light. In the films discussed above, it is clear that Hindi cinema has had slightly more than a passing concern with the diasporas and Indians living abroad – they have served as cautions signaling the dangers of Westernization in the face of growing migration, emerging transnationalism, and proliferating globalization not only in the diasporas, but also within South Asia itself.

As noted above, the rise of Bollywood as a global media ecology can be read for the relationship between globalization and the nation-state. The transformation of Hindi cinema into Bollywood occurs as the trope of the NRI (diaspora) and is used to signify not only proliferating global migration, but also the rise of neoliberalism and globalization within India. Since 1991, India has undergone an economic transformation of liberalization, privatization, and globalization.[8] These economic shifts radically changed the social and media practices of its middle-class citizen-subjects, increasingly marking them as the primary consumers and viewers within neoliberalism. These transformations impacted and proliferated media industries and fostered increasing media convergence.

The formal liberalization of the Indian economy grew in conjunction with Hindu cultural nationalism.[9] The ruling Bharata Janata Party's slogan of "India shining" emphasized a cosmopolitan techno-economic India steeped in global capitalism, located within the "new middle-class" family, and embodied by the figure of the NRI. In the face of anxieties about globalization, the nation-state wrapped itself in Hindutva and cultural nationalism in the name of protecting tradition.[10] The notion of "keeping Indian culture alive" amidst the transformation of the political economy dominated Indian cultural discourses. This manifestation of cultural nationalism became a central concern of popular Hindi cinema as well, further contributing to its growing popularity overseas. Hence, migrant and diasporic audiences found in Bollywood films a reflection of their own preoccupation with reproducing national culture and "tradition" amidst displacement. The BJP-led government that dominated this transformation (1998–2004) coincided with the emergence and rise of Bollywood's NRI genre – possibly the peak of the genre – and its heroization of the NRI.

How King Khan Conquered Bollywood and the Diaspora

As scholars have remarked (Uberoi 1998; Dwyer 2000; and Rajadhyaksha 2008), films of the mid-1990s such as *Hum Aapke Hain Kaun . . . !* and *Dilwale Dulhania Le Jayenge (DDLJ)* mark a sea-change in Hindi cinema. The movies that span the mid-1990s to early 2000s ponder and reflect upon the ambivalent and conflicting desires of the nation-state, questions surrounding gender and sexuality, and the "liberation" of these from the "repression of tradition" in the name of modernity. Gender and sexuality have long been metrics and indices by which the backwardness and belatedness of Indian modernity have been measured within colonial and Western discourses; correspondingly, the post-liberalization urban middle class has used gender and sexual politics to distinguish itself from what it deems its "traditional" non-modern counterparts. Economic liberalization and globalization have impacted the institutions of heterosexuality, marriage, and family in many ways, but Bollywood has been particularly interested in those changes located within the transforming middle class. In fact, the continuing focus on issues of gender and sexuality such as romance and love marriages, adultery, and homosexuality becomes a critical hallmark of the modern within neoliberal global India and Bollywood. The films, preoccupied with questions about the transnational space of the nation and diaspora, deploy the (trans)formation of the nuclear and conjugal couple as a way to promulgate a new global modernity. These transformations of gender and sexuality are seen as critical to the constitution of the modern transnational Indian subject. These rubrics of "new" and "modern" gender and sexuality have led to transformations within cinematic tropes. Moreover, in Bollywood, diasporic and migrant communities located in the West become distant and potentially safe laboratories for experimenting with these modern "transgressive" gender and sexual formations. Hence, gender and sexual transgressions are narrated and imaged within extraterritorial settings in order to render them within and without the nation simultaneously. One example of such a shift has been the changes in the representation of the "modern" woman, signaled through the collapse of the dichotomous characters of the "vamp" and the "maiden" that are present in films such as *An Evening in Paris*. As film scholars have argued, the vamp character has now been collapsed with the figure of the heroine, and the death of the former is no longer necessary for protecting the sanctity of the latter. Thus, the inability to recuperate and reform the sexual diasporic female subject has consequently also shifted; her metaphorical or real death is no longer necessary to the plot or to the salvation of the traditional woman.[11]

In order to accommodate this modern cosmopolitan woman, a new male NRI, too, must be imagined. The heroization of the NRI male has become a central feature of the Bollywood culture industry and it is Shahrukh Khan who has starred in this role. In over a dozen films, and even more so outside of cinema, Muslim actor Shahrukh Khan or "King Khan" has dominated Indian media in this period through television, advertising, film production, and acting.[12] Khan has successfully "Bollywoodized" himself as a transnational star, who appeals not only to Hindi cinema fans within India, but throughout the diasporas and the global south; his stardom is unparalleled globally and his fans number over a billion. Khan's repeated roles as male (Hindu) NRI have played no small part in establishing his star persona as well as establishing ideals of modern Indian masculinity. Tracing Khan's roles within the NRI genre in films such as *DDLJ*, *Pardes*, *Kabhi Khushi Kabhie Gham*, *Kal Ho Naa Ho*, *Swades* (dir. Ashutosh Gowariker), *Kabhi Alvida Naa Kehna* (dir. Karan Johar), and *My Name is Khan* (dir. Karan Johar) from the 1990s to the present tell us the story of liberalization's transformation of masculinity, family, and affect within Bollywood and the Indian nation-state. Garnering multiple film awards and box office records, many of these films have been popular both with critics and at the box office. *DDLJ*, for example, is one of the most popular films in India, the diaspora, and globally – the film has played continuously in India for over 700 weeks in Mumbai, and has been a hit in the United States, Britain, Australia, and Israel; it also may be said to be the inaugural film in establishing the norms and codes of the NRI genre.[13] Many of Khan's vehicles to stardom as the heroic NRI have been written, produced, and/or directed by just a few individuals – mainly Karan Johar and Aditya Chopra. Both Johar and Chopra have made names for themselves in Bollywood by creating urban cosmopolitan romances and family dramas that star Khan; their names have high brand recognition, signifying a hip, young cosmopolitan Bollywood for a post-liberalized urban India and its diaspora in this period.

Turning to a few of the first films within the genre – namely *DDLJ* and *Pardes* – may help illuminate how these prototypical films reflect the overarching ambivalence concerning the dangers and importance of globalization, and how these anxieties and desires play themselves out in the gender and sexual politics of the nation and the diaspora. *DDLJ* has been discussed alongside *Pardes* (see, e.g., Sharpe 2005) precisely because they both demonstrate the necessity for the female NRI to be both modern and traditional. However, although these films rely on the figure of the proper Hindu woman as the organizing principle of the nation, they are simultaneously anxious about the diasporic male subject – as the good heteronormative Hindu male NRI – who must reinvest both economically and affectively in the Hindu nation. This reinvestment is substantiated economically as well as through the figure of the Hindu bride (Mankekar 1999); this is best illustrated in *DDLJ* and the romantic relationship that develops between the upper-middle-class NRI Raj (Shahrukh Khan) and Simran (Kajol). Although Raj is Westernized, drives a fast car, drinks alcohol, and ignores his education, he, most importantly, safeguards Simran's chastity and honor during moments that are ripe opportunities for sexual activity. After a night of heavy drinking while traveling in Europe, Simran wakes up in Raj's bed. The drinking itself suggests a moral fall that leads to the far greater loss of her sexual purity (one that echoes an earlier scene in *An Evening in Paris* in which the heroine also drinks too much and is at risk of losing her honor and virginity at the hands of a "bad" diasporic male). The cost of her exposure and participation in this Western immorality is the (supposed) "loss" of her chastity. In the most quoted scene of the film, Raj toys with her, insinuating that this loss has occurred, stating "You had one too many. . . . What happened last night was what was bound to happen." Although Simran initially thinks she has become disrespectable due to "having one too many," Raj reassures her that although she believes he would take advantage of her due to his "Western" ways, he is actually "a Hindustani," and as such, "he knows what honor means for a Hindustani woman." The good Hindustani NRI is the one who protects the sanctity of the woman as nation, even in the diaspora.

Pardes deploys the doubling trope of earlier films discussed above by splitting the figure of the "bad male NRI" (the Western Rajiv) from the "good male NRI" (culturally Indian Arjun – Shahrukh Khan), rather than from the good Indian. The trope functions to make clear the necessity of male NRI morality in relation to pure homeland women. Rajiv, settled in the United States, is hyper-Americanized – a rich playboy who drinks and disrespects traditional familial values and women. He is spoilt and excessive in all the ways an Indian man can be, but should not, in diaspora. The film narrates the faults and pitfalls of his behavior through a comparison with Arjun, the NRI hero who is able to travel to America but sustain cultural values, and thus teach Rajiv how to be a good NRI. It has been arranged for Rajiv to be married to Ganga (named after the sacred river Ganges and portrayed by actress Mahima Chaudhry), a wholesome, chaste, and pure Indian woman. Both Arjun and Ganga perform their piety and loyalty through musical performance; for example, Ganga demonstrates her ability to live in the diaspora and embody "authentic" tradition and culture by performing her Indianness morally and musically, singing "I Love My India." The complex narrative in *Pardes* is not one of the woman in danger of Western contamination, but the story of how the *male* NRI must be reshaped into the moral heteromasculine NRI subject who is deserving of the homeland Hindu bride.

The need for the economic investment of the NRI is linked to the proper heteromasculinity of the NRI, who needs to be located within the (trans)national institution of the family. In *DDLJ*, Simran and Raj's love is at first threatening to the institution of marriage and the family. Simran's father longs for his homeland and, upon learning of Simran's attachment to Raj, moves the family back to his Punjabi village and completes the arrangements for her marriage to the son of a childhood friend. Being the "good" NRI, Raj returns to India in an effort to regain his Hindu wife and eventually rescue her from the Indian male who does not value her as a respectable Indian woman. But Raj's return is predicated on an economic as well as romantic return – he tells Simran's family that he wishes to open a factory, take his family's vast overseas fortunes, and reinvest in his nation. When the family learns that Raj also has intentions of marrying Simran, upheaval ensues. In the final scene, Simran's father concedes to their love, allowing Raj and Simran, along with Raj's father, to depart for England (despite the voiced interest in reinvesting and returning to India). In both *Pardes* and *DDLJ*, moral and narrative resolution can only occur upon return to the homeland. Both stage the ultimate conflict and predicate its denouement through a return to the homeland itself.[14] Hence, the genre furthers the state's discourse of economic reinvestment in the nation and simultaneously and inextricably links it to the heteronormative affiliation associated with marriage, family, and cultural return.

Tapping into this anxiety around changes to social institutions through globalization, Karan Johar's *Kabhi Khushi Kabhie Gham* (*K3G*, 2001), might be the ultimate paean to Hindu patriarchy, consumption, and cultural nationalism within the "golden age" of the NRI film; its tag line reads "it's all about loving your parents." Capitalizing on the all-star cast (Amitabh Bachchan, Jaya Bachchan, Shahrukh Khan, Kajol, Hrithik Roshan, Kareena Kapoor, and Rani Mukherjee), the film portrays what might be considered the ideal "global Indian family." Not only is the family able to overcome the obstacles associated with migration and India's entry into the global economy, but it is identified as the ideal institution to do so. The family and nation have never been so collapsed and simultaneously dispersed. As the NRI male romantic hero has become the figure of the global technoeconomy, this has meant a rewriting of the role of the patriarch within the global Indian family; it is affective, not economic, ties that bond families across time, space, and generation. Hence Amitabh Bachchan's repeated casting in the role of the patriarch relies on his stardom spanning several decades, and his ability to evoke and engender intense affective responses – *K3G* emphasizes the role of family but one in which the patriarch's role has changed.

Moreover, *K3G* reterritorializes the Indian family and nation abroad, claiming global spaces through its touristic and migrant gaze. For example, like other films that utilize panoramas of the Western landscape, *K3G* presents these scenes visually through long shots. But instead of scenes indicating displacement, longing for home, and isolation, these scenes are overlaid with visual and aural markers of Indian Hindu nationalism – clothes, dance, Hindu worship, and music. Hence, scenes of British monuments and landmarks are concurrent with the nationalist song *Vande Mataram*, women clad in salwar suits, dance, and Hindu prayer.[15] Within this film, it becomes clear that it is no longer necessary to return to the homeland – a diverse India can be found and maintained abroad.[16] Perhaps most striking is the scene in which the young son of Rahul (Shahrukh Khan) and Anjali (Kajol) teaches his entire British class to perform the Indian national anthem, *Jana Gana Mana*, evoking a respectful recognition and an appreciative ovation, if not a potent nationalism, in the British audience. Indeed, this imagining speaks to the desire of the Indian nation-state to claim the spaces of the global north as locations within a global "shining India." One might say that it heralds a globalizing India everywhere.

"New" Bollywood and NRI 2.0

After 2004, the return of the Congress Party and its coalition government to power did not dissipate the dominance of the urban cosmopolitan middle class within the political economy or the cultural imaginary. However, the necessity of a cultural nationalism emphasizing "tradition" did shift somewhat. Within the last decade of Bollywood, while tradition appears as some sort of spectacle on screen vis-à-vis ceremonies, palatial familial dwellings, and ritualized holidays, "modern" and "new" have been increasingly used to signify the aesthetics, politics, and modes of a dominant Bollywood[17] and its imagined viewer. Scholars have noted the proliferation of new and expanding genres such as horror, science fiction, action, and comedy, and the rise of the multiplex and shifting narratives that characterize this recent formation of "new" Bollywood. Moreover, "modern" is used to constitute and tag the "new middle class," but also the formation seen as critically embodying its concerns and desires – the modern and urban cosmopolitan couple. After the reification of the family within Bollywood at the turn of the century, "new" Bollywood launches a proliferation of discourses about the threats to, repression of, and anxieties of the conjugal couple, gender, and sexuality.

Moving from the rampant heroization of the techno-economic heteropatriarchal NRI male to a heightened focus on the conjugal couple, films in the mid 2000s promulgate narratives about the repression of sexuality in order to advance "transgressive" sexual and gender formations as signs of the "modern." Embedded within late capitalist middle-class aspirations and desires for participation in a post-global India and "new" modernity are apparent in replications of liberal discourses about

conjugality and sexuality, including adultery, divorce, and remarriage (*Kabhi Alvida
Naa Kehna – KANK*); premarital sex and pregnancy (*Salaam Namaste*); and homosexuality and gay identity (*Dostana*). Increasingly, an individualized, liberal notion
of sexuality is critical to conceptions of personhood, global citizenship, and modern
cosmopolitanism within media and society. Often there is an innovative use of
diaspora as an imagined space for locating these "transgressive" sexual formations. Diasporic locations are imagined simultaneously as Westernized spaces
outside the nation (as in *DDLJ* and *Pardes*) *and* as Indian cosmopolitan and urban
spaces (as in *K3G* and *Kal Ho Naa Ho*). In this regard, they are both of and outside
India, local and global, so that New York and Miami are American and stand in for
Mumbai simultaneously in films such as *KANK* and *Dostana*.

    After *Kuch Kuch Hota Hai* and *K3G*, Karan Johar[18] directed *KANK* (2006) and
produced *Dostana* (2008), both of which became emblematic of this performance
of the "modern." Set entirely in New York, in *KANK*, the fact and consequences of
adultery, divorce, and remarriage are narrativized through a relationship forged
between Dev (Shahrukh Khan) and Maya (Rani Mukherjee). Maya is married to
her childhood friend Rishi (Abhishek Bachchan), out of an obligation to his father
Sam (Amitabh Bachchan), who adopted her as an orphaned child. Dev, a talented
and famous soccer player, is married to Rhea (Preiti Zinta), who has a successful
career at a fashion magazine. Dev is hit by a car, ending his career and causing him
to resent his wife's status as breadwinner. A friendship ensues between Dev and
Maya who fall in love and have an affair, but return to their marriages out of guilt.
Eventually both marriages dissolve into divorce, and Rhea and Rishi remarry.
Absolved of their guilt and relieved of their obligations, Maya and Dev are permitted to reunite and reignite their relationship; Maya accepts Dev's proposal
in the final scene.

    While adultery is not an uncommon theme in Hindi cinema, it is typically what
happens inside the filmic plot, but outside of the camera's purview; in *KANK*, the
adultery occurs on screen precisely to "liberate" that which is (framed as) repressed.
The couple's "transgression" is at the heart of the film as it argues for the acceptance
of "modern" desires. While the mismatched couple – a protagonist with the "wrong"
partner – is a common trope in Hindi cinema, *KANK* employs this trope *within*
the institution of marriage to indicate that Maya and Dev are with the wrong partners – namely, their spouses. The film seeks to "correct" this misalignment of desire
outside of marriage and locate it firmly back within the institution of marriage and
family, one that is even affectively (rather than juridically) authorized by the film's
patriarch. On his deathbed, Maya's excessive and hedonistic adopted father and
father-in-law Sam (Amitabh Bachchan) permits her to leave her loveless marriage
with his son Rishi. Generally, heteropatriarchy's sanctioning of love and marriage
has been a frequent gauge of the social economy of gender and sexuality in Hindi
cinema. Heteropatriarchy has licensed love and marriage in various formations in
Hindi cinema, including through "feudal family romance" (Prasad 1998) and the
"arranged love marriage" (Uberoi 2002). *KANK* offers another addition to this set,
namely, that of the "sanctioned divorce and remarriage." Here, while familial obliga-

tion (Maya's obligation to Rishi and his father) plays a role in establishing the first marriage, heteropatriarchal permission is critical to dissolving the marriage, absolving Maya from the moral sin of adultery, and facilitating the second serial marriage to be possible. Hence, *KANK* imagines the possibility of adultery, divorce, and a love remarriage located intimately and distantly in the diaspora. As they meet at the start of the film on a park bench and continue to establish their relationship primarily in public spaces, it is clear that in the film, Maya and Dev can only assume an adulterous relationship and flaunt it in a public *diasporic* space, namely New York. The film locates adultery in public only within diasporic spaces. In other words, *KANK* is set in the diaspora, not because adultery does not occur within India, but because adultery is being "liberated" and proliferated into *public* middle-class spaces within the film, presumably in the service of individuals' liberty, in the form of privacy, choice, and sovereignty. At this moment, the diaspora allows this space to be imagined both in and out of the nation.

A similar argument can be made regarding the visibility of gay identity. Far more than adultery, divorce, and remarriage, same-sex desire, coded as homosexuality and gay identity, functions as a signifier of the "new" and "modern" within Bollywood. During this time Hindutva and cultural nationalism have typically associated non-heteronormative male sexualities (usually coded as "gay") with Western and diasporic (as opposed to indigenous or traditional) sexualities.[19] *Dostana*, meaning friendship, is a variation of *dosti* which is used frequently to describe some same-sex relationships between men. Directed by Taran Mansukhani and produced by Karan Johar, *Dostana* focuses on two heterosexual men pretending to be "gay" while living in Miami, Florida. Kunal (John Abraham) and Sameer (Abhishek Bachchan) find but cannot rent their dream apartment, because the owner does not want her niece Neha (Priyanka Chopra) to share it with two heterosexual men. In order to secure their ideal dwelling, they pretend to be a gay couple. In the film *Kal Ho Naa Ho*, the protagonists play up their supposed sexual intimacy and purported gayness to illicit a phobic response by their "non-cosmopolitan," "traditional" Gujarati houseworker Kantaben. Similarly, in *Dostana* the pretense of Sam and Kunal as gay acts as a foil to "traditional" (repressed and non-modern) sensibilities and as a source of humor. In short, it allows for audiences to see the acceptability of homosexuality as a critical index for the hipness, urbanity, and globality of the Indian modern subject.

While the film, like many others, uses humor to forward homosexuality in the service of heteronormativity and cosmopolitanism, an ambiguity is apparent through the performance of desire and visualization of the erotic. In the penultimate scene, Sam and Kunal are challenged to kiss each other to seek forgiveness from Neha (and the man that she loves, Abhi) for trying to sabotage their relationship. Egged (and cheered) on by the entire room, and after some resistance, they kiss. While the affect and desire of the kiss is based in coercion, guilt, and penance, the scene nonetheless picturizes the simulated act between two top Bollywood male stars on screen. This kiss is opened further to reinterpretation in the last scene of the film when Neha asks if they felt anything for each other. They defensively say no, but look at each other, remembering their kiss as they part and walk away. The film does not seek necessarily to portray and make visible a gay subject, but opens up ambiguous erotics between the men, possibly to undermine the pretense of their desire and relationship. In other words, viewers are encouraged to question whether or not that performance of love and desire did not ultimately produce affect and pleasure.

Furthermore, the film authorizes an erotic or "queer" gaze of the male Bollywood star's body and of the homosocial buddy relationship. In *Dostana*, there is a significant and "excessive" emphasis on the male body. It is important to note that the display of the male Bollywood star's body has become a key feature of advertising, star branding, and identification, and media coverage, thereby linking the male star's body with consumption and commodities within the post-liberal Indian media. In *Dostana*, this cosmopolitan and neoliberal gaze is made interchangeable with a gaze associated with gay male desire; hence the camera's lingering emphasis on Abraham's toned abdomen, pectorals, and buttocks conflates and converges sexual and material desires, linking and imbricating the globalizing of media, capital, and sexuality.

It is clear that NRI films have not only been essential to the constitution, formation, and dominance of Bollywood, but also critical to articulations of the nation and modernity within global India itself. NRI films reveal the past and recent impact of, and anxieties about, diaspora within global India. "Bollywood" captures and amplifies India's struggle with its persistent and chronic belatedness to modernity in Western terms, its subsequent identity based on a distinction from the West, and its importance as a global political and cultural presence. As Bollywood simultaneously signifies a difference from the West and a global presence, it emerges as a counterpoint in claims of new globality and modernity for the rising cosmopolitan class. In other words, its transnational idioms and regimes of signification are animated by, resonate with, and reify the new global middle class in India and its corresponding diasporas. Through the figure and genre of the NRI, Bollywood continues to maneuver and proliferate through the shifting anxieties and desires of globalization. Hence, we have argued that Bollywood globalizes (spreads across the globe), remaking transnational spaces into Indian places; at the same time, spaces within the Indian state, too, are globalized (made global and transnational) by Bollywood. While the sun may (never) have set on the British empire, today it is Bollywood that illuminates and projects a "shining India" beyond its national boundaries and across the globe.

Notes

1   See Rajadhyaksha (2008) and Prasad (2003). The term "Bollywood" has overtaken and is often used interchangeably with previous nomenclatures such as Hindi or Bombay cinema.

2   Rajadhyaksha (2008) speaks of "Bollywoodization" as a process that includes the subsumption of cinema to neoliberal global culture industries and the diasporicization and globalization of this industry.

3 Other dispersals and migrations such as those due to Partition or in the form of labor migration as guest workers are seldom narrated as diaspora or as NRI. For example, the 1947 Partition and the 1971 Indo-Pakistan war that lead to the secession of East Pakistan (and the formation of Bangladesh) resulted in the displacement of over 20 million people; this uprooting, dispersal, exile, and displacement of peoples fits the classic definition of diaspora, yet these dispersed people are neither the subject of the state's formulations of the NRI and Person of Indian Origin (PIO) nor a fragment of the national public that Bollywood seeks to address.

4 It should be noted that the film industry has begun increasingly to see diasporic audiences as a source of potential revenue. Bollywood films are often released simultaneously in India and abroad. In addition to theatrical releases, satellite television, VCR, and DVD (including piracy), and online media have allowed for elaborate and extensive distribution.

5 The film is striking in that it is set in Paris, but also includes travel to other tourist destinations including the Swiss Alps, Beirut, and Niagara Falls as part of its diegetic narrative.

6 All three films grossed well in the box office and were classified as "hits," each grossing between 1.5 and 2.25 crore rupees unadjusted. See "Top Earners 1960–1969," at http://www.boxofficeindia.com/showProd.php?itemCat=123&catName=MTk2MC0xOTY5, boxofficeindia and "Top Earners 1970–1979," at http://www.boxofficeindia.com/showProd.php?itemCat=124&catName=MTk3MC0xOTc5, both accessed March 9, 2013.

7 All translations from Hindi are ours.

8 The formal liberalization of entertainment since the late 1990s has allowed the film industry to benefit financially in the form of lower production charges and tax benefits, and has permitted filmmakers to accumulate production finance from banks and other corporate financial institutions, thereby according media industries an important and legitimate economic and symbolic status. Within this framework, film is then seen as a marker of Indian success in the international marketplace of goods, where Bollywood films compete with Hollywood ones at box offices around the world.

9 Mirroring these larger shifts in the political economy, television transformed from a development- and state-based system to a privatized and globalized system during this period. Television with its proliferation of channels became a critical medium geared towards middle-class viewers. Changes in the television industry produced and reformulated social practices, transformed public spheres and citizenship, and altered state policies. For example, television in this period became watched increasingly, though not exclusively, in the home and programming became increasingly targeted at middle-class and elite audiences. Consequently, there was a sea-change in the kinds of images that were consumed in Indian households as Indian television went from the production and broadcasting of a limited number of state television channels to the availability of privatized and globalized cable television broadcasting that spanned across foreign networks like CNN and domestic cable channels like Zee TV and Star TV. The transformations in political economy and media practices went hand in hand with shifts in the gender and sexual politics of the upper-caste Hindu middle class. With media expansion and convergence, the landscape of media and social practices changed as shifting images, narratives, and formations of sex and gender appeared on screens.

10 This period also marks the growth of the Hindutva movement in India. On December 6, 1992, the Babri Masjid in the city of Ayodhya, Uttar Pradesh, was destroyed by Hindu

nationalists, resulting in rioting across the nation. The conflict over the mosque arose because of conflicting narratives concerning the plot of land on which the mosque was built. Hindu nationalists claim that the site of the mosque is the birthplace of the Hindu god, Rama, and deployed this "history" to justify the demolition of the mosque and the subsequent violent riots. A rise in Hindu nationalism led to Atal Bihari Vajpayee – who founded the Hindu right-wing party, the Bharatiya Janata Party (BJP) – being elected as prime minister from 1996 to 2004.

11   The "modern" woman is recognizable by several traits, including her urban cosmopolitanism, her visibility in the workforce and public sphere, and her sexual role within the conjugal couple. Because women's participation in the formal workforce has also been essential for increasing middle-class income and consumption, the ideal of womanhood, too, has shifted to the figure of the urban, English-speaking, educated upper-caste Hindu woman who is often depicted as having a successful career. Scholars have also pointed out that it is often Indian middle-class women who are targeted as the new consumers of the growing neoliberal market of food, beauty, appliances, and household goods; the modern woman is one who consumes visibly. Sexual desire and performance is now demanded of the good wife-to-be as the new woman mediates, negotiates, and modulates increased visible sexualization and sexual desire. Configuring the NRI and urban Indian woman as balancing tradition and modern through her appropriately channeled and expressed sexual desires within the conjugal couple, sanctioned participation in the labor force, and high consumption of commodity goods allows for the modernization of India, but maintains national identity located within the family. Nonetheless, the national space is gendered female through the maintenance of the maidenhood of the "proper" Hindu woman. This is one of the particularly consistent and congestive aspects of Bollywood's interpellation of its national and diasporic subjects.

12   Khan started his acting career on television serials but then moved onto film with his anti-heroic and villainous roles in *Deewana, Darr*, and *Baazigar* in 1992 and 1993.

13   See "Top Lifetime Grossers," at http://www.boxofficeindia.com/showProd.php?item Cat=303&catName=TGlmZXRpbWU=, accessed March 9, 2013.

14   This lack of return to the homeland allows for the NRI to return to the homeland without resettling in India. The film *Swades* presents an idealized return of the techno-economic NRI as is discussed elsewhere; see Desai (2008).

15   A similar sense of global claiming of place may be seen in the film *Kal Ho Naa Ho* and a syncretic performance of *Pretty Woman* set supposedly in New York. Staging the song, performed by Muslim actor Shahrukh Khan in New York, is a complex claiming of space in light of India's aspirations, but also the events of 9/11 in New York. While songs are consistently associated with the private space of romance for the nuclear couple, it is also clear that song-and-dance sequences in these films emphasize a territorial gaze that claims extensive geospatial terrain as part of global India. In many of the films, these extra-diegetic scenes further the nationalism of a global India.

16   It may be possible to see these geo-imaginings as analogous to the ones that occur in *An Evening in Paris*, which reverse the touristic gaze in traveling Europe. In these cases, these foreign locales are marked as within India.

17   While Bollywood became the global face of India, diasporic filmmakers such as Deepa Mehta, Mira Nair, and Gurinder Chadha, sought to make "homeland" movies that became a part of Bollywood. Crossover transnational films such as Mira Nair's *Monsoon*

Wedding (2001) as well as more international ventures such as Danny Boyle's *Slumdog Millionaire* (2008) have become synonymous with Bollywood for Western audiences.

18   As a highly visible public figure and media moghul (including host of Koffee with Karan) with a penchant for the letter K, Karan Johar or 'KJo' himself embodies and negotiates sexually ambiguous spaces on and off screen, including rumors of his own ambiguous or "gay" sexuality and his supposed relationship with Shahrukh Khan. His films are characterized by beautiful modernity (new commodities, bright and easy consumption, a touristic camera) and aestheticized spectacles of tradition (spectacular palatial dwellings, gorgeous detailed costumes, and nostalgic and strategic casting) that are symptomatic of the modern cosmopolitanism in India.

19   Independent films like *My Brother Nikhil* have located some of these discussions *within* India and, as the title suggests, frequently reference these discussions through an urban English-speaking cosmopolitanism and usually a discourse of gay identity and rights as globalized idioms of gender and sexuality.

Filmography

An Evening in Paris, Shakti Samanta, 1967.
Baazigar, Abbas-Mustan, 1993.
Darr, Yash Chopra, 1993.
Deewana, Raj Kanwar, 1992.
Dil Chatha Hai, Farhan Akhtar, 2001.
Dil To Pagal Hai, Yash Chopra, 1997.
Dilwale Dulhania Le Jayenge, Aditya Chopra, 1995.
Dostana, Tarun Mansukhani, 2008.
Hare Rama, Hare Krishna, Dev Anand, 1971.
Hum Aapke Hain Kaun..!, Sooraj Barjatya, 1994.
Kabhi Alvida Naa Kehna, Karan Johar, 2006.
Kabhi Kushi Kabhie Gham, Karan Johar, 2001.
Kal Ho Naa Ho, Karan Johar, 2003.
Kuch Kuch Hota Hai, Karan Johar, 1998.
Monsoon Wedding, Mira Nair, 2001.
My Brother Nikhil, Onir, 2005.
My Name is Khan, Karan Johar, 2010.
Pardes, Subhash Ghai, 1997.
Purab aur Paschim, Manoj Kumar, 1970.
Salaam Namaste, Siddharth Anand, 2005.
Slumdog Millionaire, Danny Boyle, 2008.
Swades, Ashutosh Gowariker, 2004.

References

Chakravarty, S. 1993. *National Identity in Indian Popular Cinema, 1947–1987*. Austin: University of Texas Press.

Desai, J. 2004. *Beyond Bollywood: The Cultural Politics of South Asian Diasporic Film*. London: Routledge.

Desai, J. 2008. "Bollywood, USA: Diasporas, nations, and the state of cinema." In S. Koshy and R. Radhakrishnan (eds) *Transnational South Asians: The Making of a Neo-Diaspora*, pp. 345–367. New Delhi: Oxford University Press.

Dwyer, R. 2000. *All You Want Is Money, All You Need Is Love: Sexuality and Romance in Modern India*. London: Cassell.

Dwyer, R. and Pinney, C. (eds) 2002. *Pleasure and the Nation: The History, Politics and Consumption of Popular Culture in India*. New Delhi: Oxford University Press.

Ganti, T. 2012. *Producing Bollywood: Inside the Contemporary Hindi Film Industry*. Durham, NC: Duke University Press.

Koshy, S. 2008. "Introduction." In S. Koshy and R. Radhakrishnan (eds) *Transnational South Asians: The Making of a Neo-Diaspora*, pp. 1–44. New Delhi: Oxford University Press.

Mankekar, P. 1999. "Brides who travel: Gender, transnationalism, and nationalism in Hindi film." *Positions: East Asia Cultures Critique*, 7(3): 731–761.

Prasad, M.M. 1998. *Ideology of the Hindi Film: A Historical Construction*. Oxford, New Delhi: Oxford University Press.

Prasad, M.M. 2003. "This thing called Bollywood." Unsettling Cinema: A Symposium on the Place of Cinema in India, 525, at http://www.india-seminar.com/2003/525/525%20madhava%20prasad.htm, accessed March 5, 2013.

Punathambekar, A. and Kavoori, A. (eds) 2008. *Global Bollywood*. New York: New York University Press.

Rajadhyaksha, A. 2008. "The 'Bollywoodization'of the Indian cinema: Cultural nationalism in a global arena." In Punathambekar and Kavoori (2008), pp. 17–40.

Sharpe, J. 2005. "Gender, nation and globalization in *Monsoon Wedding* and *DDLJ*." *Meridians: Feminism, Race, Transnationalism*, 6(1): 58–81.

Uberoi, P. 1988. "The diaspora comes home: Disciplining desire in *DDLJ*." *Contributions to Indian Sociology*, 32(2): 305–336.

Uberoi, P. 2002. "Imagining the family: an ethnography of viewing in *Hum Aapke Hain Koun*." In Dwyer and Pinney (2002), pp. 309–329.

Virdi, J. 2003. *The Cinematic Imagination: Indian Popular Films as Social History*. New Brunswick: Rutgers University Press.

Chapter 14

West African Video-Movies and Their Transnational Imaginaries

Carmela Garritano

The narratives of transnational travel and migration that circulate under the sign of African literature tend to adopt what Françoise Lionnet and Shu-mei Shih call the "binary model of above-and-below" (2005: 7). Structured around difference, they represent Africa's relationship with the West as principally antagonistic and so organized as "a vertical relationship of opposition or assimilation" (p. 7). Examples include Buchi Emecheta's novel *Second-Class Citizen* (1974) and Chike Unigwe's *On Black Sister's Street* (2010) as well as Ousmane Sembène's early film *La Noire de* (1966) and Jean-Marie Teno's more recent *Clando* (1996). These are political narratives that write-back to the center; they tend to reiterate what Achille Mbembe, in another context, refers to as "nativist and Afro-radical narratives" – narratives that normalize the idea that "the encounter between Africa and the West resulted in a deep wound: a wound that cannot heal until the ex-colonized rediscover their own being and their own past" (2002: 635). Animated by anticolonial and other oppositional discourses, they sometimes give voice to concerns for social justice and cultural preservation and frequently "pivot on assertions of belonging" (Dawson 2010: 179).

The privileging of literary narratives as the optimal sites of interpretation for understanding Africa's entanglements with the West has rendered invisible a multiplicity of African cultural forms and expressions that do not adhere to the binary model, limiting the conclusions that we might draw about Africa's worldliness. Among these are West African popular video-movies, and in particular the genre of video-movie that I refer to as the travel movie, or the African-abroad movie (Haynes 2003). Produced and marketed in West Africa and in a European or North

A Companion to Diaspora and Transnationalism, First Edition.
Edited by Ato Quayson and Girish Daswani.
© 2013 Blackwell Publishing Ltd. Published 2013 by Blackwell Publishing Ltd.

American city that is home to a large African migrant community, these cultural products move through global cities (Sassen 2001) and media capitals (Curtin 2003), but along unofficial, highly fragmented, and privatized networks that are detached from dominant commercial networks and institutions of official or academic culture. African video-makers, addressing a popular, mass audience in Africa, have bypassed the regulatory structures of the dominant center's symbolic economy, too. Although popular video-movies explore themes similar to those taken up in literary texts, their brazenly commercial and non-ideological orientation and unapologetic deployment of aesthetics of excess and affect set them apart from realist and politicized narratives by internationally celebrated African authors and cineastes. As Jonathan Haynes remarks (2003: 23), "the international dimension of their cultural horizon is formed more by American action films, Indian romances, and Mexican soap operas than by exposure to English literature." The videos' characters lack depth and interiority, and their narratives are built on the mechanics of melodrama: "outrageous coincidence, implausibility, convoluted plotting, and episodic strings of action that stuff too many events together" (Singer 2001: 46). Their low budget and amateurish production values can be impossible to ignore, and unlike literary texts, they are noisy (Ferguson 1999). Marked by unrestrained heterogeneity, they resist ideological domestication and open up to multiple and often contradictory meanings and pleasures.

Because they neither assimilate to nor actively resist dominant culture, West African popular videos about travel and migration make visible a more variegated and complicated cultural ecology of globalization. The study of popular videos, more crucially, attends to the kinds of everyday practices "through which Africans manage to recognize and maintain with the world an unprecedented familiarity" (Mbembe 2002: 258). It is through such practices and the familiarity they express that Africans, Mbembe notes, create something unique that also "beckons to the world in its generality" (p. 258). Put slightly differently, the significance of African travel movies might be found in their expression of the desire for "global membership," a term used by James Ferguson (2006) to describe the aspirations of Africans for connection to and affiliation with the global. To seek global membership is not to imitate or assimilate to Western models. Instead, the characters of travel videos, like their makers and consumers, seek a connection to and place within "the emerging social reality we call 'the global'" (Ferguson 2006: 193). Speaking to and born of the very real aspirations to achieve equality with the center, to be "first-class" in Ferguson's apt phrase (p. 187), the movies boldly assert Africa's worldliness by drawing attention to connections between Africa and the West. They offer African audiences pleasures derived from imaginary travel to New York, London, or Amsterdam and tourist views of the cities' sites and spectacles. Focalized through the perspective of the African migrant, the spectator in Africa virtually experiences global mobility and imaginatively consumes the tourist experience by watching a narrative about the first-time Ghanaian traveler who leaves Africa in search of the prosperity embodied in the global city. In a context of scarcity, these popular forms facilitate a virtual appropriation of desired experiences and goods and provide, in the words of Mbembe (2002: 269), "a means of psychic negotiation, self-styling, and engagement with the world at large."

Modes of Production

The thriving, commercial video-movie industries in Ghana and Nigeria, collectively referred to as "Nollywood," represent the most important and exciting development in African cultural production in decades. Though the film medium failed to take root in Africa, video, since the late 1980s, has flourished. An inexpensive, widely available, and easy-to-use technology for the production, duplication, and distribution of movies and other media content, video has allowed video-makers in Ghana and Nigeria, individuals who in most cases are detached from official cultural institutions and working outside the purview of the state, to create a tremendously popular, commercial cinema for audiences in Africa and abroad: feature "films" made on video. In 2011, Ghanaian movies appeared at the rate of approximately 10 per month, while the larger Nigerian video industry, listed by UNESCO as the second largest movie industry in the world, releases a staggering 1,500 movies each year (Barrot 2009). Projected in movie theaters and video parlors in Africa, broadcast on television, streamed over the internet, distributed and pirated globally in multiple formats, West African video-movies have become among the greatest explosions of African cultural production in history.

Compared to the large number of West African video-movies produced annually, the travel-movie genre comprises a relatively small number of video productions.[1] Yet, since the appearance of travel movies in the 1990s, their titles have been among the most successful African video-movies made. According to Pierre Barrot (2009), Kingsley Ogoro's *Osuofia in London* (2003) has sold more copies than any other Nigerian movie. In Ghana, Bob Smith's *Mamma Mia* (1995) was a phenomenal success. In the Ghanaian video industry, the national industry that has been the focus of my research, the most prolific producers are Bob Smith Jr, and Socrate Safo. Both travel abroad regularly and have forged solid relationships with media professionals in the international locations where their films have been made. Bob Smith's *Mamma Mia* series was one of the earliest and most successful attempts to give Africans at home images of and stories about the European African diaspora. In 1995, Smith produced the incredibly successful *Mamma Mia* in Accra, Ghana, and Verona, Italy, where his wife lives and works and where he frequently stays for long periods of time. He followed with two sequels: *Double Trouble: Mamma Mia Part Two* (1998) and *Black Is Black: Mamma Mia 3* (2000). A few years later, Smith made another Ghana/Italy series: *Wild World: If Wishes Were Horses* (2002); *Wild, Wild World: Wild World 2* (2004); and *Wild World 3: What a World!* (2004). Smith's familiarity with Verona, his proficiency in the language and culture of Italy, his many friends and contacts in the Ghanaian community there, and his collaborative partnership with the Italian video-maker Marco Bressanelli have enabled and sustained his Ghana–Italy movie projects.[2] His example illustrates that networks of affiliations, which spread through various spheres of the foreign cities where the movies are made, make these movie projects possible. Although several producers, such as Safo, bring members of their cast and crew from Ghana, all depend on the cooperation of Africans living in the diaspora, including friends and family. Their homes, businesses, churches, and community organizations feature as locations in the movies, and producers frequently recruit members of their cast and crew from among them. *Amsterdam Diary* (2005) was one of four movies that emerged out of a collaborative effort among a group of Ghanaian actors and technicians, who, together with the director and producer Socrate Safo, carried cameras and lights to Amsterdam to shoot four videos in one month.[3] Relying on well-established contacts in Amsterdam and working cooperatively, the group videotaped Safo's *Amsterdam Diary I* and *II*, *Idikoko in Holland*, which was written and directed by Augustine Abbey, Helen Omaboe's *Twists and Turns*, and, finally, Albert Kuvodu's *Otolege*. The cost of bringing equipment and a small cast and crew to Europe was relatively an enormous expense for the producers to bear, so movie budgets were extraordinarily tight. Several actors were asked to fund part of their own trips in exchange for assistance with obtaining their travel visas. They wore their own clothes in many scenes and made do without elaborate props. Workdays were long, and the cast and crew were required to participate in and take on multiple roles in each production (Garritano 2013: 138).

The primary market for travel movies is the ordinary African who lives in Africa, a person who has never been overseas and has little prospect of ever having the means to do so. Most producers also edit, replicate, and distribute their video-movies in Ghana, where they know how the system operates and what audiences expect. Though interested in developing a large market base in the diaspora, distributing movies abroad continues to present enormous difficulties. Without access to distributors operating from within an organized distribution system, most producers rely on informal business arrangements with African marketers who travel back and forth between Africa and the diaspora regularly. Producers sell stacks of individual copies of their movies to the marketer, who then carries them overseas to be shelved next to *fufu* flour and plantains in the neighborhood African store. In recent years, a few Ghanaian producers have arranged to sell the international rights for their travel movies directly to African entrepreneurs who have the capacity and equipment to reproduce their movies in the diaspora. These are typically African music and movie stores located in African neighborhoods of large cities in Europe or the United States. Other producers have negotiated to use the African store itself as a setting in the movie.[4] The entrepreneur considers the product placement free advertising; the producer lands a free location to shoot and distribute his movie, and African audiences at home see that their "local" music, food, clothes, and other products have become part of the global cultural landscape of London or New York. As is the case in Ghana, piracy is an insurmountable problem in the diaspora. Nothing prevents duplicators from illegally copying and selling a video purchased for home use. The wide availability of African movies on the internet has further contributed to widespread piracy. The institutions that police international copyright laws disregard, or simply cannot account for, this minor cultural practice; the Ghanaian government lacks the resources to do much about piracy in Ghana let alone beyond its borders, and the producers themselves do not have the means to protect their own interests.[5]

Imaginary Travel and Virtual Tourism

Typically focalized through the point of view of a male protagonist, West African travel movies narrate the journey from Africa to a foreign city, such as Amsterdam, New York, or London. The African traveler, who is always poor and who has never been overseas, leaves home because he faces a situation of extreme economic duress and believes that he will find better opportunities abroad. These are not stories of cosmopolitan transnationals (Desai 2004) or elite flexible citizens (Ong 1999), but of Africans with little knowledge of the Western world and with little money who must resort to illegality to secure the money or papers needed to get out of Ghana. In Bob Smith's *Mamma Mia* series Kwabena Dabo has worked as a bank-teller in Ghana for nine years. When his wife Connie becomes pregnant, he decides that he must find a way to take care of his family properly, so he embezzles money from the bank in order to buy a ticket to Verona. In other movies, travelers might purchase illegal documents, as occurs in *See You Amsterdam* (2003) or *Koofori in London* (2005); pay smugglers to transport them across borders illegally, as in *Amsterdam Diary* (2005) or the Nigerian video *Europe by Road* (2004); or stow away as cargo, as seen, for instance, in *Wild World* (2002) and *Mr Ibu in London* (2004). As Haynes has noted of the Ghanaian and Nigerian travel-video narrative (2003: 27), "the process of establishing oneself abroad is presented as extremely arduous and as something that can be accomplished only with the advice and help of fellow Africans." Kwabena Dabo's plight exemplifies the point. He spends his first four days and nights in Italy in a public park in Verona, fighting off the cold and eating the *gari* he has carried in his suitcase from Ghana. He speaks no Italian, and his attempts to engage Italians walking through the park are met with cold stares and annoyed expressions. In Socrate Safo's *Back to Kotoka* (2000), Nat, a Ghanaian lawyer recently arrived in Holland, wanders the streets of Amsterdam for days, hungry, cold, and alone. His situation improves when he encounters a fellow Ghanaian, who recognizes him from home and offers support and assistance.

A spatial binary between an African city and a foreign city structures the narratives of these transnational movies. Frequent crosscuts between the two locations generate drama and suspense as resolution to a conflict in one location is withheld with a cut to the other. *Mamma Mia*, for example, cuts continually between Kwabena's hardship in Verona and Connie's slow downfall in Accra. The audience witnesses the parallel downfall of husband and wife who themselves remain unaware, until the very end of the movie, of what is happening to the other. This use of parallel editing suggests, on the one hand, great distance and disconnection between the characters, whose experiences occur without the knowledge or assistance of the other.

Yet, for the spectator, the montage indicates simultaneity, aligning the two locations in time. For the African spectator, then, the movement back and forth between Africa and the West temporally and spatially constructs a relationship of proximity between the two locations. Proximity is also indicated by the narratives in the inclusion of and frequent reference to technologies that link Africa to the diaspora. Characters visit mailboxes to receive letters and packages from abroad; they make international phone calls and send money transfers across the globe. Often, a phone call that refuses to go through or a letter that never arrives redirects the plot in unexpected or meaningful directions, emphasizing simultaneously the importance and fragility of global communication networks.

Often, the migrant's innocence or naïvety causes conflict with his African host, and in many travel movies, especially comedies, his ignorance is exploited to provoke laughter from the audience. The Nigerian comedy *Mr Ibu in London* elicits humor by playing upon Mr Ibu's ignorance of London. He doesn't know how to queue for food; he tries to cross the street and is almost hit by a car; he looks for a Nigerian newspaper at the London news stand, and his pidgin is hard for Londoners to understand. Mr Ibu cannot believe that an architectural and technological wonder like London's Tower Bridge is real. He asks if it is Mami Wata that makes it work. His host, a fellow Nigerian, assures him that it is indeed real: "It's technology," he says. He's afraid of and amazed by the London Eye, the largest Ferris wheel in Europe, and when he sees himself on the monitor of a security camera in a convenience store, he thinks he is on television. Mr Ibu's inability to read human behavior in his new context leads to his expulsion from Michael's home: Mr Ibu misinterprets Michael's wife's kindness and thinks she is in love with him. When he tries to seduce her, Michael kicks him out of the house, and he must return to Lagos.

A gendered logic of transnationality inflects most African-abroad videos. Men are represented as traveling subjects, while women seem little more than symbolic objects, whose bodies act out the movie's larger meaning. In *Amsterdam Diary*, the female protagonist Abasaa embodies the dangers and vices of the European city. She reluctantly accedes to the wishes of her mother, who advises her to use the beauty God gave her to secure a future for herself, and travels to Holland to marry a fellow Ghanaian, Kobby, the brother of her best friend Diamond. Abasaa's unhappy encounter with Amsterdam transforms her body. Homeless and unemployed, she is forced to work as a stripper and becomes addicted to drugs. Traumatized, she returns to Ghana without the ability to speak. In many transnational video-movies, the space of the diaspora is sexualized and gendered. African women living in the diaspora are bad wives or loose women. Ghanaian men, in response to their wives' provocations, are adulterous and jealous, and family ties become increasingly tenuous, signifying the homeland's weakening hold on the migrant. Perhaps indicating points of affinity with Bollywood diasporic cinema, it is marriage to a woman from home that, in many movies, sutures the male African traveling to or living in the diaspora to the homeland (see Desai 2004).

Though the Ghanaian man living abroad often looks to Africa for a wife, his Mother Africa figure, home is anything but a stable and homogenous site of origin or safety. Friends and family at home are often the source of grief for the traveler or migrant. *Amsterdam Diary* criticizes families that pressure their loved ones to go aboard. Crosscuts between Abasaa's slow downfall in Holland and her mother's excruciatingly long prayer meetings with her pastor in Ghana, where they pray to God to let Abasaa send lots and lots of money, emphasize the point. Unknown to Kwabena, the protagonist in *Mamma Mia*, Connie's life has fallen apart since his departure to Italy. She is questioned by the police about her part in the embezzlement scheme and her father throws her out of his home for disgracing him and his church. Fred, the friend to whom Kwabena has been writing letters and sending money to pass along to his wife, has been stealing the money from Connie. Overcome with despair, Connie goes into a coma and dies in childbirth. Fred, overcome with sorrow and guilt, then kills himself. It isn't until the end of the movie that Kwabena receives a letter from Ghana narrating the tragedy put in motion by his departure. In many African-abroad movies, the mother who lives in Africa signifies burdensome obligations to family and community; from back home, she reminds her son of his familial duties, which typically impede his desires for success or love. In *London Got Problem* (2006), Adam's mother calls incessantly from Ghana to ask her son for money. In *Love in America* (2008), Daniel's mother objects to his marriage to a Ghanaian woman living in the diaspora because his mother believes that their marriage will be cursed. When Daniel assures her that "this is America," a place where curses and witchcraft cannot touch him, she answers: "Tradition is tradition and you have to abide by it."

The movies typically conclude when the migrant realizes that he cannot make it overseas and must return home. The videos aim to expose the harsh realities hidden behind the myths of prosperity that lure Africans abroad, giving audiences at home melodramatic stories about the economic hardships, racism, and personal betrayals that await Africans who leave home. As a character in *Back to Ghana* (2008) says, "Auborokyire [the Akan word for 'abroad'] is hell." Ghanaians tempted by the opportunities and pleasures of life abroad are better off staying at home. Nonetheless, the appeal of the movies also relies on its audience's fascination with and desire to partake in the global modernity of the West by visiting its sites, walking its cityscapes, and consuming its food and other goods. The movies, as commodities, exploit the very desires their narratives dissuade.

The most striking, and sometimes irritating, feature of the African-abroad movie is the unsystematic deployment of the codes and conventions of classical narrative cinema. The movies deliberately violate expectations of temporal unity and spatial coherence, particularly in the placement and extended duration of location shots. Unnecessarily long takes of the foreign cityscape frequently interfere with the cause–effect logic of the narrative. Location or establishing shots grow to be scenes, spilling into and submerging the video's narrative, while the plot is put on hold for an extended look at and tour of a place or site that may have only passing relevance to the story. During these segments, the camera adopts the tourist's gaze and seems fascinated with locations for their own sake. These to-be-looked-at spaces and sites are usually associated with global travel and the global cityscape: international airports, tourist attractions, city streets, and public spaces populated by other tourists. These segments call to mind what Tom Gunning, in his (2004) work on early cinema, calls a cinema of attractions: "Rather than being an involvement with narrative action or empathy with character psychology, the cinema of attractions solicits a highly conscious awareness of the film image engaging the viewer's curiosity. The spectator does not get lost in a fictional world and its dramas, but remains aware of the act of looking, the excitement of curiosity and its fulfillment" (p.869). Displaying indifference to the movie's plot and realist illusion, these excursions into the global city "directly [solicit] spectator attention, inciting visual curiosity, and supplying pleasure through an exciting spectacle" (Gunning 1990: 58). The audience, like the main character of the movie, experiences the global city as a fascinating spectacle.

Two examples illustrate the point. *Amsterdam Diary* includes a six-minute segment that depicts in great detail Abasaa's movement through an unspecified international airport. Safo assembled this segment from actual footage he captured with a small hand-held camera that he concealed in his coat when he and the cast and crew traveled to The Netherlands. Viewers travel with Abasaa as she sits on the airplane, disembarks, walks through the airport, passes through immigration, picks up her luggage, queues for her customs interview, and, finally, leaves the airport. In Augustine Abbey's *Idikoko in Holland* (2005), one of Idikoko's Ghanaian hosts, Vera, treats him to a tour of Madame Tussaud's wax museum in Amsterdam. The camera follows the characters as they leisurely stroll through the museum, posing next to a variety of well-known African American cultural icons including Martin Luther King Jr, Oprah Winfrey, Tina Turner, and James Brown. Idikoko, enchanted by this excursion into simulacra, exclaims, "This is a nice country; I am not going back to Ghana." Leaving the museum, he and Vera feed pigeons in an open plaza, buy trinkets at a tourist boutique, and enjoy a horse-and-buggy ride through the city. Rendered mainly in long takes, these excursions through global spaces extend temporally beyond what is necessary for narrative coherence or plot development and disrupt the narrative by introducing a different temporality and by engaging the spectator directly.

Although these breaks with well-established narrative conventions might be taken as aesthetic failures or amateurish mistakes, they are, nonetheless, meaningful. Safo and Smith both explained that travel movies sell because Ghanaians in Ghana want to see how their compatriots, "their people," are faring overseas. As the camera moves through the streets of the foreign city, the spectator casts a curious and desiring gaze on the city's sites and spectacles. Here, the spectatorial investment involves, for the spectator in Africa who desires but has no way to experience life abroad, the space to occupy temporarily a transnational subjectivity. Mayfair Mei-Hui Yang (2002), in her analysis of Chinese modern mass media, uses the phrase "imaginary travel" to describe the pleasures Chinese national subjects derive from watching television programs about Chinese characters living in Japan or the United States. Likewise, African subjects might be said to "inhabit transspatial and transtemporal imaginaries" (Yang 2002: 190) as they watch other Africans navigate the journey overseas, tour famous places, and consume the experience of living or visiting else-where. Spectators identify with someone like them walking through the Red Light District of Amsterdam or visiting a McDonald's in London and share with the characters of these movies the unfamiliarity and fascination with the foreign city. As Vijay Mishra (2001) has noted in his writings about the diasporic cinema of Bollywood, imaginary travel "brings the global into the local, presenting people in main Street, Vancouver, as well as Southall, London, with shared 'structures of feeling' that in turn produce a transnational sense of communal solidarity" (p. 238). Not only do African movies bring the global into the local, however; they go further, inserting the local into the global. Travel movies create an imagined transnational community among Africans, and more, they assert African membership in the global community.

One of the ways African characters express their global membership is through consumption (Garittano 2013). In *Window Shopping: Cinema and the Postmodern* (1993), Anne Friedberg demonstrates a correspondence between the "mobilized virtual gaze" of cinema and television and other commodified forms of visual mobility, specifically the look of the tourist, who visually experiences foreign spaces, and of the shopper, who examines goods on display. Friedberg describes shopping and tourism as metaphors for cinematic and televisual spectatorship. Much like watching a dynamic world unfold on a screen, these activities bring together move-ment and visual consumption and produce "a perceptual displacement" that "defers external realities, retailing instead a controlled, commodified, and pleasurable sub-stitution" (1993: 122). African-abroad movies play upon cinema's capacity to offer, virtually, pleasures associated with mobility and consumption. The African protago-nist's introduction to the global city brings these pleasures together in the presenta-tion of an extravagant shopping excursion. These episodes present the foreign city as a consumerist space experienced through a variety of virtual mobilities and imaginary acts of consumption. Using actual locations in which real tourists shop and look, the shopping scene embeds consumption into the fabric of the everyday and allows the African spectator to take on the identity of a tourist, visually consum-ing the signs and commodity spaces of the Western city as she or he moves across its landscape. Typically, the African protagonist and his female guide, whether she is African or European, embark on this outing together, and their romance, too, finds expression as a commodity experience. To be in love in the foreign city is to consume tourist sites, foreign food, and goods as a hand-holding, heterosexual couple. In Bob Smith's *Wild World*, a shopping mall in Verona is the setting for a romantic interlude shared by Jojo, the Ghanaian tourist in Verona, and Gianna, his Italian hostess. The segment includes neither dialogue nor consequential actions. Set to cheerful Italian pop music, the characters stroll through the mall. They smile and shop, signaling to the audience that they have fallen in love.

Amsterdam Diary modifies this formula, sending Abasaa and her female Franco-phone guide through the Red Light District of the city. They walk, shop, look, buy, and eat. The montage shifts back and forth between location shots that position the two Ghanaian women in the midst of the crowds that move along the busy streets and shots that pan slowly across shop windows where the two characters stop to look at the goods for sale. The window that holds the camera's interest for the longest period of time advertises "sex for sale," and behind it are exhibited porno-graphic videos, pink vibrators, and lacy lingerie. The spectator who watches the women meander through the streets of Amsterdam virtually encounters the global cityscape as a shopper encounters a display window; it presents a range of pleasures made available to the tourist, or anyone, for a price. The appeal of the movies involves, it seems, an imaginary "visual excursion and a virtual release from the confinements of everyday life" (Friedberg 1993: 28). For the ordinary Ghanaian spectator who does not have the means to travel as a tourist nor to treat shopping as leisure, the movies provide, if only virtually, the chance to adopt a globally mobile subject position and to consume exotic and titillating pleasures from elsewhere. At once expressing and producing the desire to be mobile, the movie works in the gap between here and there.

For the Ghanaian traveler in the African-abroad movie, arrival and integration into the foreign city are continually deferred, obstructed by legal and economic barriers that prove impossible to avoid or scale. A few of the latest travel movies represent life in the diaspora differently. No longer centered on the travel under-taken by the migrant and his or her uncertain arrival in the global city, titles such as *London Got Problem* (2006), *Back to Ghana* (2008), *Love in America* (2008), *Run Baby Run* (2008), and *Abrokyire Bayie* (2009), narrate the experiences of Ghanaians who are well established in the diaspora. Turning their focus away from tourist sites and spectacles, the latest transnational movies, made by video-makers now familiar with the foreign city, and sold in larger quantities outside of Africa, normalize the experience of living aboard. As producers and directors spend more time making movies outside of Ghana and, in some cases, relocate to the European cities where they have worked, their movies, too, become more integrated into the landscape of the Western city and its African diaspora.

In these recent movies, the mise-en-scène narrows the gap between the West and Africa. No longer is the foreign city displayed as a curious spectacle, and characters rarely tour sites and amusements; in most cases, few scenes take place in exterior locations, and the cityscape merely frames the dramas happening inside domestic spaces. Many movies set in the diaspora, especially the most cheaply produced, rely on a similarly assembled montage in which an establishing shot of an exterior, urban location in a foreign city cuts to an unmarked interior space, usually a living room or kitchen, of a neatly and inconspicuously furnished home. These domestic scenes, though set in the home of Ghanaians living in the diaspora, often are shot in Ghana. In *Back to Ghana* and *U Gotta Go Home*, a compilation of multiple locations in the United States, Italy – which Smith visited on his way back to Ghana – and Ghana is presented as the New York City setting. In the first scene, set in the New York morgue where Kwabena works, an establishing shot of the morgue's exterior, identi-fied by a large sign that reads Hennepin County Morgue, was shot in downtown Minneapolis. Because Smith's crew was not granted permission to videotape in the

Minneapolis facility, scenes set inside the morgue were strung together from various unremarkable rooms, hallways, and offices along the path Smith traveled in the production of the video. The morgue's interior, where we see Smith getting dressed for work and walking down the hall, was shot in Verona, Italy, while the following scene, where Kwabena enters the temperature-controlled holding room and pulls out a drawer containing a body, was shot in Accra, Ghana. Set near the World Trade Center complex, the last scenes of the film offer the tourist-spectator a glimpse of Ground Zero, opening against the backdrop of the giant World Trade Center transit station sign. Smith explained to me that he had intended for this site to be the movie's big selling point.

Producers hoping to appeal to viewers who want to see movies about Africans living abroad have pushed this fakery to its furthest extreme, presenting movies shot entirely in African locations as if they were also set in a foreign country. The Ghanaian movie *Agya Koo in Libya* (2009) and the Nigerian movie *Love in Asia* (2007) are two examples. In these movies, global spaces in Africa are presented as global spaces abroad. *Agya Koo in Libya* (2009) relies on the most superficial Orientalist markers to encode a space as in Libya. Characters that are in Libya wear headscarves and scenes that transpire in Libya are set in the same location, the outside porch of a large house that is tiled in a Middle Eastern design. A picture of Gadhafi has been hung conspicuously on the wall. An Asian restaurant in Lagos, frequented by Asian customers and decorated in Asian decor, is put forward as actually in Asia in the Nigerian movie *Love in Asia* (2007). These tricks play upon Africa's real and imagined worldliness, exploiting the actual intermingling of the local and global that is a feature of African cities to create an imaginary, global landscape outside of Africa.

Conclusion

In their stark moral oppositions and didactic resolutions, transnational movies reaffirm values represented as jeopardized by the lure of the foreign city and its promises of prosperity and comfort. But this moral instruction is, at the same time, troubled by the flows of desire the movies activate. They produce a profound ambivalence about leaving Africa to experience global mobility, warning against the dangers of being far from Africa while putting on display the attractions of visiting and consuming a foreign city. On the one hand, they assure the viewer who does not have the means to go abroad that everything is better at home and yet, on the other hand, the pleasures they offer involve virtual travel and consumption. And underwriting this ambivalence is an assertion of global membership. The movies place Africa and Africans in the time-space of the global. In the usage coined by Nuttall and Mbembe (2008) they "world" Africa, calling attention to the technologies, means of transport, routes, commodities, and people that link the West to Africa.

Notes

1   The movies I have drawn on in this article include: *Mamma Mia Italiana*, dir. Bob Smith Jr, Ghana and Italy, 1995; *Double Trouble (Mamma Mia Part Two)*, dir. Bob Smith Jr, Ghana and Italy, 1998; *Black is Black: Mamma Mia 3*, dir. Bob Smith Jr, Ghana and Italy, 2000; *Love Brews in Toronto*, dir. Pius Famiyeh, Ghana and Canada, 2000; *Back to Kotoka*, dir. Socrate Safo, Ghana and The Netherlands, 2001; *Wild World (If Wishes Were Horses)*, dir. Bob Smith Jr, Ghana and Italy, 2002; *Wild, Wild World (Wild World II)*, dir. Bob Smith Jr, Ghana and Italy, 2002; *See You Amsterdam*, dir. Ashong Katai, HM Films Production, Ghana and The Netherlands, 2003; *Amsterdam Diary*, dir. Socrate Safo, Movie Africa Productions, Ghana and The Netherlands, 2005; *Coming from America*, dir. Harry Laud, Ghana and United States, 2005; *Koofori in London*, dir. Paa Kofi Mannoh, Ghana and United Kingdom, 2005; *Idikoko in Holland*, dir. Augustine Abbey, Ghana and The Netherlands, 2005; *Otolege*, dir. Albert Kuvodo, Ghana and The Netherlands, 2005; *London Got Problem*, dir. Albert Kuvodo, Ghana and United Kingdom, 2006. *Back to Ghana*, dir. Bob Smith Jr, Ghana and United States, 2007; *U Gotta Go Home*, dir. Bob Smith Jr, Ghana and United States, 2007; *Love Brewed in America*, dir. Socrate Safo, Ghana and United States, 2008; *Run Baby Run*, dir. Emmanuel Apea, Ghana and United Kingdom, 2008; *Agya Koo in Libya*, dir. Jones Agyemang, Ghana and United Kingdom, 2009; *Abrokyire Bayie*, dir. Albert Kuvodu, Ghana and United Kingdom, 2009.
2   Unlike other video-makers, Smith relies entirely on the resources available to him in overseas locations. Smith assembles a different crew, with its own style of video-making and levels of expertise and experience, in each location, and each crew, of course, uses different cameras, microphones, digital tape, lights, and so on. What emerges is a bifurcated narrative in which significant variations shape how the audience experiences each place. In a Bob Smith Jr production, the spectator's engagement with Italy is wholly unlike his engagement with Ghana precisely because the location and condition of the video's production inflects the materiality of the video text. For the spectator, the material conditions of the movie's production undergird the back-and-forth movement of the video narrative. The texture of each place as rendered in the movie looks and sounds unlike the other. Because Smith is the only professional actor appearing in the overseas segments of his movies, the narratives can seem out of balance, relying too heavily on Smith's character, what he says and does, while other characters, such as Smith's Italian lovers or Ghanaian friends, rarely speak and, when they do, seem to lack depth and complexity because the amateur actors who play these parts fail to offer convincing performances.
3   The discussion and analysis of *Amsterdam Diary* and other parts of this chapter draw from Garritano (2013).
4   Safo told me that he has sold the international rights to his movies for as little as 500 euros. The Ghanaian producers mail or deliver a master copy of the movie to the duplicator/distributor. The distributor then transfers the movie from digital tape to DVD and duplicates DVDs. At the time of writing, a DVD of a Ghanaian movie sold exclusively for home viewing costs about €7. In Amsterdam, the two main duplicator/distributors are Quayson K and Agenim Boateng. In London, Money Matters, Wayosi, and Kumasi Market dominate this market, while in the Bronx in New York, Africa Movie Mall distributes, and recently has even begun to sponsor, African movies.
5   Faced with these difficulties in collecting revenue for his movies overseas, Safo, who has made two movies in Amsterdam and one in New York, has concentrated his efforts

abroad on distribution. In Amsterdam, he has partnered with Sankofa TV, an Afro-centric public access station, exchanging international rights to a few of his movies for the broadcasting of others. In New York, Safo works with Sanga Entertainment (see www.smartafrican.com, accessed February 12, 2013). Sanga purchases exclusive international distribution rights for Safo's movies and, very recently, has supported his production projects in New York by giving Safo use of office space and an editing station in his building.

References

Barrot, P. (ed.) 2009. *Nollywood : The Video Phenomenon in Nigeria*. Oxford: James Currey/ Bloomington: Indiana University Press.

Curtin, M. 2003. "Media capital: Towards the study of spatial flows." *International Journal of Cultural Studies*, 6(2): 202–228.

Dawson, A. 2010. "Cargo culture: Literature in an age of mass displacement." *Women's Studies Quarterly*, 38(1): 178–193, at http://muse.jhu.edu/journals/wsq/v038/38.1-2.dawson.html, accessed February 12, 2013.

Desai, J. 2004. *Beyond Bollywood: The Cultural Politics of South Asian Diasporic Film*. New York: Routledge.

Ferguson, J. 1999. *Expectations of Modernity: Myths and Meanings of Urban Life on the Zambian Copperbelt*. Berkeley: University of California Press.

Ferguson, J. 2006. *Global Shadows: Africa in the Neoliberal World Order*. Durham, NC: Duke University Press.

Friedberg, A. 1993. *Window Shopping: Cinema and the Postmodern*. Berkeley: University of California Press.

Garritano, C. 2013. "Tourism and trafficking." In *African Video Movies and Global Desires: a Ghanaian History*, pp. 129–151. Ohio University research in international studies, Africa series 91, Athens: Ohio University Press.

Gunning, T. 1990. "'Primitive' cinema: a frame-up? or, the trick's on us." In T. Elsaesser and A. Barker (eds) *Early Cinema: Space, Frame, Narrative*, pp. 95–103. London: British Film Institute.

Gunning, T. 2004. "An aesthetic of astonishment: Early film and the (in)credulous spectator." In L. Braudy and M. Cohen (eds) *Film theory and criticism*, pp. 862–876. New York: Oxford University Press.

Haynes, J. 2003. "Africans abroad: a theme in film and video." *Africa e Mediterraneo: Cultura e Società*, 25: 22–29.

Lionnet, F. and Shi, S. 2005. *Minor Transnationalism*. Durham, NC: Duke University Press.

Mbembe, A. 2002. "African modes of self-writing," trans. Steven Rendall. *Public Culture*, 14(1): 239–273, at http://muse.jhu.edu/journals/public_culture/v014/14.1mbembe.html, accessed February 12, 2013.

Mishra, V. 2001. *Bollywood Cinema: Temples of Desire*. New York: Routledge.

Nuttall, S. and Mbembe, A. (eds) 2008. *Johannesburg: The Elusive Metropolis*. Durham, NC: Duke University Press.

Ong, A. 1999. *Flexible Citizenship: The Cultural Logics of Transnationality*. Durham, NC: Duke University Press.

Sassen, S. 2001. *The Global City: New York, London, Tokyo*, 2nd edn. Princeton: Princeton University Press.

Singer, B. 2001. *Melodrama and Modernity: Early Sensational Cinema and Its Contexts*. New York: Columbia University Press.

Yang, M.M. 2002. "Mass media and transnational subjectivity in Shanghai: Notes on (re) cosmopolitanism in a Chinese metropolis." In F.D. Ginsburg, L. Abu-Lughod, and B. Larkin (eds) *Media Worlds: Anthropology on New Terrain*, pp. 189–210. Berkeley: University of California Press.

Chapter 15

The European Salsa Congress
Music and Dance in Transnational Circuits
Ananya Jahanara Kabir

"Oye DJ, tírame la música" (Hey, DJ, throw me some music) sings Cuban-born New York resident Cucu Diamantes on her first album, *Cuculand* (Wrasse Records, 2010). As the song, "Still in Love," reveals, "este Moreno me miró que yo no pude contener" (the way this dark-haired man was looking at me, I just couldn't control myself). The tale of attraction between the Hispanic "I" and her Moreno unfolds within a recognizably Latin soundscape – until about halfway through the song, when another beat begins pushing its way through the polyrhythmic template. Faint at first, it reveals itself to the South Asian listening ear as the sounds of the *dhol* beating out a Punjabi *bhangra* rhythm (the eight-beat *kaharwa taal*). In confirmation, the song's coda has Diamantes repeating, till fade-out, in Hindi, "tu mera pyara hai" (you are my beloved one). The song's significance mutates from a transnational Cuban's electronic-accented experiment on traditional salsa to a broader experimentation with other global dance sounds originating in diaspora; the Moreno this Morena seeks seems to be a South Asian rather than a fellow Latin lover. The all-powerful DJ is both muse and conduit for the coming together of these diverse beats, and peoples, on a dance floor replete with possibilities of unpredictable, even transgressive cultural encounters. Music and dance are multiply transnationalized, although without losing the glocal significance of a Cuban singer in New York interpreting her musical heritage, which now goes by the universally acknowledged name of "salsa."

In their song "Arroz con salsa" (rice with salsa), Japan's Orquesta de la Luz (*La Aventura*, RTL International, 1994) declare that "salsa no tiene fronteras" (salsa has no frontiers). Salsa's lack of frontiers sheds light on transactions, dialogues, and

A Companion to Diaspora and Transnationalism, First Edition.
Edited by Ato Quayson and Girish Daswani.
© 2013 Blackwell Publishing Ltd. Published 2013 by Blackwell Publishing Ltd.

encounters between people and their practices that we would deem "transnational." As Diamantes' "Still in Love" suggests, salsa also helps us move away from modes of individuated analysis formulated largely through engagements with textuality, by asking us to use dance – a somatic, collective, activity – to calibrate an understanding of intercultural, transnational encounters. Formed through multiple ruptures and conjunctions – slavery, Spanish colonialism, and pan-Hispano-American movement of music and people – salsa today is transnationalized through unpredictable circuits linking global north and south. People disconnected from salsa's New World foundations and unable to understand its Spanish lyrics dance it; around its core, other non-European social dance forms from the Caribbean, Brazil, and West Africa have accrued. Anglophone, Francophone, Hispanophone, and Lusophone traditions collide on the salsa floor: Jamaican dancehall, Dominican merengue and bachata, French Caribbean zouk, Brazilian samba de gafieira, and Angolan kizomba (Sloat 2005). This eclecticism is exemplified in international "salsa congresses": intense weekends of workshops, shows, and social dancing for amateur and professional dancers.

This chapter examines the transnationalism of contemporary salsa by focusing on the Tenth Berlin Salsa Congress, October 1–4, 2010,[1] an event which drew hundreds of salseros (salsa aficionados) from around the world for three days of Latin dance, music, and merchandizing in the heart of Europe. As an "observing participant" (as distinct from a "participant observer"; see Skinner 2007: 3), I made empirical observations, participated in workshops, danced, and conversed with delegates. My experiences will be placed within a wider European context to present contemporary salsa as a subject highly congenial to scholarship on transnationalism. Salsa helps us reconsider the "transnational" as it intersects with the kinetic and somatic dimensions of knowledge production and social interaction. In thus interrupting textualized discourse (Sklar 2000; Frank 1991; Hewer and Hamilton 2009), I have been inspired by work on embodied knowledge in the Caribbean and the Americas (Taylor 2003; Benítez-Rojo 1996; Glissant 1997). Yet such scholarship emphasizes *intra*-cultural preservation. I, in contrast, investigate *inter*cultural communication through salsa, including that which involves my own, transnational Indian, dancing/analyzing self. "People dance salsa because they can't afford to go to the shrink," asseverates DJ Willy (Wilfrid Vertueux), one of Europe's premier Latin music DJs (personal interview, Berlin, October 2, 2010); his equally celebrated colleague DJ Mauri (Maurizio Gonzalez) adds, "from the pilot to the plumber, everyone is dancing salsa" (personal interview, Berlin, October 2, 2010). Salsa dancers mobilize a "kinesthetic empathy" (Sklar 1991: 7) to enter a complex embodied history of traumatic yet life-affirming postcolonial modernity. Bringing together hundreds of dancing bodies for the pure pleasure of dance, the congress does more than confirm that "globalization has led to the global export of salsa as a leisure pursuit" (Skinner 2007: 11): it is the site par excellence for this dance that "is outsider/insider music because it is owned by none and all" (Wilson 2009: 6). Through the congress, we can recast analyses of subjectivity and agency under conditions of transnationalism in terms of the Caribbean's contribution to *la alegría en el mundo* (joy in the world; Quintero Rivera 1998: 10).

From the Barrio to the Congress:
Salsa in a Transnationalizing World

A salsa congress is a gathering place for salseros to hone their dancing skills, network with other dancers, purchase salsa shoes, clothes and DVDs, and experience a salsa-related "high" over an extended weekend. Organized at hotels or convention centers, the salsa congress is big business as well as big entertainment, combining tourism with the promise of focused dance practice and exposure to the latest in salsa dance and music. These congresses began in the late 1990s in the Spanish-speaking world, hence the direct translation into English as "congress" (rather than "conference" or "convention") of the Spanish word *congreso* (Borland 2009: 467); today, another word that is used to name these events is "festival." In the last decade, the number of congresses has increased to include every corner of the globe: from Singapore to Surinam, from Gothenburg to Bangalore, from St Gall to Cairo to Sydney, congresses are everywhere and there is no logic to the location chosen other than that of it being the domicile of a salsa entrepreneur who has both local and international connections, ambition, together with the advantage of selling the location in question as having some intrinsic attractions to tempt an international salsa crowd, as well as infrastructure for their board, lodging, and dancing. The proliferation of salsa congresses reflect a "salsa boom throughout the world, a global phenomenon of music, dancing, and merchandise, which has caught up millions of devotees who live and work for their dancing nights" (Skinner 2007: 4).

This observation, made several years ago, must now be supplemented by further developments in the transnationalizing process. The internet has become the prime tool for diffusing news and publicity about congresses beyond national boundaries. Each congress has a dedicated web site via which registration of delegates, payments of fees, and searches for dance partners take place (e.g., www.salsafestival-berlin.de). Moreover, the social networking site Facebook has virally deterritorialized these interactions. As with any business, the world of salsa has made quick use of Facebook's potential for self-publicizing, especially the showcasing of photographs to multiple viewers. Typically, salsa entrepreneurs will engage a photographer to capture events; people who recognize themselves within the photographs "tag" themselves; in order to do so they will need to "friend" the site set up by the entrepreneur; on doing so, they immediately enter their circle of information, events, and publicity. This ripple effect is particularly suited to the salsa congress, which needs to engage people's memories from one year of its occurrence to the next, and is able to do so by posting photographs and videos of past congresses as well as updates, reminders, and payment deadlines for upcoming ones. The Berlin Salsa Congress regularly messages its Facebook group members with bespoke information as well as posting updates on its "profile page"; the organizers have set up country-based groups to enhance the logistics of shared travel and accommodation; and regulars at the congress are messaged individually with requests to support the congress by "sharing" news flashes about promotional prices and deadlines on their individual walls.

The salsa congress is thus part of a complex of activities that radiate outward from salsa's gradual professionalization during its movement from the barrio to the studio (Backstein 2001; Borland 2009). Little scholarly attention has been paid to it as a phenomenon, however. Its comparatively recent arrival means that it is only just attracting the notice of scholars, who "draw attention to the continuing emergence of a gamut of Salsa Congresses, Latin Dance clubs and classes springing up across the globe" in order to emphasize that "the salsa scene is worthy of investigation given its exponential growth over the last ten years" (Hewer and Hamilton 2009: 2), but who nevertheless fail to offer a detailed investigation of the congress as a manifestation of this scene. Existing monographs on salsa usually focus on salsa as a musical form rather than on salsa as dance (*pace* Waxer 2002), an emphasis which leads to the dance-oriented salsa congresses falling out of their purview. At the same time, those who do examine the development of salsa as dance concentrate on regional trends that take root in specific locations over a period of time (Borland 2009; Pietrobruno 2006; Skinner 2007), investigating the salsa club and/or salsa class as a hub for the creation of a local salsa scene. The salsa congress, in contrast, is ephemeral, itinerant, and non-local: qualities that seem of little relevance to those interested in exploring the global–local genealogies of salsa as a dance practice.

But there is much that those interested in transnationalism can learn from salsa congresses. These are sites of intercultural encounters which fuse actors and cultures from global northern and diverse southern regions otherwise separated through linguistic incomprehensibility. Their transnationalism exceeds the paradigms of postcolonial theory, which rarely considers evidence from parallel imperial-colonial histories, and which typically regards cultural innovation through north–south axes that either connect former imperial centers and decolonized metropolises or follow the colonial and postcolonial histories of slavery and diaspora. The salsa congress epitomizes how dance, in conjunction with music, can cross the boundaries laid down by imperial trajectories. In doing so, it does more than confirm the premises of transnationalism as a lens for analysing the fluid cultural and economic transactions of the contemporary world. The multiplicity of languages, cultures, affiliations, and dancing bodies that gather at salsa congresses to enjoy a participatory music tradition borne out of the specific colonial-imperial history of the Hispanic New World suggests that transnationalism cannot be explicated without thinking seriously about its relationship to modes of corporeal, collective pleasure. While challenging heuristic paradigms for thinking through postcolonialism and diaspora, the salsa congress offers transnational studies the opportunity to rethink its premises through the analysis of dance.

Surviving History through Dance:
Deep Vectors of Transnationalism

Hybridity, dislocation, and reformation underlie salsa, as is suggested by its very name (Spanish for "sauce"). First used, reputedly, by a Venezuelan disc jockey, Phidias Danilo Escalona, to denote Latin dance music in the early 1960s (Rondón 1980: 3), the term "salsa" had spread throughout Latin America by the 1970s (Waxer 2002: 4). The dance-music complex's fluid label "reflects its shifting, transnational character" (Waxer 2002: 5), but a deep history of migration subtends its transnational vectors. Salsa was created through the movement of people and rhythm cultures across Africa, the Caribbean, and the Americas. The fusion of European couple dances and lyrical styles with African rhythms and percussive traditions brought to the Caribbean through slavery created, in Cuba, the form of dance and music called *son* (Manuel 2006). The *son* fed into the dance culture of New York from the 1930s onwards, giving rise to dance crazes: mambo, cha-cha-cha; boogaloo. During the 1960s, these different traditions were redeveloped by Puerto Rican immigrants to New York to create a more codified and stylized dance form which began to be called salsa, after the new term for the music which was also rapidly getting slicker and more commercialized (Washburne 2008). By the 1990s, Pan-Latino migration to New York created "a second generation of salseros who co-opted the music of their parents, reinventing and transforming the salsa scene with sounds and expressions that better represented their own experiences as Latino youth growing up in New York City" (Washburne 2008: 6).

While the African roots of salsa can seem erased through many of these developments, the music remains fundamentally dependent on African polyrhythm and call-and-response structures. Its lyrics, too, celebrate the pull of Africa on the diasporic consciousness: as Afro-Cuban bandleader Arsénio Rodríguez, a key mover of Cuban musical traditions to New York in the 1940s, sang (Manuel 2006: 291): "yo nací de África, tal vez soy del Congo, tal vez soy del Ampanga" (I was born in Africa; perhaps I am of the Congo, perhaps of the Ampanga). These complexities of diaspora have made salsa a contested, severally claimed signifier of (Afro-)Latino identities. Salsa is widely understood "as an 'inter-Latino' and 'trans-Caribbean' music, regardless of the fact that it emerged from the cultural climate of New York City, owes much of its stylistic particularities to African American expressions (jazz and R'n'B in particular) and Cuban music practices as performed in New York in the 1940s and 1950s" (Washburne 2008: 9). There is intense inter-Caribbean competition around the claiming of salsa: the loosening of its connection with Cuba was already signified in its massive Puerto Rican investment, which was complemented by Cuba's musical and cultural isolation precisely during the period salsa was being (re)formed in New York. Alongside Puerto Rico, Venezuela and Colombia are intertwined with salsa's development; meanwhile, Cuban musicians and dancers continue to exit from or enter into "salsa" in keeping with their personal politics and predilections.

These multiple claims on salsa have parallels in the realm of dance: diverse styles of salsa dancing are available for adoption by dancers through the world. The basic difference is between a linear "cross-body" dance style, where the couples interchange their positions while remaining in a straight line, and a circular style, recognized as "Cuban," where the man and woman move around each other. Sometimes, to distinguish "Cuban" from "cross-body," the term "Puerto Rican" is used for the latter. Puerto Rican or cross-body salsa is further differentiated into On1 (also called LA style) and On2 (also called New York, or Mambo style). The difference between On1 and On2 is one of musical accent, or where one places the emphasis within the rhythmic unit of eight counts: one-two-three/five-six-seven. In On1, movement begins on the "one" and the "five"; in On2, on the "two" and the "six" (following the *tumbao* rhythm of the conga drums). In Cuban salsa, movement also begins on the "one," but most teachers of Cuban style salsa will disdain to count, preferring to use vocables (e.g., "pa-pa-PA") to emphasize the African origins of this timeline. In addition to Cuban and cross-body styles, there exists the less transnational "Colombian" style. Moreover, the Cuban style, which was historically called "casino style" in Cuba, also includes the *rueda* (wheel), where couples, rotating around each other, move in a wheel formation in response to directions which a leader calls out. The *rueda* epitomizes the Cuban style's communal, playful, and fluid feel, particularly in its idiosyncratic and imaginative calls, such as "dile que no" (Tell him "no"), "helicoptero" (helicopter), "sombrero," "Coca Cola," "panque con jogurt" (cake with yogurt), "agua" (water). In contrast, the cross-body styles emphasize dexterity through spins, fast footwork, and sharp breaks controlled by stylized movements of hands and arms.

There is virtually no scholarship on how these divergences evolved, and what they mean for the transmission and ramification of embodied histories; yet it is precisely their evolution and variegated diffusion that archive salsa's layered transnationalism. Salsa as a multiply transnational dance-music complex has been formed through intricate transactions, coded in and through its divergent dancing styles, which create a webbed connection of spaces within which the music and its embodied practices circulate. For salsa dancers of different styles, the basic grammar remains the same rhythm for the moving feet, interpreted by Puerto Rican dance styles accented numerically as "one-two-three/five-six-seven"; more immersed dancers and musicians can also recognize the hidden "clave" rhythm that structures salsa's percussive architecture. This rhythmic continuum is a crisscrossing line of affection and competition connecting the diverse developments of a shared musical heritage: it is a connective tissue that survives diaspora and transnationalism to recreate continually modes of self-expression and enjoyment. At the same time, the proliferation of these styles beyond the Americas testifies to the shaping of salsa by transnational currents of demand and supply. Who can teach what kind of salsa, and where, and the consumers for each style, are all forces that act on and determine salsa's transnationalism, even as the attitudes of non-Latino salseros towards these divergences reify and transmit stereotypes about the various Latin and Caribbean worlds with which the dance continues historically to be associated. I will now turn to the Berlin Salsa Congress to substantiate and amplify these claims.

Neither *Latinidad* nor *Cubanidad*: Salsa and a New European Cosmopolitanism

On the second night of the 2010 Berlin Salsa Congress, from around 10 p.m. onwards, spectators seated in the main arena of the fabulous venue, the Tempodrome, were treated to a dazzling array of choreographed shows by professional salsa dancers and instructors from a range of locations: Antalya, Athens, Dubai, Karlsruhe, Krakow, London, Marseille, Milan, Paris, Stockholm, Rome, Sofia, Warsaw, Utrecht, and Israel. The most applauded duo was Los Diablos of Antalya, Turkey, dancing to "Quiereme Na Ma," a song by Bogotá's La 33. Katherine Wilson asks (2009: 4): "Is an Australian *salsera* dancing to the music of a Japanese Salsa band doing anything 'Latin'?" We could apply her question to these Turkish dancers, interpreting a Colombian band at Berlin, for a highly international audience. Wilson's question follows her assertion that "with enough dedication and hard work, one can truly become an authentic *salsero*" (p. 4); yet, as she also observes, "salsa does not become 'less Latin' as it spreads around the world, but its Latin identity becomes displaced" (p. 4). Instead of looking for authenticity, we should focus on the processes of displacement and fragmentation of *latinidad* through and in dance. The Berlin Salsa Congress was emphatically *not* about proclaiming affiliations to *latinidad*. During every showcase event, the spotlight was on the 45 countries from which the participants had come, accompanied by the conference organizer and Master of Ceremonies Franco Sparfeld's reminders that this number made the Berlin Salsa Congress the most international congress in the world. There were country flags on sale and participants cheered and waved them whenever Sparfeld encouraged specific nationalities to announce their presence from the floor.

Despite this good-natured parochialism, the congress remained a resolutely transnational space. During the daytime workshops, participants conversed with each other in German, French, Dutch, Polish, Romanian, Greek, Latvian, and Italian. Teachers used mime to communicate instructions to an unpredictably multilingual mix of students. English functioned as a pidgin of sorts, with everyone speaking some form of it whenever they attempted cross-lingual communication; however, Spanish, the language of salsa lyrics, did not perform this same function. The only time it did so was at the few classes devoted to Cuban-derived dance. There were two classes on rumba, the Afro-Cuban style associated with the streets of Havana and Matanzas, which has a complex history of colonial repression, pre-Revolution stigmatization, post-Revolution fetishization, and, surviving it all, an embodied spirituality through dance repertoires associated with Afro-Cuban gods (Daniel 1991; Jottar 2009). The rumba's Afro-Cuban movements encourage salseros to re-Africanize salsa through infusing their style with a loose-limbed earthiness. This reception of rumba as a necessary space of not merely Latin, but Cuban (indeed, Afro-Cuban) "authenticity" means that the instructors are often Cuban, and the duo in charge of the rumba classes at Berlin was no exception: a Cuban and an Argentine representing Tropical Gem, a highly regarded Milanese dance company. Their very successful classes were conducted through mime, Spanish, and broken English. Spanish reappeared in the only other Cuban offering in the Congress: a class devoted to Cuban salsa taught by German Elke Ballwieser. Trained at Havana and Santiago de Cuba, and of the school that valorizes the "natural and sensual" Cuban style, with its Afro-Cuban roots, as the wellspring of all salsa forms,[2] she proclaimed her own affiliation to *cubanidad* by speaking more Spanish than English during her class.

Although the classes by Ballwieser and Tropical Gem were very well attended, the space accorded to Cuban dance forms at Berlin was minimal. Cuba, decentered but not erased, functioned as a cipher for the absent presence of "Latinness" and "Caribbeanness." It was not a contradiction that the centerpiece of the congress show-program was the premier of *El Tiempo de Maquina*, presented jointly by Tropical Gem and Flamboyan Dancers and based on the life and music of Cuban diva Celia Cruz. Born into the Afro-Cuban underclass of Havana, Cruz began her career within Havana's pre-Revolution club culture but migrated to the United States after the Cuban Revolution. Her career, which became more and more spectacular in exile, encapsulates the tense relationship between Cuban music and dance and the development of salsa. Cruz herself exploited knowingly "the ambivalence between the discourse of Cubanness for and by the exiled subject, and the transnational audiences and musical styles that have emerged, ironically, out of her own political and geographical displacement" (Aparicio 1999: 228). This irony resurfaced at Berlin when New York's Yamulee performed to Celia Cruz's song, "Tumba la caña jibarito," a lyrical sublimation of the rigors of plantation life, in impeccable New York style. These transactions between Cruz's self-declared "Cuban accent" (Aparicio 1999: 228) and its diffusion through New York to the world at large exemplify how the emergence of a transnational salsa scene out of the vicissitudes of Cuban history is refracted worldwide in salsa congresses.

At Berlin, hardly anyone was dancing Cuban style socially. Neither in the music, nor in the division of social dancing space, was there overt acknowledgment made of Cuban style as a dance form. The dance styles exhibited during social dancing were overwhelmingly cross-body – either On1 or On2, and when other rhythms were played, for example, cha-cha, they were interpreted in cross-body style. This marginalization of *cubanidad* was matched by the decisive emergence of other stakeholders marking ownership of the salsa scene. The biggest players were countries of New Europe, the Baltics and the East: with sizable contingents of Polish, Czech, Romanian, Bulgarian, Latvian, and Lithuanian dancers; as one Czech participant told me, Berlin was close enough to make annual pilgrimages to the congress possible, while a Romanian volunteer, keeping perfect clave time on a beer bottle, remarked, "we [i.e., Romanians] are Latin people." In the meanwhile, Riga has emerged as the home of Berlin's sister congress, with DJ Mauri expressing astonishment at the memory of hundreds of Latvians lip-syncing to lyrics in Spanish which they in all likelihood cannot understand (Gonzalez, personal interview, Berlin, October 2, 2010). Clearly, salsa has given post-communist European subjectivities an entry point into a hitherto denied world of expressivity, flamboyance, and fun: what is ironic, of course, is that dance and music in Cuba itself continues to respond to communism in startlingly creative ways (Moore 2006; Fairley 2006). All in all, the politics of diaspora and the histories of displacement and deracination that have ensured the dance's transnationalism seem neither visible to nor the overt concern of its new European consumers, all of whom were engaging, in Berlin, in a cosmopolitan self-fashioning via an uncomplicated apprenticeship to Latin dance.

Evolving Transnationalism at the Berlin Salsa Congress

The decoupling of live music from dance at congresses is another marker of salsa's movement away from a Latino performative and participatory tradition which thrives on the spontaneous energies exchanged between a live band, able to improvise lyrics as well as intervening instrumental sections, and a knowing audience which is as happy to listen as it is to dance. The Berlin Salsa Congress, like several other international congresses, promotes itself not through bands but through the presence of star DJs, whose careers they have consolidated. However, the DJs themselves traced the effervescence of salsa dancing to an earlier period when the consumers of Latin music were world-music aficionados, people who wanted to listen rather than being able to dance, and who were patrons of live bands. The DJs to whom I spoke in Berlin, DJ Willy and DJ Mauri, acknowledged that, with the demise of the live band, there was an attrition of interest in "the philosophy of salsa" (Gonzalez and Vertueux, personal interviews, Berlin, October 2, 2010). With the commercialization of salsa through the congresses, there was the added concern that bringing bands over to Europe from Latin America or the Caribbean would cost far more than paying for a DJ to travel from one part of Europe to another. The DJ is thus the king of the salsa congress, and it is up to him to shape the tastes and energies of the crowd through his selection of tracks. The Latin music DJ must, like any other DJ, pick up signals from the crowd; but he must also know what music will make them dance rather than simply entrance the connoisseur-listener. If the home-grown, Latino/Caribbean salsero's immersion in the tradition means a unified ability to listen as well as move, the salsa congress demonstrates how transnationalism fractures that unity into dancers that don't know how to listen, and listeners who don't know how to dance.

Does the Berlin Salsa Congress then illustrate how salsa in Europe has become completely absorbed into an intra-European relational model, which displaces and consumes cultural production from the global south in the usual mode of north–south power relations? I would nuance this picture. Firstly dance destabilizes expected power relations through its facilitation of alternative transactions in fantasy, desire, and embodied exhilaration in a collective space. Secondly, Berlin also brought together actors from diverse southern locations. I will elaborate on this point by analyzing the presence of Kaytee Namgyal of Salsa India, who is based in Bombay but is at this moment working out of Rome. Namgyal and his partner in 2010, Vanessa Diaz, who is from France (and who has worked for a year in Bombay with him), offered two bachata classes on the Saturday and Sunday mornings respectively. Bachata, a dance originating from the Dominican Republic (Pacini Hernández 1995), is not a form of salsa but provides a more sensual alternative to it, as its protocol involves more body contact than the latter. It is very popular amongst those who dance salsa both in clubs and congresses, particularly as it changes the mood on the dance floor by shifting attention from the interpretation of polyrhythm to the body's elaboration of a linear timeline via strategic hip and thigh movements. Neither as polyrhythmic nor as percussively rich as salsa, bachata's 4/4 rhythm accentuates the fourth beat, whose simplest interpretation in dance is a hip lift or twist in the opposite direction to the movement established in the three preceding beats. Although bachata is a dance from the Caribbean world, then, its rhythmic profile is distinguished by the absence of African markers.

This characteristic of bachata, together with its 4/4 rhythm and emphasis on the hip (rather than the pelvis) makes it more malleable for interpretation by non-Latino dancers, and particularly attractive to inheritors of Arabic and Indian rhythm cultures, where linear patterns divisible by four are very common (e.g., Indian *kaharwa* and *teental*; Arabic *elzaffa*). Kaytee is no exception, but his take on bachata is hardly Indianized.[3] Rather, in his workshops, Kaytee focused on what he called K-style Bachata: a personalized, signature interpretation of the dance which de-emphasizes the hips and focuses on the connection between the torso and the thighs. There are some head movements reminiscent of the French-Lusophone zouk (Guilbault 1993), and the 3 + 1 rhythmic unit of bachata is interpreted in novel ways, with breaks often stretched to three counts followed by a quick movement on the fourth. This complex response to a simple timeline is underscored by footwork, body isolation, "popping," and body breaks imported from hip-hop, another dance styles he and Vanessa favor. In fact, the duo offered a third class on "salsa hip-hop" to intermediate dancers, where this mode of body movement was imported into the salsa beat. All classes were packed and received with considerable enthusiasm. Kaytee's second bachata class received an appreciative round of applause from the participants, who were charmed by his ability to engage the audience in English, clearly a strong enough common language for them to be able to understand the stylish wit with which he conducted his class.

My partner for this class was a Turkish man who may have been Turkish German, and there were several other Germans in the group. After the class, I asked a couple – he, black, she, white – what they thought of Kaytee as a teacher. The man was an Ecuadorian living in a small Swiss town and his companion was Swiss German (Secundo Valencia, personal interview, Berlin, October 2, 2010). We spoke in a mixture of Spanish and English. Namgyal, they both agreed, was "maravilloso" (marvellous). Sure, it was "un poco raro" (a bit bizarre) that he was from India, and that an Ecuadorian would end up in a bachata class taught by an Indian, but it did not matter, because Namgyal responded to the "sentimiento" (sentiment) of the music rather than focusing on showmanship and pure "movimiento" (movement). He recognized the sensuality of the bachata and urged his students to reconnect to that element. Later that day, the Ecuadorian came up to me while we were waiting for a coffee and re-engaged me in a long postscript to the discussion (Valencia, personal interview, Berlin, October 2, 2010). "Kaytee is great," he said, "but it would be even better if he knew Spanish and could respond to the lyrics of the bachata. We respond to bachata emotionally: we dance to it but we also cry to it." In this conversation, conducted fully in Spanish, emerged the full picture of a south–south encounter: that between the Indian salsa performer and an Ecuadorian, both based in Europe, and meeting in Europe. The European venue made their interaction possible, but also brought to the notice of the "authentic" salsero the claims on Latin dance that were being made by non-Latin parties. Yet, the fact that this was not a European, "northern" claim confused his assessment of it. For the strongest critique of this self-declared indigenous salsero was directed towards the First World tourist consumer of salsa in Latin America and the Caribbean, whose desire for escape to tropical paradises, metonymically conveyed through dance, had led to the commodification of salsa "back home." This critique can also be read as an *auto*-critique of the displaced Ecuadorian self, peddling salsa in a small town in Switzerland.

South–(North)–South Encounters in the Northern Congress

Nevertheless, the transnational vectors which determine these movements of salsa also allow for interactions to take place beyond those neocolonial circuits of commodification and fetishization. Even as the Ecuadorian Swiss salsero tried to organize his conflicting thoughts about Namgyal by reminding himself of the even more ambivalent relationship between himself and the European dancer of salsa, he and I were participating in a conversation which would have not been possible outside this space. The fact that I was willing, and able, to speak in Spanish opened up a channel of another kind of person-to-person dialogue, of actors self-identifying, and mutually identifying, as from southern rather than northern affiliations. This stance was marked linguistically by my Ecuadorian interlocutor's frequent resort to the phrases *como tu sabes* (as you know) and *tu entiendes* (you understand). As I became part of his epistemological framework, as someone who is expected to share in his knowledge and his way of seeing the world, so did some other possibility, a recognition of the "Else" rather than the "Other," open up between us. I would like to see that kind of splinter inserted in the hegemonies of imperial and post-imperial histories and epistemologies as emblematic of the unexpected solidarities and understandings that can be made possible through and in dance. The salsa congress functions as a space of alternative transnationalism and new postcolonialities, where the expressive body can pay homage to alien histories of survival through enjoyment even though the individual might not think consciously at all of those histories. The task of the scholar is to construct the balance sheet out of these small gains against the not-so-small losses caused by the decentering of *latinidad*, *cubanidad* and the "Afro" in all these formulations that occurs in a space such as the Berlin Salsa Congress.

At the end of the congress' closing program on the Sunday, the London-based salsa performer and instructor Tamambo, whose Facebook page yields the name Tammam Shaibani (he is of Iraqi heritage), regaled the audience with an anecdote about his youth: "When I was a teenager, my father brought along a man with a long beard to preach to me about Islam – ok, I am of Muslim heritage – but I said, why do I need to listen to you?" Facing the audience, he cut his story to come to the point: "Look at us all here – Jews, Arabs, Turks, Cypriots, Christians, Muslims – we are all dancing, together. Our religion is salsa, not hatred." This remarkable sentiment echoed the message of the opening show by Tropical Gem, *Survivor*, which projected the dancer as the detritus and remainder of the horrors of the modern world, beginning from the Holocaust to the contemporary circulation of a mysterious virus that cannot be eradicated. If the dancer survives, it is because of the kinetic power and embodied memory transmitted through dance. Similarly, the salsa congress, with its glimpses into alternative possibilities, unexpected alignments and unspoken acts of homage, survives the often brutal, market-driven currents of transnationalism that proliferate mass consumption, standardization and hegemonic mediascapes, ethnoscapes, and financescapes (Appadurai 1990). Ironically, these very trends have ensured its emergence and continued efflorescence. As a site of south–north–south encounter, the salsa congress offers "a theoretical and performative open field of exchanges" (Lepecki 2004: 9), where dancing bodies perform kinetic rather than intellectual recollection of histories in order to bring forth momentary transnational utopias from the debris of modernity's multiple and traumatic dislocations. Pleasure and resistance oscillate as two sides of the same coin, revealing how "dance critically reconstitutes social practices while at the same time proposes ever new theories of body and presence" (Lepecki 2004: 1). In the process, the congress, for the weekend of its duration, becomes a framework not for the globalization of creole creativity (Crichlow 2009), but for the potential creolization of the world.

Acknowledgments

This chapter is based on research funded by the British Academy. I am grateful to Professor Ulrike H. Meinhof for her support and encouragement; and to Mauricio Gonzalez, Kaytee Namgyal, Franco Sparfeld, and Wilfrid Vertueux for so generously sharing with me their expertise and time.

Notes

1   Information on the current congress can be found at www.salsafestival-berlin.de, accessed March 5, 2013.
2   Elke Ballwieser de Ferriols, "Die kubanische Salsa," at http://www.asi-se-baila.de/index.php?id=35, accessed March 5, 2013.
3   For more on Kaytee, see http://www.salsa-india.com/index.php?option=com_portfolio&id=4&view=item&Itemid=100064, accessed March 5, 2013.

References

Aparicio, F.R. 1999. "The blackness of sugar: Celia Cruz and the performance of (trans) nationalism." *Cultural Studies*, 13(2): 223–236.

Appadurai, A. 1990. "Disjuncture and difference in the global cultural economy." *Public Culture*, 2(2): 1–23.

Backstein, K. 2001. "Taking 'class' into account: Dance, the studio, and Latino culture." In A. Laó-Montes (ed.) *Mambo Montage: The Latinization of New York*, pp. 449–472. New York: Columbia University Press.

Benítez-Rojo, A. 1996. *The Repeating Island: The Caribbean in Postmodern Perspective*, trans. J.E. Maraniss. Durham, NC: Duke University Press.

Borland, K. 2009. "Embracing difference: Salsa fever in New Jersey." *Journal of American Folklore*, 122: 466–492.

Critchlow, M.A. 2009. *Globalization and the Post-Creole Imagination: Notes on Fleeing the Plantation*. Durham, NC: Duke University Press.

Daniel, Y. 1991. *Rumba: Dance and Social Change in Contemporary Cuba*. Bloomington: Indiana University Press.

Fairley, J. 2006. "Dancing back to front: *Regeton*, sexuality, gender and transnationalism in Cuba." *Popular Music*, 25(3): 471–488.

Frank, A.W. 1991. "For a sociology of the body: an analytical review." In M. Featherstone, M. Hepworth, and S. Bryan (eds) *The Body: Social Process and Cultural Theory*, pp. 36–102. London: Sage.

Glissant, É. 1997. *Poetics of Relation*, trans. B. Wing. Ann Arbor: University of Michigan Press.

Guilbault, J. 1993. *Zouk: World Music in the West Indies*. Chicago: Chicago University Press.

Hewer, K. and Hamilton, P. 2009. "Salsa magic: an exploratory netnographic analysis of the salsa experience." *Advances in Consumer Research*, 36: 502–508.

Jottar, B. 2009. "The acoustic body: Rumba Guarapachanguera and Abakuá sociality in Central Park." *Latin American Music Review*, 30(1): 1–24.

Lepecki, A. 2004. "Introduction: Presence and body in dance and performance theory." In A. Lepecki (ed.) *Of the Presence of the Body: Essays on Dance and Performance Theory*, pp. 1–12. Middletown, CT: Wesleyan University Press.

Manuel, P. 2006. *Caribbean Currents: Caribbean Music from Rumba to Reggae*. Philadelphia: Temple University Press.

Moore, R. 2006. *Music and Revolution: Cultural Change in Cuba*. Berkeley: University of California Press.

Pacini Hernández, D. 1995. *Bachata: A Social History of Dominican Popular Music*. Philadelphia: Temple University Press.

Pietrobruno, S. 2006. *Salsa and Its Transnational Moves*. Lanham, MD: Lexington Books.

Quintero Rivera, Á. 1998. *¡Salsa, sabor y control! Sociología de la música "tropical."* Mexico City: Siglo XXI Editores.

Rondón, C.M. 1980. *El Libro de la salsa: Crónica de la música del caribe urbano*. Caracas: Editorial Arte.

Skinner, J. 2007. "The salsa class: a complexity of globalization, cosmopolitans and emotions." *Identities: Global Studies in Culture and Power*, 14: 1–22.

Sklar, D. 1991. "On dance ethnography." *Dance Research Journal*, 23(1): 6–10.

Sklar, D. 2000. "Reprise: On dance ethnography." *Dance Research Journal*, 32(1): 70–77.

Sloat, S. 2005. *Caribbean Dance from Abakuá to Zouk: How Movement Shapes Identity*. Gainesville: University Press of Florida.

Taylor, D. 2003. *The Archive and the Repertoire: Performing Cultural Memory in the Americas*. Durham, NC: Duke University Press

Washburne, C. 2008. *Sounding Salsa: Performing Latin Music in New York City*. Philadelphia: Temple University Press.

Waxer, L. 2002. *Situating Salsa: Global Markets and Local Meanings in Latin Popular Music.* New York: Routledge.

Wilson, K. 2009. "The space of salsa: Theory and implications of a global dance phenomenon." Unpublished conference paper: Multiculturalism, Conflict and Belonging: A Diversity and Recognition Project, September, Mansfield College, Oxford.

Part IV

Overviews and Case Studies

Chapter 16

Gender and Identity in Oral Histories of Elderly Russian Jewish Migrants in the United States and Canada

Anna Shternshis

The great wave of late Soviet and post-Soviet Jewish migration changed the landscape of Israeli culture and politics, the makeup of many North American cities, and Jewish communal life in Germany. Over the past two decades, the Russian Jewish diaspora has become the focus of numerous interdisciplinary research projects. Most of these studies, however, discuss immigrants of working age, thus primarily people under 50. Other immigrants, including some 300,000 people over 60,[1] are studied largely in the context of gerontology and nursing studies, which generally do not discuss identity change. This chapter aims to fill the gap and recommends analyzing the lives of the elderly migrants through the prism of their stories of the past and present.

I approach in-depth interviews with Soviet Jewish elders as sources of information on the relationship between the politics of relocation and identity construction. The characteristics of the respondents, selected by the "snowball" method (discussed in more detail later), combine two opposite characteristics. On the one hand, the respondents belong to the most disadvantaged group of Soviet Jewish émigrés, because of their inability to enter the workforce, a situation which has been linked to higher mortality rates compared to those who found employment (Litwin and Leshem 2008). On the other hand, almost all respondents selected for this study immigrated when they were in their sixties; they were interviewed in their eighties and nineties, and thus had lived as immigrants for over twenty years (Coleman and Podolskij 2007). Moreover, respondents report quite a high degree of satisfaction with the overall quality of their current lives.

As an ethnographer and oral historian, but also a literary scholar, I apply methods of textual analysis to the data that I collect. In analyzing self-representation, I treat

A Companion to Diaspora and Transnationalism, First Edition
Edited by Ato Quayson and Girish Daswani.
© 2013 Blackwell Publishing Ltd. Published 2013 by Blackwell Publishing Ltd.

the testimonies as stories, literary texts built in accordance with the genre, which has to include villains, heroes, obstacles, and methods of overcoming. I am less concerned with fact-checking or "what really happened" in respondents' lives, but rather see stories as narratives of construction of identity and discussion of successful coping mechanisms and strategies of acclimatization. Instead of fact-checking, I scrutinize the wording that respondents choose to express ideas and the structure of their narrative. The major result of applying this method is the revelation that the negotiation of the social meaning of gender roles plays the most important part in my respondents' self-identification.

Method

This study is based on 256 in-depth interviews with Soviet-born Jewish migrants conducted between 1999 and 2007 in Toronto, New York, and Philadelphia. I located respondents through community centers, immigrant organizations, and advertisements placed in Russian-language media. The criteria of selection included the date and place of birth (before 1930, Ukraine, Byelorussia, or Russia). Each interview was recorded and transcribed in its original language (138 in Yiddish and 118 in Russian). The interviews consisted of open-ended questions about respondents' experiences during their lives.[2] I was less interested in respondents' encounters with the medical and welfare systems, largely because these issues have already been analyzed in the existing scholarship (Litwin and Leshem 2008; Aroian *et al.*1998, 2001; Tsytsarev and Krichmar 2000; Fitzpatrick and Freed 2000; Trana *et al.* 2000; Gutkovich *et al.* 1999; and many others). Instead, I focused on the analysis of the respondents' thoughts on their cultural experiences after they have immigrated, ranging from changes in food preferences and lifestyle habits to the celebration of holidays; from the relationships with their children and grandchildren to experiences of nostalgia and entertainment choices. Most importantly, I analyzed what they thought about their own ethnic, religious, and cultural identities.

I participated in a few events organized by and for elderly Russian Jews, sat with them on benches of Brighton Beach in New York, walked and talked during their strolls in the park, and conducted some group interviews at meetings, both in the buildings of synagogues and community centers, and outside, on the streets, in a less formal environment. However, most of the data comes from the in-depth interviews conducted in the settings of the respondents' own homes. In addition to being a welcoming quiet space with unlimited supply of hot tea and home-baked goodies, the respondents' homes provided an opportunity to observe interaction with their family members and suggested clues on how to understand the testimonies.

My own identity as a Russian Jewish scholar played a role in how respondents positioned themselves during the interview. Because the conversations were recorded in Russian or Yiddish, languages predominantly associated with an insider culture, I risked missing some important information that the respondent considered obvious and not worthy of telling. However, I was able to overcome this obstacle partially by claiming ignorance because of my youth: I was in my mid-twenties when I recorded my first interviews in New York and in my mid-thirties during the last round in Toronto.

There were also tremendous benefits from the position of a cultural insider. Many respondents felt comfortable sharing their true opinions regarding government policies towards the elderly and about many inter-group dynamics. In fact, the pleasure of telling their story to someone who could truly appreciate it resulted in hundreds of referrals for other potential interviewees (Bulmer 1999: 216–217). Thus, I had the opportunity to choose among many potential interviewees in order to ensure equal representation of gender, as well as countries of origin, experiences, backgrounds, and varieties of educational experience (see Table 16.1).

No significant variation in the respondents' backgrounds was noted by country. The respondents were highly educated (50 percent had the equivalent of a college degree), and almost all had completed high school. About 55 percent of respondents were women; their relatively high percentage is explained by the longer life expectancy and more active involvement in immigrant organizations, where the respondents were sought. Many of the older migrants arrived together with their families; they had accompanied grown children who moved in search of opportunities for social and economic mobility and to avoid discrimination.[3]

Context

Russian Jews born between 1906 and 1930 in the Russian empire or the Soviet Union, and who immigrated to United States or Canada during the 1990s, were chosen as a case study for this project for two reasons. First, they constitute a large percentage of Russian Jewish migrants of the late twentieth and early twenty-first centuries. Second, the group is also distinguished by its unusual pre-immigration identity. The respondents belong to the transitional generation of Soviet-educated Jews, which combines the elements of Jewish tradition and Soviet values. In the 1930s, Soviet Jewish youth went through a process of radical cultural transformation catalyzed by the establishment of a system of secular education, anti-religious propaganda, and, above all, the political, economic, and social reforms introduced by the Soviet regime. As a result, their identity combines both Soviet anti-religious and Jewish values at the same time. The Jewish values are largely secular and are associated with affection for the Yiddish language (even if the knowledge of the language is weak), warm feelings towards Jewish holidays (though, again, lack of familiarity with their actual meanings and rituals), and general awareness of Jewish culture. Even these fluid characteristics allow us to refer to this group as the only Soviet-educated citizens who have a meaningful link to their Jewish identity, as all subsequent generations lack any content association with their Jewish identity.

In addition to being the most "Jewish" of all Soviet Jews, they can also be seen as the most "Soviet" ones. They grew up during the time of the formation of the

Table 16.1 Statistical data on respondents: Gender, place of birth, last place of residence in the former Soviet Union, and level of education

Place of residence	Number of respondents	Men	Women	Place of birth				Place of residence before immigration			Higher education
				Ukraine	Byelorussia	Russia	Poland, Lithuania, Romania	Ukraine	Byelorussia	Russia	
New York	157	81	76	76	52	11	18	68	15	39	72
Toronto	99	41	58	48	23	19	9	16	4	15	56
Total	256	122	134	124	75	30	27	84	19	54	128

Soviet state's ideology and political system. Many were members of communist youth political organizations, such as the Young Communist League (Komsomol) and the Young Pioneers. In addition, some participated actively in creating and maintaining the Soviet ideology on a grassroots level. Arguably, this was the only Soviet generation that largely internalized the values of the Soviet system and kept a generally positive attitude to it even after the Soviet Union had collapsed.

The process of immigration stirred the balance between these components of their identity, and forced many respondents to dig into their past in order to make meaningful connections with the present. For example, despite their lack of involvement in Jewish communal life before immigration, almost all of them visit synagogues and Jewish community centers in North America, and revive the knowledge of Yiddish, which they have not spoken in decades. The Soviet notions, however, also survive, but in the framework of Jewish community organizations. The memory of the past, and how it is told, ultimately gets affected by the everyday practices of the present, and thus produces a complicated picture of changing perceptions.

Findings

Fluid identities are notoriously hard to identify and analyze. The researcher is forced either to trust the respondent on their evaluations as to what is important to them, or to make informed, albeit somewhat arbitrary, decisions based on what he or she hears. While I tried to keep the questionnaire as open-ended as possible, my own presumptions and agenda have inevitably influenced the story that the respondents were telling me. I have learned from past mistakes that asking the wrong questions can lead to drawing wrong conclusions (Shternshis 2007). Similarly, direct answers to direct questions about identity tend to produce almost no results, as respondents frequently use commonplaces. In order to resolve this problem, I decided to pay less attention to my questions, and to listen to the answers as a narrative, often told despite my questionnaire or produced as an off-the-topic comment.

The respondents' process of adaptation and their current lives depended on many factors, including their health, relationship with grown children, religious beliefs and willingness to re-examine them, material conditions, and the policies towards immigrants in the country of current residence. The detailed analysis of all aspects of their testimonies deserves a book-length nuanced study. However, two themes came up in all testimonies, without exception, in all three countries. One was the participation in World War II, either by the respondent, their spouse, a family member, or even a friend. The other one was the upbringing of grandchildren. I encountered almost no differences in respondents' estimation of the importance of those two topics. Furthermore, the data revealed that while both men and women spoke about participation in the war and patterns of rearing grandchildren, all respondents agreed that the war belongs to the male sphere and the upbringing to the female, even if men were primary caregivers to their young grandchildren and women served as pilots during the war.

I began thinking about the gender identities of my respondents, and how immigration influenced them. Gradually, I collected the data on veterans' organizations and wrote an article on the importance of memory of war for community building among my respondents (Shternshis 2011). I did argue that they commemorate the war in order to fit in with the larger society, in the way that they understand it. But even then I was not able to connect the grandparenting experience and participation in the war as part of one phenomenon. And then it suddenly became clear: these two topics do not describe past achievements. Instead, they speak about the present. In fact, I came to hypothesize that gender becomes the most important factor in their contemporary lives.

One Can Count on a Colonel to Be on Time for a Prayer: Masculinity and Ethnic Identity

The respondents recall that upon arrival they were welcomed by a variety of organizations. Synagogues and Jewish community centers in the United States and Canada ran programs, often in the Russian language, specifically geared to this cohort.[4] According to the testimonies of many respondents, the welcoming programs arranged by the Jewish communities in North America resulted in a rise in their interest in Judaism and Jewish history. Retired people appreciated free language lessons and classes on Jewish history. Many became eager attenders of the adult daycare centers of New York and community programs in Toronto. However, with Judaism largely irrelevant to their culture and identity, many felt a degree of discomfort in a synagogue (Gitelman, Chervyakov, and Shapiro 2003; Gitelman 2003).

Torontonian Vitalii (b.1926) alludes to this discomfort when he speaks about his participation in his *minyan*, a ten-person quorum of Jewish men that meets for prayer every early morning: "The rabbi knows that he can trust an officer of the Soviet army to show up every morning and on time too, that is why he invited me to join the *minyan*."

A former colonel in the Soviet army with thirty years of service under his belt, Vitalii is an atheist, unfamiliar with texts of prayers and unable to read them in Hebrew. During the service he sits quietly. However, he speaks proudly and confidently of his punctuality and responsibility. In addition to a little self-irony (an atheist officer not sticking to his principles by participating in prayer), the testimony alludes to the inefficiency of the religious system of beliefs, which is allegedly unable to produce necessary punctuality and reliability. Essentially, Vitalii suggests that service in the Soviet Army made him a "better Jew" compared to the more knowledgable yet less punctual members of the *minyan*: "So what that he knows the prayer, wears a hat, and does not eat pork? I could have been him if my parents left for America when they were kids. Instead, I defended him from fascism. Doesn't it alone make me more important for Jewish people than some prayer?"

Not only does Vitalii dismiss the importance of ritual, including prayer, he also suggests that his ignoring the rules of Jewish dietary eating, and other customs, developed as a compensatory mechanism for his greater achievements. Significantly, he indirectly blames world Jewry in general, and members of the local Canadian Jewish community in particular, who expect him to fit into the norms of the community without acknowledging his sacrifices. His narrative flawlessly goes from personal choices into larger societal issues. Jewish identity ceases to be a personal choice, but rather becomes a collective responsibility, and not his own (Portelli 1991: 130). He conveys the notion of a good Jew not as a person who lives in accordance with the religious laws, but rather as the one who does "good" for the other Jews, including protecting them and standing up for their interests. He transforms the traditional, including secular, understanding of Jewish identity – and insists on its superiority.

Similar to Vitalii, other respondents share the sentiment of being a "better Jew" because of fighting in the war (Remennick 2007: 289–293, 352). This phenomenon has been noted and explained by a number of scholars. The first explanation, offered by Nina Tumarkin (1994) and Catherine Merrindale (2007), among others, is the centrality of the war in the identity of the Soviet people and their attachment to the past (see also Shternshis 2011). For all people born before 1932, the war experiences were central in shaping who they became, and in many ways determined their future career paths, worldviews, and even family lives. The memory and commemoration of the war, which since the 1970s has developed into an institution in the Soviet Union, became very personal for everyone who witnessed it (Tumarkin 1994). The second explanation traces the roots of these perceptions to the veterans who had internalized Soviet-advocated detachment between religion and ethnicity, a phenomenon which stemmed from Soviet anti-religious propaganda and other policies towards the Jews implemented during the 1920s and1930s. In my previous studies, I demonstrated that, while the policies did not result in the universally negative attitudes to religion and religious beliefs as intended, they successfully managed to divorce the connection between Jews and Judaism for all generations of Soviet Jews, including the one studied here (Shternshis 2006).

Yet, the two explanations do not explain the prevalence of the military discourse among those respondents who did not serve in the army, or the absence of such discourse among women respondents, including those who served in the army. They also do not explain why the respondents who grew up in religious families in non-Soviet areas before the war, served in the army during the war, and returned to religious observances in the immigrant period still prefer to speak about their achievements as soldiers, in contrast to their knowledge of the Jewish texts and rituals, as markers of their Jewish ethnicity. However, if we read the testimonies as texts of construction of masculinity, then suddenly, the discrepancies make sense (Cook 2007).

Socially constructed by definition, masculinity has to be constantly proved and adjusted to societal norms. In the United States and Canada, immigrants define it against the natives of their adopted country and immigrants from other places (Akhtar 1999). The testimonies of Soviet-born Jewish respondents suggest that their understanding of what it means to be a man, and a Jew, goes through a profound transformation after immigration. In speaking about their own families, they often describe Jewish men as "more like women" (Boyarin 1997). Grigorii B. (b.1913) shares: "My father was a very kind man. He was completely useless in daily life, but he was very smart, and kind. He sat all day and mumbled the words of Torah. . . . Kind of like our rabbi does here" (discussion with the author, New York, 1999).

Mikhail Z. (b.1916), who was present at this conversation (conducted on a bench in a Brighton Beach Promenade) echoes: "My father was the same. Could not earn the penny. But in the *shtetl* where we lived, he was seen as a great wise man, everyone came to him for advice" (in discussion with the author, New York, 1999).

When the respondents, both men and women, describe their fathers, the pre-revolutionary Russian Jews, they idealize them as intellectuals, wise men, loving husbands, who generally rejected violence. These idealizations fit with the ideals of traditional European Jewish masculinity, but not with the Soviet propaganda of masculinity in general and the Jewish kind in particular. Since the 1920s, the official media suggested that a new Soviet Jew is a warrior, able to fight the enemies of the Revolution and then build factories and collective farms.[5] Moreover, Jews were disproportionally represented among officers of the Red Army, especially during World War II, when 500,000 of them were enlisted and 100,000 died on the battlefield. The internal perception of Jews began to incorporate this image as a strong, responsible person, able to defend his family. Yet, the Soviet public continued to view Jews through the slogan of "Jews serving the war in Tashkent" (in the city, away from the military action of the war). Though Jews have always understood this slogan as antisemitic, they never fully internalized the perception of a Jewish man as physically strong.

After immigration, the gender identity of my respondents began to accommodate a new understanding of Jewish masculinity. Vitalii's sentiment about Soviet Jewish men being superior to those who studied the Torah during the war can be analyzed as the narrative of constructing a masculinity which would fit the local sentiments. But instead of finding things in common with other Jewish men, Vitalii emphasizes the difference. More astonishingly, he is applying the stereotypes of Jewish masculinity imposed on Jewish men in the Soviet Union to his new compatriots, and uses similar antisemitic stereotypes that used to be applied against him in the Soviet Union to describe his co-religionists in Canada. In fact, he compensates for the lack of ability to participate in rituals meaningfully by stressing his superior masculinity, the expression of which is informed by pre-immigration notions.

A Good Jewish Grandmother Never Goes to a Restaurant: Perceptions of Femininity

Like men, women respondents seem to seamlessly combine Soviet notions of femininity with the notion of what is expected of a Jew in the West. Their roles as mothers, wives, and grandmothers dominate the conversations on any topic.

Vera (b.1921 in Zaporozhe, Ukraine) came to the United States in 1989, together with her two grown daughters and their children. While the daughters were busy looking for jobs, Vera took care of her grandchildren. Now, with her grandchildren in high school, she spends all her time on the bench in Brighton Beach. I asked her why she never went to the nearby outdoor restaurant, where she could sit during rainy days, while sipping a 70 cent cup of coffee. Vera replied:

> It is not appropriate to sit in a café and do nothing all day – it is a waste of money. I don't know what all these retirees are doing in a café all day. My neighbor, she is a real American, a Jew from Poland [sic]. She has a two-year-old grandchild, so her daughter hires a nanny. A nanny! When a grandmother is still alive. Have you heard of such a thing? And what does she do? What kind of a Jewish grandmother sits and drinks coffee in a restaurant all day. . . . No wonder that so many of them do drugs, have colored hair, and wear short pants! (Discussion with the author, New York, 1999)

The contradictions in Vera's testimony reveal the details of her identity especially vividly. First, while she accuses her counterparts of wasting time and money in cafés, she herself sits on a bench all day. To her, however, spending money on coffee in a café (as opposed to making it at home) symbolizes the differences between her own and host culture. Despite the fact that Vera has spent over ten years in the United States, the restaurant culture remains foreign to her, and she uses this "field of difference" as an assertion of moral superiority over a "real American," an immigrant from Poland, who most likely arrived in the United States in the 1950s, speaks English to Vera, and is accustomed to sipping coffee in a café from both the European culture of her childhood and the American tradition. Vera, like many other respondents, refers to the immigrants who arrived decades earlier as "natives" and feels inferior to them in daily life; yet in her speech, she describes their norms as inferior to her own.

In order to assert their superiority to the society they currently find themselves in, respondents often resort to common human experiences such as methods of raising children. Differences in methods of childcare are cited as the most frequent points of intergenerational conflict, and Russian Jewish immigrants are certainly no exception to this rule (Gabaccia 1992; Remennick 1999). In the case of my respondents, their attitudes to childrearing represent an inheritance from the Soviet period, during which most multigenerational families lived in small apartments. Grandparents took care of the youngest family members when the middle generation went off to work. Even during the post-Soviet period, this practice is widespread. Russian radio and television stations, both in Russia and in diaspora, regularly host debates on who will take care of a child better – a nanny or a granny. In the case of immigrants, cherishing the old practice becomes a space which can help immigrants like Vera to compensate for their lack of integration into the local society.

It is not accidental that Vera's monologue came as a response to my inquiry about cafés. While my question was intentionally provocative (I am familiar with the generally negative attitudes of this generation towards restaurants), it did not need to be answered in such a broad, generalized way. For Vera, however, cafés represent "everything that is wrong" with American society, most importantly the free time that retired women "selfishly" enjoy away from their "duties" as grandparents and housekeepers for grown-up children. When Vera speaks about the methods of upbringing of her grandchildren, she notes:

> I will never understand local customs. They go to the supermarket, and they buy food from the can, and they give it to the child! What kind of a Jewish mother does that? Even in the Soviet Union, when everything was in shortage, I would go to the market, buy the best fruits, and manually mash them for my son. My mamma stood in lines for hours just so that we would get some meat, or an orange. We would not taste them. It was for children only. Here they do not even walk with children outside. They go to the mall, the restaurant, to the coffee shop. What about fresh air? I walked with my grandson, even when it was minus 20 [Celsius]. He had red cheeks. They go to synagogue here. They put on hats. But they hire Hispanics to look after their children. . . . Is this Jewish, I ask you? You have to be a mother first, a grandmother. God will know who is a better Jew.

Vera mentioned many other attributes of "proper" childcare. They included avoiding cold drafts, preparing warm foods for lunch, dressing with hats and boots, using physical punishment, and teaching to recite poems by heart, all, in her view missing from the American parents' repertoire and vital to the child's proper development. Needless to say, all of these characteristics came from Soviet practices of childrearing. However, Vera also attributes these characteristics to a specifically Jewish identity. For her, to be a Jew means to be a good person rather than to affiliate with Judaism, and the notion of what is "good" comes from Soviet ideology.

Soviet and post-Soviet Jews imagine a "Jewish mother" as a loving, self-sacrificing, self-sufficient, powerful individual, who also cooks very well (Shternshis 2003). In describing their mothers, many respondents emphasize their ability to survive despite the odds. Mothers skillfully run households, earn a little money on the side by sewing, selling goods on the market, or having a professional career. A mother also can cook delicious meals from scarce food supplies. Like a father, she is wise, but unlike him is physically strong and is not shy of meting out physical punishment if necessary. The only difference between the image of the pre-Revolutionary Jewish mother and the self-representation of respondents is that Soviet women were expected to work outside of the home in addition to being wonderful housewives. My respondents seem to have internalized the Soviet image of the perfect woman, which combines career aspirations and housekeeping, but it is hard to say whether it is because they are Jewish or because they were brought up in the Soviet Union. However, they do seem to articulate and praise the pre-Revolutionary characteristics of a Jewish mother, both in self-perception and in describing their own mothers and sisters.

This image has nothing to do with the North American image of the "Jewish mother" or, worse, a "JAP – Jewish American Princess," which presents Jewish women as overly materialistic, guilt-inducing, and selfish (Ravits 2000). Vera is not familiar enough with American popular culture to have learned about these images. However, her statement suggests that American Jewish women are not sufficiently caring and loving, thus not sufficiently Jewish and not sufficiently feminine. In her daily life, Vera may feel inferior to her neighbor and other American Jewish women because of their superior socioeconomic status, but she compensates for this inferiority by suggesting that the fact that these women are "better Jews" makes them "worse mothers."

Similarly to Vitalii, who compensates for his perceived shortcomings as an immigrant by self-presenting as a superior male, Vera imagines herself as a superior female – the perfect grandmother and mother. She constructs her femininity in opposition to other Jewish women, as opposed to other immigrants or non-Jewish locals. And she uses notions from the Soviet past in order to justify and to establish the points of difference and find a comfortable niche in her new society.

Gender and Elderly Russian Jewish Migrants: Summary of Findings

Immigration adds to the social and economic marginality that characterizes the lives of many among the elderly (Roberman 2007: 1038). During their immigration, Russian retired people have to embrace new medical systems, social relations, products in stores, and climates, both political and natural. Aging combined with relocating to the new country puts enormous stress on their physical and mental health. However, many of them find ways to cope by shifting their pre-immigration attitudes in order to make sense of their new countries. In the absence of possibilities to develop their careers, and, thus, their professional identities, Russian Jewish retired people put emphasis on their gender, through which they, in turn, shift their attitudes to their ethnicity.

When asked directly whether immigration has changed them, all respondents answer affirmatively. For some, the change means an improvement or downturn in their socioeconomic status. For others, it is learning to live in separate apartments from their children, getting used to new doctors, and learning to make friends at an older age. However, the major change can be charted not in their direct answers, but rather in the stories of the past that they use to make sense of their present. Some aspects of their Soviet lives, such as participation in World War II, which seemed less important during the Soviet period, become the dominant aspect for their identity.

Previous studies have argued for the importance of understanding the "migrating past" or "usable past" in analyzing the lives of immigrants of retirement age. The contribution of the analysis presented in this paper is to suggest that the most productive method of studying the usable past involves understanding how gender identity affects memory and the construction of culture among elderly immigrants. The case of Russian Jewish migrants demonstrates that Russian Jewish women and men use different points of their pre-immigration lives as cornerstones of their new identities, yet their gender identity dictates the selection of these cornerstones. Perhaps a wider application of this finding will lead to new studies of elderly immigrants, a field that desperately needs additional research.

Acknowledgment

The funding for this research came from the Rabbi Israel Miller Fund for Shoah Education, Research, and Documentation, of the Jewish Material Claims Conference against Germany (Grant #5028).

Notes

1 It is estimated that about a third of the 900,000 immigrants to Israel were over 60–65, as were 17 percent of the 600,000 immigrants to the United States and Canada, and even more among the over 120,000 Jewish immigrants to Germany. New York and Berlin are the largest centers of Russian Jewish population outside of Russia, with 320,000 Russian-speaking Jewish immigrants living in New York and around 70,000 in Berlin (see Remennick 2007: 8–62).
2 The questionnaire was roughly based on suggestions by Paul Thompson (1988).
3 For an overview of reasons of Russian Jewish migrations, see Remennick (2007).
   For the demographics of Russian Jewish diaspora, see Tolts (2004). For the summary of latest sociological research on Russian Jewish diaspora, see Remennick (2011).
4 Because older people are generally more interested in religion than younger ones (Davie and Vincent 1998; Howse 1999), my respondents visit those synagogues more often than their children and grandchildren. For more on Chabbad's work with Russian Jews, see Shneer and Aviv (2005: 36). For a popular account on Chabbad and their work around the world see Touger (2006).
5 On Soviet masculinity in fiction and cinema, see Haynes (2003); on aspects of Jewish masculinity in the Soviet Union, see Bemporad (2008).

References

Akhtar, S. 1999. *Immigration and Identity: Turmoil, Treatment, and Transformation.* Northvale, NJ: Jason Aronson.

Aroian, K.J., Norris, A.E., Patsdaughter, C.A., and Tran, T.V. 1998. "Predicting psychological distress among former Soviet immigrants." *International Journal of Social Psychiatry*, 44(4): 284–294.

Aroian, K.J., Khatutsky, G. Tran, T.V., and Balsam, A.L. (eds) 2001. "Health and social service utilization among elderly immigrants from the former Soviet Union." *Journal of Nursing Scholarship*, 33(3): 265–271.

Bemporad, E. 2008. "Behavior unbecoming a communist: Jewish religious practice in Soviet Minsk." *Jewish Social Studies*, n.s.14(2) (Winter): 1–31.

Boyarin, D. 1997. *Unheroic Conduct: The Rise of Heterosexuality and the Invention of the Jewish Man*. Berkeley: University of California Press.

Bulmer, M. 1999. *Sociological Research Methods*, 2nd edn. New Brunswick: Transaction Publishers.

Coleman, P. and Podolskij, A. 2007. "Identity loss and recovery in the life stories of Soviet World War II veterans." *Gerontologist*, 47(1): 52–60.

Cook, N. (ed.) 2007. *Gender Relations in Global Perspective: Essential Readings*. Toronto: Canadian Scholars' Press.

Fitzpatrick, T.R. and Freed, A.O. 2000. "Older Russian immigrants to the USA: Their utilization of health services." *International Social Work*, 43(3): 305–323.

Gabaccia, D.R. 1992. *Seeking Common Ground: Multidisciplinary Studies of Immigrant Women in the United States*. Westport, CT: Greenwood Press.

Gitelman, Z. 2003. "*E Pluribus Unum?* Post-Soviet Jewish identities and their implications for communal reconstruction." In Z. Gitelman (ed.) *Jewish Life after the USSR*, pp. 61–75. Bloomington: Indiana University Press.

Gitelman, Z., Chervyakov, V., and Shapiro, V. 2003. "Thinking about being Jewish in Russia and Ukraine." In Z. Gitelman (ed.) *Jewish Life after the USSR*, pp. 49–60. Bloomington: Indiana University Press.

Gutkovich, Z., Rosenthal, R.N., Galynker, I., *et al.* 1999. "Depression and demoralization among Russian-Jewish immigrants in primary care." *Psychosomatics*, 40: 117–125.

Haynes, J. 2003. *New Soviet Man: Gender and Masculinity in Stalinist Soviet Cinema*. Manchester: Manchester University Press.

Howse, K. 1999. *Religion, Spirituality and Older People*. CPA Report 25, London: Centre for Policy on Ageing.

Litwin, H. and Leshem, E. 2008. "Late-life migration, work status, and survival: the case of older immigrants from the former Soviet Union in Israel." *International Migration Review*, 42(4): 903–925.

Merrindale, C. 2007. *Ivan's War: Life and Death in the Red Army, 1939–1945*. London: Macmillan.

Portelli, A. 1991. *The Death of Luigi Trastulli, and Other Stories: Form and Meaning in Oral History*. Albany: State University of New York Press.

Ravits, M.A. 2000. "The Jewish mother: Comedy and controversy in American popular culture." *MELUS: Multi-Ethnic Literature of the United States*, 25(1): 3–31.

Remennick, L.I. 1999. "'Women with a Russian accent' in Israel: On the gender aspects of immigration." *European Journal of Women's Studies*, 6(4): 441–461.

Remennick, L.I. 2007. *Russian Jews on Three Continents: Identity, Integration and Conflict*. New Brunswick: Transaction Publishers.

Remennick, L.I. 2011. "The Russian-Jewish transnational social space: an overview." *Journal of Jewish Identities* 4(1) (January): 1–11.

Roberman, S. 2007. "Commemorative activities of the Great War and the empowerment of elderly immigrant Soviet veterans in Israel." *Anthropological Quarterly*, 80(4): 1035–1064.

Shneer, D. and Aviv, C. 2005. *New Jews: The End of the Jewish Diaspora*. New York: New York University Press.

Shternshis, A. 2003. "Choosing a spouse in the USSR: Gender differences and the Jewish ethnic factor." *Jews in Russia and Eastern Europe*, 51(2): 5–30.

Shternshis, A. 2006. *Soviet and Kosher: Jewish Popular Culture in the Soviet Union, 1923–1939*. Bloomington: Indiana University Press.

Shternshis, A. 2007. "Kaddish in a church: Perceptions of Orthodox Christianity among Moscow elderly Jews in the early twenty-first century." *Russian Review*, 66(2): 274–275.

Shternshis, A. 2011. "Between the red and yellow stars: Ethnic and religious identity of Soviet Jewish World War II veterans in New York, Toronto, and Berlin." *Journal of Jewish Identities*, 4(1): 43–64.

Thompson, P. 1988. *The Voice of the Past: Oral History*, 2nd edn. New York: Oxford University Press.

Tolts, M. 2004. "The post-Soviet Jewish population in Russia and the world." *Jews in Russia and Eastern Europe*, 52(1): 37–63.

Touger, M. 2006. *Excuse Me, Are You Jewish?: Stories of Chabad-Lubavitch Outreach Around the World*. New York: Emet Publications.

Trana, T.V., Khatutskyb, G., Aroianc, K., *et al.* 2000. "Living arrangements, depression, and health status among elderly Russian-speaking immigrants." *Journal of Gerontological Social Work*, 33(2): 63–77.

Tsytsarev, S. and Krichmar, L. 2000. "Relationship of perceived culture shock, length of stay in the US, depression, and self-esteem in elderly Russian-speaking immigrants." *Journal of Social Distress and the Homeless*, 9(1): 35–49.

Tumarkin, N. 1994. *The Living & the Dead: The Rise and Fall of the Cult of World War II in Russia*. New York: Basic Books.

Davie, G. and Vincent, J. 1998. "Religion and old age." *Ageing and Society*, 18: 101–110.

Chapter 17

The Transnational Life of Cheese

Ken MacDonald

Introduction

As you pull off the E27 – which runs north from Lake Geneva toward Zurich – and swing on to the winding road that leads up to the Château de Gruyères, it is hard to miss the signs of industrial cheese production. The box-like buildings of Fromage Gruyère SA, a facility that ripens and exports much of the world's supply of Gruyère, looms large. But these factories and warehouses stand in an odd relation to the village of Gruyères further up the road which, with its reconstructed gates, renovated chateau and cobblestone square free of cars, is a touristic homage to a medieval past. Between the factory and Gruyères sits another building that can be read as an attempt to unite the images of past and present manifest in these other two "facilities" (the village of Gruyères is most certainly a tourist facility). This site – La Maison du Gruyère – is an example of a qualifying device that can only exist in relation to a translocal if not a transnational audience. It is a cheese museum: a site designed to structure bodily movement, channel visitors through a series of sensorial encounters, and orchestrate a particular narrative of an object. It is an attempt to qualify Gruyère and to produce visitors as consumers with tastes directly articulated with the qualities the museum seeks to attach to the cheese.

In its qualifying practices, the museum does not try to hide the industrialization of production. Instead it positions that industrialization as part of a spectacular natural historical journey. This journey opens by showing visitors a very high-quality film that visually and aurally defines the cheese as an integrated expression

A Companion to Diaspora and Transnationalism, First Edition.
Edited by Ato Quayson and Girish Daswani.
© 2013 Blackwell Publishing Ltd. Published 2013 by Blackwell Publishing Ltd.

of an essentialized local knowledge, nature, and culture. It then, with the aid of audio headsets, guides them through a hall adorned with images of the natural qualities of the cheese, and scent tubes[1] that atomize and reveal those qualities. Finally it leads them into a four-sided gallery that overlooks a glass-enclosed demonstration of contemporary cheese-making. Balancing this modernist representation of industrial production is a description of the history of cheese-making in Gruyère assuring visitors that while technology may have changed, the same recipe has been used since 1655 and "the know-how of the cheese-maker and the entirely natural ingredients remain identical." La Maison du Gruyère, in its totality, and with the authority drawn from the status of a museum, creates the "social facts" of Gruyère – where it is produced, how it is made, by whom, for whom, in what quantities, with what qualities. It seeks to stabilize what is otherwise open to question.

In performing this work, La Maison du Gruyère is not unique. Travel the byways of Europe today and it is next to impossible to avoid passing close to an orchestrated encounter with representations of cheese production. Increasingly, these are funded and constructed by producers' consortiums but they attract visitors from around the world engaged in an increasingly important element of transnational cultural economies – culinary or gastronomic tourism. Like all museums, cheese museums engage in abstraction. They consolidate representations in order to produce coherence, to engage in acts of definition and circulation. Invariably they are sites that draw together and represent actors – farmers, livestock, techniques, instruments, knowledge, nature, landscape, history – otherwise so dispersed over the productive landscape and across time as to be near invisible. This dispersal makes coherent encounters with the work they do and the products they produce very difficult and haphazard, or at least it provides a different kind of coherence, one that does not suit the interests of cultural production so well. But who is the coherence for and what work does it do?

Answers to this question are multiple but it is notable that museums like La Maison du Gruyère have only appeared over the last decade or so, the same period in which efforts have been put into qualifying cheese in relation to contemporary fields of taste and in which a range of actors have been drawn together to configure and constitute a transnational cultural economy of cheese (MacDonald 2013). As narratives of an integral relation between nature, tradition, and place have become important qualifiers in the extensions of markets for cheese, it has become essential to have consolidated spaces of display – like museums, routes des fromage or cheese festivals – not only to represent particular qualities but to stabilize "the local" and to articulate new bodies of consumers with the representations that have played an important part in producing their identities as people engaged in progressive forms of consumption related to personal development.[2] Indeed, far from simply reifying glorified regional or national pasts these spaces are elements of conspicuous projects in the projection of specific transnational futures. They are expressions of how "the local" has become a key component of "the transnational" as it works to bring actors into relation across space through the configuration and shaping of fields of production and fields of taste. Commodity museums are but one manifestation of these articulations and appear as the economies they help to reproduce become more intensive (in terms of production) and extensive (in terms of market distribution). They address and articulate the interests of multiple audiences: the self-interest of producers in qualifying products; the interests of governments in realizing regional and national development objectives; and perhaps most importantly the interests of a spatially extensive constituency of consumers in searching out goods that align with a politics of distribution and consumption that emphasizes rhetorics of locality, nature, and tradition. Spaces of translation like cheese museums are not intended for people intimately familiar with the social conditions and locales of production. They are intended to produce familiarity for those who exist at a distance from the sites of production. They are a mechanism designed to produce familiarity for an unfamiliar audience.[3]

In many ways, this is not a new observation. Bourdieu (1984) and Callon, Méadel, and Rabeharisoa (2002), among others, have pointed out how processes of qualification involve a multitude of actors drawn together around the object in ways that seek to both structure and circulate a model of consumption and articulate it with the intentional organization and regulation of producers. This relies heavily on representing a cultural logics of production, and is explicitly engaged in "the objective orchestration of two relatively independent logics, that of the field of production and that of the field of consumption. There is a fairly close homology between the specialized fields of production in which the products are developed and the fields in which tastes are determined." (Bourdieu 1984: 230). Bourdieu's point here is that the cultural production of taste mediates relations and forms of production and consumption. Changes in one bring about transformations in the other, and it this orchestration that is revealed in spaces like La Maison du Gruyère.

My objective in this chapter is to describe this alignment and articulation of the fields of production and consumption as an integral component in the production of a transnational cultural economy and the work of producing familiarity and to juxtapose the integral relations between the roots of cheese – constructs of place, tradition, and nature – and the routes of cheese – the spatial extension of markets for a product simultaneously qualified as natural and cultural. Just as importantly, it is to reveal how this relation is achieved through practices of mediation. How is cheese made legible to anxious consumers and what constellation of interests and actors is responsible for extending the historically circumscribed space of circulation for cheese? In addressing these questions I draw from observations in a range of ethnographic locations – the museum, cheese festivals, and maître fromager classes – that allow insight into practices of mediation and consumption used by a range of actors. But before moving on, I should clarify what it means to speak of a *transnational* cultural economy. It is to be concerned with the production of cultures of consumption built around shared systems of communication and valuing grounded in the construction of taste that create demand for particular types or complexes of products that either exist or can be brought into existence (Callon *et al.* 2002; Crang, Dwyer, and Jackson 2003; Hughes 2000).[4] But it is equally to understand how this process is configured transnationally – both in terms of transcending ideologies of nationalism and producing sociospatial relations by drawing actors and their interests together around an object like cheese that has, through practices of qualification, become identified as transnational. Here I invoke transnationalism not simply in terms of an intensity of mobility or the multiplicity of attachment but to suggest that in being qualified as cultural, cheese, and its production, enters a field of taste that in many ways transcends historical attachments to scale – "national," "regional," "local" – even as those attachments are essential to the development of a spatially extensive web of consumers and an emergent politics of taste and distribution.

The Parochial Origins of Cheese

Walking into a cheese shop today in a city like Toronto, where I live, is a microcosmic experience. It is to walk into a small, ordered world of shelves stacked with cheeses organized by country, or even region, of origin, reducing the geographical complexity of production to the micro-globe of the cheese shelf. This shelf in the cheese shop, sagging under the burden of diverse products from just as many and diverse locales, represents a coming together of different commodity worlds in a single space. And while this selective arrangement of "the world's offerings" is usually invoked as a veil that "conceal[s] almost perfectly any trace of origin of the labor processes that produced them, or of the social relations implicated in their production" (Harvey 1989: 300), it is also a product of modernity; the outcome of a set of conditions through which emplaced elements of subsistence economies became mobile goods in global markets. Along the way, cheese, like so many other goods, has become an instrument in diverse political projects: the production of cultural identities; the promotion of regional economic development; practices of class distinction; exercises in defensive localism; and the manufacture of cosmopolitanism. This has not always been the case. To understand the utility of cheese as an instrument in these diverse projects, it is necessary, at least briefly, to consider the history of "cheese in the world," and the developments that set cheese in motion.

"Pecorino is just cheese to these people." I overheard this remark while wondering the streets of Bra, a small town in the Italian Piemonte, during Slow Food International's biennial cheese festival – an event in which the associations between producers, buyers, consumers, and distributors are (per)formed and open to view (MacDonald 2013). For all its flippancy, this comment expresses an important insight into the generic qualities of cheese in the place where it is made. To say that pecorino (a category of hard Italian cheeses made from sheep's milk) is "just cheese" is to say that when a particular group of people refers to cheese, the referent is pecorino. But it is also to say that a cheese treated with special regard in places distant from the locale of production is an "everyday" or familiar object to people who live in or near those sites.

What we might call this "origin reference" is a linguistic reflection of the fact that cheese, whatever its distant historical origins, is a local material expression of human–ecological interaction. Specific types of cheese were common to subsistence economies and while there may have been variations in production between villages or valleys based on tenure rights, people living in specific places made and ate specific types of cheese and had little exposure to alternatives. This is not to say that trade did not occur. Indeed cheeses were likely a strong medium of exchange in local markets.[5] Certain cheeses – those with a durability and capacity to age well – did indeed circulate, but this was the work of itinerant traders and not widespread networks of distribution and exchange. Jacoby (2004), for example, describes the efforts made by Venetian traders, deviating from their regular sea routes to seek out and secure a stock of Cretan cheese to feed the new consumption patterns in an eleventh-century Constantinople driven by a growing urban social elite. Similarly, cheeses from Holland were produced industrially by the eighteenth century to meet the demand of overseas markets served by a large merchant marine and navy.

But for people whose lifetime spatial horizon was limited to a few kilometers, consuming a variety of distinct types of cheese was not a common life experience. For most, the scale of cheese – the geography configured by its circulation – was circumscribed by decay. Certainly fresh cheeses did not stand much of a chance of reaching "the masses" beyond their points of production – many still do not but that is largely a function of regulatory restrictions rather than the friction due to distance. Defoe, for example, in his travels through Great Britain describes (1762: 166) stopping at an inn in Stilton with a cheese "brought to table with the mites, or maggots round it, so thick, that they bring a spoon with them for you to eat the mites with, as you do the cheese." But even harder cheeses, those that are compact and age well, were subject to destruction by mold, maggots, and mites.[6] From its inception, cheese has always been an object hurtling toward its death. Indeed, this trajectory of cheese has been translated into a quality that long defined it as perhaps necessary – a means of storing protein – but not necessarily enjoyable. Despite recent attempts to romanticize histories of the circulation of cheese (Dalby 2009; Kindstedt 2011), "in the encyclopedic works of the Middle Ages and the Renaissance, cheese is often regarded as an indigestible food, in particular old cheese" (Segal 1988: 73). These encyclopedic pronouncements were complemented proverbially – *Caseus est nequam, quia digerit omnia sequam* (Cheese it is a Peevish Elfe/ It digests all things but itself) (Oates 2003: 217) – and gave rise to a host of popular attitudes and beliefs about cheese: "the smell associated with decay and decomposition inclined people to imagine that their physical and mental health might be in jeopardy, that the substance might have a pernicious impact on the four bodily humors by means of vermin which would further exacerbate the existing putrefaction" (Bruyn 1996: 203).[7] Bruyn goes on to quote a mid-seventeenth-century Dutch academic's observation that, even though it was a common foodstuff, "a good many people are averse to eating cheese because they are convinced that it is deadly and that its consumption breeds disease that may lead to death" (1996: 204). Cheese, in the early days of nationalism, was hardly the stuff of nationalist appeal. At least outside of its place of origin, it was not necessarily an explicit object of desire, even if it was eaten as a source of protein. So, while cheese circulated, circulation was circumscribed – the friction due to distance and popular attitudes toward cheese restricted its range of travel.

The affective component of cheese had to be produced and that, for most cheese eaters today, is a function of modernity. Of course the abjection described in at least some historical texts is the perception of a class of people who could not afford to eat cheese before it reached that stage of putrefaction – before "the stench of death" had set about it. This widespread limit to consumption is an important marker in the development of class associations with particular types of cheese, associations that would cause contemporary consumers to "quake" in ignorance – for it is only people who were able to transcend subsistence limits, an elite aristocracy, who could imbue diversity with value. To use Europe as an example, it was at Court that a diversity of food was consumed. Contrary to the representations of organizations like Slow Food International, the peasant diet was restricted well into the twentieth century (Pilcher 2006). The main components of subsistence diets were locally sourced, whereas the diet of nobility was more spatially extensive. This spatial reach included the capacity to accumulate diverse types of cheese. In feudal Europe, for example, a wide trade in cheese existed. Noblemen owned dairy farms that produced large quantities of cheese and would supply cheese to Court. Cheese was also used to pay tithes to the Church and as tribute (Boisard 1992). And where cheese appears in the historical record, it is on the tables of the elite: "the name of Cheddar appears, for the first time in 1635, as that of a delicacy so much in demand at Charles I's Court in London that Cheddar cheeses were sold before they were made" (Dalby 2009: 23), effectively removing them from market distribution and restricting consumption to those with a royal affinity or deep pockets (Riley 2000). In the accumulation of regional produce from sovereign territory, the consumption of diversity is what can be seen to generate particular class associations with the consumption of cheese.

This is not to say that specific types of cheese did not take on particular class associations, but that "modern" taste was shaped to some extent through a historical association with class, status, and the ability to command the distribution of rare and fragile goods and assign them the value that accompanies exclusivity. Indeed the origin myths of well-known cheeses like Roquefort or Camembert are rife with the trope of consecration by royalty. Narratives of Roquefort, for example, often contain a reference to the royal sanction of 1411 in which Charles IV granted the people of Roquefort-sur-Soulzon the sole right to manufacture the cheese (e.g., Herbst and Herbst 2007; Masui and Yamada 1996). And the scalar leap of Camembert from local specialty to French national symbol is said to have occurred through a chance encounter in 1863 between the grandson of the supposed inventor, Marie Harel, and Emperor Napoleon III. The young man presented the emperor with one of his Camemberts and the "emperor found the cheese much to his liking; congratulated its producer; invited him to his palace . . . and requested that he deliver the product to him on a regular basis" (Boisard 1992: 7). In this single act, the relatively new *local* cheese of Camembert was consecrated and made into a *national* symbol through the favor of a more potent national symbol – the Bonapartes.

All That Is Local Melts into the Nation

That the above encounter is said to have occurred at the Surdon train station is not without significance. The concurrence of social revolution in Europe with advances in transport not only contributed to the development of an urban bourgeoisie but facilitated the creation of markets that brought a range of commodities within the reach of urban populations, and provided outlets through which the consumption of diverse foodstuffs could be experienced. With increasingly rapid access to the produce of regional markets, cheeses were made available to urban consumers in varieties and volumes never before seen. But, in many ways, cheese is an odd comestible, for it has been both a dietary staple of rural producers and a luxury food for urban elites. Cheese became a luxury food not so much because of what it was, but because of the many different forms in which it could be consumed. The capacity to consume *difference* was the mark of distinction that connoted the food as a luxury. In many ways, then, cheese was a food that, on the one hand, transcended class associations through its universal familiarity, but on the other, worked its way up the European class ladder through the capacity of the nobility to accumulate and consume a diversity of cheese from a wide spatial region. What distinguished, say, the nineteenth-century Sicilian peasant from the noble, among other things, was that while the peasant could eat pecorino made in or near his/her land; the noble could eat cheeses from across the country – "under premodern conditions, the long-distance movement of precious commodities entailed costs that made the acquisition of them *in itself* a marker of exclusivity and an instrument of sumptuary distinction" (Appadurai 1986: 44, emphasis in the original).

What is notable about the shifts following the mid-nineteenth century is that the consumption of *diversity* that had been the unique province of nobility, and its signification of power, worked its way *down* the European class ladder until it became a mark of distinction for an emergent bourgeoisie (cf. Mintz 1996). In Paris, for example, an increasing range of cheese had been appearing in city markets from the sixteenth century, but demand rose dramatically in the nineteenth century and regional cheese makers began to seek out urban-based distributors. Boisard (1992: 32) relays a tale from the diary of one Normandy Camembert producer who began shipping by train into the Paris market in 1858, and turned to the wider markets of Lille and Flanders in the 1870s. Whittaker and Goody (2001) note that while before 1840 the caves at Roquefort produced 750,000 kg per year, by 1900 that had grown to 6.5 million as the consumption of the cheese was no longer restricted to the rich and powerful. This spatial expansion, mimicked by other producers, demanded greater production, and many regions quickly saw the commercialization and industrial organization of cheese production.

But this shift did not occur without the articulation of cheese and cheese-makers with new actors who could insert their products into circuits of distribution. Producers now required middlemen – market brokers and specialty grocers, something more than simply itinerant traders – to ensure the distribution and sale of their product. To some extent, the relation between producer and retailer was reciprocal. To maintain a mark of quality distinction and to supply not simply cheese, but a *diversity* of cheese, the retailer needed to seek out new sources of product. The tale of the House of Androuët, one of Paris' primary *fromageries*, is an origin myth from the turn of the nineteenth century that heralds the structure of contemporary cheese distribution, hints at the role of the distributor and retailer in structuring consumption, and implies the importance of "the nation" in mediating that consumption:

> When Henri Androuët, who started off as a peddler for Gervais, had the idea in 1909 of making cheeses from all the regions of France available for tasting to Parisians who were unaware of their country's rich cheese heritage, the history of the house of Androuët began. Henri Androuët went into business for himself and opened his crémerie in the rue d'Amsterdam the following year. The house of Androuët was born, and with it the concept of curing as a principle of production.
>
> After the tragedy and disruption of the Great War, he developed his business, curing and aging the available cheese on the market. The banality of the products then being distributed encouraged Henri Androuët to seek out new ones, even going to visit the producers directly in order to get them. His quest for cheeses led him to crisscross France at a time when country roads were still unpaved, slowly acquiring a unique and profound knowledge of the cheeses of France, the places where they are made, and the people who make them.
>
> In the mid-1920 [sic], the fame of the house of Androuët, which by then was offering more than one hundred cheeses, had reached the point where Henri Androuët was prompted to open a tasting cellar which soon became a gathering place for cheese lovers. Around 1925, out of a desire to familiarize people with the resources of France's *terroirs*, Henri Androuët created his "cheese calendars." They listed over one hundred types of cheese, each presented under a regional or local name and accompanied by its period of full maturity. The innovative brochures were a huge success, and seeing the interest and curiosity that had been awakened in his customers, Henri Androuët opened a tasting room adjacent to his curing cellar. The cream of Paris cheese-loving society rushed there to discover traditional recipes using cheeses . . .[8]

In this origin myth Henri Androuët and his son, Pierre, are positioned as arbiters of taste, their position legitimized through the acquisition of a specialized knowledge acquired through travel to the source of the product. Of course, this history is constructed to serve the contemporary needs of the Androuët Company, which, in the last ten years, has broken its national bounds and riding the crest of "foodie" culture has established eateries in London. But the narrative plays on latent imaginaries that hold some value for contemporary consumers. In this narrative, the Androuëts are culinary pioneers of sorts. They not only source and deliver the commodity to unfamiliar consumers, but they literally teach consumption as spatial practice, invoking *terroir* as a basis of distinction between cheeses,[9] and, through their tasting rooms, set normative standards for the consumption of cheese. The role of cultural broker assumed by the Androuëts is made possible by a product set in motion, released from a cage of regional limitation not only by modern transportation technologies, but by social changes that witness the devolution of dietary habits, practices, and tastes through class hierarchies. Androuët (the firm) is obviously trying to cultivate an image of prestige, innovation, and tradition in their narrative, but the story suggests that the rise of an "appreciation" of cheese is a phenomenon associated with the development of an increasing interconnectedness in France. It speaks to the development of associations between actors and objects that bring into being new realms of circulation for cheese. It also suggests that the capacity to experience diversity was only available in the large urban centers to an educated class who could afford the product and whose capacity to engage in acts of distinction was enabled through agents like the Androuëts.

Like La Maison du Gruyère, Androuët's tasting cellar was an act of consolidation as much as comparison, bringing together in time and space that which was otherwise difficult to conceive – "French" cheese – and making it available to an aspirational class. The consumption of a diversity of cheese, along with other products associated with nationalism, became a way of establishing class boundaries through consumption and thus a mechanism for social distinction. But this act of distinction relied on learning to appreciate, via the skills of brokers like the Androuët family, "the resources of the nation's *terroirs*," a process very similar to the maître fromager and cheese appreciation classes that have sprung up all over North America in the last decade. *Terroir* is an effective mediating trope. Even as it communicates both a scale – "local" – and a condition – something typical of the locale – it allows two products of human ingenuity, cheese and "the nation," to reinforce the value of each other. Barham (2003), for example, notes that French government agents cited *terroir* as the most important of 27 concepts they use in assessing requests for *appellation d'origin côntrolée* (AOC) designation.[10] Despite its contemporary use as a mechanism of defensive localism, for the modern state, the valuation of *terroir* (and related concepts) and geographical typicality lies, at least partially, in nationalism's ability to simultaneously invoke an appreciation of diversity (diversity of regions, diversity of produce, diversity of peoples, diversity of history) and the capacity of the nation to both contain and foster that diversity. In the context of a nation, representation of regional typicality through material product is a mode of expressing the benevolent nurturing power of nationalism – in essence a statement that "we, as a nation, can maintain difference within our unity."[11] Through the consolidation of diversity cheese can become re-imagined in the service of a nation and in particular sorts of nationalisms. Charles de Gaulle, then, was being disingenuous in 1962 when he posed the oft-cited question – "How do you govern a nation with 246 different kinds of cheese?" He knew well that you govern by regulating, sanctioning, and allocating the authority of the state in ways that unify the interests of the cheese-makers; that you make the state responsible for regulating their production and distribution and you articulate each with the idea of "the nation," in this case "the nation" as a construct that unites diversity.

And, indeed, it is to the nation or more accurately, the state, that producers turn when external forces threaten to undermine the boundaries and the "value-added" of "the local." For all its cultural significance, and its supposedly detectable innate qualities, *terroir* requires codification to provide producers with protection in contemporary markets. And this protection has developed, over the past century, in the form of state-managed certification schemes such as "geographical indications"[12] and more specifically the judgment, technology, and legislation administered by the state that underpins those mechanisms. Notably, it is the state that sanctions *terroir* – the nation that sanctions the local. The nation becomes inscribed in the product partially through representations of the essential qualities of national territory but also through the regulation of technology and taste guaranteed through the authority of the state.[13]

My point in describing the process of qualifying cheese as national and the integration between representations of cheese as local and national is to define effectively the terrain of the transnational. With the interlinking of communication networks and modes of distribution in late nineteenth- and early twentieth-century Europe, cheese entered wider channels of spatial circulation. This mobility of cheese – its capacity to become "national" – was driven by the creation of new value, spurred not only by the social aspirations of a new consuming class but also by the capital interest of producers seeking out new spatially extensive markets for their products. But this could not happen without new relations of production. A new consuming class had to be provided with the knowledge of the product and the means through which to recognize and engage in acts of distinction. The emergence of tasting salons and subsequently the introduction of "the cheese course" and "cheese plates" into restaurant meals offer opportunities for this, but just as important is the circulation, beyond the nation, of people with national rather than simply local affinities.

The nation serves as a discursive device to qualify a good – cheese – but does so in a way that unifies difference through articulating localized objects with a singular transcendent ideology – the nation. The effect of unifying difference is to produce what we might think of as an "object space." Walk into most cheese shops in North America, look at the shelves and the nation figures prominently in the arrangement and presentation of cheese. The nation has become a common register – if not in the division of space on the cheese shelf then certainly through some other identifying marker such as national flags spiked into the top of a wheel – the space of goods may be international, but cheeses can be distinguished on the basis of their "national" quality. The nation has historically been an important quality in the context of the transnational circulation of cheese. This was clearly the case for North Americans. As Europe was discursively produced as a seat of culture and civilization so cheese as a part of national imaginaries came to embody these qualities. For consumers, a local appellation may have been meaningless; they had no way to position it. If referring to a cheese as Cabrales brought a blank stare, calling it Spanish Blue unearthed essentialized images of history, rusticity, tradition. This has all changed.

Cheese in Motion: Qualification for the Transnational Sphere

The cheese shops I visit in Toronto give me better access to more of the world's cheeses than those in major European cities. While shops in Paris, Torino, Zurich, or Amsterdam may carry a broader range of regional products, that selection is delimited by articulations with surrounding environments, "the nation," or some notion of what constitutes "the best cheese." This might be read as a reflection of the significant global growth in markets for fine cheese. The signs are evident in the relatively affluent sections of cities where one of the early signs of gentrification is a specialty cheese shop. It is also evident in the rise of market devices that link distribution with popular culture: cheese appreciation classes, cheese-of-the-week columns, cheese plates in good restaurants, cheese blogs, management consulting services for entrepreneurs wishing to open specialty cheese shops, and, in the ultimate sign that a product has secured a place of prestige in society, cheese now has its own consumer-oriented magazine. But, this seemingly unremarkable fact of access and distribution masks an important dimension of a transnational cultural economy – that the flows of goods, ideas, information, and the resulting scapes, are configured and mediated by the diverse interests of a host of actors drawn together by the multiple sources of value read into an object of regard (Latour 2007) – in this case cheese. Just as cheese required the alignment and articulation of certain actors to be qualified as national, becoming transnational requires specific actors to qualify cheese in ways that orchestrate the field of production and the field of consumption and to mediate relations of unfamiliarity.

The circulation of an object like cheese away from its locale of production generates the opportunity for mediating practices. Some of these are clearly logistical. Cheese needs a transport infrastructure to carry it to market, it needs traders to negotiate the relation between a single producer and a diversity of retailers, it needs the regulatory apparatus that ensures, for example, the terms of a contract between producer and trader, the certification of authenticity of the product that provides it with retail cache, or the safety of the product. But others involve mediating the "peculiarities of knowledge that accompany relatively complex, long-distance, intercultural flows of commodities" (Appadurai 1986: 41). Freeing cheese from its parochial sites of production, where discrepancies in knowledge have been overcome often by decades if not centuries of shared meaning-making, and sending it into wide circulation opens up discontinuities in knowledge at multiple points in the commodity circuit. These discontinuities produce arenas for value creation, as problems involving authenticity need to be mediated by the enactment of regulation and/or expertise designed to establish new grounds for assessing quality and for standardizing valuation.

In his discussion of the transcultural flows of commodities, Appadurai (1986) recognizes that distance (both spatially and culturally) creates conditions in which unfamiliarity can not only shape the flow of goods but also play a strong role in how they are qualified to address a politics of distribution and recognition:

"whenever there are discontinuities in the knowledge that accompanies the move-ment of commodities, problems involving authenticity and expertise enter the picture . . . as the distance between consumers and producers is shrunk, so the issue of *exclusivity* [which assigned status value to cheese when it was a means of gastro-nomic distinction] gives way to the issue of *authenticity* (p.44; my emphasis). This concern with authenticity is, in part, what lends such currency to instructive sites like La Maison du Gruyère and provenance-certifying mechanisms like Geographi-cal Indications.

These concerns also bring new sets of actors into relation: regulators and regula-tory mechanisms concerned with vouching for the safety and "authenticity" of a good destined for unfamiliar retailers and consumers; distributors, marketers, and associated practices oriented toward increasing the knowledge base of retailers and the "sophistication" of consumers; consumers and new modes of consumption shaped by engagements with diverse forms of cultural knowledge and practice (see Cook 2004). All of these, however, draw value from a politics of recognition that relies on some implied material cultural quality of the good. For example, cheese as a manifestation of durable "traditional or sustainable livelihoods," cultural knowledge or practice, or nature cannot be separated from its capacity to facilitate acts of distinction through its association with "the local," "the nation," or class (de Certeau 1986). This points to the ways in which even taste is iteratively shaped through multiple and diverse attachments to forms of qualification, and the politics of distribution and recognition, and therefore crucial to the configuration of trans-national cultural economies of goods like cheese (see also Korsmeyer 2005; Johnston and Baumann 2009).

In locales of production, the narratives and practices built around the production and consumption of cheese are understood as a process of socialization into "a culture," and consequently as a condition of producing culture. However, as pro-ducts like cheese break the parochial bounds of their production, a partial gap is opened in which a new politics of recognition and distribution becomes possible. It is in this political space that new forms of value creation are brought into being, and new modes of qualification created to mediate the encounter with new, unfa-miliar, audiences. I turn to two examples of this process that shape the orchestration of fields of production and consumption. The first is a virtual moment in the life of a social movement that seeks to redefine relations between consumers and pro-ducers in order to defend small-scale livelihoods and ways of life. The second is more obscure but is the domain of taste education.

Slow Food, *Cheese!*, and practices of qualification

The configuration of a transnational cultural economy of cheese is revealed every other year in a small town in northern Italy when actors come together to ostensibly celebrate cheese at a festival of the same name – *Cheese!*. Convened by Slow Food

International, the festival occupies the center of this medieval town and attracts over 200,000 people over a four-day run. Slow Food is an organization focused on improving the quality of food production and the enjoyment associated with eating. Born of the northern Italian Left, it grounds the defense of rurality and rural modes of production in the consumption of products that emerge from "local" ways of life, and seeks to promote this through reducing the social distance between production and consumption through the promotion of what it describes as taste education (see Leitch 2003; Peace 2008; Lotti 2010; MacDonald 2013 for descriptions and critiques). It deploys numerous devices to achieve this but primary among these are *presidia, convivia*, and the festivals that link these social forms. Presidia are organizations of producers convened around a product tied historically, economically, and culturally to a precise territory or locality and these serve as a mechanism through which Slow Food can provide technical assistance, apprenticeship training, and assistance with government regulatory systems, and promote consumption through the development of market outlets. They serve as the core of Slow Food's efforts to raise awareness of the relations between consumption decisions and the continued existence of localized "artisanal" knowledge and practice. Convivia, conversely, are local "chapters" of consumers and food professionals, and are often described in Slow Food literature as the frontline in the "defense of pleasure" which is meant to be fought by engaging in models of consumption that support presidia and presidia-like products, though given the expense of many of these products, Slow Food is often subject to a class-based critique. The third mechanism is festivals like *Cheese!* that ostensibly promote "the education of taste" and celebrate the products and social relations brought into being through the actions of presidia and convivia. In practice, however, they provide an arena for acts of qualification that seek to simultaneously create and circulate models of consumption and qualify products in ways that attach consumers, via their politics of consumption, to those products.

As a microcosmic expression of the transnational cultural economy of cheese, *Cheese!* is an effective vantage point from which to observe, document, and analyze the ways in which cultural producers like Slow Food orchestrate, mediate, and define "goods" in relation to political objectives, and the broader sociospatial effects of those practices. Like other sites of observation, it brings together actors – cheese-makers, consumers, distributors, retailers, scientists, connoisseurs – otherwise dispersed in space and opens to view relations and encounters usually hidden behind closed doors. More importantly it exposes the role of these actors in qualifying the product, an explicitly cultural act that entails delineating the meaning of goods and communicating that meaning, often through a reliance on symbolism.

Among the lanes and squares of Bra, *Cheese!* constructs a space of convention defined through defined sites. The Mercato del Formaggi convenes cheese-makers and sellers who pass out samples to the hordes of people elbowing their way through the laneways. But their main objective in coming to Bra is to establish associations with retailers and distributors needed to stabilize the circulation of their products in a transnational market. Another "stage" in Bra is the presidia booths, where as cheese-makers hand out samples and sell their goods, banners adorning their booths

seek to distinguish their cheeses even as they adhere to a standard Slow Food script
that emphasizes the qualities of nature, tradition, culture, knowledge, and place,
among others:

> Bitto cheese descends from an *ancient tradition* of *high mountain* cheesemaking. Slow
> Food created this presidium to help augment and maintain the production of Bitto
> cheese from *Alpine meadows.* Presidium members are engaged in maintaining and
> promoting a list of *traditional practices:* from the rearing of *local goats* (the cheese is
> made with 10–20% goat milk), to the rationing of pastures; from *manual milking,* to
> the use of *calècc, ancient stone huts* that serve as mountain dairies. (Booth banner,
> fieldnotes, Bra, Italy, September 22, 2007; my emphasis)

This mediating text is characteristic of Slow Food promotional materials and reveals
how particular kinds of cheese are qualified as moral objects through the assertion
of a naturalism that invokes both ecology and aesthetics and conflates them with
social relations in the form of "tradition."

This is reinforced in the other more restrictive spaces that make up the "stage"
of *Cheese!* For a fee participants can engage in programs geared toward "taste education." These include the more refined space of the Great Hall where consumers can
sample rare and award-winning cheeses from around the world; the Master of Food
classes led by a roster of Slow Food experts who relate specific associations between
product, history, and the natural and social qualities of place, and where students
can begin to acquire the knowledge required to produce themselves as culture
brokers; the Laboratori del Latte that draw together "technical experts," presidia
representatives, and small audiences into conference-like sessions focused on eso-
teric discussions of the science of cheese production; and the Laboratori del Gusto,
the taste workshops, built around the mediating practices of maître fromagers who
seek to guide participants through the "proper" practices and registers of engaging
with cheese, and quite explicitly performing the proper vocabulary "required" to
describe its qualities.

Cheese! reveals organizations like Slow Food as important nodes, mechanisms,
and actors in the development of a transnational cultural economy. In concentrated
time–space it effectively builds associations of diverse actors and interests around
consumption in ways that reveal the instrumentality of culture, nature, and history
in structuring the value of commodities. It also effectively configures a microcosm
of that cultural economy in which it becomes possible, at one "site," to observe how
the creation of value in relation to a product like cheese represents "the strategic
interests and partial knowledge with which particular actors encounter and construct a commodity at different moments in its circulation" (Foster 2006: 288).

Indeed, the entire festival can be understood to some degree as a configuration
of actors engaged in producing cheese as a transnational object. Around every
corner narratives reveal the metrics and the processes of qualification that produce
cheese as a moral good, brings "the local" into being and simultaneously "displaces"
it by situating the social relations of production in transnational circuits of regula-

tion and consumption. Ultimately these forms and practices of qualification travel out of places like Bra and wend their way into convivia where they spread among members, into the columns of food journalists, into books, into documentaries, and into cheese classes. Back in the cheese shops of Toronto I hear the same stories that I hear in Bra, passed on by distributors as they work to enroll retailers in the project of orchestrating fields of production and consumption. They also spread into the more restricted spaces and practices where "experts" learn to be experts and that work to create a shared meaning of cheese across space and seeking to resolve discrepancies in knowledge and the anxiety created as commodities like cheese travel into terrains of unfamiliarity.

Anxiety and the education of "taste"

It is by now a fairly common observation that food is never simply eaten; that "its consumption is always conditioned by meaning. These meanings are symbolic, and communicated symbolically; they also have histories" (Mintz 1996: 7). What Mintz misses here is that these meanings also have places; that the meaning of consumption (even of the same commodity) varies in time *and* space. And, in places where consumption of a commodity is a relatively new experience, there is a struggle to imbue consumption with meaning; to overcome, through the production of an expertise that can sanction authenticity, the discontinuities of knowledge that occur as commodities move.

To some extent, a frame for that meaning is latent. In North America, for example, cheese is introduced into a context in which many people know the qualities of food that they would like to consume to make statements about themselves and what is important to them. They may, for example, choose to consume products that convey certain politics, including a respect for "the natural" (cheese made using small-scale, non-industrialized production techniques), or to acquire social status. Their problem, being so physically and ideologically distant from sites of production, is that they do not know whether a cheese actually conveys these politics. They need some vehicle to certify the authenticity and accuracy of what they seek to consume. This unfamiliarity generates a particular ambivalence and ambiguity that surrounds cheese and reaches out for some kind of authoritative advice.

The way in which desire to consume is blocked by ambiguity is also not lost on those who seek to expand their markets. In the words of the former president of the French Commission for Sustainable Development:

> If we want consumers to consume "*terroir*" products and services, we need to set up procedures allowing the identification of their characteristics and to foster synergies between the action of local bodies in charge of local development and production and distribution networks. But ... one also needs to work on the demand end by advocating consumption models and life styles that contribute to personal development. In consuming "diversity", we increase our personal "diversity". Diversity encourages human

development and is thus an essential component of sustainable development. But consumers must be given the capacity to orient their consumption in this way. (Quoted in Brodhag 2000)

And therein lies the role of the contemporary broker in the production of a transnational cultural economy of cheese: the manufacture of consumption models – new cultures of consumption – framed as personal development; and the reduction of the anxiety associated with the lack of product knowledge. To an audience unfamiliar with a commodity, certain instruments have proven useful in the reduction of consumption anxiety. Perhaps the most important of these is expert guidance.

Expertise is found in many forms, but it must be enacted to be produced – experts must acquire expertise to deploy it. But that problem has been readily solved by what we might think of as pedagogical entrepreneurs who have, for the last decade, been producing such courses. Starting in the 1990s, buyers and brokers who could negotiate European marketing systems and North American regulatory regimes quickly became the control point of an expanding market, developing new supplies, "taking on regular customers among shop owners, and running 'educational' seminars to cultivate a more detailed knowledge of [cheese] among retailers, expecting that they in turn would educate their customers" (Roseberry 1996: 766). To understand this process I enrolled in a course offered in Toronto. The woman who initiated the course was herself a cheese-buyer for North American distributors and retailers. My classmates on this journey were not what I expected and included employees of some of Toronto's best restaurants, the provincially run wine outlet, food journalists, cheese distributors, buyers for grocery chains, and, ironically, people who already owned cheese shops, illustrating the degree to which deciding to invest in and open a cheese shop is another indication that the expansion of cheese consumption in North America is being constructed through the action of entrepreneurs seeking out ways to create demand and construct value (rather than an outcome of consumer demand).

Notably the mechanism put in place to teach taste in relation to cheese in North America mimics those of European brokers at the turn of the century. And this reveals the way in which taste development in support of consumption and the creation of symbolic and material value have, in many ways simply entered a phase of spatial expansion. As the product – cheese – travels through wider circuits of consumption, the modes of teaching consumption travel as well. And those who do it well are rewarded, indicating that the knowledge imparted through "experts" is embedded in what we might call networks of mutual certification. As cheese consumption expands in North America, the brokers of consumption are recognized and sanctioned by producers and exporters in production locales. For example, Steve Jenkins, a partner in New York's Fairway Market, and Kathy Strange, global cheese-buyer for Whole Foods, have both been inducted into France's Guilde des Fromagers de Saint-Uguzon, "the most celebrated association of cheesemongers and specialists in France, recognized for comprehensive knowledge and attention to the merits of French cheese. Founded in 1969 to safeguard and promote quality cheeses with a goal to create synergy around cheese production and to promote cheese consumption."[14]

Here then, the added value of personal recognition, in the form of an award used by a producer's association to validate that retailers are effectively brokering consumption, and, to paraphrase Brodhag (2000), advocating consumption models and lifestyles that contribute to personal development, and providing consumers with the capacity to orient their consumption in ways that extend the market for, in this case, French cheese, with all of its associated material and symbolic value. For markets to expand and the profitability of particular relations of production to increase, products must not only be shipped to new outlets, but, particularly in relation to commodities that aspire to an epicurean status, consumers need to internalize the product (and its mode and relations of production) as essential not only to their well-being but to their identity (Foster 2006).

Many scholars have traced the social relations and material linkages that the movement of commodities creates and within which the value of commodities emerges. But for products that come to be labeled or designated "fine" we also need to examine the movement of commodities in relation to projects that create and subsequently exploit the value of a "fine" commodity. One of the most important of these projects is connoisseurship, which, in a cultural economic context that prizes marketing and "expert knowledge," has become incredibly lucrative for the value that the positive judgment of a connoisseur can yield to a product like cheese.[15] The "right" judgment from the "right" expert can rapidly expand the geographic distribution of a cheese, producing new meaning and value for a commodity and the consumption of that commodity in a new setting. It is to define, through assertion, arrogance, and the invocation of authority, what that commodity is, or should be, for others. The point here is that connoisseurship is a practice that acts on prestige commodities to give those commodities meaning in new sites of consumption that enhances value not only for the product but also for the person who eats it.

The domination of the connoisseur's voice is strong. One evening in my maître fromager course, a fellow student was leading us through a tasting of Shropshire Blue, a British cheese that first appeared in the early 1980s. Despite its recent origin my classmate described the difficulty she had in finding an accurate history of its development and said that there were a number of stories in circulation. The instructor quickly produced Max McCalman's *Cheese: A Connoisseur's Guide to the World's Best*, and recited his history of Shropshire Blue. Whether McCalman's history or impression were accurate is beside the point. What the instructor was implicitly illustrating, in her turn to the book, was that in the development of connoisseurship "there is a structure of authority to judgments that radiate from the representative-declarative acts of some to inform those of others by a kind of inter-discursivity. . . . One quotes or cites or alludes to authority in orienting oneself to the object of aesthetic judgment" (Silverstein 2006: 483).[16]

The capacity for appreciation of a cheese, then, requires the production of an adjudicator – the connoisseur, with the ability to appreciate and distinguish between products on the basis of certain criteria and a "sense of taste." That production centers on the tasting, a major part of every class in the course:

> Eyes first, what are the *visual* cues, what is the *colour* of the *paste*? What is the *texture* of the cheese? What does that tell you about *production*? What type of rind covers the paste? What is the colour of the *rind*? What does the colour of the rind tell you about the *age*? Then the *nose*. The paste first, never the rind. Break open the paste to acquire a *fresh* scent. What do you *smell*? How do you *characterize* the *aroma*? What does the smell tell you about *production*? Now the *flavour*. No, no, we don't bite cheese, we don't chew it. We suck it. Remember, from the paste outward to the rind. A Blue cheese? Taste the white paste before the blue spores. What hits you *first*? What about *secondary* flavour? And the *finish* . . . ? (Fieldnotes, Toronto, October 2008)

Within each of these bold words are a host of descriptors – fresh, bloomy, encrusted, lactic, musty, grassy, barny, runny, supple, satiny, balanced, acidulous, livery (the list, and there *is* a list, goes on) – that are to be recorded under specific categories and referred to in the development of an aesthetic memory.

A significant component in the development of expertise and connoisseurship, then, is not simply the refinement of observation and taste, but what Silverstein (2006: 491) calls the "mastery of a register;" the development of a specific vocabulary and "a characteristic way of talking about some area of experience" that not only demonstrates knowledge of a commodity, but serves to "index one's membership in the social group that characteristically does so," and distinguish one from social groups that do not. It is the disciplining quality of this register to which my classmates and I were made subject – as we learned to discipline our palette, and translate sensory experience into language, we also learned to communicate that in ways that would satisfy the needs of diverse bodies of consumers. Gradually as the course proceeded it became clear that the aim was to realize value through overcoming discontinuities in knowledge, and anxiety produced as commodities like cheese enter new and unfamiliar terrain; providing comfort for "our clientele" and orienting their interests in ways that bring into being the consumption models and lifestyles that production and distribution networks desire. With the course completed we were set on our way replete with the tools needed to shape the field of taste.

Conclusion

Cheese museums, cheese festivals, cheese classes: all of these mechanisms speak of the work needed to produce cheese as transnational and to the value created in doing so. Value, of course is a conflicted term. But even as the forms of qualification I have described spring from and address a multiplicity of politics, they produce substantive capital gains. Cheese is not an economically trivial item. On any given day, for example, the value of Comté housed in just one of the Napoleonic-era forts above Lake Geneva used for aging the cheese can be US$118 m. Banks in Emilia-Romagna accept Parmigiano-Reggiano as collateral for production loans maintaining warehouses and a staff of cheese specialists that oversee the maturation of over 400,000 wheels worth $187.5 m wholesale. The AOC criteria that legally allow a cheese to be labeled as Roquefort have changed five times since 1925. The most recent amendment, in May 2005, reduced the minimum time that cheeses must spend in the caves of Roquefort-sur-Soulzon to 14 days, allowing producers to overcome the production bottleneck that is the defining quality of a Roquefort – maturation in the caves – and to circulate more cheese through the caves in order to realize the capital gains of an increasing market demand. Rather than sacrifice the gains of an expanded market, the association of producers changed the material conditions of the cheese – five times. Whither authenticity?

There are clearly substantive gains to be realized through the forms of qualification that help to align and orchestrate fields of production and consumption. But what I have suggested in this chapter is that there is something else at play. Cheese has a history in which meaning will always be parochial but there has been an abiding need to give meaning to cheese – just as there has been to any food as it has moved into new realms of consumption. That meaning changes as cheese travels, as it moves from places where people "know the stories" and share common understanding to places where they do not, and meaning has to be created anew. In producing that meaning afresh actors come together under structural conditions in a struggle to establish how cheese will be defined. That struggle involves the interests of farmers still trying to make a living out of producing cheese, affineurs and banks seeking to realize a return on production investments, distributors trying to command regimes of circulation, retailers trying to realize an entrepreneurial opportunity or live out the fantasy of being a "cheesemonger," cultural entrepreneurs seeking to style themselves as experts or connoisseurs, and social movements seeking to defend models of localism through the spatial extension of markets for local products. The sites I have described in this chapter are sites of such meaning-making, but they are also sites in which we can locate the production of the transnational; sites where cheese is defined through ideological formations that transcend the nation even as they have been historically subordinate to it. Qualifiers like cultural, natural, local, and traditional, for example, are no longer uniquely tethered to the nation. They transcend it, just as the actors engaged in struggles over meaning are configured in ways that transcend the nation. Even as they reside within it, their ideological and material interest in cheese connects them in ways that configure a space of transnationalism. The actors who constitute fields of production and consumption have no single unifying identity, ethnic or national, that binds them together. Their relations are drawn together and configured by cheese. But as the circulation of cheese expands and as these actors come into more regular contact physically and virtually, the grounds for new common meaning systems emerges – expressed through, for example, the standardized registers of cheese promoted in my maître fromager course – along with new sense-making and sense-giving processes. An outcome of this is that ideologies of culture, nature, and the local have come to transcend the nation because of the way they articulate with a politics of consumption rooted in a personal identity politics detached from the "nation." Even as these can reference particular locales, they have become near-universal with the capacity to link consumers across other boundaries of identity and situate them in a common politics of consumption that can simultaneously be used to qualify the objects like cheese. And even as qualifying actors shape those politics, those politics bring a transnational cultural economy of cheese into being.

Notes

1 Scent tubes contain a chemical synthesis of the smell of particular plants so that when the tube is opened by pulling up an inner sleeve the scent of say, chamomile, is released into the air.

2 That is, as moral actors engaged in acts of consumption that help to reproduce the relations of culture, place, and nature that are essential to producing the "good" qualities of the goods they consume.

3 In a city like Toronto many diasporic communities are familiar with and seek out culturally familiar goods. Indeed, it is because of this desire of many diasporic communities to reproduce cultural identity through consumption that many other residents of the city experience the opportunity to encounter these goods. But this unfamiliarity is common enough to be used by some cheese-sellers to distinguish their quality of service. Consider this press release from Nancy's Cheese, a small specialty shop in Toronto: "Cheese. It is everywhere yet can be so intimidating. Walk into a cheese shop and, for most of us, the choices are overwhelming, the names unpronounceable, the terms unfamiliar. Add to that the often impatient service at many cheese counters and customers are left quaking and rushed."

4 For example, the production of cheeses that meet the cultural demands of consumers through the attachment of qualities such as exclusiveness, uniqueness, aesthetic characteristics, and sensory profiles that can be used in social acts of performance and distinction.

5 Traces of this remain today. Unlike my cheese shop in Toronto, the shelves of the cheese shop in the village of Wengen, in Switzerland's Bernese Oberland, are weighted down with wheels of cheese from the surrounding alps. There is still a diversity, but the diversity is delimited by age and by a regional, rather than an international scale of distribution.

6 Not that this is universally seen as a bad quality. Casu Marzu, a Sardinian cheese with a long pedigree, is still made by deliberately exposing the ripening wheels to the cheese-fly (*Piophila casei*) in order for larvae to hatch inside the cheese.

7 Bruyn refers to the first chapter of Piero Camporesi's *L'officine des sens: une anthropologie baroque* (Paris 1989) – "Le fromage maudit" for reference to early medieval and modern texts that position cheese as a dangerous substance with a host of deleterious bodily effects.

8 See "The Frog Blog of Louis la Vache," at http://louislavache.blogspot.ca/2007/05/androut-matre-fromager-paris.html, accessed March 5, 2013.

9 *Terroir* is intrinsically a vague and contested term – the extra "something" that combines natural qualities with histories of human occupation, knowledge, and practice and essentially defines a regional typicality (see Trubek 2008). Despite its appeal to the ethics and aesthetics of a romantic naturalism, *terroir* is rarely treated as a social construct.

But see Tomasik (2002), Bérard and Marchenay (1995) and Guy (2003) who makes the point that before *terroir* became translated into a localized expression of national interest, it served as a rural proletarian strategy to challenge the alienating effect of capitalist-state alliances.

10 The French national Geographical Indication (GI), or certification of origin, label. Other European nations followed the French example and national GI legislation in Europe was rationalized in 1996 under the Common Agricultural Policy of the European Union, which established a hierarchy of geographical-indication legislation, the most stringent of which is the Protected Designation of Origin (PDO). Like much EU legislation, the PDO is grounded in, and works through, the legislation of member states where it previously existed, and implements new legislation where it did not.

11 It is significant, for example, that a successful AOC application in France not only legally protects the appellation as the collective property of the producers, but officially designates the product as part of the agricultural, gastronomic and cultural heritage of France (Douget and O'Connor 2003).

12 GATT Agreement on Trade-Related Aspects of Intellectual Property Rights (or TRIPS), Annex 1C, article 22, defines these as: "indications which identify a food as originating in the territory of a [member] country, a region or a locality, where a given quality, reputation or characteristic of the good is exclusively or essentially attributable to its geographical origin, including natural, human and heritage factors."

13 For example, government tasting panels, laboratory equipment required to assess whether a product satisfies minimal qualities of regional *terroir*, and the certification labels that communicate this to consumers.

14 See http://media.wholefoodsmarket.com/news/whole-foods-market-global-cheese-buyer-cathy-strange-inducted-into-prestigi/, accessed February 14, 2013.

15 Here I distinguish between previously existing ethnic or place-based identities associated with consuming cheeses connected with one's place of origin (e.g., Italians and their descendants living in Toronto seeking out regional cheeses that help to perform and reproduce an "authentic" identity away from "home") and the class identities associated with the development of connoisseurship that claims a knowledge across a *diversity* of cheeses rather than an identity associated with the consumption of a regional product.

16 In response to another student's question, "Are you supposed to eat the rind on cheese?" she responded, "Well it's really personal taste, but Max McCalman, who's *the* cheese guy, and is the cheese consultant for Artisanal in New York, never eats the rind because he thinks the taste interferes with the wines he chooses to go with them."

References

Appadurai, A. 1986. "Introduction: Commodities and the politics of value." In A. Appadurai (ed.) *The Social Life of Things: Commodities in Cultural Perspective*, pp. 3–63. Cambridge: Cambridge University Press.

Barham, E. 2003. "Translating terroir: the global challenge of French AOC labeling." *Journal of Rural Studies*, 19(2): 127–138.

Bérard, L. and Marchenay, P. 1995. "Lieux, temps, et preuves: la construction sociale des produits de terroir." *Terrain*, 24: 153–164.

Boisard, P. 1992. *Le Camembert: Mythe National*. Paris: Calmann-Lévy.

Bourdieu, P. 1984. *Distinction: A Social Critique of the Judgment of Taste*. Cambridge MA: Harvard University Press.

Brodhag, C. 2000. "Agriculture durable, terroirs et pratiques alimentaires." *Le courier de l'environnement de l'INRA*, 40, at http://www.inra.fr/dpenv/brodhc40.htm, accessed February 14, 2013.

Bruyn, J. 1996. "Dutch cheese: a problem of interpretation." *Simiolus: Netherlands Quarterly for the History of Art*, 24(2/3): 201–208.

Callon, M., Méadel, C., and Rabeharisoa, V. 2002. "The economy of qualities." *Economy and Society*, 31(2): 194–217.

Cook, I. (with others) 2004. "Follow the thing: Papaya." *Antipode* 36(4): 642–664.

Crang, P., Dwyer, C., and Jackson, P. 2003. "Transnationalism and the spaces of commodity culture." *Progress in Human Geography*, 27(4): 438–456.

Dalby, A. 2009. *Cheese: A Global History*. London: Reaktion Books.

de Certeau, M. 1986. *The Practice of Everyday Life*. Berkeley: University of California Press.

Defoe, D. 1762. *A Tour Thro the Whole Island of Great Britain. . . .* London: D. Browne.

Douget, J. and O'Connor, M. 2003. "Maintaining the integrity of the French terroir: a study of critical natural capital in its cultural context." *Ecological Economics*, 44: 233–254.

Foster, R.J. 2006. "Tracking globalization: Commodities and values in motion." In M.C. Tilley and P. Spyer (eds) *Handbook of Material Culture*, pp. 285–302. London: Sage Publications.

Guy, K.M. 2003. *When Champagne Became French: Wine and the Making of a National Identity*. Baltimore: Johns Hopkins University Press.

Harvey, D. 1989. *The Condition of Postmodernity: An Inquiry into the Origins of Cultural Change*. Oxford: Blackwell.

Herbst, S.T. and Herbst, R. 2007. *The Cheese Lovers Companion: The Ultimate A-to-Z Cheese Guide*. New York: William Morrow.

Hughes, A. 2000. "Retailers, knowledges and changing commodity networks: the case of the cut flower trade." *Geoforum*, 31: 175–190.

Jacoby, D. 2004. "Venetian commercial expansion in the Eastern Mediterranean, 8th-11th centuries." In M.M. Mango (ed.) *Byzantine Trade, 4th–12th Centuries: The Archaeology of Local, Regional and International Exchange*, pp. 371–392. Papers of the Thirty-Eighth Spring Symposium of Byzantine Studies, March, St John's College, University of Oxford.

Johnston, J. and Baumann, S. 2009. *Foodies: Democracy and Distinction in the Gourmet Foodscape*. London: Routledge.

Kindstedt, P. 2011. *Cheese and Culture: A History of Cheese and its Place in Western Civilization*. White River Junction, VT: Chelsea Green Publishing.

Korsmeyer, C. 2005. *The Taste Culture Reader: Experiencing Food and Drink*. Oxford: Berg.

Latour, B. 2007. *Reassembling the Social: An Introduction to Actor-Network-Theory*. Oxford: Oxford University Press.

Leitch, A. 2003. "Slow food and the politics of pork fat: Italian food and European identity." *Ethnos*, 68(4): 437–462.

Lotti, A. 2010. "The commoditization of products and taste: Slow food and the conservation of biodiversity." *Agriculture and Human Values*, 27: 71–83.

MacDonald, K.I. 2013. The morality of cheese: a paradox of defensive localism in a transnational cultural economy. *Geoforum*, 44(1): 93–102.

Matsui, K. and Yamada, T. 1996. *French Cheese*. London: DK Publishing.

Mintz, S. 1996. *Tasting Food, Tasting Freedom: Excursions into Eating, Culture and the Past.* Boston, MA: Beacon Press.

Oates, C. 2003. "Cheese gives you nightmares: Old hags and heartburn." *Folklore*, 114: 205–225.

Peace, A. 2008. "Terra Madre 2006: Political theater and ritual rhetoric in the slow food movement." *Gastronomica: The Journal of Food and Culture*, 8(2): 31–39.

Pilcher, J.M. 2006. "Taco bell, maseca, and Slow Food: a postmodern apocalypse for Mexico's peasant cuisine." In R. Wilk (ed.) *Fast Food/Slow Food: The Cultural Economy of the Global Food System*, pp. 69–81. Lanham, MD: Altamira Press.

Riley, G. 2000. "Cheese in art." In H. Walker (ed.) *Milk: Beyond the Dairy; Oxford Symposium On Food And Cookery, 1999 Proceedings*, pp. 287–292. Totnes, Devon: Prospect Books.

Roseberry, W. 1996. "The rise of yuppie coffees and the reimagination of class in the United States." *American Anthropologist*, 98(4): 762–775.

Segal, S. 1988. *A Prosperous Past: The Sumptuous Still Life in the Netherlands, 1600–1700.* The Hague: SDU Publishers.

Silverstein, M. 2006. "Old wine, new ethnographic lexicography." *Annual Review of Anthropology*, 35: 481–496.

Tomasik, T.J. 2002. "Certeau à la carte: Translating discursive *terroir* in *The Practice of Everyday Life: Living and Cooking.*" *South Atlantic Quarterly*, 100(2): 519–542.

Trubek, A.B. 2008. *The Taste of Place: A Cultural Journey into Terroir.* Berkeley: University of California Press.

Whittaker, D. and Goody, J. 2001. "Rural manufacturing in the Rouergue from Antiquity to the present: the examples of pottery and cheese." *Comparative Studies in Society and History*, 43(2): 225–245.

Chapter 18

Diaspora and Transnational Perspectives on Remittances

Anna Lindley

Remittances – migrants' material transfers to countries of origin – are a routine feature of diasporic and transnational lives. With large volumes of remittances traveling from relatively richer to relatively poorer countries, the 2000s saw a surge in research and policy interest in the economic impact of remittances on development processes in countries of origin. This chapter reflects on what diaspora and transnational perspectives can bring to our understanding of remittance dynamics and significance.

In particular, I will discuss the social embedding of remittances; the foregrounding of migrants' perspectives; the unsettling of conventional temporal and spatial expectations regarding remitting; and the emphasis on needs and disparities in mediating the remittance process. These points will be illustrated with examples from a range of contexts – from Serbia to Mexico to Zambia. I also use examples from my study exploring remittance dynamics from the perspectives of Somalis residing in the country of origin, neighboring Kenya, and the United Kingdom.[1]

This chapter first situates remittances in relation to global economic trends, social theory, and development policy. Second, conventional economic approaches to understanding remittance dynamics are outlined. Against this background, the rest of the chapter explores how diaspora and transnational perspectives enhance our understanding of remittance processes, particularly its social and comparative dimensions.

Situating Remittances: Trends, Theory, Policy

There are several reasons for the surge in interest in remittances. First, globalization and technological advances have greatly facilitated not only migration but also

A Companion to Diaspora and Transnationalism, First Edition.
Edited by Ato Quayson and Girish Daswani.
© 2013 Blackwell Publishing Ltd. Published 2013 by Blackwell Publishing Ltd.

international financial flows. According to World Bank data on recorded remittances, large increases have been registered during the last 20 years, and by the end of 2010, remittances to developing countries were estimated to be US$325bn (Mohapatra, Ratha, and Silwal 2010).[2] This represents a hugely significant financial flow: globally, remittances to developing countries have long outpaced Official Development Assistance and its rival Foreign Direct Investment, and have proved relatively stable in relation to other financial flows, even in the recent global financial crisis (Mohapatra *et al.* 2010). Moreover, while data collection is improving, it is thought that a large proportion of remittances still go unrecorded, due to variations in recording and classification systems and the popularity of informal remittance channels.

This recognition of quantitative significance occurred against the background of theoretical advances of the "new economics of labor migration" (NELM) in the 1980s. NELM conceptualized remittances as a strategy to maximize income, spread risk, and overcome local market constraints (Stark and Lucas 1988). In contrast to structuralist views which had tended to cast remittances as part of downward cycles of economic decline and dependency in home communities, NELM envisioned that under some circumstances, migration and remitting could help families build more profitable and sustainable local livelihoods, with numerous multiplier effects in the wider economy (Durand, Parrado, and Massey 1996).

Meanwhile, emerging sociological and anthropological perspectives on transnationalism emphasized the often intense flows of people, information, money, goods, and ideas between migrants and their home communities. Taken together, these transnational interactions and exchanges seemed increasingly to undermine the notion of communities as localized and spatially bound, pointing in some cases to the formation of transnational social fields (Levitt and Glick Schiller 2004). Flows like remittances were the "bread and butter" of transnationalism, central to understanding how migrants and family members back home constructed shared lives across borders.

These dual theoretical advances (NELM and transnational studies) coalesced with a highly receptive global development politics, as remittances rapidly became a "new development mantra" (Kapur 2003). The efforts of migrants to support family members back home seemed to epitomize the spirit of contemporary development preoccupations, appealing to diverse development actors. Neoliberal forces, focusing on macroeconomic stabilization and growth, viewed migration and remittances as a transfer of resources to poorer economies in the spirit of comparative advantage, which could foster local self-reliance in the context of the rolling back of the state. The more holistically inclined human development community saw remittances as household resources that could support education, health, and housing. Meanwhile, for advocates of participatory, grassroots-driven development, remittances represented a way in which people coped with poverty and the ravages of structural adjustment, a form of "globalization from below." Across diverse development constituencies, the search is on to find ways of maximizing the potential benefits of remittances in the developing world (Lindley 2011).

Thus, the prominence of remittances in debates about migration and development in recent years can be attributed to a combination of empirical factors (in terms of the growth of remittances as a phenomenon), theoretical factors (with change in how remittances are understood), and political factors (with the development policy climate being particularly receptive). The thrust of recent research and policy attention, however, has been largely on the impact of remittances on development processes in the home country, rather than exploring their transnational dynamics, or the perspectives of remittance-senders, to which I will turn shortly. But first, in order to appreciate the contribution of diaspora and transnational perspectives to understanding remittance behavior, it is important to consider this within the context of broader social scientific analysis of remittances, which comes primarily from economics.

Exploring Remittance Behavior: An Economic Approach

Why do migrants remit? The dominant attempt to answer this question theoretically came from NELM. This approach adapted neoclassical economics' rational choice model of migration (whereby individuals migrate in response to wage differentials in order to maximize their utility), to take into account the role of the household in migration-related decision-making processes. Conceptualizing the household as a coalition of rational economic actors, NELM understands migration as a strategy to diversify the household's income sources in response to risk or local constraints in credit, insurance, or other markets (Taylor 1999). The decision that a member of the household should migrate is based on the calculation of the costs of migration (e.g., forgone family agricultural labor, travel expenses, helping the migrant during initial periods of unemployment) and benefits of migration (e.g., regular remittances, lump-sum investment in local income generation, anticipated assistance during times of particular hardship). Thus, anticipated remittances become a central component of migration decision-making, part of an understanding – or what microeconomists term an *implicit contract* – between the migrant and the remaining family.

Against this background, four specific hypotheses were advanced regarding why migrants remitted (reviewed in Rapoport and Docquier 2005). The first motivation discussed was altruism: the idea that migrants derived utility, or satisfaction, from improving the consumption level of the members of their home-country household. Given the close-knit and reciprocal nature of relations between migrants and their families, this has also been described as "tempered altruism" and "enlightened self-interest." The second hypothesis is that migrants are motivated by self-interest to remit, in the anticipation of reciprocal assistance from the origin household – for example, inheritance, gifts, help with maintaining assets, or maintaining the migrants' standing in the home community. The third hypothesis is that remittances are a sign of a co-insurance arrangement between migrants and their families, whereby the original household, relying on sources of income that entail risks (e.g., crop failure, livestock diseases, price fluctuations, land tenancy insecurity), allocates one member to work abroad to diversify their income sources. Provided that the risks faced by the migrant in the host country labor market and those faced by the household are not positively correlated, they are able to help each other out in times of difficulty. Finally, the fourth hypothesis about why people remit is that migrants are repaying implicit or explicit loans, either for migration-related expenses, or for family members' earlier investments in the migrants' human capital such as schooling.

However, this microeconomic approach, although representing the most focused attempt to theorize remittance behavior, has some limitations. It tends to assume (1) a cohesive, co-sustaining core household as the key unit of analysis (remittances are evidence that the economic fortunes of the migrant are still bound up with this household); (2) migration determined by purely market considerations (a rational, utility-maximizing, risk-minimizing response to economic opportunity and constraint). It is a model that seems to fit the realities of some contexts better than others.

This is well illustrated by Sana and Massey's (2005) comparison of remittance behavior among Mexicans and Dominicans in the United States. They found that an NELM-based model of household diversification and investment fitted well with the patterns of migration and remittances in patriarchal rural communities in Mexico, where the traditional pattern of migration involved men migrating on a temporary basis to work in the United States, sending remittances to wives and children to cover subsistence and investments in local livelihoods, with a view to eventual return. Their findings regarding migration and remittances in the Dominican Republic were rather different, however. In an economically poorer and politically less secure setting, they observed that "migration [is] a more dramatic, less carefully planned move, with the purpose of ensuring family subsistence in the absence of viable opportunities in the home country" (Sana and Massey 2005: 512). Migrants were more likely to become permanent US residents, and they sent remittances to a wide range of relatives, reflecting distinct and more diffuse and extended household and family structures.

This example suggests that transnational and diaspora perspectives, which focus on the social embedding of transnational flows and migrants' lived experience of complex relations with homelands and host nations, have much to add to our understanding of remittances.

More than Money: The Social Embedding of Transnational Flows

Transnational perspectives draw attention not only to transnational flows, but also to the social settings in which they occur, recognizing that these social settings not only shape transnational flows, but also are in many ways constituted by such flows (Levitt and Glick Schiller 2004). Whereas NELM relies on a cohesive, co-sustaining core household in the country of origin as the key unit of analysis in explaining remittances, a transnational perspective problematizes how families are constructed in particular cultural contexts, and in transnational settings. In problematizing the household, it draws attention to the inequalities and struggles between individuals, particularly along gender and generational lines, often overlooked in microeconomic theories which risk reifying the household as a unit that takes unanimous decisions for the benefit of all members, and formulates joint, clear, and deliberate strategies (de Haas and Fokkema 2009).

"Following the money" in the Somali case illuminates complex social landscapes (Lindley 2010). It forces us to rethink conventional units of analysis, such as the household. Extended family households are routine. Polygamy is widespread. There is routine circulation of family members, goods, and money between urban homes and nomadic circuits or rural villages. Wider clan connections play an important role in socioeconomic life. These complex – and in themselves dynamic – translocal interdependencies translate (albeit unevenly) into transnational contexts. Remittances frequently involve wide-ranging family networks including siblings, uncles, aunts, cousins, nieces, nephews, and in-laws, rather than necessarily being configured around a single "origin" household run by spouse or parent. Family politics along gendered and generational lines inform remittance practices. For example, some Somali women interviewed in the United Kingdom indicated a preference for sending remittances to their female family members – say, a sister-in-law, rather than a brother – in the belief that in that way the money was more likely to be spent on family needs, rather than chewing *khat* or courting a second wife.

Situating remittances within transnational social settings like this encourages us to recognize remitting as a social as well as an economic practice. The bulk of remittance studies focus on the quantitative dimensions of remittances and often neglect to investigate their sociocultural content. What meanings do people attach to sending money? Remitting can be seen as a form of relational work: a way to maintain affectionate relationships, in the absence of other regular forms of face-to-face interaction which usually reinforce family relations (Bryceson and Vuorela 2002; Zelizer 2005). For many migrants, sending remittances is an important way to maintain a sense of familial connectedness and social well-being, as well as an altruistic sense of doing the right thing. Remitting becomes the price of still belonging. In El Salvador, migrants' families have been said to "measure affection" in remittances (Santillán and Ulfe 2006). This does not preclude the possibility that elements of altruism/enlightened self-interest, co-insurance, or debt relations might still underlie remitting. But it invites us to scrutinize more closely the nature of these relationships in particular settings.

For example, many Somali remitters expressed a sense of debt, but it was rather diffuse and indefinite. This was dramatically demonstrated when one interviewee, raised by an uncle, and now supporting four uncles and 12 aunts, explained his situation by saying philosophically: "You eat with your brother when he has money." In some instances, debts are to be transferable within family networks – as where people who had received support for their own education or migration feel that they should repay this, but instead of repaying the parents, uncles, or older siblings who originally helped them, they in turn sponsor younger family members. These observations resonate very much with the anthropological concept of generalized reciprocity, typical among kin relations, which does not imply any overt reckoning of debts, precise repayment, or definite time-frame (Sahlins 2004).

Remittance practices vary across cultural settings, may take rather distinct forms, and carry different meanings. The contemporary literature on remittances tends to focus primarily on regular flows of money, durable goods, and investments, which play a significant role in the livelihoods of recipients. Cliggett (2005) contrasts this with the practices of "gift-remitting" that dominate among Zambian rural–urban migrants. She argues that, like many rural–urban migrants in Africa, they do not have the kind of income that enables them to remit large sums, such that families can rely on them for day-to-day sustenance – indeed, the city-dwellers are often struggling to meet their own basic needs. Moreover, migration in this context tends to be more of an individual decision than a corporate household decision, so home family members do not necessarily play a big role in deciding and supporting the decision to migrate. But nevertheless, according to Cliggett, often at great cost to themselves, migrants do maintain links through intermittent gifts of cash, food, "town goods," and small luxuries. These are symbolic acts, expressing affection and remembrance of family members, part of ongoing processes of mutual recognition. By maintaining a social place in the home community, migrants can keep potential lines of assistance open. Migrants' relatives may then later be called upon to help pay bridewealth; to welcome the unemployed or retired migrant back into their homes or to work on the family farm; and to care for the migrant in their old age.

The issue of the symbolic content of remittances as acts of mutual recognition is echoed numerous times in research on international migration. But it can manifest itself differently across cultures. For example, it is widely assumed that recipients expect and/or are grateful for remittances. But this is not always the case. Bajić (2007) describes the remittances from migrant children as a "taboo" among middle-class urban Serbian parents. This is despite the fact that many of these parents invested hugely after 1991 in their children's migration to North America, Australia, and elsewhere to assure them of a better life; that the old middle class has become progressively impoverished since then; and that their children view remitting as a practical strategy to meet shortfalls in dietary, healthcare, and emergency needs that their parents' pensions do not cover. Bajić relates this resistance to accepting remittances to several class-specific cultural factors. There is a strong feeling among these parents that *they* should be the providers – and that it is undignified to accept material assistance from their children. This relates to the historical transformation of children from productive family members into the non-productive "sacred" children, taken as a sign of modernity (Bajić 2007; see also Zelizer 2005). The contrast is drawn with the young people from poor rural backgrounds who migrated as guestworkers to Austria, Italy, and Germany in earlier decades and routinely sent remittances to support their struggling families. According to Bajić, the feeling is that only "peasants" would accept remittances from their children, and that middle-class urban parents should only accept gifts of symbolic, not material value. These two factors combine to cause major embarrassment about receiving remittances, hence the parents' efforts, despite an often real need for financial assistance, to deter their children's monetary remittances, or to put the funds aside so their children can eventually have it back as inheritance. Such ethnographic examples from home communities illustrate how the form and social meaning of remittances varies across different cultural and class settings, with implications for their uses and, ultimately, their "developmental potential." But migrants' individual perspectives and situation in the host country also play into the remittance process in important ways.

From "Shadow Households" to "Superheroes": Migrants' Perspectives

Economic literature has conventionally viewed migrants as temporary, "shadow households," tied to a "core" origin household through an implicit contract, whereby the household sends the migrant and the migrant sends remittances (Caces *et al.* 1985). By contrast, a diaspora perspective highlights and problematizes the lived experience of migrants in host countries. While familial relationships and demands will surely play an important role in shaping remittance dynamics, one would expect that remittances are also shaped by the meeting of individual dispositions and host country context.

Al-Ali, Black, and Koser (2001), studying the transnational engagements of Bosnians and Eritreans in the United Kingdom, Netherlands, and Germany, make an important distinction between the desire to participate in transnational activities and the capacity to do so. For example, some migrants may desire to remit, but not be able to; others may be able to remit but have no desire to do so. Thus, while emphasizing simultaneity and connection, transnational research necessarily has to acknowledge social closure and detachment – the "limits to transnationalism" (Al-Ali *et al.* 2001; Levitt and Glick Schiller 2004). This may involve pleading poverty, or other attempts to justify the refusal to assist. For those from countries with good telecommunications this may take the form of selectively ignoring international phone calls at particular times of day, or changing one's phone number. Absence of remittances may (be taken to) imply a refusal to "recognize" relatives, or do the relational work deemed necessary to maintain a place in the family. Many Somali refugees would be shamed if they did not support their relatives – as one individual put it, he would be "struck off the family list" (Lindley 2010).

The concepts of diaspora and transnational community are useful in expanding our focus beyond the close family likely to be the main beneficiaries of remitting, to the role played by wider collectivities in encouraging and policing remitting. Strong forms of social pressure may be exerted at community level. In the Somali case, people in London also wish to avoid people "bad mouthing" them for not supporting their family, either in their home community or among Somali communities in the United Kingdom (Lindley 2010). Given the real source of support that ethnic communities offer migrants, in particular in the early years after arrival, such social disapproval can restrict access to much needed lines of assistance.

A diaspora perspective highlights the frequent marginalization of the diaspora in host countries, and therefore draws attention to the often important impact of remitting on the lives of senders. For example, research in London suggested that while some Somali remitters are secure, prospering, and well placed to send money, many others routinely struggle to meet their remittance obligations and to balance these with pursuing life in the United Kingdom (Lindley 2010). Remitting can compound poverty, and influence labor-market, savings, and investment strategies. According to one Somali interviewee: some remitters "don't live lives because of it basically. . . . Most of them, people who were working in factories, doing manual hard work, long shifts, sending money, getting the lowest incomes. Their basic wage is not much and they send to relatives." Some people are more willing to accept poorly paid manual work in unpleasant conditions and work long antisocial shifts, when they might otherwise spend time training or seeking jobs more appropriate to their skills. Meanwhile, remittance obligations often add to marital and intergenerational pressures that families (re-)negotiate in the host country setting. There are numerous other examples of migrants suffering under the strain of remittance obligations (particularly among refugees, see Al-Ali *et al.* 2001: Horst 2007, Riak Akuei 2005).

All this offers a more sober view than the sometimes rather glib celebration of migrants as new development "superheroes" in the current migration–development policy discourse. It warns us against shifting the responsibility for development in the direction of migrants, following earlier shifts from the state to the market, and the state to civil society (Faist 2008). Not only are migrants a tiny proportion of the world's population (some 3 percent), they are often employed in the most strenuous jobs, for poor pay, in terrible conditions. Many do not wish to remit – or are not able to do so. Yet they may come under tremendous pressure to do so, in ways that may conflict with their individual priorities. Diaspora and transnational perspectives also illuminate aspects of the evolution of remitting over time, and its geography, in ways that challenge conventional expectations.

Temporal and Spatial Dimensions: Reconsidering Conventional Expectations?

It is often assumed that when immigrants spend a long time in a destination country, they progressively become more integrated into that society and more detached from their country of origin. This idea draws on deeply embedded methodological nationalism, whereby the nation-state is treated as setting the dominant parameters for social analysis. The tendency to naturalize the connection between people, national territory, and identity is illustrated by the ways that migrants and refugees are often portrayed by using botanical metaphors relating to uprooting and transplanting (Malkki 1992). Mobile peoples are seen as posing a problem for state authority and development, which seeks to "fix" them to particular locations (Bakewell 2008; Scott 1998). Hence the idea that immigrants must choose – either to integrate into the host society or to return; they cannot remain living "across borders" for extended lengths of time.

This worldview is reflected in the economic literature, where it is generally assumed that where migrants do not return home, remitting will eventually decline and stop. Remitting is evidence of ongoing membership of the core household, of a coalition of rational actors, that the migrant still considers his or her fortunes largely bound up with that coalition. But over long periods of time, the economic theory goes, social ties will weaken, as individuals face competing claims on their income, from new families in the host country and the demands of building a secure future there, rather than in the country of origin (Brown and Poirine 2005).

However, diaspora and transnational perspectives have reconceptualized immigrants' lived experiences in ways that critically challenge our assumptions about integration and its effects, and alter expectations about remittance patterns over time. Importantly, diaspora and transnational perspectives question the common idea that long-term migration necessarily involved a linear process of simultaneous assimilation and detachment, rather pointing to instances where migrants maintain transnational connections over long periods of time. For example, Sana and Massey's (2005) study, cited earlier, also showed that some Dominican migrants continue to remit, particularly in response to urgent needs, long after they have settled permanently in the United States. Here the role of the situation in the country of origin, and disparities between destination and origin country, would seem to play a critical role, which will be discussed in the next section.

Moreover, integration – if it does happen over time - is not necessarily inimical to transnational activities. The limited evidence suggests that it is not necessarily a zero-sum game. For example, Marcelli and Lowell (2005) estimated the remittances of Mexicans in Los Angeles county to be inversely related, as expected, to some conventional integration metrics (e.g., education), but positively related to immigrant home-ownership in Los Angeles county. Such findings contradict straight-line assimilation theories, and seem more consistent with a transnational perspective. In sum, the "remittance decay hypothesis," widely assumed to be basic common sense, has not been systematically tested, and merits revisiting in light of emerging evidence.

There are also several ways that emerging evidence on remittances tends to contradict conventional assumptions about the spatial dimensions of remitting. There has been great emphasis on north–south remitting, on funds flowing from migrants in the global north to countries in the global south. This is what has caught the imagination of the international development community: understandably so, given the way that remittances dwarf international aid, and go directly to individuals in countries of origin. However, the existence of so-called reverse remittances from migrants' families to migrants demonstrates that it is not only a one-way flow. Families "back home" can find themselves providing migrants with travel expenses, work-permit charges, school and university fees, living expenses, and gifts. Bajić's account (2007) describes how Serbian middle-class parents who are reluctant to accept assistance often make efforts to send cash gifts to their children, thus reasserting their idea of how the relationship should be.

Moreover, recent research has highlighted the importance of south–south remitting. Ratha and Shaw (2007) estimate that while about half of migrants from developing countries reside in developed countries, half still reside in other developing countries, very often neighboring states or regional migration hubs like Saudi Arabia, Nigeria, South Africa, and Malaysia. They estimate that up to 30 percent of remittance flows to developing countries may come from other developing countries. While their remittance volumes are smaller, they may nevertheless play a substantial role in family welfare, particularly for poorer migrants more able to migrate regionally than to depart for more distant and wealthier destinations (Ratha and Shaw 2007). Besides, as the Zambian case demonstrated, even internal migration and small symbolic remittances may nevertheless perform significant roles in the lives of those involved and in society at large.

Even less discussed is the issue of remittances flowing to and within the global north. It would be interesting to explore the financial decision-making of northerners based in the global south – colonial officials, humanitarian aid workers, hypermobile businesspeople, oil workers, military and diplomatic staff – remitting to their home countries. Similarly, patterns of lifestyle migration within Europe, from the cold north to the sunny Mediterranean and associated transfers of cash, assets, and pensions remain under-researched.

Finally, not all remittances go to the country of origin: diasporic and transnational research has highlighted connections between distinct migrant destinations. This is particularly demonstrated in the context of refugee remittances, where refugees may remit to relatives displaced within the region of origin (Dick 2002; Lindley 2010; Van Hear 2006).

The tendency in the remittance literature to underplay the actually rather diverse spatial organization of remittances relates, as I have suggested, to the way in which remittances have been seen within the development discourse in recent years. Whether viewing remittances as the working out of comparative advantage and convergence, as a form of privatized development assistance, as a hard-earned transnational family livelihood, or a counter-circuit of neoliberal globalization, development thinkers and policymakers of contrasting views have been drawn to the issue of north–south remittances precisely because of the disparities between countries of destination and origin.

Comparative Contexts: Negotiating Disparities

The wish to respond to the needs of family members and others feature prominently in people's explanations of why they remit. In my research with people living in the United Kingdom who originated from the Somali territories, where admittedly the level of basic humanitarian need is among the highest anywhere in the world, the "misery" of people back home, the low wages, the lack of opportunity or hope or freedom was a constant refrain. Many explained that they sent remittances to meet quite basic needs. For example, a man from Mogadishu suggested:

> If we don't send money to Somalia, people . . . don't survive. . . . The children, if they don't go to school, they become militia, simple!. . . . If someone called me today and says my child cannot go to school because I don't have money for the school fees, I should feel guilty, if I have got money and someone told me that. Someone to die, or maybe 10p [for school fees], yeah?

Importantly, however, this comment highlights not only poverty, insecurity, and dire *need*, but also an acute awareness of *disparities* between the migrant's situation and that of the person in the country of origin. So the discussion is not only about absolute needs, it is also about *relative* positions of sender and recipient.

It is interesting that in the examples given above, of remittances in the context of Zambian rural–urban migration, and Serbian middle-class urban migration, where much lighter and symbolic forms of remitting prevailed, the disparities between migrants and non-migrants were not seen as a major issue (the Zambian rural-dwellers seemed to recognize that city-dwellers often struggled to make ends meet, and the Serbian parents proudly sought to minimize – at least discursively – the disparity between their and their children's fortunes).

But there are indeed dramatic material disparities between many origin and destination countries. Why should this matter so much to remittance-senders? First of all there is the idea from economic anthropology that: "The greater the wealth gap . . . the greater the demonstrable assistance from rich to poor that is necessary just to maintain a degree of sociability . . . [especially] where the economic gap amounts to oversupply and undersupply of customary requirements and, especially, of urgent stuff" (Sahlins 2004: 211). Thus in order to maintain social relations in the context of significant wealth gaps, particularly where one party is in great need, some form of assistance is required. Moreover, it is relatively affordable. Remitters in the West can often afford to play a significant role in the livelihoods of recipients, in a way that can continue over many years. It can be hard to justify withdrawing such support.

These north–south disparities can become progressively socially ritualized, with a tendency for migrants to view people in their home country as poor and the latter to view the former as rich. Migrants' success stories – true and otherwise – and incoming remittances (especially where they represent substantial amounts by local standards) serve to reinforce this impression. Thus the material gulf between "back home" and "out there" inscribes itself in the collective consciousness of those involved.

However, research also shows evidence in some contexts of mutual re-evaluation. In the Somali case, on the one hand people in the region have become increasingly aware of some of the problems people face overseas. On the other hand, people abroad have begun to deconstruct the poverty and insecurity of their place of origin, pointing to the pockets of stability and the relative affluence in better-off segments of society. As one Hargeisa resident put it, some expatriates who make return visits or see videos re-evaluate their "congested life," penny-pinching in the tower blocks of the cold global north, with mounting electricity and phone bills (see Lindley 2010).

Wage disparities between places of origin and destination as well as the issue of patterns of relative deprivation within migrant-sending communities have been a central element in economic migration theories. But the implications of absolute and relative disparities are often overlooked when it comes to analyzing remittance patterns. Given the frequency of global migration along steep income gradients, for example between African and European countries, this issue of disparities in shaping the remittance process would seem to merit more attention. Disparities can be conceptualized not only in terms of wealth and poverty, but also security and insecurity: elsewhere I have explored how conflict in the country of origin may shape remittance dynamics in specific ways (Lindley 2009a).

Conclusion

What does diaspora and transnational thinking bring to our understanding of remittance patterns and impact? First, it focuses our attention on the *social dynamics* of remitting, in a world that has been preoccupied with their volume and impact. Just as migrants are more than just "labor," remittances are more than just "money." They express – but also create, sustain, and modify – the transnational social formations which channel them. As such remittances are unavoidably a social practice as much as an economic transaction, making it important to pay attention to the meanings given to remittances as well as to the dollars sent. These meanings may vary significantly across cultural settings, and between different groups of migrants and their families. But they have significant implications for any attempts to leverage remittances for development purposes.

Second, a diaspora and transnational perspective illuminates migrants' perspectives on the remittance process. It problematizes the idea that migrants function simply as an economic appendage to a home-country household. This chapter has highlighted how individual dispositions and migrants' experiences in host countries mediate the desire and capacity to remit. Attentive to marginalization and abuse, this approach also makes room for discussion of the costs of remitting from migrants' perspectives, in the context of often difficult lives in the host country, and the limits to transnationalism.

Taking a diaspora and transnational perspective, thirdly, challenges some common temporal and spatial expectations about remitting. Evidence of long-term transnationalism calls us to revisit the widespread assumption that remittances decay over time, and are necessarily inversely related to integration. The focus of research might also expand to include the relatively under-researched issues of "reverse," south–north, south–south, remitting and north–north remitting.

Finally, related to the last point, this chapter, in considering remittances in relation to diaspora and transnationalism, has pointed to the contrasting contexts of migration and remitting. Beyond absolute need, disparities play a key role in shaping people's remittance practices in ways that have yet to be fully captured by comparative research.

Notes

1   This chapter draws on various previous publications, including Lindley 2009a, 2009b, and 2010.
2   The World Bank produces data on remittances, based on balance of payments information for: (1)"workers' remittances" i.e., amounts received from people resident abroad throughout the year; (2)"compensation of employees," i.e., wages, salaries, and other benefits of border, seasonal, and other non-resident workers, who formally still live in the country of origin; (3) "migrants' transfers," i.e., the net worth of the migrant transferred at time of migration or return (World Bank 2006).

References

Al-Ali, N., Black, R., and Koser, K. 2001. "The limits to transnationalism: Bosnian and Eritrean refugees in Europe as emerging transnational communities." *Ethnic and Racial Studies*, 24(4): 578–600.

Bajić, I. 2007. "The Serbian gift." *Material World*, 10, at http://www.materialworldblog.com/2007/10/the-serbian-gift/, accessed March 5, 2013.

Bakewell, O. 2008. "'Keeping them in their place': the ambivalent relationship between development and migration in Africa." *Third World Quarterly*, 29(7): 1341–1358.

Brown, R.P.C. and Poirine, B. 2005. "A model of migrants' remittances with human capital investment and intrafamilial transfers." *International Migration Review*, 39(2): 407–438.

Bryceson, D.F. and Vuorela, U. 2002. *The Transnational Family*. Oxford: Berg.

Caces, F., Arnold, F., Fawcett, J.T., and Garner, R.W. 1985. "Shadow households and competing auspices: Migration behaviour in the Philippines." *Journal of Development Economics*, 17(1): 5–25.

Cliggett, L. 2005. "Remitting the gift: Zambian mobility and anthropological insights for migration studies." *Population, Space and Place*, 11: 35–48.

de Haas, H. and Fokkema, T. 2009. "Intra-household tensions and conflicts of interest in migration decision making: a case study of the Todgha valley, Morocco." International Migration Institute Working Papers, 17, Oxford University.

Dick, S. 2002. "Liberians in Ghana: Living without humanitarian assistance." New Issues in Refugee Research, 57. Geneva: UNHCR.

Durand, J., Parrado, E.A., and Massey, D.S. 1996. "Migradollars and development: a reconsideration of the Mexican case." *International Migration Review*, 30: 423–444.

Faist, T. 2008. "Migrants as transnational development agents: an inquiry into the newest round of the migration–development nexus." *Population, Space and Place*, 14: 21–42.

Horst, C. 2007. "The Somali community in Minneapolis: Expectations and realities." In A. Kusow and S. Bjork (eds) *From Mogadishu to Dixon: The Somali Diaspora in a Global Context*, pp. 275–294. Trenton, NJ: Red Sea Press.

Kapur, D. 2003. "Remittances: the new development mantra?" In S.M. Maimbo and D. Ratha (eds) *Remittances: Development Impact and Future Prospects*, pp. 331–361. Washington, DC: World Bank.

Levitt, P. and Glick Schiller, N. 2004. "Conceptualising simultaneity: a transnational social field perspective on society." *International Migration Review*, 38(145): 595–629.

Lindley, A. 2009a. "Remittances in conflict: Some conceptual considerations." *Jahrbücher für Nationalökonomie und Statistik*, 229(6): 774–786.

Lindley, A. 2009b. "The early morning phonecall: Remittances from a refugee diaspora perspective." *Journal of Ethnic and Migration Studies*, 35(8): 1315–1334.

Lindley, A. 2010. *The Early Morning Phonecall: Somali Refugees' Remittances*. Oxford: Berghahn Books.

Lindley, A. 2011. "Remittances." In A. Betts (ed.) *Global Migration Governance*, pp. 242–265. Oxford: Oxford University Press.

Malkki, L. 1992. "National geographic: the rooting of peoples and the territorialization of national identity among scholars and refugees." *Cultural Anthropology*, 7(1): 24–44.

Marcelli, E.A. and Lowell, B.L. 2005. "Transnational twist: Pecuniary remittances and the socioeconomic integration of authorized and unauthorized Mexican immigrants in Los Angeles county." *International Migration Review*, 39(1): 69–102.

Mohapatra, S., Ratha, D., and Silwal, A. 2010. "*Outlook for remittance flows 2011–12: Recovery after the crisis, but risks lie ahead.*" *Migration and Development Brief 13*, Washington DC: World Bank, at http://go.worldbank.org/R88ONI2MQ0, accessed March 5, 2013.

Rapoport, H. and Docquier, F. 2005. "The economics of migrants' remittances." Institute for the Study of Labor Discussion Papers, 1531. Bonn: Institute for the Study of Labor.

Ratha, D. and Shaw, W. 2007. "South–south migration and remittances." World Bank Working Papers, 192. Washington DC: World Bank.

Riak Akuei, S. 2005. "Remittances as unforeseen burdens: the livelihoods and social obligations of Sudanese refugees." *Global Migration Perspectives*, 18. Geneva: Global Commission on International Migration.

Sahlins, M. 2004. *Stone Age Economics*. London: Routledge. (Originally published 1974.)

Sana, M. and Massey, D.S. 2005. "Household composition, family migration, and community context: Migrant remittances in four countries." *Social Science Quarterly*, 86(2): 509–528.

Santillán, D. and Ulfe, M. 2006. "*Destinatarios y usos de remesas. ¿Una oportunidad para las mujeres salvadoreñas?*" Serie Mujer y Desarollo, 78. Santiago de Chile: CEPAL.

Scott, J.S. 1998. *Seeing like a State: How Certain Schemes to Improve the Human Condition Have Failed*. New Haven: Yale University Press.

Stark, O. and Lucas, R. 1988. "Migration, remittances and the family." *Economic Development and Cultural Change*, 36: 465–481.

Taylor, J.E. 1999. "The new economics of labour migration and the role of remittances in the migration process." *International Migration*, 37(1): 63–88.

Van Hear, N. 2006. "'I went as far as my money would take me': Conflict, forced migration and class." In F. Crepeau, D. Nakache, and M. Collyer (eds) *Forced Migration and Global Processes: A View from Forced Migration Studies*, pp. 125–158. Lanham, MD: Lexington/ Rowman & Littlefield.

World Bank 2006. *Global Economic Prospects: Economic Implications of Remittances and Migration*. Washington, DC: World Bank.

Zelizer, V.A. 2005. *The Purchase of Intimacy*. Princeton: Princeton University Press.

Chapter 19

A Diaspora Concept That Works: Tibetan Economy and Identity in India and Canada

Timm Lau

Introduction

The Tibetan diaspora began in 1959, when the Dalai Lama's flight from the Chinese occupation of Tibet prompted an initial exodus of tens of thousands of Tibetans to India and Nepal. The Indian government under prime minister Jawaharlal Nehru decided to grant asylum to the Dalai Lama and other Tibetan refugees, and in the early 1960s the first Tibetan refugee settlements were founded in India. These settlements were administered by the Dalai Lama's Central Tibetan Administration (CTA), as well as other Tibetans who were recognized as leaders through regional or religious affiliations. Since then, many more Tibetans have trickled into South Asia from Tibet, and Tibetans have undertaken further migration to Taiwan, Australia, the United States, and Canada, as well as a number of European countries. India remains as host to the most numerous group of Tibetan migrants, estimated at 120,000; this number fluctuates because of the arrival of newcomers from Tibet each year and the return of unknown numbers to Tibet. Despite the original refugees' intention to return to Tibet once the Chinese occupation ended, in the five decades since their flight a large number of Tibetans have been born and raised in India and elsewhere. Many of these younger Tibetans have continued a difficult political struggle about the status of Tibet (see Arpi 2012 for a discussion of recent developments in the Tibetan political struggle). Positioning oneself within the Tibetan movement is an important concern for all Tibetans in the diaspora and political activities may be a part of the answer for some. However, it is the unspectacular everyday lives of Tibetans living in India and other countries around the

A Companion to Diaspora and Transnationalism, First Edition.
Edited by Ato Quayson and Girish Daswani.
© 2013 Blackwell Publishing Ltd. Published 2013 by Blackwell Publishing Ltd.

world which provide the ground for their diasporic existence, as well as the focus of this chapter. In the following paragraphs, I will introduce the themes of this chapter by introducing two Tibetans living in India and Canada.[1]

Dawa (India)

Dawa, a young man living in a Tibetan settlement in northern India, is one of the large number of Tibetans born in India. After attending a Tibetan refugee boarding school in Himachal Pradesh, he returned to his home settlement to live with his parents and his sister. In order to help make ends meet for himself and his elderly parents Dawa travels to a city in Gujarat in western India every year to undertake itinerant trade, selling sweaters during the winter months. Like thousands of other Tibetans who do this, he therefore spends a significant part of each year elsewhere in India, away from his home in the settlement. During my stay, Dawa took to visiting me occasionally late in the evening. In the setting of my rooms at night, with no one else around, he sometimes spoke frankly and highly reflectively about his personal concerns. On one such occasion, Dawa remarked upon his relationship with India: "I am a Tibetan in India and I want to have all the rights of being in India. I was born in India and I deserve the rights. Yet I am denied my rights, as a refugee. I have no rights in India." Dawa then acknowledged that he "wanted to have it both ways": he wanted to be a Tibetan, yet he was born in India and accustomed to it. Indeed, he confirmed his connection to India by saying that he very much liked it. He had traveled and seen much of India, he still traveled every year during the trade season, and he had had many pleasant and exciting experiences. Like most Tibetans in India, Dawa was also an enthusiastic follower of Bollywood films (see Lau 2010 for a discussion of Hindi film in the Tibetan diaspora in India). He told me that going back to Tibet was very difficult to imagine because he was accustomed to India, while Tibet was a place he had never seen and that he knew was very different. Raising the stakes, Dawa imagined what would happen if India did not tolerate the presence of Tibetan refugees any longer. Both potential scenarios, of having to renounce his Tibetan identity and "become Indian" or having to return to Tibet, presented insurmountable problems, as both were inconceivable to him. That night, Dawa concluded our discussion by noting that it was "very difficult to be a Tibetan in India."

Trinley (Canada)

During ethnographic research on Tibetan migration to Canada, I was invited by Trinley to interview him in his house, a large new building located in an upmarket part of the city of Calgary. Upon my arrival, he offered a choice of coffee and sweet or Tibetan tea while ushering me into the large leather sofa in his spacious living room. Trinley was a prominent member of the local Tibetan community. He had studied at the University of Calgary, where he had become an active member of the student union body before graduating, founding a company, and working for several engineering companies. Trinley explained that he had stopped working for money recently, in order to focus his energy on aiding Tibetans living in India and Canada. He had been involved in "educating" young Tibetans, speaking with them about their lives in Canada and the opportunities they had in the Canadian economy. To him, being Tibetan was both a responsibility and an asset: "Being a Tibetan, we have to ensure that our lives reflect the values associated with Tibet through our culture and Buddhism. Good things will come to us if we live that way. You see, in that way being Tibetan is like a brand. It is a positive brand if we embrace the positive qualities of being Tibetan."

According to Trinley, Tibetans in Canada could achieve successful careers while at the same time consciously living up to a high ethical standard established by the popular perception of Tibet and Tibetan Buddhism, which would in turn help them in achieving their personal and collective goals. Living in Canada, a democratic country with a strong economy, provided young Tibetans with everything they needed – it was up to them.

Both Dawa and Trinley are Tibetans who were born, raised, and educated outside of Tibet. Each of them embodies a markedly different attitude towards the Tibetan diaspora. Being a Tibetan in India presented a riddle for Dawa, as he was torn between his Tibetan roots and India as his de facto home, a place he knew and liked but in which he nonetheless perceived himself as disempowered. Trinley, on the other hand, perceived being a Tibetan in Canada as a potential position of strength, both on account of Tibetan identity being a "brand" and the relative economic strength and freedom of Canadian society. Clearly, Dawa's and Trinley's perspectives on their predicament differ markedly. I will show in this chapter that, the difference in these two perspectives notwithstanding, both are in their own ways recognizably *diasporic*. Furthermore, I will show that the experiences of economic life, in Indian local economies and in Canadian urban economies, play an important part in the construction of Tibetan perspectives on diaspora.

The Diaspora Concept and Studies of Tibetan Migration

What are the defining features of a diaspora, and how can a study of Tibetan economy and identity contribute to our understanding of the diaspora concept? Steven Vertovec warned (1997: 277) that "the current over-use and under-theorisation of the notion of 'diaspora' among academics, transnational intellectuals and 'community leaders' alike – which sees the term become a loose reference conflating categories such as immigrants, guest-workers, ethnic and 'racial' minorities, refugees, expatriates and travellers – threatens the term's descriptive usefulness." Despite this warning, and his outline of three meanings of diaspora as distinctive social form, type of consciousness, and mode of cultural production, the concept remains largely undifferentiated from other forms of migrant experience in the current literature. In anthropology, the concept of diaspora often implies the notion of a lost homeland as being central to the diasporic formation of cultural identity, centered on notions and practices which substitute and instantiate the homeland (see, e.g., Gonzalez 1992: 31; Kearney 2004: 248; Rabinowitz 1994). While seemingly distinguishing diaspora from other forms of migrant life, the prevalence of this approach has also created a hiatus in many anthropological studies, because the cultural meaning of diaspora remains undifferentiated from the social and cultural processes which create diaspora as migrant experience.

The analytical murkiness of the diaspora concept lamented by Vertovec is reflected in Tibetan studies. A brief survey of publication titles in the study of Tibetan migration since 1990 reveals that the terms refugee, exile, and diaspora are all used seemingly interchangeably to describe the same group of people.[2] Most recently, Carole McGranahan (2012) has dealt with this terminological problem by relying on chronology. For her, the term "exile" acts as an overarching umbrella category, "refugee" as a first stage of historical development, and "diaspora" as a later stage (pp.215–216). For McGranahan, the refugee stage is differentiated from the later stages, including diaspora, by being "the very difficult early decades of life in South Asia where community energy was primarily focused on subsistence," as well as by severely limited communication between Tibetans inside and outside of Tibet (2012: 215–216). The second, "growth" stage represents consolidation of Tibetan communities in India and Nepal as well as the international Tibetan political movement. Finally, McGranahan describes diaspora as the third stage characterized mainly by the further migration of Tibetans from South Asia to Asia, Australia, Europe, and North America since around the year 2000. Her distinction of a diaspora stage from a refugee stage is therefore not at first glance based on migrant experience, but rather on an externally measurable spread of Tibetans around the globe within the last decade or so. However, a smaller number of Tibetans have lived in places such as Taiwan, Switzerland, and even Canada since the 1970s. Moreover, when McGranahan invokes Tibetan experience of life outside of Tibet, it seems as though the term *exile* is made to stand in for the other stages of migrant experience (2012: 216, emphasis added):

> There is no singular experience of exile; *being a refugee or in exile or in the diaspora* is also always inflected by other things such as when one came out of Tibet or was born in exile, where one lives in the diaspora, where one's family was from in Tibet, as well as age, gender, sect, school, and what is going on in the world at any given time.

Terminological questions aside, this exhaustive list of circumstances relevant to Tibetan diasporic experience is highly useful. It displays both the connection to Tibet, as well as concern with "where one lives in the diaspora." This latter point, properly unpacked, contains within it the specifics of daily life in the host country.

Most studies of the Tibetan diaspora have generally attributed Tibet as a remote, lost homeland with central symbolic significance (see, e.g., Anand 2000; Diemberger 2002; Forbes 1989; Fürer-Haimendorf 1990; Kolås 1996; Korom 1997; Nowak 1984; Ström 1994, 1997). Tibetans in the diaspora understand that cultural and religious practice in Tibet is restrained by the Chinese authorities, and place the onus of its continuation on themselves. In this context, the symbolic presence of their spiritual leader, the Dalai Lama, has been shown to make a distinctive difference in the Tibetans' life in the diaspora in general and the struggle against cultural assimilation in particular (see, e.g., Arakeri 1998: 296–297; Forbes 1989; Fürer-Haimendorf 1990: 54; Houston and Wright 2003; McGranahan 2010, passim; Michael 1985; Subba 1988: 54; 1990: 115). The prevalent focus on cultural preservation in the literature reflects the Tibetans' own concern with cultural survival outside of Tibet. In her recent study of citizenship among Tibetan immigrants to the United States, Judith Hess (2009) uses the diaspora concept to point out the changing character of Tibetan transnational migration. She argues that Tibetan immigrants to the United States obtain citizenship but remain committed to the Tibetan cause and become "cultural ambassadors," whereas those who stay in India and Nepal remain stateless refugees out of their commitment to Tibet. Hess' focus on citizenship and activism highlights Tibetan concerns with cultural preservation and the Tibetan cause, but it does not answer the question of how diaspora as distinct from the status of refugee is formed in Tibetan migrant experience more generally, or in the absence of US citizenship, for example in India. The prevalent interest in practices of Tibetan cultural preservation and collective memory, then, has effectively mini-mized the aspect of interaction with host societies in the existing literature.

Economic activity and work present crucial social processes that enable a migrant group to construct a life-world in and with their new, post-migration surroundings. Yet, what Tibetans do for a living in the diaspora has only been mentioned in passing by a small number of studies. Annual itinerant trading with sweaters, for example, has provided the backbone of the diasporic economy for most Tibetans in India. Until my recent study of the sweater trade's importance for Tibetan belonging and non-belonging within India and its local economies, this activity had been largely ignored by academic scholars (Lau 2012). While it has been mentioned by some authors, none come close to providing an inquiry into the social relationships entailed by this trade (Arakeri 1998: 177, 194; Nowak 1984: 120–121; Ström 1994: 838–839; Subba 1990: 94). See Lau (2012) for an extended argument on the impor-tance of the sweater trade for Tibetan belonging and non-belonging within India and its local economies.

The research discussed in this chapter is concerned with the question of how regular economic activity and "work" interacts with the formation of Tibetan diasporic identities in the settings of India and Canada. In arguing for the impor-tance of economic activity in the formation of diaspora as a distinct form of migrant experience, I will explore how filling this ethnographic gap might serve to improve the diaspora concept's analytical value. The analysis of my research results presents an anthropological study of economy and identity which encompasses interaction with local host societies in the formation of diaspora, within the Tibetan transnational field. The ongoing challenge of making a living within the host society, rather than being merely a problem of refugee subsistence, will feature as a focal point in understanding how diaspora is formed as migrant experience in its respec-tive settings.

Tibetans in India

Most Tibetans in India live in refugee settlements, located throughout India but mainly in northern Indian states as well as the southern state of Karnataka. The CTA, founded by the Dalai Lama, oversees these settlements as well as social, health, and welfare services for the Tibetan communities. By Indian legislation the refugee settlements are exclusively Tibetan residential spaces, and many of them are located in proximity to the Tibetan Buddhist monasteries established in India. Most Tibetan children of secondary school age are sent to Tibetan boarding schools and live with their parents in the settlements only during school holidays. Life in the settlements predominantly revolves around Tibetan cultural and religious practices and institutions. Although their sudden flight from Tibet disrupted established patterns of residence and belonging, the Tibetans living in refugee settlements were able to form group identities which are in large part still informed by place and territory in Tibet. Along with these regional logics, prevalent hierarchical forms of leadership are also still important in the settlements today.[3] The elections of local settlement officials, for example, are inherently connected to hierarchical relationships based on status. The allegiances expressed in the election process are based on regional affiliations and the inherited hierarchical status of the leadership figures. In Tibetan sociality, it is generally of the essence to understand hierarchy and to express this understanding by behaving respectfully in the presence of elders, teachers, monks, lamas, and other persons who are in some respect one's superior. Someone showing respect and humbleness is called *ya rabs*, a person of good character – by contrast to *ma rabs*, a person of bad character. The Tibetan syllables *ma* and *ya* indicate "lower" and "higher" statuses. Therefore, the terms *ma rabs* and *ya rabs* themselves exemplify the hierarchical nature of Tibetan social concepts. This social hierarchy in the settlements is also gendered, as women are generally excluded from leading political positions. The presence of honorific registers in the Tibetan language also serves to illustrate the importance of hierarchy for Tibetan social forms. Many adults can read official Tibetan publications only with great difficulty and can become anxious and ashamed if they cannot speak well enough in front of high-status persons. The ability to speak honorific Tibetan is seen as an achievement of some distinction, this point being all the more pronounced since Tibetan culture is perceived as threatened.

While social life in the settlement revolves around Tibetan cultural and religious practices such as daily circumambulation and rituals, prayer meetings, and occasional public festivities, for many Tibetans the annual calendar also contains a significant amount of time spent in Indian local economies that are located away from the settlements. The Tibetan sweater trade started as street-hawking in the 1960s and has developed into the economic mainstay of Tibetan life in India. Whereas the early traders hawked their goods on the streets of Indian towns and villages, a concerted effort of organized traders in the 1980s enabled the construction of annual markets in many Indian cities. Today, the trade on sweater markets represents the central economic activity of Tibetan households in India. Unlike many other diasporic traders, Tibetan sweater traders do not form residential and economic enclaves in the market towns in which they do business, but return to their home settlements at the end of the trading season.

Because of their movement away from the refugee settlements, trading patterns of Tibetan itinerant traders have been described as "prolonged periods of isolation from family and community" (Ström 1994: 839), thus putting emphasis on their marginality. My ethnographic research with Tibetan traders reveals that it is inadequate to describe Tibetan itinerant traders as isolated from community, because they *form* communities. The outward form of these communities consists of associations founded by the traders of each market. The communities they incorporate are transient in that they come into being each year for the duration of the trading season, at the end of which they are suspended until the next year. In addition to the fact that they reassemble every year, the members of the market are united by further commonalities: they share Tibetan ethnicity and life in the diaspora, a common economic aim, and the experiences of the sweater trade. Their activity in Indian towns necessitates their social and economic organization as associations, in the absence of the structural and political embeddedness provided by the settlements.

We have seen earlier that hierarchy plays a central role in the Tibetan settlements. The communities of Tibetan traders are also fundamentally dependent on the organization of social hierarchy. However, by contrast to the exclusive importance of birth, descent, and gender for the negotiation of hierarchy in the settlements, ideas of education, merit, and achievement are predominant in the organization of the market associations. In the elections held among traders, they vote for those among them whom they think will be best suited as leaders. While elections for settlement officials tend to be influenced or even dominated by ideas about descent and hereditary social status, the market association elections are more exclusively based on meritocracy. Personal qualities such as skill and experience in trade and dealing with Indian officials, as well as Indian language skills were discussed with me as enabling particular candidates to be good leaders, and held up as reasons for voting for them. This did not exclude women, as I witnessed one particular female trader who had been elected as a market association leader for two consecutive terms because of her strengths in this position. This demonstrates a significant difference from the political organization and process in the settlements, where women did not play an important role in male-dominated politics. Furthermore, the decision-making process differed markedly between settlement and market. In contrast to official meetings in settlements, meetings on the market are held to facilitate an open discussion of the business at hand, in which traders actively participate. If discussions reveal that two opposing opinions prevail among the traders, a decision is made using the basic democratic device of a vote count. The meetings thus present an opportunity for participation and active decision-making by the attending traders. This differs from political processes in the settlement, in which decisions are usually made by those elected or mandated into authoritative positions, and meetings are, by contrast, held to announce the outcome of the decision. The market associations, then, represent new, democratic social organizations which are central to the Tibetan trading communities in the diaspora. While they have thus far been perceived as marginal or peripheral from a viewpoint which favors refugee settlements and exclusive Tibetan cultural practice as points of analysis, these associations present new centers of social life for a significant number of Tibetans in India and for a considerable part of their annual calendar.

In addition to this change in social organization, the trade season centrally necessitates Tibetan interaction with Indians in economic and social contexts, as the success of the trade critically depends on participation in wholesale and retail markets. The Tibetan itinerant trade in fact represents a particular form of the seasonal movement of labor which has existed in India for a long time. The socioeconomic system into which the Tibetans as niche market traders expanded successfully already existed in colonial times. By the late nineteenth century, peddlers from rural backgrounds had forged ties with urban merchants. Command of capital, credibility, and trust relationships with merchants were decisive factors for this type of trade.[4] Similarly, the Tibetan sweater trade depends crucially on the management of credit and trust relationships with sweater merchants in urban centers such as Ludhiana and Delhi (Lau 2012).

Moreover, Indian local economies are organized around deep-rooted socioeconomic ideas and norms of group belonging, which allow for both the cohesiveness of groups from the same regional and village background and the creation of group identities associated with economic activities in the labor markets in which they entered. The historical and ethnographic literature suggests that actors in Indian local economies demonstrate a proclivity to ascribe a named position to groups they perceive to function as a corporate group identifiable with a certain trade or occupation (Bayly 1978, 1983; Gooptu 2001; Falzon 2004; Robb 1993; Rudner 1994; Tarlo 1997). The classic caste description of economic organization and other group-based economic practices in India indicates this disposition to classify groups in this manner. The latter opened conceptual space for Tibetans in local market perceptions and has contributed to their new-found identity – in the Indian marketplace – as the "sweater wallahs." This identity has also helped the Tibetan market associations in their dealings with Indian municipal officials. The market associations need to renew their annual market permits, and they depend substantially on the goodwill of Indian officials to issue these permits year after year. Thus, long-term relationships established between association leaders and local officials are also essential elements in the success of the Tibetan itinerant trade.

Finally, the full ambiguity of the Tibetan itinerant trade in Indian local economies comes to the fore in the traders' relationships with customers (Lau 2012). Long-term relationships have progressively developed between traders and their customers through regular annual interactions on the market, leading to recurring visits by customers to the same market stalls, jovial and joking interactions, and invitations to Indian customers' homes. A sense of moral obligation may develop in Indian customers, who frequent the same traders every year and wish to create revenue for them, as well as in the Tibetan traders who may give favors to customers, wishing to support them on account of perceiving traits of "good people" in them. At such moments, empathetic emotional connections are displayed between traders and customers, especially where the customers – through appearance, manner, or life circumstances – mirror the Tibetans' perception of themselves as a disenfranchised group far from home. The Tibetans' fluency in Indian languages and cultural references, such as popular Bollywood songs which I once witnessed sung by a trader and her customers together, contributes to the establishment of connections. Yet, negative perceptions of customers and interactions with them in a "hostile" Indian environment are salient among the traders. As I have argued elsewhere, discursive emphasis on negative Indian traits during co-present development of long-term, trust-based relationships with Indians serves the maintenance of a separate cultural identity even as inevitable processes of rapprochement with the host society are taking place (Lau 2009).

The theme of minimized difference and potential identification is intensified in Tibetan play with identities during the sweater business season. I witnessed one young Tibetan trader in his twenties who particularly enjoyed claiming an Indian identity for himself in perfect Hindi, in face-to-face interaction with Indian customers. His sister, on the other hand, reversed the play of identity by on one occasion dressing up the two teenage daughters of their Indian landlords in the market town in Tibetan *phyu pa* dresses. This was done for an assignment at their school in which they were to present a foreign culture. She was enthusiastic about the project and taught them Tibetan phrases, even taking rare time off from her market duties to accompany them to school on the day to make sure their dresses were fitting properly. Although it was not, as in her brother's case, she who experimented with Indian identities, her enthusiasm in "lending" Tibetan identity-markers to the two Indian teenagers is significant. That young Tibetan traders in India play with identities is significant because, despite strong and antagonistic identity politics which emphasize difference, it demonstrates that these differences are de-emphasized at other times.

Tibetans in Canada

Since Tibetans first migrated from South Asia to North America in the 1990s, the United States and Canada have increasingly replaced India and Nepal as centers in the Tibetan diasporic imagination. Roused by tales of economic success and superior lifestyle, the majority of young Tibetans in India and Nepal would invariably prefer to migrate rather than remain in the settlements which have haphazardly become their home. While in India the contrast between hierarchical social organization in the settlements and meritocratic organization on the markets is highlighted by the recurrent movement of the itinerant traders between these settings, the economic positioning of Tibetans in Canadian cities rests on the latter's urban social geography. In the Canadian cities of Calgary and Toronto, Tibetans generally live dispersed throughout the city. Only the Queen Street/Bathurst Street area in Toronto provides a hub of Tibetan restaurants and some residential concentration. The TD Canada Trust bank, for example, has recognized this demographic and hired Tibetans to provide customer service in their local branch, where they are able to easily converse with their Tibetan customers who may not speak English very well. Nonetheless, urban living in Canada is clearly characterized by the absence of the dichotomizing contrast in social-geographic and economic spaces presented by the refugee settlements/market towns dyad in India. Although some Tibetans find work with Tibetan employers, for example in Tibetan restaurants, the majority follow more individual economic trajectories within the opportunities provided by the Canadian host society. In Canada, Tibetans are economically active in such diverse occupations as restaurant- and shop-owner, engineer, photographer, graphic designer, caregiver, or travel agent. Social or economic organizations comparable to the trade associations founded by Tibetans in India are not established in Canada.

In interviews about their economic trajectories in Canada, Tibetans in Calgary and Toronto generally stressed the importance of networking. On the one hand, Tibetans helped other Tibetans who had newly arrived in Canada by finding them jobs with their own past or present employers. This networking amongst Tibetans was very common and seen as an essential part of Tibetan sociality in Canada: no Tibetan arrival in Canada was "left alone" in their new environment. The centrality of finding a first job, and the role of Tibetan networks in achieving this, was readily acknowledged by all my informants. The networks of Tibetans in Canada extend across North America and back to South Asia. Many Tibetans came to Canada through the United States, traveling up through the border and applying for asylum upon arrival. Lasting connections between Tibetans in different localities in North America as well as South Asia are maintained, and the inherent networking capacities actualized, through new technologies readily available in Canadian urban environments. Social networking on the internet and on smart phones, through services such as Facebook, are foremost amongst them. Communication and information thus travel the globe electronically in the Tibetan diaspora, and money does the same. Remittances from Canada and the United States are highly significant markers of the global transnational relationships established between Tibetans in North America and South Asia. New buildings erected by Tibetan families in their settlements in India were often financed with money sent back from North America. The points of origin of remittances indicate that economically also, North America provides the center to a South Asian periphery.

Some Tibetan informants in Canada directly referenced the importance of global networks for their economic activity. Importantly, the positions of center and periphery in this context are not fixed but flexible. For one informant working as a photographer, for example, the demise of North American print media meant that India, the place he had left to come to Canada, once again became an important center for his career trajectory. There was less and less work for him in North America, while his previous employer in India went from strength to strength, and he considered returning to India to take up work there again. Another Tibetan informant utilized his knowledge and network of Indian trade contacts to start a new business in Toronto. His business in an up-market retailing area of the city sold Indian and Tibetan jewelry, garments, and other luxury items to, presumably, wealthy Canadian customers and tourists. His previous experience in manufacturing goods in India, as well as the extensive network of business contacts he accumulated during decades of economic activity in India, were absolutely essential to his ability to start his Canadian business.

Research in Canadian urban centers highlights the importance of individual Tibetan economic trajectories in urban economies, as well as networking activities and transnational connections. In Canada, transnational connections to the Indian subcontinent provide important economic pathways for some Tibetans, as well as the potential for shifts of center–periphery relationships in their economic careers. Tibetan informants in Canada directly referenced the importance of global networks for their economic activity. Very importantly, however, they also referenced these global networks in discussing their sense of identity in the diaspora. The question "where are you from?" held multiple possible answers for Tibetans in Canada: they had lived in a Canadian city for a certain amount of time; they had lived in one or more of the many Tibetan settlements in India before this; they had visited a Tibetan boarding school in another location in India for a long period of their lives; and some of them were born in Tibet before being sent to India for education by their families. The connections one had with other Tibetans through shared experiences, and the instantiations of these connections, for example through shared economic or political projects, wallposts and messages on Facebook, or other means of exchange and indications of belonging, made for a much easier and in some ways more direct answer to the question of identity. "Work," however, was a central concern for my Tibetan informants in Toronto and Calgary in this context also. This term included volunteering for charitable organizations, most often in the context of the Tibetan movement but sometimes outside of it. As one of my informants in Toronto put it: "I volunteered for non-profit organizations when I studied. This was important to me and it still is . . . my work in publishing is great and I enjoy doing it, but it is not everything to me. It is important to do service for others, in Tibetan culture, and as a Tibetan I feel it is important to do this."

My research suggests that Tibetan identities emerging in the Canadian context are more translocal than localized, and incorporate new understandings of Tibetan cultural identity. As my informant Trinley's statement in the introduction to this chapter demonstrates, such understandings may reflect an entrepreneurial inflection in which identity may even be explicitly seen as a kind of "brand." Furthermore, both paid and unpaid activities, such as volunteering for charitable organizations, are understood as "work." This work is in turn understood also to "do work" on one's identity as a Tibetan person in the diaspora. Tibetan identity and economic activities in Canada, as well as their respective construction, are thus understood to be interconnected by Tibetans themselves.

Conclusion

Engseng Ho's (2006) study of the Hadrami diaspora deals with a people who have been dispersed across the Indian Ocean for hundreds of years, rather than recently displaced. However, his specific approach to studying Hadramis presents an important point of overlap with my study of the Tibetan diaspora. Ho discusses the transregional space in which Hadrami groups live, and the historical importance of the journeys of goods, emissaries, pilgrims, and religious adepts. He points out that different sets of social relations travel along these routes, making for a "nonhomogeneous surface," and that points along the circuit "serve as a node in different circuits, being central in one but peripheral in another" (p. 120).

The interplay of center and periphery in different circuits is apparent in the Tibetan diaspora in India and Canada. In India, the refugee settlement/market town dyad presents a shifting center/periphery relationship: in the settlement, substitutes for the Tibetan homeland provided by the CTA, Tibetan monasteries, and other institutions are squarely at the center and the Indian host society at the periphery. During the itinerant trade, however, the annually re-established market associations, trade activities, and interaction with the Indian host society become central, whereas what determined life in the settlements becomes more peripheral. This shift in center/periphery relationships is also evident in the changing emphasis on difference between Tibetan and Indian, leading to a de-emphasizing play with identities on the market. But the shift is perhaps most clearly seen in the changing importance of hierarchies of gender and inherited status: they are central in the settlements, but become peripheral and replaced by capabilities and achievements in trade activities, which take center-stage on the markets.

As Ho also describes for the Hadrami diaspora (2006: 121), regional destinations in the transnational Tibetan diaspora can create potentials that allow mobile actors to benefit from a kind of geographical arbitrage between them. This arbitrage is enabled by flows of knowledge and information as much as the flow of goods. Here, again, nodal points may become central or peripheral, such as when the retreat of previously central print media in North America shifted the economic center for one informant back to India.

My research on the Tibetan diaspora in India and Canada demonstrates that a focus on interaction with host societies as well as transnational flows allows for the investigation of simultaneous and diverse centers in diasporic constellations. In the specific interactions which constitute a diasporic lifeworld, illustrated by the Tibetan itinerant trade in India and economic activities in Canada, the local may at times provide the center and the original homeland or its substitutes the periphery, and there may be multiple centers of diasporic existence. The analysis of these elements illuminates the paradoxical co-presence of "here" and "there" typical of diasporic formations, and the identities created within them. This point complements the existing strengths of cultural analysis in diaspora studies, which places an emphasis on the homeland. Such studies show that emerging diasporic practice concerns the creation and maintenance of difference in the face of inevitable social relationships with the local "here," by individually and collectively identifying with "there." Once developed, such practice maintains diasporic identities by engendering the important forms of cultural preservation relating to the "lost homeland." However, both identification with the homeland and relationships to local society have to be made and remade anew. Relationships with the local have to be remade precisely because they are a source of diaspora as social form and experience. This is true even where these relationships have existed for generations, as they are always in flux and subject to change. In other words, the particular qualities which make a subject diasporic in a certain place and social group change over time just as the ways of relating to local society change. Approaching diaspora formation in this way explains why diasporic difference is "a process of continual renegotiation in new circumstances of dangerous and creative coexistence" (Clifford 1997: 276).

Including the importance of local social interaction to the formation of diaspora, then, serves to clarify the concept by separating the social and historical processes that constitute diaspora from its cultural meaning. Diaspora as distinct from the state of being a refugee and other forms of migrant experience exists only where relationships with the host society have developed to a sufficient extent, making it possible for the latter to shift from periphery to center, from "strange" to local, and from the absence of home to a kind of home. Hence, relationships with the local host society are of great consequence in the formation of diaspora, because they are constitutive of diasporic consciousness as distinct from other forms of migrant experience.

Notes

1 Fieldwork for this chapter in India took place during 15 months in 2004/2005, supported by the Wenner-Gren Foundation's Dissertation Fieldwork Grant and the Reginald Smith Research Studentship at King's College, Cambridge. Fieldwork in Canada (Calgary and Toronto) took place in 2010/2011, supported by the AXA Research Fund's Postdoctoral Research Fellowship. I have anonymized the personal names of my informants.

2 For "refugee" see Diehl 1997; Grent 2002; Klieger 1997; Prost 2006; Subba 1990. For "exile" see Frechette 2004; Huber 2001; McGranahan 2005. For "diaspora" see Anand 2000, 2002; Calkowski 1997; Klieger 2002; Korom 1997; Ström 1997; Yeh 2002.

3 As Carole McGranahan states (2005: 573), "despite homogenizing and hegemonizing efforts, regional affiliations and allegiances to both lay and religious district leaders, such as village chiefs and lamas, retain both practical and symbolic importance in exile." See Lau (2008) for an extended argument on Tibetan hierarchical sociality and the importance of the Tibetan emotional concept *ngo tsha* in its reproduction.

4 Historical work by de Haan (1993) and Gooptu (2001) shows that this system accommodated seasonal movement of labor such as incoming labor migration to cities during the winter months, as well as diverse forms of labor which included street-hawkers and petty traders. The clearest indication that small-scale peddling of goods was a common economic activity in India is given by Bhattacharya (2003).

References

Anand, D. 2000. "(Re)imagining nationalism, identity and representation in the Tibetan diaspora of South Asia." *Contemporary South Asia*, 9(3): 271–287.

Anand, D. 2002. "A guide to Little Lhasa in India: the role of symbolic geography of Dharamsala in constituting Tibetan diasporic identity." In C.P. Klieger (ed.) *Tibet, Self, and the Tibetan Diaspora*, pp. 11–36. Proceedings of the Ninth Seminar of the International Association for Tibetan Studies, Leiden: Brill.

Arakeri, A.V. 1998. *Tibetans in India. The Uprooted People and their Cultural Transplantation.* New Delhi: Reliance Publishing House.

Arpi, C. 2012. "Turning points in the Tibetan Movement – the latest shift: From Dharamsala to Eastern Tibet." In *Current State of Affairs in Tibet: Reasons? Papers Presented at the Conference – A Report.* Tibet Series II, 2012/4, New Delhi: FNVA.

Bayly, C.A. 1978. "Indian merchants in a 'traditional' setting: Benares, 1780–1830." In A. Hopkins and C. Dewey (eds) *The Imperial Impact: Studies in the Economic History of Africa and India*, pp. 171–193. London: Athlone Press for the Institute of Commonwealth Studies.

Bayly, C.A. 1983. *Rulers, Townsmen and Bazaars: North Indian Society in the Age of British Expansion, 1770–1870.* Cambridge: Cambridge University Press.

Bhattacharya, N. 2003. "Predicaments of mobility: Peddlers and itinerants in nineteenth-century northwestern India." In C. Markovits, J. Pouchepadass, and S. Subrahmanyam (eds) *Society and Circulation*, pp. 163–214. Delhi: Permanent Black.

Calkowski, M.S. 1997. "The Tibetan diaspora and the politics of performance." In F.J. Korom (ed.) *Tibetan Culture in the Diaspora. Proceedings of the Seventh Seminar of the International Association for Tibetan Studies*, pp. 51–58. Wien: Verlag der Österreichischen Akademie der Wissenschaften.

Clifford, J. 1997. *Routes – Travel and Translation in the Late Twentieth Century.* Cambridge, MA: Harvard University Press.

de Haan, A. 1993. "Migrant labour in Calcutta jute mills: Class, instability and control." In P. Robb (ed.) *Dalit Movements and the Meanings of Labour in India*, pp. 271–301. Delhi: Oxford University Press.

Diehl, K. 1997. "When Tibetan refugees rock, paradigms roll: Echoes from Dharamsala's musical soundscape." In F.J. Korom (ed.) *Constructing Tibetan Culture: Contemporary Perspectives*, pp. 122–159. Quebec: World Heritage Press.

Diemberger, H. 2002. "The people of Porong and concepts of territory." In K.Buffetrille and H. Diemberger (eds) *Territory and Identity in Tibet and the Himalayas. Proceedings of the Ninth Seminar of the International Association for Tibetan Studies*, pp. 33–55. Leiden: Brill.

Falzon, M.-A. 2004. *Cosmopolitan Connections: The Sindhi Diaspora, 1860–2000.* Leiden: Brill.

Forbes, A.A. 1989. *Settlements of Hope: An Account of Tibetan Refugees in Nepal.* Cambridge, MA: Cultural Survival.

Frechette, A. 2004. *Tibetans in Nepal. The Dynamics of International Assistance Among a Community in Exile.* New York: Berghahn Books.

Fürer-Haimendorf, C. von 1990. *The Renaissance of Tibetan Civilization.* Oracle, AZ: Synergetic Press.

Gonzalez, N.L. 1992. *Dollar, Dove and Eagle: One Hundred Years of Palestinian Migration to Honduras.* Ann Arbor: Michigan University Press.

Gooptu, N. 2001. *The Politics of the Urban Poor in Early Twentieth-Century India.* Cambridge: Cambridge University Press.

Grent, N. 2002. "Polyandry in Dharamsala: Plural-husband marriage in a Tibetan refugee community in northwest India." In P.C. Klieger (ed.) *Tibet, Self, and the Tibetan*

Diaspora: Voices of Difference. Proceedings of the Ninth Seminar of the International Association for Tibetan Studies, pp. 105–138. Leiden: Brill.

Hess, J.M. 2009. *Immigrant Ambassadors: Citizenship and Belonging in the Tibetan Diaspora.* Stanford: Stanford University Press.

Ho, E. 2006. *The Graves of Tarim: Genealogy and Mobility Across the Indian Ocean.* Berkeley: University of California Press.

Houston, S. and Wright, R. 2003. "Making and remaking Tibetan diasporic identities." *Social & Cultural Geography*, 4(2): 217–232.

Huber, T. 2001. "Shangri-La in exile: Representations of Tibetan identity and transnational culture." In T. Dodin and H. Räther (eds) *Imagining Tibet: Perceptions, Projections and Fantasies*, pp. 357–372. Boston, MA: Wisdom Publications.

Kearney, M. 2004. *Changing Fields of Anthropology: From Local to Global.* Lanham, MD: Rowman & Littlefield.

Klieger, P.C. 1997. "Shangri-La and hyperreality: a collision in Tibetan refugee expression." In F.J. Korom (ed.) *Tibetan Culture in the Diaspora. Proceedings of the Seventh Seminar of the International Association for Tibetan Studies*, pp. 33–51.Vienna: Verlag der Österreichischen Akademie der Wissenschaften.

Klieger, P.C. 2002. "Engendering Tibet: Power, self, and change in the diaspora." In P.C. Klieger (ed.) *Tibet, Self, and the Tibetan Diaspora: Voices of Difference. Proceedings of the Ninth Seminar of the International Association for Tibetan Studies*, pp. 139–154. Leiden: Brill.

Kolås, Å. 1996. "Tibetan nationalism: the politics of religion." *Journal of Peace Research*, 35(1): 51–66.

Korom, F.J. 1997. "Introduction. Place, space and identity: the cultural, economic and aesthetic politics of Tibetan diaspora." In F.J. Korom (ed.) *Tibetan Culture in the Diaspora. Proceedings of the Seventh Seminar of the International Association for Tibetan Studies*, pp. 1–8. Vienna: Verlag der Österreichischen Akademie der Wissenschaften.

Lau, T. 2008. "Understanding Tibetan shame and hierarchy through emotional experience in fieldwork." In L. Chua, C. High, and T. Lau (eds) *How Do We Know? Evidence, Ethnography and the Making of Anthropological Knowledge*, pp. 157–178. Newcastle-upon-Tyne: Cambridge Scholars.

Lau, T. 2009. "Tibetan fears and Indian foes: Fears of cultural extinction and antagonism as discursive strategy." *vis-à-vis: Explorations in Anthropology*, 9(1): 81–90.

Lau, T. 2010. "The Hindi film's romance and Tibetan notions of harmony: Emotional attachments and personal identity in the Tibetan diaspora in India." Special issue, *Journal of Ethnic and Migration Studies* 36(6): 967–987. Reprinted in M. Svašek (ed.) *Emotions and Human Mobility: Ethnographies of Movement.* London: Routledge, 2012.

Lau, T. 2012. "Sweater business: Commodity exchange and the mediation of agency in the Tibetan itinerant sweater trade in India." In M. Svašek (ed.) *Moving Objects, Moving Subjects: Transnationalism, Cultural Production and Emotions*, pp. 96–116. Oxford: Berghahn Books.

McGranahan, C. 2005. "Truth, fear, and lies: Exile politics and arrested histories of the Tibetan resistance." *Cultural Anthropology*, 20(4): 570–600.

McGranahan, C. 2010. *Arrested Histories: Tibet, the CIA, and Memories of a Forgotten War.* Durham, NC: Duke University Press.

McGranahan, C. 2012. "Mao in Tibetan disguise: History, ethnography, and excess." *HAU: Journal of Ethnographic Theory*, 2(1): 213–245.

Michael, F. 1985. "Survival of a culture: Tibetan refugees in India." *Asian Survey*, 25(7): 737–744.

Nowak, M. 1984. *Tibetan Refugees: Youth and the New Generation of Meaning*. New Brunswick: Rutgers University Press.

Prost, A. 2006. "The problem with 'rich refugees': Sponsorship, capital, and the informal economy of Tibetan refugees." *Modern Asian Studies*, 40(1): 233–253.

Rabinowitz, D. 1994. "The common memory of loss: Political mobilization among Palestinian citizens in Israel." *Journal of Anthropological Research*, 50: 27–44.

Robb, P. 1993. "Meanings of labour in Indian social context." In P. Robb (ed.) *Dalit Movements and the Meanings of Labour in India*, pp. 1–67. New Delhi: Oxford University Press.

Rudner, D.W. 1994. *Caste and Capitalism in Colonial India*. Berkeley: University of California Press.

Ström, A.K. 1994. "Tibetan refugees in India: Aspects of socio-cultural change." In P. Kvaerne (ed.) *Tibetan Studies. Proceedings of the 6th Seminar of the International Association for Tibetan Studies*, pp. 834–847. Oslo: Institute for Comparative Research in Human Culture.

Ström, A.K. 1997. "Between Tibet and the West: On traditionality, modernity and the development of monastic institutions in the Tibetan diaspora." In F.J. Korom (ed.) *Tibetan Culture in the Diaspora. Proceedings of the Seventh Seminar of the International Association for Tibetan Studies*, pp. 33–50. Vienna: Verlag der Österreichischen Akademie der Wissenschaften.

Subba, T.B. 1988. "Social adaptation of the Tibetan refugees in the Darjeeling–Sikkim Himalayas." *Tibet Journal*, 13(3): 49–57.

Subba, T.B. 1990. *Flight and Adaptation: Tibetan Refugees in the Darjeeling–Sikkim Himalaya*. Dharamsala: Library of Tibetan Works and Archives.

Tarlo, E. 1997. "The genesis and growth of a business community: a case study of Vaghri street traders in Ahmedabad." In P. Cadène and D. Vidal (eds) *Webs of Trade: Dynamics of Business Communities in Western India*, pp. 53–84. New Delhi: Manohar.

Vertovec, S. 1997. "Three meanings of 'diaspora', exemplified among South Asian Religions." *Diaspora*, 6(3): 277–299.

Yeh, E. 2002. "Will the real Tibetan please stand up! Identity politics in the Tibetan diaspora." In P.C. Klieger (ed.) *Tibet, Self, and the Tibetan Diaspora: Voices of Difference. Proceedings of the Ninth Seminar of the International Association for Tibetan Studies*, pp. 229–254. Leiden: Brill.

Chapter 20

Cell Phones and Transnationalism in Africa

Wisdom J. Tettey

Introduction

The total number of international migrants in the world has increased over the past decade from about 150 million in 2000 to about 214 million in 2010, indicating that one out of every 33 persons today lives in a country other than that of their birth, compared to one out of every 35 a decade earlier (IOM 2011). An estimated 19.3 million Africans live outside their countries of origin, comprising almost 2 percent of the continent's total population (UN 2009). The annual rate of growth of Africa's migrant stock, between 2005 and 2010, stood at 1.7 percent (UN 2009). Simultaneous with the growth in the geographical dispersion of people from their places of origin is the phenomenal jump in the rate at which information and communication technologies (ICTs) are spreading. Consequently, we are seeing a convergence of these processes as ethnoscapes intersect with technoscapes in transnational circuits. This convergence is helping to compress time and space among various geographical areas and peoples and revolutionizing communicative practices within those spaces.

One technology that has contributed in unexpected and unprecedented ways towards bridging the physical, social, political, and emotional distance between places of domicile and places of origin, is the cellular phone. Overall, 90 percent of the global population, including 80 percent of those in rural areas, now has access to mobile networks, with 143 countries providing 3G services, in 2010, compared to 97 three years earlier. The International Telecommunications Union estimates (ITU 2010) suggest that 2010 would end with global subscriptions to mobile cellular subscriptions standing at about 5.3 billion. According to the organization (2010: 3),

A Companion to Diaspora and Transnationalism, First Edition.
Edited by Ato Quayson and Girish Daswani.
© 2013 Blackwell Publishing Ltd. Published 2013 by Blackwell Publishing Ltd.

The total number of SMS sent globally tripled between 2007 and 2010, from an estimated 1.8 trillion to a staggering 6.1 trillion. In other words, close to 200,000 text messages are sent every second. . . . Assuming an average cost of USD 0.07 per SMS, in 2010 SMS traffic is generating an estimated USD 812,000 every minute (or around USD 14,000 every second). In 2009, SMS revenue accounted for 12% of China's largest mobile operator's total revenue. The Philippines and the United States combined accounted for 35% of all SMS sent in 2009.

Much of the growth in mobile telephony, just as is the case with international migration, is taking place in the developing world. While mobile cellular telephony is registering marginal growth, and reaching saturation point, in the developed world, the overall picture shows that "the developing world is increasing its share of mobile subscriptions from 53% of total . . . at the end of 2005 to 73% at the end of 2010," with the expectation that penetration rates in those countries would hit 68 percent at the end of 2010 (ITU 2010: 2). It needs to be acknowledged that these trends are not uniform and that the remarkable expansion in access to cellular technology in Asia (particularly in China and India) belies differences within the developing world. This recognition does not, however, diminish the extensive growth in other regions. Thus, while Africa's expected penetration rate of 41 percent by the close of 2010 is still a far cry from the global estimate of 76 percent (ITU 2010), there is no denying the fact that the expansion of cellular services on the continent is nothing short of phenomenal.

The extent of the cellular phone revolution in Africa is brought into sharp relief by comparing the above data to available statistics for the internet. At 9.6 percent in 2010, Africa's internet penetration rate not only lags behind the global average of 30 percent, but also the developing country average of 21 percent (ITU 2010). Data for fixed broadband lines also reveal the extent to which they pale in comparison to mobile phones. In contrast to the mobile phone penetration rate of 41 percent in Africa, the corresponding figure for fixed broadband subscription was a miniscule 1 percent in 2010. In addition to inadequate infrastructure which imposes constraints on expansion of, and access to, these services, high costs of broadband services also make them unaffordable for a significant number of citizens. As the ITU (2010: 7) observes, "in 2009, an entry-level fixed (wired) broadband connection cost on average 190 PPP$ per month in developing countries, compared to only 28 PPP$ per month in developed countries. This has significant implications for the uptake of ICT services, which is much higher for lower-cost mobile cellular compared to higher-priced fixed broadband."

In view of the increasing distance that migration has created between those who emigrate and their compatriots at home, the networks of diaspora existence that emerge, and the facilitating role that new ICTs, particularly cell phones, are playing to connect people, it has become "necessary to evaluate not only the use of mobile phones among immigrant communities but also to assess the communicative practices and appropriation of ICTs on the other end of the transnational connection" (Benítez 2006: 191). Various studies show that as mobility outside people's immediate environs grows, communication technologies like the cell phone have not only become convenient but imperative in some instances (see Alonso and Oiarzabal 2010; Thompson 2009). Johanson and Denison (2011), in their study of the Chinese diaspora in Italy, conclude that the technology is a survival device that facilitates both a network of compatriots in virtual form and the transfer of resources to their homeland (see also Stern and Messer 2009). This chapter examines the extent to which the African diaspora, and its links with home, reflects the dovetailing of ethnoscapes and technoscapes. It does so by exploring the intersections of trans-nationalism, cellular phones, and the communicative forms that they generate as well as their impact at the individual and societal levels.

Understanding the Context for the Cell Phone Revolution in Africa

As noted above, Africa has seen significant expansion in cell phone use and services, with Etzo and Collender (2010: 659) arguing that "only superlatives seem appropriate to describe the mobile phone 'revolution' – its impact and its potential – in Africa." Indeed, observers of the cellular phone market agree that the continent is the current global leader in the technology's rate of adoption, with subscription rates outstripping any other region over the last several years (Etzo and Collender 2010; Brady, Dyson, and Asela 2008: 388; Scott *et al.* 2004). Jack and Suri (2010: 1) observe that:

> Mobile phone technology has reduced communication costs in many parts of the developing world from prohibitive levels to amounts that are, in comparison, virtually trivial. Nowhere has this transformation been as acute as in sub-Saharan Africa, where networks of both fixed line communication and physical transportation infrastructure are often inadequate, unreliable, and dilapidated. While mobile phone calling rates remain high by world standards, the technology has allowed millions of Africans to leap-frog the land-line en route to 21st century connectivity.

There are several reasons for the extensive leapfrogging that the continent has enjoyed in the area of cellular telephony. These include expensive and inadequate fixed lines, widespread deregulation of the telecommunications industry in many countries, the ingenuity of Africans in facilitating access to, and use of, the technology, and the development of innovative business models and marketing ideas by cell phone companies that are efficacious and appropriate for the African context. Part of the reason for the unprecedented spread of the technology is the fact that service providers did not limit themselves to the conventional practice of targeting urban areas, but cultivated a large clientele base in rural and remote communities as well (Scott *et al.* 2004, ii). Brady and her colleagues (2008: 388) capture these developments very well when they note that:

The high cost of fixed-line services and their absence in many remote communities, combined with the deregulation of the telephone market has fueled this unexpected exponential growth. . . . New design approaches in Africa have also demonstrated that the screens of mobile devices can be designed to be usable by illiterate or semi-literate people with strong visual-pictorial cultural traditions. . . . Moreover, Africans have devised practices which overcome the challenges of the high cost of mobile phones relative to average income and rechargeability issues where electricity supplies are limited. Village entrepreneurs make a living by levying community members for the use of their mobile phone on a per use basis, while other entrepreneurs with spare car batteries (recharged at the nearest town with an electricity supply) will power up mobile phones for a fee.

Based on the evidence provided above, it is no wonder that some analysts "conclude . . . that phones (especially mobiles) are already part of African culture and are not just for the elite" (Scott *et al.* 2004: 1).

One of the reasons for the cell phone's role in qualitatively enhancing the ability of geographically dispersed members of a particular network or community to interact in such hitherto unimaginable, but increasingly common, ways is the relatively low costs that callers incur. As has been noted in other contexts, "increasing access to inexpensive international telephone calls has been instrumental in the very formation of what we now call transnational families" (Şenyürekl and Detzner 2009: 809; see also Stern and Messer 2009: 670). Friends, relatives, and members of other social networks are, therefore, not only able to stay in touch, but are able to do so more frequently than would have been the case under other communication regimes, such as those based on fixed phone lines or the postal system.

While fixed phone lines have the capacity to provide some of the services that are available on the cell phone (e.g., multiway calling, speaking phones, etc.), they are unable to match the near ubiquity and ease of access that characterize their wireless counterpart. The fixed-line infrastructure in many African countries is limited in geographical scope and carrying capacity. The continent had 1.6 fixed telephone lines per 100 inhabitants in 2010, compared to a world average of 17.1 (ITU World Telecommunications/ICT Indicators Database 2010, 14th edn).[1] As a result of this limitation and the corruption that characterizes installation of the service, many ordinary citizens are unable to avail themselves of it. Furthermore, the cost of maintaining the service seems to quickly get out of the reach of many people who are lucky enough to get them installed. The situation is made worse by the unreliability of the lines due to poor maintenance by some telecom providers. In the context of poor services, many subscribers are shifting to cell phones, which have the convenience of portability without the burden of fixed costs that come with land lines. In the words of Donner (2009: 91), "as technologies go, mobile phones are quite flexible. GSM and CDMA networks provide coverage to homes, to workplaces, even to the wilderness. People carry handsets with them as they move from place to place and between social situations." Moreover, the fact that incoming calls are generally free means that one can own a phone without incurring more than the initial subscription cost and the minimum amount needed to keep it active. It is for the foregoing reasons that cell phone subscription in Africa significantly dwarfs landline subscriptions. In 2010 there were 41.4 cell phone subscriptions for every 100 people compared to only 1.6 landlines for the same number of inhabitants (ITU World Telecommunications/ICT Indicators Database 2010, 14th edn).

As staggering as the data on cell phone subscriptions are, it is worth mentioning that the sociology of cell phone use in Africa is such that the number of people who use the phone is much larger than subscription numbers might suggest. This is because while the phone may be owned by an individual, the ecology of those who use it to make or receive calls is more extensive. This reality is captured by the following observation in the Grassfields of Cameroon:

> MTN and Orange, the two leading network providers in Cameroon, offer a very limited or no network in Zhoa. One of the few spots where it has been possible to access the Orange network for a few years now is right in front of Shehu Usmanu's shop. . . . His shop has become the village phone booth.
>
> He charges FCFA 300 per call, and says that as many as seven people a day come to make calls. He receives many calls and SMS messages for onward transmission to fellow villagers, requesting them to come and wait for calls at a specified time or sometimes simply exchanging news and information with family and friends. (de Bruijn, Nyamnjoh, and Angwafo 2010: 273)

The cell phone's advantage over other forms of ICT, in bridging the physical distance created by migration, goes beyond fiscal accessibility. It also transcends the constraints of illiteracy because interactants are able to communicate verbally using languages with which they are conversant. Thus, unlike internet-enabled platforms such as email or Skype, which require conversance in the major international languages and a basic level of computer literacy, cell phones are relatively unconstrained by these factors. Many illiterate Africans are adept at dialing numbers themselves or can have numbers of their contacts programmed on their handsets with speed dials that they can easily figure out. It is also the case that many transnational calls are initiated by members of the diaspora and so the recipient only needs to press the color-coded and/or easily identifiable answer button and they are in communication with the caller.

Social Networks and Absent Presences in Transnational Circuits

Cell phones have transformed transnational communication through the redefinition of "presences" and "absences" and the increasing exercise of post-corporeal agency (Pertierra 2005). Prior to the cell phone revolution, physical absence meant that migrant communities were, to a very large extent, unable to engage in synchronous interaction with their relatives and others within their social circles left behind in their countries of origin. Messages had to be sent by regular mail or relayed through third parties, with attendant delays, filtering, or loss of confidentiality. They were effectively largely disembedded from the web of social interactions that constituted the milieu of their previous lives. With the coming of cell phones, and their commonplace use, however, interactants can now overcome these constraints. While they are still physically removed from each other, lack of propinquity does not necessarily translate into absence, as they can be brought into many activities that may be taking place outside their immediate physical environment. The cell phone has thus enabled "the agency of the absent. To understand this agency we have to treat it as the outcome of a process in which distance is created; in which displacement is controlled; in which something is kept present whilst also being lost" (Callon and Law 2004: 10). As Vertovec points out (2004: 222): "Whereas throughout the world non-migrant families commonly have discussions across a kitchen table, now many families whose members are relocated through migration conduct the same everyday discussions in real time across oceans." In fact, it is not uncommon now to see several members of an African family sit or stand around a cell phone, at each end of the home–diaspora circuit, engaging in a conversation which various individuals are expected to contribute to or have a stake in. This communicative practice has been made easier by the speaker function of the cell phone which enables the replication of a common mode of conversation in Africa – simultaneous and multiple aural and verbal engagement among interactants. Multiway calling functions have also allowed multi-site conversations that bring together people located in more than two physical spaces. Someone in London, for example, is able to call a relative in Accra (Ghana), and have both of them linked to another relative in Doha (Qatar). The technology has, indeed, become a "social glue of migrant transnationalism" (Vertovec 2004) and facilitates speedy assembly and mobilization of multiple parties to an issue.

The cell phone is allowing people in transnational spaces to engage directly with, respond more quickly to, and keep up with developments in their places of origin in a manner that they could not do before the advent of the possibilities offered by the cell phone. Their absent presence is demonstrated, for example, when they take part in medical decisions regarding a loved one back home or funeral arrangements for a departed relative (see Gastaldo, Gooden, and Massaquoi 2005). The opportunity to participate in these decisions is valued significantly by many Africans in the diaspora who express frustration about decisions that are made by others, sometimes presumably on their behalf, the financial burden of which is disproportionately borne by them. As will be discussed later, cell phone technology also presents opportunities for financial transfers to be made more expeditiously in support of such decisions.

While the emotional dimension of the transnational experience is as old as the phenomenon of migration itself, its contemporary expression among Africans separated by physical space has been enhanced by the deterritoriality of interaction that cell phones have enabled. These expressions take various forms, including a text message or phone call through which a person engages another for emotional succour as he/she goes through the vicissitudes of life in a different country, shares the joy of a positive experience, or seeks spiritual advice on what to do. For a lot of Africans negotiating their existence in a new location, sometimes with no local network of support or a social circle, links with home are their best way of maintaining emotional and psychological balance (see Horst and Miller 2005).

Prior to the advent of cell phones, these migrants were compelled to deal with their emotional and psychological needs by themselves, or wait for extensive periods of time to get a response to a letter detailing their circumstances. In the absence of a listening ear or during the drudgery of waiting for the mail, the situation may exact a toll on their lives. With the convenience of the cell phone, they can engage with their trusted relatives and friends for emotional sustenance immediately they have an issue to deal with. On the other side of the divide, those left at home can also lean on their friends and relatives in the diaspora with a phone call or a text message when circumstances warrant. The following words from a mother in Harare, Zimbabwe, illustrate how the spatio-temporal compression made possible by cell phones has facilitated emotional connections:

> My son went to London in 2000 and I have not met him since. However, my cell phone keeps me in touch with him and if there is a problem here I can phone or text him a message. When he sends me money he communicates with me using the cell phone. The cell phone has brought me closer to my beloved son. (Kwaramba 2010)

The flip side to the emotional catharsis made possible by the cell phone is a new regime of anxieties that result when various parties are unable to get through to each other for whatever reason. Whereas relatives could, in the past, go about their lives for extended periods without being concerned that they had not heard from each other, the era of the cell phone has made them uncomfortable with lulls in communication. They wonder what is wrong and worry when they do not hear from each other over periods of time that would not have elicited such reactions in the past.

The circumstances under which some Africans leave their countries of origin, such as without proper documentation, result in many sojourners remaining incommunicado for significant periods of time as they go through the travails of navigating their new worlds. Illegal immigrants may wander the transnational circuit with no sense of rootedness for a long time during which they are either unable or unwilling to contact relatives except, at best, through letters. The itinerant nature of their existence means that relatives are unable to get in touch with them at specific locations. Now with cell phones and SIM cards that can be easily purchased in various locations around the world, these individuals are not only able to maintain regular contact with people back home, if they so choose, but can also get in touch with other compatriots or acquaintances in their new locations, thereby harnessing some social capital for their survival in these new locales. In those cases where they choose not to contact relatives, for one reason or the other, the latter can still seek them out by working through a network of associates who may pass on the phone number of someone who knows, or is likely to know, where they may be. These possibilities, therefore, take away from the anonymity or autonomy that these sojourners might want for themselves.

The multi-step nature of migration for many Africans, the challenges of emigrating, the pressure of settling when they arrive in their destination countries, or the difficulty of combining parenting with the quest for survival, means that many families get separated as one member seeks opportunities for the betterment of the whole. This situation has led, for example, to a variant of the satellite/astronaut-children phenomenon whereby people in the diaspora are compelled to parent from afar (Constable 2009; Dreby 2007). Migrants leave their children in the care of the remaining parent or, where both parents are abroad, in the care of relatives or friends. As Gastaldo and her colleagues argue (2005: 7), "the decision to leave children behind or the act of sending children back home to be cared for commonly by a maternal grandmother is a transnational migration strategy" that is employed within many immigrant communities as they negotiate the demands of parenting and the exigencies of economic survival.

The implications of prolonged separation from children or spouses can put severe strains on relationships and or deny these transnational families the privileges and advantages that come with living together (Parreñas 2001, 2005). While the cell phone cannot be said to have fully restored the responsibilities, joys, and intimacies of physical co-presence, there is no denying the fact that it has enabled family members to "connect with one another in deeply meaningful ways" (Şenyürekl and Detzner 2009: 811). Children have a better opportunity to hear a parent's voice or exchange images regularly; both can contact each other more readily and more often than was the case before cell phones; and parents can more directly share in the upbringing and development of their children without being physically present. Clearly, "mobile phones are innovatively implicated in the new conditions of global labour which have an affective as well as economic character, and that go to the heart of people's lives" (Goggin and Clark 2009: 592).

Beyond filial and platonic intimacies, cell phones have also become a catalyst for transnational liaisons and romantic relationships (Pertierra 2008). Relationships have been started and nurtured over cell phones, particularly among those Africans for whom the privileged marriage market is constituted by potential mates who come from their places of origin (see Skrbiš 2001; Grabska 2010). These individuals are linked to a recommended male or female by a matchmaker in their home or diaspora social circles. They then begin interacting via phone calls and SMS, and sharing images either using cell phones or complementary platforms with intent to determine whether to pursue a more serious relationship. If there is mutual agreement to proceed, the cell phone becomes the means for sustaining the relationship until such time that there is a physical meeting. The cell phone has also become the tool for sustaining relationships among those who have been separated from romantic partners by migration.

Having analyzed the possibilities that cell phones have offered for building and enhancing transnational social networks and relationships, it is critical that we explore the implications as well. A down side to the opportunities presented by this technology is the erasure of one of the criteria used by Western immigration officials when establishing relationships between those based in the diaspora and their relatives when it comes to visa applications for sponsorship or visits. Some immigration offices ask for correspondence between relatives (mostly defined by old communication platforms such as letters or birthday cards) that not only prove relationship but provide evidence of a continuous, sustained, and cordial one. While records of text messages can potentially serve this purpose, they may not always do so, and there may not be evidence of voice-based phone interactions either.

As noted earlier, people can communicate via cell phones without necessarily owning them, and so may not retain any SMS records. Furthermore, because many transnational conversations are voice-based and it is relatively less expensive to make calls from abroad using phone cards, the originating party in the diaspora may not have records of interactions. The new technology may, thus, impose non-financial costs on families as they engage with immigration authorities. It is important that these authorities come to appreciate the dynamics of the technological changes shaping transnational interactions among families and adjust their evaluation systems accordingly.

Notwithstanding advances to connectedness that cell phones have produced, it is important not to lose sight of the fact that, for some, it "remains an object of ambivalence, bringing unforeseen burdens and obligations" (Horst 2006: 143). Among these is the removal of the cordon that distance and constrained communication provided prior to the cell phone revolution. In the past, many Africans in the diaspora did not have to worry about being notified of quotidian happenings in their communities of origin (e.g., deaths, illnesses, and births of people not closely related to them) and expectations of them to fulfill related social obligations. With access to relatively cheap cell phone rates, and the regularity with which conversations with home take place, they are now informed of such events and their knowledge puts an obligation on them to meet expectations (see de Bruijn *et al.* 2010: 274). As Pettigrew observes (2009: 699), "mobile phone texters are in 'perpetual contact' . . . and are virtually accessible at any given time; however, accessibility seemingly diminishes freedom. . . . [consequently], forces of autonomy and connectedness exist in dialectical tension with one another."

Another manifestation of this tension is "flashing." Many Africans in the diaspora, express frustration about the phenomenon of "flashing" whereby a caller hangs up before the receiver is able to respond and the former expects the latter to call back. While this frustration is also expressed domestically, the cost to the receiver abroad who chooses to respond is much more prohibitive. Ease of access for people at home has, therefore, led to loss of autonomy and a sense of compulsion to return calls, with attendant financial burdens on the part of those located abroad. As Donner observes (2009: 96), "through missed calls and 'please call me' messages, families and other call partners can redistribute the costs of phone calls towards those most able to pay."

Cell-phone-enabled transnational romances are also upsetting the social structure within some African communities as members of the diaspora, usually males, win the hearts of local females with their relatively better socioeconomic status and promises of a better life abroad, and shower them with gifts. Local young men, who may be struggling with socioeconomic deprivation, then find themselves to be uncompetitive in the marriage market. The resulting tensions are captured by Grabska (2010: 479) in the following revelation by one of her Sudanese research subjects (Kakuma, a young Dinka man in Kenya):

> You see fighting in the [refugee camp in Kakuma]? It is because of the "lost boys" from America who come to marry and fight over girls. They cause a lot of trouble. Before they went to America, there were no problems. Now, they come and take girls, often by force, and pay too much so the rest of us [in the camp] cannot [afford to] marry.

I am not contending that asymmetrical power dynamics in the marriage market, and the resultant tensions, are created by cell phones. Rather what I am suggesting is that cell phones have made it easier for romantic relationships to develop and be nurtured across geographical boundaries, with extensive insertion of socioeconomically better-off suitors into an environment of general deprivation, thereby creating imbalances in romantic opportunities. Furthermore, matchmakers benefit from the largesse of the diaspora suitor as they facilitate these distal encounters. The technology is, thus, playing "a central role in the commodification of intimacy and in shaping new movements and geographic and electronic landscapes of intimacy for individuals who are otherwise geographically dispersed" (Constable 2009: 53).

Transnational Remittances and Entrepreneurship

One of the significant contributions that migrants continue to make to their countries of origin is in the area of remittances. The International Organization for Migration (IOM) disclosed that even though the proportion of migrants relative to the global population has been stable for the last decade, the amount of money they remit home has increased substantially, even in the midst of the global financial crisis of the last couple of years. Developing countries' share of these transactions increased from US$83 bn in 2000, representing 63 percent of the world's total, to more than US$316 bn in 2009, constituting 76 percent of the global total (IOM 2011). It needs to be pointed out that these figures do not reflect the total amount of remittances since many migrants send money home through informal means that are not captured by these statistics. The remarkable contribution of remittances to the economies of countries of origin is vividly illustrated by the IOM's estimation that "formal and informal remittances to developing countries could be as much as three times the size of official development aid" (IOM 2011).

Remittances from African migrants reflect the larger context in the developing world. According to a 2009 statement by the Governor of the Bank of Kenya, that country's diaspora "remits an average of US$50 m each month through the formal channels such as commercial banks and authorized international money transfer entities" (Central Bank of Kenya 2009: 4). It is estimated that annual remittances from Somali émigrés total between US$750 m and US$1 bn, making the country the fourth most remittance-dependent country in the world, with those transfers constituting 20–50 percent of its GDP (Hassan and Chalmers 2008). These transfers have helped keep private sector economic activities afloat in the midst of a war-ravaged environment (Maimbo 2006).

An African-pioneered innovation in the use of cell phones for money transfers has not only expanded options for Africans in the diaspora who want to send money home, but it has also made it more convenient for recipients to access funds more securely, more readily and more confidentially. That innovation is M-Pesa, a mobile banking and money transfer system which was first introduced in Kenya in 2007 by Safaricom (a local cell phone company connected to the Vodafone Group), with support from the United Kingdom's Department for International Development. Since then, similar initiatives have been launched in other countries in Africa and elsewhere. Examples of services targeting Africans in the diaspora include the Zimbabwe-focused multi-platform called Mikemusa and the US-based Shaka Mobile. This is how Mikemusa works:

> To send funds customers will simply enter the recipient's name and phone number, the amount to be sent, and pick a secret passcode for the recipient. Senders can also enter a personalized text message which will be automatically sent to the recipient's phone along with the transfer confirmation. The SMS only contains notification and is not instrumental to the payout transaction. . . .
>
> In Zimbabwe, the recipient presents at the cashout point where they are asked to provide their identification card and passcode. The recipient can withdraw all or a portion of the funds they received using their cell phone for secure authentication. The recipient will then present to our pay out partners NMB (National Merchant Bank) who will process payout of remitted funds using our m-cash 1600 terminal, or online terminal. (Mobile Money Africa 2010a)

Within the first two years of its operations, M-Pesa's customer base far exceeded the pool of customers who had accounts with Kenya's traditional banks (Etzo and Collender 2010), with Jack and Suri (2010) suggesting that by August 2009 there were 7.7 million subscriptions and about 38 percent of the country's adult population was enrolled. While a significant portion of M-Pesa transactions are domestic, it is worth noting that there is a transnational dimension to total transactions. Members of the diaspora either make direct transfers to recipients in Kenya or are involved in a process of serial transfers whereby remittances are initially sent to a contact person in the country by traditional means and then forwarded to the ultimate recipient using M-Pesa. The Governor of the Central Bank of Kenya disclosed at the launch of M-Pesa's international money transfer service, in October 2009, that virtually everyone on the Safaricom platform has an M-PESA Account. The service is used to transfer Ksh 1.35 billion per day, a tremendous success by any measure. The launch of the international leg of the M-PESA money transfer service is therefore a natural progression in the value chain. . . . Millions of people have been brought out of obscurity, because their cell phone gadgets have the ability to facilitate instant access not only to financial services, but also to the rest of the marketplace. It has also redefined space and time; information and funds can move from London to Lodwar in a fraction of time.

This service will enable inbound international person to person transfers by the Kenyan Diaspora in the United Kingdom to regularly remit money to Kenya faster, reliably and possibly cheaper in the long run. It is hoped that this service will encourage members of the Kenyan Diaspora who would normally prefer informal remittances channels to migrate to the use of this reliable, albeit convenient platform to send money home. (Central Bank of Kenya 2009: 2–3)

There are several reasons for the huge success of mobile transfers. They offer speedy transfer of funds, avoid the insecurity and loss of privacy and confidentiality that comes with using intermediaries, surmount the regulatory barriers and inconveniences of the traditional banking system and, by and large, seem to cost less (see Money Matters Africa 2010a; Yujuico 2009: 64). Furthermore, by getting money directly to the intended individual, there is a strengthening of autonomy in the reception and use of those funds by the recipient (Hamel 2009: 20). Scott and his colleagues argue that (2004: 7)

accelerating the introduction of pro-poor electronic accounts and using mobile technology for remittances will strengthen social safety nets, make local markets more dynamic (diversification of goods and produce), and increase the flow of remittances, especially the transfer of small amounts. Given that charges on remittances to Africa are of order $1.5 billion a year, the potential financial benefit of introducing cheaper systems is huge.

Even in cases where remittances follow traditional routes (e.g., the carrying of physical cash on behalf of others by people traveling back home; bank wire transfers; money transfer companies such as Western Union; or *Hawalla* networks) there is usually a follow-up phone call that alerts the recipient and provides whatever information is needed to receive the money.

Another remarkable convenience provided by the cell phone is the ability of diaspora members to pay for goods and services in their countries of origin from their locations of domicile, either for themselves or on behalf of relatives and friends at home. One such service is offered by the organization Mukuru.com which allows Zimbabweans in the diaspora "to transfer money over mobile phones. For instance, gas fueling can be paid over the internet from anywhere to anybody with a mobile phone in Zimbabwe, then the petrol station owner gets his money back through vouchers" (Crisscrossed 2007). In Kenya, M-Pesa services enable members of the diaspora to fulfill their financial obligations to various agencies without having to

358

Wisdom J. Tettey

be there in person or delegate to an intermediary. These include payment of utility and other bills. According to one user:

> Mpesa is such a revolution in Kenya. It fills in the gap created by the (near) absence of a credit card system. It is actually a debit system. I work outside Kenya but I am able to pay for my bills and also remit money home using Mpesa. I transfer cash from my bank account to my Mpesa account then transact all my business "just like home." (Dizikes 2010)

The indisputable success of mobile banking and transfer platforms is borne out by the interest shown by Western Union, arguably the world's largest money transfer company. It has entered into agreements with several African banks and phone companies around the world to offer these services, using its network of 21,000 agents located in 49 African countries and a global network that spans 200 countries with 435,000 agents (Mobile Money Africa 2010b).

Transnational entrepreneurship by individuals and groups in the diaspora is also being facilitated by cell phones as they are able to keep in touch with business partners or employees much more regularly (see Chen 2006). People with investments at home can also more closely follow how these are going by monitoring these investments and those assigned to take care of them. Someone investing in a building project, for example, can receive frequent feedback from a third party about progress of work that someone else is supposed to be overseeing. This surveillance system helps to curb horror stories where people in the diaspora send money home for buildings that are never (fully) constructed, and yet are told that everything is fine, only for them to return home to find out that they have been duped.

While we tout the positive contributions that the transnationalism–cell phone nexus is making to the lives and livelihoods of Africans, it is important to recognize that this revolution also has the potential to accentuate social and economic disparities within communities in countries of origin. After all, there are still significant numbers of Africans who are without access to cell phones or any other type of technological platforms that enable them to take advantage of the potentials of ICTs (Etzo and Collender 2010: 665). As Stern and Messer point out (2009: 670), it is important that we

> consider the consequences of digital inequality and technological access on the types of social capital that are provided by family networks. Indeed, if financial considerations inhibit one's opportunity to maintain one's family network, thus decreasing its breadth, their potential for maximizing social capital and familial support (structural or emotional) is limited, compared with those with greater access to the media multiplexity.

The relative ease of transferring money, plus the exponential growth in cell phone access in countries of origin, also imposes tremendous pressure on members of the diaspora community as they negotiate a multiplicity of financial demands and obligations in the in-between spaces that they occupy.

Concerns about the political impact of such social capital is not lost on political actors, particularly in conflict areas, who fear that financial flows could be used to undermine their authority. It is these concerns that led Al-Shabaab, the Al-Qaeda-related rebel group in Somalia, to impose a ban on Zaad and Sahal mobile banking services run by telecommunications companies in the country. The group contends that the services pose a "great hazard to the economy of Somalis and accused an unnamed company in the United States of being behind the service. The group said the unnamed service wanted to take over the economy of the world by using MMT (Mobile Money Transfer). Al Shabaab argued that use of Somali shillings declined in recent months because of the mobile service" (Mobile Money Africa 2010c).

Transnationalism and Glocalization of Politics

Laguerre (2005) argues that people who leave their countries of origin, particularly politicians, do not exit its politics but rather engage with it through what he calls a metaphor of circulation. Access to an extensive network of cell phones has transformed the nature of that circulation in dramatic ways, in terms of the currency and speed of engagement with the politics of home, opportunities for political articulation, mobilization, aggregation, and action toward resource mobilization.

Rarely do Africans in the diaspora have conversations with people at home without touching on the political economy of their homeland. As part of their exercise of emotional citizenship vis-à-vis their homelands, they are interested in what is going on, especially since conditions there have a direct impact on relatives left behind as well as their own connections to the country, whether these are current investments or future plans. In fact, networks of political concern, interest, and influence traverse the deterritorialized boundaries of the state, such that the best conduits for accessing political goods may go through people in the diaspora. As Lyons and Mandaville (2010) note:

> If someone in rural Liberia wishes to appeal to the central government in Monrovia for support, the closest social link may be to use a cell phone to call a relative in Philadelphia known to have political connections in the capital. Geographic distance does not prohibit political influence; physical distance matters less for patron-client relationships than social proximity. Neo-patrimonialism has gone global.

Whereas the importance of cell phones in African elections have been recognized (see Tettey 2009a), their role in transnational political strategy formulation and resource mobilization between diasporan Africans and their compatriots at home has not received much attention. There is, however, evidence that such interactions go on and have been significantly enhanced by cell phones. During Ghana's 2008 elections, for example, this author spoke to a number of Ghanaians in the diaspora who were involved in political campaigns at home as advisors, fundraisers, and communication strategists. Their preferred mode of communication with their counterparts at home was the cell phone, because they could reach these individuals anywhere on the campaign trail or during the elections. In fact, one of the most volatile periods during that election season was a recorded cell phone conversation, purported to be between a European-based Ghanaian woman to a minister in the incumbent government, in which she outlined strategies for undermining the elections in order for the governing party to retain power (Ghanaweb 2008). Even though the credibility of the recording is still contested, the incident reflects recognition that many Africans in the diaspora are very much engaged with the politics of home through ICTs, albeit to different degrees (Tettey 2009b).

One contribution of cell phones to civic engagement is "crowd-sourcing" (www.ushahidi.com/; http://www.executionchronicles.org/close-up12-rotich.htm) or "crowd-voicing" (Economist 2011), whereby ordinary citizens connect with relatives or colleagues either domestically or abroad, to pass on information related to events unfolding in their countries. When post-election violence erupted in Kenya and Côte d'Ivoire, in December 2007 and December 2010, respectively, many of their citizens in the diaspora stayed in touch with their relatives via cell phones to find out how they were doing, serve as conduits for getting information out about human rights abuses, and so on. A number of the commentators on media networks in Western countries were citizens of these nations, and their commentaries were based on information that they had received through various channels, including cell phone conversations with contacts in their places of origin. The same pattern followed the dramatic events in Tunisia and Egypt in early 2011 in spite of efforts in the latter to deny access to cell phone services for a while.

As Qiu (2008: 39) observes, mobile telephony can be "a catalyst to civil society formation at times of emergency," echoing Castells and colleagues' idea of a "mobile civil society" (2007: 185). The Kenyan crisis was, thus, the birthplace of Ushahidi (meaning testimony or witness in Kiswahili), an interactive mapping network which has since been deployed in other crisis situations such as Haiti during the 2010 earthquake, and in South Africa the same year, during the xenophobic attacks on other African nationals. Ory Okolloh, a Kenyan activist and lawyer educated in the United States and based in South Africa, is credited with founding the network which has now developed into a not-for-profit organization. It operates by having people send messages (via SMS, email, etc.) about events, needs, and locations to a mobile operator, from where they are transferred to a website to be translated, mapped, and categorized, sometimes by members of the diaspora (Nesbit and Janah 2010). It is worth bearing in mind that cell-phone-enabled political engagement is not necessarily always in the service of political freedom, democratic governance, or human rights. "For instance, in the wake of Kenya's 2007 elections, text messages were used to coordinate mass political terror along ethnotribal lines, reifying divisions considered antithetical to liberal nationalism" (McIntosh 2010: 337).

It is not uncommon these days for Africans in the diaspora to be called on the phone by journalists regarding political issues about which they are knowledgable. These calls could be live, on electronic news or talk programs, or interviews for later broadcast or publication in print media. Some of these calls take place via cell phones. There are also instances where calls are initiated by members of the diaspora to media programs and organizations at home, to provide information that they consider relevant to the political discourse in their countries of origin. It is instructive to note that some members of the Ghanaian diaspora whose cell phones have Ghanaian SIM cards received a text message from the country's Constitutional Review Commission in December 2010 as part of the Commission's

> text-in (SMS) campaign, aimed at getting more people to share their views on these proposed amendments. . . . "[F]rom the comfort of your office, your home, your bedroom, your car, during the day or in the still of the night, you can make your views known." Contributors are urged to share their views on the subjects by texting their SMS messages to short code 1992 on all networks. (Joy News 2010)

While long-distance nationalism pre-dates the introduction of cell phones, analyses of contemporary expressions of such political engagement show that "the effectiveness of emotionally intense ethnic and nationalist attachments greatly benefit from these networks" of ICT connectivity (Skrbiš 2001; Tettey 2009b). In their analysis of the relationship between the Somali diaspora and socioeconomic development in their country of origin, David and Ghedi (2009: 99) observe that:

> Today, nearly all of Somalia is linked to the world by sophisticated telecommunications networks. For example, mobile phones have replaced radio communications as the necessary tool for the Somali remittance system. In the larger towns, there are competing mobile phone networks, and private companies coordinate services with local authorities to provide 24-hour electric power, many through investments by the diaspora.

Conclusion

With the combination of transnationalism and mobile phone technology, "societies increasingly exist more in social relations than in a place *per se*. Geographical location is playing a lesser role in determining a person's feeling of belonging than social relations in many cases" (de Bruijn *et al.* 2010: 270).What the foregoing analysis demonstrates is that the cell phone has significantly transformed transnational communicative practices, among Africans, since it was first used in the Democratic Republic of Congo in 1987 (Etzo and Collender 2010: 660). It is one of "those technologies that distribute actors, even those who stay at home, through time and space. The new technologies of communication multiply such distributions and links between different spatiotemporal contexts" (Callon and Law 2004: 10). It is clear that Africans have appropriated cell phone technology in very innovative ways to facilitate social, financial, and political transactions between the local and the global, and are indeed pace-setters with regard to some of these innovations, such as M-Pesa and Ushahidi. As one blogger notes with regard to mobile transfers,

"Africans in general have pioneered the use of cellphones to transfer value by using airtime as a virtual currency" (Crisscrossed 2007).

The African diaspora community has also been a catalyst for technological change by supporting the expansion of cell phone adoption. They have done so by providing friends and relatives with handsets or other services that facilitate long-distance communication. Hamel notes (2009: 27) that in one Senegalese village, for example, "local migrants who left to work in Italy . . . used their income to purchase telephones and fund the installation of electricity and telephone services in their communities back home."

In tandem with the advantages of the technology is a reconfiguration of relationships resulting from a new array of demands and obligations, with accompanying pressures, that could have been avoided in earlier times. The complex, multilayered components of the technology's impact vis-à-vis home–diaspora linkages, therefore, need to be acknowledged and the dialectical tensions underlying the intersectionalities of the two phenomena must be incorporated into any critical analysis of their conjuncture.

Note

1   For current statistics see http://www.itu.int/ITU-D/ict/statistics/, accessed March 12, 2013.

References

Alonso, A. and Oiarzabal, P.J. (eds) 2010. *Diasporas in the New Media Age: Identity, Politics, and Community*. Reno: University of Nevada Press.

Benítez, J.L. 2006. "Transnational dimensions of the digital divide among Salvadoran immigrants in the Washington DC metropolitan area." *Global Networks*, 6(2): 181–199.

Brady, F., Dyson, L.E., and Asela, T. 2008. "Indigenous adoption of mobile phones and oral culture." In F. Sudweeks, H. Hrachovec, and C. Ess (eds) *Proceedings: Fifth International Conference on Cultural Attitudes Towards Communication and Technology*, pp. 384–398. Perth, Australia: Murdoch University.

Callon, M. and Law, J. 2004. "Introduction: Absence–presence, circulation, and encountering in complex space." *Environment and Planning D*, 22(1): 3–11.

Castells, M., Mireia, F.-A., Qui, J.L., and Sey, A. 2007. *Mobile Communication and Society: A Global Perspective*. Boston, MA: MIT Press.

Central Bank of Kenya 2009. "Address by Prof. Njuguna Ndung'u, Governor Central Bank of Kenya, during the official launch of M-Pesa international money transfer service at Safaricom House, Tuesday, October 13." Nairobi: Bank of Kenya.

Chen, W. 2006. "The impact of internet use on transnational entrepreneurship: the case of Chinese immigrants to Canada." In P. Law, L Fortunati, and S. Yang (eds) *New Technologies in Global Societies*, pp. 197–220. Singapore: World Scientific Publishing.

Constable, N. 2009. "The commodification of intimacy: Marriage, sex, and reproductive labor." *Annual Review of Anthropology*, 38: 49–64.

Crisscrossed 2007. "4 examples of innovative phone use in Africa," at http://www.crisscrossed. net/2007/08/29/4-examples-for-innovative-mobile-phone-use-in-africa, accessed February 18, 2013.

David, B. and Ghedi, A.J. 2009. "Historical Somali migration and the Somali workforce at home and in the diaspora." In T.L. Weiss (ed.) *Migration for Development in the Horn of Africa: Health Expertise from the Somali Diaspora in Finland*, pp. 95–106. Helsinki: International Organization for Migration.

de Bruijn, M., Nyamnjoh, F., and Angwafo,T. 2010. "Mobile interconnections: Reinterpreting distance, relating and difference in the Cameroonian Grassfields." *Journal of African Media Studies*, 2(3): 267–285.

Dizikes, P. 2010. "Banking on mobile money." MITNews, February 23, at http://web.mit.edu/ newsoffice/2010/mobile-money-0223.html, accessed February 18, 2013.

Donner, J. 2009. "Blurring livelihoods and lives: the social uses of mobile phones and socio-economic development." *Innovations* (winter): 91–101.

Dreby, J. 2007. "Children and power in Mexican transnational families." *Journal of Marriage and Family*, 69: 1050–1064.

Economist 2011. "Mobile services in poor countries: Not just talk." *The Economist,* January 27, at http://www.economist.com/node/18008202, accessed February 18, 2013.

Etzo, S. and Collender, G. 2010. "The mobile phone 'revolution' in Africa: Rhetoric or reality?" *African Affairs*, 109(437): 659–668.

Gastaldo, D., Gooden, A., and Massaquoi, N. 2005. "Transnational health promotion: Social well-being across borders and immigrant women's subjectivities." *Wagado: A Journal of Transnational Women's and Gender Studies*, 2: 1–16.

Ghanaweb 2008. "Please listen to Radio Gold now!!!" at http://discussions.ghanaweb.com/ viewtopic.php?t=95609&sid=5af48a77ff0e267977de51b4e23c013b, accessed February 18, 2013.

Goggin, G. and Clark, J. 2009. "Mobile phones and community development: a contact zone between media and citizenship." *Development in Practice*, 19(4): 585–597.

Grabska, K. 2010. "Lost boys, invisible girls: Stories of Sudanese marriages across borders." *Gender, Place and Culture*, 17(4): 479–497.

Hamel, J.-Y. 2009. *Information and Communication Technologies and Migration.* Human Development Research Paper 39 (August). New York: United Nations Development Program.

Hassan, M.A. and Chalmers, C. 2008. *UK Somali Remittances Survey.* London: Department for International Development.

Horst, H.A. 2006. "The blessings and burdens of communication: Cell phones in Jamaican transnational social fields." *Global Networks*, 6(2): 143–159.

Horst, H.A. and Miller, D. 2005. "From kinship to link-up: Cell phones and social networking in Jamaica." *Current Anthropology*, 46(5): 755–778.

IOM 2011. "Global trends," International Organization for Migration, *Migration Satellite: Global Migration Observer,* at http://www.migrationsatellite.com/migration/global-trends, accessed March 5, 2013.

ITU 2010. *The World in 2010: ICT Facts and Figures – the Rise of 3G.* Geneva: International Telecommunications Union, at http://www.itu.int/ITU-D/ict/material/FactsFigures2010. pdf, accessed February 18, 2013.

Jack, W. and Suri, T. 2010. "The economics of M-Pesa," at http://www.mit.edu/~tavneet/M-PESA.pdf, accessed February 18, 2013.

Johanson, G. and Denison, T. 2011. "Mobile phones, diasporas and developing countries: a case study of connectedness among Chinese in Italy." In J. Steyn, J.-P. Van Belle, and E.V. Mansilla (eds) *ICTs for Global Development and Sustainability: Practice and Applications*, pp. 176–188. Hershey, NY: Information Science Reference.

Joy News 2010. "Constitution review commission releases top 25 proposed amendments," *Joy News*, December 24, at http://www.modernghana.com/news/309876/1/constitution-review-commission-releases-top-25-pro.html, accessed March 12, 2013.

Kwaramba, F. 2010. "Cell phones changing lives of people." *The Zimbabwean*, at http://www.thezimbabwean.co.uk/index.php?option=com_content&view=article&id=36321:cell-phones-changing-lives-of-people&catid=35:opinion-a-analysis&Itemid=31, accessed February 18, 2013.

Laguerre, M.S. 2005. "Homeland political crisis, the virtual diasporic public sphere, and diasporic politic." *Journal of Latin American Anthropology*, 10(1): 206–225.

Lyons, T. and Mandaville, P. 2010. "Diasporas shape politics." *Khaleej Times*, November 22, at http://www.khaleejtimes.com/DisplayArticle08.asp?xfile=data/opinion/2010/November/opinion_November118.xml&section=opinion, accessed February 18, 2013.

Maimbo, S.M. (ed.) 2006. *Remittances and Economic Development in Somalia: An Overview*. Social Development Papers: Conflict Prevention and Reconstruction 38, November. Washington DC: World Bank.

McIntosh, J. 2010. "Mobile phones and Mipoho's prophecy: the powers and dangers of flying language." *American Ethnologist*, 37(2): 337–353.

Mobile Money Africa 2010a. "MobileMoney is finally a reality for Zimbabwean diaspora." Press release, at http://mobilemoneyafrica.com/details.php?post_id=57, accessed March 5, 2013.

Mobile Money Africa 2010b. "Western Union will be the central hub for MobileMoney in Africa – Interview with Khalid Fahid," at http://mobilemoneyafrica.com/details.php?post_id=114, accessed February 18, 2013.

Mobile Money Africa 2010c. "Al Shabaab bans mobile banking service in Somalia," at http://mobilemoneyafrica.com/details.php?post_id=301, accessed February 18, 2013.

Nesbit, J. and Janah, L.C. 2010. "Directing relief efforts and creating jobs through text messaging." *Innovations*, 5(4): 69–72.

Parreñas, R. 2001. "Mothering from a distance: Emotions, gender, and intergenerational relations in Filipino transnational families." *Feminist Studies*, 27(2): 361–390.

Parreñas, R. 2005. "Long distance intimacy: Class, gender and intergenerational relations between mothers and children in Filipino transnational families." *Global Networks*, 5(4): 317–336.

Pertierra R. 2005. "Mobile phones, identity and discursive intimacy." *Human Technology: An Interdisciplinary Journal on Humans in ICT Environments*, 1(1): 23–44.

Pertierra R. 2008. "Computer-mediated-interactive-communication-technology (CMICT) & the anthropology of communication: a Philippine example." *Telektronikk*, 2: 68–76.

Pettigrew, J. 2009. "Close relationships: Text messaging and connectedness within close interpersonal relationships." *Marriage and Family Review*, 45: 697–716.

Qiu, J.L. 2008. "Mobile civil society in Asia: a comparative study of people power II and the Nosamo movement." *Javnost: The Public*, 15(3): 39–58.

Scott, N., Batchelor, S., Ridley, J., and Jorgensen, B. 2004. *The Impact of Mobile Phones in Africa*. London: Commission for Africa.

Şenyürekl, A.R. and Detzner, D.F. 2009. "Communication dynamics of the transnational family." *Marriage and Family Review*, 45: 807–824.

Skrbiš, Z. 2001. "Nationalism in a transnational context: Croatian diaspora, intimacy and nationalist imagination." *Revija za Sociologiju (Sociological Review)*, 3/4: 133–145.

Stern, M.J. and Messer, C. 2009. "How family members stay in touch: a quantitative investigation of core family networks." *Marriage and Family Review*, 45(6): 654–676.

Tettey, W.J. 2009a. "News media and governance reform: Sub-Saharan Africa." In P. Norris (ed.) *Public Sentinel: News Media and Governance Reform*, pp. 277–304. Washington, DC: World Bank.

Tettey, W.J. 2009b. "Transnationalism, the African diaspora and the deterritorialized politics of the internet." In O. Mudhai, W. Tettey, and F. Banda (eds) *African Media and the Digital Public Sphere*, pp. 143–163. New York: Palgrave Macmillan.

Thompson, E.C. 2009. "Mobile phones, communities and social networks among foreign workers in Singapore." *Global Networks*, 9(3): 359–380.

UN 2009. "Trends in international migrant stock: the 2008 revision." United Nations Department of Economic and Social Affairs, Population Division, at http://www.un.org/esa/population/migration/UN_MigStock_2008.pdf, accessed February 18, 2013.

Vertovec, S. 2004. "Cheap calls: the social glue of migrant transnationalism." *Global Networks*, 4(2): 219–224.

Yujuico, E. 2009. "All modes lead to home: Assessing the state of the remittance art." *Global Networks*, 9(1): 63–81.

Chapter 21

Home-Making in the Diaspora
Bringing Palestine to London
Michelle Obeid

This chapter discusses the experience of a Palestinian family, whom I call Gazāwi,[1] in the aftermath of their displacement from Gaza to London. The chapter looks at the process of emplacement in a new country by trying to understand the everyday practices of creating a new home in a new location. How do new places become endowed with meaning? What sort of efforts and agencies are required along the way? And how does one's past life contribute to creating the present and the future? The story of this family is not unique. Rather, it exemplifies the predicament of people on the move who find themselves dealing with unforeseen contingencies. "Home," "roots," and "land" feature very much in the everyday discourses of family members who see their return to Palestine as imminent. This, however, does not stop them from engaging with the array of possibilities that their new location holds. The family I worked with actively engaged in creating new socialities that added meaning to their lives. In this chapter, I am interested in unpacking the projects that "root" migrants in new places. My aim is to understand the specificities of the diasporic condition and its relationship to home and home-making. To proceed, however, one might begin with animating both concepts: "diaspora" and "home."

A Palestinian Diaspora?

In recent literature, scholars have begun to problematize the use of the category "diaspora" to describe Palestinians living abroad. Drawing on Hanafi's (2005: 98) contention that Palestinians are "partially diasporic," Peteet (2007: 629) pushes the

A Companion to Diaspora and Transnationalism, First Edition.
Edited by Ato Quayson and Girish Daswani.
© 2013 Blackwell Publishing Ltd. Published 2013 by Blackwell Publishing Ltd.

critique further to remind us that "uncritical invocations of diaspora risk minimizing the range of traumatic conditions that fuel displacement and the way these shape sociocultural formations and subjectivity." Peteet calls for a disaggregation (theoretical and ethnographic) of diaspora which would allow a better understanding of the violence and the political and economic upheavals that other terms such as "refugee," "internally displaced," or "forced migrant" may communicate. This, of course, does not apply to Palestinians alone but rather is a point of discussion for theorizing diaspora at large, considering the elasticity the term is allowed in recent literature. It is not the categories *per se* that preoccupy Peteet. Rather, she advocates for a "critical politics of mobility" that "critically examines and ethnographically grounds its use of diaspora" (2007: 630). Making a slightly different argument, yet maintaining a critical approach to categories of mobility, Jansen and Lofving's (2009) volume takes issue with treating people as "'representatives' of 'types' of displacement" (such as forced versus voluntary) as these, they argue, tend to create moral judgments (deserving and undeserving), not to mention that the boundaries between "forced" and "voluntary" migration are themselves questionable (p. 8).

The Gazāwis provide a very good example of the futility of choice-based labels. They are a Palestinian family of nine. Six of the children, as well as the parents, moved to London at different times over the course of ten years. Among the nine of them, they combine an assortment of legal statuses: student residencies, asylum claims, refugee statuses, and British citizenship. Their arrival stories range from being smuggled across various borders for one brother to traveling on a business-class ticket for another. For all of them, however, the premise of their displacement, despite its logistical execution, relates to the living conditions they were subjected to in their home town Gaza as a result of the structural and actual violence inflicted on the Palestinians by the Israeli state. A main repercussion of the blockade on Gaza, for example, has been the closure of a thriving business that the Gazāwis owned in the Erez Industrial Zone (on the border between Israel and Gaza). Other drivers were life-threatening events during the Israeli war on Gaza in 2008 and its aftermath, and the overwhelming sense of entrapment inflicted on the general population of residents. If we take Kelly's argument (2009: 26) about displacement, that it "is never simply a physical movement across space, but also involves transformations in the political, spatial and economic practices through which people are related to place," then the displacement of the Gazāwi family may have started long before their move to London. Certainly, family members identify their predicament at individual, family, and collective levels as *muhajjarin* (displaced) or *mushattatin* (dispersed), which to them reflects the plight of Palestinians as a people.

Scholars of Palestine worry that the label "diaspora" may negate both the internationally recognized legal category and the identity of "Palestinian refugee" thus deflecting attention from their struggle for self-determination (Peteet 2007). But Hanafi (2005: 106) reconciles this tension by asserting that "a refugee remains a refugee even if she/he adopts the nationality of the host country." My aim here is not necessarily to discredit the use of categories – our main tools as social scientists – but rather to acknowledge the loss of complexity that may come about with deploying certain categories, especially in the Palestinian case. Hence to understand what displacement and emplacement meant for the Palestinian family that I worked with, I take on board the call for an ethnographic examination of mobility which requires that we look at the actual lived experience of moving persons, as "ordinary people" (whether their migration was "forced" or not) who are agentive actors embedded in social, political, and historical contexts (Jansen and Lofving 2009: 8).

What Is "Home"?

A key issue in discussions around diaspora is the notion of the home or homeland. For Palestinians, the homeland constitutes not only a collective memory but also a defining feature of an ongoing political demand – articulated through the "right of return" (Khalidi 1992) – that constitutes the discourse of Palestinian leadership. But an uncritical assumption of a tie to the homeland presupposes "an . . . already constituted ethnic or national group at departure and in exile" (Peteet 2007: 629), in other words an essentially unchanging territorialized identity. Scholars of diaspora and displacement challenge the "fetishization" of the homeland or "origin" (Axel 2002; Clifford 1994) and urge us to look beyond the sedentarist bias (Malkki 1995) that tends to naturalize the relationship between locality and belonging. We need to consider ways of rethinking celebratory approaches towards rootedness that have dominated the literature (Stepputat 2002: 202) without flattening out the oppressive processes that characterize displacement and without dismissing that there *are* links between place and belonging. Deterritorializing identities, then, can be done while at once taking into account people's attachments to notions of the homeland and discourses of return (Jansen and Lofving 2009) – or "the myth of return" (Al-Rasheed 1994). A reasonable start might be to ask how the home that one left behind might feature in shaping the everyday processes of creating home in a new context. And what sort of efforts, strategies, and affects are involved in making a home?

Anthropologist Ghassan Hage (2009: 471) takes physical mobility to be hugely tied to "existential mobility," which he argues is often associated with "forward movement, viability and the future." The process of home-making, then, is forward-looking in as much as it entails longing for a lost past. In his influential essay *At Home in the Entrails of the West*, Hage (1997: 102–103) proposes that home-building is an affective construct: it entails "the building of the *feeling* of being 'at home.'" He identifies four key feelings that are crucial to this affective process: the feeling of security which relates to being a willful subject in one's home; the feeling of familiarity through "maximal spatial knowledge" of one's place; the feeling of community through possessing "maximal communicative power," and the feeling of "a sense of possibility" where one can "perceive opportunities of a 'better life.'" So in order to understand how these "feelings" are created, a study of "home" (or home-making) is best approached as an empirical question (Jansen and Lofving 2009). What sort of context enables (or disables) the production of these feelings? How do people "produce locality" (Turton 2005: 275) in new places and how might this process draw on continuities with "homes" left behind? Turton's suggestion is helpful here as he argues that places become endowed with meaning as a *product* of social activity rather than being merely a stage for them (2005: 275). What are these social activities and how are they produced on an everyday level?

In this chapter, I explore ethnographically the experience of the Gazāwis in creating home in their new location. I suggest that the process of home-making incorporated the engagement with what I consider to be "projects of rootedness." By this I mean purposeful activities that demand a long-term commitment and produce attachments that root persons in a particular place. For the Gazāwis, this project crystallized with opening a Palestinian café that was to ground the family spatially, financially, emotionally, and politically as it gradually became a site for the reproduction of Palestinian-ness, a space where Palestine was made visible in London and where a political message was reproduced. Although all the members of the Gazāwi family were involved in this project, I focus on the parents whose case typifies the contingencies inherent in mobility. Below, I discuss the context which embedded the Gazāwi parents in a new locality in which they had to rebuild home, family, and nation.

A Family Reunited

In this section, I explore the "sense of possibility" that emanates from the predicament of being displaced in *ghurba* – a term that literally means estrangement and is used by Arabs to imply exile or a diasporic existence. Beyond the Gazāwis' sense of yearning for their house, relatives, friends, and life left behind in Gaza, London provided a site in which the "centre of gravity" (Hanafi 2005), a meeting point for a dispersed family, could be repositioned.

Settling in London had never been an option for the Gazāwi parents. For Umm and Abu Bashir, London was a city that they had been visiting for six years in order to check on their four sons who had migrated consecutively. It was there that they attended their eldest and second eldest sons' graduations and two marriages. As more of their children migrated to London, it became a familiar yet transitory place. But on one of their usual visits to see their sons in 2007, the couple was unexpectedly stranded in London due to the heightening of the blockade that the Israeli state had enforced on Gaza, which involved the closure of all border crossings, prohibiting the passage of goods and people. With not much choice, and succumbing to their sons' pleas, the parents applied to stay in the United Kingdom and were granted a five-year residence permit based on a humanitarian appeal. Not surprisingly, at first the couple envisaged their move as a liminal and temporary phase that would soon end with the opening of the borders. But a few months into their stay, the Israeli war on Gaza broke out, making the idea of return seem more distant. Frustrated at first and troubled by the fate of their house and business back home, the couple accepted that they might have to stay longer than they had intended as the months went by. Particularly after the arrival of two more daughters and their families who applied for asylum and joined the family by 2010, London shifted from being a place of exile for the Gazāwis to a place that is endowed with significance (Feld and Basso 1996) as it allowed for the uniting of a family fragmented by *ghurba*.

Increasingly, the parents became more involved in the lives of their children. Once reunited, the family began to reinstate habitual practices that had once taken place, thus [re]creating everyday sociality and familiarity with each other and with the new place: shopping with daughters, cooking big meals, calling each other several times a day, discovering markets and shopping centers, going together to a doctors' appointment, looking after grandchildren, and so on. But it was particularly the project of the café that enhanced the process of "rooting," facilitated by enablers that advanced a sense of continuity through activities, aspirations, and sentiments that were in place before the move to London. The most immediate one was turning an everyday activity, making Palestinian food, into a business. Food is heavily associated with "home" and home-made food was the niche that the café was after. The marketing of Palestinian food, produced in the home, made the café "the first of its kind in the UK offering real home-made Palestinian cuisine in the heart of London," as the menus boasted. Umm Bashir described the process as fairly straightforward. All she had to do was standardize her usual recipes by measuring and noting down the ingredients accurately. As soon as the menu was decided, issues relating to presentation, service, and marketing developed as they went along.

The second enabler relates to the fact that embarking on a business was not alien to Umm Bashir who had built a good reputation for herself back in Gaza as one of the few businesswomen running a factory in the Erez Industrial Zone. Umm Bashir considers herself to be an active and resourceful person who has the ability to negotiate gender divisions in a highly masculinized space. While her children were growing up, she turned her skill in sewing to a small business in which she sold home-tailored clothes to neighbors on her street. Over time, these orders exceeded the capacity for home production so she used some of the family savings to open a factory. By the time Erez closed in 2004, she had 100 staff members working under her management. Her business manufactured garments to international clothes companies based mainly in Europe. The consequences of the closure of Erez were dire on the Gazan economy and residents, the Gazāwis included. But as soon as the family started to recuperate, Umm Bashir invested in a spa salon of "European standards," having ordered top-of-the-range beauty equipment immediately before she and her husband made their visit to London with unforeseen consequences. So the transferability of Umm Bashir's entrepreneurial skills, handy in the new context, provided a sense of purpose and continuity with her old life back home. The parents were no longer guests at their sons' houses but have now regained their older role as decision-makers and providers.

The third, and perhaps more important enabler, was establishing a new livelihood that is family-centered, one that relies on family labor and is oriented toward its future security. Although the Gazāwi sons were established in their careers, the parents wanted a base for the children to fall back on. Particularly, they were concerned for their youngest son who had not yet found his feet in the United Kingdom.

Unlike his elder brothers who graduated in London and secured good jobs, the youngest, Khalid, was never interested in higher education before migrating. By the time he turned 18, Khalid had withdrawn from university and become more drawn to political activism. Soon he began to despair about the prospects of his future in Gaza. Eventually, he made his way to London and claimed asylum. But his case took longer than ten years, not least due to the UK dispersal policy for asylum-seekers and refugees (see Sales 2002; Hynes 2006),[2] which "dispersed" Khalid to northern cities away from his brothers and their social circles. Without the legal right to work as an asylum-seeker, Khalid needed a social network through which to find informal work. So he kept relocating to London, having to reapply several times. In the meantime, he ended up moving from one job to another in the informal catering industry where he worked for several Arabic restaurants in West London. Although his three brothers lived in the same city and supported him morally (and sometimes financially), Khalid's parents became increasingly worried about his future. Their idea was to capitalize on his learned skills in catering and support him until he could run the café successfully. The parents also had in mind his elder brother who worked for a five-star hotel in the food and banqueting section; they held high hopes of using his expertise to develop the business well enough for him potentially to relinquish "the employee" status and focus entirely on the family business. The investment in a Palestinian café, therefore, carried the promise of more than just an economic safety net and involved a strategy for cohesion among the brothers.

The Gazāwi family worked hard on this project with various degrees of participation from its members. Although the parents' imminent return to Gaza loomed over the different stages of the project, the everyday execution of it intensified the link between kinship, home-making, and belonging (see Mallet 2004) and drew the parents into an emplaced life in London. "Who would have thought the Gazāwis would end up in London!" exclaimed Umm Bashir in a discussion with me about her previous work in Gaza.

At Home in the Café

In this section, I discuss the simultaneous establishment of a new family home and business. This process contributed to the emplacement of the Gazāwi family in the space of the café and gave way to the weaving of a web of social relations that extended to their neighborhood. A description of the spatial arrangement will shed light on the sense of familiarity that was generated with this process.

The café and the new Gazāwi living accommodation were part of the same property, with the café being on the top floor and the home in the basement. In order to access the family home downstairs, the Gazāwis had to go through the main street entrance into the centre of the café and take the stairs to the lower floor. The lower part of the property did not have a kitchen which meant that to prepare their own food the family had to use the café kitchen, separated from customer tables and chairs by a display fridge. This arrangement is due to the fact that the space used to be a shop with a massive warehouse that stocked secondhand clothes. The owner was not doing well and wanted to shut his business. The time was right as the Gazāwi parents began to feel they were overburdening one of their married sons who hosted them. Umm Bashir saw an opportunity in this property which she believed she could turn into a habitable flat with some restructuring. Also, if they were going to establish a business, living close enough would spare them the commute. In addition, paying one rent for the whole place seemed like a financially astute idea. With the correct permits, the underground floor was turned into two double bedrooms, a bathroom, and a spacious living room. A year later, a small single bedroom and a small bathroom were added. The new furnished accommodation allowed two unmarried sons (including the youngest, Khalid) to move in, followed by one daughter who joined the family later and the son who worked in a hotel but lived on the other side of town with his wife and two children. On a regular weekday, six adults and two children lived in the flat and the number was increased by six more on weekends, when the eldest daughter and her family eventually moved to a nearby street in London. This arrangement reminded the family of "how they used to be" back in Gaza, together under the wing of their parents (despite sometimes tense dynamics that emerged due to the restriction of the space).

The location of the kitchen was crucial in the amalgamation of home and café. It was not uncommon to see members of the family going into the kitchen in their pyjamas to make a latte, to fry an egg, or even to heat some food from the display fridge. Umm Bashir would prepare the main food for the café in the morning. This same food was consumed by the whole family at different times of the day. Aside from the menu of the café, Umm Bashir started making a daily special, which was often a dish that one of her children requested. The family either ate in the café on the top floor or carried the food down to the living room if it was busy. There were particular times when the café was busier than usual such as dinnertime on weekdays and lunchtime on weekends. At these times, Umm Bashir's grandchildren were banned from going upstairs. But often, the youngest two would be found running around tables, charming some customers while annoying others. It was difficult to convince the children that the café was not their "home." For them, the adult version that the café was a "business" seemed artificial. In fact, little Mohammad once asked me if we also had a till in our kitchen where we keep the money to buy sweets. When the entire family was on site, they would have their big family weekend lunches after peak time, occupying almost half the space, considering that there were ten tables in the café. As one daughter commented to me, amused by the noise emanating from their table, "you can see we have opened the café for us [the family]. The café is really the 'salon' of our house!"

Although the above comment was made in jest, it rang true since a lot of the entertaining undertaken by members of the family on a daily basis, such as receiving friends and neighbors, was done in the upstairs space. The children teased Abu Bashir for treating the outside seating in the café as his balcony in Gaza, often shouting out invitations to passers-by to come in for coffee or tea. They teased him even more for forgetting that they were running a business and exercising his hospitality when he really needed to be charging people for their drinks! For bigger events like birthdays, engagement celebrations, or even Ramadan dinners, the café would shut early and host family parties that involved special meals, loud music, and *dabke* (Palestinian dance).

Outside of the café itself, the Gazāwis created a network of social relationships. Some of these were with other Palestinians dispersed around London. But on an everyday level, most of these relationships were emplaced in their very mixed neighborhood and were built around the café. The shops in the vicinity were owned by a diversity of people: a Moroccan owned a butchery, an Englishman a fishery, an Indian a fruit-and-vegetable shop, and a Portuguese a bakery. A fellow Palestinian owned the next-door Italian restaurant. Apart from some special Arabic ingredients that they ordered from Arab shops, the Gazāwis bought most of the café supplies from these neighbors thus embedding the café in the neighborhood economy; an aspect that strengthened neighborly ties. These shop-owners and their families would often be seen in the café during the day and at some of the Gazāwi family festivities. As Umm Bashir joined an adult ESOL (English for Speakers of Other Languages) class offered at the end of the road, new friendships were formed with more neighbors. One of her classmates, a Lebanese refugee familiar with the food of the region, was even offered a part-time job in the café, making special savory pastries twice a week. This "social field" facilitated a sense of familiarity outside of the house/café and exemplifies the "modes of incorporation" that Glick Schiller and Çaglar (2006: 614) referred to when they argued for an approach that looks beyond migrants' interactions with their own "community," ethnic, or national group. The sense of feeling at home for the Gazāwis was fostered by the familiarity created in the home, through their work in the café and through the economic and social relationships they forged on their immediate street.

Making Palestine Visible

For the Gazāwis, remembering and asserting their national identity as Palestinians was crucial in developing a sense of familiarity and, more importantly, in imbuing their new life with meaning. "Being Palestinian," and showing it, was a defining factor in their new setting and in their daily exercise of home-making. In this section, I discuss how the café was used as a site to promote Palestinian-ness and to make a particular image of Palestine visible in London through a variety of activities.

The "Palestinianness" of the café cannot escape a first-time visitor. It is affirmed at first through the materiality of the place and the sensory experience it exudes. Framed Palestinian embroidery pieces, including one of the Palestinian flag, together with photos and heritage items adorn the walls. A massive hand-painted canvas of Al-Aqsa Mosque decorates one wall. A local artist who is a Palestinian supporter and a regular customer at the café had donated it to the family. Beside the display fridge is a wall-size map of historical Palestine. Outside at the entrance, a massive banner hangs on top of the door and welcomes the visitor with the name of the café, Al-Zaytuna, which means "olive." The name was carefully chosen as the family picked one of the symbols of Palestinian people's tie to their land. Following the name on the banner is the motif of the café, "the taste of Palestine." Through the visuals, the symbols, the aroma of falafels, and other spices wafting from the kitchen and through the taste of food, the visitor is promised a sensory experience that would transport her to Palestine. The deployment of heritage paraphernalia and traditional photos of a place is not uncommon in Arabic restaurants in London. This trend is used in the various Lebanese, Iraqi, Egyptian, and other restaurants in areas like Edgware Road where there is a concentration of Arabic restaurants. Others also use names that evoke "tradition" or a glorified past. The niche the Gazāwis were after, however, was the "uniqueness" of the Palestinian experience as they claim to be the only café in London that not only offers Palestinian food, but does so in a "home-made" fashion; in their case, quite literally.

The intertwinement of home and nation – the combination of uniquely offering a national/ethnic cuisine and one that is produced at home – comprises a significant claim to "authenticity." This is recognizable through the common distinction between mass-produced food (or restaurant food) and one that is produced at home which "makes it exude that specifically homely goodness: intimations of sound nutrition, careful choice of ingredients and careful labour (of love)," particularly love associated with "mothers' cooking" (Hage 1997: 101). Indeed, the regulars knew Umm Bashir would come out to greet them in her broken English and enjoy the compliments about the tastiness of her food. The atmosphere created by the Gazāwi family, Abu Bashir's welcoming invitations and jokes, seeing the family consume that same food ("it's so good we eat it ourselves"), and the children running around increased the homeliness of the culinary experience.

For Palestinian customers, and perhaps for the Gazāwi family itself, the food prepared and consumed at Al-Zaytuna had affective powers. Food, both as material and symbol (Wilk 1999), is well known to transport people (especially ethnic and diasporic groups) to different times and places through triggering "experience or meaning in reference to the past" (Holtzman 2006: 363). Food elicits feelings of nostalgia. But nostalgic orientations are not necessarily only about the past. For the Lebanese migrants in Australia, for example, expressions of nostalgia in themselves provided a feeling of "being there *here*" (Hage 1997: 109). So what seems like a yearning for the past can contribute very much to the creation of the present and the future. Cooking, consuming, and selling Palestinian food on an everyday level may have been an expression of longing for the Gazāwis and their few Palestinian customers. But these activities were also about setting an agenda in the present and engaging with a political message that was fundamental to being Palestinian in the diaspora: primarily, the Gazāwis were (re)creating a "national cuisine."

Food has been known to be used among various groups to assert or often invent national identities (Holtzman 2006; Wilk 1999; Avieli 2005). Drawing on Anderson's (1983) "imagined communities," scholars agree that national dishes are more often than not imagined, invented, or fabricated (Avieli 2005). Yet, there remains a propinquity between food and national identity. The "invention" of a Palestinian cuisine is based principally on the creation of a context in which consumption of that same familiar food bears new significance and meaning. Moreover, the "cuisine" itself may be reconfigured when elevated to the status of national representation, particularly outside of Palestine.[3]

Many of the dishes offered on the menu of Al-Zaytuna were known items common to the majority of other Arabic restaurants, especially the Lebanese. These included the *mezze* (starters) such as hummus, falafel, and salads (for a discussion of food boundaries see Zubaida and Tapper 1994). Items of the sort (which are common to the whole region and beyond, considering that they are served in Turkish and Greek restaurants in London) had the status of being "Palestinian" by the mere fact of being prepared at a Palestinian home by Palestinian cooks. Aside from these, the café offered some daily main dishes as its exclusive Palestinian specialty. These included the "Palestinian breakfast," one of their bestselling items, two main hot dishes comprised of traditional "*kidra*" rice (rice cooked in a special clay pot) with chicken or fish and *musakhan*, another traditional dish made out of bread, chicken marinated with sumac and olive oil, and caramelized onion. The café served a "dish of the day" that changed on a daily basis and was made up of a stew with rice, a meal that Palestinians normally have at home rather than at the restaurant. In addition, the café offered two main home-made desserts and ready-made *baklawas* bought from a Lebanese supplier. The café also had a special catering menu for parties and events and offered special food usually associated with Palestinian feasts and weddings: *kharuf* (stuffed lamb), *mansaf* (rice, bread soaked in dried yoghurt broth, and chunks of lamb), *fatteh* (rice, bread saturated with stock and served with chicken), and *maqlubeh* (fried vegetables cooked with rice and lamb and served "upside down," as the name of the dish implies).

What is interesting about this selection is that each of the above-listed dishes on the café menu is marketed as "traditional Palestinian food," despite the fact that all were modernized versions and that hardly any of the ingredients were from Palestine. The "Palestinian breakfast," for instance, was modeled on the "English breakfast" found in many restaurants in London. The dish has several portions of different items on one plate – a serving style that differs from the way the Gazāwi family consumes it, with each item in one bowl. Rather than having eggs, sausage, fried tomatoes and beans, this breakfast platter contained hummus, falafel, two types of Palestinian omelettes, and a salad, all served in generous portions on a big platter. The *kidra* rice was cooked in a normal pot and served in the clay pot only on special occasions, when the café was booked for private events or Ramadan dinners. As for the *musakhan*, it was cooked and served in a pragmatic manner that suited its high demand in the café. Rather than layering the bread, chicken, and onions over a tray and baking it, the dish was turned into individual wraps served with a portion of hummus and salad. Another version was devised which replaced the chicken with *hallumi* cheese and *za`tar* (dried thyme) to cater for vegetarians. These traditional dishes were "modernized" in terms of preparation, service, and consumption. Nevertheless, they were sold and consumed as national "traditional" dishes, presented to the patron "as they used to be" (or would have been) in Palestine. Here, immediately an image of the past is invoked. This, as mentioned above, is not necessarily merely an exercise of nostalgia.

Howell (2003: 217) argues that the modernization of *mansaf*, which became the Jordanian national meal, entailed a "process whereby the dish [was] simultaneously 'disembedded' from its domestic moorings and reconfigured as a sign, a symbol of national particularity and unity." *Mansaf* became a symbol sold to audiences that ranged from other Jordanians, to foreign governments, Iraqi refugees, and, above all, tourists. The creation of a national dish, she argues, fits into Jordan's efforts as a contemporary nation-state to carve out for itself "distinctive politics, history, culture, economy, and cuisine" (Howell 2003: 238). Howell's ethnography confirms Mintz's (1996) classical argument that the creation of national cuisines tends to take place in contexts where representation is imperative. Thus, the process itself then becomes about narrating, imagining, and construing a past with a particular audience in mind. Like the Jordanians, the Gazāwis were also turning the Palestinian dishes they were familiar with into commodities that were simultaneously symbols of "Palestinianness," though they were actively re-embedding these into the domestic sphere through marketing them as "home-made," hence doubly emphasizing the "authenticity" of the experience that was to be consumed in their café. As Mintz (1996) suggested, the audience for the Gazāwis was multifarious, comprising tourists, locals, Arabs, government officials, and an idea of a British/international public. It was common knowledge that Edgware Road was a more attractive destination for Arab patrons, though Al-Zaytuna did have its own Arab and Palestinian customers. But the location of the café near a touristic area that hosts one of the biggest markets in West London meant that aside from the regulars, a turnover of new patrons was frequent.

Through catering to this wide public, the Gazāwis were presenting a political message transported through the consumption of food and the space of the café.[4] The national cuisine presented a picture of Palestinian culture and history that was otherwise obscured from the world by the Israeli occupation. The "authentic" national cuisine that the Gazāwis were (re)creating in London rose above the Israeli occupation but also overrode contemporary divisions within Palestinian society. It was the traditional food with which Palestinians, regardless of where they ended up physically and politically, were familiar. Their presentation did not distinguish between regional food in Palestine (for example, some dishes were specifically Gazan). Nor did it admit reconfiguration or modernization in the diaspora. This national cuisine, instead, was a trope of Palestinian unity as an imagined nation and people before (and despite) *shatat* (exile). This was further confirmed by some events that brought together Hamas and Fateh supporters, who would consume the national cuisine to celebrate Id, for example. It was a representation of a constructed state of being, of "other things being equal."

De Cesari (2010: 633) argues that "restoring the Palestinian past is [itself] an act of defiance." Practices around heritage, for example, are not merely about preserving the old. Rather, she suggests, Palestinians use heritage and the trope of the past as "a technology of presence." Like the Jordanians discussed by Howell, the Gazāwis were deploying their national cuisine as a representation of the Palestinian nation to an international audience in a capital where public opinion is imagined to affect world politics. This indicates especially that Palestinians, as well as their leadership, are well aware that change within Palestine can only be done through lobbying outside of it (Bashara 2008).[5] The Gazāwis deployed the national cuisine and presented it in a space with material reminders of historical Palestine: authentic food, the flag, the map, and images of *fellahs* (peasants) dressed in embroidered clothing, and heritage items.[6]

The more people accepted this representation through the consumption of their cuisine (and the café), the more their nation seemed to be endorsed. This was even more significant when high-profile patrons visited the café, even if their aim was a multicultural culinary experience as opposed to a political agenda. Examples of this include reservations made by staff of embassies or a Labour Party dinner booked at the café for 30 people. The most revealing example is a couple of random visits by prime minister David Cameron, who lived nearby. Although not particularly famous for his pro-Palestinian policies among the Palestinian community of London, his visits prompted a lot of attention by the Gazāwis who made sure to take photos with him, enlarge them, and hang them next to the Palestinian flag and later post them on their website. His public stances towards the colonialist practices of the Israeli state were irrelevant. His presence in the café was credited to their efforts of making Palestine visible in London. "Let them all know that even the Prime Minister himself is for Palestine. He came and ate here with his family and came back," commented Khalid. The Gazāwi family aimed to educate their British and international customers that Palestine was on the map, that it is a civilized and cultured place. Consuming Palestinian food was a sign that the patrons supported this image and by default the plight and cause of Palestinians.

The Gazāwis eventually set out to expand the presence of their national cuisine outside of the spatial boundary of their café. In particular, festivals which had representations of other nationalities were a target. Through networks with a very active Palestinian community in London, the café began to take part in international festivals. Umm Bashir and her daughters, dressed up in the traditional Palestinian *thob*, along with Khalid and other available family members, would proudly exhibit their national cuisine in front of a Palestinian flag at their designated Palestine stall. At a more local level, the Gazāwis took pride in convincing their borough council to add a Palestinian representation in their Annual Cultural Festival of 2010. This festival boasts multiculturalism and bringing together "different people of the world" to celebrate music, dance, and food. The unprecedented participation of the Palestinians was an indicator of the degree to which the Gazāwis now felt emplaced in their neighborhood on one hand and the extent to which they were contributing to putting Palestine on the radar of audiences in London on the other. The creation of a Palestinian national cuisine in the context of London shows us how, in Holtzman's words (2006: 363), "real or perceived resilience in foodways speak to understandings of the present and imaginings of the future through reference to mythic or historicised conception of past eating."

Conclusion

This chapter has explored in brief the experience of a Palestinian family in emplacement. My aim is to take seriously the recommendation in the recent literature for an analysis that focuses "not only [on] memories of social and geographical belonging but also forward-looking practices of attachment to . . . place" (Jansen and Lofving 2009: 2). The Gazāwi family undertook new projects that rooted them in London, despite their persistent aspirations to return to Palestine. Particularly, opening a Palestinian café required commitments that reconfigured familiar socialities and embedded them in new ones. The Gazāwis, like other migrants, embarked on creating a "sense of familiarity," which I suggest was forged through reconfiguring home, family, and nation in the diaspora. Al-Zaytuna café became home for the Gazāwi family, previously fragmented by the Israeli occupation. But it also became home for a political project mediated through the creation of a "national cuisine" that turned the Gazāwis into "spokespeople" in a capital considered to be a hub for world politics. The café became a site for enacting a politics of presence by making Palestine visible and by deploying food as a tool for telling (and experiencing) a narrative of a Palestine beyond occupation and divisions. This chapter, therefore, hopes to contribute to the ongoing discussions that aim to understand "diaspora" and "home" in their ethnographically emergent contexts and to approach people on the move with a lens that pictures them as agentive actors seeking "a sense of possibility" for a better life.

Acknowledgments

Ethnographic fieldwork was conducted with the "Gazāwi" family in London between January and December 2011. The research was done under the fellowship of the Centre for the Advanced Study of the Arab World, University of Manchester, to whom I am grateful.

Notes

1 All names in this chapter are pseudonyms, including the name of the cafe.
2 This policy introduced in 1999 aimed to relocate asylum seekers and refugees to cities in the north of England and Scotland in order to lift the pressure of London and the south of England.
3 The same argument stands for changes in a dish within the same country (see for example Howell 2003).
4 Clark (2004: 29) shows how contemporary punks in Seattle politicised food through their "punk cuisine" and used their café scene as a space to contest American mainstream power relations based in "white-male domination over nature, animals, and people around the world."

5 Bishara cites a British study that shows that 9 percent of polled newsreaders in Britain knew Israelis were the occupiers of the Palestinian territories and that the settlers were Israeli rather than Palestinian.
6 See Swedenburg (1990) for a discussion of the image of the Palestinian "peasant" as a national signifier.

References

Al-Rasheed, M. 1994. "The myth of return: Iraqi Arab and Assyrian refugees in London." *Journal of Refugee Studies* 7(2/3): 199–219.
Anderson, B. 1983. *Imagined Communities: Reflections on the Origins and Spread of Nationalism*. London: Verso.
Avieli, N. 2005. "Vietnamese New Year rice cakes: Iconic festive dishes and contested national identity." *Ethnology*, 44(2): 167–187.
Axel, B.K. 2002. "The diasporic imaginary." *Public Culture*, 14(2): 411–428.
Bishara, A. 2008. "Watching US television from the Palestinian street: the media, the state, and representational interventions." *Cultural Anthropology*, 23(3): 488–530.
Clark, D. 2004. "The raw and the rotten: Punk cuisine." *Ethnology*, 34(1): 19–34.
Clifford, J. 1994. "Diasporas." *Cultural Anthropology*, 9(3): 302–338.
De Cesari, C. 2010. "Creative heritage: Palestinian heritage NGOs and defiant arts of government." *American Anthropologist*, 112(4): 625–637.
Feld, S. and Basso, K.H. (eds) 1996. *Senses of Place*. Santa Fe: School of American Research Press.
Glick Schiller, N. and Çaglar, A. 2006. "Beyond the ethnic lens: Locality, globality, and born-again incorporation." *American Ethnologist*, 33(4): 612–633.
Hage, G. 1997. "At home in the entrails of the West: Multiculturalism, ethnic food and migrant home-building." In H. Grace, G. Hage, L. Johnson *et al. Home/World: Space, Community and Marginality in Sydney's West*, pp. 99–153. Annandale: Pluto Press.
Hage, G. 2009. "A not so multi-sited ethnography of a not so imagined community." *Anthropological Theory*, 5(4): 468–475.
Hanafi, S. 2005. "Rethinking the Palestinians abroad as a diaspora: the relationships between diaspora and the Palestinian territories." In A. Levy and A. Weingrod (eds) *Homelands and Diasporas: Holy Lands and Other Places*, pp. 97–122. Stanford: Stanford University Press.
Howell, S. 2003. "Modernizing Mansaf: the consuming contexts of Jordan's national dish." *Food and Foodways: Explorations in the History and Culture of Human Nourishment*, 11(4): 215–243.
Holtzman, J.D. 2006. "Food and memory." *Annual Review of Anthropology*, 35: 361–378.
Hynes, P. 2006. "Summary of findings: the compulsory dispersal of asylum seekers and processes of social exclusion in England." London: Middlesex University, at http://www.esrc.ac.uk/my-esrc/grants/PTA-026-27-1254/outputs/Download/ed56f72c-6fef-40b3-9252-14c556fad7c3, accessed March 8, 2013.
Jansen, S. and Lofving, S. (eds) 2009. *Struggles for Home. Violence, Hope and the Movement of People*. New York: Berghahn Books.
Kelly, T. 2009. "Returning to Palestine: Confinement and displacement under Israeli occupation." In Jansen and Lofving (2009), pp. 25–41.

Khalidi, Rashid. 1992. "Observations on the right of return." *Journal of Palestine Studies*, 21(2): 29–40.

Malkki, L. 1995. "Refugees and exile: From refugee studies to the national order of things." *Annual Review of Anthropology*, 24: 495–523.

Mallet, S. 2004. "Understanding home: a critical review of the literature." *Sociological Review*, 52(1): 62–89.

Mintz, S. 1996. *Tasting Food, Tasting Freedom: Excursions into Eating, Culture and the Past*. Boston, MA: Beacon Press.

Peteet, J. 2007. "Problematizing a Palestinian diaspora." *International Journal of Middle East Studies*, 39: 627–646.

Sales, R. 2002. "The deserving and the undeserving? Refugees, asylum seekers and welfare in Britain." *Critical Social Policy*, 22(3): 456–478.

Stepputat, F. 2002. "The final move? Displaced livelihoods and collective returns in Peru and Guatemala." In N.N. Sorensen and K.F. Olwig (eds) *Work and Migration: Life and Livelihoods in a Globalizing World*, pp. 202–223. London: Routledge.

Swedenburg, T. 1990. "The Palestinian peasant as national signifier." *Anthropological Quarterly*, 63(1): 18–30.

Turton, D. 2005. "The meaning of place in a world of movement: Lessons from long-term field research in southern Ethiopia." *Journal of Refugee Studies*, 18(3): 258–280.

Wilk, R.R. 1999. "'Real Belizean food': Building local identity in the transnational Caribbean." *American Anthropologist*, 101(2): 244–255.

Zubaida, S. and Tapper, R. (eds) 1994. *Culinary Cultures of the Middle East*. London: I.B. Tauris.

Chapter 22

Imagining Transnational Futures in Vanuatu

Maggie Cummings

Hey, today is another day, another life, another stage of living in Vanuatu. People die everyday and the weather changes everyday. Everything is money and nothing goes without money, money flows everywhere in Vanuatu.

So, how will I care for my child for a better future? How long will it take for my government to be stable. Friends we are already half way to the golden jubilee, now its our 31st anniversary and I still have a piece of bread in my hand, nothing to say, nothing to talk about but its only about that piece of bread I had since I was born.

Fans, this is class six, not Diploma or Masters Degree but CLASS SIX from Dokowia this time, this 31st anniversary with a piece of bread but not Beef stew and rice from a food stall. RELAY AND REMEMBER PREPARE FOR A BETTER FUTURE. (CD liner notes from Dokowia's *Volume 5: L.S.B.-Class 6*)

The idea of global "flows," popularized in Arjun Appadurai's essay "Disjuncture and Difference in the Global Cultural Economy" (1990), is now nearly synonymous with transnationalism in contemporary academic and popular discourse, and provides a convenient shorthand for a vast array of social, political, and economic phenomena. In contemporary Vanuatu, as evidenced in the liner notes (from a local hit CD) included above, novel social, political, and economic phenomena are also glossed in terms of flows – specifically, the flow of money. However, the author enlists the idea of "flow" to describe contemporary life in a way that is culturally specific, and shares little in common with the academic shorthand. Life in Vanuatu has always involved "flows" – of people, substances, and goods – but the "Better Future" liner notes (as I will call them) clearly express misgivings about the ubiquitous flow of cash in and around the country today. The author highlights a key

A Companion to Diaspora and Transnationalism, First Edition.
Edited by Ato Quayson and Girish Daswani.
© 2013 Blackwell Publishing Ltd. Published 2013 by Blackwell Publishing Ltd.

problem in Vanuatu: money does *not* flow everywhere, but it certainly is increasingly true that "nothing goes without money," and that, as my ni-Vanuatu (indigenous) friends repeatedly told me throughout my fieldwork, "money changes everything." The liner notes reference the unfettered flow of money, yet, in doing so, evoke the opposite – the problems, such as poverty, hunger, and despair, that arise when money does not flow, or flows in ways that benefit some and disadvantage others. The author's exhortation to remember to "prepare for a better future" speaks to a fear, one widely shared in Vanuatu, that, as cash becomes increasingly important to everyday social and economic life, the future may not be any better than the present.

One of the most socially and financially transformative means by which money "flows" into and throughout Vanuatu is through its participation in New Zealand's Recognised Seasonal Employer (RSE) scheme, which employs temporary migrants from several Pacific islands as seasonal horticultural workers. This chapter is an exploration of the hopes, fears, and aspirations of ni-Vanuatu men and women for their individual and collective futures in the wake of the recent introduction of the RSE. The scheme, which began in 2007, presents new, almost unprecedented opportunities for short-term transnational migration and relatively reliable wage labor for ni-Vanuatu, and these opportunities in turn present tantalizing new possibilities for the future. Here, I am particularly interested in exploring the ways in which ni-Vanuatu understandings of gender, mobility, and labor shape the ways in which they imagine the various possibilities of future flows – of both money and people – presented by the RSE.

The insights into transnational aspirations that I explore here are based on ethnographic fieldwork with returned RSE workers and their families conducted during two separate two-month field-trips, in 2008 and 2011. I also draw on insights from my earlier fieldwork, conducted before the implementation of the RSE, in 2001–2002. During the two more recent trips, I was interested in hearing not only about the workers' experiences living and working overseas, but also about how they envisioned their futures relative to their work lives – as one of the explicit goals of the RSE program is to change ni-Vanuatu lives for the better through the advent of a robust remittance economy. It is worth noting that the perspective I present here is the view from the national capital, Port Vila, where I conducted most of my fieldwork. One of the key goals of the RSE program is to give rural ni-Vanuatu more chances to participate in the wage-labor and cash economies, and many participants migrate directly from rural villages to New Zealand and back (McKenzie, Martinez, and Winters 2008). However, it is also the case that Port Vila is a magnet for ni-Vanuatu looking for paid labor (often with little success), both inside and outside the country, and the town plays a significant symbolic and literal role in local understandings of the relationship between mobility and wage labor.

In focusing on hopes, dreams, and fears for imagined futures, I take my ethnographic cue from my informants, who, like the author of the "Better Future" notes, frequently expressed concern about their future prospects and the prospects of their children. I take my theoretical cue from Henrietta Moore's *Still Life: Hopes, Desires,*

Satisfactions (2011). Moore suggests that, for social scientists, the time has come to "think again" about global capitalism and globalization, and how they shape "the worlds we share with others." She argues that, too often, our analyses focus on pessimism and loss and implicitly (or explicitly) "invoke the ghostly spectre of change understood as the erosion of ways of life" (Moore 2011: 5). She wonders, "What would the terrain of enquiry look like if we began from elsewhere, if we were to focus instead on the enabling and animating aspects of hopes, desires, and satisfactions" (p. 25)? According to Moore, such a shift in focus might enable us to understand the social change associated with globalization (and, by association, the global flows that characterize transnationalism) not as something that happens *to* the people whose lives we study, but rather, something that they themselves *do*, participate in, drive, and shape through their own choices, actions, feelings, and theories. In order to expand our understanding of social change in all its contemporary forms, we need to think about what Moore, following Foucault (1998) calls the ethical imagination: "the way in which technologies of the self, forms of subjectification and imagined relations with others lead to novel ways of approaching social transformation" (2011: 15). For Moore, a focus on the creative possibilities of the ethical imagination is a way to "think again," and to think beyond the pessimism and loss paradigm when making sense of globalization, culture, and agency (2011: 206n3).

Moore's conceptualization of the ethical imagination is of particular interest to me because ni-Vanuatu themselves oscillate, in their own theorizations of the challenges of the present, between characterizing social change in terms of cultural loss and a hopeful, if cautious, insistence that a better future, one that remains culturally "authentic," is possible. The "Better Future" liner notes exemplify this productive tension: on the one hand, they make reference to the paradigmatic signs of cultural loss and the problems associated with rapid urbanization and the increasing significance of the cash economy: the high cost of living in urban areas, the inadequacy of the education system, and the ubiquity of government corruption. On the other hand, the liner notes suggest a formidable tenacity (everything changes, as it always has) and even optimism – if listeners "relay" the message, and choose wisely, their children will have a better future.

What insights might be gained through a focus on ni-Vanuatu imaginings of transnational futures? As Moore argues (2011: 21), anticipation, or "the alterity of the future," is the terrain on which hopes, desires, and satisfactions take shape. Anticipation, though forward-looking, is grounded, necessarily, in the conditions and knowledge of the present. The way that ni-Vanuatu anticipate the future, and try to bring it to fruition on their own terms, tells us much about the present. Focusing on the future provides one way to answer the question I pursue here: what does the abstract phenomenon of "transnationalism" mean to ni-Vanuatu, and what new kinds of knowledge and experiences does their engagement with transnationalism enable?

Below, I begin by providing relevant background: a brief cultural history of Vanuatu and a description of the RSE. I go on to discuss two case studies, each related to the introduction of transnational labor through the RSE, which exemplify the ni-Vanuatu ethical imagination at work. The first explores the new possibilities opened up for culturally appropriate feminine comportment. The second focuses on the way that men are making sense of the new "kinds" of manhood that the RSE makes available to them. I conclude with a discussion of the way that ni-Vanuatu today are "changing the conversation" (Lindstrom 1990) about what it means to be ni-Vanuatu, to be a migrant laborer, and to be part of this particular transnational flow.

About Vanuatu

Vanuatu is a Y-shaped archipelago comprised of 82 islands in the southwest Pacific. Formerly known as the New Hebrides, Vanuatu achieved independence in 1980 from Britain and France, who had jointly ruled as a condominium government since 1906. The national languages are English, French, and Bislama, the pidgin lingua franca, but most ni-Vanuatu also speak one of the more than 100 vernacular languages as their mother tongue.

According to the 2009 census, Vanuatu's population was 234,023, approximately 44,000 of whom live in the national capital, Port Vila. Situated on the central island of Efate, Port Vila is the largest urban center (Luganville, on the northern island of Espiritu Santo, has 13,000 inhabitants), and is often referred to simply as "town." The population of Vanuatu has grown at a rate of 2.3 percent per year since 1999, but urban growth is outpacing growth in rural areas (at 3.5 percent and 1.9 percent per year respectively), as more and more ni-Vanuatu flock to the urban areas in search of employment. Nonetheless, the population is still overwhelmingly rural (76 percent), and most ni-Vanuatu make a living through subsistence agriculture supplemented by intermittent forays into the cash economy (by selling copra, for instance) (Vanuatu National Statistics Office 2009).

The indigenous Melanesian people refer to themselves as "ni-Vanuatu" – the people "of the place." In the years following independence, creating and maintaining a strong sense of shared national identity among the archipelago's diverse cultural groups was important. This national identity is neatly encapsulated in the country's motto, *Long God Yumi Stanap* (we stand united under God), which is often accompanied by a coat of arms that features a (male) paramount chief in traditional regalia. Ni-Vanuatu are devout Christians, but have incorporated Christianity into what they call *kastom*. The term refers to local beliefs and cultural practices, but more importantly, as Lissant Bolton has put it (2003: xiii), it is "the word that people in Vanuatu use to characterise their own knowledge and practice in distinction to everything they identify as having come from outside their place." In my experience, everyday talk about *kastom* among ni-Vanuatu draws heavily upon a series of binary dichotomies in which the first term is considered authentic, the second inauthentic, and a potential threat to ni-Vanuatu traditional culture. Such oppositions include tradition/modernity, Melanesian/foreign, rural/urban, elders/youth, Christian/heathen, and men/women. *Kastom* frequently is discussed as being rooted in, or providing a link to, the past. However, as John Taylor (2010) argues, the most successful embodiments of *kastom* are those that are Janus-faced, drawing on the past and pointing the way to the future as well. Any understanding of transnationalism, and particularly the RSE, and the futures it potentially engenders, must necessarily take into consideration the role that *kastom* plays in the ethical imagination, as well as the way that *kastom* is itself being re-imagined.

The Recognised Seasonal Employer (RSE) Scheme

With one notable exception, the RSE is the first large-scale opportunity of its kind, in which ni-Vanuatu are able to migrate overseas for labor in significant numbers. During the late nineteenth and early twentieth centuries, thousands of ni-Vanuatu (and other Pacific islanders) were "recruited," sometimes by coercion or misinformation, to work as indentured laborers on the sugar plantations of Fiji and Queensland, Australia (Miles 1998: 112–117). The practice of indentured-labor migration, known as "blackbirding," introduced ni-Vanuatu into the "global flow" of transnational migrant labor. It played a crucial part in the creation of a pan-archipelago (and Pan-Melanesian) identity; blackbirding gave rise to Bislama (when ni-Vanuatu from different islands needed to talk to each other). In other words, transnational flows of migrant labor have long been central to ni-Vanuatu identity (and livelihood). Furthermore, the Pacific island labor trade set the stage for practices of gendered migration that continue to this day, with "men taken away to work, and women left in their places in Vanuatu's villages" (Jolly 1987: 121). The collective memory of the blackbirding period as a dark time in the nation's history also inflects contemporary understandings of, and apprehensions about, opportunities for transnational labor migration under the RSE, regardless of the actual labor and recruiting conditions in New Zealand today.

Since the end of the Pacific labor trade, there have been few opportunities for ni-Vanuatu to participate in the flows transnational labor migration. There is no ni-Vanuatu diaspora to speak of, only 1.5 percent of ni-Vanuatu live overseas (World Bank 2008). Until the inception of the RSE, migration has been mostly inter-island, and circular – between rural island and plantations, or between villages and town, and back again, with migrants in search of wage labor, education, or excitement.

After two years of consultation between various stakeholder governments and agricultural industries, the RSE was officially launched in April 2007, with employers and migrants first being able to take advantage of the scheme in September 2007 (Bailey 2009: 1). The goal of the program was to "ease labor shortages in New Zealand's horticulture and viticulture industries and at the same time aid economic development in the Pacific Islands" (Gibson and McKenzie 2010: 3). The scheme was conceived as a way of meeting New Zealand's development commitments to the Pacific region. It allows for temporary immigration of up to 5,000 migrants per year from the Pacific Island Forum states. Ni-Vanuatu represent a significant portion of these migrants; for instance, in 2008, 1,700 workers were recruited from Vanuatu (ILO 2009: 6). These workers are paid New Zealand minimum wage (a portion of which goes to their recruiting agent, if they had one); plus room and board and half of their return airfare (the other half of which is paid by their employer).

The scheme was introduced, and is now lauded, as a "triple win," one in which the host country, sending countries, and the workers all benefit. New Zealand benefits with a pool of labor that is more reliable than the steadily shrinking rural population or the backpacker community; for Vanuatu (and other Pacific participants), the benefit is an increase in gross national product due to remittances; for workers, the scheme provides a chance to gain new skills and to earn more money than they could at home. The high hopes for the RSE clearly revolve around the potential for remittances to increase the standard of living; however, as we have seen, the flow of money into and throughout Vanuatu may raise as many problems as it solves. At the very least, it seems likely that the success of the RSE looks very different from the perspectives of the various stakeholders. For instance, Rochelle-Lee Bailey conducted interviews and participant observation with ni-Vanuatu worker in the vineyards of Central Otago. In her (2009) analysis, which draws on the work of Tanya Basok (2002) with Mexican guest-workers in Canada, the success of the scheme, from the employers' perspective, requires the "unfreedom" of the workers. RSE workers are unfree in that they are unable to leave their employment and seek other work if dissatisfied. They are bound, by their contracts, to work for the employers stipulated on the visas and contracts. They are reliant on their employers for room, board, and airfare. Moreover, as I discovered during my own fieldwork, they must "behave" well during their contracts (not questioning authority, for instance), or they will receive poor evaluations, and not be offered a subsequent contract.

The necessity of unfreedom for RSE "success" raises questions about what success, or, in Moore's terms, satisfaction, might look like for ni-Vanuatu participants in the scheme. How do ni-Vanautu pursue their hopes and dreams in this context? How might their achievement of "satisfactions" of their own choosing shape the future and meaning of transnational migrant labor itself? The case studies below suggest some possibilities.

Case 1: What Women Want

In order to understand the terrain of transnationalism in the ni-Vanuatu ethical imagination, it is necessary to understand the cultural significance and interconnections of gender, place, and movement. As noted above, ni-Vanuatu have long migrated throughout the archipelago for work, but this kind of migration is closely associated with, and practiced by, men. Women's *kastom* place is in the village and in the home. Ni-Vanuatu attempts to make sense of, and ethically engage with, the RSE scheme necessarily draw on local discourses and practices of gender movement and place-making. This was abundantly clear from the very outset of the program, especially in the kinds of speculative, apprehensive, and hopeful stories and gossip that circulated about the RSE shortly after it began. Here, I describe the ethical imagination at work: the ways in which ni-Vanuatu attempted to make sense of the RSE in the period immediately following its first season.

In June 2008, I returned to Port Vila to conduct fieldwork for the first time since 2001–2002, when my research had focused on the cultural politics of gender, morality, urbanization, and social change. My intent was to reconnect and follow up with the young women who had been my friends and ethnographic informants. During my earlier trip, these women were *ol yangfala gel* ("young people" or "youth" in Bislama) – unmarried, childless women in their late teens and early twenties. Our conversations focused on the moral panic surrounding urbanization, modernization, and rapid social change in Port Vila. Youth, and especially young women, were the object of this moral panic. Young, single, urban-dwelling women were accused of destroying *kastom* through immodest comportment: wearing sexually provocative and "foreign" clothing such as shorts or pants, moving about freely in town, and evading the tighter strictures of male authority – chiefs, pastors, and male kin – in rural villages. These young women were constantly compared to the "ideal" ni-Vanuatu woman: the *mama* (mother). The *mama* is a modest, ideally rural-dwelling, churchgoing, married mother who is respectful of Christian and *kastom* forms of male authority, and who can be recognized by her respectful island dress. Mamas forge a connection to the nation, to *kastom*, and therefore to the past, by bearing children, and are respected for producing the future citizens of Vanuatu. Young urban-dwelling women, as I have argued elsewhere (Cummings 2005, 2008) are considered dangerous not only because they are matter out of place (living in the bright lights of the big city, rather than in the island communities to which they are tied through kinship and *kastom*), but because they are also, figuratively speaking, "matter out of time." Disconnected from or threatening to the past, they are often told by their elders that their value to the nation and the state is in their future role as mothers of future citizens.

Not surprisingly, these young women spoke longingly of their futures – futures in which they would marry, have children, and be able to command the respect accorded to mothers; yet they were apprehensive about having to give up their relative freedom and submit more fully to their husbands', pastors', and chiefs' authority. They were also uncertain how they would manage marriage and motherhood while still making a living: unemployment is high in Port Vila, and the job market is being increasingly feminized (through domestic labor and the service and tourist industries). Often, married women bring home the bacon, fry it in the pan, and play the role of docile, respectful wife, as well. My friends dreamed of a future in which they might live in Port Vila and prosper, but no longer be called "trouble" and be accused of destroying *kastom*. My goal in 2008, therefore, was to see how "the future" was working out for my informants, all of whom had married and had at least one child, if not several, in the years since I had seen them.

When I arrived in June 2008, the first intake of RSE workers had just returned from New Zealand. Port Vila was abuzz with talk and speculation, both hopeful and wary, about the potentially life-transforming possibilities enabled by participation in the RSE. All my conversations about "the future," and about what had changed in Vanuatu in the six years since my first visit, inevitably turned into discussions of the RSE. Women's hopes and fears about the scheme, and the aspirations, strategies, and, sometimes, resignation, that it inspired, were expressed along familiar gender lines. Social change in Vanuatu is often discussed in highly gendered terms – good modernization is that which maintains the status quo of gender relations – with women remaining respectful of male authority, and men continuing to earn that respect as responsible, breadwinning heads of households. Troublesome social change challenges male authority, or results in men giving in to too many temptations and becoming irresponsible. This was clearly the cultural and ethical terrain upon which ni-Vanuatu imagined the benefits and pitfalls of the RSE. However, it was also a space of potential – a space in which the women I knew felt that they might open up, rework, and challenge gender norms. In general, much of the uncorroborated *toktok blong rod* (gossip) about the newly returned RSE workers focused on their properly gendered comportment; especially in terms of sexuality and kinship obligations (and marital obligations, in particular). During my 2001–2002 fieldwork, young women, especially those who lived in town, worked, and were relatively free to move around Port Vila as they chose, were often accused of being peripatetic and, by association, promiscuous; young men, if accused of anything, were accused of spending all their money (or, at least, what little they had) on kava or alcohol. What did I hear most frequently about the newly returned RSE workers in 2008? That the women were running amok, being promiscuous and getting pregnant; and that the men were (mis)spending their hard-earned money on alcohol instead of on their families. One of the first things that I heard about the RSE program was that "for every team that comes back, five women are pregnant, and five men are divorcing their wives." Listening to the *toktok blong rod* suggested, at least at first, a dearth of imagination in the "ethical imagination": these were exactly the same kinds of stories I heard about men, women, mobility, and comportment before the RSE was introduced (although the shift in action to a transnational stage certainly added to the anxiety and consternation evidenced in the stories).

However, in addition to gauging public sentiment about the RSE, I also interviewed men and women who had just returned from New Zealand (the men were on seven-month terms; the women were on three-month terms, which their ni-Vanuatu recruiting agents had deemed more appropriate and less harmful to family life). Although their stories were much more mundane than the *toktok* (no pregnancies, no promiscuity, no drunken spending sprees), they nonetheless spoke of their experiences in highly gendered, and contentious, terms. For instance, all but one of my male informants had wives; but each said that they felt that women should not be allowed to go overseas. Women should stay home and take care of their families. Besides, they said, the work was too hard, the weather too cold, and women would be too quick to "let go of *kastom*" and follow "New Zealand ways."

The women I spoke with, on the other hand, felt that *they* were far better equipped than ni-Vanuatu men to go to New Zealand. For one thing, they claimed, often with glee, that their work was "the easiest work they'd ever done." Grading and packing fruit in a packhouse for eight hours per day was much easier than cooking, cleaning, taking care of one's children and working in a tourist shop. Women told me that recruiters should give married mothers first priority, because women are better at managing and saving money, as they do not "drink" their wages, and always put their earnings toward their children's school fees. Men, one woman told me, are just "too prone to temptation" to be trusted when there is so much money at stake. Women, she said, are so accustomed to having their every move scrutinized in Port Vila, that they do not "misbehave" while they are away, even if there are no relatives or chiefs there to watch them. This self-surveillance hints at what each of my women informants lamented was the worst thing about having participated in the RSE: gossip and rumors about their sexual comportment while they were away. During my initial fieldwork on gender, comportment, and social change, young women envisioned the future with apprehension, but also hopefully – as a possible end of the predicaments of their youth, and especially the end of being blamed for the perceived loss of *kastom*. However, they now find themselves faced with a new (yet similar) predicament, one which seems to be exacerbated by the introduction of the RSE.

Nonetheless, there are satisfactions to be found; satisfactions that arise in some-what unexpected places. One of my RSE interviewees told me candidly that she had used her time abroad to "refreshem mi" – to "start fresh" with her husband, whose adultery in Port Vila had prompted her to sign up for a three-month contract in New Zealand. When she came back, she said, he had missed her terribly. He was also very impressed, rather than threatened by, her breadwinning capabilities, and he had a new respect for her. She said she feels appreciated, and that they are much happier now. They had plans to sign up together for the next intake of migrant workers, so that they could save enough money to buy some land and build a house in town. Her story demonstrates the way that hope, in the unlikeliest of circum-stances, animates an experience of transnational migration that is understood not in terms of loss or pessimism, but satisfaction and possibilities for a better future (one which nonetheless does not entail a denial of, or rupture from, ni-Vanuatu family values).

However, as one friend put it, even after only one intake, it was clear that "RSE i no save stap nao" ("the RSE is here to stay"). In addition to hope, satisfaction, and apprehension, many ni-Vanuatu approach the country's entry into this new trans-national flow of people, labor, and money with resignation. The RSE is here to stay, and any imagining of a "better future" will include (directly for some, indirectly for others) the RSE, whether or not they are able to find satisfaction within the new flows it enables. For young women, this means balancing a genuine respect for *kastom* with an equally genuine (indeed, pressing) need for the various "satisfac-tions" enabled by the RSE: access to greater (cash) wealth with which to feed, clothe, and educate their families, as well as greater freedom and control over their own mobility. The RSE measures success for the Pacific islanders who participate in the scheme in terms of development, but success looks rather more nuanced when viewed from the perspective of ni-Vanuatu migrants and their families. These women were keen to embrace the transnational future, but for them, transnational labor opportunities are not simply a path to economic development. Rather, such opportunities require the creative, yet culturally intelligible, engagement of the ethical imagination, in order to ensure that their own desires and hopes shape the novel social transformations at hand.

Case 2: Transforming Masculinities

Feminine comportment may be one of the ethical "issues" that animates ni-Vanuatu understandings of what it means, and feels like, to live in a transnational world and, in particular, to participate in the RSE scheme, but that is not to say that cultural understandings of masculinity are not significant as well. Men make up the majority (as high as 82 percent) of the ni-Vanuatu participants in the scheme (Gibson and McKenzie 2010: 6), and recruiters, working in conjunction with employers as well as chiefs and pastors from Vanuatu, aim to find men who are "honest, hard-working, who obey orders, who show respect, and do not drink alcohol excessively" (Gibson, McKenzie, and Rohorua 2008: 8). During my fieldwork in 2008, the RSE was yet new, and speculation about its potential was tentative; but by 2011, ni-Vanuatu understandings of the scheme had started to coalesce, and the RSE was more thoroughly ensconced in local imaginings of both collective and individual futures. However, this is not to say that opinions and experiences of the RSE were in any way uniform, but rather that the RSE had become "good to think with" about broader patterns of social transformation, especially as they related to men, masculinity, and work.

In the mental soundtrack of my fieldwork in Port Vila in 2011, the hit single *Class Six* by Dokowia (whose liner notes are so telling), features prominently. I heard *Class Six* several times every day – on the radio, in buses and taxis, playing on teenagers' mobile phones, and at the kava bars. The song, which is simultaneously catchy yet bleak, also evokes the paradoxical mix of frustration and hope, loneliness and solidarity that the sense of impending but unknowable change creates. It is a heartbreaking ballad about being under-educated and underemployed in Port Vila. The song's protagonist laments his inability to get meaningful or reliable employment after having been "pushed out" of school after Year Six (the end of elementary school in Vanuatu) because his parents could not pay his school fees. He confesses his jealousy and disappointment when he sees former classmates, those who were able to finish school, driving trucks or working at the bank. When he can get work, it is temporary, on a construction site, and the boss is breaking labor laws – but the protagonist does not know because he only finished Year Six. Worse yet, he does not have enough money to eat takeaway, or to watch football on satellite. Indeed, as he laments in the chorus, he can barely afford urban, "modern" staples like rice and bread because "Praes blong raes i go antap, praes blong bred i go antap" (The price of rice is going up, the price of bread is going up). He is, essentially, an SPR (*Sperem Pablik Rod*; someone with little to do but "hit the road"). SPR is the label given to so-called wayward youth who, because they are unemployed, "hit the road," wandering around aimlessly, looking for work and killing time, window-shopping and causing trouble (Mitchell 1998). *Class Six* was undeniably the most popular song of the season, and seemed poised to become an anthem of sorts.

The popularity and evocativeness of *Class Six* provides an apt starting point for a discussion of men's experiences of and ethical engagements with the RSE in particular. After all, one of the key goals of the RSE, from the development perspective of New Zealand, at least, is to provide skills training ("upskilling") to the unskilled segment of Vanuatu's population and potential workforce. "Unskilled" and "Class Six leaver" are nearly synonymous, and most of the ni-Vanuatu participants in the scheme did, in fact, have fewer than six years of education (McKenzie *et al.* 2008: 16). The popularity of the song speaks to widely shared concerns about the difficulties of making ends meet in Port Vila. Moreover, it reflects a growing concern that different kinds of work (or, at least, different levels of success at finding and keeping waged employment) are creating new kinds, or categories, of people, and of men in particular (for instance, those who can afford bread and rice, and those who cannot). Here, I want to focus specifically on the ways in which different forms of labor are understood to produce different kinds of men, thereby suggesting different possibilities for the future as well. How does the RSE build upon existing work-made boundaries between kinds of men (or men with different "skills")? What new kinds of masculinity are emerging in the wake of this new industry? To answer these questions, I want to focus on just two possible "ways" of being a ni-Vanuatu man today: *man blong garen* (garden) and *man blong mane* (money).

Walking around town in 2011, refamiliarizing myself with old haunts, I passed a group of three men in bright orange work-vests who were picking up and bagging the trash from the sides of the roads. I called out a "good morning" and one man, Henry, waved me over. We started chatting, and when I said I was interested in work, he lit up. He was from Havana Harbour, about 30 minutes' drive outside of Port Vila. He had caught a bus into town that morning in hope of being able to pick up some temporary work for Port Vila municipality, as he had done in the past. Fortunately, the sides of the road needed to be cleaned up for "the finance people" (a conference of foreign investors who were to be spared from seeing the worst of Port Vila's trash-management problems). He described how he would stay with relatives in Man Ples, one of the peri-urban settlements, while he was working; and would send or take any money he made home to buy food and clothes for his family. He introduced me to his workmates, Peter and Sam, and suggested we sit down in the shade under a nearby tree. Peter, the oldest of three, was in town from the northern island of Pentecost, working a one-year contract for the municipality, and sending his money home to the village; Sam was in his thirties, and, like Henry (who was in his forties), he had come into town from the other side of the island to try to find temporary work.

Peter and Sam were more reticent than Henry; or they were, until I asked about the RSE. Although none of the men had participated in the scheme, they had strong opinions about it, and about the kind of men who went to New Zealand (or perhaps the kind of men they were upon their return). There are two kinds of men in

Vanuatu, Sam said: *ol man blong garen* (those who know how to work the land) and *ol man blong mane* (literally, money's men). He explained that the problem in Vanuatu in general, and especially in town, is that people do not want to work the land any more, or do not know how. They've become lazy, he said. The RSE can be a good thing, but the men agreed among themselves that many people end up coming back without any money because they spend it all on clothes or alcohol. Sam went on to say that the problem is that people go to New Zealand to make money, but end up wanting all of the *stuff* that foreigners have, and spend all their money, and then come back and have to sell their land in order to keep buying the kind of consumer goods that they want. They become, in other words, *ol man blong mane*. He described himself (and his co-workers), on the other hand, as *ol man blong garen*: certainly, he works in town when he gets a chance, but that is only because school fees and clothes and rice are necessities, and they cost money. But he knows how to garden, and understands the importance of a connection to land maintained by working it; he is teaching his children to garden, and making sure they speak their vernacular language (not just Bislama). Sam said that it is true that life is hard, and you have to find money, because you need money for many things; but, he said, money isn't everything. Men who go to New Zealand to make money for the sole purpose of being *ol rabis man* (rubbish men; no good), for causing trouble and for spending money on stuff, have been seduced by money, and have come to mistakenly think that money *is* everything.

There are two things worth noting here. This depiction of RSE workers (which I frequently heard from ni-Vanuatu who had never participated in the scheme themselves) bore little resemblance to returned workers' own characterizations of their transnational labor experience. Although many the RSE workers that I interviewed would sheepishly admit to having spent more money than they should have on alcohol, clothes, and electronics, they certainly did not think of themselves as *ol man blong mane*. Rather, it was New Zealanders who were ruled by money. As one young man put it, "Everything is money there! You can't do anything if you don't have money. It's all they care about! They think you can eat money." Indeed, many young men cited this as the reason they were happy to be home (and, for some, the reason that they had little interest in returning for a second season) – they did not care to spend any more time in the land of money.

The second point to note is how closely Sam's description of *ol man blong mane* resembles the SPR: young, itinerant, unconnected to the land, and eager to consume the accoutrements of Western-style modernity. In fact, many of the men that I spoke to who had gone to New Zealand (especially the ones who were from town, not from a village), said that they *were* basically SPRs before they went overseas. Upon returning from New Zealand, with money in their bank accounts, yet still no prospects for work at home, they were now like SPRs, but not quite. They were on the cusp of something new, but they were not sure what. This uncertainty seemed to manifest itself in men's plans for the money they had saved – every man I talked to said that he wanted to buy land (or go back to family land in the islands) and to build a concrete house. However, few had taken the plunge yet – opting, instead, to stay in town, spending their money, until they decided whether or not they would leave to go back to New Zealand for another season. They had not yet decided whether they could envision a future where their well-being and livelihood required ongoing ties to the land of money, however appealing it might be in the short term.

There is clearly ambivalence, not least among recently returned RSE workers themselves, about what "kind" of men the workers will become. The categories on offer – *man blong mane, man blong garen*, SPR, or Class Six-er – draw upon existing cultural norms about gender, about urban and rural life, and about what kinds of knowledge are valuable. These categories are still in the process of becoming meaningful and are not yet set in stone. However, the RSE itself provides yet another possibility, through its focus on "skills training" and "upskilling." As it turns out, these RSE-based skills *are* changing things, but not necessarily as either the New Zealand government or the employers might have predicted.

What, exactly, are these new skills? Men, who usually work outdoors, rather than in the packhouses, learn skills specific to agricultural work in orchards and vineyards. They learn how to tell if fruit is ripe; how to recognize different varieties of fruit (apples, for instance); they learn how to grade the fruit they pick. The RSE is intended to "build capacity" and "transfer skills" to unskilled workers in Vanuatu, but it is not entirely clear how these skills could be put to work at home (where the requirements of gardening are very different, and where fewer and fewer men have access to garden land in any case). However, there are many other, implicit skills being cultivated through the RSE. When I asked young men what kinds of skills they had learned during their contract, they rarely mentioned anything that actually had to do with the work itself; rather, they felt that the skills that they had spent the most time and effort acquiring had been those "skills" that made them docile, unfree workers. Informants spoke of learning about time management, because, "you have to learn to work against the clock; it's not like 'Vanuatu time' anymore." Moreover, they learn "good hygiene" because "the farmers get really upset if you don't meet their standards." Returned workers also told me that they had learned to do their own work-related paperwork (rather than entrusting it to a recruiter or an orchard manager). This was not just a matter of self-sufficiency. They learned that "you can't complain about it [your paycheque] if it's wrong, or they'll say you're a troublemaker. So you have to figure it out quickly or you'll be ripped off or won't be asked to come back next season." Finally, but perhaps most tellingly, one informant told me the most important (and most difficult) skill: "You learn how to listen to the boss. Sometimes they give instructions that don't seem to make sense, but you learn to just do what they say."

My male informants spoke just as hopefully as their female counterparts about the possibilities that the RSE afforded them for changing their circumstances (by ensuring their future ability to buy land, build homes, and provide for their children, for instance). Men's hopes and dreams, like women's, were tempered by a sense of trepidation, even resignation ("you just have to learn to do what they say"). However, like women, ni-Vanuatu men are finding satisfaction where they can, and in ways that will clearly shape their transnational futures. Let me share one last anecdote that suggests that ni-Vanuatu men are not in too much of a hurry to become docile workers, no matter how much they want to earn wages, and even if they are resigned to tolerating temporary and cyclical "unfreedom" while they are overseas. My friend Colin told me emphatically that, "More than anything else, what the company wants is to find men that will shut up and work. They prefer people from the islands who don't know English or even Bislama, because they can't complain." What skill were his colleagues quickest to learn, according to Colin? "Everybody learns to speak English, and fast. We want to work, but we don't want to be pushed around and ripped off." I spoke to many men (and women, for that matter), who had, in fact, learned English while they were overseas. However, many also expressed the same approach to their vernacular languages as Sam: they continued to speak it at home and teach it their children.

Conclusion: Changing the Conversation

Men's desire to learn English to mitigate their unfreedom, coupled with their desire to ensure the ongoing use and value of various vernacular languages, exemplifies a key feature of the ethical imagination vis-à-vis the RSE, one that answers my original question about the new kinds knowledge enabled through local engagements with transnationalism. They are tentatively, but hopefully, "changing the conversation" (Lindstrom 1990). Lindstrom uses the idea of changing the conversation to discuss the circulation of knowledge, and the power it enables, on the southern island of Tanna; it is useful here for thinking about how ni-Vanuatu make sense of, and engage with, the flows of transnationalism in ways that allow them to pursue their own satisfaction.

Drawing on Raymond Williams' distinction between alternative and oppositional knowledge (1980: 40), Lindstrom defines oppositional knowledge as statements that cannot be tolerated or accommodated because they "make no sense in dominant cultural terms" (1990: 198). Alternative statements of meanings, values, opinions, and attitudes, on the other hand, may be "unexpected, surprising, unpredictable, or deviant [but] remain within the compass and oversight of ruling knowledge" (p. 198). Alternative statements, in other words, are not about abandoning an old conversation, or starting a new one entirely, but, rather, changing the conversation. One of the reasons that an approach to understanding transnational migration that focuses on pessimism and cultural loss does not fit in this case is that the RSE, though new, is part of a longstanding conversation about the proper *kastom* relationship between gender, mobility, and labor. Men like Colin and his workmates, in an effort to succeed in the RSE without becoming completely unfree, have literally changed the conversation by learning to communicate with their employers in English. They are also in the process of carving out a new, as yet undefined, kind of manhood – no longer SPRs, they hope to buy land of their own, and to occupy a category somewhere between *man blong garen* and *man blong mane*. The young women I knew are also changing the conversation: in a situation that potentially exacerbates their fears for the future (that they will have less freedom of movement, be unable to provide for their families, or be unable to earn respect, except as mothers), they, too are carving out a niche for themselves: as respected wives and mothers who wisely earn money and invest it in their families, maintaining *kastom* while also taking advantage of new opportunities. It would be overstating the case to say that "all it takes is a little imagination" for ni-Vanuatu to achieve their hopes, desires, and satisfactions. However, the ethical imagination in Vanuatu, characterized by a respect for *kastom* that is both past- and forward-looking, creates possible paths to a "better future" that are enabled and animated by ni-Vanuatu experiences and understandings of transnationalism today.

References

Appadurai, A. 1990. "Disjuncture and difference in the global cultural economy." *Theory, Culture and Society*, 7(2): 295–310.

Bailey, R.-L. 2009. "Unfree labour? Ni-Vanuatu workers in New Zealand's Recognised Seasonal Employer Scheme." MA dissertation, School of Social and Political Sciences, University of Canterbury, New Zealand.

Basok, T. 1999. "Free to be unfree: Mexican guest workers in Canada." *Labour, Capital and Society*, 32(2): 192–221.

Bolton, L. 2003. *Unfolding the Moon: Enacting Women's Kastom in Vanuatu*. Honolulu: University of Hawaii Press.

Cummings, M. 2005. "Who wears the trousers in Vanuatu?" In A. Meneley and D. Young (eds) *Auto-Ethnographies: The Anthropology of Academic Practices*, pp.51–64. Toronto: Broadview Press.

Cummings, M. 2008. "The trouble with trousers: Gender, *kastom*, and sexual culture in Vanuatu." In L. Butt and R. Eves (eds) *Making Sense of AIDS: Culture, Sexuality, and Power in Melanesia*, pp.133–149. Honolulu: University of Hawaii Press.

Foucault, M. 1998. "Ethics: Subjectivity and truth." *Essential Works of Michel Foucault, 1954–1984*, ed. P. Rabinow. New York: New Press.

Gibson, J. and McKenzie, D. 2010. "The development impact of a best practice seasonal worker policy: New Zealand's Recognised Seasonal Employer Scheme (RSE)." *Working Papers in Economics*, 10(8): 1–30.

Gibson, J., McKenzie, D., and Rohorua, H. 2008. "How pro-poor is the selection of seasonal migrant workers from Tonga under New Zealand's Recognized Seasonal Employer Program?" World Bank Policy Research Working Paper, 4698, August 1. Washington, DC: World Bank. ILO 2009. *Decent Work Country Programme Report Vanuatu 2009–2012*. Port Vila: International Labour Organisation.

Jolly, M. 1987. "The forgotten women: a history of migrant labour and gender relations in Vanuatu." *Oceania*, 58(4): 119–139.

Lindstrom, L. 1990. *Knowledge and Power in a South Pacific Society*. Washington, DC: Smithsonian Institution Press.

McKenzie, D., Martinez, P.G., and Winters, L.A. 2008. "Who is coming to Vanuatu under the New Recognised Seasonal Employer (RSE) program?" *Working Papers in Economics* 9/08, Department of Economics, University of Waikato, Hamilton.

Miles, W.F.S. 1998. *Bridging Mental Boundaries in a Postcolonial Microcosm: Identity and Development in Vanuatu*. Honolulu: University of Hawaii Press.

Mitchell, J. 1998. *Young People Speak: A Report on the Vanuatu Young People's Project*. Port Vila: Vanuatu Cultural Centre.

Moore, H.L. 2011. *Still Life: Hopes, Desires and Satisfactions*. Malden, MA: Polity Press.

Taylor, J.P. 2010. "Janus and the Siren's call: Kava and the articulation of gender and modernity in Vanuatu." *Journal of the Royal Anthropological Institute*, 16(2): 279–296.

Vanuatu National Statistics Office 2009. "Census summary," at http://www.vnso.gov.vu/index.php/surveys/census-2009, accessed March 8, 2013.

Williams, R. 1980. *Culture and Materialism*. London: Verso.

World Bank 2008. *Migration and Remittances Factbook 2008*. Washington, DC: World Bank.

Chapter 23

Global Cities and Transnational Circulations

Singapore and Hong Kong

Rajeev S. Patke

Introduction

A city is a site for collective human habitation; it is also an agglomeration of energies which consumes resources, produces value and waste, and participates in the mobilization of humans and ecosystems, goods, capital and services, information and technologies, cultural modes and practices. It is the locus for a negotiation between what Arjun Appadurai describes as "sites of agency" and "fields of possibility" (1996: 31). Cities are in constant flux: what they appear to be at any given moment in time depends on the gaze of the beholder. What a city can signify also depends on what one brings to it and what one looks for in it. Cities mediate between the regional and the global, the national and the transnational. Cities also act as agents and symptoms of globalization. How they do it depends on an understanding of what Henry Yeung (2010) describes as their "coming into being," in which "processes and mechanisms internal to global cities are coupled in strategic ways with the transnational network relations beyond these cities."

More than half the human population of the planet is now urban. During the last century, human population density has grown at a faster rate in Asia than in other parts of the world. Asian cities have increased in population, economic activity, demographic transformations brought about by migration, consumption of natural resources, and damage to the natural environment at a rate that is probably more rapid than in other parts of the world. Seven of the ten largest human agglomerations of the world are currently in Asia. Cities in East and Southeast Asia have undergone changes in urban lifestyles and cultural practices at a rate that matches and sometimes exceeds that of cities in South Asia. The very notion of a city is being

A Companion to Diaspora and Transnationalism, First Edition.
Edited by Ato Quayson and Girish Daswani.
© 2013 Blackwell Publishing Ltd. Published 2013 by Blackwell Publishing Ltd.

transformed radically by the growth of linked city complexes such as that of Tokyo, the Pearl River Delta region, Seoul, and Metropolitan Manila. In comparison, Hong Kong and Singapore stand out for their relatively modest size, their disproportionately large global clout, and their capacity to slip urban discourses that see global cities as linked to one another more firmly than to the nations in which they are situated. A description of their unique and shared features sheds a very specific kind of light on the diversified nature of transnational circulations and the role of contemporary cities in global formations.

Singapore and Hong Kong are continually self-transforming cities, as unlike as cousins, who seek recognition as global cities on the basis of transnational flows of resources and outputs they command, their ideal locations as protected deepwater ports, their intense and adroit extraction of economic leverage from continually updated technologies of production and circulation, their ambition to create service centers with a global reach, and their desire to provide an urban experience that can mediate between the regional and the cosmopolitan, free of religious intolerance or violence, with ethnic tensions largely repressed by the unwavering equation between economic prosperity and the dream or chimera of urban happiness. They differ in climate and history, in how they demonstrate their commitment to late modern capitalism, and in how they have been governed: laissez-faire in Hong Kong (certainly until 1997, and with qualifications since then), and closely supervised by effectively a one-state government in Singapore since 1965. They share a common spirit of "Chinese commercial entrepreneurialism" (Hamilton 1999: 27), whose implementation has been influenced by the kinds of governance they have received and by the contingencies of their geopolitical positioning. Through chance as well as design, and despite complex links to a large hinterland, each has retained for itself a degree of autonomy remarkable in the history of major urban development. Each has also managed – thus far – to circumvent limitations of space and scarcity of natural resources by making capital out of a highly motivated workforce and sizable inflows of diasporic immigrants and foreign investments. Despite the tropical weather, Singapore has relied upon treaties with Malaysia for a large portion of its drinking water; diversifying this reliance in the twenty-first century by turning to reprocessed water and desalination.

The island has no natural oil resources, and yet its government established oil refining in the island state and became the world's third-largest trading and petroleum-refining center by the late 1980s. Hong Kong too has no natural resources, and imports all its fossil fuels, yet both cities remain among the busiest ports in the world, sharing that honor with Amsterdam (and more recently, Shanghai). In each, the transnational dimension bears an ironic relation to the idea of nation: Hong Kong bypassed the idea in 1997 when the post-1842 British Crown Colony became a Special Administrative Region of the People's Republic of China. Singapore, a British colony since the early nineteenth century, arrived at nationhood in 1965 – with reluctance – only because it was forced out of the Malay Federation as a result of ethnic politics. It has since developed the idea of a city-state on a model that resembles a tightly organized company more than the template common to the nation-centered metropolises of Asia.

Hong Kong and Singapore grew into major ports under British colonialism, a process that entailed the capacity to attract capital and labor in the ever-expanding service of commerce and trade. In Singapore, the inflow of migrants has been determined largely by economic factors, and its ethnic profile is predominantly Chinese (comprising descendants of Chinese migrants from the southern and coastal parts of southeast China), with Malays, Indians, and Eurasians as the minorities. In Hong Kong, economic motivation has been reinforced by political developments in mainland China, especially the Maoist takeover of 1949, and the resulting exodus of Chinese business from Shanghai and hundreds of thousands of refugees from southern China to Hong Kong.

The origins, cultural profiles, and professional skill-sets of transnational migrants coming into Singapore and Hong Kong have kept changing over time, but the fact of migratory urban growth has remained a constant in both cities. Hong Kong differs from Singapore in one respect concerning migration: while more often than not Singapore has been the destination for those who migrated there, Hong Kong has served as destination as well as "jumping-off and return point" (Wickberg 1999: 35) for those departing mainland China, whether in the nineteenth or the twentieth century. Starting with a few hundred people at the beginning of the colonial period, each grew rapidly through the nineteenth century. Mid-nineteenth-century Singapore and Hong Kong had populations below and above the 100,000 mark respectively; by 1900, Singapore had a population of approximately 200,000 and Hong Kong over 800,000. By 1950, Singapore had crossed the 1 million mark and Hong Kong was approaching 2 million. By the turn of the century, Singapore had crossed the 4 million mark and Hong Kong was over 7 million (Lahmeyer 2006).

Compared to most other cities with a comparable growth in population during the modern period, the proportion of people who were born overseas and migrated to Singapore or Hong Kong has been high in relation to the number of people born in either city. Likewise, both cities remain a temporary home for a high percentage of transient foreigners. By 2000, the number of expatriates living in Hong Kong had crossed the half-million mark, of which over half had come to Hong Kong from Asian countries, and the remainder from other parts of the world. In Singapore, "foreigners constitute approximately 30 percent of Singapore's total employment, giving Singapore the dubious distinction of having the highest proportion of foreign workers in Asia" (Yeoh and Yap 2008: 183). In terms of overall contemporary profiles, the CIA *World Factbook* (2010a) indicates that Hong Kong has a current population of 7.05 million, a GDP of US$301.8 bn, exports of $321.8 bn, and foreign investments of $858.2 bn (at home) and $811 bn (overseas). The same source (CIA 2010b) indicates that Singapore has a current population of 4.66 million, a GDP of $243.2 bn, exports of $274.5 bn, and foreign investments of $275.2 bn (at home) and $190.8 bn (overseas). Such brute facts (for which other sources cite slightly different numbers) are of course only part of the picture.

Each city is linked by trade both to adjacent regions and to global partners. It is widely recognized that the two cities went through specific forms of transformation to arrive at their current trade positions. In Singapore, the first phase "lasted from 1965 to 1980 and effectively encompassed the evolution of a manufacturing economy thoroughly embedded in what has become known as the New International Division of Labor" (Smith 2001: 436). Its second phase, described by the government as a second industrial revolution, "aimed at replacing 'down-market,' labor-intensive manufacturing industry with high-tech industry, a range of producer services and a regional investment profile" (Smith 2001: 436). In recent years, Singapore has made a conscious effort to develop trade and investment links with India, despite the known problems of dealing with a country beset by a labyrinthine bureaucracy. As with its investments in China, this policy is a consequence of the increasing economic power of the two Asian giants, and the need for a small city-state to maintain close transnational ties with their burgeoning economies, markets, and pools of human talent. Compulsive long-term planning and an uncanny ability to anticipate global economic changes has been a hallmark of the rise of Singapore to its current global position. After the economic damage sustained as a result of World War II, and the closed-door policies adopted by the People's Republic of China from 1949, Hong Kong has reinvented itself several times, accommodating swiftly to changing economic and political circumstances, and ensuring the role of principal agent of capitalist trade linkages throughout the region: "Hong Kong played the same role in the economy of China as it did in the economies of Southeast Asia. In the early twentieth century, organizing their commercial activity largely through Hong Kong, the Cantonese were the largest group of businessmen in Shanghai, and they largely controlled the distribution of imported sundry items throughout China" (Hamilton 1999: 23–24).

The capacity to adapt has continued to characterize Hong Kong since 1997, and although many residents started leaving the island from the early 1980s (with Canada as the most preferred destination), the period since 1997 has shown that Hong Kong continues to play a vital role in terms of its intensified relation with the manufacturing centers that have sprung up in the Pearl River Delta, for whom it serves as principal investor and conduit. Hong Kong has had a more widespread regional and global reach than Singapore, since it draws a large part of its economic energy from the two-way flows it generates through its geographical proximity to mainland China. Its administrators have also exhibited a more freewheeling attitude towards economic planning, a temperamental and historical predilection endorsed and encouraged throughout its long colonial history. It is an option which postcolonial resource-scarce Singapore has not been able to afford. The manner in which the two cities are embedded in global trade networks differs significantly, as noted by Chiu, Ho, and Tai-lok (1997: 11): "Hong Kong and Singapore are linked up with the global economy and 'internalized' differently – while the former plays the role of OEM (original equipment manufacturing) manufacturer within the international commercial subcontracting network, foreign direct investments assume a dominant position in the latter."

Singapore is smaller in size and overall scale of economic activity than Hong Kong. However, the two share several features: each is highly urbanized, with little or no unemployment, hardly anyone living below the poverty line, and none of the ethnic violence that is almost endemic in most other parts of the developing world. That provides a significant difference between these two cities and the living conditions of most other Asian mega-cities and the urban conditions common to the large nations to which each is adjacent. Each has a per capita GDP that is among the highest in Asia, and comparable to that of the most advanced urban populations of the world. Each is predominantly Chinese in ethnic terms (with Cantonese as the primary language in Hong Kong, and English as the primary language in Singapore since independence), although, as Wang Gungwu points out, the Chinese in Hong Kong, Macao, and even Taiwan have been seen by mainland Chinese as *tongbao* (compatriots), whereas the Chinese who settled in Singapore, and other locations more distant from mainland China, are seen as *huaqiao* (overseas Chinese) (Wang 1999: 120–121).

Both Hong Kong and Singapore are severely restricted in space, and the urban density is very high, with a severe limit to the scope for further demographic expansion, with implications for urban development as well as immigration policies for the future. Singapore is distinguished from Hong Kong in having had a government-sponsored housing policy in place since 1960 which has ensured that every citizen has access to subsidized housing, a provision for which there is no equivalent in Hong Kong. Both cities have grown through waves of migration from the neighboring regions over more than a century. The influx of human resources has played a major role in the growth of the labor force: some of it has settled, some of it remains transient, producing complex and ever-changing dynamics between the settled and the non-settled parts of the labor force.

In terms of population, the two cities are dwarfed by many other Asian cities from China and India, and by Seoul and Tokyo in the Far East. In terms of economic productivity, however, they are a significant force in the region and beyond. Their geographic location has proved decisive in giving each a historical role to play in the growth of trade and commerce in Southeast and East Asia. Their advantages as natural ports occupying strategic locations along networks of trade routes has ensured for both cities long histories of mercantile growth. In both cities, the spirit of entrepreneurship established during the colonial period was sustained and built upon in the postcolonial period, with varying degrees of control and support from the state apparatus.

Both cities have continued to grow steadily throughout the period from the end of World War II, and especially from the 1960s. Each has shown a high degree of adaptability to changing regional and global circumstances; each has become adept in creating a unique role for itself in terms of trade and commerce, and in attracting regional as well as global investments. Each provides a diversity of cultural practices and traditions. Each has developed to its present globalized condition by developing and adapting in relation to a mainland it is related to but distinct from, both economically and culturally. Each is also remarkable in the degree to which the state-sponsored narrative that the people are its chief resource has been realized through the combination of administrative policy as well as the spirit of individual economic entrepreneurship. To what degree, and precisely how, can one situate either city in relation to contemporary discourses of the global city?

The Idea of a Global City

The idea of a global city has become far less exclusive since it was introduced into the discourse of urban change by Saskia Sassen. Her (1991) work was one among many indicators of the increasing attention devoted to the phenomenon of urban growth by city planners, geographers, sociologists, economists and cultural theorists, whose attempts to get a handle of choice on the phenomenon led to many preceding formulations such as Lewis Mumford's "megalopolis" (1938), J. Friedmann's "world city hypothesis" (1986), and the population-based notion of the megacity, for which a number such as 8 or 10 million generally suffices (placing Hong Kong at 48 and Singapore at 50, as of January 2013, according to the online reference site, *The Principal Agglomerations of the World*, http://www.citypopulation. de/world/Agglomerations.html). In 1991, it seemed plausible for Sassen to reserve the applicability of the term *global city* to New York, London, and Tokyo, with specific reference to the role they had acquired in the global economy through "the combination of spatial dispersal and global integration" (pp. 3–4). In 2006, she qualified the earlier position by suggesting that the "global city is not a descriptive term meant to capture a whole city," instead, she preferred to delimit the idea as referring to "the partial and specific structuration of the global inside the urban" (p.x). Since the 1990s, global rankings have become an obsessive consideration for academics as well as city planners.

Beaverstock, Smith, and Taylor, for instance, compiled a roster of cities in 1999, on the basis of what they termed "global competence," which they determined by singling out for assessment four services: accounting, advertising, banking, and law. Since 2008, the Japan-based *Global Power City Index* (see below) has devised its own method of ranking cities in a global hierarchy, and it singled out New York, London, Paris, and Tokyo as the top four mega-cities for 2010, while Singapore made it to fifth in their 2009 ranking (Mori Memorial Foundation 2010). The ranking for the top five in 2011 was: New York, London, Paris, Tokyo and Singapore (Mori Memorial Foundation 2011). By 2011, the idea of a global city has come to apply to many more cities: precisely which and how many depends on the criteria used to define the term. Taking account of differences in disciplinary perspectives, the consensus surrounding the idea of a global city suggests an urban agglomeration complexly meshed into and significantly responsible for a large part of the transnational circulation of goods and services, human and natural resources, information, media, and technology, as well as many of the cultural values and practices which sustain and change, as well as depend upon and lead to, the complex system of interdependencies that are entailed in the idea of globalization.

Size has a role to play in creating a global city, as well as economic productivity and the political or cultural leverage that comes in specific circumstances with economic power; but the consensus on how to define a global city comes under strain when it comes to specifying the combination of criteria and the relative weight given to constituent features in the definition of a global city. A brief contrast among some recent surveys is therefore useful in focusing specifically on whether and how Hong Kong and Singapore might qualify for recognition as global cities, keeping in mind a growing trend among students of urbanism to recognize that economic prominence needs to be balanced with ecological, cultural, and livability factors in describing and evaluating global cities.

In 1950, the three most populous cities in the world were New York, London, and Shanghai. By 1975, Tokyo had virtually tripled its population and exceeded that of New York, while the third most populous cities were Mexico City and Shanghai, with London's population remaining roughly where it had been in 1950. In 2011, the idea of a global city overlaps, but only partially, with the idea of a mega-city, since the latter term is based solely on the size of the population while the former prioritizes transnational linkages and globalized flows over sheer numbers.

Beaverstock, Smith, and Taylor (1999: 446–449) divide approaches to the idea of a global city into five categories: first, "early proponents of world city research . . . identified the strategic domination of certain world cities in the world-system by analysing and ranking the locational preferences and roles of multinational corporation (MNC) headquarters in the "'developed" world'"; a "second approach centered upon the decision-making corporate activities and power of MNCs, in the context of the new (spatial) international division of labour discovered in the late 1970s"; a "third approach has firmly associated the cities within the urban hierarchy with their propensity to engage with the internationalisation, concentration and intensity of producer services in the world economy; "a fourth approach identifies major cities and their relative positions through rankings of international financial centres"; a fifth approach, which the authors promote, treats "world cities as particular 'postindustrial production sites' where innovations in corporate services and finance have been integral to the recent restructuring of the world-economy."

More recently, a study from the United States, conducted by the journal *Foreign Policy*, the management consultancy firm A.T. Kearney, and the Chicago Council on Global Affairs, has generated *The Global Cities Index*, which lists 65 global cities (Foreign Policy 2010). The top of the latest such list includes four Asian cities, and also shows among other things, that size matters only in relation to the scale of economic activity, with the top ten ranks going to New York, London, Tokyo, Paris, Hong Kong, Chicago, Los Angeles, and Singapore, in that order.

The Global Cities Index rates cities on the basis of the combined effect of five dimensions: business activity (including capital markets, the number of *Fortune* Global 500 firms headquartered there, and the volume of the goods that pass through the city), human capital (how well the city acts as a magnet for diverse groups of people and talent), information exchange (how well news and information is dispersed about and to the rest of the world), cultural experience (the level of diverse attractions for international residents and travelers), and political engage-ment (measures the degree to which a city influences global policymaking and dialogue). Whether these five dimensions suffice, and how they might be defined or redefined remain open questions, though it seems evident that there is a fair degree of agreement that some combination of economic, demographic and cul-tural factors are key elements in the network of circulating energies that signify the global scope and reach of a city.

Another recent approach originating from the Institute of Urban Strategies at the Mori Memorial Foundation in Japan provides a slightly more rounded idea of what it takes for a city to claim being global in their *Global Power City Index*. The aim is to evaluate cities on the basis of a set of "six main functions representing city strength (Economy, Research and Development, Cultural Interaction, Livability, Ecology and Natural Environment, and Accessibility), and four global actors who are leading the urban activities in their cities (Managers, Researchers, Artists, and Visitors) and one local actor (Residents)." The combination of criteria leads to a ranking of global cities on the combined effect of a number of factors, giving a far more complex profile of what makes different cities attractive to different walks of life. Thus, while managers might be interested in features such as potential for business growth and infrastructural support for business, a researcher might be interested in the kind of research culture a city provides, artists might look for an environment where the public and the city management encourage the arts, a visitor might be more interested in tourist attractions and quality of entertainment, and those who make the city their home might look for features such as medical benefits and the quality of the environment at work and in terms of housing.

The criteria used by the four types of "actors" are as follows: for the manager, accumulation of enterprise and business; for the researcher, quality of research institutions; for the artist, cultural stimulus; for the visitor, cultural appeal and opportunities; and for the resident, economic environment. Though different scoring methods give different rankings, by general consensus New York, London, and Tokyo retain the position of global influence they were given in Sassen's (1991) book. The latest edition of the *Global Power City Index* (Mori Memorial Foundation 2011) ranks the top ten cities in the following order: New York, London, Paris, Tokyo, Singapore, Berlin, Amsterdam, Seoul, Hong Kong, and Sydney. By now, the idea of a global city has evolved from an exclusive demographic count and a notion of economic centrality within global networks or a limited set of professional and economic parameters affecting services to a more balanced idea of assessment that recognizes that complex urban environments must achieve high standards in pro-viding for a combination of needs affecting industry, art, culture as well as the business of daily living if a city is to be regarded as sustainably global.

Transnational Flows: Singapore and Hong Kong

No city becomes global without becoming a significant part of the networks and mobilizations through which all contemporary transnational energy systems have their being, with cities as their conduits and magnets. The inflow and outflow of the urban transnational can be described as a complex mesh with several discursive dimensions: human, natural, economic, technological, and cultural. Religion is one of the oldest and most decisive of transnational forces: it came in three waves to Southeast Asia: Hindu, Muslim, and Christian. Today, the medieval Hindu influence has largely faded into history. The Islamic influence, which began to take hold decisively from the thirteenth century CE, has proved lasting, especially in Malaysia, Indonesia, and the southern parts of the Philippines. It constitutes a minority in Singapore, and an even smaller one in Hong Kong. Christianity was the most recent of the world religions to arrive in the region. Christian missions came to Singapore in the 1820s and to Hong Kong in the 1840s, often with educational goals in mind in addition to their proselytizing. Colonial administrators were at best supportive, and at worst neutral to these missions. While Buddhism, Taoism, and Confucianism are the primary religions in Hong Kong (with 10 percent Christian according to the *CIA World Factbook* 2010a), in Singapore the current religious profile of the resident population is more mixed (CIA 2010b): Buddhist 42.5 percent, Muslim 14.9 percent, Taoist 8.5 percent, Hindu 4 percent, Catholic 4.8 percent, other Christian 9.8 percent, other 0.7 percent, none 14.8 percent. Two things stand out in terms of the transnational influence of religions in Singapore and Hong Kong: the state apparatus remains committed to multi-religious tolerance and secularism. Religion retains significance for worshippers, but at the level of private and communal experience, without the public edge or prominence it acquires in many other urban contexts within and outside Asia.

The second transnational force is migration. Singapore and Hong Kong came into being as colonial ports enriched by successive waves of migrants, predominantly by ethnic Chinese, mainly from the southern provinces of China. British colonialism added to the mix both in terms of Eurasians, and in terms of indentured labor, imported from economically undeveloped parts of India to clear the swamps in Singapore, and work for the empire in building roads and railways, and in running plantations of rubber and palm oil in British Malaya: "between 1852 and 1937 . . . 1,189,000 [Indians went] to Malaya" (Lal 2004: 83). Contemporary Singapore and Hong Kong can be described as dual gateways, encouraging migrations to and from the region, although as the steady increase in their population testifies, their power to attract migrants has been greater than their capacity to induce people to leave for other destinations, a feature that changed briefly but dramatically in the case of Hong Kong when pre-1997 fears of what might happen to business and living conditions once the British colony had reverted to China induced many Hong Kong citizens to migrate to destinations such as Canada, the United States, Australia, and Singapore.

Transnational migration can be distinguished between unskilled and skilled labor, and between transients and immigrants. The large majority of unskilled or semi-skilled transient workers live in the global city in a mode that is temporary, marginalized, and alienated: tolerated for the work that citizens would rather not undertake, but denied parity with citizens in matters of housing, healthcare, and amenities. Since they can be ejected at short notice, their experience of living in a global city partakes of the fate of the mythical Tantalus, making them distant cousins to their ghostly ancestors: slaves, and indentured laborers.

In pragmatic terms, cheap labor serves the global city as the humble means to grand ends. The Singapore government relaxed its immigration policies soon after independence as the need for imported labor became apparent, and it has moved progressively towards administrative controls which ensure that highly skilled workers drawing higher salaries have a better chance to make the transition from temporary workers on time-specific contracts to permanent residency and citizenship. As living standards have improved, and with a common pattern of double-income middle-class families, since 1978 Singapore has come to rely on domestic workers ("maids" in local parlance), drawn from neighboring regions for household chores, especially the Philippines, Indonesia, Thailand, and Sri Lanka: "In December 2009, it was reported that there were 856,000 migrants in low or semi-skilled manual jobs. This includes 196,000 women employed as live-in domestic worker" (HOME 2011). For a total island-wide population of approximately 5 million, this is a high percentage.

The percentage in Hong Kong is also high according to a report by Philip Bowring (2011): "In Hong Kong's case there are some 250,000 such temporary workers, mostly from the Philippines and Indonesia, and they constitute 7 percent of the working population." Yet the transnational culture of these domestic workers, the tensions created by frequent cases of abuse by employers, and the interstitial spaces these transient workers inhabit in spatial and social terms, add a complex and often disregarded and repressed dimension to the quality of life in Singapore and Hong Kong as aspiring global cities. Yeoh, Huang, and Willis (2000) note three features of the relation between this phenomenon and transnational global flows: "the increased international mobility of female labor," the degree to which gendered processes underpinning global cities "pivot on ideologies of the family," and the failure of "gendered processes fuelling transnational flows in and out of global cities" to "transform the civil sphere" (pp. 155, 156).

Transformation in Technologies, Media, and Cultures

The transnational is a form of mediation; it is also a form of the intermediate and the intermediary. Nothing mediates and serves as intermediary better than new technologies and new media: both Singapore and Hong Kong are notable for their obsessive interest in and compulsive use of both. Their connectivity by submarine communications cables makes them significant players in global financial transactions. Their ports are amongst the most up to date; their telecommunications and internet connectivity are among the most advanced, just as their internal metropolitan rail systems (the MRT in Singapore, the MTR in Hong Kong) are among the most efficient. Their airports have had a central role to play in making each a major transit point and destination for air travel. This infrastructure equips the two cities with a diversified and developed agency for regional flows and a sizable share of the global traffic in humans, goods, services, and data, with the one qualification that unlike Hong Kong and most of the rest of the world, Singapore does not permit private access to TV reception by satellite dish, and tries, after a fashion, to carry out surveillance on and prosecute the more obviously gross forms of trafficking in material on the internet, a task that is as laudable as it is self-stultifying in the age of untrameled mobilities.

The transnational dimension to the global reach of a city is never more clearly manifest than in how it produces, circulates, and consumes cultural processes and products. Manufacture is not confined to goods; it extends to conscious and inadvertent forms of self-imaging. A global city is continually implicated in the process of imaging: either for transnational business, tourism, and/or settlers and denizens, or as part of the promotion of an achieved urban identity. One way of addressing these processes is through what Ulf Hannerz (1996: 6) described as contemporary urban actor roles: "In the transnational arena, the actors may now be individuals, groups, movements, business enterprises." He identifies four types of actor as playing major parts in the making of contemporary world cities: (1) educated professionals, (2) "various Third World populations," (3) "people concerned with culture," and (4) tourists (pp. 129–131). As far as tourism is concerned, both Hong Kong and Singapore have become prominent targets, despite their limited resources in terms of landscape, historical artifacts and relative newness of galleries, museums and other exhibition venues.

The situation is changing rapidly: Macao, Hong Kong's neighbor, has matched and exceeded Las Vegas in the capacity to attract the dedicated gambler, the tourist-as-gambler, and the gambler-as-tourist; in 2010, Singapore launched its own version of an integrated resort, built at a cost exceeding S$8 bn, despite internal misgivings about what licensed gambling might do to the work ethic of a predominantly Chinese population innately drawn to gambling. Both cities have seen a burst of activity in the regional and international art auction markets, in art curatorship, and the setting up of new museums or the refurbishing of old ones. Both cities have secured a strong presence on the part of Western auction houses such as Sotheby, and money deposited in Singapore banks by rich nationals from neighboring regions can now be spent not only on expensive property but on art objects.

The import of global (and more specifically) Western high culture is increasingly prominent and heavily subsidized by public (and sometimes private) funding: Singapore's Esplanade theater was launched in 2002 at a cost exceeding US$600 m, and serves as the showpiece venue for an assortment of regional and international art events, with Western classical music and theater playing a prominent role in the city's competition with cultural counterparts in Kuala Lumpur and Hong Kong. A music conservatory set up through private endowments now vies with the premier training schools in the United States and United Kingdom to attract young classical musicians of the region to train in Singapore. The urban topography of both cities continues to change dramatically as various international styles of architecture and housing spread their imprint across what was once a more distinctively regional repertoire of architectural styles. The rise in property prices in both cities is phenomenal, regardless of the pressure this places on ordinary citizens in Hong Kong and government subsidized housing in Singapore.

An aggressive positioning under way in both cities to provide host venues for an assortment of international sporting events (for example, the inclusion of Singapore in the Formula 1 racing calendar since 2008, and the hosting of the Youth Olympics in 2010) is symptomatic of how the images these cities project of their alleged global status becomes a self-fulfilling prophecy. But Ackbar Abbas' memorable description (1997: 4) of a culture of disappearance which he regards as characteristic of Hong Kong begins to find a counterpart in the gradual mutation of Singapore's region-specific diversity into a hypermodern kind of cosmopolitanism: "a tendency towards timelessness (achronicity) and placelessness (the international, the parasitic), a tendency to live its own version of 'the floating world.'"

Place and time are reconfigured in a complex yet readily communicable form by the film medium. Films that establish the taste by which they will be admired introduce their own unique ethos into the flow of transnational imagery. New technologies and media have a central role to play in such circulations. What shipping, airlines, and cables have done for Hong Kong and Singapore in terms of providing ease of access and mobility to people and goods, cinema has done with the martial-arts film industry in Hong Kong, from the 1960s to the present time. What began as a very region- and culture-specific industry has since become a transnational force to reckon with. As Meaghan Morris remarks (2005: 1, 2): "Hong Kong films are watched, copied, collected, discussed, pirated, re-made, parodied and appropriated in many different viewing situations all over the world," making "Hong Kong cinema a benchmark of achievement, a site of inspiration and cross-cultural borrowing, a model for emulation and a target of rivalry." The paternalistic management policies adopted since independence by the government in Singapore did not see as affordable the development of a film or television industry with the degree of freedom enjoyed by the entertainment industry in Hong Kong. However, there are signs in contemporary Singapore that film-making is catching on among young film directors.

Literary refractions from Singapore and Hong Kong generally tend to qualify, question, or undercut the global scale of urban ambitions, with rare and influential exceptions such as Edwin Thumboo's "Ulysses by the Merlion" (1976) which ushers in a modern transnational Ulysses whose travels bring him to a modern Singapore so that the hero from the mythical West can be confronted by the Eastern city's ambitions:

> Peoples settled here,
> Brought to this island
> The bounty of these seas,
> Built towers topless as Ilium's.
>
> They make, they serve,
> They buy, they sell.
>
> (Thumboo 1993: 80–81)

The poet Lee Tzu Pheng is more quizzical and self-questioning about endorsing what the poem "Bukit Timah, Singapore" calls the city's "megalopolitan appetite," and the poem "'My Country and My People'" describes as one of its dehumanizing consequences: "milli-mini flats/for a multi-mini-society" (Lee 1980, in Pang and Lee 2000: 49–50, 51–52). An even more skeptical poet, Arthur Yap, notes laconically that in "the calculus the city is reckoned on," "credulity is a bigger commodity than credibility" (Pang and Lee 2000: 107, 108). This local tradition in writing offers a muted but articulate form of resistance to the urban planners' will to globalism, treating the belated and hence urgent modernization of Singapore as a site for energies whose propulsion is deeply ambivalent between the creative and the destructive. Boey Kim Cheng's "The Planners" (1992) is bitter about the city's accomplishments:

> The country wears perfect rows
> of shining teeth.
>
> Anaesthesia, amnesia, hypnosis.
> They have the means.
> They have it all so it will not hurt,
> so history is new again.
>
> (Pang and Lee 2000: 37)

The view from Hong Kong differs slightly: the writers neither welcome nor fear urban change. They note its happening, and they busy themselves getting used to it. Edmund Blunden, writing as far back as 1962, is droll about change in his poem "On Lamma Island":

> This quiet place is changing as we all do.
> Builders have new ideas, shoppers too.
> Even pigsties pass from old to new.
>
> (Xi and Ingham 2003: 241)

More than three decades later, Louise Ho, herself, like Blunden, a transnational writer, is more matter-of-factly affirmative in her poem "Island" (1997):

> We are a floating island
> Kept afloat by our own energy
> We cross date lines
> National lines
> Class lines
> Horizons far and near
>
> We are a floating island [. . .]
>
> (Xi and Ingham 2003: 298)

Literary writing from both cities responds to the transformation of their home cities with a good deal of acumen, always alert and sensitive to the social consequences of massive and rapid urban transformations. When cities become global – writers remind us – what is gained in the materiality of tall towers and bustling tourism is paid for in the dematerialization of memory, and the homogenization of personal and communal histories into the single monotone of an urban drive always pitched at the level of economic prosperity and technological advancement rather than spiritual well-being or conducive living environments.

References

Abbas, A. 1997. *Hong Kong: Culture and the Politics of Disappearance*. Minneapolis: University of Minnesota Press.

Appadurai, A. 1996. *Modernity at Large: Cultural Dimensions of Globalization*. Minneapolis: University of Minnesota Press.

Beaverstock, J.V., Smith, R.G., and Taylor, P.J. 1999. "A roster of world cities." *Cities* 16(6): 445–458; doi: 10.1016/S0264-2751(99)00042-6.

Bowring, P. 2011. "Foreign workers welcome, but no permanent residents, please." *Yale Global Online*, November 11, at http://yaleglobal.yale.edu/content/foreign-workers-welcome-no-permanent-residents, accessed March 8, 2013.

Chiu, S.W.K., Ho, K.C., and Tai-lok L. 1997. *City-States in the Global Economy: Industrial Restructuring in Hong Kong and Singapore*. Boulder, CO: Westview Press.

CIA 2010a. "Hong Kong." *The World Factbook*, at https://www.cia.gov/library/publications/the-world-factbook/geos/hk.html, accessed February 20, 2013.

CIA 2010b. "Singapore." *The World Factbook*, at https://www.cia.gov/library/publications/the-world-factbook/geos/sn.html, accessed February 20, 2013.

Foreign Policy 2010. "The global cities issue." *Foreign Policy*, September/October, at http://www.foreignpolicy.com/issues/current, accessed February 20, 2013.

Hamilton, G.G. 1999. "Hong Kong and the rise of capitalism in Asia." In G.G. Hamilton (ed.) *Cosmopolitan Capitalists: Hong Kong and the Chinese Diaspora at the End of the Twentieth Century*, pp. 14–34. Seattle: University of Washington Press.

Hannerz, U. 1996. *Transnational Connections: Culture, People, Places*. London: Routledge.

HOME 2011. *Shadow Report to 49th Session*. Human Organization for Migration Economics, at http://home.org.sg/downloads/CEDAW_ShadowReport_Jul2011.pdf, accessed February 20, 2013.

Lahmeyer, J. 2006. *Population Statistics*, at http://www.populstat.info/populhome.html, accessed February 20, 2013.

Lal, B.V. 2004. "People in-between: Reflections from the Indian indentured diaspora." In S.-L. Wong (ed.) *Chinese and Indian Diasporas: Comparative Perspectives*, pp. 69–93. Hong Kong: University of Hong Kong.

Lee, T.P. 1980. *Prospect of a Drowning*. Singapore: Heinemann Asia.

Mori Memorial Foundation 2010. *Global Power City Index 2010*. Institute of Urban Strategies, The Mori Memorial Foundation, at http://www.mori-m-foundation.or.jp/english/research/project/6/pdf/GPCI2010_English.pdf, accessed February 20, 2013.

Mori Memorial Foundation 2011. *Global Power City Index 2011*. Institute of Urban Strategies, The Mori Memorial Foundation, at http://www.mori-m-foundation.or.jp/english/research/project/6/pdf/GPCI2011_English.pdf, accessed February 20, 2013.

Morris, M. 2005. "Introduction: Hong Kong connections." In M. Morris, L.L. Si, and C.-K.S. Chan (eds) *Hong Kong Connections: Transnational Imagination in Action Cinema*, pp. 1–18. Hong Kong: Hong Kong University Press/Durham,NC: Duke University Press.

Pang, A. and Lee, A. (eds) 2000. *No Other City: The Ethos Anthology of Urban Poetry*. Singapore: Ethos Books.

Sassen, S. 1991. *The Global City: New York, London, Tokyo*. Princeton: Princeton University Press.

Sassen, S. 2006. "Foreword." In M.M. Amen, K. Archer, and M.M. Bosman (eds) *Relocating Global Cities: From the Center to the Margins*, pp. ix–xiii. Lanham, MD: Rowman & Littlefield.

Smith, D.W. 2001. "Cities in Pacific Asia." In R. Paddison (ed.) *Handbook of Urban Studies*, pp. 419–450. London: Sage Publications.

Thumboo, E. 1993. *A Third Map: New and Selected Poems*. Singapore: Unipress.

Wang, G. 1999. "Chineseness: the dilemmas of place and practice." In G.G. Hamilton (ed.) *Cosmopolitan Capitalists: Hong Kong and the Chinese Diaspora at the End of the Twentieth Century*, pp. 118–134. Seattle: University of Washington Press.

Wickberg, E. 1999. "Localism and the organization of overseas migration in the nineteenth century." In G.G. Hamilton (ed.) *Cosmopolitan Capitalists: Hong Kong and the Chinese Diaspora at the End of the Twentieth Century*, pp. 35–55. Seattle: University of Washington Press.

Xi, X. and Ingham, M. (eds) 2003. *City Voices: Hong Kong Writing in English, 1945 to the Present*. Hong Kong: Hong Kong University Press.

Yeoh, B.S.A. and Yap, N. 2008. "Gateway Singapore: Immigration policies, differential (non) incorporation, and identity politics." In M. Price and L. Benton-Short (eds) *Migrants to the Metropolis: The Rise of Immigrant Gateway Cities*, pp. 177–202. Syracuse, NY: Syracuse University Press.

Yeoh, B.S.A., Huang, S., and Willis, K. 2000. "Global cities, transnational flows and gender dimensions: the view from Singapore." *Tijdschrift voor Economische en Sociale Geografie*, 91(2): 147–158.

Yeung, H.W.-C. 2010. "Globalizing Singapore: One global city, global production networks, and the developmental state." Unpublished keynote address at the Creating Cities: Culture, Space, and Sustainability: The City, Culture, and Society (CCS) Conference, Ludwig Maximilians University, Munich, Germany, February 25–27.

Chapter 24

Diaspora and Discourse
The Contrapuntal Lives of Mexican Non-Migrants
Hilary Parsons Dick

Introduction

Si a mi me daría la oportunidad de ir a Los Estados Unidos con mi familia, pues sí, ya mejor allá. Porque aquí se sufre mucho. Aquí lo que se gana no alcanza para nada, no mas para puro comer y mal comidos. Mal comidos y creo que allá – pues allá tambien se sufre, ¿verdad?. . . tambien se sufre. Pero creo que allá se mantiene mejor. Mejor para los niños que son los que se van, pues ahorita, para arriba.

[If I were given the opportunity to go to the United States with my family, well yes, really [it's] better there. Because here one suffers *a lot*. Here what one earns isn't enough for anything, only to just eat and [one is] *not well fed*. Not well fed and I think there – well, there one also suffers, right? . . . . one also suffers. But I think that there one maintains oneself *better*. Better for the children, who are the ones who now are building lives.][1] ("Rosario," a Mexican non-migrant)

Most people are principally aware of one culture, one setting, one home; exiles are aware of at least two, and this plurality of vision gives rise to an awareness of simultaneous dimensions, an awareness that – to borrow a phrase from music – is *contrapuntal*. (Said 2000: 186; emphasis in original)

Said's provocative "Reflections on Exile" (1984) captures a process that many scholars of diaspora and transnationalism argue characterizes the lives of mobile and displaced populations: their present lives unfold with a "contrapuntal awareness" of lives inhabitable in some other space and time (Basch, Glick Schiller, and Blanc 1994; Clifford 1994; Malkki 1995). But these populations are not the only ones who live contrapuntally. Images of lives realizable "beyond here" – such as the opening image of a life in which one can maintain oneself better in the United States – are

A Companion to Diaspora and Transnationalism, First Edition.
Edited by Ato Quayson and Girish Daswani.
© 2013 Blackwell Publishing Ltd. Published 2013 by Blackwell Publishing Ltd.

also mobile, entering also into the discursive practices of non-migrants, as we see in the opening quotation from a conversation I had with "Rosario," one of my friends and research participants in Mexico. The practices through which people articulate and take stances on counterpoint lives are a central way in which the processes of contemporary globalization, like transnational migration, become concrete and salient (Appadurai 1996; Gupta 1992; Larkin 2002; Dick 2010a). What distinguishes people's engagement with the processes of globalization, then, is not that some people live contrapuntally while others do not. Rather, it is the relationships people form with contrapuntal lives. What kinds of claims do they make on those lives – do they see them as accessible or unfurling beyond a border that cannot be crossed?

Drawing on ethnographic fieldwork in Uriangato, a small Mexican city with several migration pathways to the United States, this chapter examines the production of contrapuntal lives in the discourse of Mexican non-migrants like Rosario. I use the term *non-migrant* to refer to the family and friends of migrants who dwell close to the active practice of migration. As I have explored elsewhere (Dick 2012, 2010a, 2010b), working-class Uriangatenses regularly engage in "migration discourse": talk, such as Rosario's opening words, about the prospects of migration, through which they articulate contrapuntal lives. The expression of contrapuntal lives is routinized by a representation of space and time – a *chronotope* (Bakhtin 1996: 84), found throughout Uriangatense migration discourse. Consider Rosario's words in the opening quotation to this chapter, in which she produces a common here–there framework contrasting lives realizable *aquí*/here in Mexico to those realizable *allá*/there in the United States. Like the terms "here" and "there," which only become meaningful in opposition, so too does this framework represent Uriangatense lives in Mexico as meaningful only in relief to Uriangatense lives in the United States. These lives are inextricably linked; or, as one of my research participants put it, "one goes there with a dream of doing something here." This framework restricts the contrapuntal lives people can claim to those available across one border in the United States, even though there are migration pathways from Mexico to several other countries (Mize and Swords 2011: 215–234; Paz 2009).

This here–there framework is part of a widely distributed "cultural chronotope" (Agha 2007b; Lempert and Perrino 2007) that relies on a modernist binary which configures the United States as a land of socioeconomic mobility and progress, but also of moral dissolution, and Mexico as a land of morality and family, but also of socioeconomic stagnation. Therefore, the contrapuntal lives of Uriangatense non-migrants are expressed in close dialogue with national imaginings, as are many transnational and diasporic social formations (Eisenlohr 2006; Werbner 2004). In analyzing the modernist chronotope, I employ the concepts "transnationalism" and "diaspora" as ways of thinking through the relationships non-migrants form to contrapuntal lives. Transnational paradigms presuppose a territory inflected by single geopolitical border (Clifford 1994: 304), emphasizing continual cross-border movements that create a sense of simultaneity, as if people are living in more than one nation-state at a time (Basch *et al.* 1994; Rouse 1991). As such, they position contrapuntal lives as accessible. To some extent, the modernist chronotope expresses just this sort of transnational sensibility: lives "here" and "there" are rendered across one border as co-constitutive and, therefore, as unfolding simultaneously. Over the last twenty years, scholars of Mexico–United States migration have overwhelmingly described this sort of cultural formation as "transnational" (e.g., Farr 2006; Hirsch 2003; Rouse 1991, 1992; Smith 2006).

However, the modernist chronotope problematizes transnational images of simultaneity across borders, suggesting a more diasporic orientation. Diasporic paradigms presuppose the construction of social worlds across many possible borders (e.g., Das 2008; Werbner 2004), while also delineating an impassible barrier between one's present life and "home," locating that home in a distant past or a remote future (Clifford 1994). The contrapuntal lives of diaspora, therefore, are inflected by longing, alienation, and loss and are consequently positioned as never fully accessible. Indeed some have argued (Schmidt Camacho 2006) that the militarization of the Mexico–United States border since the early 1990s (De Genova 2002; Durand and Massey 2003) has made transnationalism increasingly difficult, constructing a situation of diasporic semi-exile for Mexicans in the United States. As such arguments suggest, the construction of transnational and diasporic relationships are ongoing "political" achievements that critically reflect on people's present circumstances – and on whether, and how, they think that it is possible to transform those circumstances (Eisenlohr 2006: 228; Werbner 2004: 896). But what kind of political commentary is expressed through the Uriangatense modernist chronotope?

The modernist chronotope does more than contrast the United States and Mexico; it entails two morally freighted "ideal Mexicos" – one which urges the embrace of tradition; the other, the embrace of progress. For working-class Uriangatenses, these two ideal Mexicos are part of a single national imagining that constructs "being moral" as an essential feature of "being Mexican." Consequently, these Mexicos must be integrated, so that tradition and progress are realized simultaneously. However, it is nearly impossible for working-class people to achieve such integration in their actual lives because the opportunities for socioeconomic mobility in Uriangato do not allow them to "progress." Therefore, the contrapuntal lives of working-class non-migrants are expressions of a fractured, diasporic social position in Mexico, characterized by an impassible divide between the lives they feel morally compelled to lead in order to "be Mexican," and the lives to which they can actually lay claim. Therefore, diaspora is not just a possible response to physical displacement from home; it can also be a product of alienation from home, even for people who never leave home. My central argument, then, is that the contrapuntal lives of Uriangatense non-migrants reveal a "diaspora at home" that articulates a trenchant critique of the failures of class mobility in Mexico, as I will show through an analysis of the modernist chronotope, the practices of home-building in Uriangato, and Rosario's relationship to both.

In the following, I first provide a broad overview of the modernist chronotope and its associated contrapuntal lives and national imaginings, detailing their moral freighting through a discussion of family life in Mexico. I then offer an examination of the practices and ideational significance of home-building, through which working-class people's thwarted efforts to integrate the "two Mexicos" is poignantly exemplified. In this section, I argue that the conditions of possibility for "diaspora at home" critiqued by Uriangatense migration discourse have been generated by three dramatic socioeconomic transformations, which have unfolded in Uriangato since the 1970s: the growth of a local textile industry, the nuclearization of families, and the rise of large-scale migration to the Unites States. Finally, I offer a close textual analysis of a bit of speech from a conversation I recorded in Uriangato with Rosario and her husband "Fernando." In this conversation, the dream of home acquisition and its deferral to a remote future are dominant themes that repeatedly arise as Rosario and Fernando grapple with "diaspora at home." The excerpt I analyze was articulated by Rosario; I detail the discourse features, especially pro-nominal usage and verb tense, Rosario uses to take stances on images of her actual and contrapuntal lives. This analysis allows me to illustrate how individual actors actively relate themselves to the diasporic social positioning articulated though migration discourse and, in so doing, critically evaluate their present lives.

Fieldwork on Uriangatense Migration

Uriangato is a *municipio* (county): the next level of government in Mexico after states, typically encompassing one urban center and a handful of satellite rural communities called *ranchos*. In the early 2000s, the municipality of Uriangato had a population of 53,000; the majority (46,000) lived in its urban center (Aranda Ríos 2000: 25). My fieldwork was part of a two-year ethnography in Uriangato and Pennsylvania. My research focused on families, for Mexico–U.S. migration is over-whelmingly shaped by family life (Hondagneu-Sotelo 1994; Massey *et al.* 1987; Hirsch 2003; Smith 2006). Rosario is a member of one of the families around which I organized my fieldwork. I spent extensive social time with her and her relatives, not only recording dozens of conversations, but engaging in a range of activities, from preparing food to attending weddings. Through this, I became familiar with the routine stances taken by Rosario and her relations toward diaspora at home. I centered my fieldwork in Uriangato on a working-class neighborhood, where I also lived. While I built relationships with several middle-class people, my point of ori-entation was this neighborhood and its residents because U.S.-bound migration out of the urban center is concentrated there.[2]

A Tale of Two Mexicos: The Contrapuntal Lives of Non-Migrants

The two ideal Mexicos discussed above are articulated through the central themes of migration discourse: *siguiendo adelante* (getting ahead) and creating *vida bonita* (a "beautiful" life) (Dick 2010a). The literal translation of bonito/a is "beautiful," but its use in Mexican Spanish conveys that the people or activities thus described represent that which is morally upright (Stack 2003). The primary way in which working-class Uriangatense non-migrants create a *vida bonita* is through the realization of a specific kind of family life rooted in the realization of a concept of personhood I call "role constituted" (Dick 2010b: 95). Role-constituted personhood situates the essence of humanity in the successful occupation of co-constitutive social roles (mother and child; husband and wife), which endure beyond any one individual. One creates a *vida bonita* by sacrificing personal ambitions in the service of the mutual obligations associated with these roles (cf. Farr 2006; Hirsch 2003, Rouse 1995). In migration discourse, most working-class Uriangatenses readily assert that this form of personhood renders life in Mexico morally superior to life in the United States. The idea that Mexico is morally superior to the United States has been part of Mexican nationalist discourse since the late nineteenth century (Bartra 1992; Lomnitz-Adler 1992, Lomnitz 2001), and it is promoted in the Catholic Church discourse (Lester 2005) to which Uriangatenses are routinely exposed (Dick 2010a). Thus, the theme of creating a *vida bonita* entails a national imagining that roots "being Mexican" in traditional values and practices, especially those of role-constituted family life. Not surprisingly, much of the migration discourse of non-migrants involves debates over whether relations in the United States have abandoned their commitments to the *vida bonita*, becoming *desobligados* (disobliged): a contrapuntal imagining that suggests they have become immoral and "un-Mexican."

The ideal Mexico of the *vida bonita* is countered by the second dominate theme of migration discourse, which, together with the theme of creating a *vida bonita*, makes up the core contrast of the Uriangatense modernist chronotope: getting ahead. For working-class Uriangatenses, "getting ahead" means being socioeconomically mobile. The theme of "getting ahead" is pervasive in Mexico, most notably in nationalist discourses and their promotion of "progress" (Bartra 1992; Dick 2010a; Lomnitz-Adler 1992; Tenorio-Trillo 1996; Castellanos 2010; Messing 2002; 2007: 259, 266–268). These discourses forward a national imagining that portrays Mexico as behind and needing to catch up, specifically to standards of living set by the United States. This imagining informed economic development programs in Mexico throughout the twentieth century (Walsh 2004), including in Uriangato where, starting in the 1970s, the municipality began a process of industrialization, reducing its investments in agriculture and eventually becoming one of Mexico's most productive textile centers (Lattanzi Shutika 2011). The growth of the textile industry made Uriangato one of the more prosperous municipalities in the region, expanding local possibilities for socioeconomic mobility.[3]

Uriangatenses describe the transformation of the municipality's farming class into an industrial working class through the theme of "getting ahead." Consider the following statement made by Fernando in my conversation with him and Rosario:

Pues, como digo, antes no, no – la gente no pensaba en el futuro. No pensaban en el futuro, y en sobresalir – tratar de sobresalir. Y ahora sí. La gente de antes – yo sí lo veía: casitas de piedra y con cartones y todo eso. Sí. Y ahora, ya no. Ya tratan de superarse un poquito más, y piensan más. Quieren vivir ya más . . . mejor.

[Well, as I say, before no, no – people didn't think about the future. They didn't think about the future, and in improving, in trying to improve. And now yes. People from before – I myself used to see: stone houses and with cardboard and all of that. Yes. And now, not anymore. Now people try to improve themselves a little bit more, and they think more. They want now to live more . . . better.]

Fernando constructs a temporal framework contrasting the life of Uriangatenses "then and now," which is commonly replicated not only in working-class interpretations of industrialization, but also in migration discourse (Dick 2010a: 280–281). Although such statements do not make overt claims about morality, they do entail morally laden presuppositions about the value of "progress" that are quite typical of narratives of modernity (Keane 2007; Miller 1994; Napolitano 2002). Before it did not matter if people were satisfied with houses of stone and cardboard because they did not know any better; but now they do. So, now only the ignorant and lazy dwell in such homes, and their putative unwillingness to "live better" is a moral failing. The realization of the morality of progress relies on a concept of personhood that situates the essence of humanity in the unique, intrinsic characteristics of individuals, what I call "autonomous personhood" (Dick 2010b: 95). To progress, one's moral duty is to become autonomous of role-constituted obligations and actualize those characteristics, thus "improving oneself" (cf. Keane 2007; Mahmood 2005). As Fernando suggests, "improving oneself" in working-class Uriangato means, above all, displaying that one is not poor – that one is socioeconomically mobile and can achieve ever-higher standards of living. And, in "improving themselves" thus, Uriangatenses not only help themselves get ahead; they help their nation as well.

Getting ahead and creating a *vida bonita* offer distinct visions of "being Mexican" that are based in alternative orientations to time (cf. Alonso 1994). One requires people to "think about the future," urging Mexicans to "get ahead"; the other requires living in a present made alive by its connections to the past, urging countrymen to actualize the traditions of role-constituted family. Although these orientations are starkly different, working-class Uriangatenses do not represent them as competing options, but as equally important moral imperatives: you must get ahead while creating a *vida bonita*. That is why I describe "getting ahead" and "creating a *vida bonita*" as the lynchpins of a single chronotope – one that locates the heart of "being Mexican" in the integration of the moralities of progress and tradition. But as I show in the next section, such integration is challenging for working-class Uriangatenses because the political economy generated by Uriangato's industrialization has denied them the opportunities that facilitate the ongoing pursuit of progress. As part of this, the fulfillment of the role-constituted family life has become intimately bound up with aspirations for socioeconomic mobility that far outpace the actual possibilities for such mobility. Consequently, many working-class Uriangatenses face a seemingly impassable barrier separating them from a life they have a nationally inflected moral obligation to fulfill. This separation creates a diaspora at home, an alienation between "being working-class" and "being Mexican."

Diasporic Home-building: Working-Class Mobility
Dreamed and Deferred

A key site where working-class Uriangatenses express and negotiate diasporic alienation is in the practice and ideational valuation of home-building. Working-class
Uriangatenses view home-building as the central site where the traditional morality
of family life is created and maintained. This view is part of a widespread cultural
construct in Mexico that contrasts "the home" and "the street," positioning "home"
as the source of social order; without home, that order is destabilized (Hirsch 2003;
Hyams 2003; Mendoza-Denton 2008). At the same time, a shift toward family
nuclearization in Uriangato, which coincided with industrialization (a pattern
found across Mexico, see Hirsch 2003), has changed the aspirations of home-
building. Before the 1970s, most homes in Uriangato were family compounds in
which parents shared residence with their unmarried children and their sons'
nuclear families. Since the 1970s, however, the proper development of family life –
creating a nurturing and stable environment inside of which partners can raise
moral children – has become contingent on couples being able to own a single-
family home (Dick 2010b: 99–104; cf. Hirsch 2003). If a couple does not have their
own home, they risk being seen as not fulfilling their obligations as parents, and
thus risk moral failure.

But the dream of home-ownership is difficult to achieve for working-class people.
Because most banks in Mexico will not grant mortgages to people who do not
already own a home, it is largely impossible for working-class Uriangatenses to
purchase a new home outright; instead, they build homes piecemeal as they are able
to save the money for construction (cf. Miller 1994). Yet, most of the jobs in which
working-class people are employed in Uriangato's textile industry are seasonal and
"off the books," so many workers do not receive the benefits accorded to them by
the law, such as overtime pay and health benefits. This makes it challenging to save
money for anything, especially a major capital expense like a home. Because of this,
many working-class Uriangatenses argue that the barriers to class mobility for *obreros
como nosotros* (laborers like us) are insurmountable: while – they argue – the Mexican
economy functions well for middle- and upper-class people, *they* must go to the
United States to get ahead. As such, Uriangatense migration discourse articulates a
critical commentary on the failures of Mexico's economy and the socioeconomic
binds they create.

These failures have also encouraged large-scale migration out of urban Uriangato
to the United States, most of it – until recently – by men who migrated seasonally
without their families in order to access the capital needed for home construction
in Mexico. As has been documented in locations throughout Mexico (Hirsch 2003;
Lattanzi Shutika 2011; Massey *et al.* 1987; Smith 2006), families with access to remittances sent by migrant loved ones in the United States generally build larger and
more elaborate homes, which changes local housing standards (Alarcón 1992; Stark
and Taylor 1991). If in the 1970s, most families in Uriangato lived in single-story

abodes, often with each nuclear family sharing a bedroom, now working-class families aspire to homes influenced by US home-building – not only that each nuclear family have its own home, but that each home have two or three stories, a living room, dining room, and separate bedrooms for the parents and every child (Hirsch 2003; Pader 1993). As a result, the moral imperative to build a home for stable family life is now linked to the aspiration to build ever-more luxurious and atomized living environments. Paradoxically, then, the migration meant to help working-class people circumnavigate the barriers to class mobility in Mexico has fortified those barriers by facilitating a perpetual increase in living standards that makes it more unlikely that most working-class people will be able to "get ahead" – a paradox made especially poignant in light of the fact that many migrants are not able to earn enough in the United States to meet these standards (cf. Massey and Sánchez 2010).

Thus, in summary, the industrialization of Uriangato has created the conditions of possibility for diaspora at home by producing a sociocultural and political economic context that places value on "getting ahead," while powerfully constraining working-class people's ability to get ahead and be "moral Mexicans." But these conditions do not a diaspora make; diasporas are political commentaries on such conditions. In the preceding analysis, I have shown that the modernist chronotope that orders the expression of contrapuntal lives in migration discourse does, indeed, produce such a critique. I outlined some of the widely distributed claims of this critique, particularly the proposition that "workers like us" must go to the United States to get ahead. As I have explored in other work (Dick 2010a, 2012), while any working-class Uriangatense would recognize this proposition, and the critical commentary it entails, not all of them accept or agree with it. Fernando, for example, represents himself as someone who once embraced it, but who now believes that, with hard work, his family can "get ahead" in Mexico. Rosario, on the other hand, still strongly agrees with the proposition that one must go to the United States in order to get ahead, advocating that her family embrace a contrapuntal life. Hence there are differences in how working-class people negotiate the integration of the two Mexicos. In the following section, I explore how Rosario engages with this process.

Diaspora at Home – Rosario's Discourse

Rosario and Fernando's extended family, like those of most working-class people, has migration experience. Of Rosario's 11 siblings only she and two sisters have not been to the United States. Fernando himself once migrated to Utah for a little over a year to work in construction, with the goal of saving money for a home in Mexico. But, as he put it, "I could not realize my dream." His employment was insufficient to support the expenses of a transnational life: two residences, trips across the border. Then he was involved in a car accident, which produced a record of legal violation that bars him from eligibility for US visas.[4] After the accident, he returned to Uriangato and has not migrated since. In the decade following his return, he and Rosario have worked in vain to acquire the capital needed for home construction; meanwhile, their children have become teenagers, raised in one rental home after another. Through our recorded conversation, Rosario endeavors to integrate the two ideal Mexicos by elaborating a social positioning I found to be commonly articulated by married female non-migrants. She would like to migrate in order to get ahead; however, she would only do so with her husband and children, in service of building their life, and especially their home, in Uriangato. As I have explored elsewhere (Dick 2010b), presenting the desire to migrate as in the service of family development is a key way in which working-class women maintain their respectability while contemplating potential departures to a land seen to corrupt morality and "Mexicanness." But family migration is not an option for Rosario.

Both Fernando and Rosario talk about a time before Fernando's migration when they dreamed of obtaining visas that would allow them to migrate legally as a family. This is no longer possible because of Fernando's car accident, and Fernando will not migrate with his family illegally – for him, it is too dangerous to be morally defensible. As such, Rosario's contrapuntal life – a life in the United States as a family – rests on the other side of her husband's unwillingness for them to migrate together. This was the case for many women non-migrants I knew, and it mirrors the experience of women in other parts of Mexico, where the wills of family members more actively constrain women's migration (Dick 2010a, Hondagneu-Sotelo 1994; Hirsch 2003). Women like Rosario who want to migrate as a family, but whose partners do not share that desire, are placed in a double-bind that is iconic of diaspora at home: they want to migrate to get ahead, but cannot do so without fracturing their moral standing as good family women and authentic Mexicans. Rosario's efforts to integrate the two Mexicos, and their failure, can be revealed through an analysis of a different kind of chronotopic framing – the "event chronotopes" that emerge over the course of unfolding talk (Agha 2007b: 321).

All talk has a spatiotemporal organization, as people employ discourse features, such as "here and there," that situate representations of themselves and others in time and space (see, e.g., Agha 2007a; Eisenlohr 2006; Inoue 2004; Lempert and Perrino 2007). Such acts of locating are not just descriptive; they create internally coherent structures that allow speakers to formulate stances on those representations, accepting some as embraceable possibilities in the present and others as ruptured dreams. As such, the analysis of event chronotopes is a useful way to see how actors encounter and evaluate the diasporic social positioning discussed above. In Figure 24.1 I offer a micro-analysis of two discourse features that help produce an event chronotope in a bit of speech articulated by Rosario: pronouns and verb tense. Before the following excerpt, Rosario has been describing how difficult it is to save enough money to build a house in Mexico.

By attending to pronominal use in this excerpt, we see three images of Rosario emerge. The first one is of her alone in lines 1, 2, and 4, constructed through the first person singular subject pronoun *yo* (the Spanish equivalent of "I"), and also entailed in verb endings, such as "-o" at the end of *digo* (I say), labeled "R_1." The second one is of her with her children in lines 3 and 4, constructed through the first

Line	Spanish	Translation
1	Y es eso de que yo … sí, le digo a el –	And it's that I$_{R\_1}$ … yes, I$_{R\_1}$ tell him –
2	Hubo un tiempo en que a el le decía que nos *llevara*.	There was a time when I$_{R\_1}$ used to tell him that he should take us $_{R\_2}$ [to the United States].
3	Pero por lo mismo – no nos llevó porque todo … pues, como el platicaba, verdad?, tuvo unos problemas allá. Por eso no nos llevó.	But because of that same – he didn't take us $_{R\_2}$ because all … well, like he was saying, right?, he had some problems there [with his brother]. That's why he didn't take us $_{R\_2}$.
4	Pero yo le decía que "nos llevara para los dos ponernos a trabajar y ya hacer una casa aquí [para] que cuando ya nos enfadara, ya tenemos a donde llegar."	But I$_{R\_1}$ used to say to him, "You should take us$_{R\_2}$ so the two [of us]$_{R\_3}$ can put ourselves$_{R\_3}$ to work to build a house here. So that when we$_{R\_3}$ get fed up, now we have a place of our own."

Figure 24.1   Rosario's discourse

person plural object pronoun *nos* ("us" in English) (R_2). And the third one is of her and Fernando as a couple in line 4, also constructed through the use of *nos*, as well as the first person plural subject pronoun verb ending -*emos* in *tenemos* ("we have") (R_3). R_1 is "biographical" in that Rosario depicts herself to have actually occupied this version of herself. R_2 and R_3 are both biographical and contrapuntal. The biographical couple, for example, is entailed in the conversations that she implies she and Fernando had about migration through the instances of reported speech in lines 1, 2, and 4. The contrapuntal couple is depicted in line 4, where she paints a picture of the two of them working together in the United States to build a house in Mexico. The referent of the final "we" at the end of line 4 is ambiguous – it potentially represents her and Fernando, her and her children, as well as all of them as a unit. This multi-referentiality creates an entailment that suggests that it is only through the actualization of a contrapuntal life that their family can be fully unified in Mexico.

These visions of Rosario express the two ideal Mexicos through her evocation of two widespread cultural images of family life and womanhood in Mexico. The first image is of the mother as an intercessor who speaks to the husband on behalf of her children, in this case to convince him to take everyone to the United States (line 2), implying that Fernando has the final say on whether or not they migrate (cf. Hondagneu-Sotelo 1994). Here Rosario invokes traditional patriarchal ideals of family life that posit the family as like a church hierarchy, with a patriarchal head (father/priest/God), leal subjects (children), and a female advocate for her subjects (mother/Virgin Mary) (cf. Rouse 1995). But she also constructs a competing image of a wife in "companionate marriage": an image of family life as built on the equal partnership of a couple that shares mutual love and cooperation and works together to build their family, as Rosario depicts in line 4. This ideal has been increasingly taken up by Mexican couples since the 1970s, informing the processes of family

Line	Tense	Speech		
1	Present R_1	And it's that I … yes, I tell him –		
2	I_Past R_1, R_2	There was a time when I used to say him that he should take us [to the United States].		
3	P_Past R_2	But because of that same – he didn't take us because all … well, like he was saying, right?, he had some problems there. That's why he didn't take us.		
4	I_Past R-1	But I used to say to him,		
	Present R_2 R_3		Direct reported speech	"You should take us so the two [of us] can put ourselves to work to build a house here. So that when we get fed up, now we have a place of our own."

Figure 24.2   Temporal framing in Rosario's discourse

nuclearization, including the drive to acquire a home of your own (Hirsch 2003; Gutmann 2007). It is also bound up with notions of "progress" associated with getting ahead, and it is frequently used in talk about migration as a way for men and women to show that they are "modern" (Hirsch 2003; Napolitano 2002). But these images of family life are not on equal footing. Consider how Rosario grounds these images in time and space, and therefore in relationship to herself, through the verb tenses she employs (Figure 24.2).

Notice, first, the rupture between lines 1 and 2: in line 1, Rosario starts to use the simple present tense to suggest an image of ongoing conversations between her and Fernando; we can infer based on the statements that follow that these conversations pertained to her desire for them to migrate as a family. But she cuts herself off – this image is not quite right. She begins again in line 2, using a past tense not found in English: the "imperfect past" ("I_Past"), employed, for example, in the verb ending "-ía," as in *a el le decía* ("I used to say to him"). Generally used to suggest continual actions in the past, the imperfect tense can also suggest a time period or epoch. By using this tense in lines 2 and 4, Rosario creates a sense that there was a past era during which the dream of going to the United States was very much alive for her, during which she regularly advocated for it. This past era is interrupted in line 3, where Rosario employs the "preterit past" (P_Past). This tense is used to emphasize the definitive completeness of past events: he had problems in the United States; he didn't take us. When placed inside the ongoing usage of the imperfect, as it is in this excerpt, the preterit past creates a sense of interruption – one event was ongoing, when another came in and caused events to shift course. In this case, Fernando's problems are depicted as fracturing her connection to her contrapuntal life; if once she believed that life to be a tangible option, now it is inaccessible to her. Through this depiction, she is offering an image of the kind of life she would like to have in Uriangato: her family getting ahead, with a home of their own. Thus, the event chronotope that erects a temporal barrier between her actual and contrapuntal life serves as a critical commentary on her present circumstances, which make even the life she would have in Uriangato diasporically contrapuntal – belonging to a remote past to which she cannot return.

Conclusion

Finally, then, the articulation of contrapuntal lives functions as a form of evaluation of the kinds of lives to which non-migrants believe they can lay claim in Uriangato. Through this, they articulate a diasporic social positioning that highlights the cruelty of a political economy that helps inculcate in working-class people a desire to get ahead – one deeply integrated with being authentically, morally Mexican – while providing socioeconomic opportunities that may give them a taste of class mobility, but that deny them the ability to realize the kinds of perpetual mobility mandated by narratives of progress. For this reason, many Uriangatenses turn to migration to the United States; tellingly, patterns of large-scale migration out of urban Uriangato did not exist before the expansion of the textile industry, which suggests that there is an important link between the rise of this industry and the thwarted socioeconomic aspirations of working-class people. Though, as we have seen, the effort to circumnavigate barriers to socioeconomic mobility in Mexico through physical mobility to the United States only recreates diaspora at home for all but a handful of migrants and their families. Thus, the articulation of a diasporic social positioning by working-class Uriangatenses calls into question the morality of progress: what is so moral about getting ahead, about "improving yourself" if it separates you from family, from home, and even from your own life?

Many of the middle-class people I knew in Uriangato also pose this question – not because they reject the morality of progress, but because they question the way working-class people endeavor to progress. They are critical of "migrating to get ahead," both as a proposition and as a practice, arguing that it is evidence of the greed and laziness of working-class people, qualities they suggest bring working-class people's commitment to nation into doubt. Middle-class Uriangatense rejection of "migrating to get ahead" offers a different kind of morality tale, which constructs the socioeconomic struggles of poor and working-class people not as evidence of structural inequalities generated by local and transnational political economies, but as individual moral failings: if you cannot get ahead, it is your fault. Such individualist moralities are widely used – not only in Mexico, but the United States as well – to justify the neglect of reforms that might alleviate structural inequalities, in favor of those that punish the poor for being poor. Some argue (e.g., Wacquant 2009) that the success of individualist moralities are a central feature of the global economic transformations of the late twentieth century, of which the industrialization of Uriangato and its associated patterns of migration are but one example. In such a discursive and political economic context, the critical commentary expressed by the diasporic social positioning of working-class Uriangatenses becomes especially important and especially urgent for us to hear.

Acknowledgments

As ever, I owe a debt of gratitude to the people in my field sites: without your time, friendship, and words there would be no chapter. I extend thanks to the members of my Arcadia University writing group, Jennifer Riggan, Dina Pinsky, Peter Siskind, and Maryam Deloffre, who provided patient, productive feedback on an early draft. I am grateful for Michele Koven's and Alejandro Paz's generous and insightful comments on a later draft. The 2011 American Anthropological Association Meetings panel, Temporalities of Transnationalism and Diaspora, which I co-developed with Alejandro, was also a source of insight for my ideas. This chapter benefited from the excellent editorial work of my research assistant Allison Martinez-Davis; I am thankful for the Arcadia University Faculty Development Award that allowed me to employ Allison. Finally, I thank Ato Quayson and Girish Daswani for inviting me to contribute to this volume. Any flaws in the article are my responsibility.

My fieldwork was generously funded by a Fulbright Garcia-Robles grant; two Mellon Foundation Population Studies grants; and the University of Pennsylvania's Department of Anthropology.

Notes

1 All translations are by the author. All personal names are pseudonyms, employed to protect my research consultants.
2 While the Mexican census, CONAPO, put the number of households across the municipality with members in the United States at 52 percent in the early 2000s, a survey I conducted of 170 randomly selected households in Plan de Ayala (see Dick 2006) showed that 85 percent of households in the neighborhood have members in the United States.
3 Uriangato's Office of Economic Development places the average daily salary in Uriangato at 200 pesos per day, more than double the national average of 80 pesos per day.
4 This is a result of the increase in penalties on undocumented immigrants who break other US laws, including traffic violations; these provisions were enacted in the Illegal Immigration Reform and Immigrant Responsibility Act of 1996 and amplified in the Patriot Act of 2001 (see Massey, Durand, and Malone 2002; Massey and Sánchez 2010: 75–76).

References

Agha, A. 2007a. *Language and Social Relations: Studies in the Social and Cultural Foundations of Language*. Cambridge: Cambridge University Press.
Agha, A. 2007b. "Recombinant selves in mass mediated spacetime." *Language and Communication*, 27: 320–335.

Alarcón, R. 1992. "Nortenización: Self-perpetuating migration from a Mexican town." In J. Bustamante, C. Reynolds, and R.A. Hinojosa (eds) *US–Mexico Relations: Labor Market Interdependence*, pp. 302–318. Stanford: Stanford University Press.

Alonso, A.M. 1994. "The politics of space, time, and substance: State formation, nationalism and ethnicity." *Annual Review of Anthropology*, 23: 379–405.

Appadurai, A. 1996. *Modernity at Large: Cultural Dimensions of Globalization*. Minneapolis: University of Minnesota Press.

Aranda Ríos, G. 2000. *Monografía de Uriangato*. Uriangato, Mexico: Municipal Government of Uriangato.

Bakhtin, M. 1996. *The Dialogic Imagination: Four Essays*. Austin: University of Texas Press.

Bartra, R. 1992. *The Cage of Melancholy: Identity and Metamorphosis in the Mexican Character*, trans. C.J. Hall. New Brunswick: Rutgers University Press.

Basch, L., Glick Schiller, N., and Blanc, C.S. 1994. *Nations Unbound: Transnational Projects, Postcolonial Predicaments, and Deterritorialized Nation-States*. Amsterdam: Gordon & Breach.

Castellanos, M.B. 2010. *A Return to Servitude: Maya Migration and the Tourist Trade in Cancun*. Minneapolis: University of Minnesota Press.

Clifford, J. 1994. "Diasporas." *Cultural Anthropology*, 9(3): 302–338.

Das, S. 2008. "Between convergence and divergence: Reformatting language purism in the Montreal Tamil diasporas." *Journal of Linguistic Anthropology*, 18(1): 1–23.

De Genova, N. 2002. "Migrant 'illegality' and deportability in everyday life." *Annual Review of Anthropology*, 31: 419–447.

Dick, H.P. 2006. "What to do with 'I don't know': Elicitation in ethnographic and survey interviews." *Qualitative Sociology*, 29(1): 87–102.

Dick, H.P. 2010a."Imagined lives and modernist chronotopes in Mexican nonmigrant discourse." *American Ethnologist*, 32(2): 275–290.

Dick, H.P. 2010b. "No option but to go: Poetic rationalization and the discursive production of Mexican migrant identity." *Language and Communication*, 30(2): 90–108.

Dick, H.P. 2012. "Words of passage: Discourse and the imagined lives of Mexican migrants." Unpublished MS.

Durand, J. and Massey, D.S. 2003. "The costs of contradiction: US border policy 1986–2000." *Latino Studies*, 1: 233–252.

Eisenlohr, P. 2006. *Little India: Diaspora, Time, and Ethnolinguistic Belonging in Hindu Mauritius*. Berkeley: University of California Press.

Farr, M. 2006. *Rancheros in Chicagoacán: Language and Identity in a Transnational Community*. Austin: University of Texas Press.

Gupta, A. 1992. "The song of the nonaligned world: Transitional identities and the reinscription of space in late capitalism." *Cultural Anthropology*, 7(1): 63–79.

Gutmann, M. 2007. *The Meanings of Macho: Being a Man in Mexico City*. Berkeley: University of California Press. (First published 1996.)

Hirsch, J.S. 2003. *A Courtship after Marriage: Sexuality and Love in Mexican Transnational Families*. Berkeley: University of California.

Hondagneu-Sotelo, P. 1994. *Gendered Transitions: Mexican Experiences of Immigration*. Berkeley: University of California Press.

Hyams, M. 2003. "Adolescent Latina bodyspaces: Making homegirls, homebodies, and homeplaces." *Antipode*, 35(3): 536–558.

Inoue, M. (ed.) 2004. "The history of ideology and the ideology of history." Special issue, *Journal of Linguistic Anthropology*, 14(1): 1–109.

Keane, W. 2007. *Christian Moderns: Freedom & Fetish in the Mission Encounter*. Berkeley: University of California Press.

Larkin, B. 2002. "Indian films and Nigerian lovers: Media and the creation of parallel modernities." In S. Newell (ed.) *Readings in African Popular Fiction*, pp. 18–36. Bloomington: Indiana University Press.

Lattanzi Shutika, D. 2011. *Beyond the Borderlands: Migration and Belonging in the United States and Mexico*. Berkeley: University of California Press.

Lempert, M. and Perrino, S. (eds) 2007. "Temporalities in text." Special issue, *Language of Communication*, 27(3): 205–335.

Lester, R. 2005. *Jesus in Our Wombs: Embodying Modernity in a Mexican Convent*. Berkeley: University of California Press.

Lomnitz, C. 2001. *Deep Mexico, Silent Mexico: An Anthropology of Nationalism*. Minneapolis: University of Minnesota Press.

Lomnitz-Adler, C. 1992. *Exits from the Labyrinth: Culture and Ideology in the Mexican National Space*. Berkeley: University of California Press.

Mahmood, S. 2005. *Politics of Piety: The Islamic Revival and the Feminist Subject*. Princeton: Princeton University Press.

Malkki, L. 1995. *Purity and Exile: Violence, Memory, and National Cosmology among Hutu Refugees in Tanzania*. Chicago: University of Chicago Press.

Massey, D.S., Alarcón, R., Durand, J., and González, H. 1987. *Return to Aztlan: The Social Process of International Migration from Western Mexico*. Berkeley: University of California Press.

Massey, D.S., Durand, J., and Malone, N.J. 2002. *Beyond Smoke and Mirrors: Mexican Immigration in an Era of Economic Integration*. New York: Russell Sage Foundation.

Massey, D.S. and Sánchez, M.R. 2010. *Brokered Boundaries: Creating Immigrant Identity in Anti-Immigrant Times*. New York: Russell Sage Foundation.

Mendoza-Denton, N. 2008. *Homegirls: Language and Cultural Practice among Latina Youth Gangs*. Oxford: Wiley Blackwell.

Messing, J. 2002. "Fractal recursivity in ideologies of language, identity and modernity in Tlaxcala, Mexico." *Texas Linguistic Forum*, 45: 95–105.

Messing, J. 2007. "Multiple ideologies and competing discourses: Language shift in Tlaxcala, Mexico." *Language in Society*, 36: 555–577.

Miller, D. 1994. *Modernity, an Ethnographic Approach: Dualism and Mass Consumption in Trinidad*. Providence, RI: Berg.

Mize, R.L. and Swords, A.C.S. 2011. *Consuming Mexican Labor: From the Bracero Program to NAFTA*. New York: University of Toronto Press.

Napolitano, V. 2002. *Migration, Mujercitas, and Medicine Men: Living in Urban Mexico*. Berkeley: University of California Press.

Pader, E. 1993. "Spatiality and social change: Domestic space in Mexico and the United States." *American Ethnologist*, 20: 114–137.

Paz, Alejandro. 2009. "The circulation of Chisme and rumor: Gossip, evidentiality, and authority in the perspective of Latino labor migrants in Israel." *Journal of Linguistic Anthropology*, 19(1): 117–143.

Rouse, R. 1991. "Mexican migration and the social space of postmodernism." *Diaspora*, 1(1): 8–23.

Rouse, R. 1992. "Making sense of settlement: Class transformation, cultural struggle and transnationalism among Mexican migrants in the United States." *Annals of the New York Academy of Sciences*, 645: 25–52.

Rouse, R. 1995. "Questions of identity." *Critique of Anthropology*, 15: 351–380.

Said, E. 2000. "Reflections on exile." In E. Said, *Reflections on Exile and Other Essays*, pp. 173–186. Cambridge, MA: Havard University Press.

Schmidt Camacho, A. 2006. "Migrant melancholia: Emergent discourses of Mexican traffic in transnational space." *South Atlantic Quarterly*, 105(4): 831–861.

Smith, R.C. 2006. *Mexican New York: Transnational Lives of New Immigrants*. Berkeley: University of California Press.

Stack, T. 2003. "Citizens of towns, citizens of nations: the knowing of history in Mexico." *Critique of Anthropology*, 23(2): 193–208.

Stark, O. and Taylor, J.E. 1991. "Migration incentives, migration types: the role of relative deprivation." *Economic Journal*, 101: 1163–1178.

Tenorio-Trillo, M. 1996. *Mexico at the World's Fairs: Crafting a Modern Nation.* Berkeley: University of California Press.

Wacquant, L. 2009. *Punishing the Poor: The Neoliberal Government of Social Insecurity.* Durham, NC: Duke University Press.

Walsh, C. 2004. "Eugenic acculturation: Manuel Gamio, migration studies, and the anthropology of development in Mexico, 1910–1940." *Latin American Perspectives*, 31: 118–145.

Werbner, P. 2004. "Theorizing complex diasporas: Purity and hybridity in the South Asian public sphere." *Journal of Ethnic and Migration Studies*, 30(5): 895–911.

Chapter 25

The Scales of Justice
Reflections on Representation and
Responsibility in a Transnational Frame
Kevin Lewis O'Neill

> *The pictures will not go away. That is the nature of the digital world in which we live.*
>
> Susan Sontag (2004)

This chapter addresses three interrelated sets of texts and images to say something about the ways in which broad social forces reframe ethical sensibilities. Each set emerged in the year 2004, capturing media and scholarly attention. They emerge from the Abu Ghraib prison scandal; Mel Gibson's *The Passion of The Christ*; and *The Blindfold's Eyes*, the spiritual autobiography of a Guatemalan torture survivor, Sister Dianna Ortiz. These sets of texts and images prompt reflection about how transnational processes shift the scales of responsibility not simply from the local to the global but also from the abstract to the personal. To whom am I responsible? The answer to this question has never been clear but has become less obvious in a world of interconnected and interdependent transnational spaces. While Judith Butler (2007) has argued brilliantly that the camera became a part of the torture at Abu Ghraib, these three sets of images and texts (when read in and through each other) have the potential to implicate the viewer as well, rendering him or her, as per Stanley Fish, "surprised by sin" (1988).

The first part of this chapter establishes that a peculiar narrative emerged from major English language media, one that interpreted images from Abu Ghraib and from *The Passion of The Christ* as pornographic. *New York Times* columnist Frank Rich (2004a) described *The Passion of The Christ* as being "constructed like nothing so much as a porn movie, replete with slo-mo climaxes and pounding music," while

A Companion to Diaspora and Transnationalism, First Edition.
Edited by Ato Quayson and Girish Daswani.
© 2013 Blackwell Publishing Ltd. Published 2013 by Blackwell Publishing Ltd.

radio host Rush Limbaugh (2004) announced (on the *Rush Limbaugh Program*, May 6) that the images from Abu Ghraib looked like "standard good old American pornography." This reading victimizes the viewer rather than the tortured, depicting the images as dangerously impressionable. The second part of this chapter destabilizes this interpretation with an appreciation of how both sets of images have been read in postwar Guatemala, the site of my own extended fieldwork on religion, violence, and human rights. With men and women having been crucified during Guatemala's genocidal civil war, and with hundreds of extrajudicial executions defining Guatemala's postwar context, neither Gibson's movie nor images from Abu Ghraib have been likened to or mistaken for pornography in any consistent way. Instead, they have been read as torture – with an unequivocal concern for those men and women dragged from their friends and family only to be humiliated, beaten, and murdered. In response to these two very different ethical imaginations, the third part of the chapter draws on the spiritual autobiography of Sister Dianna Ortiz to read each set of images as complete with a liturgical structure that recognizes the viewer as a qualified participant in state-sponsored torture. Released at roughly the same time as *The Passion of The Christ* and the Abu Ghraib prison scandal, Ortiz's autobiography makes the viewer, to quote Fish, "simultaneously a participant in the action and a critic of his own performance" (1988: xiii). Ortiz suggests that the viewer participates in the torture because he or she watches and says not a word.

While bolstered by extended ethnographic fieldwork, this chapter treads at the level of critical reflection to join a growing conversation in "ordinary ethics" – that is, "an ethics that is relatively tacit, grounded in agreement rather than rule, in practice rather than knowledge or belief, and happening without calling undue attention to itself" (Lambek 2010: 2). "Ordinary ethics" is an ethnographic project that (perhaps predictably) works diligently to negotiate the different scales at which ideas of responsibility and justice form. Yet, the bounds of culpability continue to change. In this chapter alone, a series of worldwide processes cut interpretative communities in unexpected ways, making ethics itself a multi-scalar practice. These processes include the War on Terror, transnational media networks, global Catholicism, postwar efforts at peace and reconciliation, and a capacious notion of the pornographic. A study of ethics today, in the end, demands what George Marcus (1995) has called a multi-sited approach that not only follows "the people," "the thing," or "the conflict" but also has a sense of responsibility for it. *To whom am I responsible?* This chapter, in the end, visits different scales of interpretation to highlight the diverging ethical perspectives that emerge in an era of transnational social relationships.

Viewer as Victim

In 2004, news reports of what is now known as the Abu Ghraib prison scandal circulated the internet, print media, and cable programming.[1] These reports were replete with brutal photos of abuse and torture – of naked men covered with feces, with bags over their heads and electrodes stuck to their bodies. At the same time, just as this international scandal raised the specter of state-sponsored torture, public debate intensified over Mel Gibson's *The Passion of The Christ*. Released only weeks before the Abu Ghraib prison scandal and complete with its own images of anguish, the movie sparked debates over the representation of violence in popular culture.[2] Interestingly, these two sets of images tended to miss each other at the level of analysis.[3] Although they coexisted within the same news cycles, the closest they came to intersecting was when placed one after the other on CNN Headline News or when published within the same section of the *New York Times*. The problem with this missed point of contact is that the images from Abu Ghraib and *The Passion of The Christ* are so hauntingly comparable. *The Economist's* May 8, 2004, cover depicts an Abu Ghraib prisoner assuming the position of the crucified, gingerly balanced on a block with his arms outstretched. The *Washington Post* printed a different photograph of a naked prisoner, with one leg placed over the other and with his arms parallel to the prison floor. Covered in fecal matter, his body forms a T (White, Davenport, and Higham 2004). Each of these images invokes Christ's passion. *Harper's Magazine*, making the correlation even more obvious, quotes a correspondence between Private Sabrina Harman and a friend months before the Abu Ghraib scandal: "I cant [sic] get it out of my head. I walk down the stairs after blowing the whistle and beating on the cells with a [baton] to find 'The taxicab driver' handcuffed backwards to his window naked with his underwear over his head and face. He looked like Jesus Christ" (Wypijewski 2006: 47). The resemblance between the two sets of images proved to be uncanny at times.

Beyond content and composition, these two sets of images also share a curious interpretation. Both have been read as pornographic. Christopher Hitchens (2004a), contributing editor to *Vanity Fair*, called Mel Gibson's *The Passion of The Christ* an "exercise in lurid sadomasochism" for those who "like seeing handsome young men stripped and flayed alive over a long period of time." Hitchens would also comment in a piece for *Slate Magazine* that Gibson's movie relies almost entirely on "sadomasochistic male narcissism" (2004b). This comment struck a chord with Frank Rich (2004a) of the *New York Times*, prompting him to announce: "Of all the 'Passion' critics, no one has nailed its artistic vision more precisely than the journalist Christopher Hitchens." The floodgates then opened, the archive tells us, spilling forth a kind of panic about pornography.[4] Columnists throughout North America and Western Europe began to agree that "Gibson's film is a roaring two hours of orgiastic blood-letting and homoeroticism" (Halley 2004), "a crude work of pornographic iconography" (Clarke 2004) that "plays like the Gospel according to the Marquis de Sade" (Ansen 2004). Others made comparisons between *The Passion of The Christ* and the pornographic movie *Deep Throat* (Persall 2004). One critic simply stated that the movie is a "dark and bloody spectacle of fundamentalist pornography" (Pevere 2004a), adding elsewhere, "what graphic sex is to the use of the body in hardcore porn, graphic violence is to the destruction of the body in *The Passion of The Christ*" (Pevere 2004b). The movie, it has been said, is "an orgy" of gore (Christopher 2004).

This narrative is striking, to be sure, but for those familiar with *The Passion of The Christ*, this reading makes some sense. The movie has no dramatic intrigue, no suspense, and no surprise ending. Just like a pornographic movie, *The Passion of The Christ*'s plot is thin; everyone knows how the story will end well before it begins. Before the film went into production, before moviegoers planted themselves in their seats, Jesus would die by the end. It was also relatively obvious what this slow, painful death would look like, even if many were surprised by the graphic extent to which Gibson took his movie. Jesus would be stripped, tortured, and then crucified, with nails driven into his hands and feet. Soldiers would also plunge a spear into his side. What drives this movie, much like pornography, is not so much a storyline or character development, but rather the viewer's presumed fascination with the body and what is done to it repeatedly, at times mechanically. Gibson's movie, in so many words, pivots on a simple curiosity with the ploddingly slow penetration of a body. As one *Passion of The Christ* critic mentions: "Again and again, we're exposed to the clinical repetition of a single act, until an alleged act of passion comes to seem boring and passionless. Is that not a definition of pornography?" (Groen 2004). To this effect, Gibson employs cinematic tropes familiar to the porn industry: scenes in slow motion, a driving soundtrack, and hyperbolic crescendos.

A generous historian might understand this critical interest in the pornographic as suggestive of the fact that Christ's passion has long been read as an erotic event. The history of Christianity is rife with devotees who describe Christ's wounds, especially Jesus' spear-pierced side, as like a vagina; the faithful have also portrayed Christ maternally with breasts, and, at other times, as radiantly handsome – as crucified and dejected but magnificently svelte (Bynum 1982; Atwood 1997; Fogelman 2003). Biblical scholars have also written at length about how the faithful yearn for Christ just as lovers brood for each other's bodies (O'Neill 2010). Gregory of Nyssa, writing in the fourth century, explained that "the most acute physical pleasure" and "erotic passion" are symbols that "teach us the need for the soul to reach out to the divine nature's invisible beauty and to love it as much as the body is inclined to love what is akin to itself" (McGinn 2001: 157). Gregory's interpretation is not without cause, given how some of the most celebrated saints have longed for Christ. St Teresa of Ávila famously wrote in the sixteenth century (1991: 275) that "the great love of God" often left her "utterly consumed," "penetrated to [her] entrails," and made her "utter several moans" for both the "intense pain" and its "sweetness." For the faithful, pain mixes with divine pleasure. Christ's passion is oftentimes their passion.

Yet the critics' palpable anxiety spoils any chance that they have stumbled upon a kind of devotional sensibility. Many of these critics seem afraid of the movie. In fact, if one reads closely what critics have written about *The Passion of The Christ*, there is a sustained concern for what Gibson's explicit rendering of torture might do to the viewing public. One such critic comments that "Gibson's film is sado-porn and will appeal to the same audience of ghoulish teenagers whose dollars fuel the slasher-film industry" (Hoyt 2004). Another article even goes so far as to quote a professor of criminology who notes that he has seen the damage that "graphic, violent imagery implanted in people's heads can do" (Cridlin 2004). Yet another commentator tells us: "You are in for one of the most unremittingly cruel movie going experiences ever" (Pevere 2004c). What is of interest is that these critics are concerned for the viewing public – for *our* heads, *our* children, and *our* ghoulish teenagers. These images spark concern and empathy for *us* – not Him. David Denby of the *New Yorker* asks (2004): "How will parents deal with the pain, terror and anger that children will doubtless feel as they watch a man flayed and pierced until dead?" This is a distinct kind of concern echoed, surprisingly, by critics of the Abu Ghraib prison scandal.

Observers read the photos from Abu Ghraib as "imitating the kinds of behaviour portrayed in cheap porn movies" (McMillan 2004: 18), as a "pornographic mix of raunch and violence" (Seaquist 2005) and as "a low-budget re-enactment of Salo Pasolini's notorious film based on The 120 Days of Sodom by the Marquis de Sade" (Smith 2004). CBS News reported that the images "amounted to hard-core porn," noting that guards ordered prisoners to expose themselves, masturbate on demand, and simulate oral sex with each other (CBS 2004). Yet the actual content of the photographs is just one source of the media's panic. The images' very stylization is another – how, for example, soldiers photographed their subjects, what poses they found meaningful, what relationship between the dominator and the dominated they found most humiliating. To this, one journalist wrote, "it was US Supreme Court Justice Potter Stewart who famously admitted he couldn't define what pornography was, but that 'I know it when I see it.' Like everyone else who's viewed the sickening images taken at Abu Ghraib prison, I've seen it" (Kingston 2004). Several other media sources developed these observations, noting not only that the content of the images was pornographic, but that their social life seemed to rely on pornographic economies. A "pornographic culture," one critic explained, "has clearly influenced the soldiers" (Viner 2004). The suggestion is that these images "were being traded within the military like homemade pornography" (Bischoff 2004) and that they "owed their humiliating compositions to an obvious familiarity with porn generally and internet porn in particular" (Knight 2005). With seeming ease, a narrative emerged from major English language media that these images were pornographic. And, much like the panic that circled Gibson's *The Passion of The Christ*, the narrative suggested that the images from Abu Ghraib were dangerous. "As if the pictures were the problem," Frank Rich wrote (2004b), "rather than what they reveal."

Along with the idea that the content and composition of the images were pornographic, there appeared the equally suggestive idea that the function of the images was somehow pornographic as well. An editorialist from the *Washington Times* writes, "It is difficult to understand what useful journalistic purpose was served by the new photographs. . . . Whether the motivation was meretricious, partisan or antiwar, it was meant to excite rather than to elucidate – and thus was journalistic pornography." The images, the article contends, "do not shed any light on the central question of who directed the abuse of detainees at Abu Ghraib prison" (Washington Times 2004). In fact, it explains, the images tell us nothing about Abu Ghraib. They do not demonstrate the motivations behind these acts of torture; they do not display their relative value to the War on Terror, and they do not show a degree of emotional ambivalence. They simply allow the viewing public to watch with "voyeuristic cruelty" (Blacker 2004). Rather than educate, the images titillate. Without reason, and for the sake of nothing more than spectacle, they bring our attention to tortured bodies in all their nakedness and vulnerability.

These images' pornographic dimensions have also been compounded by remarkable moments of slippage. A striking example came with the *Boston Globe*'s publication of what eventually turned out to be staged pornographic photos of supposed US soldiers raping supposed Iraqi women. These were actually images from a hardcore pornography website that were somehow mistaken for Abu Ghraib photos. The *Boston Globe* quickly retracted them, admitting simply (and rather sheepishly) that "A photograph on Page B2 yesterday did not meet Globe standards for publication. . . . Images contained in the photograph were overly graphic, and the purported abuse portrayed had not been authenticated" (Boston Globe 2004). This mistake, along with Rush Limbaugh's declaration that the images seemed like "standard good old American pornography," inspired Susan Brison, a philosophy professor at Dartmouth College, to write a rather smart article in the *Chronicle of Higher Education*. In it, she asks a provocative question: What are we to make of the fact that porn looks like actual torture and actual torture looks like porn (Brison 2004)?

Brison's question is as difficult to answer as it is thought-provoking, precisely because pornography and torture are so much a part of the American everyday. Their familiarity can blur an analytical vision, begging a comparative perspective to see these images (as well as torture and pornography's cultural contours) anew. This is why the next section shifts to Guatemala, where Gibson's *The Passion of The Christ* and the Abu Ghraib prison scandal received a great deal of critical attention.[5] Yet the very kind of panic that one finds in major English language media did not emerge in postwar Guatemala. Instead, a tragic familiarity with state-sponsored torture and postwar violence provoked a very different kind of interpretation.

Guatemala's Crucifixion

In postwar Guatemala, neither Gibson's movie nor images from Abu Ghraib have been likened to or mistaken for pornography. Much of this has to do with Guatemala's civil war, which began after the failure of a nationalist uprising by military officers in 1960, and ended with a United Nations-mediated peace process (1994–1996). The Oslo Accord, signed in 1994 as part of this peace process, initiated the Historical Clarification Commission (CEH), a project created to investigate human rights violations and to make recommendations on how to promote peace in postwar Guatemala. According to the CEH, more than 200,000 people died or disappeared as a result of the armed conflict, of which more than 80 percent were Maya; furthermore, 93 percent of these human rights violations could be connected to the state. The CEH (1999) establishes in light of the United Nations Genocide

Convention that the Guatemalan state committed acts of genocide against Maya people. The Roman Catholic Church's truth commission report, titled *Never Again* (REMHI 1999), also documents how state forces and paramilitary groups were responsible for the vast majority of civilian deaths, disappearances, and tortures – with the strongest waves of repression best characterized as acts of genocide. The testimonies that line the Church's report are graphic: fetuses pulled from wombs, men castrated, women gang-raped. They are testimonies that weave Guatemala's tortured history through Christ's passion narrative, making Christ's crucifixion Guatemala's crucifixion (O'Neill 2005). Bishop Juan Gerardi, a Church leader and human rights activist, was beaten to death due to his work with the Church's truth commission report, only one day after its release (Goldman 2007). The day before his murder, he announced:

> The thousands of testimonies of the victims and the recounting of the horrific crimes are today's manifestations of the figure of the "suffering servant of Yahweh," brought to life in the people of Guatemala. "Behold my servant", says Isaiah, ". . . many were afraid of him. He was so disfigured he was beyond human semblance, and his form beyond that of sons of man. He has borne our grief and carried our sorrows, yet we esteemed him stricken, smitten by God and afflicted." (REMHI 1999: xxv)

Gerardi's remarks represent only a small moment in a larger postwar narrative, one that reads the suffering of a tortured country as a promise for eventual resurrection. The Church's report notes: "Despite the profound sorrow with which we have heard these testimonies of human suffering, the memory and image of Christ crucified anew, we can do no less than hope that by renouncing this dark past of horror, and with our determination to rebuild our country, a new climate of hope will emerge" (REMHI 1999: xxix). Of ultimate importance here is how state-sponsored torture becomes imagined alongside (but more often than not through) the passion narrative. While not every testimony published in the Church's report involves Christian images (the Catholic Church itself acknowledges that only 9 percent of testimonies collected make biblical references; REMHI 1999: 277), the report's testimonies nonetheless deliver poignant and powerful examples of Christ's passion framing state-sponsored torture, providing an interpretative framework for both survivors and perpetrators. Three testimonies begin to animate this point:

> What we have seen has been terrible: burned corpses, women impaled and buried as if they were animals ready for the spit, all doubled up, and children massacred and carved up with machetes. The women too, murdered like Christ. . . . Before murdering her, they nailed her to a cross they had made. They stuck huge nails into her hands and chest, then they put her inside the house to burn her up. They found her burned, still on the cross; her son was beside her, also burned – badly burned. . . . Have you ever seen the crucifixion? Well here, very nearly, was Jesus Christ; there was a man, there was half of a man – the most horrendous thing I have ever seen – a man totally disfigured. He already had worms, he had no teeth, no hair, his face was disfigured, he was hanging, I mean, by his hands. (REMHI 1999: 9–10, 79, 153)

Here, Christ's passion becomes axiomatic,[6] providing both order and meaning to the seeming disorder of genocide. The critically acclaimed photographer Jonathan Moller, an artist who has documented Guatemala's post-genocidal context, both captures and participates in this framing, delivering an image that resonates with these testimonies. This image is of a crucifix; it comes from a small church in San Juan Cotzali – a small town hit hard during the genocide. Jesus hangs both broken and hobbled on his cross while dozens of names surround him. Each name marks someone murdered during the civil war. And, above this display, there reads simply but powerfully: "And they gave their lives like Christ." Moller's (2004) work embodies the Church's own reading of Guatemala's genocide.

One of the most powerful passion narratives to emerge from wartime Guatemala, however, does not come from popular religious expression or from the truth commission reports. It comes from the spiritual biography of Dianna Ortiz. Ortiz is an Ursuline missionary from the United States who was kidnapped in 1989 by Guatemalan security forces operating under the direction of a US official. Blindfolded, burned with cigarettes 111 times, and gang-raped – impregnated with a fetus she eventually aborted – Ortiz was filmed by her torturers, allowing the photographic gaze, as per Butler (2007), to become a part of the torture. By way of the camera, they made Ortiz's clandestine torture chamber public. Just as Abu Ghraib prison guards allowed photography to deepen the effect of torture with an implied viewership, Guatemalan security forces intensified Ortiz's humiliation by prompting Ortiz to consider those who might one day view her anguish. Her family? Her friends? Her sisters in Christ? "Well, you know, we have the photos of you, and the videos," Ortiz's captor told her. "Those could be embarrassing" (Ortiz 2004: 33). These perverted promises kept her silent for years.

Ortiz, however, eventually wrote a memoir; it is a stirring spiritual biography that oftentimes reads as in lock-step with Christ's own passion and resurrection. As Ortiz writes, her pain is Christ's pain; his resurrection is her resurrection. Ortiz reflects (2004: 132): "Jesus also was tortured, and he cried out on the cross, 'My God, my God, why have you forsaken me?' When I was first taken down into the basement of that building in Guatemala I asked myself the same question – why had God abandoned me?" Unlike Gibson's reading of Christ's crucifixion, the very one that critics liken to pornography, Ortiz's own telling of torture bends her memoirs away from the sensational and towards the reflective. She writes that on the first Good Friday following her release, the day that officially commemorates Jesus' crucifixion, she thought to herself, "why are we adoring an act of torture, lingering on each detail, as if in the act of torture itself there is some kind of glamour?" (p. 49). For Ortiz, there is no glamour in Jesus' death. For Ortiz, any representation of Jesus' passion that could be understood as pornographic, as the product of Hollywood style or as a sadomasochist romp through the Bible, would fall short of capturing torture's brute force. This is why Ortiz parallels her experience of torture with Jesus' crucifixion, even going so far as to model her moments in a Guatemalan torture chamber after the Stations of the Cross, the Church's formal meditation on Jesus' final hours:

Jesus meets his mother. . . I see my mother, as I saw her when José left me in the dark, before the interrogation started. . . . I traveled in my mind or with my spirit and found her in her bedroom, lying on her side, facing the wall. She is sobbing. . . . *Veronica wipes the face of Jesus*. . . . I remember Alejandro bringing the wet cloth near my face. *Jesus is stripped of his garments*. . . . I am not reflecting, but remembering when and how each piece of my clothing was removed. (2004: 50)

Ortiz gains strength from knowing that "if Jesus could rise, break out of that tomb of darkness and still live, maybe that was a journey we were all supposed to make, not after life, but here on earth – a journey from darkness to light, from numb half-life to full consciousness" (p. 145). Again, Christ's passion is Ortiz's passion.

Important to this analysis is not simply the idea that Ortiz's memoir models a different kind of interpretation than the panic detailed in the first part of this chapter, but also the historical fact that Ortiz's story collides with the Abu Ghraib prison scandal itself. The first paperback edition of Ortiz's *The Blindfold's Eyes* was released in 2004 – at roughly the same time as Gibson's *The Passion of The Christ* and as the images from Abu Ghraib became public. For Ortiz, neither set of images titillates. Neither set appears orgiastic, or even a threat to those supposedly ghoulish teenagers who sustain the slasher film industry. The images from Abu Ghraib haunt her with good reason. Ortiz remarks in an interview, "I've heard people say that what happened in Abu Ghraib is an isolated incident, and I have to just shake my head and say, are we on the same planet? Aren't you aware of our history? Isn't history taught in the classroom about the role of the US government in human rights violations?" (Pilger 2007). Ortiz adds elsewhere: "I could not even stand to look at those photographs [from Abu Ghraib]; neither could many of the other torture survivors, especially those of us from Latin America . . . because so many of the things in the photographs had also been done to me" (Ortiz 2005). Ortiz's own account of torture makes it so very strange that the images from either Gibson's *The Passion of The Christ* or the Abu Ghraib prison scandal could be read as pornographic. The empathetic distance that exists between these two interpretations is stunning. While major English-language media lingered on a concern for the viewing public – on how these graphic images might affect our children, our minds, ourselves – Ortiz authors a very different interpretation, one that extends empathy towards the victims of torture while also (the following section notes) prompting a moment of reflection about the viewing public's complicity in these acts. This is a yet unexplored perspective that owes its salience to an array of sources, one of which is the passion narrative's own structure and content.

Self-Recognition

Mel Gibson's *The Passion of The Christ* tells the story of Jesus' final hours – how he was arrested in the Garden of Gethsemane by Roman soldiers, condemned to death by Pontius Pilate, beaten and flogged, marched to Golgotha under the weight of his cross, and finally nailed to that cross. Folded into this narrative are two aspects that indict the movie's model viewer for Jesus' very torture and crucifixion. Both come when Jesus appears before Pontius Pilate for the second time. Gibson's film follows the biblical text closely, narrating that Pontius Pilate could find no basis for Jesus' execution. The movie, thus, places Pilate in conversation with chief priests, community leaders, and a growing mob. Pilate pleads, "You brought me this man as one who was inciting the people to rebellion. I have examined him in your presence and have found no basis for your charges against him. Neither has Herod, for he sent him back to us; as you can see, he has done nothing to deserve death" (Gibson and Fitzgerald 2004). The crowd, nevertheless, insists that Jesus must be killed. As part of custom, Pontius Pilate offers the crowd a choice to release one prisoner – either Jesus or Barabbas, a known murderer. The crowd responds in unison. They choose Barabbas (Matthew 27: 18–21). "With one voice," Gibson and Fitzgerald's screenplay notes (2004), "they cried out, 'Away with this man! Release Barabbas to us!'" (Luke 23: 18–19). Yet, before Jesus takes up his cross, Pilate announces one last time: "Look, I am bringing him out to you to let you know that I find no basis for a charge against him." Gibson's screenplay then narrates Jesus' fate: "When Jesus came out wearing the crown of thorns and the purple robe, Pilate said to them, 'Here is the man!' As soon as the chief priests and their officials saw him, they shouted, 'Crucify! Crucify!'" (Gibson and Fitzgerald 2004). Pilate ultimately acquiesces to the crowd. Jesus dies.

Important here are the two moments when the crowd decides Jesus' fate. The first is when they shout down Pilate's hesitations and the second is when they decide for Barabbas' freedom over Jesus' life. These are poignant moments that are stressed by liturgical representations of the passion narrative and that Gibson's movie highlights by way of strategic camera shots, ones in which the viewer is meant to feel as if a part of the crowd. These cinematic conventions, such as a first person perspective, dramatize and intensify the viewer's identification with the crowd. Gibson's cinematic effort is not original, however. In Christian liturgies that commemorate Jesus' passion, it is common for the parish or the congregation – those men and women in the pews – to play the part of the mob. The liturgy prompts the congregation to dismiss Pilate, to choose a murderer's freedom over Jesus' life. Men and women, young and old, every year, in churches that range from the Pentecostal apocalyptic to the Roman Catholic, read from scripts. They announce: "Crucify him. Crucify him." Latin American communities of faith often bring these liturgical moments to life. These parishes re-enact the passion narrative, making the story into a play, a performance, and even a pilgrimage. In Guatemala during Holy Week, during the early hours of Good Friday, processions snake through the towns. Framed by dirges and thick plumes of pungent incense, parishioners dress as Roman soldiers. They shoulder enormous floats; each represents a different Station of the Cross. Crowds follow. The faithful watch their fellow parishioners carry Jesus to his death. The faithful participate in the execution of their savior. "*Qué sufre*" (How he suffers), an old Guatemalan woman once whispered to me as Jesus' float passed us slowly. Important is the fact that the woman noted how Jesus *suffers* – not *suffered*. Passion becomes event.

This kind of participation, liturgically speaking, implicates those who watch Jesus' torture, crucifixion, and death. The very structure of the narrative invokes complicity. The faithful are meant to watch, to form a mob, to voice their own desire for Jesus to be crucified. Each person of faith is meant to reflect over the moment in which they choose Barabbas over Jesus. Mel Gibson's *The Passion of The Christ* self-consciously follows suit. With shaky camera-work, as if the viewer is herself jostled by the crowd, the moviegoer watches Jesus' suffering, stands shoulder-to-shoulder with those who spit at him. The movie's very structure, its very effort at hyperrealism, prompts the moviegoer to watch silently in her or his seat while others curse and kick at Jesus. "I think people don't usually say much after the film," Gibson explained in an interview. "They can't really talk, which is a good reaction, I think, because they are introspective – which is what I hoped to achieve: introspection" (Neff and Struck 2004). The passion narrative makes the viewer complicit, provokes the viewer to become a participant. The liturgical reasons for this are innumerable; yet, the one that proves most insightful here is the observation that acquiescence is a kind of complicity – that silence is approval. Not only is the moviegoer – in the case of Gibson's film – meant to plead with Pilate to kill Jesus, but the very structure of each and every passion play, of each and every Station of the Cross, also intends the believer to watch in silence, to say not a word while Jesus suffers an unthinkable death. Ingeniously, Gibson allows the North American moviegoing experience, the obligation to watch every movie in complete silence so as not to disturb fellow moviegoers, to highlight this liturgical strategy. The viewer watches idly as a man is tortured beyond recognition. Passion plays envelop the viewer, and Gibson's movie works to single out each ticket-holder, saturating each one with a level of culpability.

This liturgical move, for centuries, has provided fodder for spiritual reflection – on original sin, on grace, on what it means to be a Christian. Mel Gibson's movie simply leans on hundreds of years of reflection to make a long-argued point about the human condition – about viewership and victimhood. It is a liturgical move akin to what Stanley Fish discovers in his seminal reading of John Milton's *Paradise Lost* (2005). Fish, we might remember, argues that the act of reading *Paradise Lost* invokes a moral struggle within the reader, one that makes him or her attracted to Milton's Devil more so than to Adam, Eve, and God. The poem's very structure, Fish suggests, uses narrative techniques to call attention to the reader's distance from God, his or her fall from grace, his or her attraction to evil over goodness. Milton's *Paradise Lost* renders the reader surprised by sin. Similarly, Gibson's movie, following the structure of a Christian passion play, surprises the faithful by placing each moviegoer amid the crowd, amid the cursing, amid the blood. "I want people to understand the reality of the story," Gibson noted, "I want them to be taken through an experience. I want them to feel" (McClure 2004). Gibson wants each moviegoer to feel complicit in Jesus' execution – even if only because he or she watches in silence.

Dianna Ortiz (2004) makes this very point while meditating on Jesus' crucifixion. Her emphasis is on the viewer's culpability – what it means to watch silently: "I watch [in my mind] each spike driven in [Jesus' hands]. People are standing around. They can't look away. They feel horror but stand and watch in silence or mutter a few words of praise about his courage. His side is pierced with a spear – he is tortured, slowly murdered. The onlookers acquiesce" (p. 50). Ortiz adds during a larger conversation about her own torture and whether she should bring the Guatemalan government to court on human rights charges: "The thought hits me like lightening [sic]: like them, I'm a silent witness, too. I thought I could get away with the affidavit as my only testimony and then begin life anew, forgetting what I'd seen and heard in the basement prison" (p. 50). She could not and does not. Her memoir stands as a testimony to her willingness to act, to her bravery, to her being noisy during moments that asked her to watch in silence. She speaks out – by pressing her case within the Guatemalan judicial system, by exposing the genocidal dimensions of Guatemala's civil war to an international human rights community, by writing her story against a structure that asks her to acquiesce.

There is a lesson to learn from Ortiz, one that can be applied to the images from Abu Ghraib, if only because these images share a familial resemblance with those from Mel Gibson's *The Passion of The Christ*. While there are very good reasons not to read the images from Abu Ghraib as parroting a Christian narrative, not to suggest that the tortured are Christ-like (Sentilles 2008), this thought experiment does have purchase – if only because so many of the perpetrators at Abu Ghraib subscribe to Christian imaginations. To quote (again) Private Sabrina Harman: "[I find] 'The taxicab driver' handcuffed backwards to his window naked with his underwear over his head and face. He looked like Jesus Christ" (Wypijewski 2006: 47). To some (but surely not all), those tortured at Abu Ghraib did look like Jesus Christ.

The lesson is that these photos from Abu Ghraib, when read in light of Mel Gibson's *The Passion of The Christ*, envelop the viewing public and, therefore, shift the bounds of ordinary ethics itself. With shaky camera-work, as if the viewer is him or herself jostled by the crowd, the viewer watches as prisoners at Abu Ghraib suffer; the viewer stands shoulder-to shoulder with those who grab, beat, and spit at the incarcerated. The photos' very structure, moreover, prompts the viewer to watch silently in her seat while others curse and kick. The photos from Abu Ghraib, in short, make the viewer complicit. They provoke the viewer to become a participant. Just like Gibson's *The Passion of The Christ*, the photos from Abu Ghraib, in the words of Ortiz, render the viewer a silent witness. And, following Fish's (1988) work on *Paradise Lost*, this culpability can evoke a moral struggle within the viewer, one that makes the viewer reflect over her or his role in state-sponsored torture – over her relationship to the tortured. The photos' very structure, as per Fish, employs techniques (even if unintentionally) to call attention to the viewer's own fall from grace – to a sin that should surprise us all.

Notes

1   A dense literature has formed around these images. They include the work of Steven Strasser (2004), Mark Danner (2004), Seymour M. Hersh (2004), and S.G. Mestrovic (2007).

2   The scholarly response to *The Passion of The Christ* has been significant. Central to my interpretation of the movie has been a cluster of publications, including the work of Timothy K. Beal and Tod Linafelt (2006), Zev Garber (2006), and Paula Fredriksen (2006).
3   For scholarly attention paid to both sets of images, see, for example, the work of Steven C. Caton (2006), Sarah Sentilles (2008), and Alessandro Camon (2004).
4   Seemingly innumerable references discuss *The Passion of The Christ*. Some of the more thoughtful include articles written by James Carroll (2004), Joe Queenan (2004), A.O. Scott (2004), and Ann Hornaday (2004).
5   See, for example, Spanish-language publications from Conrado Alonso (2004), Gustavo Adolfo Montenegro (2005), Dina Fernández (2004), Crista Kepfer (2004), Irina Barreno (2004), and José Raúl González Merlo (2004).
6   For a better sense of the term "axiomatic," see the work of David M. Schneider (1968) and Victor Turner (1967).

References

Alonso, C. 2004. "Horrores en Irak." *Prensa Libre*, May 12.
Ansen, D. 2004. "So what's the good news?" *Newsweek*, March 1.
Atwood, C. 1997. "Sleeping in the arms of Christ: Sanctifying sexuality in the eighteenth-century Moravian Church." *Journal of the History of Sexuality*, 8(1): 25–51.
Barreno, I. 2004. "Más pasión, menos pasión." *Prensa Libre*, April 7.
Beal, T.K. and Linafelt, T. (eds.) 2006. *Mel Gibson's Bible: Religion, Popular Culture, and* The Passion of The Christ. Chicago: University of Chicago Press.
Bischoff, D. 2004. "Iraq pornography makes this . . . America's dirty war." *Star-Ledger*, May 19.
Blacker, T. 2004. "Pictures that reflect the depravity of the internet age." *The Independent* (London), May 14.
Boston Globe. 2004. "For the record." *Boston Globe*, May 13.
Brison, S.J. 2004. "Torture, or 'good old American pornography'?" *Chronicle of Higher Education*, 50(39): B10.
Butler, J. 2007. "Torture and the ethics of photography." *Environment and Planning D*, 25(6): 951–966.
Bynum, C.W. 1982. *Jesus as Mother: Studies in the Spirituality of the High Middle Ages*. Berkeley: University of California Press.
Camon, A. 2004. "American torture, American porn." *Salon*, June 7, at http://dir.salon.com/story/opinion/feature/2004/06/07/torture, accessed February 21, 2013.
Carroll, J. 2004. "An obscene portrayal of Christ's passion." *Boston Globe*, February 24.
Caton, S.C. 2006. "Coetzee, Agamben, and the passion of Abu Ghraib." *American Anthropologist*, 108(1): 114–123.
CBS 2004. "Congress sees shocking new pictures of Iraqi prisoner abuse." *The Early Show*, reporter D. Martin, first broadcast May 13.
CEH 1999. *Memoria Del Silencio. Guatemala: Comisión para el Esclarecimiento Histórico*. Guatemala City: Comisión para el Esclarecimiento Histórico.
Christopher, J. 2004. "Feel his pain." *The Times* (London), March 25.
Clarke, R. 2004. "New films." *The Independent* (London), March 27.

Cridlin, J. 2004. "Kathleen Heide." *St Petersburg Times* (Florida), April 6.

Danner, M. 2004. *Torture and Truth: America, Abu Ghraib and the War on Terror*. New York: New York Review of Books.

Denby, D. 2004. "Nailed: Mel Gibson's 'The Passion of The Christ." *New Yorker*, March 1.

Fernández, D. 2004. "Sádicos en Irak." *Prensa Libre*, May 24.

Fish, S. 1988. *Surprised by Sin: The Reader in Paradise Lost*. Cambridge, MA: Harvard University Press.

Fogelman, A.S. 2003. "Jesus is female: the Moravian challenge in the German communities of British North America." *William and Mary Quarterly*, 60: 295–332.

Fredriksen, P. (ed.) 2006. *On The Passion of The Christ: Exploring the Issues Raised by the Controversial Movie*. Berkeley: University of California Press.

Garber, Z. (ed.) 2006. *Mel Gibson's Passion: The Film, the Controversy, and Its Implications*. West Lafayette, IN: Purdue University Press.

Gibson, M. and Fitzgerald, B. 2004. *The Passion of The Christ: Screenplay*. Los Angeles: Icon Productions.

Goldman, F. 2007. *The Art of Political Murder: Who Killed the Bishop?* New York: Grove Press.

Groen, R. 2004. "The greatest gory ever told." *Globe and Mail*, February 25.

Halley, G. 2004. "Mel's Passion is a pornography of violence." *Sunday Independent* (Ireland), March 28.

Hersh, S.M. 2004. *Chain of Command: The Road from 9/11 to Abu Ghraib*. New York: HarperCollins.

Hitchens, C. 2004a. "Why I detest *The Passion of The Christ* . . . with a passion." Christopher Hitchens: Politics, War and Religion Blog, February 27.

Hitchens, C. 2004b. "Schlock, yes; awe, no; fascism, probably: the flogging Mel Gibson demands." *Slate Magazine*, February 27, at http://www.slate.com/articles/news_and_politics/fighting_words/2004/02/schlock_yes_awe_no_fascism_probably.html, accessed March 8, 2013.

Hornaday, A. 2004. "Less than the gospel truth." *Washington Post*, February 25.

Hoyt, D. 2004. "Gibson's 'Passion of The Christ' should appeal to ghoulish teens who fuel slasher-film industry." *San Francisco Chronicle*, March 7.

Kepfer, C. 2004. "Lágrimas al ver La Pasión." *Prensa Libre*, March 19.

Kingston, A. 2004. "Porn of another kind." *National Post* (Canada), May 11.

Knight, I. 2005. "Porn by any other name." *Sunday Times* (London), May 8.

Lambek, M. 2010. *Ordinary Ethics: Anthropology, Language, and Action*. New York: Fordham University Press.

Marcus, G. 1995. "Ethnography in/of the World System: the emergence of multi-sited ethnography." *Annual Review of Anthropology*, 24: 95–117.

McClure, H. 2004. *Making* The Passion of The Christ. Los Angeles: Icon Productions.

McGinn, B. 2001. "The language of inner experience in Christian mysticism." *Spiritus: A Journal of Christian Spirituality*, 1(2): 156–171.

McMillan, J. 2004. "Tawdry sexual culture is society's new curse." *Scotsman*, August 7.

Merlo, J.R.G. 2004. "Sufriendo pasiones ajenas." *Prensa Libre*, April 6.

Mestrovic, S.G. 2007. *The Trials of Abu Ghraib: An Expert Witness Account of Shame and Horror*. London: Paradigm.

Milton, J. 2005. *Paradise Lost*, ed. Philip Pullman. New York: Oxford University Press.

Moller, J. 2004. *Our Culture Is Our Resistance: Repression, Refuge and Healing in Guatemala*, at http://www.jonathanmoller.org/portfolio1.htm, accessed February 21, 2013.

Montenegro, G.A. 2005. "Fuera de control." *Revista D*, September 11.

Neff, D. and Struck, J.J. 2004. "'Dude, that was graphic': Mel Gibson talks about *The Passion of The Christ.*" *Christianity Today*, February 23, at http://www.christianitytoday.com/movies/interviews/2004/melgibson.html?start=1, accessed February 21, 2013.

O'Neill, K.L. 2005. "Writing Guatemala's genocide: Christianity and Truth and Reconciliation Commissions." *Journal for Genocide Research*, 7(3): 310–331.

O'Neill, K.L. 2010. "I want more of you: the politics of Christian eroticism in postwar Guatemala. *Comparative Studies in Society and History*, 52(131): 131–156.

Ortiz, D. 2004. *The Blindfold's Eyes: My Journey from Torture to Truth.* Maryknoll, NY: Orbis Press.

Ortiz, D. 2005. "Sister Dianna Ortiz details her abduction and torture by US-backed Guatemalan military." *Democracy Now! The War and Peace Report, October 12*, at http://www.democracynow.org/2005/10/12/sister_dianna_ortiz_details_her_abduction, accessed March 12, 2013.

Persall, S. 2004. "A blood feast of American film." *St Petersburg Times* (Florida), January 30.

Pevere, G. 2004a. "Our critics' opinions on the original release." *Toronto Star*, September 2.

Pevere, G. 2004b. "A dark and bloody spectacle." *Toronto Star*, February 25.

Pevere, G. 2004c. "The Passion of The Christ 18A." *Toronto Star*, March 12.

Pilger, J. 2007. *The War on Democracy.* Documentary film, dir. Chris Martin, pres. John Pilger. London: Lionsgate.

Queenan, J. 2004. "Christ, you know it ain't easy." *Guardian*, March 27.

REMHI 1999. *Guatemala, nunca más; Interdiocesan Project for the Recovery of Historical Memory*, Volumes I, II, III, IV. Guatemala: Archbishop's Office. (Originally published in Spanish, 1998.)

Rich, F. 2004a. "Mel Gibson forgives us for his sins." *New York Times*, March 7.

Rich, F. 2004b. "It was the porn that made them do it." *New York Times*, May 30.

Schneider, D.M. 1968. *American Kinship: A Cultural Account.* Chicago: University of Chicago Press.

Scott, A.O. 2004. "Good and evil locked in violent showdown." *New York Times*, February 25.

Seaquist, C. 2005. "Abu Ghraib and the mirror." *Christian Science Monitor*, February 11.

Sentilles, S. 2008. "'He looked like Jesus Christ': Crucifixion, torture, and the limits of empathy as a response to the photographs from Abu Ghraib." *Harvard Divinity Bulletin* 36(1): 32–38.

Smith, J. 2004. "The Iraq abuse scandal: How could she? Why would she?" *Independent on Sunday* (London), May 9.

Sontag, S. 2004. "Regarding the torture of others." *New York Times*, May 23.

Strasser, S. (ed.) 2004. *The Abu Ghraib Investigations: The Official Reports of the Independent Panel and the Pentagon on the Shocking Prisoner Abuse in Iraq.* New York: Public Affairs.

Teresa of Ávila. 1991. *The Life of Teresa of Jesus; The Autobiography of St Teresa of Ávila*, trans. E.A. Peers. New York: Doubleday.

Turner, V. 1967. *The Forest of Symbols: Aspects of Ndembu Ritual.* Ithaca, NY: Cornell University Press.

Viner, K. 2004. "Comment & analysis: the sexual sadism of our culture, in peace and in war." *Guardian*, May 22.

Washington Times 2004. "Journalistic pornography." *Washington Times*, May 24.

White, J., Davenport, C., and Higham, S. 2004. "Videos amplify picture of violence." *Washington Post*, May 21.

Wypijewski, J. 2006. "Judgment days: Lessons from the Abu Ghraib courts-martial." *Harper's Magazine*, February.

Chapter 26

Greek Settler Communities in Central and South Asia, 323 BCE to 10 CE

Rachel Mairs

Alexander advanced with his army to the Hellespont and transported it from Europe to Asia. He personally sailed with sixty fighting ships to the Troad, where he flung his spear from the ship and fixed it in the ground, and then leapt ashore himself the first of the Macedonians, signifying that he received Asia from the gods as a spear-won prize. (Diod. Sic. 17.17.1-2.[1])

In twenty days [Alexander] fortified the city which he was projecting, and settled in it some of the Grecian mercenaries and those of the neighboring barbarians who volunteered to take part in the settlement, as well as the Macedonians from his army who were now unfit for military service. (Arr. *Anab.* 4.4.)

Alexandria the Farthest

In 334 BCE, Alexander the Great led his armies across the straits which separated Europe from Asia, and into the lands of the Persian empire. Five years later, in 329 BCE, he established the most distant and remote of the many garrisons and eponymous cities which he founded along the route of his campaigns: Alexandria Eschate – Alexandria the Farthest – on the river Jaxartes, at modern Khujand in Tajikistan.[2] Although no full contemporary accounts survive, later historians such as Arrian, who wrote in the second century CE, were able to draw on sources now lost. In Arrian's *Anabasis* (Expedition) *of Alexander*, we find many descriptions – some

A Companion to Diaspora and Transnationalism, First Edition.
Edited by Ato Quayson and Girish Daswani.
© 2013 Blackwell Publishing Ltd. Published 2013 by Blackwell Publishing Ltd.

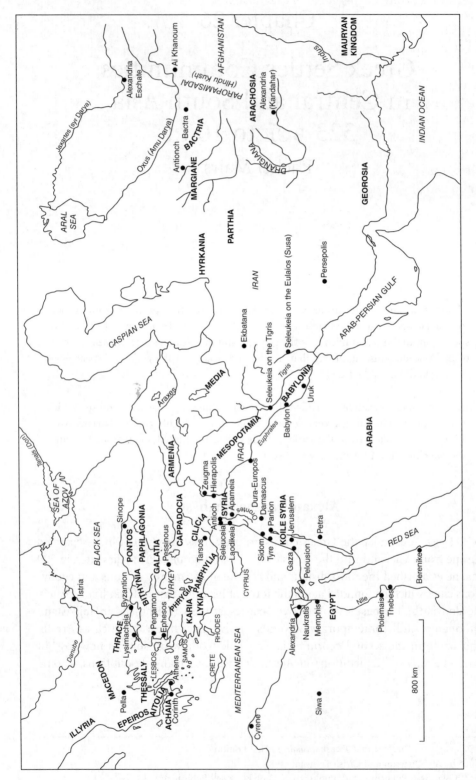

Figure 26.1 Map of the Hellenistic world

detailed, some simply remarks made in passing – of the processes by which Greek colonial outposts were established, and the composition of their populations (Fraser 1996). The most famous Alexandria, in Egypt, was an entirely new foundation, a metropolis which grew and flourished over the following centuries. But this city was not representative of the settlements created by Alexander in the course of his rapid, blitzkrieg campaigns through the Persian empire. More often, he left garrisons in existing cities, under the command of one of his officers. He also frequently retained in office Persian officials who had been amenable to him, perhaps aware of the dangerous and destabilizing rupture of socioeconomic structures and bonds of political loyalty which might come from cutting the nobles off from their lands.

Alexander was capable of being a pragmatist. What he was not – or at any rate never had the opportunity to demonstrate himself to be – was an administrator. Alexander subdued, at least temporarily, a great deal of territory in a relatively short period of time, but after his death at Babylon in 323 BCE, his generals and surviving family members engaged in decades of war, diplomatic machination, and assassination, before some formal and stable parceling out of the dead king's "spear-won" territory was achieved. My focus here is not on the complex political history of these successor states, but on the social history of the Greek communities established in the aftermath of conquest.

Some later Greek writers viewed Alexander as having been engaged in a kind of *mission civilisatrice*. Plutarch's essay *On the Fortune or Virtue of Alexander the Great* claims (328 E–F) that "Alexander founded over 70 cities among barbarian tribes, sprinkled Greek institutions all over Asia, and so overcame its wild and savage manner of living. . . . Alexander's victims would not have been civilised if they had not been defeated" (Austin 1981: 18–20). What the evidence reveals is naturally something rather more complex. At Alexandria Eschate, according to Arrian, Alexander spent just 20 days building fortifications, and the population of the new city comprised Greek mercenaries from his army, local "barbarians" who "volunteered," and demobilized Macedonians who were no longer fit for active service. Over the following years, in Alexandria Eschate and other Greek garrison-settlements of Central Asia, both local populations and the Greek settlers themselves rebelled against Alexander's political heirs. At times this was even in concert with one another, giving the enterprise an ironic "cross-community" aspect: "Fusion, harmony and brotherhood did not suddenly replace years of mutual animosity; the Greeks with Athenodorus wanted to leave, and the native peoples wanted nothing better . . ." Thus, the only cooperation between Greeks and 'barbarians' thus far was for the purpose of ridding each group of the other's company (Holt 1988: 83).

Much though all concerned may have desired otherwise, the Greeks stayed. Greek-ruled kingdoms survived in Bactria – present-day northern Afghanistan, southern Uzbekistan, and Tajikistan – until the mid-second century BCE, and in northwestern India perhaps as late as the turn of the Common Era. In these territories, Greeks and locals intermarried and developed their own distinctive cultures, while remaining in contact with, and considering themselves to be part of, a wider Greek world.

The Hellenistic *Oikoumene*

Military colonies were left across the vast extent of the defeated Achaemenid Persian empire, from Egypt to India. Some of these settlements scarcely outlived Alexander himself; others received ongoing, large-scale immigration, and were attractive destinations for Greek émigrés.

The ancient Greek experience is frequently referenced in the introductions to recent works on diasporas (Cohen 1997: 2, 83–84; Dufoix 2008: 38–41). I would like to take the opportunity, in the context of the present work, to offer a more extended case study of one chapter in the long history of Greek diasporas, the post-Alexander Hellenistic settlements of Central and South Asia. The term *Hellenistic* – as opposed to "Hellenic" – carries a range of implications. It may be understood in a purely chronological and geographical sense, pertaining to the Greek-dominated states of the eastern Mediterranean and Near East, ruled by descendants of the generals of Alexander until the death of the last Hellenistic dynast, Cleopatra VII of Egypt, in 30 BCE. But it also hints at something about the cultures and identities of these kingdoms and their inhabitants, that in their diversity they are very different from the old world of Archaic (*c.*800–480 BCE) and Classical (up to 323 BCE) Greece. The Hellenistic Greek diaspora presents its own particular historical and cultural context, different in direction, magnitude, constitution, and socioeconomic and political impetus from the circumstances, for example, of Archaic Greek colonization in the Mediterranean and Black Sea.[3]

In modern studies of the Hellenistic world, the term "diaspora" is not commonly used in a more than colloquial sense, and indeed in ancient Greek sources this metaphor of "scattering" into exile or colonization is most strongly associated with the Jewish diaspora (Gruen 2002). Nevertheless, historians and archaeologists of the Hellenistic world have often engaged very actively with the wider social sciences in their efforts to understand the various implications of population mobility and cultural interaction in their own regions and periods of specialization. This involves theoretical engagement, and the search for models, analogies, or simply resonant themes in more recent historical case studies, especially those provided by the (initially) European colonial and imperial projects of the Age of Discovery through to the neocolonialism of the early twenty-first century (a classic example is Will's 1985 *anthropologie coloniale* of the Hellenistic world). My purpose here is not to measure the Hellenistic Greek experience against any particular, prescriptive criteria of what does or does not constitute a "diaspora," although I shall consider several features often identified as characteristic of diaspora communities as I outline my case study. In addition, I should like to introduce some concepts and terminology particular to the Hellenistic world, by way of introduction to the mechanisms of Greek population movement and settlement in the period after Alexander, and their contemporary context and reception.

Areas of Greek settlement in the Mediterranean, North Africa, and the Near East constituted the *oikoumene*, the inhabited, civilized, Hellenized world – a world which, of course, expanded considerably in the wake of Alexander's conquests (Geus 2003: 232–245). Within the *oikoumene*, among Greeks and persons of Greek descent, there was some notion of a common origin, common customs, and ongoing connections with a Greek homeland, and with each other. The fifth-century BCE Greek historian Herodotos offered one influential definition of Greekness (*hellenikon*) as existing in "our common blood, common tongue, common cult places and sacrifices and similar customs" (8.144.2; trans. and further discussed by Hall 2002: 189). In the following section, I shall consider the extent to which the Greek settlements of Central and South Asia belonged to, and interacted with, the wider *oikoumene* on these terms.

Rhetorically, the new lands might be conceptualized as *doriktetos ge* "spear-won land," just as Alexander had claimed Asia by hurling his spear into the ground as he leapt ashore after crossing the Hellespont, and indeed the mechanisms of the early Hellenistic Greek settlement produced, in some places, landscapes and power structures resonant of a military occupation. Although the influx of a substantial Greek settler population, and the arrival of new political masters in the royal dynasties descended from Alexander's generals, brought changes to the conquered lands, Hellenistic systems of administration developed from and built on the precedent of Persian-era practices and institutions (on the Seleucid empire, see Aperghis 2004).

By far the best-documented Hellenistic kingdom is Egypt, under the dynasty of the Ptolemies, whose government, administration, and society we can reconstruct to a degree unimaginable for Central and South Asia. The reason is that the dry climate of Egypt has preserved a vast number of personal and official documents written on papyrus, in which we can trace the impact of the influx of Greek immigrants on the villages, the countryside, and their inhabitants. As well as garrisons, soldiers were billeted in private homes, with all the potential for conflict and intimate encounter which this might afford. Retired or demobilized soldiers were rewarded with a land grant (*kleros*) which the holder (*klerouchos*), initially at least, passed to his heirs with an obligation of future military service (Falivene 2009). Census documents of the third century BCE, written in both Greek and the indigenous Egyptian language, reveal a population where ethnicity mattered – Greeks paid taxes at preferential rates – but where the connections between an individual's descent, language use, official "ethnic" classification and personal identity might already fail to "line up" in any straightforward manner (Clarysse and Thompson 2006). Intermarriage (almost always between Greek men and Egyptian women) was common, and Greek status was passed along the male line.

The Graeco-Bactrian and Indo-Greek Kingdoms

The Hellenistic Greek diaspora had a characteristic often considered as important to the definition of a modern diaspora: multiple destinations. Although they share many common features, derived from the circumstances of their foundation and ongoing interconnections, the Greek colonies in the lands conquered by Alexander must also be understood on their own terms. Egypt was indeed a land of opportunity, but the experiences of the first and subsequent generations of the Greek émigré community in Bactria will have been very different. Although they were in a position of military dominance, there had been an element of compulsion to the settlement, and in the early years, as I have already noted, they took advantage of every opportunity to leave. Greeks and Macedonians joined Alexander's army for opportunities to profit and advance themselves, and there was also – in public rhetoric at least – a desire for revenge on the Persian empire for what Greece had suffered during the Persian Wars of the first half of the fifth century BCE. The soldiers' aim was to accrue wealth and go back home, or to find a "better life" under benevolent masters such as the Ptolemies, who could provide good pay, land grants, and favorable tax regimes. Bactria's charms were less immediately obvious.

Over the course of the third century BCE, a local Greek dynasty under a father and son both named Diodotos established Bactria's effective independence from the other Hellenistic states (Holt 1999). Until around the middle of the second century BC, when the Graeco-Bactrian kingdom was destroyed by a combination of outside invasions and civil war, the Greek kings of Bactria grew wealthy and powerful from Bactria's agricultural and mineral resources, and its position on trade routes between India, the Near East, and Central Asia (Strabo 11.11.1). In the early second century BCE, Bactrian Greek kings such as Demetrios and Menander invaded northwestern India, establishing a second wave of Greek colonies in the Indian subcontinent.

Throughout this period, the Greeks of Bactria maintained an ambivalent relationship with the Greek "motherland" and the wider *oikoumene*. On the one hand, Greek ethnic and cultural identity, and direct ties to the Greek world, were important to the descent community and were openly asserted and celebrated. At the city of Ai Khanoum, on the river Oxus in northeastern Afghanistan, a shrine in the center of the city contained a Greek inscription of ethical maxims from the symbolic center of the Greek world, at Delphi (Robert 1968):

> These wise sayings of earlier men, the words of well-known men, are enshrined in the holy Pytho [at Delphi]. There Klearchos copied them faithfully, and set them up here in the sanctuary of Kineas, blazing from afar.
>
> > As a child, be well-behaved.
> > As a youth, be self-controlled.
> > As an adult, be just.
> > As an elder, be wise.
> > As you come to the end, be without grief.
> >   (Trans. adapted from Holt 1999: 175)

Ai Khanoum was a major city in the Bactrian heartland, but the Greek language and Greek culture also thrived in some more out-of-the-way places. Kandahar, in southern Afghanistan, ancient Arachosia, was the site of one of the conqueror's many Alexandrias – in this case an addition to an already important Persian provincial center. Arachosia's political history was more turbulent than that of Bactria:

following its conquest by Alexander, it passed under the control of the Indian Mauryan empire, then was conquered again by the Greeks of Bactria (Bernard 2005). Because it has not been thoroughly excavated, we know rather less about the Greek community at Kandahar than about that of Ai Khanoum. In recent years, however, some important material has come onto the antiquities market, such as a Greek verse inscription which originally stood on the wall of a roadside tomb outside the city. The language is educated and refined, and the writer marks out his own name in an acrostic:

> *Stele of Sophytos*: The irresistible force of the trio of Fates destroyed the house of my forefathers, which had flourished greatly for many years. But I, Sophytos son of Naratos, pitiably bereft when quite small of my ancestral livelihood, after I had acquired the virtue of the Archer [Apollo] and the Muses, mixed with noble prudence, then did consider how I might raise up again my family house. Obtaining interest-bearing money from another source, I left home, keen not to return before I possessed wealth, the supreme good. Thus, by travelling to many cities for commerce, I acquired ample riches without reproach. Becoming celebrated, I returned to my homeland after countless years, and showed myself, bringing pleasure to well-wishers. Straightaway I built afresh my paternal home, which was riddled with rot, making it better than before, and also, since the tomb had collapsed to the ground, I constructed another one and, during my lifetime, set upon it by the roadside this loquacious plaque. Thus may the sons and grandsons of myself, who completed this enviable work, possess my house.
>
> *Acrostic*: Through Sophytos the son of Naratos. (Trans. adapted from Hollis 2011)

Sophytos had received an excellent Greek literary education, and there are hints in his poem that this included the traditional grounding in the works of Homer. In places, he uses obscure Homeric vocabulary, and even makes an allusion to the famous opening lines of the *Odyssey*, where the Muse is asked to sing of Odysseus' journeys to many cities and among diverse peoples. The home to which Sophytos returns from his travels, however, is Kandahar, not a Greek island; and his own name, like that of his father, is not Greek.

The case of Sophytos reminds us that, whatever the strength of their physical and emotional connections to a Greek homeland, the communities of Greek culture and descent in the easternmost reaches of the *oikoumene* also developed along their own lines. Some, at least, of the first generation regarded themselves as sojourners rather than settlers. Among subsequent generations, it is difficult to say what, if any, symbolic capital was attached to the notion of an eventual return to Greece. Bactrians of Greek heritage were the dominant local group, but, as in contemporary Egypt, Greek status did not require that both of an individual's parents should have been Greek. Alexander settled Bactria with soldiers, not families; the region was not a popular posting; and it is unlikely that there was much in the way of ongoing immigration from the Greek world. Intermarriage between Greek soldiers and local women, whether indigenous Bactrians, or members of the old Persian imperial diaspora, should be assumed to have been all but universal.

The offspring of these unions (with no personal experience of their Greek "motherland" other, perhaps, than the origin myths contained in tales from their fathers and grandfathers), created and inhabited a society and culture which would have seemed foreign to a visitor from the Greek Mediterranean. The architecture and material culture of Ai Khanoum, for example, owe far more to Persian and local Bactrian traditions than to Classical Greek models. The great court of the city's central palace quarter is lined with Corinthian columns, a Greek-style semicircular theater is set into the slopes of the upper city, and athletes and scholars might exercise and promenade in a fine gymnasium on the banks of the Oxus. But the plans of the palace and main temple derive from the Near East, and the residential district inside the city walls contains houses designed to respect the local climate and prevailing winds. The relationship between material culture and ethnic identity is a complicated one. Ethnicity may certainly be expressed through and be predicated upon elements of material culture, dress, architecture, and so forth, but with ancient populations it is naturally difficult to identify *which* elements. In the city of Ai Khanoum, the Greek language and cultural traditions (theater, intellectual and sporting pursuits in the gymnasium) were maintained, and connections to Delphi and the Greek world were celebrated and enshrined in stone. What I would suggest we might see at work here is the development of a Greek identity in which certain other forms of material culture and cultural expression have had their ethnic force neutralized, allowing Greek ethnic boundaries to be maintained and patrolled, while incorporating greater cultural diversity (Mairs 2008).

Politically, however, there were tensions in relations with the "motherland." Long after the Diodotids had established their independence in the mid-third century BCE, Greek rulers of Bactria continued to resist any attempt by other kings of the *oikoumene* to bring them back into the political fold of the Hellenistic empires. In 206 BCE, the Seleucid king Antiochos III laid siege to the Graeco-Bactrian king Euthydemos at his capital, Bactra. The episode is described by the Greek historian Polybios, who records that Antiochos soon realized that he was caught in a stalemate, and gladly received an envoy from Euthydemos (Polyb. 11.34: 6–14). In support of his claim to legitimate kingship, Euthydemos maintained that he was not a rebel, but had overthrown rebels (the Diodotids). But his most powerful tool of persuasion was a threat: while he and Antiochos, two Greek kings, continued to quarrel with one another, hordes of nomads were gathering and would overwhelm them both if they did not come to an agreement. Antiochos made peace. The episode reveals how a Greek king of Bactria, over a century after the initial settlement under Alexander, might both assert a common Greek identity with another Hellenistic king, and defy attempts to be brought into his empire.

Although other regions of the Hellenistic world are far better documented in historical sources, surviving contemporary documentation, and the archaeological record, the Greek-ruled kingdoms of Bactria and neighboring regions provide interesting case studies of Greek diaspora communities which existed in only intermittent communication with the Greek homeland, and resisted political interference from other Greek diaspora states. This isolationism – a matter both of policy and of practical necessity – coexisted with an enduring emotional and ideological attachment to the "old country" and, it may be assumed, a sense of belonging to the new lands, polities, and societies of the areas of Greek settlement in Central and South Asia.

Conclusion: The Heirs of Alexander

Indian sculptures or Indian buildings, however, because they reflect a foreign influence or betray a foreign origin are not the less, but perhaps the more interesting to ourselves, who were borne to India upon a crest of a later but similar wave and who may find in their non-Indian characteristics a reminiscence of forms, which we already know in Europe and of a process of assimilation with which our own archaeological history has rendered us familiar. (Speech by Lord Curzon, Viceroy of India, at the Annual Meeting of the Asiatic Society of Bengal, February 7, 1900, quoted in Ray 2007: 107)

A curious – but not entirely unexpected – footnote to the history of the Greek settler communities in Bactria and India is their adoption as cultural and ideological predecessors by a later imperial diaspora in the region: the British soldiers and administrators who came to India under the East India Company and the British Raj. Many British residents in the Indian subcontinent identified strongly with the Classical Graeco-Roman past, and an intuitive progression from this identification was to draw comparisons between Alexander and his Greek successors in the east, and the British in India. There was a very practical aspect to such investigations: amateur historians would set out with the works of Classical historians such as Arrian and Quintus Curtius Rufus in their hands to trace Alexander's routes in the Indus valley and hill country of the northwest frontier. In a 1901 issue of the *Geographical Journal*, Colonel Sir Thomas Hungerford Holdich, the retired Superintendent of Frontier Surveys, reviewed a compendium of excerpts from the Classical sources translated by J.W. McCrindle (1901). Holdich writes from the perspective of "intelligent travellers" and recommends that (1901: 611): "part of it, at any rate, should be a familiar addition to the personal equipment of the Indian frontier official; for it is on the frontier chiefly that the light of antiquity is required to assist in unravelling the ethnographical problems of the present." One of Holdich's few reservations about the book is that a frontier official on the move may find it too large and heavy, and here he also expands on his views about the relationship between an unchanging, ahistorical India and two foreign diaspora communities which came to dominate it:

The book is consequently heavier and not quite so handy as its predecessors in the series, of which the adaptability of each separate volume to the capacity of an ordinary pocket, and its small consideration as an additional weight to a traveller's baggage, were by no means a contemptible attribute. The value of the series lies hardly more in the accuracy of translation and the scholarship exhibited by its author than in its ready accessibility to those political, military, and commercial wanderers whose business leads them into the remoter corners of our Indian Empire, and who can verify for themselves, as they go, the extraordinary accuracy of some, at least, of those old-world records of the changeless East. It is with the help of such practical scholars as McCrindle that the unwritten history of a country which has never produced a historian can be gradually unfolded by men whose knowledge of Greek literature probably ends with the Greek version of the New Testament. (Holdich 1901: 610)

This is Alexander's "civilizing mission" redux. Although Holdich is well aware that most of Alexander's notional British heirs were not scholars, he trusts both the potential of the Classical sources to give accurate testimony about the "changeless East," and that modern sojourners are continuing – and validating – a long history of European settlement *in* India and Orientalist control of knowledge *about* India.

The accounts of British explorers are not restricted to attempts to rerun the campaigns of Alexander. They record other claimants to the title of Alexander's heirs, in the mountains of Nuristan and the Hindu Kush, among groups whose "European" fair coloring and divergence from the languages and customs of their neighbors (as "kafirs" or infidels) made them a source of fascination for British travelers. It is difficult to establish the point at which these communities began to believe or claim themselves to be the descendants of Graeco-Macedonian colonists, and whether this was in fact under the influence of Islamic or modern European traditions about the campaigns of Alexander in the region. What is clear is that the idea has long been attractive to Europeans, and has at times been enthusiastically taken up by the communities themselves. In Rudyard Kipling's 1888 novella *The Man Who Would Be King*, two British army deserters attempt to set themselves up as kings of Kafiristan, by pretending to be sons of Alexander. (The connection is made more explicit in the 1975 film, directed by John Huston and starring Michael Caine and Sean Connery.) In 1833, the British adventurer Alexander "Bokhara" Burnes recorded his encounter with "the reputed descendants of Alexander the Great" in the *Journal of the Royal Asiatic Society*, and noted that there was a local tradition of this descent: "In speaking of the existence of Grecian colonies in the remote regions of Central Asia, said to be descended from Alexander of Macedon, it is necessary to premise, that I am not indulging in speculation, but asserting a lineage of various tribes of people, that is claimed by themselves, and merits therefore our attention" (Burnes 1833: 305). On his own investigations into the "Origin of the Kafir of the Hindu Kush," some decades later, Holdich (1896: 49) carried with him earlier editions of McCrindle's "excellent translations" which possessed "the invaluable attribute of portability."

The fantasy of lost tribes of Greeks in the mountains of Pakistan and Afghanistan has proven difficult to dissipate, despite the improbability of undiluted Greek genetic material or customs persisting over more than two thousand years. It plays to the ongoing fascination with the ancient forerunners of modern European (and American) military and colonial ventures in South and Central Asia (Holt 2005), and is doubtless also for some a convenient fiction. For the "lost tribes" themselves, there are certain rewards to be earned from perpetuating claims to descent from

Alexander, or allowing them to be perpetuated. Reasserted connections to the "mother country" bring a raised international profile and investment from Greek NGOs (Rickett 2011).

The historical Hellenistic Greek diaspora in Bactria and India ceased to exist as a culturally distinct and politically dominant community before the turn of the Common Era. Within a very few years of the initial military settlement in the region, in the late fourth century BCE, it had already begun to develop along lines independent from the other Hellenistic states of the Mediterranean littoral, with which it remained in contact and to which it asserted some connection. The "imagined community" of the eastern Greek diaspora, however, proved much longer-lasting and in some quarters endures even to the present day.

Notes

1 I cite Greek and Roman historical works, as is common convention, according to the abbreviations used in the OCD (2003). Unless otherwise specified, translations are given from the editions published in the *Loeb Classical Library*, which provide the original text with a facing English translation.
2 I do not provide full references to the modern scholarly literature on the history and archaeology of the Greek settlements in Central Asia and India, for which the reader may consult Mairs (2011).
3 On the Hellenistic world, see further Green (1990) and Erskine (2003). Austin (1981) provides a collection of ancient sources in translation, including extracts from the works of Greek and Roman historians, inscriptions and documentary texts.

References

Aperghis, G.G.M. 2004. *The Seleukid Royal Economy: The Finances and Financial Administration of the Seleukid Empire*. Cambridge: Cambridge University Press.

Austin, M.M. 1981. *The Hellenistic World from Alexander to the Roman Conquest: A Selection of Ancient Sources in Translation*. Cambridge: Cambridge University Press.

Bernard, P. 2005. "Hellenistic Arachosia: A Greek melting pot in action." *East and West*, 55(1–4): 13–34.

Burnes, A. 1833. "On the reputed descendants of Alexander the Great, in the valley of the Oxus." *Journal of the Royal Asiatic Society of Bengal*, 2: 305–308.

Clarysse, W. and Thompson, D.J. 2006. *Counting the People in Hellenistic Egypt*, Volume 1: *Population Registers (P.Count)*; Volume 2: *Historical Studies*. Cambridge: Cambridge University Press.

Cohen, R. 1997. *Global Diasporas: An Introduction*. London: UCL Press.

Dufoix, S. 2008. *Diasporas*. Berkeley: University of California Press.

Falivene, M.R. 2009. "Geography and administration in Egypt (332 BCE–642 CE)." In R.S. Bagnall (ed.) *The Oxford Handbook of Papyrology*, pp. 521–540. Oxford: Oxford University Press.

Fraser, P.M. 1996. *The Cities of Alexander the Great*. Oxford: Clarendon Press.

Geus, K. 2003. "Space and geography." In A. Erskine (ed.) *A Companion to the Hellenistic World*, pp. 232–245. Oxford: Blackwell.

Green, P. 1990. *Alexander to Actium: The Hellenistic Age*. Berkeley: University of California Press.

Gruen, E.S. 2002. *Diaspora: Jews Amidst Greeks and Romans*. Cambridge, MA: Harvard University Press.

Hall, J.M. 2002. *Hellenicity: Between Ethnicity and Culture*. Chicago: University of Chicago Press.

Holdich, T.H. 1896. "The origin of the kafir of the Hindu Kush." *Geographical Journal*, 7(1): 42–49.

Holdich, T.H. 1901. "Review: Dr McCrindle's 'Ancient India.'" *Geographical Journal*, 18(6): 609–611.

Hollis, A.S. 2011. "Greek letters in Hellenistic Bactria." In D. Obbink and R. Rutherford (eds) *Culture in Pieces: Essays on Ancient Texts in Honour of Peter Parsons*, pp. 104–118. Oxford: Oxford University Press.

Holt, F.L. 1988. *Alexander the Great and Bactria: The Formation of a Greek Frontier in Central Asia*. Leiden: Brill.

Holt, F.L. 1999. *Thundering Zeus: The Making of Hellenistic Bactria*. Berkeley: University of California Press.

Holt, F.L. 2005. *Into the Land of Bones: Alexander the Great in Afghanistan*. Berkeley: University of California Press.

Mairs, R. 2008. "Greek identity and the settler community in Hellenistic Bactria and Arachosia." *Migrations and Identities*, 1(1): 19–43.

Mairs, R. 2011. *The Archaeology of the Hellenistic Far East: A Survey. Bactria, Central Asia and the Indo-Iranian Borderlands, c.300 BC–AD 100*. Oxford: BAR.

McCrindle, J.W. 1901. *Ancient India as described in Classical Literature being a collection of Greek and Latin texts relating to India, extracted from Herodotus, Strabo, Diodorus Siculus, Pliny, Aelian, Philostratus, Dion Chrysostom, Porphyry, Stobaeus, the Itinerary of Alexander the Great, the Periêgêsis of Dionysius, the Dionysiaka of Nonnus, the Romance history of Alexander and other works*. Westminster: Archibald Constable & Co.

OCD 2003. *Oxford Classical Dictionary*, ed. S. Hornblower and A. Spawforth, rev. 3rd edn. Oxford: Oxford University Press.

Ray, H.P. 2007. "Alexander's campaign (327–326 BC): a chronological marker in the archaeology of India." In H.P. Ray, and D.T. Potts (eds) *Memory as History: The Legacy of Alexander in Asia*, pp. 105–121. New Delhi: Aryan Books International.

Rickett, O. 2011. "Culture Kalash in Pakistan." *Guardian*, April 16.

Robert, L. 1968. "De Delphes à l'Oxus: Inscriptions grecques nouvelles de la Bactriane." In *Comptes-rendus de l'Académie des inscriptions et belles-lettres*, 1968: 416–457.

Will, E. 1985. "Pour une 'anthropologie coloniale' du monde hellénistique." In J.W. Eadie and J. Ober (eds) *The Craft of the Ancient Historian: Essays in honor of Chester G. Starr*, pp. 273–301. Lanham, MD: University Press of America.

Chapter 27

Parts and Labor
The Commodification of the Human Body
Monir Moniruzzaman

"*Selling a kidney is like running for a* sonar horin *or golden deer – an illusion.*"
Hiru, a 38-year-old kidney seller in Bangladesh (Moniruzzaman 2010)

The human body has long been commodified in diverse forms. From slavery and prostitution to the organ trade, the body, particularly its parts and labor, is being turned into materials for economic exploitation (Sharp 2000). Marxist analysis exemplifies how the ruling class controls the means of production and thus exploits the working class by extracting their surplus value of labor. In modern times, the body is stripped of spare parts to extend the lives of the affluent few, through the "miracle" success of biotechnology and the rise of the neoliberal economy. This stark exploitation of the human body raises a serious ethical question: should the body be treated as a collection of spare parts with price tags within a supply-and-demand market model? This chapter examines the current form of exploitation of the impoverished underclass, whose bodies become sites for organ harvesting.

Western biomedicine has a long history of modifying human bodies and improving their function and form through the incorporation of devices, products, and extensions. From prosthetic legs to eyeglasses to hearing aids, biomedicine has aspired to improve and repair bodies through reconstruction and redesign. In the twentieth and twenty-first centuries, this trend towards repair and redesign has been fueled by biotechnology, which facilitates the transplantation of cells, skin, and, in the last 50 years, organs themselves (Moniruzzaman 2006: 179). The rapid progress of biotechnology creates a high demand for reusable parts, turning not only human cadavers but also living bodies into a lucrative industry (Kimbrell 1993). A human cadaver is currently worth more than US$230,000 on the open market, as about 150 of its parts can be reused (Hedges and Gaines 2000; Sharp 2006: 11). The living human body is also fragmented into saleable major organs (kidney, liver, and cornea), soft tissues (bone marrow, ligament, and skin), reproductive products (sperm, ova, placenta, and fetal tissues), as well as blood, plasma, hair, and even the whole body (Hogshire 1992; Roach 2003; Sharp 2006: 11). Today, we witness the global "human body shop" expanding as a by-product of the scientific endeavor; nonetheless, this trend is highly questionable, both ethically and socially.

This chapter particularly focuses on organ transplantation, which has created an illegal trade in human body parts – mostly kidneys, but also liver lobes, single corneas, single lungs, and part pancreas. At present, the waiting list for an organ transplant is increasing more quickly than the legal supply of donors. To reduce the escalating waiting time, wealthy recipients create new paths to harvest "fresh" organs from the bodies of impoverished populations living densely in developing countries. The World Health Organization calculates that about 10 percent of the 63,000 kidney transplants carried out worldwide every year involve commercial transactions (Garwood 2007: 5). The emergence of a "black market" of organs, which was recognized more than two decades ago, raises serious ethical questions. Is it right to purchase an organ, even if the organ sought provides longevity? Is the sale of one's organ a justifiable means of fighting poverty? Universal human rights and social justice issues are also relevant here, as modern medical procedures such as organ transplantation often justify a system for prolonging the lives of "haves" over the lives of "have nots."

The commodification of human body parts is recurrently understood as both a macroeconomic and macro-historical phenomenon, as it is embedded in the larger system of exchange and extraction across differences of wealth and encompasses the broad dynamics of both developed and developing countries. As Nancy Scheper-Hughes notes (2000: 193), the flow of organs follows the modern route of capital: from south to north, from Third World to First World, from poor to rich, from black and brown to white, and from female to male. The historical relationship of conquest, colonization, and extraction has shaped the transformation of actual Third World bodies into raw materials in their own right. At the same time, these processes need to be examined in terms of the microeconomic, political, and cultural contexts in which organ commodification takes place. By exploring the ethnographic details of organ trade in a local setting, this chapter examines how such practice constitutes serious violence against the poor, generates extreme suffering, and violates longstanding cultural practices about the human body.[1]

Organ Trade in Bangladesh

Abul, a poor 32-year-old Bangladeshi farmer, sold one of his kidneys to a wealthy American citizen (a Bangladeshi-born US resident) in a renowned hospital in Singapore. Abul's testimonies reveal the processes and experiences of selling his kidney that document the labyrinth of exploitation that kidney sellers face in the process of selling their body parts, and from which they suffer severely afterwards. Abul's odyssey for organ selling is divided into three sections: pre-operative, operative, and post-operative.

Pre-operative

Excruciating poverty forced Abul to sell one of his body parts. When Abul came across a Bengali newspaper advertisement seeking a kidney donor, he was tempted to donate one of his body parts due to the lucrative offers (i.e., monetary reward, job offer, and/or overseas visa) made in exchange for that donation. An example of such a newspaper advertisement posted by a potential recipient is shown in Figure 27.1.

Even though Abul had limited knowledge about organs in the body, he hastily contacted the buyer, imagining that he would soon be able to resolve the ongoing economic hardship he was facing. Over the phone, the buyer asked Abul about his tissue-typing report, but Abul did not know where and how to have his tissues examined. His first attempt was fruitless.

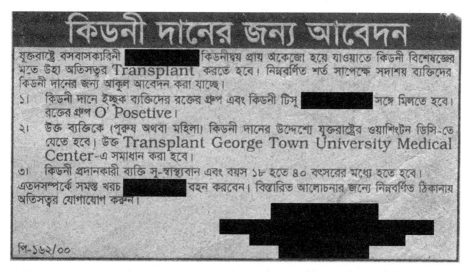

Figure 27.1 *The Daily Ittefaq*, January 4, 2000. Translation: Request for Kidney Donation. Both kidneys of a USA resident, [name], are damaged. Kidney specialists advise her to transplant a kidney immediately. A heartfelt request is made to the good persons who can donate a kidney with the following criteria. 1. The interested donor's blood group and the tissue must be matched with those of [name]. Blood group O+. 2. The donor (male or female) must travel to Washington, DC, USA, for the donation. The transplant will be performed at Georgetown University Medical Center. 3. The donor must be in good health and between 19 and 40 years of age. All the relevant expenses will be covered by [name]. To discuss details, contact urgently the following address [name, address, postal code, telephone]

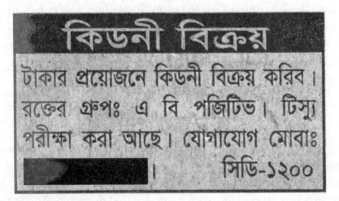

Figure 27.2   *The Daily Ittefaq*, April 27, 2005. Translation: Kidney Sale. For financial reasons,
I will sell a kidney. Blood group: AB+. Tissue test is done. Contact [cell phone no.]

Abul started searching for organ classifieds that are published regularly in Bengali
national newspapers. About two months later, he found another advertisement that
matched his blood group. He contacted the buyer, but a few weeks later was notified
that the buyer had successfully matched his tissues with another donor. By this time,
Abul was frustrated; he placed an advertisement in *The Daily Korotoa*, a regional
newspaper published in the northern part of Bangladesh. Figure 27.2 is an example
of a classified ad posted by a potential seller. More than a dozen potential buyers
called Abul, but no deal resulted, as Abul was not interested in trading his kidney
with those who lived far away.

He republished his advertisement; a potential recipient living close by contacted
him. When they met with each other, the recipient attempted to convince Abul to
"donate" his kidney by portraying "kidney donation" as a "noble act" that saves lives
and does not harm the donor. The recipient promised to pay Abul 100,000 Taka
(US$1,500) in exchange for his kidney and bear all the expenses involved in trans-
plantation (i.e., Abul's transportation, accommodation, and hospitalization).
Unfortunately, the recipient died shortly afterwards, as he was not able to arrange
for the high cost of transplantation.

Abul became caught up in searching organ classifieds. This time he contacted
another buyer, who was a middleman but posed as a recipient in the newspaper
advertisement. Figure 27.3 is an example of such classifieds, published by an organ
broker in Bangladesh. This advertisement was published by a broker who was
seeking donors from various blood groups. As the broker instructed, Abul borrowed
some money from a local moneylender and traveled to Dhaka to have his tissue-
typing done at the Bangladesh Institute of Research and Rehabilitation in Diabetes,
Endocrine, and Metabolic Disorders (BIRDEM), the major tissue-typing center in
that country. A week later, the broker collected the Human Leukocyte Antigen
(HLA) report and informed Abul over the phone that his tissue did not match the
potential recipient's. The broker shrewdly promised Abul to match his tissues with
an affluent recipient without delay.

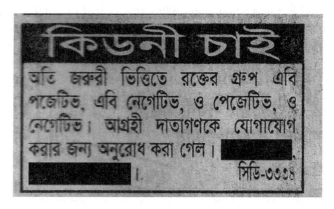

Figure 27.3 *The Daily Ittefaq*, September 26, 2003. Translation: Kidney Wanted. Kidney for the blood groups of AB+, AB-, O+, O- are needed urgently. Interested donors are requested to contact [telephone numbers]

While still waiting to hear back from the broker, Abul went to the tissue-typing unit at BIRDEM and asked a clerk about trading his kidney. The clerk made a phone call to Dalal, a major kidney broker in Bangladesh. Dalal came to BIRDEM and cunningly told Abul a story about *the sleeping kidney*. The story goes like this: A person has two kidneys: one works and the other one sleeps. If one kidney is infected, the other kidney automatically starts working. But if one kidney is damaged, the other one will be damaged, too, because of the polluted blood. Therefore, everybody can be healthy with only one kidney. During the operation, the doctor first starts a donor's sleeping kidney with medicine. The "newly awakened" kidney stays in the donor's body, and the "old" kidney is removed and given to the transplant recipient. In this manner, selling a kidney is presented as a win–win situation.

Dalal matched Abul's tissues with a wealthy recipient within a few weeks. At first, Dalal introduced Abul to the recipient's business manager, a proxy. The proxy arranged the HLA examination for Abul along with 15 other potential donors on the same day. After receiving all the test results and consulting with a kidney specialist, the proxy asked Abul and three other donors to come to Dhaka again. All of these donors went for other medical tests as well, based on the test results, Abul was chosen as the key potential donor. The proxy immediately told Abul to dress up and come to Dhaka to finalize the deal.

In a luxurious business office, the proxy introduced Abul to his boss, the father of the person needing a kidney transplant. The recipient's father asked Abul about his family details and reasons for selling the kidney. After this brief meeting, the father asked Abul to stay in Dhaka for a couple of weeks to undergo further medical examination. However, within a few days, Abul became impatient staying in a hotel and wanted to go back to his village. The recipient's father invited Abul for dinner at his palatial mansion. However, Abul had to give two syringes of blood to a laboratory assistant just before the dinner. The father told Abul that his son was living in the United States but was being admitted to an excellent hospital in Singapore for kidney transplantation. The father stated that only Abul could save his son's life; in return, the man pledged to support Abul for the rest of his life. The man also promised to pay Abul a substantial amount of money, and instantly gave him 3,000 Taka (US$50) as a gift. When Abul expressed fears about the surgery, the man guaranteed that the operation was 100 percent safe, saying that Abul would be in the hands of world-renowned medical specialists. The man also mentioned that going to Singapore would be fun, as Abul could visit new places and experience different food. To establish the commodified kinship, the man called Abul his nephew and asked him to visit his house regularly.

Abul had photographs taken wearing a studio coat and tie. The recipient's family forged legal documents and helped Abul to apply for a passport. When Abul received his passport, he saw that his new name was Abdus Sohhan, for he was being identified as the recipient's nephew. After receiving his visa, Abul received 5,000 Taka (US$70), as well as clothing and suitcases from his recipient's family. One gloomy morning, Abul, the recipient's father, and the proxy left for Singapore – Abul's first-ever airplane ride. When the plain began taxiing, Abul started to weep. He felt as if he was facing a noose before being hanged.

Operative

In Singapore, Abul had to deposit his passport into the proxy's hands. This ensured that Abul could not return to Bangladesh without giving up his kidney. The first thing Abul did upon arrival was to meet with his recipient. The recipient was so relieved to see Abul that he promised to maintain a lifelong relationship with his donor. Beginning the next day, Abul regularly visited a luxurious hospital to undergo various medical tests. When all the tests were completed, a medical board interviewed Abul and his recipient to verify their relationship. According to the Singaporean law, donors and recipients must be closely related; for this reason, the recipient prepared Abul again and again to lie during the interview. Abul managed to convince the medical board that he was donating a kidney to one of his family members. He gave the board the forged documents and lied endlessly during the interrogation: for example, when a board member asked whether he was married, Abul answered that he was a bachelor, which he was not.

Abul was admitted to the hospital a few days later. He was worried, wondering whether he would survive the surgery. The recipient encouraged Abul, saying that he was saving a life – a noble act, indeed. But Abul could not close his eyes; he was constantly thinking about his family. When he entered the operating room, he was reciting *Innalillah*, the verse from the Koran that Muslims pray when they see a corpse pass by.

After the operation, Abul woke up to an intolerable sharp pain. The first thing he noticed was the rough incision, about 20 inches long, on his abdomen. He did not know that if the recipient had paid only US $200 more, the surgeons could have used laparoscopic surgery, which requires an incision as small as 3 inches.

About a week later, Abul was released from hospital. The recipient's family gave him gifts, including a gold chain, a watch, a charger light, and a few children's toys. They also gave him US$500 and promised to pay the rest of the money after returning to Dhaka. They told him he could stay in Singapore, but as an illegal worker; he decided instead to go back to his family. When the plane touched Bangladeshi soil, Abul re-entered his old life with a damaged body.

Post-operative

Abul was under constant psychological pressure to hide his scar from his family. When his wife noticed the long scar, Abul had to disclose his actions. His wife became angry, but in due course, Abul convinced her to sell one of her kidneys, too, arguing that it was a safe and lucrative act.

In total, Abul received 140,000 Taka (US$2,000) for selling his kidney. The recipient's father told Abul that the market price of a Bangladeshi kidney is 100,000 Taka ($1,400), but he was open-handed because Abul was cooperative and compassionate to the man's son. Even though Abul received a better deal, he spent most of it paying off debt; the rest of it went towards opening up a livestock farm. Yet, Abul could not escape poverty by selling his kidney. Eventually, he asked his recipient's father for a job, as was promised; the man bypassed Abul's plea, stating that there was no vacancy in his office.

Abul's health deteriorated significantly in the post-vending period. He regularly experienced an acute burning sensation while urinating; once, the pain was so severe that the recipient's family admitted him to hospital. Abul did not receive any biannual post-operative health checkup, which the recipient had also promised. Whenever Abul needed medication, it was usually out of his reach. In the end, Abul realized that selling a kidney did not turn the wheel of his fate.

Abul was one of the 33 kidney sellers (30 male and three female) whom I interviewed during my risky fieldwork in Bangladesh, which was carried out mainly between 2004 and 2005. Gaining access to kidney sellers was the most arduous task in undertaking this fieldwork. Most Bangladeshi sellers did not disclose their actions to family members – not even to spouses or parents – as the organ trade is outlawed and is considered a disgraceful and humiliating act there. I successfully located these sellers only after gaining the trust of a kidney broker – my key informant and intermediary in this research. Conducting interviews with kidney sellers was the primary method of my data collection. I spent an average of 10 hours with each seller. All interviews were unstructured and narrative-based, comprising about 1,500 pages of written transcripts.

My ethnography (Moniruzzaman 2010) reveals that Bangladesh serves as an emerging but growing organ bazaar sustained by mostly domestic and some overseas recipients (almost all of whom are Bangladeshi-born foreign nationals). According to my estimates, about 250 kidneys are trafficked each year from poor Bangladeshis to wealthy recipients; their transplants are performed within Bangladesh and abroad. In 1999, Bangladesh passed the Organ Transplant Act to outlaw this trade, yet in that country's national newspapers, not only kidneys, but also livers, corneas, and any other transplantable parts of human body are regularly advertised to buy or sell. A variety of organ brokers have expanded their network and run the business for a hefty fee. Local medical specialists claim that the Transplantation Act is "strictly maintained" in their motherland. Meanwhile, organ buyers (both recipients and brokers) trick or force poor citizens to sell their body parts and then spitefully deceive and deprive them, paying as little as $600 for their kidneys. The absence of a cadaveric organ donation program in Bangladesh, a country where 78 percent of the people live on less than two dollars a day, further enhances the trade in human organs.

Violence Against the Poor

Bangladeshi kidney sellers – all of whom are poor – are victims of "structural violence," a term coined by Johan Galtung in 1969. Galtung notes that this form of violence is silently built into social structures and social institutions that systematically prevent individuals from achieving their full potential (1969: 168). Structural violence is often recognized as physical and psychological harm that constrains the "capabilities of each person," resulting from exploitative economic, political, and social systems (Sen 1998: 2). Paul Farmer closely links structural violence to "social injustice" and "social machinery of oppression," which are embedded in a "larger matrix of culture, history, and political economy" that fosters human rights abuses and extreme suffering (2004: 307; 2005: 29–30; Farmer *et al.* 2006: 1686). My ethnography witnesses how and to what extent poor Bangladeshis are subject to structural violence, which raises serious ethical question about social justice.

In the People's Republic of Bangladesh, excruciating poverty forces many poor people to turn to the organ trade. About 35 million poor people (nearly one quarter of the population) face the violence of needless hunger, which is an outcome of structural violence manifested through colonial exploitation, neoliberal readjustments, and severe corruption – what Amartya Sen (1982) calls a human-made disaster (see also Hartman and Boyce 1998). Inevitably, poor Bangladeshis are suffering from harrowing health conditions: a staggering 77 percent of them lack minimal requirements for a healthy human existence. About 50 percent of women have chronic energy deficiency and 2 million children are suffering from acute malnutrition (UN 2009). Nevertheless, fewer than 56 million poor people in Bangladesh have access to basic health services beyond immunization and family planning (UNESCAP 2002: 1). To make matters worse, socioenvironmental factors, such as arsenic poisoning, air pollution, pesticide use, and smoking tobacco contribute to an alarming number of organ maladies. Regrettably, the majority – the economic underclass – is at the greatest risk of kidney failure, yet they die prematurely without receiving dialysis, let alone a transplant.

A kidney transplant is one of the most expensive medical procedures for Bangladeshis. Even in a public hospital there, the cost of kidney transplant and post-operative care for two weeks starts at about 225,000 Taka (US$3,200). It is virtually impossible for most Bangladeshi poor people to collect this amount of money in their lifetime. Therefore, they literally beg for money in local newspapers and take other steps to receive a transplant. For example, a brother of a kidney transplant recipient who died from organ rejection just one month after the operation told me: "All of our family members tried our best to save my brother's life. We sold our land and jewelry, and borrowed money from the bank to arrange transplantation. But we could not save my brother and we are still paying off our debt." Additionally, the healthcare for organs in Bangladesh is concentrated in two major cities; most poor people do not have access to organ care at all. Currently, the service of transplantation fulfills the needs of less than 1 percent of the population – the wealthy minority. Meanwhile, the poor die in silence, knowing that they could have saved their lives through an organ transplant. Transplantation is not just a new technology, it is a life-saving procedure. These ethical questions therefore arise: "Miracle" technology for whom? Who suffers from organ maladies, but who receives care?

The poor are not only deprived; at the same time, their body parts are being extracted through structural violence. My ethnography illustrates how Bangladeshi buyers (both recipients and brokers) create a desire for the sellers, most of whom do not understand the function of the kidney but are tempted to "donate" because of the buyers' fraudulent claim that kidney "donation" is a safe, lucrative, and noble act. Once the sellers are recruited, buyers cunningly lure them through deception, manipulation (even coercion), and misinformed consent, and then cheat them when the game is over. The deception is so rampant that not only brokers, but also most recipients, do not pay the full amount they had promised to the sellers. These are stark examples of structural violence that directly impairs kidney sellers' physical and psychological integrity (see the discussion later in this chapter), as well as perpetuating physical violence against the poor – a serious violation of justice.

Structural violence facilitates organ harvesting, even though it is a gruesome exploitation of the poor. In this deal, the rich are beneficiaries, while the poor are mere suppliers of body parts. The sellers carry lifelong risks of having had an organ removed, while the rich recipients prolong their lives at the poor's expense. Yet, wealthy and middle-class Bangladeshi recipients take extreme and unethical steps to purchase an organ. For example, Umma Habiba Dipon, a 27-year-old middle-class Bengali fashion designer, arranged a charitable art exhibition and a musical concert in Dhaka in 2006. With the funds she raised, Dipon purchased a kidney from a poor Pakistani. Like Dipon, most other Bangladeshi recipients who can afford to do so unscrupulously extract kidneys from the bodies of the poor instead of obtaining kidneys from family members. I have also seen how a wealthy 72-year-old Bangladeshi recipient (a member of the Islamic fundamentalist party, which forbids the sale of organs) purchased a "fresh" kidney from a 22-year-old slum-dweller; however, this would-be recipient died just before the operation. Some other Bangladeshi recipients purchased a second kidney after the first transplant failed. These grim realities of structural violence beg fundamental questions. Why harvest organs from the underfed bodies of the poor? Should not the poor have an equal right to keep their organs intact inside their bodies?

Suffering of Sellers

Structural violence not only perpetuates a serious violation of justice, but also generates extreme suffering for impoverished kidney sellers. Empirical studies note that kidney sellers' health deteriorated, their economic condition worsened, and their social integrity was seriously impaired after they sold a kidney. While the medical community addresses the harm done to kidney sellers solely in relation to the physical impact of the procedure, the psychological, economic, and social suffering also make this trade highly problematic.

Selling a kidney has numerous negative impacts on health, particularly on sellers' physical abilities. The 33 Bangladeshi sellers whom I interviewed typically experienced pain, weakness, weight loss, and frequent illness after selling their kidneys. Similarly, in India, 50 percent of the 305 sellers reported persistent pain at the nephrectomy site; 33 percent complained of long-term back pain (Goyal *et al.* 2002: 1589–1591). In Pakistan, 32 of the studied kidney sellers also experienced tiredness, dizziness, and shortness of breath, while three of them had elevated blood pressure readings or had blood or protein in their urine as a result of having one kidney (Moazam, Zaman, and Jafary 2009: 33–34). In another study there, 239 sellers further reported fatigue, fever, urinary tract symptoms, dyspepsia, and loss of appetite (Naqvi *et al.* 2008: 1446). In Iran, 300 sellers reported a deterioration of between 22 percent and 58 percent in their general health after nephrectomy (Zargooshi 2001: 1790).

The medical community also notes the deterioration in the kidney donors' health. There are reported cases where kidney donors die (as do recipients) as a result of donation; the risk that the donor could die due to surgery has been put at 1 in 3,000 (0.03 percent; Bruzzone and Berloco 2007: 1785). One analysis found that since the inception of the United Network of Organ Sharing/Organ Procurement and Transplantation Network (UNOS/OPTN) database 0.04 percent of kidney donors have become transplant candidates themselves, some within four years of donation (Davis and Delmonico 2005: 2103). Medical personnel further claim that donors have a higher risk of developing chronic kidney disease in the long term (Naqvi *et al.* 2008: 1444). It is also evident that donors commonly experience an alarming incidence of hepatitis, a disturbingly high incidence of hypertension, presence of noticeable hemorrhage, and evidence of impaired kidney function, compared to the controls (Danovitch 2008: 1361). In addition, the risks of donor-transmitted viral diseases, such as HIV/AIDS, as well as infection and malignancy, are high (Chapman 2008: 1343). Importantly, the risk of death or disease as a result of having only one kidney could be much higher among sellers compared to donors. Even though no long-term study among kidney sellers exists to date, it can be anticipated that the health of sellers is seriously compromised due to living in hunger and malnutrition, while donors are sustained by medical facilities, caring families, and a sense of fulfillment. Consistently, published studies demonstrate that the bodily health impacts that result from selling a kidney are alarming, yet almost none of these sellers received the promised post-operative care – not even one appointment.

Selling a kidney also has a serious economic impact on sellers. A total of 78 percent of Bangladeshi sellers reported that their economic condition deteriorated in most cases after the surgery; many sellers lost their jobs and were still unemployed, while other were able to work fewer hours because they had only one kidney. As a result, some Bangladeshi sellers (15 percent) have already engaged in organ brokering. Similarly, Indian sellers also reported that their average family income declined by one third; the number of them living below the poverty line increased after trading (Goyal *et al.* 2002: 1589–1591). Another study reported that most Indian sellers sold their kidney to pay off their debt, but were back in debt again after the operation (Cohen 1999: 152). In Pakistan, 88 percent of vendors reported no economic improvement after the operation (Naqvi *et al.* 2007: 934; see also Moazam *et al.* 2009: 33). Moldavian and Filipino sellers also faced unemployment after they returned to their villages (Scheper-Hughes 2003: 220). Again, in Egypt, 81 percent of vendors spent the payment within five months of nephrectomy, mostly to pay off financial debts, rather than investing it in quality-of-life enhancements (Budiani-Saberi and Delmonico 2008: 927). Iranian sellers likewise reported that vending caused serious negative effects on employment for 65 percent of the studied vendors; their income declined by between 20 and 66 percent (Zargooshi 2001: 1790). All of these studies point out that sellers' economic conditions worsened or remained unchanged after they sold a kidney.

Furthermore, sellers experience devastating social suffering for selling their body parts. Bangladeshi sellers usually do not disclose their actions due to the high social stigma placed on selling organs; as a result, 79 percent of them become socially isolated. Similarly, Pakistani sellers expressed feelings of profound shame at having sold a kidney and added that people in the community made fun of them (Moazam *et al.* 2009: 35). Moldavian and Filipino sellers were also being labeled as "weak" and "disabled" by their employers and girlfriends; if they were single, nobody would agree to marry them, since people generally believe that someone who has only one kidney would not be able to support a family (Scheper-Hughes 2003: 220). Iranian sellers also reported that vending increased marital conflict for 73 percent of sellers, of whom 21 percent divorced following the surgery (Zargooshi 2001: 1790). Overall, such extreme suffering of kidney sellers is intensified by structural violence.

Against Embodied Self

Organ commodification is inherently reprehensible, as it proceeds against long-standing cultural, existential, and ethical practices. As Scheper-Hughes notes (2003: 204), the trade in body parts violates "modernist and humanist conceptions of bodily holism, integrity, and human dignity," as well as "cultural and religious beliefs in sacredness of the body." The following discussion demonstrates that living without a kidney is not just a physical alteration, but a disembodiment and infringement of the self.

We live within our body and self. The body and self are tied together in such a way that organs are not just exchangeable objects, but rather are living parts of a person (Fox and Swazey 1992: 207). Embodiment theories can prove helpful to understanding how organ commodification creates a crisis in the existential ground of body, self, and culture, making this practice highly problematic. Selling organs is considered a very undignified, humiliating, and stigmatized act in many societies (Scheper-Hughes 2003; Moazam *et al.* 2009; Cohen 1999). During my fieldwork in Bangladesh, I found out that seller Mofiz's sister died of a heart attack after finding out about his kidney selling, which is seen as a disgusting and disgraceful act there (Moniruzzaman 2010). Due to the major social stigma attached to selling body parts, most of my interviewed sellers hide their action from their family members and friends; those whose actions have already been revealed are living in social isolation, shame, and agony. These sellers reveal that most of them feel disembodied due to selling their body parts.

Following Islamic precepts, 32 of the Bangladeshi sellers I interviewed (all but one is Muslim) considered that selling body parts is reprehensible because it permanently and deliberately alters bodily integrity. Because Islam emphasizes the need to maintain the integrity of the body at burial, religious leaders object to the selling of any body parts, although they sanction organ donation as a gift of life (Abouna *et al.* 1990). Many sellers said that their action is an infringement of bodily integrity; they regret not being able to return their whole body to God in the afterlife. Some sellers also reflected that due to selling body parts, they are unable to follow the Islamic principle of *Tawhid*. *Tawhid* encompasses that Allah is one, and the only one, who created everyone from a single soul; thus, everyone has the same fundamental essence. All existences, which are essentially monistic, must answer to Allah, guided by the principle of *Tawhid*, which can be achieved in unity through the harmony of spirit and body (Scheper-Hughes and Lock 1987; Tober 2007). Since sellers capitalized the essence of God and violated their bodily integrity, they would not be able to achieve *Tawhid*, they believed. Few sellers were also puzzled about intra-religious organ exchange, believing that this jeopardized the harmony of their bodily integrity. For example, Hindu seller Hiru, who was circumcised to establish the commodified kinship with his Muslim recipient, believed that he destroyed the integrity and holism of both bodies – his own and his recipient's. These sellers shared "an imagined sense of original wholeness," which is unique to humans and exists in many cultures (see Papagaroufali 1996: 241).

In addition, organ commodification raises culturally varied issues concerning the body and property rights. In contrast to Western discourse on individual property rights over the body, Bangladeshi kidney sellers commonly considered God to be the owner of their body, and their body parts his gifts. They believe they only have stewardship of "God's gifts" and do not have authority to treat body parts as personal possessions (see similar discussion on other Islamic societies in Tober and

Budiani-Saberi 2007; Moazam 2006). As a result, Bangladeshi sellers regretted selling God's gift and considered their action as *haraam*, or forbidden by their faith.

Further, organ commodification is highly challenging because it violates human dignity (see WHO 1991: 1–8; Declaration of Istanbul 2008: 1–10). As Edward Keyserlingk notes (1990: 1005):

> Human organs have a special status due to their intimate relation with persons. Furthermore, in life the body as an organic whole is a good, since it is the center and means of awareness and vehicle of communication. It is this link between self and body that grounds bodily inviolability. These characteristics make the body and its parts properly the subject of altruism and gift giving rather than commercial sale. To respect these characteristics of persons is to respect human dignity. Organ sales, in contrast, treat the body as a collection of spare parts, independent of the body's intimate relationship to the life of a person. Organ sales thereby violate human dignity.

On a similar note, many Bangladeshi sellers I interviewed pointed out that selling a body part signifies a self without dignity. They argued that organ commodification is the most disgraceful act a human can commit – a completely inhumane and immoral act – excepting murder or suicide. After selling their kidneys, they lost their self-respect, intrinsic worth, and moral judgment; as seller Sodrul stated, "I always feel very small inside, as if I am living like an insect in a dark drain, as well as refrain from looking directly into people's eyes, and my head is always down" (Moniruzzaman 2010). Some sellers also mentioned that they lost their human identity for selling their kidney; they described themselves as "worse than animals" or "sub-humans."

Taken altogether, organ commodification is deeply problematic, as it proceeds against embodied practices of bodily integrity, body ownership, and human dignity that are existentially grounded in many cultures. As a result, Bangladeshi sellers suffered from disembodiment, as their body has become other to the self – not only through cultural practices that devalue it, but also through ontological impairment of being in the world (see Murphy 1987).

Sellers' narratives also reveal that they experience profound psychological and psychosocial suffering, particularly in relation to their selfhood, which constitutes a damaged self. Many sellers reflected that kidney commodification jeopardizes the homeostatic balance of their body and self. Post-vending, they sensed that their new body exists in binary opposition to their old body. For example, some sellers mentioned that they are living in a damaged, incomplete, and weaker body, as opposed to a normal, complete, and stronger body, as they had done before. These sellers felt as if lacking a part of their body split their entire body, which eventually turned them into a "half human" (see Moazam *et al.* 2009: 34), and by extension, their self had become disordered.

By losing a body part, sellers' ontological experience is also disconnected from reality. For example, seller Jobbar said, "When I sleep on the left, I cannot feel my kidney is on my right and vice versa. I could feel a kidney is here and it is not in there. I sensed its existence and non-existence" (Moniruzzaman 2010). Some sellers also felt that they have an entire body, but when they see the scar, they realize something is missing under their belly; they are momentarily back in the operating room. These sellers felt like those amputees who have the illusion that they still possess a missing arm or leg, as Merleau-Ponty illustrated in reference to the "phantom limb" (1962; Murphy 1987: 99).

Most sellers feel as if they are living in nothingness. Every year, they vividly remember their operation day – "the death day," as one of them called it. Every day, they live with the fear of dying sooner because they have only one kidney; seller Mofiz often recites a verse from the Koran – *Inna lillahi wa inna ilayhi raji'oon* (to God we belong and to him we will return) – a verse Muslims recite when they hear any news of death or see a corpse passing by (Moniruzzaman 2010).

All sellers felt that they had an integrated selfhood with their recipients. By sharing flesh and blood, seller and recipient become one body, one person, one being. As seller Manik stated, whenever he met with his recipient, he felt "oneness" with him, as if his body was within his recipient's body. No wonder some sellers feel strange when their recipient dies: they cannot comprehend how one of their body parts could have died when they themselves are still alive. How can they remain in the existential life once their kidney goes to the afterlife? They feel as if they are here, but some of their body parts are there, which is akin to "bodiless living." These ontological and embodied sufferings cultivate a damaged self (Moniruzzaman 2010).

All the Bangladeshi sellers I interviewed tended to withdraw from their family, friends, and society and live in social isolation. They suffered from grave sadness, disgrace, hopelessness, and crying spells. In their frustration, some of them became addicted to drugs. Meanwhile, seller Mofiz often sat down, speechless, in a dark place, and thought about committing suicide (Moniruzzaman 2010; see also Zargooshi 2001: 1796; Moazam *et al.* 2009: 33).

In summary, commodifying organs is exploitative, unethical, and harmful. The structural violence against the poor offers vital grounds to rebut this trade. In addition, the widespread suffering, harm, and risk associated with kidney selling are deeply disturbing, which gives substantial reasons to oppose this practice. The cultural practices against organ commodification also warn us that human body parts are not an alienable form of properties; rather, such a practice damages the embodied self.

Conclusion

In this chapter, I have documented how the human body becomes the site of a novel form of exploitation for the advancement of new medical technologies. While we have experienced diverse forms of body commodification throughout centuries (e.g., slavery, prostitution, and organ harvesting), the recent medical practice of organ extraction creates profound violence, harm, and suffering to the impoverished population. Yet, some liberal bioethicists propose a regulated organ market (i.e., the Iranian model), arguing that such a system would save the lives of dying patients and lessen the exploitation of organ sellers (Radcliffe Richards 1996; Cherry 2005; Taylor 2005; Matas 2008; Hippen 2005). In contrast, I argue that an organ market is not an Aladdin's lamp that would change all the existing economic inequality and political disparities; rather, such a market would escalate structural violence against the poor, causing them even greater suffering.

When Richard Titmuss (1970) compared the system of human blood donation in the United Kingdom, where all blood for transfusion is given by unpaid volunteer donors, to the system in the United States, where some blood is donated and some bought by commercial blood banks from the poor (who typically sell their blood to earn money), he argued against the US system of blood commercialization. Titmuss rejected the typical arguments about the efficiency of the market and concluded that the British blood collection system works better than the American one. As he observed, the American system leads to chronic shortages, wasted blood, higher costs, and a greater risk of contaminated blood. Following ethical reasoning, Titmuss also argued that a market in blood exploits the poor. He further lamented that turning blood into a market commodity erodes people's sense of obligation to donate blood, diminishes the spirit of altruism, and undermines the "gift-giving relationship" as an active feature of social life. Here Titmuss suggested that once people begin to view blood as a commodity, they are less likely to feel a moral responsibility to donate it; the decline in voluntary blood donation in America is attributed to the rise of commercial blood banks, as he argued (Titmuss 1970; Sandel 2012).

Surely, the human organ market does not speak to the lives of the economic underclass, but rather seriously discriminates against them. Such a market promotes bodily inequality and facilitates preying on and profiting from the poor. Since the poor are already subject to widespread structural violence, we need to ensure justice for them rather than harvesting organs from their malnourished bodies. At the very least, the poor deserve to keep their body parts, which are essential for their physical survival. In addition, the practice of organ commodification raises ethical, cultural, religious, and legal questions about the close relationship between the body and the self. Such a practice constitutes severe damage to self, infringement of body integrity, invasion of body ownership, and violation of human dignity. It has serious implications for the definition of what it means to be human, and more generally for life as it should be lived (Fox and Swazey 1992). It also threatens the integrity of species, of humanity itself, and of individual bodies (Sharp 2006). The market approach not only would be likely to destroy both cadaveric and altruistic organ donation, but also raises slippery-slope questions, such as: How far we can go? Can we cut off a leg or a hand from the poor, assuming that one of these body parts is adequate for them? The commodification of human body parts is profound exploitation and dehumanization of the poor that until now has been unseen in human history.

Note

1   The names of all interviewees have been changed to protect their identities.

References

Abouna, G.M., Kumar, M.S.A., Samhan, M. *et al.* 1990. "Commercialization of human organs: a Middle Eastern perspective." *Transplantation Proceedings*, 22: 918–921.

Bruzzone, P. and Berloco, P. 2007. "Ethical aspects of renal transplantation from living donors." *Transplantation Proceedings*, 39(6): 1785–1786.

Budiani-Saberi, D. and Delmonico, F.L. 2008. "Organ trafficking and transplant tourism: a commentary on the global realities." *American Journal of Transplantation*, 8(5): 925–929.

Chapman, J. 2008. "Should we pay donors to increase the supply of organs for transplantation? No." *British Medical Journal*, 336 (June 14): 1343.

Cherry, M. 2005. *Kidney for Sale by Owner: Human Organs, Transplantation, and the Market.* Washington, DC: Georgetown University Press.

Cohen, L. 1999. "Where it hurts: Indian material for an ethics of organ transplantation." *Daedalus*, 128(4): 135–164.

Danovitch, G. 2008. "Who cares? A lesson from Pakistan on the health of living donors." *American Journal of Transplantation*, 8: 1361–1362.

Davis, C.L. and Delmonico, F.L. 2005. "Living-donor kidney transplantation: a review of the current practices for the live donor." *Journal of the American Society of Nephrology*, 16: 2098–2110.

Declaration of Istanbul 2008. "Organ trafficking and transplant tourism." Convened by the Transplantation Society and International Society of Nephrology, Istanbul, Turkey, April 30–May 2.

Farmer, P. 2004. "An anthropology of structural violence." *Current Anthropology*, 45(3): 305–325.

Farmer, P. 2005. *Pathologies of Power: Health, Human Rights, and New War on the Poor*, 2nd edn. Berkeley: University of California Press.

Farmer, P., Nizeye, B., Stulac, S., and Keshavjee, S. 2006. "Structural violence and clinical medicine." *PLoS Medicine*, 3(10): 1686–1691.

Fox, R.C. and Swazey, J.P. 1992. *Spare Parts: Organ Replacement in Human Society.* Oxford: Oxford University Press.

Galtung, J. 1969. "Violence, peace, and peace research." *Journal of Peace Research*, 6(3): 167–191.

Garwood, P. 2007. "Dilemma over live-donor transplantation." *Bulletin of the World Health Organization*, 85(1): 5–6.

Goyal, M., Mehta, R., Schneiderman, L., and Sehgal, A. 2002. "Economic and health consequences of selling a kidney in India." *Journal of American Medical Association*, 288: 1589–1593.

Hartman, B. and Boyce, J.K. 1998. *A Quiet Violence: View from a Bangladesh Village*, 7th edn. London: Zed Books.

Hedges, S.J. and Gaines, W. 2000. "Donor bodies milled into growing profits." *Chicago Tribune*, May 21: A1, A16–17.

Hippen, B. 2005. "In defense of a regulated market in kidneys from living vendors." *Journal of Medicine and Philosophy*, 30: 593–626.

Hogshire, J. 1992. *Sell Yourself to Science: The Complete Guide to Selling Your Organs, Body Fluids, Bodily Functions and Being a Human Guinea Pig.* Port Townsend, WA: Loompanics Unlimited.

Keyserlingk, E. 1990. "Human dignity and donor altruism – are they compatible with efficiency in cadaveric human organ procurement?" *Transplantation Proceedings*, 22: 1005–1006.

Kimbrell, A. 1993. *The Human Body Shop: The Engineering and Marketing of Life.* San Francisco: HarperCollins.

Matas, A. 2008. "Should we pay donors to increase the supply of organs for transplantation? Yes." *British Medical Journal*, 336: 1342.

Merleau-Ponty, M. 1962. *Phenomenology of Perception.* London: Routledge & Kegan Paul.

Moazam, F. 2006. *Bioethics and Organ Transplantation in a Muslim Society: A Study in Culture, Ethnography, and Religion.* Bloomington: Indiana University Press.

Moazam, F., Zaman, R.M., and Jafarey, A.M. 2009. "Conversations with kidney vendors in Pakistan: an ethnographic study." *Hastings Center Report*, 39(3): 29–44.

Moniruzzaman, M. 2006. "Moving human and non-human body parts: a review of the history of organ and tissue transplant." *Eastern Anthropologists*, 59(2): 179–193.

Moniruzzaman, M. 2010. "'Living cadavers in Bangladesh: Ethics of the human organ bazaar." PhD dissertation, University of Toronto.

Murphy, R.F. 1987. *The Body Silent: The Different World of the Disabled.* London: Norton.

Naqvi, S.A.A., Ali, B., Mazhar, M. *et al.* 2007. "A socio-economic survey of kidney vendors in Pakistan." *Transplant International*, 20: 934–939.

Naqvi S.A.A, Rizvi, S.A., Zafar, M.N. *et al.* 2008. "Health status and renal function evaluation of kidney vendors: a report from Pakistan." *American Journal of Transplant*, 8(7) July: 1444–1450.

Papagaroufali, E. 1996. "Xenotransplantation and transgenesis: Immoral stories about human-animal relations in the West." In P. Descola and G. Palsson (eds) *Nature and Society: Anthropological Perspectives*, pp. 241–255. New York: Routledge.

Radcliffe Richards, J. 1996. "Nepharious goings on: Kidney sales and moral arguments." *Journal of Medicine and Philosophy*, 21(4): 375–416.

Roach, M. 2003. *Stiff: The Curious Lives of Human Cadavers.* New York: Norton.

Sandel, M. 2012. "What money can't buy: the moral limits of markets." New York: Farrar, Straus & Giroux.

Scheper-Hughes, N. 2000. "The global traffic in human organs." *Current Anthropology*, 41(2): 191–224.

Scheper-Hughes, N. 2003. "Rotten trade: Millennial capitalism, human values, and global justice in organs trafficking." *Journal of Human Rights*, 2(2): 197–226.

Scheper-Hughes, N. and Lock, M. 1987. "The mindful body: a prolegomenon to future work in medical anthropology." *Medical Anthropology Quarterly*, 1: 6–41.

Sen, A. 1982. *Poverty and Famines: An Essay on Entitlement and Deprivation.* Oxford: Oxford University Press.

Sen, A. 1998. *Commodities and Capabilities.* Oxford: Oxford University Press.

Sharp, L. 2000. "The commodification of the body and its parts." *Annual Review of Anthropology*, 29: 287 328.

Sharp, L. 2006. *Strange Harvest: Organ Transplants, Denatured Bodies, and the Transformed Self.* Berkeley: University of California Press.

Taylor, J.S. 2005. *Stakes and Kidneys: Why Market in Human Body Parts are Morally Imperative*. Aldershot: Ashgate.

Titmuss, R. 1970. *The Gift Relationship: From Human Blood to Social Policy*. London: Allen & Unwin.

Tober, D.M. 2007. "Kidneys and controversies in the Islamic Republic of Iran: the case of organ sale." *Body and Society*, 13: 151–171.

Tober, D. and Budiani, D. 2007. "Introduction: Why Islam, health, and the body?" *Body and Society*, 13: 1–14.

UN 2009. "2 million children wasting in Bangladesh." United Nations News Center, March 30.

UNESCAP 2002. "Population program and reproductive health including family planning program in Bangladesh." United Nations Economic and Social Commission for Asia and the Pacific, Bangladesh Country Report, at www.saarcgenderinfobase.org/includes/showFile.php?id=77, accessed March 8, 2013

WHO 1991. "Guiding principles on human cell, tissue, and organ transplantation: a report on developments under the auspices of WHO 1987–1991." Geneva: World Health Organization.

Zargooshi, J. 2001. "Quality of life of Iranian kidney 'donors'." *Journal of Urology*, 166: 1790–1799.

Chapter 28

Diaspora Activism and the Politics of Locality

The Armenians of France

Hakem Al-Rustom

Surp Mesrop School at Its Thirtieth Anniversary

In late May 2008, the Armenian community of Alfortville, a Parisian *banlieue* (suburb), was celebrating the thirtieth anniversary of the 1978 establishment of the Armenian school of Surp (Saint) Mesrop in the neighborhood. Alfortville has been receiving Armenian migrants since the 1920s, and in addition to the school, the city has an Armenian culture center, the Armenian church of Saints Peter and Paul (established in 1929 by the first wave of Armenian refugees from Anatolia), a Protestant Armenian church, and a plethora of social and political clubs. In the coffee houses so essential to the everyday life of the neighborhood, patrons speak Western and Eastern Armenian in addition to Turkish.

The anniversary festivities took place between Thursday May 29 and Sunday June 1, 2008, at L'Espace Culturel of Alfortville and consisted of a four-day exhibition of artwork by the pupils of the school. As is the case with all formal events in the Armenian community, the inauguration of the exhibition was attended by the local mayor, René Rouquet, and the hierarchs of the Armenian Apostolic Church in France (not to be confused with the Armenian Catholic church, which is in communion with Rome). On this occasion, a representative from the Armenian embassy was also present. The omnipresent Armenian members of the mayor's team, who work closely with him and were on his election list, facilitated the interactions between the mayor and the community.[1]

The opening speaker was Mr. Sarkisyan,[2] an Armenian member of the mayor's team who is from Istanbul, sits on the board of the Surp Mesrop School, and is active in the administration of the church. Speaking in French, he emphasized the

A Companion to Diaspora and Transnationalism, First Edition.
Edited by Ato Quayson and Girish Daswani.
© 2013 Blackwell Publishing Ltd. Published 2013 by Blackwell Publishing Ltd.

school's important role in maintaining the Armenian language in the diaspora, especially given that the school is named after Surp Mesrop, the saint who created the Armenian alphabet in 411 CE in order to translate the Syriac bible into Armenian. He then thanked the mayor and the people of Alfortville for the moral and financial support they provide to the school. Mayor Rouquet followed with a short talk which he opened with: "Today, the twenty-ninth of May, is an important and happy day. On this day, in 1998, the French Parliament acknowledged the Armenian Genocide of 1915." The comment about the genocide came as a surprise to me and to many in the audience, who fell silent for a few seconds before breaking into fervent applause. Later, I realized that Rouquet was behind the bill that publicly acknowledged the genocide in France in 1998. Rouquet then echoed Sarkisyan's comment about the importance of the school in preserving the Armenian language and went on to praise Armenians' contributions to all aspects of Alfortville's history and life.

In another community event two days later, on May 31, the director of the school said that language links people with their history. Language also creates a special identity for a group: "Only an Armenian could speak Armenian. When I speak Armenian in public, others immediately ask me "*Hay es?*' (Are you Armenian?)." She spoke of the importance of the Armenian language to the 700,000 Armenians in France, saying that Armenian is not a "foreign" language but an integral part of France.[3]

Indeed, the pictures of the school's activities that were exhibited that day portray the pupils of Surp Mesrop celebrating French Catholic customs such as Santa Claus parties before December 25; whereas the Armenian Christmas is celebrated on January 6, the same day as the Catholic celebration of the Epiphany, Mardi Gras (Ash Wednesday), and Mi-Carême (the "mid-Lent" on the third Thursday of the Catholic Lent), none of which are traditional Armenian religious and social customs. The school's mission is reflected in Sarkisyan's comment to me when I referred to the Armenian migrants from Turkey as Turkophone Armenians: "We have no Turkophone Armenians," he insisted, "we only have Armenians! In the school we teach the pupils how to be Armenian and French – Armenians who are fully integrated into French society." Our conversation was then interrupted by someone who asked him a question in Armenian, at which point the two carried on a 15-minute conversation in Turkish, using only a few Armenian words.

The celebrations of the thirtieth anniversary of the Surp Mesrop School ended with a concert at the Pôle Culturel, the main auditorium of Alfortville. The performance of folk, classical, and nationalist Armenian songs was billed as one of the major events of the season, and only a handful of seats remained empty. Sitting in the middle row were the mayor, the Armenian archbishop of France, and the notables of the community, well dressed in dark suits and ties. Before the concert started, the presenter welcomed the mayor and the archbishop and gave a 10-minute talk about the important historic links between Armenia and France, "We consider Armenia a province of France. Don't forget that the last Armenian king was exiled in Paris [in 1393]. As there are regional languages in France, like Provençal and Breton, Armenian too is a regional language."[4] The performance was by Ensemble

Naïri, directed by Haïk Davtian (who is from Armenia), and included 150 participants. It was a Pan-Armenian event; the participants and audience were Armenians
from France, Turkey, Lebanon, Syria, Greece, and Armenia. No matter what their
country or territory of origin, everyone raised their voices in the final songs of the
concert that expressed nationalist sentiments for Yerevan, the capital of the post-
Soviet Republic of Armenia.

Moments like the Surp Mesrop anniversary invite further enquiry because of the
importance of the local political context in forging diasporic identities and in
shaping patterns of assimilation in the host society (Schwalgin 2004). Between
remembering the genocide that took place in Anatolia and singing for Yerevan in a
French auditorium lies the diasporic activism and the politics of locality of the
Armenians in France. Diaspora formation involves both *roots* and *routes,* to use Paul
Gilroy's (1993) pun, embracing where people come from and where they settle.[5]
Forced and voluntary migration patterns often have sociohistoric roots, with
migrants and refugees choosing their destinations based on geographic proximity,
language, and cultural ties, colonial history, and other factors. The genocide that
took place in the early years of Turkish nationalism rendered Anatolian Armenian
survivors displaced individuals inside of Turkey and exiles outside of it. The establishment of the Republic of Turkey over Anatolia and the arrival of Armenians in
France as *apatride* (stateless) left Armenians in a liminal state in both the place of
origin (the homeland) and destination (the host country).

Pierre Bourdieu uses the Greek term *atopos,* "of no place" or "out of place," to
describe the state of the immigrant. This term, which Bourdieu originally used
to describe the Algerian migrant's experience in France, encapsulates the Armenian
predicament in both Turkey and France. Bourdieu (2004: xiv) describes the state of
the immigrant as "neither citizen nor foreigner, not truly on the side of the Same
not really on the side of the Other, he exists within that 'bastard' place, of which
Plato also speaks, on the frontier between being and social non-being. Displaced,
in the sense of being incongruous and inopportune, he is a source of embarrassment." This chapter locates the Armenian diaspora politics in France in the context
of three homogenizing national projects: Turkish nation-state building, French
republicanism, and Armenian diaspora institutions.

Migrating to France

Given the large numbers and long history of migration to France, immigrants have
been conspicuously absent from the historiography of France, and that "immigration [became] 'external' to past and present-day French society" (Noiriel 1996: 27,
30). Despite, or maybe because of, the fact that France has the longest tradition of
migration of any European country, migration has been regarded in France throughout history as problematic, not only by the French government, which saw the
presence of the migrant workers as temporary, but also by historians and sociologists writing in the country. Immigration was cast within a gloomy narrative of

misfortune and poverty that had forced the migrants to leave their homes. The literature on the North African migrants in France, for example, invokes themes such as uprootedness, solitude, and even madness (Noiriel 1996: 27). In addition, French politicians have frequently assigned negative labels to immigration: Michel Poniatowski equated it with "occupation," thereby marking the immigrant as an enemy, while President Valéry Giscard d'Estaing (president 1974–81) called it an "invasion," casting the immigrant as a barbarian (Kastoryano 2002: 17). Though much of the literature focuses on France's negative view of North African migrants, the stigma that went hand in hand with the image of the migrant was not attached solely to North African migrants; the French also stigmatized Armenians, seeing them as "threatened by assimilation" and engaged in a struggle to "preserve their originality" (Ternon 1983, quoted in Noiriel 1996: 28). As a result, the Armenian community was seen as a threat to French republican assimilation policies.

The French Revolution added an essential element to the French model of immigration, which is the defence of "human rights." For that reason, from the nineteenth century until World War II, France has welcomed the largest number of refugees of any European country.[6] Consequently, unlike many other migrant communities, Armenians arrived in France with two important legal conditions: they were refugees and *apatride* (stateless) persons. The latter designation was problematic because Armenians had no home country to which they could return, and thus they were destined to remain in France.[7] Their condition was complicated by the Turkish government's refusal to take responsibility for the refugees who had left the cities and villages of Anatolia during and after World War I (Mandel 2003: 32, 51, 224–225; Marashlian 1999).

Armenians' refugee status, however, has benefited them in France because refugees were regarded more favorably than migrants in pursuit of economic betterment and jobs – "as if political persecution was the only 'excuse' native Frenchmen could accept for immigration" of foreigners into France, Noiriel suggests (1996: 260). For example, despite the small number of Spanish migrants to France who were refugees, scholars have devoted much more attention to this small group than to the larger group that included economic migrants. Similarly, only those Italian migrants considered to be escaping fascism were well regarded, and Armenians were perceived solely in the reflective light of Missak Manouchian, who played an important role in the French anti-Nazi resistance – known as the Manouchian Affair (Noiriel 1996: 260).

French Diplomacy and the Making of the Armenian Refugees Problem

The expulsion of Armenians from their ancestral homeland in Ottoman Anatolia or Western Armenia (now Turkey) and their resettlement in France should be understood as the cumulative outcome of the Turkish nationalist policies and French imperial interests in the Arabic-speaking Ottoman provinces (a detailed treatment of the Armenian question in post-World War I diplomatic treaties, especially the Treaty of Lausanne of 1923, is presented in chapter 3 of Al-Rustom 2013). On the Turkish side, there were centrally planned systematic massacres and deportations during World War I that amounted to genocide as defined by the Convention on the Prevention and Punishment of the Crime of Genocide of 1948.[8] By the end of World War I, most surviving Armenians found refuge in the neighboring Arab Ottoman provinces of Syria, Aleppo, and Mosul, while France hosted 65,000 Armenian refugees, about 30 percent of the total (Mandel 2003: 21).[9]

In the aftermath of the Treaty of Sèvres, which divided Ottoman Anatolia among the European powers, France – whose army was occupying greater Syria and parts of southern Anatolia bordering Syria – signed the Treaty of Ankara on October 20, 1921, with the Turkish revolutionists represented by the Grand National Assembly of Turkey (TBMM) headed by Mustafa Kemal (later Atatürk).[10] In this treaty, France ceded the southern Anatolian cities of Antep, Maraş, and Urfa to the Turkish revolutionists, and in return the Turkish revolutionists acknowledged French rule over Ottoman Syria.[11] This treaty enabled France to secure its hold over Syria and insured that the Sykes–Picot agreement which envisioned the division of greater Syria (including Lebanon and Palestine), and Iraq with Britain would be no longer challenged by Turkish territorial claims. Meanwhile, it facilitated the expulsion of the majority of the Armenian population of southern Anatolia and the expropriation of their property by the Turkish revolutionists. In the months following this agreement, and immediately before the foundation of the Republic of Turkey on October 19, 1923, the TBMM issued laws that canonized the permanent exile of Armenians.[12]

It is in this context that Armenians arrived in France as *apatride* refugees and were required to travel with a document stating *But de son voyage: il ne peux pas retourner* (reason for travel: he cannot return) (Hovanessian 1995). This document had two possible legal implications. First, it did not allow Armenians to return to Anatolia, and deprived them of all legal right to the properties they had left behind – thus fitting in with the Turkish nationalist policies and the instated laws of the TBMM. Second, it created a legal framework for Armenians to stay in France since they "could not" go back to their native villages and cities. At the same time, France gave Armenians citizenship in the French mandate of Lebanon, which was carved out of the Ottoman Syrian provinces. Many Armenian refugees had escaped to the newly created French mandates from the territories ceded by France in the Ankara Treaty (Suny 1993: 219), and the treaty had made their return to Anatolia from Syria and Lebanon legally and pragmatically difficult. By giving the refugees legal frameworks to live in the countries of their exile, the French government absolved the Turkish state from responsibility to repatriate and/or compensate the Armenians who fled its territory during and after World War I.[13]

Armenians in France: From Refugees to Diaspora

Armenians in France therefore became the "orphans of the nation" (a description used by a French journalist at the time; see Mandel 2003: 21–22) since the Ottoman empire was replaced by the nation-state of Turkey, and Ottoman Armenians were not allowed to return to their Anatolian villages, then subject to demographic and spatial Turkification projects. Anatolian Armenians thus experienced a rupture in their "geocultural landscape" and were purged from their ancestral homeland in a process that I call *denativization*.[14] Meanwhile, Armenians, like other immigrants in France, were subjected to policies of assimilation by the French state. Even those French officials who were aware of the extermination policies that Armenians had survived did not have sympathy for or interest in Armenians' desire to preserve their Armenianness. On the contrary, French officials distrusted the refugees' lack of nationality, questioned their loyalty, and wanted to "remove any sign of ethnic distinctiveness as rapidly as possible" (Mandel 2003: 21–22). Coupled with anti-refugee sentiments in France during the economic crisis of the 1930s, this relegation of Armenians to *apatride* status shaped the way they integrated into French society.

Genocide and Diaspora

It is common to divide the Armenians into two groups: those living in the ancient homeland and those living in the widely spread diaspora. However, the diaspora is far from monolithic, not only because of the diversity of its populations but also because of the lands of origin and destination. Furthermore, Armenians tend to differentiate between two categories within the broader category of diaspora: the first is the *kaghutahayutiun*, the Armenian trade colonies that existed as early as the sixth century CE; the second is the *spiurk* (the diaspora), the recent dispersal in the aftermath of the genocide (Björklund 1993: 338).[15] The genocide therefore constitutes the "founding event" (Ter-Minassian 1994: 220) or "founding moment" (Panossian 2006: 242), of the diaspora – a "critical event" (cf. Das 1997) that marks Armenian history and a temporal divide between what was experienced before and after the event.

The meaning and understanding of the Armenian diaspora was thus transformed radically; being an Armenian in the diaspora meant being a survivor (Panossian 2006: 228, 236). It was no longer a diaspora of merchants, laborers, fortune-seekers, intellectuals, and political exiles; it is rather a nation in exile, a community of victims and descendants of refugees (Panossian 2006: 239). In the shadow of the genocide, Armenian culture can no longer be taken for granted. Armenians are expected to make sacrifices for the family, local community, and nation to prevent assimilation into the host culture, a phenomenon known as "white genocide." After the independence of Soviet Armenia, such sacrifice became oriented towards the Republic of Armenia on behalf of its national interests (Schwalgin 2004: 84; for a comparative study of the role the genocide plays in forming the Armenian experience in the United States, see Bakalian 2011: 347–60, in Cyprus, see Pattie 1997, and in Greece, see Schwalgin 2004: 84). The genocide and its denial became central to contemporary Armenian identity and political engagement in the diaspora. Consequently, Armenians became "a nation of victims" first by the violence of mass killings, then by the denial of the latter by the Turkish state (Panossian 2006: 236). For Armenians, the genocide was also a strong "equalizer" of Armenian identity within heterogeneous diaspora communities (Libaridian 1981). How, then, did this diverse diaspora integrate as a community in France, a country whose republican ideology opposes ethnic and religious communal identity?

Communitarianism and the French State

The French nation-state's aspiration for demographic homogeneity has been reflected in many of the government's policies, such as those regarding national language, national education, and military service (Weber 1976). The French republican ethic was to seek homogenization by removing all markers of distinctiveness from public visibility. For this reason, homogenization policies have been perceived as "cultural destruction" by immigrant and regionalist groups in France (Silverstein 2004: 234–235). In addition to education and language, *laïcité* (secularity) has been foundational in defining the French national community. Yet Etienne Balibar has argued that French *laïcité* does not mean the absence of the sacred from politics and public life, rather the "sacralisation of the state," in which the French civic state replaces Catholicism with its own rituals, such as civic festivals, and new categories of time and space (quoted in Silverstein 2004: 143). Balibar's argument sheds light on why the French assimilation model calls for homogenization and simplification and hence why "groups defined according to criteria of 'ethnic' or national origin have not been tolerated." However, this general statement about the French model has an important exception: when an ethnic group does not appear to have a communal ethnic identity, this lack of unity insures its assimilation through the lens of the French state and its national concerns (Noiriel 1996: 259–260), as is the case with the Armenians in France.

The issue of extra-national ethnic and/or religious identity that appears to be visible and communal has manifested itself in issues such as Muslim headscarves (see Bowen 2007: ch. 7; Silverstein 2004: 144) and the attitude of the French state with regard to acknowledging language diversity in the country. Taking the latter example, while France hesitantly signed the European Charter for Regional and Minority Languages in May 1999 (it was made available for signature in November 1992), the government accompanied its signature with a declaration to the Charter stating its understanding that the "aim of the Charter is not to recognize or protect minorities but to promote the European language heritage" and that the usage of the term "groups" (referring to speakers of a language) "does not grant collective rights to speakers" (Government of France 1999). Whether to allow a diversity of languages and cultures is a contested topic in France, and the issue has an important genealogy that sheds light on the republican model followed by the state. As far as the French state is concerned, the protection of languages is practiced for the sake of either "European heritage" or the "heritage of France" but not as a means of preserving communal identity or individual or collective *rights*. It is thus treated as an issue of history, culture, and heritage that stands apart from contemporary politics and is considered a means of future socialization of communities living within the French Republic.

Yet France's unwillingness to acknowledge any linguistic or religious community is limited to the level of official discourse. Practically, French state officials appeal to "communities" within the republic in their public discourses. Government officials use expressions such as "Algerian community," "Muslim community," or "Armenian community" and thank or consult "representatives of the relevant communities" (Kastoryano 2002: 34). The communal attributes used in the state's discourse and policies push heterogeneous communities towards developing a homogeneous communitarian identity. They come to be regarded as *a community* in France and become solidified under the French state, even as these communities negotiate a place – be it integration or assimilation – in French society.

"Stateless" Power

In the European Union member states, the regulatory power over populations that was traditionally a monopoly of nation-states is being diminished (Tölölyan 1996). As a result of this devolution of state power, larger space has been made available for diasporas, migrant communities, and native ethnolinguistic communities to exist and express themselves subnationally, in addition to making new claims on nation-states.

Diasporas are often regarded as posing challenges, if not a threat, to nation-states, because the very "construction of diasporas is fundamentally about the effort to assert and sustain very particular social boundaries across space and time, to 'make oneself at home in the world' through an avowal of membership in an ethnonational collectivity" (Amit 2002: 264).[16] Consequently, diasporas have become both subnational and transnational communities (Tölölyan 1996: 26). This dual state of affiliation allows diasporas to forge identities that challenge the standardized and often rigid national borders, filial belongings, and exclusive power of the state in areas such as capital, labor, ideas, information, cultural commodities, and belonging (Tölölyan 1996: 4).

While most post-Ottoman national movements developed their exclusive nation-states and propagated their national history and language through the schooling system and media, Armenians in the diaspora have pursued similar ends through non-state institutions, a phenomenon that Tölölyan calls "stateless power" (1991; 2001: 7).[17] This concept positions the hegemony exercised by diaspora institutions against the misconceptions that diaspora is antistate, open, cosmopolitan, transnational, and capable of offering flexible and multiple identities. Rather, diasporas are not boundless, and one cannot associate their perceived openness with cosmopolitanism (Amit 2002: 264). Diaspora scholarship therefore should not neglect the power exercised by diasporas nor their ability to propagate nationalism through their institutions (Tölölyan 2001: 7–8). As such, it is important to consider the similarities between nation-states and diaspora institutions in the case of Armenians in France. In the amassing of stateless power, the (re)production of culture and of contesting visions of collective identity is a quotidian, persistent, and costly activity, conducted not just by a few individual aesthetic producers but also by larger groups of journalists, intellectuals, teachers, scholars, activists, artists, performers, and entertainers, some of whom are associated with . . . organisations and institutions that offer material support and make ideological claims. (Tölölyan 2001: 4–5)

These institutions therefore constitute "a diasporic civil society that nurtures and sustains the public sphere of debate and cultural production" (p. 5).

Some diaspora institutions influence political events in the host nation and dominate major communal institutions. In a Foucauldian sense, they have both productive and prohibitive power. They exercise productive power by extending social services and producing meaning and identity through discursive means, as well as by administering pedagogy in Armenian language, national history, and folk music and dance (Tölölyan 2001: 27). Such reproductive measures carry within themselves prohibitions against a critical view of past events and alternative modes of being Armenian. This stigma against such expressions was mostly visible when imposed on the Armenian post-1970 migrants from Turkey because of the Turkified or Kurdified culture, lack of knowledge of the Armenian language, and the fact that they do not articulate their Armenianness through speaking and advocating for genocide recognition because of the political culture in which they were raised in post-genocide Turkey.

Essentially, then, the Armenians in France had to navigate the terrain between the French republican requirement of assimilation and the homogeneity (re-Armenianization), demanded by the Armenian diaspora institutions (Ter-Minassian 1994: 211). In this context, it is vital to recall Mr. Sarkisyan's comment about Surp Mesrop School's mission: "In the school we teach the pupils how to be French and Armenian; Armenians who are fully integrated in French society." In response to the first goal, Armenians practiced self-imposed assimilation into French culture, and to the second, they participated in the reproduction of Armenian culture. Armenians therefore swing between visibility and invisibility, between the two extremes of assimilation and re-Armenianization – the former in public, the latter in private.[18]

Unlike headscarves and Muslim piety in French public spaces, Armenian ethnic markers are not perceived by the French state as a salient threat to the French republican ethic, because the "success" of the Armenians as a migrant community in France must be attributed to neither their break from the Armenian cultural traditions nor their adoption of French values, language, and mannerisms. Rather, it is due to a "process of identity negotiation" which expressed itself through meeting all the French social and professional needs for a successful integration, while at the same time maintaining links with their group and culture of origin (Andesian and Hovanessian 1998: 69).

It was understood that Armenians should not show any sign of communal affiliation, especially in public. The French republican model does allow for asserting one's specific identity, but only in the private sphere, within the walls of houses and the gates of Armenian churches and community institutions (Mandel 2003: 96–103). However, the distinction between private and public is often blurred. Just as host countries reshape migrants, diaspora communities influence their new habitus. For example, Armenians have left many *marquage ethnique* (ethnic markers) in France, especially around communal spaces and memorials. Armenian churches (some built in a noticeably Armenian architectural style), schools and cultural centers carrying recognizably Armenian names and written in the Armenian script, monuments for genocide victims, signs over restaurants and grocery shops, Armenian toponyms on streets and gardens, in addition to epitaphs in Armenian script in communal cemeteries (Ter-Minassian 1994: 211) are all examples of the visibility of Armenian ethnic distinctiveness in the French public space.

French-Armenianness: Genocide and "Nativist" Discourse

Among the important displays of Armenian cultural history in France is the public commemoration of the genocide. Commemorative events take place every year on April 24 in Paris, and in other communes of France on the closest Sunday to that date. In Paris, the events take place at three symbolic locations: the Armenian Cathedral, seat of the Armenian Apostolic Bishop of France; the tomb of the Unknown Soldier at the Arc de Triomphe (where the French victims of the two world wars are commemorated); and then a demonstration from the Arc, passing in close proximity to the Turkish embassy, and ending at the statue of Soghomon Gevorki Soghomonyan (1869–1935), known as Komitas, an Armenian priest, musicologist, and composer, which is the official memorial site of the Armenian genocide in Paris (Figure 28.1). Demonstrators hold flags of France and the Republic of Armenia, and oppose the inclusion of Turkey in the European Union until the Turkish state recognizes the genocide.

Although the first public commemoration of the genocide was in 1919 (Panossian 2006: 237), and subsequent commemorative events took place, as in Marseilles in 1927 (Mandel 2003: 8, 213), the year 1965 was a turning point. The fiftieth anniversary of 1915 shifted Armenian communities – to use Tölölyan's terms – from post-genocide exilic nationalism to diasporic transnationalism, and thus the mobilization for the recognition of the genocide became a trait of the Armenian diasporic state, experience, identity, and *raison d'être*.[19]

The aftermath of the Nuremberg trials did not give Armenians the recognition they sought. However, in 1965, demands for official recognition of and recompense for the horror of the Armenian genocide exploded for several reasons. First, 1965 marked the fiftieth anniversary of the beginning of the massacres, reminding many Armenians of how long they had waited for recognition, trials, or reparations. In fact, the file of Ottoman Armenians had not been opened since the totally ignored Treaty of Sèvres of 1920. In addition, the increased Russification of Soviet Armenia and the assimilation of the Armenians in Western Europe and North America would soon culturally annihilate those who survived the genocide. It was therefore a time

Figure 28.1 The Komitas statue at the site of the genocide memorial in Paris, 8th arrondissement. The Mayor of Paris places flowers in front of the statue, while others place individual red flowers around it (Photo courtesy of the author)

of despair and of the opening of existential questions about the future of Armenians in Soviet Armenia and the diaspora. Second, the perpetrators of the genocide had not been brought to justice. The crime of the Young Turk government, the predecessor of the Turkish state, had passed without recognition, punishment, or compensation, at a time when Turkey was a member of NATO and an important ally for the Western bloc during the height of the Cold War (Björklund 1993: 346).

"Mort pour la France"

The two ritual events I discussed above – the celebration of Surp Mesrop's anniversary and the commemoration of the genocide – reveal the discourse adopted by some of the influential institutions that essentially *nativized* Armenians, and rendered the Armenian language a "regional" (rather than a migrant) language in France. The term *native* in English refers to aboriginal characteristics or the ability to trace ancestry to a particular place. Some institutions that represent Armenians in the political arena have used terms such as "regional" and "provincial" to anchor Armenians in France, claiming that they are part of the historic fabric of French society (unlike any other migrant or refugee group) and have been since well before World War I. Armenians thus historicize their presence in the host country to assert that they were part of France before the group of refugees arrived in the early 1920s, and thereby reduce the sense of this influx as a problem for the French state. The genocide anniversary activities in Paris suggest that the official commemoration of the genocide is not an ethnic marker of a group affiliation but an event with an important French national context. How did the Armenian diaspora in France bring about this official and public commemoration of the genocide, an event that after all took place outside of France and was only remotely related to French national history or concerns?

On April 23, 1965, the French daily *Le Monde* ran an article on its front page entitled "Un tragique cinquantenaire: le massacre des Arméniens en Turquie" (The fiftieth anniversary of a tragedy: the Armenian massacres in Turkey) written by Frédéric Feydit, a French historian and a member of the Armenian Academy of St Lazar in Venice, Italy. After Feydit presented a historic survey of Armenian history, the article concluded by stating that as citizens of France, Armenians are the most loyal, and their loyalty was demonstrated by the number of Armenians who died for France *(mort pour la France)* during the two World Wars, some of whom had not even been granted French citizenship at the time (Feydit 1965: 1, 6).

Many genocide memorials in France commemorate not only the Armenians massacred by factions in the Young Turk government at the time but also the Armenians who died while fighting in French armies. In keeping with Feydit's points in his *Le Monde* article, a closer look at the Komitas statue reveals that it fulfills this dual function. An inscription on the left side reads, "Homage to Komitas, composer, musicologist, and to 1,500,000 victims of the Armenian genocide of 1915 perpetrated by the Ottoman Empire"; on the right side are the words, "For the memory of the Armenian combatants engaged voluntarily and those who resisted. Died for France" *(mort pour la France)*.

This spirit was also reflected during the parliamentary debate about public recognition of the genocide on May 26, 1998. The mayor of Alfortville, René Rouquet, was the rapporteur for the parliamentary foreign affairs commission. As the first speaker during the session, he presented the historic and political arguments in favor of formal recognition of the genocide. Next, Jean-Pierre Masseret, the secretary of state for war veterans, endorsed Rouquet's position on recognition. Masseret emphasized France's role in welcoming the survivors of the 1915 *événements* (events) and their children. He referred to Armenians as *la communauté française d'origine arménienne* (the French community of Armenian origin), thereby downplaying Armenians' foreign origins and highlighting their sacrifices for the French state. The community, he said, "has given all its best to France, and it fought for freedom and human dignity, which are cardinal virtues of the Republic." He added that as the minister responsible for war veterans, he knew "the contribution that the [French] community of Armenian origin brought to this fight with the price of their own

Figure 28.2   Located at the entrance of the Armenian cathedral in Paris, the statue of an Armenian soldier dressed in French military uniform. The French inscription reads: "1914–1918 / For the Armenian volunteers of the French army / died for France" (Photo courtesy of the author)

blood," and he then mentioned additional instances in French history when Armenians fought for French causes (Assemblée Nationale 1998: 3–4).

A few months after the genocide commemoration events, I expressed my puzzlement to an Armenian companion about the inclusion of Armenian soldiers who died while fighting within the French armies (Figure 28.2). Krikor was the first Armenian I met in Paris; he is originally from Istanbul, had trained as an engineer, had been an activist in leftist politics in Turkey at the peak of the anticommunist strife in the 1970s, and immigrated to Paris in 1978. His remark was similar to comments I've heard from other Armenians: "Do you think that Armenians had a choice in that? Do you think it would have been possible for them to gain such acknowledgement from the French state and to construct such memorials without a mention that there are Armenians who fought and died for France? I don't think it would have been possible otherwise."[20] To adapt to French social and political culture, Armenians have conformed to the French republican ethic by assimilating into French society in such a way that their difference would not be seen as a threat.[21]

Western Armenian as a "Native" Language?

As Eugene Weber (1976) demonstrates, language homogeneity was, and still is, a cornerstone for the "unity of the republic" which is expressed in "republican civic nationalism" (Kastoryano 2002: 27). Article 2 of the constitution of the fifth French Republic states that the language of the republic is French. France shifted gears and started to recognize multiplicity in its society in the early 1980s when François Mitterrand (president 1981–1995) proclaimed, in a famous speech during his election campaign (delivered on March 14, 1981 in Lorient, Brittany), that French citizens have "le droit à la différence" (the right to be different). Since then, terms such as "multiracial," "multicultural," "plural," and "pluricultural" have been added to the official French political lexicon (Kastoryano 2002: 26). This shift positioned language diversity in political debates in France; however, it was meant to give rights to France's native linguistic communities, and *not* immigrants.

This spirit fueled the letter written by the mayor of Alfortville to allow the use of Armenian language in schools. A proposal submitted to the French state on February 2, 1983 by the previous mayor of Alfortville, Joseph Franceschi (serving 1965–1988), suggested using Armenian in state exams. The letter stated (quoted in Ananian 2008: 32–33) that

> The efforts made in favour of respecting regional identities, we should not forget that there are ethnicities whose identity should be equally respected. . . . This is the case of the important Armenian community in France. . . . The number of the survivors, of what no one fails to consider as the first genocide of the 20th century, have found refuge on our soil. The majority of them, as well as their descendants, have acquired French nationality. They participate actively in the life of our country and many among them . . . have in the dark hours of our history, united in the resistance against the Nazi oppressor.

As in the debate on the genocide bill in the National Assembly, the mayor's argument was based primarily on the Armenians' experience of genocide and their participation in French national causes. In this way, he was able to solidify his argument and make the case for the exceptional treatment of Armenians and the Western Armenian language in France.

Other measures have been taken in response to Mitterrand's policy shift. The government established Le Conseil national des langues et cultures régionales (the National Council for Regional Languages and Cultures) by a decree in 1985, and in 2001, the department responsible for the French language, known as La Délégation générale à la langue française, was expanded to include, in addition to French, the category "languages of France." This change was reflected in its official name, which became La Délégation générale à la langue française et aux langues de France (DGLFLF). The DGLFLF divides the languages of France into two categories, the first being *langues régionales*, which are either dialects or languages that are native to particular regions of France; the second being *langues non-territoriales*, which include languages that are non-native (i.e., migrant) to France under which Western Armenian is acknowledged.[22] As it now stands, the French parliament has revised the constitution to officially recognize "regional languages" but *not* non-territorial (i.e., immigrant) languages by adding article 75-1, which states: "Les langues régionales appartiennent au patrimoine de la France" (regional languages are part of the heritage of France), in the *Loi constitutionnelle de modernisation des institutions de la Vème République*, ratified on July 23, 2008.

Within this context one can understand the claim of the director of the Surp Mesrop School and the host of the concert at the Pôle Culturel auditorium when he said that the Armenian language is "native" to France. Being refugees with no hope of return posed a challenge to Armenians: on the one hand, the host societies insisted on their assimilation or integration, and on the other, Armenian community leaders called for commitment to an Armenian identity and cause (Panossian 2006: 296). Forced assimilation has left Armenians with perpetual anxiety that after this great rupture in history, their identity, language, and culture might be lost through dispersion and assimilation (Panossian 2006: 236–238), migration (Pattie 1997: ch. 7), or marrying *odars* (non-Armenians) (Pattie 1997: 169–170; Bakalian 2011: 393), an outcome that some Armenians describe as "white genocide" or "ethnocide" (Ter-Minassian 1988: 232; Schwalgin 2004: 72; Björklund 1993: 342).

Some commentators have argued that in France, "assimilation leads to the 'disappearance of foreignness'" (Jacqueline Costa-Lascoux, quoted in Kastoryano 2002: 30). The reluctance of the French state to acknowledge the right to express one's difference (Tölölyan 1996: 26) has pushed Armenians to look for an alternative to the stark choice between assimilation and expression of their ethnic difference. The statues of Komitas and the Armenian soldier in French military uniform both represent paths to integration in French society and reflect the special recognition the French state has granted to Armenians to express their cultural specificities. Armenians have expressed their difference adaptively, becoming part-and-parcel of France by making themselves resemble native subnational groups within the country. The Armenian soldier communicates the message that Armenians, like other good French citizens, fought and died for French causes; Komitas highlights the fact that as genocide survivors, Armenians have lost their homeland and have nowhere to return to. The two statues therefore emphasize Armenians' distinctiveness from other migrant groups, especially those whom the French state perceives to be "unassimilable," such as Arabic-speaking Muslims.[23]

Conclusion

This chapter has argued that the successful integration of the Armenian diaspora in France is due to two factors: the first being their integration into French life in public while maintaining one or more aspects of Armenian cultural specificity in private. Hence, Armenians did not pose a threat to the French state because they did not seek to express Armenian affiliation in public or turn their ethnic affiliation into a communitarian one. The second is their success in appealing to the French political elites through their participation in French national causes, particularly the French resistance to Nazi occupation. The fact that their integration was achieved within the French secular model, which retains the distinction between the private and public, meant that the acknowledgment and public commemoration of the genocide was not viewed as threatening to the French Republic.

The French state still does not officially regard Western Armenian as a regional language, but starting with Mitterrand's presidency, the government has taken special measures to promote Armenian language and culture because of the specificity of the Armenian genocide and the loss of Anatolia as a homeland. In fact, Mitterrand was the first French president to speak publicly about the genocide, mentioning it in a speech in Vienne, Isère, in January 1984, where he said, "It is not possible to erase the traces of genocide that hit you. These must be inscribed in human memory" (Assemblée Nationale 1998: 3). Since then, Armenian diaspora institutions have furthered their "stateless power" to pressure the French state to take action in two main arenas: to designate formally the Young Turks' mass annihilation policies as "genocide," and to institute measures to promote Armenian language and culture in France.[24]

The public events I discuss above reveal the dynamics of negotiating between the French state and the Armenian diaspora institutions: the Armenian diaspora shows loyalty to France and to the French state, while the state acknowledges the existence of the Armenians as French citizens who have a special need to protect their language and culture, particularly because they have survived genocide, which the state commemorates publicly. For this reason, the way in which Armenians, or any other migrant group, appeal to the politics of French society tells us about France itself and sheds light on how migrants experience and adapt to its specific political culture.

Acknowledgments

This chapter is dedicated to the memory of Peter Loizos (1937–2012), teacher and friend. An early version of it was presented at the Workshop on Diaspora and Activism in Europe at the London School of Economics in September 2008, and has benefited from the comments of the participants, especially Armine Ishkanian and Daphne Winland. My gratitude goes to Riva Kastoryano for hosting me as a visiting scholar at the Centre d'études et de recherches internationales of Sciences Po, in Paris, where this chapter was completed in the summer of 2011, and to the Global Public Policy Network/Partnership Mobility Bursary that made this visit possible. I thank Martha Mundy for her generous feedback and support. Claire Mouradian and Kéram Kevonian guided me in understanding the French context. Raymond Kevorkian shared with me his encyclopedic knowledge and the resources of the Bibliothèque Nubar in Paris. I am especially indebted to Sinem Adar, Veronique Benei, Melissa Bilal, Aram Kerovpyan, Maud Mandel, Susan Pattie, Ara Sarafian, Sossie Kasbarian, Khachig Tölölyan, and Altuğ Yılmaz for their generosity of time

2 The name "Black Carib" is used here to refer to events and documents taken from the colonial period; "Garifuna" is used when referring to recent and contemporary discourses and practices.
3 Eleggua, Ogun, Chango, Oya, Obatala, Ochun, and Yemaya.

References

Anderson, A. 1992. "Alexander Anderson and the Carib War in St. Vincent (ca. 1798)." In P. Hulme and N.L. Whitehead (eds) *Wild Majesty: Encounters with Caribs from Columbus to the Present Day*, pp. 217–230. Oxford: Clarendon Press.

Appiah, K.A. 1992. *In My Father's House: Africa in the Philosophy of Culture*. New York: Oxford University Press.

Apter, A. 1992. *Black Critics and Kings: The Hermeneutics of Power in Yoruba Society*. Chicago: University of Chicago Press.

Barnes, S.T. 1997. *Africa's Ogun: Old World and New*, 2nd edn. Bloomington: Indiana University Press.

Benitez-Rojo, A. 1996. *The Repeating Island*. Durham, NC: Duke University Press.

Brandon, G. 1993. *Santería from Africa to the New World: The Dead Sell Memories*. Bloomington: Indiana University Press.

Brown, D.H. 1999. "Altared spaces: Afro-Cuban religions and the urban landscape in Cuba and the United States." In R.A. Orsi (ed.) *Gods of the City*, pp. 155–231. Bloomington: Indiana University Press.

Brown, D.H. 2003. *Santería Enthroned: Art, Ritual, and Innovation in an Afro-Cuban Religion*. Chicago: University of Chicago Press.

Brown, K.M. 1991. *Mama Lola: A Vodou Priestess in Brooklyn*. Berkeley: University of California Press.

Brown, K.M. 1999. "Staying grounded in a high-rise building: Ecological dissonance and ritual accommodation in Haitian Vodou." In R.A. Orsi (ed.) *Gods of the City*, pp. 79–103. Bloomington: Indiana University Press.

Brown, K.M. 2003. "Making Wanga: Reality constructions and the magical manipulation of power." In H.G. West and T. Sanders (eds) *Transparency and Conspiracy: Ethnographies of Suspicion in the New World Order*, pp. 233–257. Durham, NC: Duke University Press.

Brown, P.R.L. 1981. *The Cult of Saints: Its Rise and Function in Latin Christianity*. Chicago: University of Chicago Press.

Butler, K.D. 2001. "Defining diaspora, refining a discourse." *Diaspora*, 10(2):189–219.

Campo, O. 1995. "Brevia: the Supreme Court and the practice of Santería." In A.M. Stevens-Arroyo and A.I. Perez y Mena (eds) *Enigmatic Powers: Syncretism with African and Indigenous Peoples: Religions Among Latinos*, New York: Bildner Center for Western Hemisphere Studies.

Chevannes, B. 1994. *Rastafari: Roots and Ideology*. Syracuse, NY: Syracuse University Press.

Chevannes, B. 2001. "Jamaican diasporic identity: the metaphor of Yaad." In P. Taylor (ed.) *Nation Dance: Religion, Identity and Cultural Difference in the Caribbean*, pp. 129–138. Bloomington: Indiana University Press.

Clifford, J. 1994. "Diasporas." *Cultural Anthropology*, 9: 302–338.

Cohen, R. 1997. *Global Diasporas*. Seattle: University of Washington Press.

Dufoix, S. 2008. *Diasporas*, trans. W. Rodarmor. Berkeley: University of California Press.

Edwards, B.H. 2003. *The Practice of Diaspora: Literature, Translation, and the Rise of Black Internationalism*. Cambridge, MA: Harvard University Press.

England, S. 1999. "Negotiating race and place in the Garifuna diaspora: Identity formation and transnational grassroots politics in New York City and Honduras." *Identities*, 6(1): 5–53.

Gilroy, P. 1993. *The Black Atlantic: Modernity and Double Consciousness*. Cambridge, MA: Harvard University Press.

Gilroy, P. 2000. *Against Race: Imagining Political Culture Beyond the Color Line*. Cambridge, MA: Harvard University Press.

Gonçalves da Silva, V. 1995. *Orixás da Metrópole*. Petrópolis: Editora Vozes.

Gordon, E.T. and Anderson, M. 1999. "The African diaspora: Toward an ethnography of diasporic identification." *Journal of American Folklore*, 112(445): 282–296.

Hall, S. 1996. "New ethnicities." In *Stuart Hall: Critical Dialogues in Cultural Studies*, ed. D. Morley and K.-H. Chen, pp. 441–450. London: Routledge.

Hepner, R.L. 1998. "Chanting down Babylon in the belly of the Beast: the Rastafarian movement in the metropolitan United States." In N.S. Murrell, W.D. Spencer, and A.A. McFarlane (eds) *Chanting Down Babylon*, pp. 199–216. Philadelphia: Temple University Press.

Herskovits, M.J. 1990. *The Myth of the Negro Past*. Boston, MA: Beacon Press. (Originally published 1941.)

Johnson, P.C. 2005. "Three paths to legal legitimacy: African diaspora religions and the state." *Culture and Religion: An Interdisciplinary Journal* 6(1): 79–105.

Johnson, P.C. 2007. *Diaspora Conversions: Black Carib Religion and the Recovery of Africa*. Berkeley: University of California Press.

Klimt, A. and Lubkemann, S. 2002. "Argument across the Portuguese-speaking world: a discursive approach to diaspora." *Diaspora*, 11(2): 145–162.

Levitt, P. 2001. *The Transnational Villagers*. Berkeley: University of California Press.

Martin, S. 2011. "Mario Balotelli points the way to a new Italian society," *Guardian*, November 22, at http://www.guardian.co.uk/commentisfree/2011/nov/22/mario-balotelli-points-way-italian-society, accessed March 1, 2013.

Matory, J.L. 2005. *Black Atlantic Religion: Tradition, Transnationalism, and Matriarchy in the Afro-Brazilian Candomblé*. Princeton: Princeton University Press.

Mattoso, K.M. de Queirós. 1989. *To Be a Slave in Brazil, 1550–1888*, 2nd edn, trans. A. Goldhammer. New Brunswick: Rutgers University Press.

McAlister, E. 1998. "The madonna of 115th Street revisited: Vodou and Haitian Catholicism in the age of transnationalism." In R.S. Warner and J.G. Wittner (eds) *Gatherings in Diaspora: Religious Communities and the New Immigration*, pp. 123–160. Philadelphia: Temple University Press.

Mintz, S. and Price, R. 1992. *The Birth of African-American Culture: An Anthropological Perspective*. Boston, MA: Beacon Press. (Originally published 1976.)

Murphy, J.M. 1988. *Santería: An African Religion in America*. Boston, MA: Beacon Press.

Olmos, M.F. and Paravisini-Gebert, L. 2003. *Creole Religions of the Caribbean: An Introduction from Vodou and Santería to Obeah and Espiritismo*. New York: New York University Press.

Ortner, S. 1984. "Theory in anthropology since the sixties." *Comparative Studies in Society and History*, 26: 126–166.

Palmié, S. 1996. "Which centre, whose margin? Notes towards an archaeology of US Supreme Court Case 91-948, 1993 (Church of the Lukumí vs. City of Hialeah, South Florida)." In O. Harris (ed.) *Inside and Outside the Law: Anthropological Studies of Authority and Ambiguity*, pp.184–209. New York: Routledge.

Palmié, S. 2002. *Wizards and Scientists: Explorations in Afro-Cuban Modernity and Tradition*. Durham, NC: Duke University Press.

Pierucci, A.F. and Prandi, R. 2000. "Religious diversity in Brazil: Numbers and perspectives in a sociological evaluation." *International Sociology* 15(4): 629–641.

Prandi, R. 1991. *Os Candomblés de São Paulo*. São Paulo: Hucitec/EDUSP.

Richman, K. 2005. *Migration and Vodou*. Gainsville: University Press of Florida.

Sansone, L. 2003. *Blackness Without Ethnicity: Constructing Race in Brazil*. New York: Palgrave Macmillan.

Sewell, W.H. Jr 1999. "The concept(s) of culture." In V.E. Bonnell and L. Hunt (eds) *Beyond the Cultural Turn: New Directions in the Study of Society and Culture*, pp. 35–61. Berkeley: University of California Press.

Sheffer, G. 2003. *Diaspora Politics: At Home Abroad*. Cambridge: Cambridge University Press.

Shepperson, G. 1966. "The African abroad or the African diaspora." *African Forum: A Quarterly journal of Contemporary Affairs*, 2: 76–93; reprinted in T.O. Ranger (ed.) *Emerging Themes of African History*, pp. 152–176. London: Heinemann, 1968.

Smith, J.Z. 1987. *To Take Place: Toward Theory in Ritual*. Chicago: University of Chicago Press.

Thornton, J. 1998. *Africa and Africans in the Making of the Atlantic World, 1400–1800*, 2nd edn. Cambridge: Cambridge University Press.

Tölölyan, K. 1996. "Rethinking diaspora(s): Stateless power in the transnational moment." *Diaspora*, 5(2): 3–36.

Tuan, Y.F. 1977. *Space and Place: The Perspectives of Experience*. Minneapolis: University of Minnesota Press.

Tweed, T.A. 1997. *Our Lady of the Exile: Diaspora Religion at a Cuban Catholic Shrine in Miami*. New York: Oxford University Press.

Vásquez, M.A. and Marquardt, M.F. 2003. *Globalizing the Sacred: Religion Across the Americas*. New Brunswick: Rutgers University Press.

Vertovec, S. 2000. *The Hindu Diaspora: Comparative Patterns*. London: Routledge.

Waters, M.C. 1999. *Black Identities: West Indian Immigrant Dreams and American Realities*. New York: Russell Sage Foundation/Cambridge, MA: Harvard University Press.

Weber, M. 1978. *Economy and Society*, ed. G. Roth and C. Wittich. Berkeley: University of California Press.

Werbner, P. 2000. "Introduction: the materiality of diaspora – between aesthetic and 'real' politics." *Diaspora*, 9(1): 5–20.

West, C. 2001. *Race Matters*, 2nd edn. New York: Vintage Books. (Originally published 1993.)

Zane, W.W. 1999. *Journeys to the Spiritual Lands: The Natural History of a West Indian Religion*. New York: Oxford University Press.

Chapter 31

Diaspora Tourism
The Heritage of Slavery in Ghana
Ann Reed

Introduction

Since the early 1990s, the Ghana government and various tourism stakeholders have developed heritage tourism that recounts the history of the transatlantic slave trade. The establishment of Ghana's slavery heritage memoryscape can be traced to efforts to refurbish Cape Coast Castle and Elmina Castle into attractive tourist destinations and promoting Pan-African-oriented festivals – PANAFEST (Pan-African Historical Theatre Festival) and Emancipation Day – as routinized events in the tourism calendar. Ghana has officially promoted itself as "the Gateway to Africa," particularly for diaspora Africans (primarily African Americans and Jamaicans, and defined in this context as people of African descent whose ancestors were forced to migrate as a result of the transatlantic slave trade) since 1998 when Emancipation Day – a Caribbean holiday marking the abolition of slavery in the British colonies – was first commemorated in Ghana.

The *National Tourism Development Plan for Ghana* identified African Americans as an important niche market for roots tourism (GMOT, UNDP, and WTO 1996: 137), as they were thought to view Ghana as a primary ancestral homeland owing to the high number of forts associated with the transatlantic slave trade found along its coastline. Approximately 10,000 African Americans visit Ghana annually (Mensah 2004; Zachary 2001: 1), and diaspora Africans reportedly comprise 60 percent of Ghana's tourist trade (Benson and McCaskie 2004: 111n3). Tourism policymakers believed the Ghanaian economy would stand to gain the most by focusing on African Americans – the diaspora group thought to have the most disposable income. However, as I describe below, some resent being labeled by the Ghana state as tourists and would rather be recognized as returnees. Although there are other important diaspora groups in Europe, the Caribbean, and South America who participate in tourism to Ghana I will limit my discussion to African Americans in this chapter.

In considering the critical intersection where diaspora and globalization meet, this chapter discusses the nexus of Ghana government agendas, diaspora traveler desires, and contexts that shape cultural flows relevant to pilgrimage tourism. As people, ideas, media, goods, and capital circulate globally, new relationships between people and places are continually made and remade. Are there differences in the meaning of travel for a one-off tourist, an annual pilgrim, and a one-time tourist who decides to settle permanently? What constitutes a successful return to a home-land center? What factors challenge a successful return? How do historical circum-stances and the traveling of cultures affect meanings of travel? Based on participant observation of pilgrimage tourist destinations and Pan-African festivals and forums, as well as interviews with African Americans and Ghanaians carried out for approxi-mately 21 months between 1999 and 2011, I address these questions by reflecting upon the play of local, national, and transnational influences in shaping the interac-tions between diaspora Africans and Ghanaians as well as the shifting meanings of place and roots.

The Diaspora African Call to Ghana

Ghana has long been a compelling destination for Anglophone diaspora Africans because of its relative peace, the fact that English is spoken widely, and the histories of both the slave trade and Pan-Africanism. Between the late 1950s and 1966, Kwame Nkrumah attracted political activists interested in transnational anticolonial and civil rights struggles. Such renowned individuals as George Padmore and C.L.R. James (both Trinidadian but based in London), Norman Manley (future prime minister of Jamaica), Louis Armstrong, Maya Angelou, Martin Luther King Jr, and Malcolm X either visited or resided in Ghana during this period (Gaines 2006: 5–6). After Ghana became the first sub-Saharan African country to gain independence in 1957, President Nkrumah encouraged the professional class of diaspora Africans – pri-marily from the United States and the Caribbean – to bring their skills to aid in the development of Ghana and Africa more broadly. Doctors, lawyers, dentists, teachers, writers, artists, technicians, and architects, among others, responded to his call, and some African Americans found living in Ghana to be a welcome respite to living in the United States under Jim Crow and institutionalized racism.

I hesitate to describe African Americans – or even more problematic, diaspora Africans – as a single cultural group. As Abu-Lughod (1991) has argued, not only can generalizing about cultural groups lead to reductionist misrepresentations, it can promote the idea that cultural groups are marked by overdetermined assump-tions of discrete difference and not by commonality. It is more useful to think about how cultural groups are constructed with fluid and flexible boundaries and how these constructions have real-world consequences. This obviously is also an extremely relevant insight for diaspora groups. In contrast to constructions of a common (singular) heritage, diaspora groups can and do change cultures. This can create difficulties when real cultural differences reveal that the expectations of cultural homogeneity between homeland and diaspora are unfulfilled. Such expectations are often deployed, by both homeland and diaspora groups, although for different reasons and within various contexts. Other misunderstandings can arise when the differing heritage narratives of homeland and diaspora groups compete with one another in public culture.

Roughly one thousand African Americans live and work in Ghana today (Zachary 2001: 1). During my 2001–2002 fieldwork, it was suggested to me that there were two distinct groups comprising the African Americans living in Ghana: one was there primarily for lucrative employment opportunities (e.g., people employed at the US embassy or in the mining industry). These expatriates would presumably return to the United States after their employment ended, feeling no particular reason to remain resident in Ghana. The second type of African American group was more politically activist and Left-leaning (e.g., more likely to champion the diaspora African-driven causes of reparations and repatriation). According to my interviews with African Americans resident in Ghana, they share commonalities about why they are drawn to live in Ghana. Most have had a lifelong interest in Africa, a perception that Africa is home, and a longing to fulfill the dream of coming home. In many cases, their first encounter with traveling to Africa was as part of an educational tour group. Several of the African Americans I interviewed reported bringing their own tour groups of students, teachers, co-workers, religious congregants, family members, or friends to Ghana and other African countries. Malkia Brentu used to bring groups from Detroit, Cleveland, New York, and Philadelphia twice a year to Ghana or West Africa. She told me she never made a penny from it. Her organized tours would always have a set theme, such as African drumming and dancing or cultural retentions between black families in West Africa and those in the United States. After their initial more educational and touristic visits to the continent, many of those I interviewed decided to settle in Ghana, where they have established businesses and development projects. This raises a few pertinent questions. First, where does the notion that Africa is home come from? Second, in what ways are the initial tours structured? I elaborate upon these ideas in the next section.

Africa as Home and the Structure of a Homeland Tour

While, on the one hand, all members of the *homo sapiens* species can think of Africa as home if we accept the notion that human origins can be traced from the Rift Valley, diaspora Africans probably have something else in mind when they think of Africa as home. Heritage is more to the point here, if we think of our tendency to mark distinct ethnic identity through dress, hair styles, music, foodways, linguistic

patterns, religious beliefs, or political persuasions. For example, we can think of
Peter Tosh's (1977) lyrics:

> Don't care where you come from.
> As long as you're a black man, you're an African.
> No mind your nationality.
> You have got the identity of an African.

These frame a sense of ethnic identity no matter where one travels in the world.
Likewise, we tend to meditate upon particular cultural memories and historical
frames that we believe make us who we are. Ray (2001: 9) argues that Americans of
the late twentieth century have been particularly interested in this project of reclaiming one's unique ethnic identity as an inheritance that counters an American
ambivalence over striking a balance between finding community and expressing
individualism. Continuing into the early twenty-first century, we have witnessed
enduring interest in origin stories, genealogy, and folk memories if we consider the
popularity of web sites like www.ancestry.com or television programs such as PBS's
Faces of America and NBC's *Who Do You Think You Are?* We listen intently about
the family origins of a particular celebrity, to learn about achievements and scan-
dals, and if the person has old enough connections to the United States, we might
hear about ties to slavery – whether one had an ancestor who was enslaved, owned
slaves, or agitated against slavery. It is also interesting that there is a biological
memory (one of my key informants referred to this as "genetic recall") emphasis to
all of this; ancestry is supposed to define contemporary cultural values, although
that is in disregard to the realities of culture change discussed above.

Part of what structures a homeland tour to Ghana is what diaspora visitors hear
by word of mouth about the experience, what they see on YouTube, Facebook, or
other web sites that depict pilgrimage tours to Ghana as well as imagining what
one's African ancestors might have endured in the enslavement process. Diaspora
memories of the transatlantic slave trade are shaped by numerous sources that
comprise a pastiche of fictional and non-fictional accounts, for example: Stephen
Spielberg's film, *Amistad*; Alex Hailey's book and television series, *Roots*; slave narratives by Frederick Douglass and Olaudah Equiano; *Atlantic Slave Trade* by Philip
Curtin; *How Europe Underdeveloped Africa* by Walter Rodney; and Wikipedia. Of
course, there is no set canon of sources that may inform one's experiences, and
encountering these images and ideas happens over one's lifetime and is not always
consciously recorded, but the fact that it is expected that *slavery* is the dominant
experience in thinking about Africa means that this is a common lens through
which connections are perceived. This is true not only in popular culture, but also
in academic discourse – Gilroy uses the image of the slave ship as the common
denominator in theorizing the hybridity of diaspora groups he calls the black Atlantic (1993: 12–17). Ships signify not only the idea of diaspora Africans forced into
exile as commodities, but also represent the possibilities of emancipation demonstrated in Back to Africa movements, and I might add that ships (or airplanes)

delivering returnees on contemporary homeland tours are also intended to bring about redemption. Tying in the imagery of the ship with history and popular culture of diaspora Africans, Gilroy notes three common themes in the history of Black Atlantic political thought (1993: 208):

> the notion of a return to a point of origin. . . . the condition of exile or forced separation from the homeland . . . in these circumstances, the memory of slavery becomes an open secret and dominates the post-slave experiences that are interpreted as its covert continuation. . . . the idea that the suffering of both blacks and Jews has a special redemptive power, not for themselves alone but for humanity as a whole.

These ideas resonate, individually or together, with the reasons why many diaspora African travel to Ghana.

Sankɔfa

Michael Herzfeld writes (1997: 27) that iconicity is the principle of signification derived from resemblance, which "seems natural and is therefore an effective way of creating self-evidence." *Sankɔfa* serves as an icon for diaspora Africans interested in connecting to Africa as a motherland; this relates to Gilroy's first diaspora theme above as return to point of origin. It is one of many Akan adinkra symbols, pictorial images traditionally made from carved calabashes dipped in dye and used as stamps on funeral cloth. *Sankɔfa* is glossed contemporarily as "going back to the source to retrieve what was lost," or "going back to your roots," and illustrates iconicity as its meaning has been reified through the mass production of *sankɔfa* T-shirts and wood carvings, as well as the title of the popular film (*Sankofa*) that serves as a cautionary tale for what happens when an African American woman loses sight of her African heritage (she is transported back in time and is enslaved on a Caribbean sugar cane plantation). This film reinforces Gilroy's second and third diaspora themes above, namely that the memory of slavery endures and overshadows post-slave experiences, yet has redemptive power.

These ideas are not limited to commodities and media forms, however. They are also commonly expressed by pilgrimage tourists. Contemporary African American visitors to Cape Coast and Elmina castles have utilized the notion of *sankɔfa* in their guestbook entries to show how important making a pilgrimage to the castle is, as in the following excerpt: "My Ancestors died here and I am a descendant of one of the survivors. Returning to the place of my heritage is a blessing always; to be manifested today and tomorrow. Remembering, reaffirming and reconnecting with the past to move forward – SANKOFA!!!"

Though Cape Coast and Elmina castles have been at the heart of Ghana's slavery heritage, over time other recognized pilgrimage tourism sites have developed. The year 2001 marked the first time a pilgrimage was made to northern Ghana as part of the biennial PANAFEST celebration. This pre-PANAFEST pilgrimage was undertaken by 14 African Americans to a slave-route site at Paga-Nania in the Upper East region.

Local Ghanaian guides showed the delegation trees to which slaves were tied and a burial ground used for slaves. Pe Charles Awiah Awampaga II, paramount chief of the Paga Traditional Area, said the site had been kept to remind "our brothers and sisters in the diaspora of the wickedness of man and also to create the awareness that they have relatives back home in Africa, especially Ghana" (quoted in Zangina 2001: 12). In his public address at the PANAFEST 2001 opening ceremony in Elmina Castle's forecourt, James Small relayed the significance of his group's pilgrimage to sites along the slave route (extracted from my fieldnotes):

> . . . . We got to realize in Paga that there are extraordinary sites, where our people experienced being captured, being held in slave markets. We got to come down on the road, through Tamale to Kintampo, into Kumasi, and yesterday coming to River Pra, stopping to have libations poured before we crossed the river. And then participating at Assin Praso in a magnificent durbar, and then going to the mass graves of many of those who were killed at Assin Praso at a point of exchange where they tried to escape. Today we are here in front of this extraordinary dungeon-fort that was the first to be established on our homeland. But in our hearts, being the children of those who were enslaved in diaspora – sent to South America, Caribbean, North America – we understand that those were not *our* ancestors, but our *common* ancestors. And we are very clear that there is no guilt for Africans who live on the continent to hold, any greater than the guilt for those of us who live away to hold. What PANAFEST and Emancipation have allowed for us to do, is to forgive ourselves and to bring about the healing necessary to unite our cultural nations and political nations so that this will never happen again. . . . Only in the past, can you find completed ideas, completed principles, completed concepts, completed notion of peopleness, completed ideas of family, completed concept of self, that you can draw upon in the present to build your future. Sankɔfa is more real than we understand. We do not want to forget the past. We will forever remember the past, and we want the world to know – we never gave up, we never gave up, neither in Africa, nor abroad.

Both quotations above stress kinship and unity between Africans and diasporans, while Small goes further, to invoke the concept of sankɔfa in order to stress that remembering the past is absolutely critical to forging a positive future, resulting ultimately in Pan-Africanism, recognizing Africans and diasporans as part of the same family, and healing the historical wounds of alienation brought about by slavery. Once again, we see Gilroy's (1993) three main themes of black Atlantic political thought expressed in Small's recounting of the pilgrimage to Paga Nania: a return to one's African origins, the memory of slavery that recalls a forced separation from the homeland, and using painful memories as a strategy for redemption.

Goals of Homeland Tours

In the film, *Through the Door of No Return* (1997), filmmaker Shirikiana Aina retraces her African American Pan-Africanist father's footsteps back to Ghana, where he intended to repatriate before his life was cut short in 1972. As the camera shows Elmina Castle illuminated by only a few lights and from the ocean side of the structure, Aina repeatedly asks the question, "Do they remember us?" The imagery and the question frame the imperative of diaspora African homeland travel to Ghana: reconnecting with a motherland that is extremely difficult to trace owing to the nature of the transatlantic slave trade which purposefully divided families or ethnic groups that spoke the same language, or included the horrors of rape by slave masters and selective breeding with other Africans intended to bring about the desired qualities in a slave. So many individuals have mingled over the generations and so much time has passed, that the painful possibility exists that diasporans may not be remembered – as descendants from a particular family line or as members of a specific ethnic group. This is especially frightening if the afore-mentioned biological-memory concept is applied to identity; one's identity is in danger of being erased. On the other hand, for African Americans who see Ghana merely as a foreign country, kinship ties might either be unimportant or fortunate, accidental, touristic discoveries.

A central place in Aina's film is taken by Imahküs Njinga Okofu, an African American resident in Ghana and proprietor of One Africa, which specializes in offering tours of Cape Coast and Elmina castles for diaspora Africans. Their com-memorative ceremony is named "*Thru the Door of No Return – The Return*," and follows the structure of a ritual in which participants gather in the dungeon to light candles and are told what injustices captives were made to endure there. Sometimes local Ghanaian actors dress up like slaves and wail in the dungeons for those on the pilgrimage tour. Participants call out the names of great (transnational) African leaders in tandem with family members who have passed away. Later they go through the Door of No Return, where they are told that in some cases African captives would have seen the ocean for the very first time and would have been terrified to board ships to embark upon the Middle Passage, never to see Africa again. The presentation concludes with the reminder that now there is the Door of Return from the ocean side leading back into the castle; this is meant to underscore the idea that African captives were never meant to return back to mother Africa, but that now, as descendants, those on tour can reclaim an African homeland and identity. The significance of this message is meant to highlight the strength of the enslaved ancestors who persevered hardship and the pride of their descendants, who against all odds are now able to make the journey back home.

In the film, Okofu explains that she offers these tours to educate diaspora Afri-cans about how Africa is their home, that they are part of the African family, and that they should never forget about what happened during the transatlantic slave trade: "How can we allow someone to forget *our* holocaust? Over 100 million dead. It's no joke." During the film several African Americans who had been on the tour comment on how profound and moving the experience was for them. One middle-aged woman comments that upon attending One Africa's tour of Elmina Castle, "When we came here and it was dramatized, and we really, really lived it. There's nothing like it." The web site for One Africa (2011) lists testimonials by several

African Americans who found the tour to be a transformative experience: "The Door of no Return experience for me was a cleansing, redemptive and continually renewing experience that has transformed me from an African-American to an African born in America. I was able to embrace those ghosts that haunted me now as ancestors." The resounding message captured both in the web site and the film is that diaspora Africans really have to go to Ghana's castles in person and take part in this commemorative ceremony in order to fully appreciate the embodied experience and come home.

While African Americans prioritize connecting with Ghana as a meaningful homeland in whatever way possible, whether it is through commemorative tours or by fostering friendships with Ghanaians, the vast majority of Ghanaians are more interested in tapping diaspora Africans as a vehicle for economic betterment. The public speeches of PANAFEST and Emancipation Day convey the urgency for Africans of the continent, mainly Ghanaians, and Africans of the diaspora, mainly African Americans and Jamaicans, to join forces as a unified collective committed to the uplift of Africa and Africans everywhere. In their official PANAFEST and Emancipation Day speeches, representatives of the state typically welcome home brothers and sisters of the diaspora while simultaneously reminding them to invest in Ghana, start businesses, and share technical skills. During his PANAFEST 2001 address, a traditional chief spoke in Fante (a local dialect), saying that he would pray that all of his people should marry foreigners, a suggestion that was met with laughter by some Ghanaians in the audience. This chief did not specify whether the foreigners should be black or white, just that he envisioned Ghanaians marrying foreigners to promote economic development. His earnest statement was lost on the non-Fante speakers in the audience; however, even if he had monetary gain primarily in mind, we should consider that marriage between groups promotes not only economic ties but social integration as well.

Some of the key players in PANAFEST have involved individuals in intercultural marriages. For example, Efua Sutherland, the Ghanaian playwright and poet who originated the idea for PANAFEST to celebrate the performing arts and cultures of Africans and diaspora Africans, was married to African American political activist William Sutherland, and they had three children. The couple established Tsito Secondary School in the rural trans-Volta region in order to promote education in traditional culture tied to modernization and village development through encouraging a cooperative farm, sugar and soap manufacturing, and vegetable oil production (Gaines 2006: 105). Nathanya Halevi Kohain is the current executive director of the PANAFEST Foundation, and is also an entrepreneur, educator, and ordained rabbi in the African Hebrew faith. He has lived in Ghana for over two decades and has a blended family with his Ghanaian wife, Mabel Tamakloe-Halevi. During my last visit to Ghana in 2011, we sat in the restaurant they run; their staff is exclusively Ghanaian, and they have many Ghanaian friends with whom they socialize on a regular basis. We talked about how their youngest son is now attending one of the most prestigious secondary schools in Ghana. Rabbi Kohain is clearly well integrated into the local community and has fulfilled the vision of being part of the

African family, yet coming home to Ghana has not been without its challenges. Perhaps the most obvious sign that this integration does not come easily for many pilgrims and repatriates is the conflict over the term *oburoni*.

Perceptions of African Americans and Afro Caribbeans

The Akan term *oburoni* inevitably crops up in the public discourse about the degree to which diaspora Africans belong to Africa and should be considered Africans. This term literally means, "one who comes from beyond the horizon," but is now glossed as "foreigner" or "white person."

Many diaspora Africans have suggested that Ghanaians replace *oburoni* with terms that are not at all related to "foreigner" or white person. In 2000, at an academic conference at the Kwame Nkrumah University of Science and Technology (KNUST) located in Kumasi, an African American scholar proposed that Ghanaians begin employing the neologism, *sankɔfani*, as a term of reference for diaspora Africans. She reasoned the term *oburoni* is offensive to diaspora Africans and that *sankɔfani* or "one who goes back to the source to fetch what was lost" is more appropriate. Some of the Ghanaian scholars present at the conference quickly explained that calling someone *oburoni* is not meant to be an insult, but is done either in a matter-of-fact manner or jokingly. Ghanaians themselves sometimes call one another *oburoni* if they have a fair complexion, Western education, speak English, hold a white-collar job, travel abroad, or exhibit features associated with foreign cultures. This shows the difficulties that occur when diaspora groups expect that they still share a culture with homeland groups, but homeland groups perceive cultural changes that create real social and economic differences.

Cape Coast residents have a wide range of opinions about the extent to which diaspora Africans are kin or foreigners, and their comments reveal a complex, multi-layered picture of belonging. Cape Coasters often responded to my questions that they considered African Americans *both* their brothers and sisters *and* foreigners. Many Ghanaians find no contradiction in accepting both relationships, perhaps because they (unlike Americans), make no assumptions about ancestry defining contemporary culture.

Some Ghanaians told me they do not consider African Americans to be *oburoni* in their physical appearance because they have black skin, but when they speak, their language betrays them and makes them *oburoni*. Cape Coasters suggested that economic class, hairstyles, clothing, and language reveal ways in which diaspora Africans are different from Ghanaians.

At the same time, some Ghanaians listed cultural similarities that they have in common with diaspora Africans, especially Afro-Caribbeans; puberty rites, naming ceremonies, food, and words are thought of as areas of cultural retention or cultural commonality. A few Cape Coasters said that African Americans behave "more African" than Ghanaians do. In Ghanaian society, the youngest generation of Ghanaians, in particular, is perceived to have uncritically adopted Western cultural values. Some Ghanaians believe encouraging tourism of African Americans and Jamaicans to Ghana would revitalize elements of "traditional" African culture. However, these same Ghanaians express fears that unsavory elements of Western culture creep into Ghana through tourism. One local said:

> Economically, it would be beneficial to us to bring in money and ideas. . . . We can help some of our people to appreciate some of our own traditions. Ghana's youth are virtually Americans. People visiting want to take up our traditions – African Americans have had traditional weddings here. The youth look up to Americans, [so it can help if they] start picking up culture. [On the other hand, some] come in, and the culture and ideas they bring in is a bit foreign – in terms of drugs and sex. In Ghana, sex is protected. . . . We used to not have anything like AIDS. I think some of these things were brought in by tourists.

Cultural Dissonance and Economic Difference

Real and perceived class differences between African Americans and Ghanaians lead to cultural dissonance and divergent goals. While many African Americans are interested in cultivating a social bond with Ghanaians based on shared African identity, Ghanaians focus more on the potential economic returns of relationships with rich foreigners. Part of the problem is that there is little opportunity for inter-action between most African American tourists and Ghanaians. African American tourists traveling to Cape Coast and Elmina are typically on a tight schedule that includes a quick visit to the castles before being whisked back to the capital city of Accra. Visitors seldom have the opportunity to walk around town or get acquainted with any of the local people in more than a superficial way.

Despite their limited interaction, African Americans and Ghanaians forge some-times opportunistic and sometimes meaningful relationships with one another. The project of consciousness-raising and sensitivity training happens at a variety of levels from individual conversations to radio programs to public addresses at PAN-AFEST and Emancipation Day. A local Ghanaian reasoned, "There should be a deliberate effort to conscientize people – Ghanaians of all ages – so when tourists come, they'll know what to do."

On the individual level, savvy Ghanaian children approach African American tourists and tell them they look just like one of their family members. The children hope to get some money out of the encounter – either by begging or selling trinkets for cash, or by collecting addresses and later requesting money for school, books, or toys. At the same time, African Americans remind Ghanaians that they are returning home to Africa and should not be called *oburoni*. A Cape Coaster explained:

> When they come and we make them happy, they tell friends back home about their experiences in Ghana and try to convince them to come down to establish businesses

here. I have seen some black Americans who are resident at . . . a suburb of Cape Coast. They have so enjoyed their stay here to the extent that if you tell them that they are black Americans, they get annoyed. They say they are Ghanaians.

Perceptions on Pilgrimage Tourism in Ghana

A few African Americans have pointed out to me that the African Americans who come to Ghana primarily for sightseeing and not for reclaiming an African identity are the same people who have "assimilated into the white world" or have been "enculturated into enjoying Western culture." According to this logic, African Americans who have assimilated into dominant American culture contrast sharply with Africans born in America wanting to make the pilgrimage home. Rabbi Kohain explained the significance of this journey for the latter group:

> I see it as a pilgrimage exercise, that Africa or Africans in the diaspora, to those who are very African centered, this is nothing less than Mecca or Jerusalem in terms of wanting to get back home to the motherland. . . . [For African Americans] the fact that *that* living hell in America during the time of capture, enslavement in America – "I can only balance that if I can only get home." And, it's almost turned into – kind of like a metaphorical or allegorical ideal that it's like going to heaven. . . . So, it's not like a normal trip for an African traveling out of the diaspora.

The late Gladys Rice, who migrated from Detroit to live in Ghana, said that most African Americans do not know exactly where they come from – all they know is that their ancestors left the shores of Africa and that the castles represent a starting point to reconnect with their heritage. She linked her first visit to Gorée Island in Senegal and the castles in Ghana to the memory of African American sharecroppers struggling to get by, and the fight for civil rights. Her experience of growing up in poverty in the United States inspired her mission to treat sick children in Ghana. Like several other African Americans residing in the greater Cape Coast area, she felt her calling in Ghana was helping to alleviate poverty. She and another African American migrant to Ghana ran a local free clinic that provided basic health care and medical supplies for the community.

Local Ghanaians and African Americans may not necessarily agree about the reasons for uniting under the Pan-Africanist banner. Ghanaians focus on practical matters of economic return generated through castle tourism, PANAFEST, and Emancipation Day. African Americans seek a deeper social connection with Africa as their homeland to build the foundation for a collective African family. There is room for addressing both practical concerns of collectively solving problems faced by African Americans and Ghanaians and promoting Pan-African identity. Targeting an issue, such as poverty alleviation, would help to address a practical problem, and although these issues may have little to do with tourism, but instead suggest longer-term, deeper investments that some diaspora Africans are ready to make in Africa, tourism is still the vehicle which initially brings African Americans to Ghana.

Tourism for Development

During the 2000 KNUST academic conference mentioned above, an African Ameri-can audience member stood up during the question-and-answer session and said, "I know I'm being political here, but we are *never* tourists when we come here!" What she had in mind was that when diaspora Africans come to Ghana, they have a mission, a purpose that is intended to promote positive, grassroots community development during their stay. In 1985, the late Asantehene – Otumfuo Opoku Ware II – established the role of Nkɔsuohene/hemaa, or development chief. Since the 1990s, hundreds of diaspora Africans and an unspecified number of white Ameri-cans, British, Germans, Dutch, and Ghanaians have been enstooled as Nkɔsuohene (Bob-Milliar 2009: 541–542). A Nkɔsuohene is responsible for promoting commu-nity development and is called upon by the local traditional chief to contribute funds and/or technical skills for such projects as: providing electricity and clean drinking water; building schools, clinics, roads, and public toilets; promoting educa-tion and health care.

Conferring the title of Nkɔsuohene on foreigners has been fraught with increas-ing controversy over time, as tourism development has spurred contractors who solicit potential *Nkɔsuohenes* in what has been called a money-making scheme. Several African Americans have been "snatched" and enstooled as development chiefs without fully understanding the attendant responsibilities and the institution of chieftaincy in Ghana. In December 2001, I attended a symposium on the topic in Elmina sponsored by the district office of the Centre for National Culture. During the forum, Nana Kwamina Ansah, chief of Eguafo and now president of the Central Regional House of Chiefs, explained his personal position on the issue:

> Different factors go into selecting a chief: money, background, and even gender. . . . He is valuably nominated and enstooled or enskinned, with appropriate family lineage – which simply put, means royal. Anyone who is considered for a chief title, must come from a royal family and be put forth by the kingmakers. My family got rid of our own local slave to be an international slave during the transatlantic slave trade. If you are a descendent of this slave and return today to be enstooled, this would be an unholy link with the original ancestors. You would be a puppet in our traditions and customs. Maybe they can parade somewhere, but culturally the links are not there. Not all Ghanaians can be made chiefs, not even all those who distinguish themselves. This giving chieftaincy to foreigners is an insult to the institution. Instead we can name libraries, clinics, and schools after them – not delving into the spiritual side of our culture.

In my interview with another traditional chief, he interpreted *Nkɔsuohene* as merely an honorary title:

> Yeah, I have made one [African American as Nkɔsuohene]. I was so much against it from the very beginning. But chief has been defined differently. So what you hear and

you see strictly by these African Americans are *honorary*. Now they say a chief is somebody who must come from that lineage, related or appointed by the queen mother, and he must pass through the normal process. He must come from a special clan – what we call the royal family. . . . So, that Afro-American has no lineage here, has no family as it is appropriate for this. So what we make them is honorary . . . the late Asantehene said that, "We have sons and daughters who are ready to contribute to the development of an area." And so that is Nkɔsuohene. . . . It gives them the opportunity to serve, but with this sort of post. It gives them some sort of status that they can have direct contact with the chiefs and people of the area.

Consensus is lacking when it comes to maintaining a firm policy on the issue of conferring chieftaincy on foreigners. These chiefs differ in precisely *how* diaspora Africans should be acknowledged for their development assistance – through a library name or through an official title. If we consider their words critically, three key themes emerge from the above quotes: (1) that the institution of chieftaincy should remain intact and sacred; (2) that people who contribute to community development should be recognized; and (3) that when the issue of kinship and ancestry comes up, traditional chiefs either maintain that African Americans have no lineage or that their lineage is that of a slave's. These chiefs' assumptions contrast totally with the idea of African Americans claiming a homeland in Ghana through ancestry that is commonly deployed in public speeches during PANAFEST and Emancipation Day by Ghanaian state representatives and find resonance in diaspora African tourists, pilgrims, and repatriates. For diaspora repatriates, ultimately, these points relate back to the question of whether or not they are accepted by Ghanaians into the African family – not merely symbolically, but literally.

Conclusion

Principles like sankɔfa and representations of Ghana's slavery heritage destinations are taken for granted and embedded in cultural practice in such a way as to construct Ghana as a homeland center for diaspora Africans. My interviews with African Americans and analysis of their visitor remarks demonstrate that some see their journeying to Ghana as an act of redemption, one that completes a cycle of return that their ancestors were unable to make. To many African Americans, they are realizing a pilgrimage to a homeland center and engaged in an embodied experience that signals triumph against all odds to self-actualize a connection with their African homeland. They may be the one representative from their family, church, or town to embark on the pilgrimage, and as such carry the burden of representing the broader black community.

PANAFEST/Emancipation Day 2012 was cancelled due to the sudden death of President John Atta Mills just as it was about to commence in July. The official PANAFEST 2012 itinerary was slated to include sites in the North, like Paga Nania Slave Camp (PANAFEST Foundation 2012), that have historically received less attention than Cape Coast and Elmina castles in the South. A private Accra-based tour company operated by an African American expat organized a post-PANAFEST 2012 atonement ceremony in Salaga featuring descendants of slave raiders ritually washing the feet of diasporans as a sign of apology, wreath laying at a grave site in honor of those who perished during the slave trade, and a healing feast between the descendants of slave raiders and the descendants of the slaves (Land Tours 2011). The description of this atonement ceremony on the tour company's web site states that the ritual was devised by the villagers out of a genuine interest in righting the wrongs of the past (Land Tours 2011). Of course, the ceremony also takes place within the context of a packaged tour that requires participants to pay a fee to the tour operator. Paying in advance for a pilgrimage tour and framing the ceremony as a ritual that is grounded in healing, rather than a commercial enterprise, highlights the notion that it is a sacred encounter.

In addition, the movement to incorporate sites in the hinterlands with more complicated stories of resistance, capture, trade, and transport alongside the coastal castles used to hold captives before embarkation is significant. It raises questions about how not only physical features but also rituals associated with them help to structure the meaning of pilgrimages. Is the tour group one that was formed back home with known individuals, or cobbled together at the destination site in mixed company? Is it comprised of only diaspora Africans? Do participants interpret the significance of their travel to Ghana in similar ways? Is the visit to a remote place? Is it visited infrequently or only on special occasions? If a pilgrimage site is not of the mass tourism variety or the tour is held at a time when other visitors are absent, it might appear more sacred. What is the story that goes along with the site? How are meanings conveyed in person and transmitted to increasingly wider audiences (e.g., through media channels and by word of mouth)?

The relevant spaces and discourse associated with Ghana's slavery heritage have been reterritorialized, compelling us to continually re-examine in practice "the politics of community, solidarity, identity, and cultural difference" (Gupta and Ferguson 1997: 37). Over time, these places have come to mean different things for diaspora groups – whether they are tourists, annual pilgrims, or repatriates – and for Ghanaian groups – whether they are inspired by embracing Pan-African nationalism or not. As speakers and performers at PANAFEST and Emancipation Day promote the rhetoric of African solidarity, some audience members are bound to be more attentive than others. While diaspora Africans are moved by the warm welcome delivered in official durbars, they may also be disappointed by the mixed messages encountered in their interaction with everyday Ghanaians. At the same time, Ghanaians may view diaspora Africans as wealthy investors with the capacity for improving the economy, long-lost family members and comrades in contemporary political-economic struggles, or even both simultaneously. Constructions of Ghana's slavery heritage are likely to continue to shift over time. This instability is evident in some of the disjunctures surrounding the promotion of Ghana's pilgrimage tourism, notions of connection to and alienation from Africa, and questions over cultural meanings.

References

Abu-Lughod, L. 1991. "Writing against culture." In R.G. Fox (ed.) *Recapturing Anthropology: Working in the Present*, pp. 137–162. Santa Fe: School of American Research Press.

Benson, S. and McCaskie, T.C. 2004. "Asen Praso in history and memory." *Ghana Studies*, 7: 93–113.

Bob-Milliar, G.M. 2009. "Chieftaincy, diaspora, and development: the institution of Nkɔsuohene in Ghana." *African Affairs*, 108(433): 541–558.

Gaines, K.K. 2006. *American Africans in Ghana: Black Expatriates and the Civil Rights Era*. Chapel Hill: University of North Carolina Press.

Gilroy, P. 1993. *The Black Atlantic: Modernity and Double Consciousness*. Cambridge, MA: Harvard University Press.

GMOT, UNDP, and WTO 1996. *National Tourism Development Plan for Ghana (1996–2010)*. Integrated Tourism Development Programme (GHA/92/013), Accra: Ghana Ministry of Tourism, United Nations Development Program, and World Tourism Organization.

Gupta, A. and Ferguson, J. 1997. "Beyond culture: Space, identity, and the politics of difference." In A. Gupta and J. Ferguson (eds) *Culture, Power, Place: Explorations in Critical Anthropology*, pp. 33–51. Durham, NC: Duke University Press.

Herzfeld, M. 1997. *Cultural Intimacy: Social Poetics in the Nation-State*. New York: Routledge.

Land Tours 2011. "Detailed itinerary: PANAFEST 2012, atonement experience." Land Tours Ghana Limited, at http://www.landtours.com/panafest_atonement2012.asp, accessed March 13, 2013.

Mensah, I. 2004. "Marketing Ghana as a Mecca for the African-American tourist," *GhanaWeb*, June 10, at http://www.ghanaweb.com/GhanaHomePage/features/artikel.php?ID=59447, accessed March 1, 2013.

One Africa 2011. "Thru the door of no return – the return." One Africa Resort, at http://www.oneafricaghana.com/index.php?option=com_content&view=article&id=47&Itemid=70, accessed March 1, 2013.

PANAFEST Foundation 2012. "Schedule for PANAFEST 2012," at http://www.panafestghana.org/op.php?id=28, accessed March 13, 2013.

Ray, C. 2001. *Highland Heritage: Scottish Americans in the American South*. Chapel Hill: University of North Carolina Press.

Through the Door of No Return. 1997. Dir. S. Aina. Washington, DC: Mypheduh Film, Inc.

Tosh, P. 1977. "African." *Equal Rights* album. Sony Music Entertainment.

Zachary, G.P. 2001. "Tangled roots: For African-Americans in Ghana, the grass isn't always greener." *Wall Street Journal*, March 14: A1.

Zangina, C. 2001. "African-Americans on pilgrimage." *Ghanaian Times*, July 28: 12.

Chapter 32

The Transnational Politics of the Techno-Class in Bangalore

T.T. Sreekumar

The rise of a "new" Indian middle class in the late 1980s and early 1990s has been the subject of much academic debate, with a great deal of the literature revolving around how to define the middle class (Sridharan 2004), its relation to liberalization, including its contradictory effects (Fernandes 2000a), consumption patterns, including the moral and cultural effects of consumerism (Lakha 1999; Beinhocker, Farrel, and Zainulbhai 2007), the role of the media in propagating certain images of the middle class (Fernandes 2000b), and the impact of globalization (Lakha 1999), to name a few.[1] Another area of great interest has been the role of the middle class in democratic processes (Varma 1998; Datta-Ray 2002; Palshikar 2003; Ram-Prasad 2007).

The Indian middle class play an important role in the country's democracy, not only as appropriators of democratic spaces, through their hegemonic shaping of their image of India – in conjunction with local and global capitalist interests (Palshikar 2003), but also in their emerging role as professional and cultural intermediaries in the civil and political societies in India, that is, as a new techno-class in an emerging knowledge economy. The positioning of the nation-state as a unit of analysis for citizenship, identity, and social change has come into question in recent years. Anthias (2010: 222) refers to the "hegemony of the nation-state paradigm" that is so strong that it subsumes even conceptualizations of transnationalism, hybridity, and multiculturalism, and manifests itself as "methodological nationalism" (Wimmer and Glick Schiller 2002). Asking whether the nation can be transcended through transnational processes, Anthias warns that, contrary to expectations of more equitable relations, negative forces such as racist imaginings can occur within broader international frameworks. At the individual level, Mau (2010) refers to the phenomenon of individual cross-border interactions and

A Companion to Diaspora and Transnationalism, First Edition.
Edited by Ato Quayson and Girish Daswani.
© 2013 Blackwell Publishing Ltd. Published 2013 by Blackwell Publishing Ltd.

mobility as *social transnationalism*, noting that this does not necessarily negate national identity or create cosmopolitan citizens. It does, however, transform the relationship between society and the state. In examining the analytic link between "diaspora" and "transnationalism," Faist (2010) makes the distinction that both terms are associated with processes that cross borders, but while the former refers to groups living outside of a homeland, the latter is often used to denote the durable ties that migrants maintain across countries. The focus on migrants as important social agents in transnationalism studies allows us to examine not only their impact on the countries they migrate to, but the impact that their return, and continued transnational connections, has on their home countries. In fact, transnational practices play a critical role in shaping feelings of belonging after migrants return home (De Bree, Tine, and De Haas 2010), and in the digital age, the sense of agency in building community through choice and circumstance that is developed under diasporic conditions is often manifested in the "active participation, production, and redefinition of self through consumption and communication" (Gajjala 2010: 211). Transnational elites may live in a world of their own, in gated communities that are reproducing themselves in globalized cities worldwide (Pow 2011). These elites are thus physically removed from lower levels of society even as their transnational links have a strong influence in shaping the spatial contexts of the latter. This chapter attempts to address the gap in the literature regarding the increasing visibility of the transnational professional and cultural intermediaries in the civil and political societies in Third World mega-cities like Bangalore, a dimension that is critically significant in contextualizing and conceptualizing the new techno-class as a new social force to be reckoned with.

This chapter attempts to address the issue by partly drawing on the notion of heterotopias (Foucault 1986; Lefebvre 1991, Saldanha 2008). It explores the intertwining meanings of an aggressive advertisement campaign in the metropolitan city of Bangalore (*DNA Daily*'s inaugural advertisements for its Bangalore edition labeled "I Believe in Bangalore") and the activities of an urban social movement in Bangalore called Janaagraha (literally, "people's desire") to understand the political and social appeal of a new transnational techno-class in influencing the imagination of spatial ordering in a Third World mega-city. Heterotopias can be usefully understood as spaces that are not private or public, but "necessarily collective or shared spaces" (Dehaene and De Cauter 2008). Therefore, in exploring the role of the *DNA*'s "I Believe in Bangalore" campaign in reimagining the city and the compelling and mostly contested interventions of Janaagraha for reordering spatial organization of the city, I employ the notion of heterotopias as a contested space that is at once real (i.e., an existing geographical place) as well as imagined (i.e., as a *future anterior*).

"I Believe in Bangalore"

The promise of Bangalore, implicit in the growing concentration of science and technology institutions and public sector industries in the city, has loomed large in the national imagination from the early phase of decolonization. Jawaharlal Nehru, India's first prime minister, described it as a city of the future, particularly as it did not carry the burden of history, unlike the Presidency cities (Nair 2005). The sudden influx of IT companies into the city in the late 1990s gave it an international reputation as the "Silicon Valley" of India, and resulted in the emergence of a new transnational class of knowledge workers who soon began to take an interest in the city's civic and political realms. Bangalore is thus often lauded for the role of its civil society, known for its vibrant networked participation, as an important "stakeholder" in the urban agenda and for making the state more accountable to its citizens (Madon and Sahay 2000; Nair 2005; Sudhira, Ramachandara, and Bala Subrahmanya 2007).

The transnationalization of the new techno-class in Bangalore has been appropriately noted in the literature. Madon (1997: 234) has argued that the prosperity ushered in by rising industrial productivity, fueled by the growth of high-tech industries, has given the city a cosmopolitan look, with the conspicuous presence of a rising middle class in the central parts of the city and in other expensive areas beyond the city center. As in other cities in the developing world, the impact of globalization on Bangalore has been striking in terms of its cultural impact, particularly in relation to the city's (middle- and upper-class) youth and issues of identity (Saldanha 2002). The emigration of large numbers of young persons from across the country to Bangalore's IT and related industries has given Bangalore the image of being a "young city."

Based on this general impression of Bangalore as a city characterized by its "IT wealth, a cultural bent, a spiritual home for fashion, its coffee shops and pubs, and the highest number of rock bands in the country" (Joshi 2008), Mumbai-based *DNA* newspaper marked its entry into the Bangalore market in 2008 with the highly publicized "I Believe in Bangalore" campaign. The campaign was divided into seven phases, with each new phase being revealed every week or two. The first phase had hoardings with the image of a city resident alongside the words, "I Believe in Bangalore."

In the first phase of the campaign, one of the representative posters shows a young lady standing in a pose that draws the eye to her pregnant state, with the slogan "I Believe in Bangalore" on a brightly colored backdrop behind her. The combination of purple and orange is striking, but not a radical departure from the color combinations of traditional Indian garments. This and the badly painted wall that takes up a large part of the photograph seem to point to the present state of the city. That the woman is pregnant conveys a sense of looking forward – the belief she places in the ability of the city to provide for her unborn child is an investment in its future. The graffiti-like spray-painted splotch of black against which the slogan appears is the one feature of the picture that hints at a departure from the traditional. The young woman may be wearing a dress (as opposed to a sari or other traditional Indian garment), but it is a conservative dress, and with her long hair, gentle expression, and demure pose, she signals a belief in the Bangalore of the present as well as the future.

While that got people talking, the second teaser phase had these people saying, "I Believe in Bangalore because Bangalore is in my DNA." In contrast to the first phase billboards, a sample from the second phase showed a young woman in pose and outfit that are recognizably modern and urban. Her hands on hip and thigh, chin held high, expression resolute, wearing tight jeans and t-shirt, hair let loose, and beads slung around her neck all combine to convey not just youth and modernity, but an attitude of rebellion and resistance against tradition and the past. Apart from "DNA" being the name of the newspaper, its use in the slogan references its original meaning of genetic building blocks. This positions modern Western-educated youths as having access to the cultural roots of the past even while it highlights their claim on the city's future.

The third phase was launched with interesting facts about the city's heritage and modernity fused with launch news of the newspaper. For instance, one hoarding shows a woman with the copy entitled "Bangalore Is the Spiritual Home of the Indian Fashion Industry." Another points out that "India's first air-taxi couldn't have taken off from anywhere else," while yet another humorously notes that "Bangalore is a city of parks. Software parks." Subsequent phases focused on involving the youth in the creation of the campaign, thanking Bangaloreans for "a stupendous response"; and the final phase announced the actual launch of the newspaper. The campaign intended to create a buzz, not just about the newspaper launch, but about the city itself; to create a "Bangalore fever," and tap the sentiments of the youth to make it an ongoing celebration of the city (Joshi 2008; Khandelwal 2008). According to the organizers, the campaign was aimed at deflecting increasing criticism of and negative publicity about Bangalore, particularly of its ailing infrastructure and deteriorating law-and-order situation, by giving citizens, especially the usually soft-spoken locals (*Kannadigas*), a chance to voice their faith in the city by highlighting its positive aspects (Joshi 2008).

The voicing of pride in Bangalore's achievements is particularly salient for two reasons: firstly, the rapid urbanization of Bangalore has resulted in haphazard development and urban bottlenecks, in addition to perpetuating urban–rural divides (Sastry 2008), which have deeply impacted the quality of life of its citizens. Secondly, the hastening of migration into the city as a result of the IT boom has resulted in a change in the composition of the population, and consequent struggles to shape and reshape the Bangalorean identity, based on issues of region, religion, language, caste, and class, to name a few. These identity struggles have undoubtedly been exacerbated by the increasing participation of the city in the global knowledge economy (albeit the peripheral fringes). Relevant to this is the argument that the type of hi-tech peripheral growth experienced in Bangalore results in "enclave development," within which the benefits accrue disproportionately to a closed circle of elites, particularly those with transnational linkages to the larger diaspora (Boas, Dunning, and Bussell 2005). This also ties in with my earlier observation about the impact of globalization on the construction of identities among youth, and the disposition towards a Western youth culture, especially among those who have the money to engage fully with the West, and the subsequent gulf between these "global" youth and "local" (for which read lower-middle-class) India (Saldanha 2002). I argue that the *DNA* campaign, unmindful of, or deliberately underplaying, these various fissures in Bangalore society, tapped into an imagined space of a transnational, unified, homogenous, and conspicuously middle-class Bangalore, with the ultimate hope that by appealing to the residents' love for the city, they could transfer the consumer's attention to the newspaper. While the campaign was successful in its attention-grabbing gimmicks, and in evoking a sense of pride in the city, a cursory glance at the blogosphere reveals two critical issues: firstly, the view that some of the topics covered by the campaign appeared to be an outsider's view of the city, and did not adequately reflect – or address – the more urgent issues affecting citizens' quality of life, notably traffic snarls, power (electricity) cuts, and inflation. A blogger's response was typical (Bhat 2008): "I found some of the lines defensive: 'Even New York has traffic jams.' Firstly, shouldn't that be 'New York has traffic jams too'? For the average Bangalorean [sic] to be told to accept traffic jams as part of life because other bigger, iconic cities have traffic jams too is not a positive message."

The blogger was alluding to the billboards during Phase 3, such as "one day the mayor of Silicon Valley will be a Bangalorian: I believe in Bangalore" and "Even New York City has traffic jams: I believe in Bangalore." The transnational Bangalore does not any more consider Singapore as its destiny – it is New York. The issue of infrastructural bottlenecks, as mentioned earlier, is a sore point with city residents, many of whom blame the new IT-related workforce for adding to the city's woes. Secondly, while newcomers undoubtedly believe in Bangalore for all the benefits it offers them, original Bangalore residents (or "natives") are increasingly made to feel that they are outsiders in their own city, the landscape of which is ever changing and gradually becoming more unidentifiable with their past.

This is an interesting departure from the previously imagined closeness of Bangalore with newly industrialized Asia to more advanced global cities. The transition is negotiated in one of the posters where a slogan asks, in a challenging tone "If Sepang can host a F1 race, why can't Bangalore?" Formula 1 racing is held in many cities around the world, and it is significant that Malaysia is highlighted in the slogan rather than a Western country like Germany or the United Kingdom. Unlike the other pictures in the campaigns that seek to associate Bangalore with highly developed countries, this one compares (in a manner that could be seen as dismissing and perhaps even insulting) Bangalore with a country that is positioned as less advanced, and thus asserts that if such a country can be deemed worthy of hosting a sporting event as high profile and exclusive as the F1 race, then certainly Bangalore is in an even better position to do so with its modernity and affluence. (Hosting Formula 1 requires a significant investment in infrastructure.) The assumption embedded in this slogan is that viewers know where Sepang is, and what Malaysia represents in terms of a developmental trajectory. The focus on a luxury sport is significant in a country that is known, among other things, for its level of poverty.

There are no more human models in the fourth phase – only the distinctive purple and orange stripes, the *DNA* logo, and the "I Believe in Bangalore" motif. In addition, there is the question, printed in white along the lower purple stripe, "What's in Bangalore's DNA?" Focus has now shifted from the DNA of the people in the city to the DNA of the city itself. The play on words – begun in Phase 2 – continues in this phase. Each poster presents two choices with checkboxes – not necessarily obvious ones. But the format of two options where the assumption is that one must be preferred over the other is indicative of a technocratic turn in the campaign – viewing the poster puts the viewer in mind of filling in a form. In one of the posters, the choice given is between "9 a.m. to 5 p.m." and "9 p.m. to 5 a.m." This is a subtle choice that may not immediately strike a viewer as significant. But the priming effect of previous phases may have trained viewers to understand that they are expected to choose the second option, such that a vibrant night life is more a part of Bangalore's preferred culture than a stolid, ordinary workday. It is possible that both choices are preferred, highlighting the city as one that works hard to build its future, as well as one that has arrived in the future and thus has developed the confidence and affluence to enjoy the resultant prosperity. Several such spurious dichotomies were suggested in a subsequent campaign. For example, the choice between "inspire" and "expire" is clear – as the latter implies dying out or fading away, as opposed to being creative and invigorating. "Merge in" versus "stand out": again the priming effect of previous phases makes it clear that Bangalore's vibrancy and energy mean that distinctiveness is in its DNA. "Adapt" versus "change" thus is not such a clear choice at first glance, but the second option appears more in line with the take-charge philosophy of the campaign that advocates innovation and celebrates transformation, rather than adapting to existing conditions. In the board "Silicon Valley" versus "Bangalore" the viewer sees that the answer to the question "What is in Bangalore's DNA" is "Bangalore" itself, a sort of self-reflexive positioning that has an empowering effect, removing the need for an external source of legitimacy and affirmation. Rather than being the Silicon Valley of India, Bangalore is only and completely Bangalore, sufficient in itself as an icon of technology and the future. Finally, "Marriage" versus "Live in" appears to be a conversation starter rather than anything else, bridging the construction of Bangalore as a future city with the anticipated controversial content of the publication.

A critical analysis of the campaign reveals its overwhelmingly transnational and middle- to upper-middle-class character, reflected in its language as well as its images. Pictures of young people dominated the campaign; in fact, the picture of a young, pregnant lady can even be construed as representing the future of the city, by pinning its hopes on the next generation. Another important observation, I think, is that the models appear to be sufficiently affluent, their attire as well as interests are reflective of a Westernized or globalized citizen, equally at ease with his or her local and global identities. The billboards highlight the various achievements of Bangalore in terms of its modernity, and vis-à-vis its Western counterparts, to the neglect of the city's local (read traditional) heritage and culture.

In a sample picture from the fifth phase, the background has morphed into a room with clean, smoothly painted walls and windows that look as though they could be in a modern house anywhere in the Western world, even though the message by now is clear that the ubiquitous modernity has a definite local placement in Bangalore, a city that matches up to global standards. The "I Believe in Bangalore" slogan is diminished, both in size and placement next to the *DNA* logo, in keeping with the campaign's movement towards bringing the newspaper to the forefront while its construction of Bangalore as a modern and youthful global city is normalized, and therefore moved to the background. A young lady is in a yoga pose, stretching upward towards the light. Yoga is a traditional Indian concept, but has become a part of exercise regimens worldwide, accepted particularly enthusiastically by affluent Western countries and modified to suit their interests and needs. The modern exercise apparel marks this practitioner as one who may be approaching the discipline from a Western perspective. Yoga becomes a symbol of Bangalore's transnational links when used in this manner. The two options "believer" and "non-believer" with checkboxes appearing next to them appears to invite the viewer to choose, yet with its subsuming of the traditionally Indian into the by now inevitably and naturally transnational, there is no choice at all. There is nothing left to disbelieve, as everything exists at the same time – past and future, local and global, Indian and Western.[2]

Social Space and the New Techno-Class in Bangalore

The 1990s witnessed a change in the nature of citizens' participation in city affairs in Bangalore, with rising middle-class modes of civic activism, as reflected in the emergence of citizens' groups and NGOs that have increasingly turned into owners of rights or "stakeholders," participating in the management of the city (Nair 2005; Sudhira *et al.* 2007). The gradual abdication by the state of its developmentalist roles and its redistributive functions, and the ascendance of the market (and notably, I add, the emergence of the knowledge economy) have given rise to a new parastatal managerial elite, embodied in institutional innovations such as the Bangalore Agenda Task Force (BATF) and Janaagraha (Sudhira *et al.* 2007). The story of BATF, although a failed experiment, is illustrative in this regard. Constituted as an advisory body with enormous executive powers, with members drawn mostly from the so-called secessionists, it replaced conventional spaces of the traditional civil society in Bangalore in dictating directions for urban governance in the city. The members of the BATF exercised overwhelming influence in the processes of policy making for urban infrastructure, which brought the new social class in conflict with representatives of the traditional civil society of the urban poor and subaltern groups.

Janaagraha also has its own shares of embarrassment in its encounters with the organizations for the slum-dwellers and urban poor, notably its unceremonious withdrawal from the Greater Bangalore Water and Sewerage Project (GBWASP) in 2006, amidst allegations of its attempts to "privatize" water, and with allegations of elitism and a middle-class bias dogging its activities. The increasing visibility of these techno-elites in the Indian context, particularly in the urban context, has been accompanied by an unprecedented exertion of political authority by these social classes in influencing social and economic policies of both local and provincial governments.

While mainstream descriptions harp on the innovativeness and good intentions of the BATF and Janaagraha, in academic literature they have been variously critiqued: for the hegemony of the capitalist class (Nair 2005); for the creation of an "exclusive citizenry" that bypasses political systems and exclude elected representatives (Ghosh 2005; Nair 2000); and for an institutionalized form of "middle-class activism" that serves as a "Trojan horse" to depoliticize and dilute claim-making by poorer groups (Benjamin 2005). Scoones (2007) notes the increasing importance of the professional, urban middle class (including the unusual access and influence of the Indian diaspora) as a lobby group in Bangalore, whose mood is followed carefully by the urban-based English language media, and which exerts disproportionate influence on political discourse. The challenge, thus, has to be seen in conjunction with the need to conceptualize the subject position of an emerging techno-class in India and contextualize its political role.

The new techno-class and the transnational elite in urban India are increasingly participating in social action, turning themselves effectively into an agency of change, altering the terms and substance of the relationship between market, state, and civil society by rearticulating their self-representation and not infrequently suggesting that their civil and political initiatives are in fact "people's" movements. Several civic associations and "virtual" as well as "real" interest groups and communities of action and discourse with members from this new social class have proliferated in India. Their actions range from passive "net presence" to active real-life confrontation with the state and its agencies. Through in-depth interviews with prominent activists, volunteers, employees, state officials, and politicians associated with civic organizations, as well as an investigation of the spatial practices of Janaagraha, in particular, the case study reported in the following section examines the role of the techno-class, as exemplified by Janaagraha, in the transformation of the social space in Bangalore.

Janaagraha: Understanding the Contestations of Space

Founded in December 2001, Janaagraha is a "citizens' movement" in Bangalore, based on the fundamental premise that participatory democracy is central to good governance.[3] At the core of its philosophy of constructive engagement lie the twin pillars of "practical patriotism" – a process wherein citizens can contribute to democracy, even for a few hours a month, through a "balance between a person's job, their family, their entertainment, and their desire to make a difference in society at large" – and "professional volunteerism," which entails holding people accountable for the commitments they make in the voluntary service of the country.

Since its inception, Janaagraha has described itself as a citizens' *movement* and not an organization *per se*: a distinction that differentiates it from the myriad number of NGOs working on civic issues in the city. According to one of our informants, who is a close insider of the movement, three key features distinguish Janaagraha from other civil society organizations (CSOs): (1) it was not initiated by the government; (2) it does not adopt a confrontationist attitude; and (3) it views itself as providing solutions. To the contrary, another informant from the conventional civil society pointed out that grassroots organizations adopt strategies of both confrontation and collaboration in their interactions with the government, and that their confrontational strategies mark the biggest difference between themselves and Janaagraha. The differences between the functioning of Janaagraha vis-à-vis other NGOs/CSOs, in terms of approaches/strategies, as well as in its language and priorities, are particularly stark in terms of its interventions with regard to the urban poor.

While grassroots organizations work with poorer communities as a whole and at a personal level, embracing multiple issues that affect the disadvantaged, Janaagraha adopts a more focused – and therefore, a more limited – approach in its interaction with the urban poor. As our informant notes: "in Janaagraha already it is planned . . . only ward works and drainage problem, how the people will participate," indicating that another fundamental difference between other grassroots NGOs and Janaagraha is that while the former "have to listen to their [urban poor] demands, problems and issues, here [Janaagraha] it is [sic] they have to participate for our agendas." This points to the question of demand generation in the work that is being done in largely middle-class organizations such as Janaagraha, that is, whether it is genuine demand from within the area/population or forced/planned demand coming from outside. Furthermore, this raises the issue of priorities of the urban poor versus the priorities of Janaagraha, which appear to be relatively fixed for Janaagraha, rather than those for grassroots NGOs, which are more flexible. This was a challenge for the urban poor dealing with Janaagraha, as their immediate priorities would not be undertaken in meetings.

Deliberately or otherwise, the marginalization of the urban poor in governance debates by Janaagraha and the larger body to which it was affiliated, the BATF, has been a recurring critique of these institutional innovations. The good governance intentions of Janaagraha and the BATF notwithstanding, these forums are critiqued, as mentioned earlier (Benjamin 2005; Ghosh 2005; Nair 2000, 2005), for the creation of a parallel form of governance. One of our informants, a politician and member of the state legislative assembly from one of the constituencies from Bangalore, admits that while his experience in BATF "was good," he disapproves of Janaagraha's strategy of bypassing elected representatives such as himself: "That's the problem, see, there must be a difference between representative and such NGOs, ultimately you are a reflection of the society, and elected member is the replica of the society, and my experience is more than your theoretical knowledge and I have to deal with my people, I can't bypass the needs of my people." He is also critical of the BATF for having been "too fast," "biased," and for "ignoring the poor," and attributes the subsequent trust deficit to the lack of coordination between the task-force and elected representatives, despite their similarity of purpose. Pointing out that "there was absolutely no opportunity [for elected representative to influence the BATF agenda]; it was more of an executive corporate," he stressed that the role of IT and elite groups should be restricted to an advisory, and not policymaking, role in city governance.

Transnational Professionals and the Changing Face of Civil Society

The role of transnational professionals in governance, then, is a disputed one: while elected representatives attest to the "private agendas" that the BATF policymaking process attempted to be pushed forth, the members of the new techno-class defend their social role as historical and inevitable. Our informant from the former ranks of the BATF highlighted the integrative role of the taskforce, and noting that one of its major successes was that it gradually achieved some sort of continuity in governance, which "has never happened in the history of governance [in Bangalore]," and that the involvement of professionals in governance resulted in a scientific basis for BATF activities, based on meticulously designed opinion polls and prior research. He also disagreed with criticisms that the BATF overrode the democratic decision-making process, arguing that firstly, they derived their authority and legitimacy directly from the (then) chief minister (S.M. Krishna), and secondly, that their processes involved efficiency gains. While the notion of efficiency gains is reflective of the priorities of corporate governance, he insists that their role (as professionals in the BATF) was an advisory one, and that the supremacy of the system, in its approval of their plans, remained intact.

The resulting effort was "City Connect," a programme based on the core belief that "corporate India needs to come to the table and play a positive collaborative role in urban India." With focus on road and transport issues, the objective of City Connect is not just a fully formed public transportation system, but a transformation in "the entire quality of life" in cities. He is also keen to avoid an acrimonious relationship with the government, and to make it a mutually beneficial "partnership":

> I am saying that there is a business interest to make this happen, so we came up with City Connect, but the City Connect platform is an inclusive platform by design, it brings to place NGOs, industry associations, and welfare association. We put this platform together and worked with the government and jointly identified projects, some are fast track, quick kind of projects, some are reform projects which will take a longer time; we will enable this. And for this to work, it is a partnership thing, and the first thing is that I will not get into a blame game with the government, this is about collaborating and working with the government and not to blame."

Thus it can be clearly seen that there is increasing evidence of linkages between NGOs and the IT sector. The activists of the traditional civil society point out a change in civic activism in Bangalore (in terms of its character, language, etc): "Several times I have visited Bangalore and I found that there are new social movements coming up basically initiated by IT professionals, I wanted to see how they have impacted." In this case, the term "professional" is clearly used to refer to those in the IT (or a related knowledge-intensive) industry. This is corroborated by Dasgupta (2008), who notes the network established between the IT industry and some NGOs in Bangalore, both of which are overwhelmingly middle class in their composition. Referred to as "the third force" by Heitzman (2004), these NGOs now work in tandem with IT entrepreneurs to reform governance and renew citizenship. Citing the example of the partnership between IT major Infosys and Janaagraha, Dasgupta (2008) points out that in the instance of the IT entrepreneurs and the middle-class NGO leadership the notions of experts (Horrocks 2009) and expertise are delinked.

Thus, while Janaagraha (as representative of the new techno-class in Bangalore) is often lauded for its innovativeness and its commitment to participatory urban governance, it has also been at the receiving end of a constant stream of criticism for its (predominantly middle- and upper-middle-class) composition (resulting in allegations of promoting an institutionalized form of middle-class activism to the detriment of the poor, as well as strident critiques of its "elitist" nature); motives (taking over political and economic decision-making); procedures (planning strategies that appear to disadvantage poorer groups); and linkages with government and big businesses that have resulted in what critics call a "parallel process of governance," particularly an IT–NGO nexus in the city's governance (see Benjamin 2005; Dasgupta 2008; Ghosh 2005; Nair 2005).

Janaagraha's active efforts to engage the discourses on the social space in Bangalore are reflected in its numerous references to *shaping the city*. It is in its efforts to "shape" the city, its demands focused on collective consumption, and in its political mobilization in relationship to the state, particularly local government, that I refer to Janaagraha as an urban social movement (USM). Castells (1983: 305) defines USMs as "urban-oriented mobilizations that influence structural social change and transform the urban meanings." In his development of this definition, Castells had in mind struggles oriented around the following categories: improved collective consumption, defense of cultural-territorial identity, and local government as a target for political mobilization, reflecting the atmosphere of social change of the 1960s and 1970s (Mayer 2006). In analyzing the spatiality of Janaagraha's activities, I refer to several of their publications, wherein the ward works campaigns, for example, are described as harnessing the energy of citizens, as "the most permanent stakeholders in building the shape and character of their city, as well as in determining the quality-of-life it provides" (Clay 2004: 3). The spatial component of these campaigns is evident at both a macro- and micro-level. At the micro-level, each ward was broken down into smaller, recognizable areas or neighborhoods and participants identified problems in the area of a ward that they resided in, allowing them to "connect" more easily to a *familiar space*, rather than the entire ward, at least at the initial stage of issue identification (Clay 2004: 19).

Conclusions and Discussions

Spivak (2000: 11) has argued that electronic capitalism enables the most successful to secede from the rest of the society: "This secessionist culture or subject of the virtual mega city is not only diversified in the usual race-class way alone, but also capital-fractured in agency – between active and passive, or, if you like, 'control' and its antonym, although that is already too crude when the movement is electronic." Members of the secessionist culture will have excellent links in India, will be often traveling to India and are "free to be globally mobile in skills, with corresponding aspirations." They would live in India but would earn a salary in US dollars and would travel abroad incessantly. According to Spivak (2000: 11), "If such persons seem to live only virtually in the real space called Bangalore, the words 'real' and 'virtual' belong to an earlier semiotic."

The same social class in India has been positively described as "New Barbarians," following Nietzsche. Citing Nietzsche (1968), Angell and Ezer (2006: 165) point to the emergence of new social forces, as "from the margins, previously unnoticed, arises a group of ruthless, pragmatic, and amoral opportunists that will overturn the current table of values ... to exploit those around them." But they are quick to highlight the fact that "exploitation" does not mean in this context "a corrupt or imperfect or primitive society: it pertains to the *essence* of the living thing as a fundamental organic function, it is a consequence of the intrinsic will to power which is precisely the will of life" (Nietzsche 1990: 194, cited in Angell and Ezer 2006: 165).

Proposing that a "New Barbarian" spirit is alive in India, Angell and Ezer (2006: 170) argue: "In the literature on contemporary society – particularly from Indian scholars – a major theme emerges: that of a rising 'middle class.'" This middle class is characterized as hardworking and fiercely patriotic, yet self-centered. Its members show little concern for the poor and take advantage of opportunities that the "flexible" political system affords them. Angell and Ezer (2006: 170) differ with these writers and argue that Indian scholars "exhort the middle class to change their ways and adopt a more Judeo-Christian morality." In contrast, Angell and Ezer "stand with Nietzsche and celebrate the rising Indian middle class ... for the nonjudgmental, these New Barbarians are profoundly Nietzschean, and worthy of admiration" (p. 70). In other words, the practical patriotism of the transnational techno-class has to be celebrated.

One important aspect missing in these analytics is an assessment of the increasing visibility of these professional and cultural intermediaries in the civil and political societies in India. The "secessionists" and the "new barbarians" in urban India are increasingly participating in social action, turning themselves effectively into an agency of change, altering the terms and substance of relationship between market, state, and civil society by rearticulating their self representation and not infrequently suggesting that their civil and political initiatives are in fact "people's" movements.

The notion of public space and spatiality as proposed by Lefebvre (1991) and Foucault (1986, originally published 1967) in particular can be usefully applied to examine the "I Believe in Bangalore" campaign, and its implications for an (imaginary) transnational middle-class politics in Bangalore. The revolutionary notion of space as more than just a physical or mental construct is put forth by Lefebvre where he asserts that "*(Social) space is a (social) product*" (1991: 26, emphasis in original). The reading of space as consisting of the lived space of social practice is suggested by Lefebvre's threefold understanding of spatiality, his "conceptual triad" (1991: 33). Lefebvre's attempt to define the perceived realm of physical space as produced and reproduced through spatial practices is based on the notion that "[s]paces are labored and played into existence" (Saco 2002: 5). Lefebvre cites representations of space as the dominant space in any society, being

> the coherent and totalizing scientific ideologies of space (blueprints) propounded by urbanists, architects, planners, and social engineers and instantiated in the layout of cities, buildings, streets, bridges, factories, and even so-called private suburban domiciles. It is for this reason that Lefebvre associates the representations of space with the producers of space. He locates the users of space within the realm of less coherent spaces of representation. (Saco 2002: 6)

Saco also adds that because these lived spaces are, in part, products of hegemonic representations of space, Lefebvre (1991: 39) labels these as "dominated – and hence passively experienced." Despite the primacy of ideological effects, Lefebvre argues (1991: 30) for the role of creative appropriations in a lived space, suggesting that these are spaces "which the imagination seeks to change and appropriate." In other words, "spaces of representation may include quasi-surreal spaces where the point is not so much to give meaningful order, but rather to disrupt, postpone, and even overturn meaning" (Saco 2002: 6), making lived spaces potential sites of resistance.

When Foucault (1986) introduced the term *heterotopia* in a lecture for architects, he was referring to various (actual) institutions and places that interrupt the apparent continuity and normality of ordinary everyday space – that is, "heterotopias" as literally "other places" (Dehaene and De Cauter 2008). However, at other times, he also referred to heterotopias as both a real and an imagined or constructed space (Tan 2009). Saco (2002: 16) suggests that we make sense of this apparent contradiction between imaginary and actual sites of heterotopias by simply dealing with them as different kinds of sites: one set predominantly linguistic (composed of words) and the other set predominantly non-linguistic (composed of things). The intertwining meanings of an aggressive advertising campaign and the activities of an urban social movement in Bangalore encapsulate the way in which a new techno-class with transnational links has come to influence the imagination of spatial ordering in a Third World mega-city.

Social movements for better urban governance, such as Janaagraha, are typical examples of such involvement. Their demands ranged from "Singaporianization" of Bangalore to radical pro-globalization policy shifts. Such civic associations, "virtual" as well as "real" interest groups, and communities of action, discourse and reproduction of heterotopias, with active involvement from the techno-class, that have emerged in the mega-urban spaces in India do not appear to be transient phenomena. Apparently, they are here to stay. Their actions range from passive "net presence" to active real-life confrontation with the state and its agencies. In the Indian and particularly in the urban context, these social classes have begun to exert an unprecedented political authority influencing the social and economic policies of both local and provincial governments. The conflict between the new techno-class and old civil and civic society actors are manifested in a spectrum of confrontations ranging from public policy controversies to intense land struggles. The outcomes of these conflicts will have an impact on the way in which the practical patriotism of the new techno-class will evolve in future.

Acknowledgments

The author wishes to thank Milagros Rivera Sánchez, and Shobha Vadrevu for useful suggestions on a previous draft. Thanks are also due to Anuradha Rao for critical inputs, discussions and research assistance.

Notes

1   Fernandes (2000a), however, terms the rise of this "new" middle class as an "invention," pointing out that the "newness" involves a discursive production of a new image of the middle class rather than the entry of a new social group into this class, and rests on the invention of the new middle class as the social group which is able to negotiate India's new relationship with the global economy in both cultural (a new cultural standard based on consumption) and economic terms.

2   The campaign concludes with the slogans "Thank you, Bangalore for a stupendous response!" and "Great news. *DNA* now in my Bangalore" emphasizing that the readers of the publication have accepted the new transnational vision of Bangalore constructed by the ad campaign, an assumption that residents have internalized this constructed image of Bangalore.

3   In this section I have relied on information provided by a wide group of informants during several interviews conducted during the fieldwork period 2008–2009. They included NGO activists, bureaucrats, politicians, journalists, and IT professionals. I interviewed a total of 42 informants.

References

Angell, I.O. and Ezer, J. 2006. "New barbarians at the gate: the new spirit emerging in India." *Information Society*, 22(3):165–176.

and spirit in discussing the issues presented here and beyond. Any shortfalls remain solely my own responsibility. All French translations are by the author.

Notes

1   The election for the post of the mayor is done by presenting the team of the mayor, whose members often appear on election posters. During the 2008 municipality elections, candidates from all parties had Armenians on their lists. While the ruling UMP candidate was himself Armenian, the majority of Armenians voted for the current mayor René Rouquet, who has been in office since 1988.

2   All names have been changed to protect the identity of my interlocutors.

3   Various studies give a much lower number: Tölölyan (2001) estimates that there are 250,000 Armenians in France, and Andesian and Hovanessian (1998: 61) estimate 300,000. The Armenians diaspora website however gives the higher estimate of 450,000 (http://www.armeniadiaspora.com/population.html, accessed February 28, 2013).

4   The last Armenian kingdom in Cilicia fell in 1375, and the last king was exiled in Paris in 1393.

5   I am indebted to Melissa Bilal for bringing this point to my attention in the context of Armenian diaspora.

6   The reception of migrants and refugees also continued until the 1970s when France welcomed one immigrant for every 1,000 inhabitants, a rate that is only comparable to the United States. The Federal Republic of Germany hosted 0.05 per 1,000, while Britain and Sweden had 0.03 per 1,000 each. The French state, however, has always imposed its law on newcomers (Noiriel 1996: 258–259).

7   Similarly, the Armenian stateless refugees in Greece were regarded as a threat and were not granted Greek citizenship until 1968. Such negative reception of the refugees in Greece was also shared by the Rum-Orthodox refugees who arrived in Greece from Anatolia following the exchange of population stipulated by the Lausanne Treaty (Schwalgin 2004: 79–80; cf Hirschon 1998).

8   This Convention gave the legal definition to the crime of genocide as defined by the lawyer Raphael Lemkin, who supported his definition by citing the mass annihilation of Ottoman Armenians in 1915 as a prime example (Auron 2004: 9).

9   This predicament was not unique to Ottoman Armenians. The aftermath of World War I witnessed the disintegration of the three multi-ethnic empires: the Romanov, the Hapsburg, and the Ottoman. This has turned millions into minorities, refugees, internally displaced persons, and subjected many to various forms of sociopolitical demographic engineering (Mazower 1998: 41–75). In the 1920s, the number of refugees in Europe has been estimated as 9.5 million (Mandel 2003: 19). For a discussion of the refugee problem after the demise of the Ottoman empire, see Loizos (1999).

10   The TBMM (Türkiye Büyük Millet Meclisi) was the de facto ruler of the Ottoman empire starting on April 23, 1920, and later became the Turkish parliament when the Republic of Turkey was established in 1923.

11   In the early Republic period the names of those cities were modified by adding suffixes to reflect their purportedly heroic role in the Turkish war of independence: they became *Gazi*antep, *Kahraman*maraş, and *Şanlı*urfa – *Gazi* meaning "conqueror," *Kahraman* "heroic," and *Şanlı* "glorious."

12   These are: Law of April 20, 1922 with regards to the confiscation of property of the Armenians who left the Cilicia region; Law of April 25, 1923 which extends the confiscation to all Armenians whatever the motives or date of their departure from Anatolia; the Law of September 1923, of which Article 2 prohibits the return of Armenians to Cilicia and the eastern provinces of Anatolia. Furthermore, upon establishing the Republic of Turkey, the citizenship law did not allow those who were outside of Turkey to return and become citizens of the republic. For a detailed discussion on the abandoned and confiscated Armenian property in Anatolia, see Onaran (2010) and Üngör and Polatel (2011).

13   In his study on the Armenians of Syria and Lebanon, Migliorino (2008) contextualizes their post-genocide resettlement in the two states, where the French Mandate authorities granted them various degree of cultural autonomy in the 1920s. Such autonomy facilitated the "(re)construction of a new, post-Genocide Armenian world in the Levant," through the constitution that included them in the parliamentary system in both countries. Capitalizing on such autonomy, the refugees established institutions (political parties, associations, schools, media, etc.) that enabled both the preservation and development of Armenian culture in both states (Migliorino 2008: chapter 2).

14   "Geocultural landscape" is Ella Shohat's description of the predicament of Arab Jews *(Mizrahim)* who migrated to Israel, especially Iraqi Jews (2006: 204). For a detailed treatment of *denativization* as an analytical concept that explains the overall Ottoman Armenian experience, see Chapter 1 of Al-Rustom (2013).

15   Marseilles and Paris had pre-genocide Armenian merchants and intellectuals, who constituted the population of the "colonies." In 1910 their number in France was around 2,000 (Andesian and Hovanessian 1998: 66). The word diaspora and its Armenian equivalent *spurk* share the same Indo-European root *spr* from which words such as spore, sperm, spread, and disperse are also derived (Tölölyan 1996: 10).

16   In countries where pluralism is tolerated, such as the United States, or part of the state structure, such as Syria and Lebanon, diasporas do not pose a perceived threat as is the case with countries that do not allow extra-national collectivities. Unlike France, Armenians in the United States arrived in a society that is tolerant of ethnic subcommunities and religious pluralism (Bakalian 2011: 393–94), and those in Lebanon and Syria were encouraged to maintain their cultural distinctiveness (Migliorino 2008).

17   The need to find other means of gaining power became especially important when the project of establishing an Armenian state in Anatolia failed during the Lausanne conference, and the Republic of Armenia became a Soviet republic, see Al-Rustom (2013).

18   This perspective of balancing integration and assimilation in the host society is shared in other Armenian diaspora communities. For example at the Armenian Assembly National Conference in 2004, the president of pan-diaspora Armenian General Benevolent Union said the following about Armenian hyphenated identity: "Being Armenian–American does not mean that they are 50% Armenian and 50% American. No – it means that they are 100% Americans, who feel a strong and full commitment to their Armenian identity" (quoted in Kasbarian 2009: 87).

19   In discussing this shift, Tölölyan (2001) makes a distinction between the *exilic,* the "ethnic" identity of the first generation of refugees and the *diasporic,* the identity that evolved as later generations forged new identities and settled permanently in new places. Similarly, Bakalian (2011: 393–394) differentiates between "traditional Armenianness" and "symbolic Armenianness." The former refers to those born in the Middle East and

Soviet bloc who learned the Armenian language and were raised in an Armenian (sub) culture in their home societies. The latter, on the other hand, is the "Armenianness" of those born in the diaspora (such as the United States, the focus of Bakalian's study) where the symbolic identity is a matter of choice and does not necessarily mean that they know the language or were raised in an Armenian milieu.

20 Similarly, to honor 26,000 Algerian colonial subjects who died for France during World War I, a mosque in Paris was constructed (Silverstein 2004: 131).

21 Andesian and Hovanessian (1998: 60–61) say that Armenians are considered the most integrated foreign community in French social life. See also the examples discussed in Mandel's (2003) study and Hovanessian (1995) on the settlement of the first Armenian refugees in France.

22 A list of these languages is available on http://www.dglf.culture.gouv.fr/lgfrance/lgfrance_presentation.htm, accessed February 28, 2013.

23 See Silverstein's (2004: ch. 2) ethnography on the Berber/Arab divide and the degree of their different abilities to assimilate into French culture as perceived by the French political elites and policymakers.

24 Mitterrand took other positive measures towards migrants, including the legalizing of illegal immigrants, and the supporting of associations with the aim of strengthening and diversifying civil society in France (Silverstein 2004: 132, 240).

References

Al-Rustom, H.A. 2013. "Anatolian fragments: Armenians between Turkey and France." PhD thesis, Department of Anthropology, London School of Economics.

Amit, V. 2002. "Armenian and other diasporas: Trying to reconcile the irreconcilable." In N. Rapport (ed.) *British Subjects: An Anthropology of Britain*, pp. 263–280. Oxford: Berg.

Ananian, S. 2008. *30 Ans Ecole Bilingue Saint Mesrop, Alfortville 1978–2008*. Alfortville: Collection Alfortville-Mémoires.

Andesian, S. and Hovanessian, M. 1998. "L'arménien: Langue rescapée d'un génocide." *Vingt-Cinq Communautés Linguistique de la France*, Volume 2: *Les langues immigrées*. Paris: L'Harmattan.

Assemblée Nationale.1998. "'Reconnaissance du Génocide Arménien.' Séance du 29 Mai." *Journal Officiel de la République Française*, Paris.

Auron, Y. 2004. *The Banality of Denial*. Piscataway, NJ: Transaction Publishers.

Bakalian, A. 2011. *American Armenians: From Being to Feeling Armenian*. Piscataway, NJ: Transaction Publishers.

Björklund, U. 1993. "Armenia remembered and remade: Evolving issues in a diaspora." *Ethnos*, 85(3/4): 335–360.

Bourdieu, P. 2004. "Preface," trans. D. Macey. In A. Sayad, *The Suffering of the Immigrant*. Cambridge: Polity Press. (First published 1999.)

Bowen, J.R. 2007. *Why The French Don't Like Headscarves: Islam, the State, and Public Space*. Princeton: Princeton University Press.

Das, V. 1997. *Critical Events: An Anthropological Perspective on Contemporary India*. Oxford: Oxford University Press.

Feydit, F. 1965. "Un tragique cinquantenaire: Le massacre des arméniens en Turquie." *Le Monde* (Paris), April 23.

Gilroy, P. 1993. *The Black Atlantic: Modernity and Double Consciousness*. London: Verso.

Government of France 1999. "List of declarations made with respect to treaty No. 148," at http://conventions.coe.int/treaty/Commun/ListeDeclarations.asp?NT=148&CM=1&DF=&CL=ENG&VL=1, accessed February 26, 2013.

Hirschon, R. 1998. *Heirs of the Greek Catastrophe: The Social Life of Asia Minor Refugees in Piraeus*. New York: Berghahn Books.

Hovanessian, M. 1995. *Les Arméniens et leurs territoires*. Paris: Autrement.

Kasbarian, S. 2009. "Whose Space, Whose Interests? Clashes within Armenian Diasporic Civil Society." *Armenian Review* 51(1–4): 81–109.

Kastoryano, R. 2002. *Negotiating Identities: States and Immigrants in France and Germany*. Princeton: Princeton University Press.

Libaridian, G. 1981. "The changing self-image of the Armenian in the Ottoman empire: Rayahs and revolutionaries." In R.G. Hovannisian (ed.) *The Image of the Armenian in History and Literature*, pp. 155–170. Los Angeles: Undena Press.

Loizos, P. 1999. "Ottoman half-lives: Long-term perspectives on particular forced migrations." *Journal of Refugee Studies*, 12(3): 237–263.

Mandel, M. 2003. *In The Aftermath of Genocide: Armenians and Jews in Twentieth-Century France*. Durham, NC: Duke University Press.

Marashlian, L. 1999. "Finishing the Genocide: Cleansing Turkey of Armenian survivors, 1920–1923." In R.G. Hovannisian (ed.) *Remembrance and Denial: The Case of the Armenian Genocide*, pp. 113–145. Detroit: Wayne State University Press.

Mazower, M. 1998. *Dark Continent: Europe's Twentieth Century*. New York: Vintage.

Migliorino, N. 2008. *(Re)constructing Armenia in Lebanon and Syria: Ethno-Cultural Diversity and the State in the Aftermath of a Refugee Crisis*. New York: Berghahn Books.

Noiriel, G. 1996. *The French Melting Pot: Immigration, Citizenship, and National Identity*. Minneapolis: University of Minnesota Press.

Onaran, N. 2010. *Emval-i Metruke Olayı: Osmanlı'da ve Cumhuriyette Ermeni ve Rum Mallarının Türkleştirilmesi*. Istanbul: Belge Yayınları.

Panossian, R. 2006. *The Armenians: From Kings and Priests to Merchants and Commissars*. New York: Columbia University Press.

Pattie, S.P. 1997. *Faith in History: Armenians Rebuilding Community*. Washington, DC: Smithsonian Institution Press.

Schwalgin, S. 2004. "Why locality matters: Diaspora consciousness and sedentariness in the Armenian diaspora in Greece." In W. Kokot, K. Tölölyan, and C. Alfonso (eds) *Diaspora, Identity, and Religion: New Directions in Theory and Research*, pp. 72–92. Abingdon: Routledge.

Shohat, E. 2006. *Taboo Memories, Diasporic Voices*. Durham, NC: Duke University Press.

Silverstein, P. 2004. *Algeria in France: Transpolitics, Race, and Nation*. Bloomington: Indiana University Press.

Suny, R.G. 1993. *Looking Toward Ararat: Armenia in Modern History*. Bloomington: Indiana University Press.

Ter-Minassian, A. 1988. "Les Arméniens de France." *Les Temps Modernes*, 504–506, July–September: 189–234.

Ter-Minassian, A. 1994. "Les Arménien de Paris depuis 1945." In A. Marès and P. Miza (eds) *Le Paris des étrangers depuis 1945*, pp. 205–240. Paris: Sorbonne.

Ternon, Y. 1983. *La cause arménienne*. Paris: Seuil.

Tölölyan, K. 1991. "Exile Governments in the Armenian Polity." In Y. Shain (ed.) *Governments-In-Exile in Contemporary World Politics*, pp. 166–187. London: Routledge.

Tölölyan, K. 1996. "Rethinking *diaspora(s)*: Stateless power in the transnational moment." *Diaspora* 5(1): 3–36.

Tölölyan, K. 2001. "Elites and institutions in the Armenian transnation." *Diaspora*, 9(1): 107–136.

Üngör, U.Ü. and Polatel, M. 2011. *Confiscation and Colonization: The Young Turk Seizure of Armenian Property*. London: Continuum.

Weber, E. 1976. *Peasants into Frenchmen: The Modernization of Rural France, 1880–1914*. Stanford: Stanford University Press.

Chapter 29

The Muslim Brotherhood and the Transnationalism of Islam

Meena Sharify-Funk and Ali Albarghouthi

Introduction

What is transnational Islam? Is it new? Is it hostile, or friendly? In a post-9/11 environment of heightened anxiety about all things Islamic, the first two questions are almost inseparably intertwined with the third. For some, the idea of transnational or global Islam evokes deepseated images of a perennially threatening Islamic Other that has once again come knocking on Western gates, resurgent today in a globalization of terrorism and violence. For others, adding the word "transnational" to Islam signifies not so much an amplification of radicalism or militancy as an opportunity for "reformist" forces to finally unseat "traditional" orthodoxies. In both cases efforts to characterize transnational Islam are driven less by careful analysis than by prevailing fears and wishes, and preconceptions.

What is missing from popular treatment of transnational Islam is recognition that the complexity of the transnational supports the spread of multiple, even opposite, interpretations of Islam. Far from being merely an enabling force for purveyors of violence or a revolutionizing conduit for progressive religious ideas, contemporary transnationalism is providing fresh means of expression for a full spectrum of Islamic ideas and subcultures. Furthermore, while contemporary media are indeed having an impact on the manner in which religious ideas are articulated, transnationalism itself is not new to the Islamic experience, and is rather a deeply embedded dimension of communal life that is taking on new meanings in the present context. As the examples in this chapter seek to illustrate, the transnational gives no inherent advantage to extremism or reformism, and can bolster "traditional" authority as well as new forms of religious interpretation and leadership.

A Companion to Diaspora and Transnationalism, First Edition.
Edited by Ato Quayson and Girish Daswani.
© 2013 Blackwell Publishing Ltd. Published 2013 by Blackwell Publishing Ltd.

In Islam, the transnational is simultaneously old and new. As Oliver Roy explains (2006: 109), "Muslims throughout history have experienced forms of globalization, through travel, pilgrimage or the widespread use of Arabic and of a common teaching curriculum." At the same time, modern trends are indeed having an impact on religious conversations and movements, creating opportunities for multiple currents of belief and opinion to reconstitute themselves within the "distant proximities" (Rosenau 2003) of contemporary life. While roots of the transnational can be found deep in Islamic experience, examination of diverse cases reveals that ideas and structures of the past can be replicated or reconfigured in surprising ways as contemporary movements engage or contest new trends in social, political, and cultural life.

After a brief overview of ways in which contemporary scholars are integrating consideration of the transnational into their analyses of Islamic culture and thought, this chapter examines forms of transnationalism in the contemporary Muslim religious experience that highlight ways in which voices of orthodoxy are being rearticulated, manifesting both continuity and discontinuity with traditional forms of religious transnationalism. Particular attention will be given to a scholar-activist, Yusuf al-Qaradawi, whose fame and influence have been greatly augmented by satellite television, as well as to Egyptian televangelist Amr Khalid and to the Muslim Brotherhood.

Renegotiating the Sacred: Impact of Contemporary Transnationalism

Like other world religions, Islam has been and continues to be defined by the transcultural, transnational, and the global. In the last ten years or so, more scholars of Islam have attempted to understand and describe the transnational or transcultural nature of Muslim public experience in the twentieth and twenty-first centuries. This emerging literature is ushering in new ways to imagine Muslims (both men and women) and Muslim public spheres (from sub-Ummahs or "local imaginaries" to the larger global Ummah) as being constituted in variety of "trans"-phenomenal negotiations. Whether it is the space of relations amongst nations ("the transnational"), or the space amongst cultures ("the transcultural"), or the space amongst different localities ("the translocal"), scholars of Islam are emphasizing the processes of "trans" identity or, in other words, of living in a pluralistic world shaped by direct as well as mediated encounters with multiple contexts of meaning.

For these scholars, the localities of the world cannot be adequately represented by a two-dimensional map with definitive borders and boundaries; rather their character would be better conveyed by a multidimensional map of conglomerated, fluid, intercontextual realities, in which different localized zones of daily life overlap and interpenetrate with others. In such a world, traditional zones of experience such as the "Islamic" or "Western" milieus are no longer monolithic or isolated realities, but rather composites of religious, cultural, and political as well as ethnic contexts. These contexts, which form individual identities, are multiple and overlapping.

They are constantly involved in dynamic processes of relationship and conversation – conversations which reflect the inescapable complexity of the contemporary world that all Muslims (including the laity, academicians, and clergy, as well as political figures) encounter. These conversations do not inevitably lead to harmony or agreement, but they do have a profound effect on identity, encouraging individuals to reimagine Self and Other in ways that support either a solipsistic or a dialogical orientation.

The transnational has become not only an "intensification of the "public space" (Mandaville 2003) but also a form of "public space" that enables Muslims to transcend isolation and derive inspiration for actions in their own local realities. It is beyond the nation (not to mention the family and the tribe) and yet is bounded to the same extent as the internet: it is an open network that is constituted by those who actively engage in dialogue and participate. Inherent in transnationality is the active exploration of new frontiers and a tendency to dwell in "the space in between" the states that define geopolitical boundaries, and thereby to inhabit interstatial space. For some, transnational engagement provides a means of escaping local marginalization, to become part of a parallel conversation that is "distanced" from mainstream cultural expression and yet also empowered by the creation of stronger and more intensely communicative bonds across space.

Mandaville (2003: 276) defines the transnational as referring to "a wider range of social formations and transactions which are structured across the borders and spaces of nations, but which do not necessarily entail a primary role for sovereign governments." Contemporary transnationalism involves increasing movement of people and ideas across borders due to (1) changes in the labor markets and ease of travel; (2) the emergence of global cities which rise above the national to play a key role in a global economy; and (3) the development of new information and communication technologies and new media that enable the exchange of ideas across borders (Mandaville 2007). These trends have significant ramifications for religions and religious identities. In many respects current communication technologies and experiences of mass migration are amplifying forms of identity and experience that have long been encouraged by world religions such as Islam, which have always been shaped by conversations that encourage identification with a larger "we" transcending locality, and which are also constituted by conversations – amicable as well as dissonant – with those who define themselves as members of another religious or ideological community. At the same time, these technologies and experiences of migration are also introducing new experiences, concepts, and cultural forms into religious discourse, increasing the pluralism of popular religious thinking and inducing renegotiations of sacred meaning.

The Transnational in Traditional Islam

While contemporary transnationalism has been accompanied by accelerated cultural change and profound contestation over what constitutes "authentic" Islam, there are grounds for claiming that a "transnational" ideal has been present within Islam from the beginning. Contrary to the notion that Islam is somehow a religion "of the desert," Islam's beginnings as a religious movement can be traced to the complex social environments of Mecca and Medina – important trading cities of Western Arabia in which diverse tribes came into contact with one another and from which they engaged the larger world. A central theme of the Qur'an and the Hadith literature is that Muslims should constitute a trans-tribal and trans-racial community – a community within which the presence and legitimacy of other religious communities is acknowledged and accommodated.

The prophet of Islam, Muhammad, started his mission and received his first revelation of the sacred book of Islam, the Qur'an, in the city of Mecca. This was the center of Arabia. Nestled between its hills lay the *Kaba*, the sacred mosque, and the Arabs believed the entire city of Mecca to be a sacred sanctuary in the midst of the lawlessness of many parts of the Arabian Peninsula. Mecca, therefore, was the epicenter of religious activity and a hub of trade and culture. This cosmopolitan center of Arabia was destined to be the birthplace of the new transnational religion, which would soon elevate the city to global prominence as a pilgrimage destination (Hajj, see below).

The Qur'an framed its message in universal language directed to all humanity: "Say: O people I am the messenger of God to all of you" (7:158). It sought to replace the older order of tribal affiliation and the concomitant blood feuds with a religious bond that transcends lineages and stresses religious merit. Tribalism and even Arabo-centrism – "an Arab is no better than a non-Arab except if more pious," Muhammad is reported to have said – gave way to a new religious construction: the *ummah*. This new community of believers was supposed to de-emphasize the natural differences of color and blood, even space and time, and convene based on religious loyalty and spiritual inclinations. Differences, except for religious ones, should be shed for the sake of all believers becoming one: "This *ummah* [community] of yours is one and I am your Lord so be mindful of me" (23:52). This new social realignment, despite practical complications, helped create a society that was open – practically at times and only ideally at others – to other races and cultures.

When the new Muslim community had to flee Mecca for Medina, the move, dubbed *hijrah* or migration, was immortalized as the archetypal sacrificial movement in search of purity and renewal. *Hijrah* represented a physical and symbolic "shift in the very basis of social affiliation and polity" (Mandaville 2007: 208). From the time it transformed the persecuted Muslim minority in Mecca into a community in charge of its own affairs in Medina, *hijrah* entered the Muslim vocabulary as both a physical and a figurative edifying movement. In Medina, Islam became established as the basis for a new polity, which would eventually become a truly transnational, multiracial, and multicultural religious community bound together by shared norms, beliefs, practices, and rites of migration.

Practices that have for centuries bound Muslims together across great distances are taking on new significance in the modern transnational context. Ramadan, for

example, has increasingly transcended mere localized observance, becoming a powerful bonding experience for Muslims worldwide. Announcements of the beginning
of Ramadan and its religious rituals are transmitted almost instantaneously across
the globe. One could be living in Rio de Janeiro and yet follow the prayers from
Mecca, or stay in Barcelona and watch the latest religious programming from Yusuf
al-Qaradawi or Amr Khaled (see below). And if a Muslim were to land in a different country during this month, he or she could step into a mosque and be
immediately drawn into the "spirit" of Ramadan: enhanced spirituality and socialization. *Salah*, the five daily prayers, provide similar familiarity and connection
across space.

From the beginning, the obligation to perform *Hajj* (pilgrimage to Mecca) elevated travel to a duty in the new faith, with profound consequences for the transmission of religious ideas and the blending of Muslim peoples. As one of the five
pillars incumbent upon every able-bodied Muslim, *Hajj* has for centuries brought
Muslims together from the far corners of the earth to assemble in Mecca on a yearly
basis, and interact with a multitude of languages and cultures they had not experienced before. In the modern context this experience has been intensified, with air
travel making what was once an arduous and lengthy trek accessible to far more
individuals. While this has created enormous logistical and crowd-management
challenges for civil authorities, the essential character of the *Hajj* experience remains
the same. Malcolm X's famous account of his own multiracial *Hajj* experience is
representative of the impact that pilgrimage-based encounters have long had on
Muslim self-understandings of faith and community.

The long and sometimes dangerous premodern *Hajj* journey produced travel
narratives that prefigured the renowned *rihlah* (travel) narratives of ibn Jubayr and
ibn Battutah (Gosch and Stearns 2008), and provided Muslims with an opportunity
not just to fulfill a concrete religious obligation but also to visit new destinations
and enhance religious knowledge through encounters with scholars. Travel provided
a means to advance learning and preserve knowledge, meritorious even if it were
to take one to the ends of the earth. A popular *hadith* (saying) of Muhammad
enjoins believers to "seek knowledge even if it be in China," and historically many
Muslim sojourners used pilgrimage as a vehicle for their scholarly endeavors. Indeed,
the many volumes of non-Qur'anic sayings attributed to Muhammad were profoundly expedited by pilgrimage across great distances: *hadith* collection and compilation was achieved mostly through the crisscrossed travels of the *ulama* between
the metropolises of Baghdad, Damascus, Cairo, Cordoba, and Samarkand. These
cities became in effect world cities, not only in the economic sense, but also in the
field of ideas and the dissemination of knowledge.

The sojourns of scholars made *hadith* collection a transnational affair, one that
enshrined travel and pushed it to the frontiers. Contemporary *hadith* scholar
Mohammad Akram Nadwi's groundbreaking encyclopedia (over 40 volumes long)
documents more than 8,000 women scholars of *hadith* (*muhaddithat*) dating back
over 1,400 years. Karimah bint Ahmad ibn Muhammad ibn Hatim al-Marwazziyah
was the most famous *muhaddithah* to teach in Mecca, where many people, including

several prestigious imams, would travel from afar to hear her *hadith* narrations. She traveled extensively from her home in Kushmihan in the pursuit of knowledge, to Isfahan, Jerusalem, and then Mecca, where she eventually settled. She strictly adhered to the practice of maintaining authenticity of texts by insisting they be compared with the originals, and was thus respected for her accuracy and attention to detail in narration (see Nadwi 2007).

Rites of travel made the *ulama* (religiously learned individuals) of Islam a transnational cognitive and social network that "transcended all ethnic and linguistic divides" (Roy 2006: 109). Relying on the common tongue of Arabic as the currency of religious knowledge, scholars could easily find employment as jurists in lands quite distant from their birthplaces. Drawing legitimacy from the transmission of authoritative religious knowledge, the *ulama* acted as the political check to the power of the caliph and became the guardians of orthodoxy and orthopraxis in communal affairs. They instructed students, received inquiries from, and saw their ideas carried to the far reaches of, the Muslim empire. The spread of the *Maliki* Sunni legal schools to Andalusia and the *Shafii* school to Indonesia happened even though their eponyms never set foot in these areas.

Yusuf al-Qaradawi: The Scholar Activist

Recent generations have seen great changes in the social, political, and intellectual contexts of Muslim religious institutions, creating discontinuities without fundamentally altering the transnational character of Islamic learning and preaching. Dramatic increases in literacy have made religious writings much more readily available to the newly literate masses, creating a broader audience for authoritative teachings while also enabling new modes of content delivery. New technologies from broadcast television and radio to satellite TV and the internet have further impacted the processes of disseminating religious knowledge, providing traditional and revivalist figures with new means of inserting their teachings into contemporary social milieus. Few have been more adroit in this endeavor than Yusuf al-Qaradawi.

Yusuf al-Qaradawi (b. 1926) is an *azhari* scholar through and through. His journey with al-Azhar, the oldest and most prominent Islamic mosque-university in Egypt, started with elementary school and culminated with a PhD in 1973 (see www.qaradawi.net). Donning at all times the garb of *azhari* scholars, Qaradawi has achieved a prominence which cannot be understood without the legitimacy that a thousand-year-old institution gives to him. Yet this is not the sole reason why he stands out. What distinguishes Qaradawi is a preoccupation with the issues of the day and an activism that stretches to institution building. His ability to combine roles that seldom mix makes him a highly effective scholar-activist.

Qaradawi's rise to global stardom came in partnership with the Qatari news channel, al-Jazeera, where he regularly appears on the religious program *al-Shariah wa al-Hayah* (Sharia and Life). Yet his claim to fame and influence precedes and transcends that. Qaradawi enjoys a wide appeal as an author. Responsible for more than 80 publications, his first major publication *al-Halal wa al-Haram fi al-Islam* (The Lawful and the Prohibited in Islam), has gone through 40 editions and was translated into more than 11 languages. It owes its popularity to its accessible language, which made it a favorite among lay Muslims, and to its message of Islamic exceptionalism advanced through interreligious comparisons. This work may have foreshadowed Qaradawi's interest in European and American Muslims, for he wrote it in response to concerns over Muslims adjusting to life, and possibly losing their religion, in the West (Soage 2010). His PhD dissertation on the role of *Zakah* (obligatory religious charity) in solving social ills was among the few dissertations in al-Azhar to deal with contemporary issues, and it launched his career as a consultant on several boards in the budding field of Islamic finance (Graf and Skovgaard-Petersen 2009). Several of his books show him to be one who does not shy away from politics or hot topics. He challenged socialism in Egypt in the 1960s with a series of books under the main title *Hatmiyyat al-Hall al-Islami* (The Necessity of the Islamic Solution), and combated later secularist interpretations with such works as *al-Islam wa al-Almaniyyah: Wajhan li Wajh* (Islam and Secularism: Face to Face), *al-Tatarruf al-Almani fi muwajahat al-Islam* (Fundamentalist Secularism Confronts Islam), and *Shariat al-Islam Salihah li al-Tatbiq fi Kull Zaman wa Makan* (The Shariah of Islam is Suitable for Application at all Times and Places). A look at some of his other publications – *Ghayr al-Muslimin fi al-Mujtama al-Islami* (Non-Muslims in Muslim Society), *al-Islam wa al-Unf* (Islam and Violence), *Nahnu wa al-Gharb* (We and the West), *Awlawiyyat al-Harakah al-Islamiyyah fi al-Marhalah al-Muqbilah* (The Priorities of the Islamic Movement in the Future), *al-Baba wa al-Islam* (The Pope and Islam), and *al-Hukm al-Shari fi Khitan al-Inath* (The Islamic Ruling on Female Circumcision) – underscores the political and social foundations of Qaradawi's traditionalism and his global outlook.

It may come as no surprise to learn that the Muslim Brotherhood, and Hasan al-Banna in particular, had a profound influence on Qaradawi, who has often spoken in glowing terms of Banna and his ideas, and was in fact sentenced to jail repeatedly for his membership in the organization. Qaradawi's move to Qatar signaled a new chapter in his life, for it is from there that his (transnational) institution building and international fame took off. He founded the Islamic studies department in the nascent Qatar University, and soon after established and chaired the College of Shariah and Islamic Studies, as well as the Sunnah and Sirah Research Center at Qatar University, which he heads today. He was also instrumental in founding the European Council for Fatwa and Research (ECFR; see www.e-cfr.org) and the International Union of Muslim Scholars (IUMS; see www.iumsonline.net), and continues to preside over both institutions. The stated goal of the ECFR is to be sensitive to the specific needs of European Muslims; it brings together European Muslim scholars to deliberate on legal issues and consider the special needs and circumstances of Muslim minorities in Europe. The IUMS, on the other hand, is more global in scope. Its aim is to organize Muslim scholars from across the world and harvest the power of institutions in effecting change. It also aspires to be ecumenical, recognizing the sectarian diversity of Muslims by including Shia and Abadi representatives on its board of trustees. As its head, Qaradawi is afforded a global title and connections that allow him to speak on behalf of Muslim religious leadership worldwide.

The turns that Qaradawi's life has taken are atypical of *azhari* religious scholars. His early membership in the Muslim Brotherhood allowed him to benefit from its networks, and his later distance from the organization gave him wider appeal as an independent. Convinced that Islam was under attack, Qaradawi worked tirelessly to push back and present the Islamic alternative. Among the many threats he identifies, he describes globalization as "the imposition of American political, economic, cultural and social supremacy over the rest of the world" (Soage 2010: 23). It is Islam, he argues, that promotes a globalization committed to equality of all humans, because it is not a secular or materialist globalization but an ethical one anchored in its relationship to the divine.

Qaradawi's ascent to regional and even global notoriety has not come without controversy, particularly among progressive and feminist Muslims concerned about his neo-traditional teachings and among those who find his commentary on political affairs (e.g., his firm support for Hamas in the Israeli–Palestinian conflict) provocative and troublesome. Nonetheless, his religious views reflect highly influential currents within contemporary Muslim thought, and are valued by those who find his teachings responsive to their immediate concerns as they confront social change. Qaradawi's relative independence from national religious establishments – commonly viewed as subservient to the state – gives his voice added credibility and resonance.

Amr Khaled: The Contemporary Preacher Superstar

The same technological and social changes that have made Christian televangelism an influential medium in North America have also provided scope for entrepreneurial religious preachers in predominantly Muslim lands such as Egypt. While Qaradawi has played this role in a way that reflects traditional forms of religious authority, some have found ways to fill this newly available media niche without relying on institutional Islamic training or donning traditional Muslim garb. Few have accomplished this more effectively than the Egyptian preacher Amr Khaled.

Like Qaradawi, Khaled is a global phenomenon with a mass following. His web site (www.amrkhaled.net) touts itself as the most popular personal web site in the world, with more than 2 million visitors every month, and his Facebook page has 1.5 million friends. He attracts more viewers than Oprah Winfrey (the comparison itself is telling), and "his videos have racked up 26 m hits on YouTube" (BBC News 2010). *Newsweek* and *Time* magazines have repeatedly chosen him as one of the most influential personalities in the world, and he is "by far the most popular religious preacher in the Arab world" (Esposito and Mogahed 2008: 121). As a featured speaker in the Reviving the Islamic Spirit (RIS) conferences in Canada and the United States, attended by thousands, it is safe to say that his reach now extends far beyond the Arab world.

Khaled's first claim to fame came as a preacher to the upper and middle classes in Egypt, successfully mixing demands for religious piety with a this-worldly ethos that applauds material success. And as his base expanded through record sales and satellite TV shows, Khaled maintained his emphasis on practicality and an Islamic message embracive of modern life. To be a good Muslim for Khaled does not mean that one has to shun art and culture, indeed they have always had their place in Islamic civilization and should be part of any future Muslim renaissance. One can also be fashionable and modest at the same time without any contradiction, and can have fun along the way too. Khaled's concern is with Muslim youth: he uses their language and seems to have tapped into their dilemma. Torn between idealized past and bitter realities, between Islamic authenticity and material attraction, Khaled offers a synthesis and charges the youth with the responsibility of changing their society despite the obstacles. He asks them through his programs and projects to take the initiative and be the vanguard of social change, to go out and find something to do. Khaled adopts the language and problems of young people and injects them with hope; he reassures them that Islam can make them great again, but for that they don't need to abandon the trappings of modern culture.

Khaled's message resonates with some governments and organizations in the Middle East and beyond. He received several official government speaking invitations, partnered with the regional United Nations agencies and the World Health Organization in the Middle East, and was identified by the Tony Blair government as one of the voices of moderate Islam that the British government would want to support to bolster its fight against terrorism. Yemen recently heeded this recommendation and its president invited Khaled in December of 2010 to offer a message of moderation that can combat extreme interpretations of Islam. Khaled delivered the Friday *khutbah* (sermon) in Saleh Mosque in the capital for around 70,000 congregants. Despite parallels between Khaled and Qaradawi – both regionally identified as voices of moderation and sponsored by heads of states – Khaled's political stance differs from Qaradawi's direct and blunt political commentary. For Khaled, state politics seems almost peripheral and auxiliary to religious renewal and social service, a stance that diverges from the political path of the Muslim Brotherhood. Reform for Khaled is non-confrontational: it is not about the political process or governments or about competing ideologies. Khaled manages to maneuver the anxieties of political actors by emphasizing openness, dialogue, and peaceful change within existing political structures. His message to Muslim minorities in the West adds to this the burden of integration into their societies and becoming the best model citizens they can be.

Transnational Networking: Muslim Brotherhood and Advocacy Organizations

"Superstar" teachers and preachers such as al-Qaradawi and Khaled are by no means the only orthodox face of transnational Islam; Muslim charities, missionary (*dawa*) societies, advocacy groups and social movements are also active in the contemporary scene. No modern Islamic movement has been more influential within and across national boundaries than the Muslim Brotherhood, a transnational phenomenon that began as a revivalist answer to British colonialism and to the rapidly advancing secularization of a Muslim society. From its roots in Egypt the Brotherhood soon established branches throughout the Middle East, and now has affiliated groups and constituencies among Muslim communities on every continent, including Europe and North America.

Hasan al-Banna (1906–1949) may have foreshadowed the new religious leadership embodied by Amr Khaled, yet his greatest legacy lies in creating a truly transnational organization, comprising one of the largest Muslim reform movements in the twentieth and early twenty-first centuries. Reflecting the intentions of its founder, the organization continues to play pivotal political, social, and religious roles in many countries of the Middle East and the Western Muslim diaspora, and exhibits the transnational–local negotiations of contemporary Muslim movements that contest the nationalist secular premises of the modern nation-state system.

Though Banna was not a member of the *ulama*, his father was. Shaykh Ahmad Abdul Rahman al-Banna al-Saati studied at one of the largest mosque colleges in Egypt, Ibrahim Pasha Mosque, and spent more than thirty years working on his magnum opus: a collection of *hadith* of over 20 volumes (Kramer 2010). Shaykh Ahmad took care to emphasize the religious education and morality of his children, and Hasan al-Banna grew up surrounded with religious instruction and sensibility. He seems to have also had an inclination towards activism early in his life when he joined in his early teens a society for the observance and inculcation of Islamic moral practice. A second major influence on Banna, without discounting the influence of Sufism, is the pan-Islamic anticolonial reformist discourse of Jamal al-Din al-Afghani (d.1897) and Muhammad Abduh (d.1905). Banna was an avid reader of *al-Manar* magazine – the reform mouthpiece edited by Abduh's student Rashid Rida (d.1935) – which he attempted to restart after Rida's passing. Banna was also closely linked to another famous reformer, the Syrian Muhibb al-Din al-Khatib, and the Muslim Brotherhood organization that Banna founded in 1928 was modeled after al-Khatib's Young Men's Muslim Association (YMMA) (Commins 2008). Yet it speaks to Banna's organizational skills and vision that he was able to create an entity that not only outlasted its model but made serious inroads into Egyptian society.

Banna's goal was to translate reform ideas into reality. He believed that the failure of past reformers, such as al-Afghani, Abduh, and Rida, was mainly in their inability to take their ideas to the people in a manner that reflected the comprehensive and holistic nature of Islam. Banna's mission was to take what had so far been an elite intellectual project and translate it into a clear and practical plan for the masses. From Abduh, he inherited his desire to take Islam back to its foundational, simpler purity and circumvent matters of dispute and dissention. Banna spoke of his vision as an amalgam of different Muslim schools of thought, Salafi (literalist) and Sufi (mystical), and he used to discourage preoccupation with speculative matters, usually of little relevance to everyday life. He would urge his followers instead to focus on daily programs of worship and moral edification (a possible influence of Sufism) as well as civil and political activism that mirrored the activism of al-Afghani. Islam, for Banna, was a comprehensive system, not a private hidden ritual, and the program of the Brothers was to demonstrate that: it combined religion with politics, had economic and social goals, and imagined itself as an aesthetic, cultural, and recreational project. To sustain this effort, Banna introduced hierarchy and bureaucracy into his nascent organization, gleaning this from his past experience with hierarchy in the Hasafiyya Sufi order and the increased bureaucratization of Egyptian society. He developed an organizational model for creating new branches and recruiting members, created networks of provincial branches, and linked them all to the Cairo headquarters over which he presided.

The institutional model coupled with the spirit that Banna infused into his organization helps explain its success in transplanting itself into other countries and continents. The activism and focus on a simple Islamic message centered on unity proved to be a successful combination. It enabled the Brotherhood to provide basic Islamic services to the Muslim diaspora, which in turn helped them attract more recruits and expand their organization. Their social services and political involvement, arising from their understanding of Islam as comprehensive, raised their public profile as the spokespeople of Islam and transformed them into major religio-political actors. Interaction with the local environment, most importantly, helped indigenize the movement wherever it went.

Despite the fact that Banna and his successors continue to inspire the Muslim Brotherhood worldwide, the Brothers' organizations operate independent of each other in each country (Rubin 2010), and have at times drawn criticism for involvement with opposition activities. Even within the Middle East itself, significant differences developed between chapters of the Brotherhood reflective of differences in the national environments. The wide resonance the Muslim Brotherhood's core message (reassertion of core Islamic principles, reform of Islamic thought, rejection of inauthentic social norms, refusal to imitate the West or passively accept Western political tutelage) resulted in the movement becoming an umbrella for diverse activists and subgroups, some of which diverged from the non-violent strategy of Islamic resurgence espoused by Banna, particularly when faced with brutal state repression, as in the case of Sayyid Qutb (1906–1966). Nonetheless, the broad mainstream of Brotherhood movements in Egypt and elsewhere advocates a voluntary rather than coercive reassertion of Islamic principles.

It is instructive to understand the relationship between the local and the global in the thought of Banna and the Brotherhood and their attempt at alternative definitions. In a letter sent to the king of Egypt and the Sudan, and various Muslim leaders, Banna explained how Islam represents the path to true national greatness (Euben and Zaman 2009: 58). Yet Banna was quick to differentiate between an Islamic nationalism that is connected to God and thus is concerned with human welfare and other secular modern nationalisms that are nothing but "chauvinism" and "false pride." For Banna, Islam offered a different and expansive conception of the fatherland.

According to the Islamic understanding, the fatherland comprises: (1) the particular country first of all; (2) then it extends to the other Islamic countries, for all of them are a fatherland and an abode for the Muslims; (3) then it proceeds to the first Islamic Empire. . . . (4) Then the fatherland of the Muslim expands to encompass the entire world. . . . Thus did Islam reconcile the sentiments of local nationalism with that of a common nationalism. . . . (Euben and Zaman 2009: 61–62)

As Mitchell notes (1993: 264), "this is not nationalism in the Western sense of the word." The geographical boundaries of the nation-state are compromised here by a vertical relationship with God anchored in spirituality (not materialism) and the shared origin of all humans, and by a horizontal relationship with other humans that recognizes an expanded moral responsibility. The focus on the nation-state turns out to be not an end in itself but a step towards strengthening larger and more meaningful structures. Banna understood nationalism as one brick in a wall: if the brick is weak, the entire wall is weak. Thus, the Brothers ought to work for the betterment of their local environment. But the brick makes sense only within the wall, or else it is misguided and lost. In this vision, the Brotherhood combines a focus on the local with the transnational, understands each in light of the other, and uses each to strengthen the other. The local and the transnational identities unsettle each other and keep the boundaries porous and shifting.

One of the local manifestations of the Muslim Brotherhood in the West is the Muslim Association of Canada or MAC (www.macnet.ca). The organization promotes itself on its web site as part of the vision of al-Banna and the Muslim Brotherhood.

MAC's modern roots can be traced to the Islamic revival of the early twentieth century, culminating in the movement of the Muslim Brotherhood. This movement influenced Islamic activities, trends and intellectual discourse throughout the world including those of Muslims who came to Canada in search of freedom, education and better opportunities. MAC adopts and strives to implement Islam, as embodied in the Qur'an, and the teachings of the Prophet (peace be upon him) and as understood in its contemporary context by the late Imam, Hassan Albanna, the founder of the Muslim Brotherhood. MAC regards this ideology as the best representation of Islam as delivered by Prophet Muhammad (peace be upon him).

This introductory 2010 quote from MAC's website was rephrased in 2012, seemingly reflecting the greater scrutiny the Brotherhood were under in the wake of the Arab Spring. Though the newly redacted paragraph is less emphatic, it nevertheless still reflects the allegiance of the organization to the ideas and ideals of al-Banna.

MAC's roots are deeply enshrined in the message of Prophet Mohammad. Its modern roots can be traced to the vigorous intellectual revivalist effort that took hold in Muslim societies starting in the early twentieth century. This revival aimed at reconciling faith with the challenges of modernity and providing a clear articulation of balance and moderation in understanding Islam. In the Arab world, this revival culminated in the writings of the late Imam Hassan al-Banna and the movement of the Society of Muslim Brothers (commonly known as the Muslim Brotherhood). Al-Banna's core messages of constructive engagement in society, focus on personal and communal empowerment, and organizational development had a deep impact on much of the Muslim world.

With 11 chapters across Canada, MAC proclaims that its national goals are best met through emphasis on the local work of community building, education, and individual edification. This strategy provides a strong base for the national organization, which in turn can come back to strengthen individual chapters.

Another of MAC's public goals and a balance that it seeks to strike is integration into Canadian society while preserving a distinct religious identity. One of MAC's biggest events, illustrative of its vision of integration, is the biannual Eid (festival) prayer in downtown Toronto (see www.gtaeid.com). More than simply a religious prayer event that is said to be the largest in Canada – the web site claims 10,000 attenders – the event also serves public relations purposes. Non-Muslim guests at the event have included the premier of the province of Ontario, the mayor of Toronto, and various government ministers. Religion, politics, and entertainment thereby coalesce, presenting MAC's Muslims as one of the distinct colors of the Canadian mosaic, or as the web site puts it, "as a community in Canada that is an essential, integral and vibrant part of this society yet maintaining its religious attributes as a community of believers with distinct needs and values." While MAC is but one of many Muslim communities in Canada – some of which, for example the Ismailis, express themselves quite differently – it provides an intriguing example not only of transnational Islamic networking, but also of the complex identity negotiations that Muslims and other minority religious communities undertake within a diaspora context.

Conclusion

Transnational social organization has deep roots in the Islamic experience, and is now being reconfigured within a contemporary Muslim experience permeated by new media and information technologies, extended by diaspora–homeland relationships, and animated by the search for stable identity within a context of globalization. While the preceding examples by no means exhaust the rich diversity of contemporary Islamic transnationalism, they do illustrate recurrent patterns identified by Mandaville (2003). First, the intensified transnationalism of the current era is leading Muslims to "reimagine" their collective identity. Increased interaction among Muslims from diverse cultural and national contexts is fueling a renewed search for fundamental principles, calling traditional syntheses into question but not undermining the idea of authoritative tradition. The result of this search is neither uniformity nor runaway pluralization, as diverse voices interact in a changing context of conversation. Second, Muslim transnationalism has opened new doors for participating in public discourse, facilitating the emergence of new religious authorities that compete with the traditional *ulama*. Although some contemporary Muslim voices critique globalization quite vigorously, their discourse and patterns of networking are nonetheless impacted by it. New "Muslim public spheres" are emerging, providing scope for different opinions to be discussed and debated as well as for novel forms of religious expression, such as televangelism and internet preaching. Third, nation-states face mounting challenges in their efforts to shape the contours and content of Islamic discourse, as individuals and ideas alike cross borders with increasing ease. Muslim communities in the West and changing Muslim societies in traditional Muslim heartlands are increasingly part of a shared public sphere within which ideas and images can be transmitted instantaneously. Finally, contemporary Muslim transnationalism has enabled far-flung Muslim communities to articulate Islamic contestations or alternatives to the prevailing globalism.

While Islamic authenticity is a core value and goal of the individuals and movements surveyed in this chapter, it remains true that the conversations in which they engage and the answers they produce are inescapably plural and not inherently anti-Western. The popularity of Yusuf al-Qaradawi and Amr Khaled, for example, owes at least as much to each figure's responsiveness to the demands and challenges of the current era as to either individual's reputation for erudition. Like the Muslim Brotherhood, they are actively involved not in the advocacy of an "anti-modernity" (as regards science and technology) but rather in the shaping of an "alternative" or "Islamic" modernity that renews a sense of continuity with past teachings while also opening a horizon to the future. In this respect, efforts to reconstruct orthodoxy within a modern transnational context echo the past, while also providing scope for adaptation and innovation.

References

BBC News 2010. "Superstar Muslim preacher Amr Khaled battles al-Qaeda." *Newsnight*, December 7, at http://news.bbc.co.uk/2/hi/programmes/newsnight/9264357.stm, accessed February 28, 2013.

Commins, D. 2008. "Hasan al-Banna." In A. Rahnema (ed.) *Pioneers of Islamic Revival*, pp. 125–149. London: Zed Books. (Originally published 1994.)

Esposito, J.L. and Mogahed, D. 2008. *Who Speaks for Islam? What a Billion Muslims Really Think.* New York: Gallup Press.

Euben, R. and Zaman, M.Q. (eds) 2009. *Princeton Readings in Islamist Thought: Texts and Contexts from al-Banna to Bin Laden.* Princeton: Princeton University Press.

Gosch, S.S. and Sterns, P.N. 2008. *Premodern Travel in World History.* New York: Routledge.

Graf, J. and Skovgaard-Petersen, B. 2009. *Global Mufti: The Phenomenon of Yusuf Al-Qaradawi.* New York: Columbia University Press.

Kramer, G. 2010. *Hasan al-Banna.* Oxford: Oneworld Publications.

Mandaville, P. 2003. *Transnational Muslim Politics: Reimagining the Umma.* New York: Routledge.

Mandaville, P. 2007. *Global Political Islam.* New York: Routledge.

Mitchell, R.P. 1993. *The Society of the Muslim Brothers*. Oxford: Oxford University Press. (Originally published 1969.)

Nadwi, M.A. 2007. *Muhaddithat: Women Scholars of Islam*. Manchester: Interface Publishers.

Rosenau, J. 2003. *Distant Proximities: Dynamic Beyond Globalization*. Princeton: Princeton University Press.

Roy, O. 2006. *Globalized Islam: The Search for a New Ummah*. New York: Columbia University Press.

Rubin, B. (ed.) 2010. *The Muslim Brotherhood: The Organization and Policies of a Global Islamist Movement*. New York: Palgrave Macmillan.

Soage, A.B. 2010. "Yusuf al-Qaradawi: the Muslim Brothers' favorite ideological guide." In Rubin (2010), pp. 19–38.

Chapter 30

Religions of the African Diaspora

Paul Christopher Johnson

Defining the Category

Diasporic religions are composed on the one hand out of memories about space – places of origins, about the distances traversed from them since a time of exile, and physical or ritual returns imagined, already undertaken, or aspired to in the future. On the other hand it is about how those memories arise *in* space, out of a given repertoire of the available and the thinkable. Memories are summoned from a position, a place of emigration, a destination. Diasporic religious agents recollect the past through territorial and temporal ways of seeing, and from particular sites. Diasporic ways of seeing are made and reproduced in ritual performances, among other modes, as those are assembled from the new site's materials and repertories, its niches and needs, its plausible guiding ideas. In the ritual juxtapositions of objects and persons in space, horizons of memory are called to conscious reflection. Diasporic religious actors "make history" even as they forge the future, by projecting present events, and their present selves, against the horizon of another territory and time, a horizon that is itself also in motion.

African diasporic religions are often conceived of as those religions that were practiced on the great continent before being carried to new shores, often by force, in the bodies of Africans enslaved during the Atlantic trade that lasted roughly from 1450 to 1850. The old research question was the question of continuity between the religions of Africa itself and the religions of Afro-descendants in the Americas and the Caribbean. This question drove two generations of scholarship that sought to measure and evaluate the degree of Africanness that was retained in various New

A Companion to Diaspora and Transnationalism, First Edition.
Edited by Ato Quayson and Girish Daswani.
© 2013 Blackwell Publishing Ltd. Published 2013 by Blackwell Publishing Ltd.

World religions, albeit not under the rubric of diaspora *per se*. The dominant pioneering figure was the anthropologist Melville Herskovits. In Herskovits' view (in a work first published 1941), New World African religions could be plotted on a continuum or scale of fidelity. According to this scale, the practices of the "Bush Negroes" (Saramaka) of Suriname were "most African"; Vodou of Haiti was quite African; the traditions of the Gullah of the South Carolina coastal islands only slightly African (Herskovits 1990: 16). Certain religious practices were valorized as relatively pure, others as diluted, mixed, or "syncretized." Ironically, this attempt to quantify degrees of "Africanness" replicated the use of blood quantities in nineteenth-century racial categories to define degrees of blackness. It also elided the inventiveness of African diasporic cultures, foregrounding instead the discourse of authenticity and valuing sameness over time above innovation. By now it is clear that we need a different approach to the study of the religions of the African diaspora.

My own approach to African diaspora religions defines them as those clusters of religious discourses and practices that actively invoke the territory of Africa as a horizon of memory, authenticity, and sacred authority – whether Africa is physically known, imagined, or ritually created – and that take the distance from that idealized place as a problem that can at least partly be addressed in ritual. This means that African diaspora religions can be, and are, performed by persons not of African descent, but the practices must be understood as making reference to Africa or Africanness. Such a perspective can be contrasted with a rival definition of African diaspora religion that would define the category as those religions that persons of African descent perform, whatever those religions might be.

To accept the first point of view, as I recommend here, implies that the diasporic condition is relative, and fluid: one can be more or less religiously diasporic, or diasporically religious, in one's practice and consciousness. By becoming diasporic, joining the African diaspora through religion, practitioners do not just seek a past that waits to be discovered, but rather take part in actively creating African, Afro-American, and Afro-Caribbean pasts and futures. The key analytical move here is to view diasporas as not simply given by biological descent or by historical fiat, but rather as a possible subject position, a way of seeing adopted to varying degrees. This doesn't deny the ways that the range of available subject positions is constrained by the politics of recognition – by race, most notoriously, especially in the case of the African diaspora. Consider, on this score, the case of the famous Italian soccer player, Mario Balotelli, who heard chants of "There are no black Italians!" from opposing fans when his team visited Turin in 2009 (Martin 2011). Here was an *imposed* African diasporic consciousness, as Balotelli was instructed by white Italians that he must by necessity name Africa rather than Italy as his horizon of identity, even though he was Italian born and bred. And yet there is agency even within this imposed politics of recognition; Balotelli may acknowledge or refute such taunts. The point is that we should reframe the issue of African diasporic consciousness as a matter of culture rather than of nature, and call attention to the agency of religious actors as they activate an African horizon through ritual performance.

By joining a diaspora and becoming diasporic, a given religious group begins to view itself against new horizons that change the configuration and meaning of its religious, ethnic, and even racial identifications in the present. We should consider the African diaspora not only as the "retention" of something – the program of Herskovits – but also as a process of creation, and addition. Scholars of diasporic situations ought to consider the conditions under which groups join the African diaspora, adopt it, create it or, as in the case of Balotelli, have it abruptly inscribed onto them, as well as those contexts in which diasporic religious consciousness is retained.

Multiple Diasporic Horizons

Many African diasporic religions are comprised of multiple diasporic horizons; they are doubly or even triply diasporic. For the Garifuna in Central America, for example, the standard of authentic religious practice was that of the former homeland in St Vincent, a small island located in the Windward Islands, Lesser Antilles. It is from St Vincent that ancestors return to take part in ritual events performed on the beaches of Honduras. Many Garifuna who have emigrated to New York, however, have now come to a consciousness of themselves as African, such that the former horizon of authenticity and roots now lies in the shadow of an additional diasporic horizon, that of Africa (Johnson 2007). Still other Garifuna view the Central American coast as the homeland. The three different diasporic horizons serve different roles and to some degree are in tension with one another as anchors of different identifications, creating dynamism that precludes closure. The Central American diasporic horizon links them with Honduran Amerindians for certain purposes, especially around issues of contested land rights (England 1999). The St Vincent horizon aids the Garifuna in prosecuting and processing their historical relation and resistance to British colonialism, as well as current restitution claims against Great Britain for their forced deportation from St Vincent in 1797. The African diasporic horizon helps Garifuna in New York to find common cause with other African Americans, and to reimagine their story in a global, and cosmopolitan, frame.

The Garifuna example shows how a single group can simultaneously view itself against multiple diasporic horizons; or, put differently, strategically shift between discourses of diasporism and indigenism (Matory 2005: 109). This is especially true for religions of the African diaspora, many of which formed in the Caribbean and the Americas during the Atlantic slave trade, before being carried by migrants to Europe and North America in the late twentieth century. Through this process, religions like Vodou, Santería, Rastafari, and Candomblé became doubly diasporic, as their practitioners in New York, Paris, London, or Miami look not only to Africa but also to the Caribbean as powerful homelands from which they are displaced.

Such doubly diasporic religions are comprised of complex spatial memory-performances that activate sentiments of affiliation or attachment to multiple sites.

They are spatial in multiple senses: They are carried by emigrants *through* space, they are reinscribed *in* space (at least if they are to be maintained over time), and they are *about* space. The third point is less self-evident then than the first two, so let me clarify. The memory-performances giving ritual form to horizons of the past are not only transported from a homeland to a new world, but are in their content also about the processes of exile, transport, and transmission. In many African diasporic religions, ritual performances are not "diasporic" only because they were once indigenous to Africa and then were carried to a new land, but also because their very content is about those crossings. Ancestral spirits travel to possess the bodies of ritual performers in the present by repeating epic migratory journeys undergone by ancestors themselves. In one key lineage of Brazilian Candomblé called *Ketu,* for example, many Yoruba *orixás,*[1] originally from southwest Nigeria, are summoned to reappear and dance in the bodies of their initiates. Oxôssi is the patron deity, as he was the royal divinity of the city-state of Ketu. Although the political entity of Ketu no longer exists in Nigeria, that place lives on as a spatial memory in the experiences of participants in the religion of Brazilian Candomblé. In that sense, African diasporic religions are those traditions that ritually animate spirits who arrive from Africa as living indexes or incarnations of territorial and historical presence.

Contested and Emerging Diasporas

The African diaspora signifies different things to different ethnic groups that deploy it, is activated by different kinds of ritual events, and is animated by different kinds of ancestral spirits as ciphers of distinct historical and territorial presence. The pressures that arise in the attempt to discern common sources of deep affinity can cause social rifts and identity transformations as often as solidarity or common cause. As the sociologist Mary Waters showed (1999), for example, Anglophone Caribbean blacks in the United States often try to separate themselves from African Americans. They stress their "West Indianness," and are conscious of maintaining their distinctive accents so as not to be too easily conflated with their African American proximal hosts, who are perceived as holding low social status (Waters 1999: 57, 103, 151, 332). Haitians in New York sometimes bank on the prestige of French to accomplish the same sort of distancing (McAlister 1998). A Haitian woman in New York may under certain circumstances feel, be identified as, or self-introduce herself as "African American," "African," "Caribbean," or "French"; but all of these are likely to be suspended during a Vodou ceremony in Brooklyn in favor of an authentic "Haitianness," since that is the diasporic mode most befitting the occasion. That same person might the next day attend a Neighborhood Watch group, or a protest against police brutality, and there identify as black. Or she may visit a Cuban botánica, a store selling popular ritual tools like icons and candles, and, while chatting with a Cuban *santero* bask in the conviviality of a common understanding of African diasporic religious affiliation. All of this suggests that the consciousness of taking part in a common African diaspora may be a more fragile and contingent state than it is sometimes assumed to be.

As testimony to the historical process required to produce the African diaspora, or the lack thereof, consider again the example of the Garifuna, historically named by Europeans "Black Caribs."[2] At the end of the eighteenth century, they were despised by other groups of African descent that resided on the same island of St Vincent, slaves brought by British colonists. The Black Caribs were disparaged as "flatheads" for allegedly applying boards to children's foreheads to elongate them and thereby distinguish them from African slaves, a practice adopted from Carib Indians (see Anderson 1992: 229, written *c.*1798). Several Black Caribs owned African slaves who were forced to produce export crops like tobacco. In the Carib Wars leading to the Black Caribs' deportation in 1796–1797, African slaves and Black Caribs fought against each other rather than in alliance. Though we might imagine these rival groups as cells of a single diaspora organism, in the biological sense of descent from Africa, they clearly did not conceive of, or conduct, themselves as co-agents with shared concerns. There existed as yet no diaspora culture.

Diaspora, then, is a process rather than a state: "diaspora-ization," to take Stuart Hall's awkward neologism (1996b: 447), entails a shift in consciousness and a conversion of identifying practices. Scholars of African diasporic religions should ask, therefore, under what conditions do such conversions to diasporic consciousness occur? How does a "local" religion change when it engages the broader nexus of a diaspora? What are the specific cultural transmissions where shifts in sentiment occur, such that we could begin to speak not only of theories, but also of ethnographies of diaspora-ization (Gordon and Anderson 1999; Palmié 2002)? Finally, why does "diaspora-ization" guarantee so little consensus once the shared marker is adopted?

African Diasporic Situations as Catalysts of Religion

Diasporas are discursive artifacts that are not merely descriptive, but also expressive and constructive; they express desires and call new social formations into being (Butler 2001; Klimt and Lubkemann 2002; Tölölyan 1996; Sheffer 2003). As Khachig Tölölyan stressed, the adoption of "diaspora" is a moniker that wields power and makes things happen (1996: 19). Similarly, Brent Edwards followed Stuart Hall to suggest that diasporas are articulations across gaps that, like the articulations of hip or knee joints, allow for forward motility (2003: 15). When religious social actors join a diaspora, they shift their own horizons of self-understanding toward a given identification in order to make something happen.

Among other things that diasporas do, I suggest, is that *they make religions*. First, diasporas force the hand of religious discourses and actions. Formerly "natural" or unspoken parts of the social environment and its quotidian routine, religious words and acts now become the object of conscious selection. They must be planned for, allotted space, and deliberated and settled upon. Which ideas and rituals must at all costs be recollected, retained, and revived, and which can be set aside? By what criteria? Who decides? For groups in exile or emigration, religion is reified by being dislodged from its embedded, unspoken status to becoming a discrete object of contemplation and contest (P. Brown 1981; J. Smith 1987; Cohen 1997; Levitt 2001). As John Thornton (1998: 235) described the recreation of African religions in the Americas, "the merging of religions requires something more than simply mixing forms and ideas from one religion with those of another. It requires a reevaluation of the basic concepts and sources of knowledge of both religions in order to find common ground." This critical re-evaluation can have the effect of accelerating religious sentiments, discourses, and practices.

Second, diasporas make religions in the sense that they demand public recognition and summon new versions responding to that need. The most obviously public (and mobile) medium of transmission is that of texts. Though once-indigenous religions becoming diasporic do not inevitably become text-based religions, they must at least become to a certain degree "public." Their relative security in the hostland – their legitimacy as a recognized and protected "religion" whatsoever – depends upon managing a persuasive presentation (Vertovec 2000: 149). Going public entails the expansion of cultural products' articulation, such that they are perceived as both legible and relevant, or at least tolerable, to a broader audience. When indigenous religions become diasporic they must become at least modestly more cosmopolitan in their appeal – available and recognizable to audiences that did not produce them, and that may be distant in time and space from the initial site of their production. Newly arrived religions may remain "under the radar" in a hostland for a certain period, but their long-term endurance requires the acquisition of stable institutional niches; this in turn demands the rationalization of their style in previously unknown ways. This was the case, for example, with the Afro-Cuban religion of Santería. Once a secret religion of immigrant communities in Miami and New York, in the last decade it has acquired greater long-term security as a religion by publicly facing, and surviving, legal scrutiny of its practice of animal sacrifice, by marshaling a thoroughgoing defensive theology, and by reinventing itself as a "church" (Campo 1995; Palmié 1996; Johnson 2005).

Third, diasporas make religions in the sense that they generate a spatial trail, an itinerary of horizons which, by signifying golden ages of organic integrity and autonomy, present multiple horizons of memory for adherents. Emigrants spatially and ideologically replant rituals in new sites of attachment. Haitian devotees of Vodou as emigrants to New York found a new social niche at the Church of Mount Carmel in Brooklyn (McAlister 1998). Cubans, including practitioners of Afro-Cuban Santería, reoriented themselves to the shrine of Our Lady of Charity in Miami (Tweed 1997). Cuban American *paleros* and *santeros* rewrote the entire city maps in accord with their own analogical logic of religious correspondences (D. Brown 1999, 2003). By reattaching their religious practices to new sites, those objects and practices signify within a new system of relations, shifting the "meanings" they communicate (Ortner 1984; Sewell 1999; Vásquez and Marquardt 2003).

Fourth, diasporas make religions in the sense of catalyzing new forms, sources, sites, and brokers of the sacred. David Brown asked a Cuban priestess of Santería in New York how she continued her work without the same territorial resources as at home. She gave an example: "You have to find a mountain [to revere Obatala, the Yoruba/ Afro-Cuban sky-god]. Where will I find a mountain in New York City? You have to find a similarity, Riverside Drive, you stand at the base of it [the rocks] and to you that's a mountain" (1999: 169). She hooked the Afro-Cuban god, Obatala, onto Riverside Drive in New York, via a chain of associations. Yet this apparently simple substitution ("rocks by Riverside Drive" for "mountain") doesn't just allow the ritual action to occur; it opens paths for manifold new possible significations.

Even as some features of diasporic religion can be transferred to new sites, remembered spaces become sacralized as pivots of imagined communities. Religion and commerce may become strongly linked in diasporic situations. Continuity with the homeland is brokered by merchants of material goods who sell the "authentic" to those who perceive themselves to be in exile. In this commerce of memory across distance, the putatively *pure* and *original* are rendered valuable commodities, such that diasporas and "purist" claims about origins are intimately linked (Matory 2005: 116). Anthropologist Karen Richman (2005: 119, 128) has even argued for the case of Haiti and Vodou that diasporas make religions in the sense that a whole new class of ritual specialists arose in the homeland to mediate absent migrants' suddenly problematic relation to the authentic spirits of the homeland left behind.

Sites of African Diasporic Religious Attachment

Diasporas are social products that must be rehearsed, represented, and refreshed; they do not spring up or endure automatically; rather, they demand continuous, long-enduring effort. This work of diaspora is enjoined not only in large religious performances that are consciously and ideologically diasporic but also in small habitual acts – a "quotidian diaspora" (Werbner 2000) – often without any special awareness of it. A Jamaican Rastafarian in diaspora knows full well the colors her hat should bear to keep that identity "in mind" both for observers and for herself, though, again, it will not typically be a matter of reflection. Diasporas are sentimental communities but also "habit communities." Sentiments of affiliation are quickened by repeated appeals to the senses in certain kinds of acts and events – religious rituals, musical performances, home-style meals.

Emigrant carriers of Caribbean religions arriving in US cities must discover, select, and stabilize agreed-upon new places of devotion, and accomplish this task in relation to a cityscape already thoroughly parsed and designated. The establishment of African diasporic religions depends on contexts of reception, and sites of potential institutionalization. McAlister's (1998) study of the use of the church of Our Lady of Mount Carmel at 115th Street in East Harlem, for example, shows how Haitians' use of the site for pilgrimages in honor of the Vodou deity Ezili Danto depends, in part, on the Italian American community's assent and welcome. The influx of Haitians is viewed positively by the site's older users because the Haitians have buoyed and revitalized what was once a dying ritual precariously maintained by a waning Italian American constituency. Thus Vodou was "hooked onto" a new site in Harlem. When Rastafarians rename North America as "the heart of Babylon," and thereby cast Jamaica and Africa into relief as authentic centers (Hepner 1998: 209), or refer to Miami as "Kingston 21" and Brooklyn as "Little Jamaica," Rastafari is "hooked onto" North America through language. This is equally so when practitioners of Santería make the Statue of Liberty their own as a site of the Afro-Cuban *oricha* Olokun, god of the sea, or visit the East and Hudson Rivers as the domain of Ochun, goddess of fresh waters and femininity (K. Brown 1999: 169). Similarly, when the Garifuna began to establish a presence in the New York African diaspora religious scene, they did so in part by calling on the resources of places like the African Diaspora and Caribbean Culture Center on West 58th Street. Though the Center was established by an Afro-Puerto Rican *santera* Marta Moreno Vega, and though it serves primarily as a Santería resource center, the Garifuna were welcomed as an expansion of the Center's broad purpose. It offered both propitious and familiar hooks – Spanish, a broad-based clientele of people of color, and a religion based in material exchange leading to spirit possession – and the space for newcomers corroborating that broad religious profile.

African diasporic religions are transformed as they are accommodated in new sites and populations. Among the most dramatic transformation is the racial democratizing of African diasporic religions. For example, white Brazilians may become liturgically "African" through initiatory procedures of the Afro-Brazilian religions of Candomblé or Umbanda – though their willingness to do so depends, presumably, on the ability to shift the codes in other contexts at will. Though the structures of feeling comprising black culture were originated within communities of African descent, they are no longer the exclusive property of those groups (Gilroy 1993: 3). Then too, as the discourse of diaspora seeks to simplify the identity problem of origins, it complicates others. Candomblé claimants to African diaspora identity cannot help but note that half the practitioners of the religion are not of African biological descent at all (Prandi 1991; Gonçalves da Silva 1995; Pierucci and Prandi 2000; cf. Palmié 2002: 197–198). This raises an important question: Does being *of* or *in* the African religious diaspora imply only a liturgical consensus acknowledging African origins, or something more?

The spatial dislocations and relocations of diasporic situations, in other words, present religious crises, but such crises call forth creative responses and religious innovations through the freedom *from* previous determinations of place (Tuan 1977: 152).

Fusions and Fissures: The Particularity of African Diasporic Culture

The distinguishing feature of the African diaspora in comparison to other diasporic identifications is that it is framed in relation to the issue of race. And yet, though

the African diaspora and alternative descriptors like the "black Atlantic" are sometimes used interchangeably, there is at best an elective affinity between black identity
and African diasporic culture, including religion. In fact, in important respects the
two identifications are at odds, with black identity standing as at once a cipher of
cosmopolitan modernity and postmodern decay, and African diasporic cultural
identity often standing as a cipher of ancient origins and roots. Nevertheless, they
sometimes operate in tandem, especially in the US urban context that serves as
the seedbed for African diasporic religious culture's most recent and strident
formulations.

The idea of the African diaspora has been present for a long time, since the
second half of the nineteenth century in the words of Delaney, Blyden, Garvey, Du
Bois, and Padmore. But the "African diaspora" did not yet exist in those precise
terms (Appiah 1992; Gilroy 1993). While it was long argued that the first specific
instance of "African diaspora" in print was penned by George Shepperson (1966),
Stéphane Dufoix recently noted (2008: 11–13) at least two earlier occasions of its
appearance, one by Charles Victor Roman in 1916, the other by Alfred Métraux in
1951. Additional cases are certain to be found. Nevertheless, it was during the late
1960s that "the African diaspora" began to enter common usage and gain momentum in academic circles.

At the very moment that the "African diaspora" was entering widespread circulation, the contingencies and fissures of that united front were revealed by the post-
1960 migratory wave. The variety of Caribbean groups that arrived en masse in
the United States and Europe bore disparate ethnic, racial, and religious self-
understandings, and with the sudden co-presence and confrontation between Lusophone, Hispanophone, Francophone, and Anglophone groups, all presenting claims
on, or resistance to, the new nomenclature, the African diaspora's heavy links to a
monolithic primordial Africa were strained. Moreover, actual relations with the
continent of Africa were more variable than political mobilizations of the first half
of the twentieth century suggested.

The idea of Pan-African unity was replaced with notions of hybrid communities
of "black," and imagined communities of "African" identifications, both conceived
as relatively fluid signifiers, adapted differently in distinct national-state venues –
such that putative genetic and organic bonds were replaced by late modern signifying chains. The African diaspora was redefined as a derivative of shared suffering
under slavery and subsequent racialist, and often racist, regimes – the sublime slave
(Gilroy 1993) on the "repeating island" (Benitez-Rojo 1996). Here was a common
political project of resistance, and partially shared structures of feeling. It was not
essentialized in race, ethnicity, or territory, but rather in history; it was claimed
to have relative stability based in shared experiences of subjugation and racial
terror (Mintz and Price 1992; Appiah 1992; Gilroy 1993, 2000; Clifford 1994;
West 2001).

Membership in African diasporic religions, it followed, was not an identification
merely given through "hard" racial or ethnic essences. It was rather acquired through
cultural processes – what Weber called "conscious monopolistic closure" around

certain features – that entail a kind of conversion of consciousness (quoted in Sansone 2003: 10).

Many scholars observe that this is not so much a recent phenomenon as a centuries-long condition that began with the fictive kin networks of the slave trade itself. For example, Katia Mattoso wrote of the existential indeterminacy for enslaved Africans disembarked in Brazil (1989: 127):

> But try to imagine what it must have been like for a Muslim to find himself in a group of slaves practicing an animistic religion, or for a Bantu to join a community where Yoruban influence dominated, or, even more complicated, for a creole slave to confront black religions whose meaning he no longer understood. All these individuals must have been forced to find some compromise, to grope toward a modus vivendi in which unresolved contradictions must have produced constant tensions.

Calibrating the Various Diaspora Conversions

In studying the religions of the African diaspora, we are dealing with not one, but three different social phenomena: (1) diaspora in the form of relatively shared cultural dispositions across multiple sites, to the eye of an outside observer, which may or may not exist as an internalized consciousness by religious actors; (2) diaspora as an internalized conversion of consciousness, the subjective self-understanding as being of a diaspora, whether or not a multi-sited cultural resemblance empirically exists; and (3) diaspora as "diaspora" and hence ideology, a discursive artifact articulated in speech and in the public sphere in order to achieve desired effects.

The three forms are inter-calibrated with each other in complex ways, which is why it may be worthwhile to keep them analytically distinct. For example, until the 1950s, the Garifuna were "in" the African diaspora in sense 1, but not in senses 2 or 3. When they did enter the diaspora in the second and third senses, the first sense was shifted; the underlying "set of shared cultural dispositions" was tilted and reified in a particular version of it, the Yoruba model. Next, the discourse of diaspora (sense 3) is distinct from senses 1 and 2. Claims of the durable continuity of a group in one territory with another, more or less distant one, may actually increase in the face of evidence calling such continuity into question. Diaspora discourse may expand in the frequency and stridency of its articulation in consequence of the perceived enfeebling, or even absence, of actual bonds of culture or sentiment. As such, the discourse of diaspora and the actual empirical relationship between disjoined communities must be seen as separate though overlapping social phenomena. Moreover, as we will see in the example of Brazilian Candomblé below, there are users of the diaspora concept in senses 2 and 3 who are not of African descent at all, yet who, through religion, begin to identify themselves as such.

In the Brazilian religion, Candomblé, we witness not the complexity of how to draw boundaries circumscribing the African diaspora, but rather the problem of how to know what the identification means once it is discursively affirmed. Imagine that a set of prominent houses of Candomblé view themselves as constituent parts of a broader entity called "African diaspora religion," as is indeed the case. If made strongly enough, this claim steers such groups into conflict with other houses of Candomblé, the members of which understand themselves as distinctly and markedly "Brazilian" and who remain uninterested in the purging of Catholic and spiritist elements – features that many regard as part-and-parcel of "authentic" Candomblé – which such active re-Africanizing would require. In this case, a transnational ethnic location of the religion as purely African competes with a national ethnic location, mirroring a century of scholarly debates on the relative "Africanness" versus creole "Brazilianness" of religions like Candomblé.

The example indicates how African diasporic religious forms are contested, unstable, and contingent, not only in terms of when and how they come into being, but also what they imply once established. Candomblé of Brazil has been nationalized, and become trans-racial through its wide dissemination in the public sphere. By contrast, Garifuna ancestor religion, discussed earlier, has narrowed such boundaries, purging possible Amerindian genealogy to become more purely African. Joining the African diaspora through religion in the former case implies a *liturgical* investment in practicing a religion from Africa, regardless of the racial identities of practitioners. In the other, Garifuna case, it entails a serious ethno-racial investment in becoming *ancestrally* African.

African Diaspora as Meta-Religion

Despite the variability in the configuration of these three idioms of diaspora in any given religion, diasporic situations allow previously distinct and separate religions to engage each other, begin to forge cross-referential religious identifications, and collectively build an African diaspora meta-religion. The religions begin to be read against, and recombined with each other. Spiritual Baptist migrants from St Vincent are influenced by Trinidadian religious style in Brooklyn, and may even adopt the Yoruba *orishas* in their practice (Zane 1999: 167–169, 175). Santería takes on a Puerto Rican style in the Spanish Harlem barrio as *santerismo*, combined with Espiritismo to reduce the wide range of *orichas* to "Seven African Powers"[3] (Murphy 1988: 48; Brandon 1993: 107–108). For many New York practitioners of Afro-Cuban religions, distinct homeland religious lineages of the *orichas*, Palo, the *muertos* (dead ancestors) and Espiritismo are combined in ritual practice, remaking the religious grammar by using techniques of code-switching. The same ritual act or object can be discursively framed in relation for different contexts and objectives (Barnes 1997; D. Brown 1999, 2003; Chevannes 1994, 2001; K. Brown 1991, 1999, 2003; Richman 2005; Olmos and Paravisini-Gebert 2003). The *orishas* may be especially invoked in relation to questions of "roots," tradition, and Africanness, compared with the Palo *ngangas* or *muertos*, marshaled toward all-too-human missions of money or lust (Palmié 2002). The ancestral spirits (*muertos*) are discursively invoked for family concerns, while the discourse of Espiritismo may be viewed as effectual in contexts calling for "scientific" debates or ecumenical religious comparisons on topics of evolution, spiritual cleansing, or reincarnation.

Stylistic crossovers in ritual practice are now also common fare: at a Garifuna ceremony I attended in the Bronx, a woman in a possession trance behaved in a manner neither I nor any Garifuna present had ever witnessed. She picked up burning candles to pour hot wax on her chest and shoulders, perhaps to prove her trance or give evidence of the power of the possessing spirit. Such demonstrations are non-existent in Garifuna homeland possession, but occur in Vodou, and indeed she later indicated having learned the new expression at a Haitian rite.

But such code-switching between once distinct religions especially occurs in relation to second-order verbalizations. Among the various groups who begin to view and identify themselves collectively as "African diaspora" religious practitioners, and therefore members of a single supra-ethnic religious style, it is now common to hear commentaries comparing the various sub-religions and their deities, and crediting them with distinct values: Santería for its attention to lineage and its divination specialists (*babalawos*); Vodou for its pageantry and the dramatic "heat" of its possession dances; Palo for its speed and ruthless efficiency; the Garifuna for their rustic authenticity, and so forth.

This relatively new global superform, *African diasporic religion*, raises new horizons of self-understanding and shared history, and offers new possibilities of solidarity and legitimacy. Scholars of particular traditions should ask, however, what the consequences are for "local" practice, and for specific religious traditions, when they adopt and engage this religious superform and try to adapt to its norms.

Notes

1   Defining the *orisha* (Cuban *oricha*, or *ocha*), the deities originally of the Yoruba religion of southwest Nigeria, is a notoriously difficult enterprise, but at very least it can be asserted that there is a strong euhemerist strain: the deities of the Yoruba are great ancestors later divinized. In this vein, one of the first attempts at defining the Yoruba gods came from William Bascom in 1938: "An orisa is a person who lived on earth when it was created, and from whom present day folk are descended. When these orisas disappeared or "turned to stone," their children began to sacrifice to them and to continue whatever ceremonies they themselves had performed when they were on earth. This worship was passed on from one generation to the next, and today an individual considers the orisa whom he worships to be an ancestor from whom he descended" (quoted in Apter 1992: 150). In this sense orishas were patron deities of regional dynasties. They were also forces of various domains of nature and culture. In the New World, the orishas became classifying archetypes of people, including all their faults. For example, the Afro-Cuban thunder-god Chango is just, but also a philanderer; the creator of humans, Obatala, is wise, but also aged and fragile; Ochun of rivers is beautiful, but suffers a nouveau riche greed; the iron-god who clears the paths, Ogun, is brave but also bullheaded, and so on.

Anthias, F. 2010. "Nation and post-nation: Nationalism, transnationalism and intersections of belonging." In P.H. Collins, and J. Solomos (eds) *The SAGE Handbook of Race and Ethnic Studies*. London: Sage Publications.

Beinhocker, E.D., Farrel, D., and Zainulbhai, A.S. 2007. "Tracking the growth of India's middle classes." *McKinsey Quarterly*, 3: 51–61.

Benjamin, S. 2005. "The lifestyle advertisement and the Marxist manifesto as Trojan horses in a city of stealth," at http://www.isst-india.org/PDF/Lifestyle%20Advertisement.pdf, accessed March 1, 2013.

Bhat, L. 2008 "Daily news and analysis: daily new addition, Bhatnaturally," at http://www.bhatnaturally.com/advertising/daily-news-analysis-daily-new-additon/, accessed March 1, 2013.

Boas, T., Dunning, T., and Bussell, J. 2005. "Will the digital revolution revolutionize development? Drawing together the debate." *Studies in Comparative International Development*, 40(2): 95–110.

Castells, M. 1983. *The City and the Grassroots: A Cross-Cultural Theory of Urban Social Movements*. Berkeley: University of California Press.

Clay, E. 2004. *Shaping Vibrant Cities. Neighbourhood Vision Campaign 2003: A Citizens' Platform for Participatory Ward Planning*. Bangalore: Ramanathan Foundation.

Dasgupta, S. 2008. "Success, market, ethics: Information technology and the shifting politics of governance and citizenship in the Indian silicon plateau." *Cultural Dynamics*, 20(3): 213–244.

Datta-Ray, S.K. 2002. "India's two cultures, the rich and the poor." *New York Times*, April 23, at http://www.nytimes.com/2002/04/23/opinion/23iht-edray_ed3__0.html?pagewanted=1, accessed March 1, 2013.

De Bree, J., Tine, D., and De Haas, H. 2010. "Post-return experiences and transnational belonging of return migrants: a Dutch-Moroccan case study." *Global Networks*, 10(4): 489–509.

Dehaene, M. and De Cauter, L. 2008. "Heterotopia in a postcivil society." In M. Dehaene and L. De Cauter (eds) *Heterotopia and the City: Public Space in a Postcivil Society*, pp. 3–9. London: Routledge.

Faist, T. 2010. "Diaspora and transnationalism: What kind of dance partners? In R. Bauböck and T. Faist (eds), *Diaspora and Transnationalism: Concepts, Theories and Methods*. Amsterdam: Amsterdam University Press.

Fernandes, L. 2000a. "Restructuring the new middle classes in liberalizing India." *Comparative Studies of South Asia, Africa and the Middle East*, 20(1/2): 88–104.

Fernandes, L. 2000b. "Nationalizing 'the global': Media images, cultural politics and the middle class in India." *Media, Culture and Society*, 22(5), 611–628.

Foucault, M. 1986. "Of other spaces," trans. J. Miskowiec. *Diacritics*, 16(1): 22–27. (Originally published 1967.)

Gajjala, R. 2010. "3D Indian (digital) diasporas." In A. Alonso and P.J. Oiarzabal (eds) *Diasporas in the New Media Age: Identity, Politics, and Community*. Reno: University of Nevada Press.

Ghosh, A. 2005. "Public–private or a private public? Promised partnership of the Bangalore Agenda Task Force." *Economic and Political Weekly*, November 19: 4914–4922.

Heitzman, J. 2004. "Network city. Planning the information society in Bangalore." New York: Oxford University Press.

Horrocks, I. 2009. "'Experts' and e-government: Power, influence and the capture of a policy domain in the UK." *Information, Communication and Society*, 12(1): 110–127.

Joshi, D. 2008. "Daily news and analysis: Outdoor is in its DNA." *Afaqs*, August 5, at http://www.afaqs.com/perl/media/story.html?sid=21826, accessed March 1, 2013.

Khandelwal, P. 2008, "DNA uses outdoor to foray into Bangalore." *Campaign India*, January 13, at http://www.campaignindia.in/Article/225052,dna-uses-outdoor-to-foray-into-bangalore.aspx, accessed March 14, 2013.

Lakha, S. 1999. "The state, globalisation, and Indian middle-class identity." In M. Pinches (ed.) *Culture and Privilege in Capitalist Asia*, pp. 252–276. London: Routledge.

Lefebvre, H. 1991. *Production of Space*, trans. D. Nicholson-Smith. Oxford: Blackwell.

Madon, S. 1997. "The information-based global economy and socio-economic development: the case of Bangalore." *Information Society*, 13(3): 227–244.

Madon, S. and Sahay, S. 2000. "Democracy and information: a case study of new local governance structures in Bangalore." *Information, Communication and Society*, 3(2): 173–191.

Mau, S. 2010. *Social Transnationalism: Lifeworlds Beyond the Nation-State*. New York: Routledge.

Mayer, M. 2006. "Manuel Castells' *The City and the Grassroots*." *International Journal of Urban and Regional Research*, 30(1): 202–206.

Nair, J. 2000. "Singapore is not Bangalore's destiny." *Economic and Political Weekly*, 1512–1514.

Nair, J. 2005. "The promise of the metropolis: Bangalore's twentieth century." New Delhi: Oxford University Press.

Nietzsche, F. 1968. *The Will to Power*, trans. R. J. Hollingdale. London: Penguin Books.

Nietzsche, F. 1990. *Beyond Good and Evil*, trans. R. J. Hollingdale. London: Penguin Books.

Palshikar, S. 2003. "Whose democracy are we talking about? Hegemony and democracy in India." In R. Vora and S. Palshikar (eds) *Indian Democracy: Meanings and Practices*, pp. 127–164. Thousand Oaks, CA: Sage Publications.

Pow, C.P. 2011. "Living it up: Super-rich enclaves and transnational elite urbanism in Singapore." *Geoforum*, 42(3): 382–393.

Ram-Prasad, C. 2007. "India's middle class failure." *Prospect Magazine*, September 30: 138, at http://www.prospectmagazine.co.uk/2007/09/indiasmiddleclassfailure/, accessed March 1, 2013.

Saco, D. 2002. *Cybering Democracy: Public Space and the Internet*. Electronic Mediations, 7, Minneapolis: University of Minnesota Press.

Saldanha, A 2002. "Music, space, identity: Geographies of youth culture in Bangalore." *Cultural Studies*, 16(3): 337–350.

Saldanha, A. 2008. "Heterotopia and structuralism." *Environment and Planning A*, 40(9): 2080–2096.

Sastry, G.S. 2008. "Emerging development issues of Greater Bangalore." ISEC working paper 194, Institute for Social and Economic Change, Bangalore.

Scoones, I. 2007. "The contested politics of technology: Biotech in Bangalore." *Science and Public Policy*, 34(4): 261–271.

Spivak, G S. 2000. "Megacity." *Grey Room*, 1(1): 9–25.

Sridharan, E. 2004. "The growth and sectoral composition of India's middle class: Its impact on the politics of economic liberalization." *India Review*, 3(4): 405–428.

Sudhira, H.S., Ramachandra, T.V., and Bala Subrahmanya, M.H. 2007. "City profile: Bangalore." *Cities – International Journal of Urban Policy and Planning*, 24(5): 379–390.

Tan, K. 2009. "Makeshift heterotopia(s): Tent cities in North America." Paper presented at the Austrian Association of American Studies annual conference, October 22–25, University of Graz.

Varma, P.K. 1998. *The Great Indian Middle Class*. New Delhi: Viking.

Wimmer, A. and Glick Schiller, N. 2002. "Methodological nationalism and beyond: Nation-state building, migration and the social sciences." *Global Networks*, 2(4): 301–334.

Index

debt, 113, 116, 320–321

De Cesari, Chiara, 376

decolonization, 59, 128, 141, 145–146

Defoe, Daniel, 297

de Gama, Vasco, 196

de Gaulle, Charles, 301

de Haan, Arjan, 342n4

Deleuze, Gilles, 56

Demetriou, Madeleine, 71

Democratic Republic of Congo, 42, 362

denativization, 478, 483–484, 490n14

Denby, David, 432

Denison, Tom, 348

Denmark, 167

Dernersesian, Angie Chabram, 65

Desai, Kieran, *Inheritance of Loss*, 142

Diamantes, Cucu, 263–264

Dias, Bartolomeu, 195–196

diaspora, concept of, 2–3, 8–9, 127, 233,
   332–333
   as distinct from transnationalism, 12,
      70–72
   etymology, 8, 127, 146, 446, 490n15
   geographical turn, 89
   meanings, 332–333, 366–377
   and urban studies, 89–90
   yearning for homeland, 111, 142, 185, 333
   see also diaspora studies

Diaspora, Migration and Identities
   Program, AHRC, 7

diaspora formation, 3–4, 342
   and nation-states, 5, 146
   reason for, 80

diaspora institutions, 480–481

Diaspora journal, 7

diaspora studies, 5, 6–7, 70–71, 126, 128,
   367, 480

diaspora tourism, 524–537

diasporic imaginary, postcolonial, 139–156
   defining, 142, 146–148, 151, 155n9
   and identity, 148

diasporic literature, 152–153
   see also Commonwealth literature

diasporic return *see* return migration

diasporic space, concept of, 4, 146–147

Dick, Hilary Parsons, 33

Dilwale Dulhania Le Jayenge (*DDLJ*,
   Chopra), 234–235, 237, 238, 240

displacement, 19, 89, 149–151, 245n3,
   367, 412

Diyanet, 133

DNA Daily, 540, 541–543

Dogville (2003), 95, 96

domestic workers, 43
   colonial, 193, 98, 199, 203
   enslaved, 201, 218
   feminine role, 14, 387
   immigrant, 14, 43, 65, 116, 406
   labor migration, 14, 43, 65, 406
   medieval, 165
   power dynamics, 14
   racial segregation, 195
   workplace, 14

Dominican Republic, 110
   colonial, 145
   diaspora, 110, 132–133, 324
   migrant remittances, 319, 324
   results of migration, 110, 319
   Westernization, 110

Donner, Jonathan, 349, 354

Dostana (Mansukhani), 242, 243–244

Dove, Mabel, 207

Driessen, Henk, 214–215, 219–220, 221

drugs trade, 110

Dubai syndrome, 112

Du Bois, W.E.B., 107
   Souls of Black Folk, 147

Dufoix, Stephanie, 146, 517
   Diasporas, 7–8

Duhani, Said Naum, 228n10

Dutch East India Company (VOC), 203,
   205

Dutch empire, 193, 201, 205
   interracial relations, 202–203

East African Asians, 74, 130

East African slave trade, 166

East Asia, 178
   return migration to, 173, 174, 176–178

Eastern Europe
   ethnic minorities, 146, 173–174, 175,
      177, 178
   migrants, in London, 99
   salsa participants, 270

East India Company *see* British East India
   Company

Madagascar, 193
Madiano, Mirca, 109, 114
mail order brides, 109
Maison du Gruyère, La, 293–294, 304
Malaysia, 145, 325, 398, 543
  colonial, 11, 145
  Islam, 405
Malinowski, Bronislav, 32, 33
Malintzin, 196
Malkki, Liisa H., 41
Mamma Mia video series (Smith), 251,
  253–254, 255
Manchester School of Anthropology, 31,
  108
Mandaville, Peter, 359, 496
mangeteers, 112
Manouchian, Missak, 476
Marcelli, Enrico, 324
Marcus, George, 429
  Writing Cultures, 30
market associations, 336, 337
marriage
  arranged, 109, 207n3, 353, 355
  companionate, 421–422
  interracial, 192, 195, 196, 198–199, 201,
    205, 207n3, 207n4
  and labor migration, 389
  second, 117
  transnational, 43, 109, 112, 354–355,
    449–450, 531
Marseilles, 42, 482, 490n15
Martinez-Alier, Verena, 198
Marx, Karl, 108
Marxism, 155n1
masculinities, 238, 240, 285–286,
  389–391
mass media, 54–66
  broadcast, 60–61
  conglomerates, 63
  and cultural dissemination, 14
  and diasporas, 11–12, 54–55, 56
  ecologies, 56, 58
  professionalization, 61
  and resistance, 66
  sensationalist, 62
  studies, 54
  technologies, 13, 58, 61, 64

see also film; internet; music; printing;
  television; video-movies
Masseret, Jean-Pierre, 484
Massey, Douglas, 319, 324
material culture, 12, 14, 94, 148, 450
  see also architecture; home-building
Matory, Lorand, 163, 169
  Black Atlantic Region, 156n9
Mattoso, Katia, 518
Mau, Steffen, 539–540
Mauritius, 37, 145, 166, 168, 169
Mbembe, Achille, 249, 250, 251, 259
McAlister, Elizabeth, 515
McCalman, Max, *Cheese*, 309
McCrindle, J.W., 451–452
McGranahan, Carole, 333, 342n3
Mecca, 497, 498
media studies, 54
medical care, 321, 335, 405, 534, 535
  colonial, 169, 199
  and organ donation, 455–456,
    459–465
  see also mental health
Medina, 497
Mediterranean region, 14–15, 214–215
  Greek colonization, 446–447
mega-cities, 397–398, 401, 402, 540
  see also global cities
"melting pot," migrant, 12, 14, 108, 218
  see also assimilation
Memmi, Albert, 207
mental health, 289, 297
Merkel, Angela, 16
Mesrop, Surp (Saint), 474
Messer, Chris, 358
Methodists, Ghanaian, 114
methodological individualism, 116, 119
methodological nationalism, 5, 75–76, 109,
  119, 323, 539
  critique of, 35, 108, 141
  dominance of, 139–140, 144
  and mobility, 140–141
  term, 75, 91, 108
Mexican migrants, 418–424
Mexico
  census, 424n2
  economic development, 416–417

Washington Times, 432
Waterbury, Myra, 81
Waters, Mary, 512
Weber, Eugene, 486
Weber, Max, 108
West, Carolyn, 197
West African culture, 57–58
    diasporic translation, 57–58
    literary texts, 249–250
    video-movies, 249–260
    see also British West Africa; French West
        Africa
Western Armenian language, 486–487,
    488
Westernization, 110, 407–408, 542
    see also globalization
Western Union, 358
Wild World series (Smith), 253, 257
Williams, Eric, 164
Wilson, Katherine, 269
Wimmer, Andreas, 75, 91
Witwatersrand, South Africa, 195
women
    colonial wives, 192–193
    colonized, 190, 192, 193
    entrepreneurial, 370
    eroticism, 118
    and families, 114–115, 118, 420
    gender stereotypes, 43, 235, 246n11,
        286–290, 335, 336, 387–388, 389
    and household labor, 43
    Indian, film portrayals of, 235
    labor migration, 386–389, 420
    respectability, 194, 239–240, 387, 388, 420
    sex workers, 43
    sexual abuse of *see* rape
    skills, 200–201, 205

slaves, 166, 193–194, 196, 197, 201
    young, 387, 389
    see also domestic workers; gender issues
Wordsworth, William, *The Prelude*, 150
work ethic, 178, 407
work permits, 109
World Bank, 34, 328n2
world cities *see* global cities
world-systems theories, 34
World War I, 476–477, 491n20, 489n9
World War II, 108, 488
    aftermath, 93, 140
    soldiers, 283, 286, 484–485
World Wide Web *see* internet
Wright, Richard, 60

Yahoo Messenger, 115
Yang, Mayfair Mei-Hui, 256
Yap, Arthur, 409
Yemen, 502
Yeoh, Brenda, 406
Yeung, Henry, 397
Yiddish
    diasporic language, 280, 281, 283
    literature, 156n13
yizker bikher, 148
yoga, 545
Yoruba people, 156n9, 169–170
    religious practices, 512, 515, 518, 519,
        520n1
Young, Robert, 59, 145
Young Turk Revolution, 224–225, 477

Zambia, 321, 326
Zionism, 55, 68
Žižek, Slavoj, 65
Zoroastrians, Indian, 126